- **Dynamic Study Modules** help students study chapter topics and the language of MIS on their own by continuously assessing their knowledge application and performance in real time. These are available as graded assignments prior to class, and are accessible on smartphones, tablets, and computers.

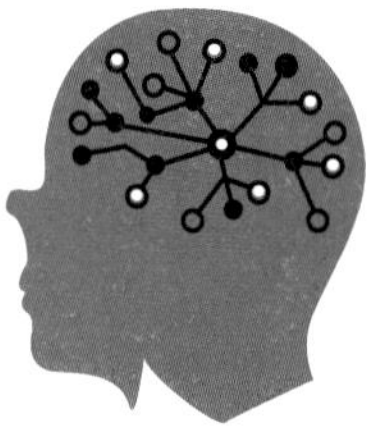

- **Learning Catalytics™** is a student response tool that helps you generate class discussion, customize your lecture, and promote peer-to-peer learning based on real-time analytics. Learning Catalytics uses students' smartphones, tablets, or laptops to engage them in more interactive tasks.

- The **Gradebook** offers an easy way for you and your students to see their performance in your course.

  Item Analysis lets you quickly see trends by analyzing details like the number of students who answered correctly/incorrectly, time on task, and more.

  And because it's correlated with the AACSB Standards, you can track students' progress toward outcomes that the organization has deemed important in preparing students to be leaders.

- **Pearson eText** enhances learning — both in and out of the classroom. Students can take notes, highlight, and bookmark important content, or engage with interactive lecture and example videos that bring learning to life anytime, anywhere via MyLab or the app.

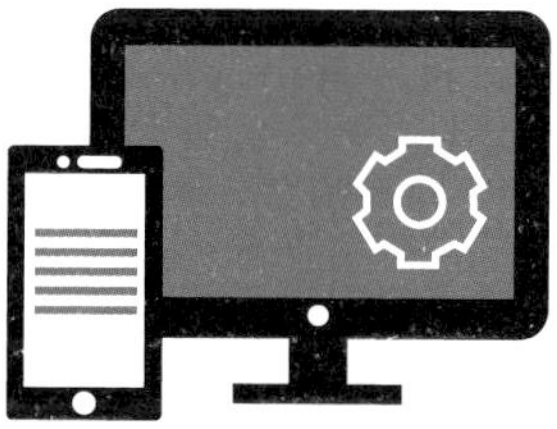

- **Accessibility (ADA)**—Pearson is working toward WCAG 2.0 Level AA and Section 508 standards, as expressed in the **Pearson Guidelines for Accessible Educational Web Media.** Moreover, our products support customers in meeting their obligation to comply with the Americans with Disabilities Act (ADA) by providing access to learning technology programs for users with disabilities.

  Please email our Accessibility Team at **disability.support@pearson.com** for the most up-to-date information.

- With **LMS Integration**, you can link your MyLab course from Blackboard Learn™, Brightspace® by D2L®, Canvas™, or Moodle®.

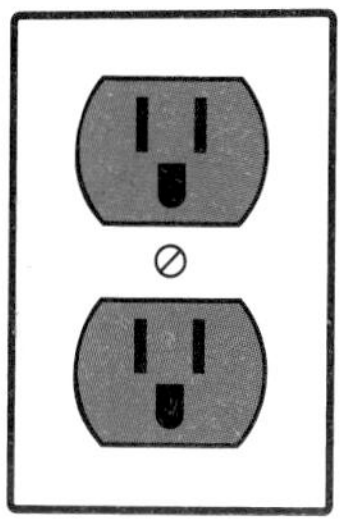

http://www.pearsonmylabandmastering.com

Integrating Business with Technology

By completing the projects in this text, students will be able to demonstrate business knowledge, application software proficiency, and Internet skills. These projects can be used by instructors as learning assessment tools and by students as demonstrations of business, software, and problem-solving skills to future employers. Here are some of the skills and competencies students using this text will be able to demonstrate:

Business Application skills: Use of both business and software skills in real-world business applications. Demonstrates both business knowledge and proficiency in spreadsheet, database, and Web page/blog creation tools.

Internet skills: Ability to use Internet tools to access information, conduct research, or perform online calculations and analysis.

Analytical, writing and presentation skills: Ability to research a specific topic, analyze a problem, think creatively, suggest a solution, and prepare a clear written or oral presentation of the solution, working either individually or with others in a group.

*** Dirt Bikes Running Case in MyLabMIS**

Business Application Skills

Business Skills	Software Skills	Chapter
Finance and Accounting		
Financial statement analysis	Spreadsheet charts	Chapter 2*
	Spreadsheet formulas	Chapter 10
	Spreadsheet downloading and formatting	
Pricing hardware and software	Spreadsheet formulas	Chapter 5
Technology rent vs. buy decision	Spreadsheet formulas	Chapter 5*
Total Cost of Ownership (TCO) Analysis		
Analyzing telecommunications services and costs	Spreadsheet formulas	Chapter 7
Risk assessment	Spreadsheet charts and formulas	Chapter 8
Human Resources		
Employee training and skills tracking	Database design	Chapter 12*
	Database querying and reporting	
Manufacturing and Production		
Analyzing supplier performance and pricing	Spreadsheet date functions	Chapter 2
	Data filtering	
	Database functions	
Inventory management	Importing data into a database	Chapter 6
	Database querying and reporting	
Bill of materials cost sensitivity analysis	Spreadsheet data tables	Chapter 11*
	Spreadsheet formulas	
Sales and Marketing		
Sales trend analysis	Database querying and reporting	Chapter 1
Customer reservation system	Database querying and reporting	Chapter 3
Customer sales analysis	Database design	
Marketing decisions	Spreadsheet pivot tables	Chapter 11
Customer profiling	Database design	Chapter 6*
	Database querying and reporting	

Customer service analysis	Database design Database querying and reporting	Chapter 9
Sales lead and customer analysis	Database design Database querying and reporting	Chapter 12
Blog creation and design	Blog creation tool	Chapter 4

Internet Skills

Using online software tools for job hunting and career development	Chapter 1
Using online interactive mapping software to plan efficient transportation routes	Chapter 2
Researching product information Evaluating Web sites for auto sales	Chapter 3
Analyzing Web browser privacy protection	Chapter 4
Researching travel costs using online travel sites	Chapter 5
Searching online databases for products and services	Chapter 6
Using Web search engines for business research	Chapter 7
Researching and evaluating business outsourcing services	Chapter 8
Researching and evaluating supply chain management services	Chapter 9
Evaluating e-commerce hosting services	Chapter 10
Using shopping bots to compare product price, features, and availability	Chapter 11
Analyzing Web site design	Chapter 12

Analytical, Writing, and Presentation Skills*

Business Problem	**Chapter**
Management analysis of a business	Chapter 1
Value chain and competitive forces analysis Business strategy formulation	Chapter 3
Formulating a corporate privacy policy	Chapter 4
Employee productivity analysis	Chapter 7
Disaster recovery planning	Chapter 8
Locating and evaluating suppliers	Chapter 9
Developing an e-commerce strategy	Chapter 10

Thirteenth Edition

Essentials of Management Information Systems

Kenneth C. Laudon
New York University

Jane P. Laudon
Azimuth Information Systems

Pearson

330 Hudson Street, NY NY 10013

Vice President, IT & Careers: Andrew Gilfillan
Senior Portfolio Manager: Samantha Lewis
Managing Producer: Laura Burgess
Associate Content Producer: Stephany Harrington
Portfolio Management Assistant: Madeline Houpt
Director of Product Marketing: Brad Parkins
Product Marketing Manager: Heather Taylor
Product Marketing Assistant: Jesika Bethea
Field Marketing Manager: Molly Schmidt
Field Marketing Assistant: Kelli Fisher
Cover Image: RedlineVector/Shutterstock; bluebay/Shutterstock
Vice President, Product Model Management: Jason Fournier
Senior Product Model Manager: Eric Hakanson
Lead, Production and Digital Studio: Heather Darby
Digital Studio Course Producer: Jaimie Noy
Program Monitor: SPi Global
Full-Service Project Management and Composition: Katie Ostler, Cenveo® Publisher Services
Printer/Binder: LSC Communications
Cover Printer: Phoenix
Text Font: 10.5/12.5 Times NR MT Pro

Acknowledgments of third-party content appear on the appropriate page within the text.

Library of Congress Cataloging-in-Publication Data

On file with the library of Congress.

1 18

Pearson

ISBN 10: 0-13-480275-6
ISBN 13: 978-0-13-480275-6

About the Authors

Kenneth C. Laudon is a Professor of Information Systems at New York University's Stern School of Business. He holds a B.A. in Economics from Stanford and a Ph.D. from Columbia University. He has authored twelve books dealing with electronic commerce, information systems, organizations, and society. Professor Laudon has also written over forty articles concerned with the social, organizational, and management impacts of information systems, privacy, ethics, and multimedia technology.

Professor Laudon's current research is on the planning and management of large-scale information systems and multimedia information technology. He has received grants from the National Science Foundation to study the evolution of national information systems at the Social Security Administration, the IRS, and the FBI. Ken's research focuses on enterprise system implementation, computer-related organizational and occupational changes in large organizations, changes in management ideology, changes in public policy, and understanding productivity change in the knowledge sector.

Ken Laudon has testified as an expert before the United States Congress. He has been a researcher and consultant to the Office of Technology Assessment (United States Congress), Department of Homeland Security, and to the Office of the President, several executive branch agencies, and Congressional Committees. Professor Laudon also acts as an in-house educator for several consulting firms and as a consultant on systems planning and strategy to several Fortune 500 firms.

At NYU's Stern School of Business, Ken Laudon teaches courses on Managing the Digital Firm, Information Technology and Corporate Strategy, Professional Responsibility (Ethics), and Electronic Commerce and Digital Markets. Ken Laudon's hobby is sailing.

Jane Price Laudon is a management consultant in the information systems area and the author of seven books. Her special interests include systems analysis, data management, MIS auditing, software evaluation, and teaching business professionals how to design and use information systems.

Jane received her Ph.D. from Columbia University, her M.A. from Harvard University, and her B.A. from Barnard College. She has taught at Columbia University and the New York University Stern School of Business. She maintains a lifelong interest in languages and civilizations of Asia.

The Laudons have two daughters, Erica and Elisabeth, to whom this book is dedicated.

Brief Contents

Complete Contents

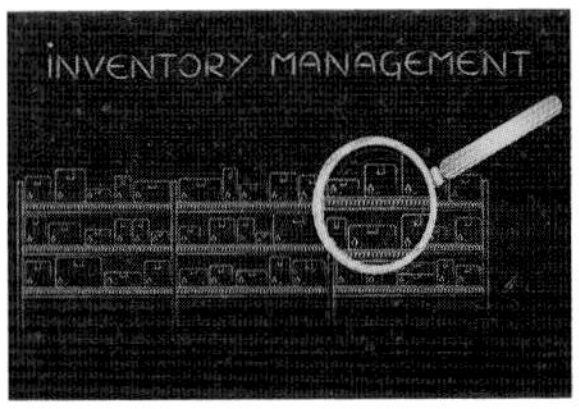

INVENTORY MANAGEMENT

Business Cases and Interactive Sessions

Here are some of the business firms you will find described in the cases and Interactive Sessions of this book:

Chapter 1 Business Information Systems in Your Career

The Grocery Store of the Future: Look at Kroger
Can You Run Your Company with Your iPhone?
UPS Competes Globally with Information Technology
Did Information Systems Cause Deutsche Bank to Stumble?

Chapter 2 Global E-business and Collaboration

Enterprise Social Networking Helps Sanofi Pasteur Innovate and Improve Quality
Data Changes How NFL Teams Play the Game and How Fans See It
Cisco IX5000: What State-of-the-Art Telepresence Can Do for Collaboration
Social Business: Full Speed Ahead or Proceed with Caution?

Chapter 3 Achieving Competitive Advantage with Information Systems

Verizon or AT&T: Which Company Has the Best Digital Strategy?
Digital Technology Helps Crayola Brighten Its Brand
Carter's Redesigns Its Business Processes
Walmart Versus Amazon and the Future of Retail

Chapter 4 Ethical and Social Issues in Information Systems

The Dark Side of Big Data
Volkswagen Pollutes Its Reputation with Software to Evade Emissions Testing
Will Automation Kill Jobs?
Facebook Privacy: Your Life for Sale

Chapter 5 IT Infrastructure: Hardware and Software

PeroxyChem's Cloud Computing Formula for Success
Wearable Computers Change How We Work
Computing Takes Off in the Cloud
Is BYOD Good for Business?

Chapter 6 Foundations of Business Intelligence: Databases and Information Management

Data Management Helps the Charlotte Hornets Learn More About Their Fans
Kraft Heinz Finds a New Recipe for Analyzing Its Data
Keurig Green Mountain Improves Its Data Management
How Reliable Is Big Data?

Chapter 7 Telecommunications, the Internet, and Wireless Technology

RFID Helps Macy's Pursue an Omnichannel Strategy
Net Neutrality: The Battle Continues
Monitoring Employees on Networks: Unethical or Good Business?
Google, Apple, and Facebook Battle for Your Internet Experience

Chapter 8 Securing Information Systems

Hackers Target the U.S. Presidential Election: What Happened?
WannaCry and the SWIFT System Hacking Attacks: Theft on a Worldwide Scale
How Secure Is BYOD?
U.S. Office of Personnel Management Data Breach: No Routine Hack

Chapter 9 Achieving Operational Excellence and Customer Intimacy: Enterprise Applications

Skullcandy Rocks with ERP in the Cloud
Logistics and Transportation Management at LG Electronics
Kenya Airways Flies High with Customer Relationship Management
How Supply Chain Management Problems Killed Target Canada

Chapter 10 E-commerce: Digital Markets, Digital Goods

YouTube Transforms the Media Landscape
Uber: Digital Disruptor
"Socializing" with Customers
A Nasty Ending for Nasty Gal

Chapter 11 Improving Decision Making and Managing Knowledge

Can Big Data Analytics Help People Find Love?
Does IBM's Watson Have a Future in Business?
Will Robots Replace People in Manufacturing?
GE Bets on the Internet of Things and Big Data Analytics

Chapter 12 Building Information Systems and Managing Projects

Girl Scout Cookie Sales Go Digital
Developing Mobile Apps: What's Different
Snohomish County Public Utility District Implements a New Human Resources System
The Philly311 Project: The City of Brotherly Love Turns Problems into Opportunities

Preface

We wrote this book for business school students who wanted an in-depth look at how today's business firms use information technologies and systems to achieve corporate objectives. Information systems are one of the major tools available to business managers for achieving operational excellence, developing new products and services, improving decision making, and achieving competitive advantage. Students will find here the most up-to-date and comprehensive overview of information systems used by business firms today. After reading this book, we expect students will be able to participate in, and even lead, management discussions of information systems for their firms.

When interviewing potential employees, business firms often look for new hires who know how to use information systems and technologies for achieving bottom-line business results. Regardless of whether you are an accounting, finance, management, operations management, marketing, or information systems major, the knowledge and information you find in this book will be valuable throughout your business career.

What's New in This Edition

CURRENCY

The 13th edition features all new opening, closing, and Interactive Session cases. The text, figures, tables, and cases have been updated through September 2017 with the latest sources from industry and MIS research.

NEW FEATURES

- **New Career Opportunities** section in each chapter, identified by shows students specifically how this book can help them find a job and build their careers. The last major section of each chapter presents a description of an entry-level job for a recent college graduate based on a real-world job description. The job requirements are related to the topics covered in that chapter. The job description shows the required educational background and skills, lists business-related questions that might arise during the job interview, and provides author tips for answering the questions and preparing for the interview.
- **New Conceptual Videos** collection includes 45 conceptual videos of 3 to 5 minutes in length. Ken Laudon walks students through three of the most important concepts in each chapter using a contemporary animation platform. Available only in the MyLabMIS digital edition
- **New Video Cases** collection: 28 video cases (two or more per chapter) and 10 additional instructional videos covering key concepts and experiences in the MIS world. The video cases illustrate how real-world corporations and managers are using information technology and systems. Video Cases are listed at the beginning of each chapter.
- **Learning Tracks:** 53 Learning Tracks in MyLabMIS for additional coverage of selected topics. This edition includes new Learning Tracks for case-based reasoning and fuzzy logic.

NEW TOPICS

- **Updated coverage of artificial intelligenc (AI):** Chapter 11 has been rewritten to include new coverage of machine learning, natural language systems, computer vision systems, and robotics, reflecting the surging interest in business uses of AI and "intelligent" techniques.

- **Big Data and the Internet of Things:** In-depth coverage of big data, big data analytics, and the Internet of Things (IoT) in Chapters 1, 6, 7, and 11. Includes big data analytics, analyzing IoT data streams, Hadoop, in-memory computing, non-relational databases, data lakes, and analytic platforms.
- **Cloud Computing:** Updated and expanded coverage of cloud computing in Chapter 5 (IT infrastructure) with more detail on types of cloud services, private and public clouds, hybrid clouds, managing cloud services, and a new Interactive Session on using cloud services. Cloud computing also covered in Chapter 6 (databases in the cloud), Chapter 8 (cloud security), Chapter 9 (cloud-based CRM and ERP), Chapter 10 (e-commerce), and Chapter 12 (cloud-based systems development).
- **Social, Mobile, Local:** New e-commerce content in Chapter 10 describing how social tools, mobile technology, and location-based services are transforming marketing and advertising.
- **Social Business:** Expanded coverage of social business, introduced in Chapter 2 and discussed in throughout the text. Detailed discussions of enterprise (internal corporate) social networking as well as social networking in e-commerce.
- Machine learning
- Natural language processing
- Computer vision systems
- Robotics
- Chatbots
- Blockchain
- Data lake
- Distributed database
- DevOps
- FinTech
- Near field communication (NFC)
- Native advertising
- Platforms
- Software-defined storage (SDS)

The 13th Edition: The Comprehensive Solution for the MIS Curriculum

Since its inception, this text has helped to define the MIS course around the globe. This edition continues to be authoritative but is also more customizable, flexible, and geared to meeting the needs of different colleges, universities, and individual instructors. Many of its learning tools are now available in digital form. This book is now part of a complete learning package that includes the core text, Video Case Package, and Learning Tracks.

The core text consists of 12 chapters with hands-on projects covering the most essential topics in MIS. An important part of the core text is the Video Case Study and Instructional Video Package: 28 video case studies (two to three per chapter) plus 10 instructional videos that illustrate business uses of information systems, explain new technologies, and explore concepts. Videos are keyed to the topics of each chapter.

In addition, for students and instructors who want to go deeper into selected topics, there are 53 Learning Tracks in MyLabMIS that cover a variety of MIS topics in greater depth.

THE CORE TEXT

The core text provides an overview of fundamental MIS concepts using an integrated framework for describing and analyzing information systems. This framework shows information systems composed of people, organization, and technology elements and is reinforced in student projects and case studies.

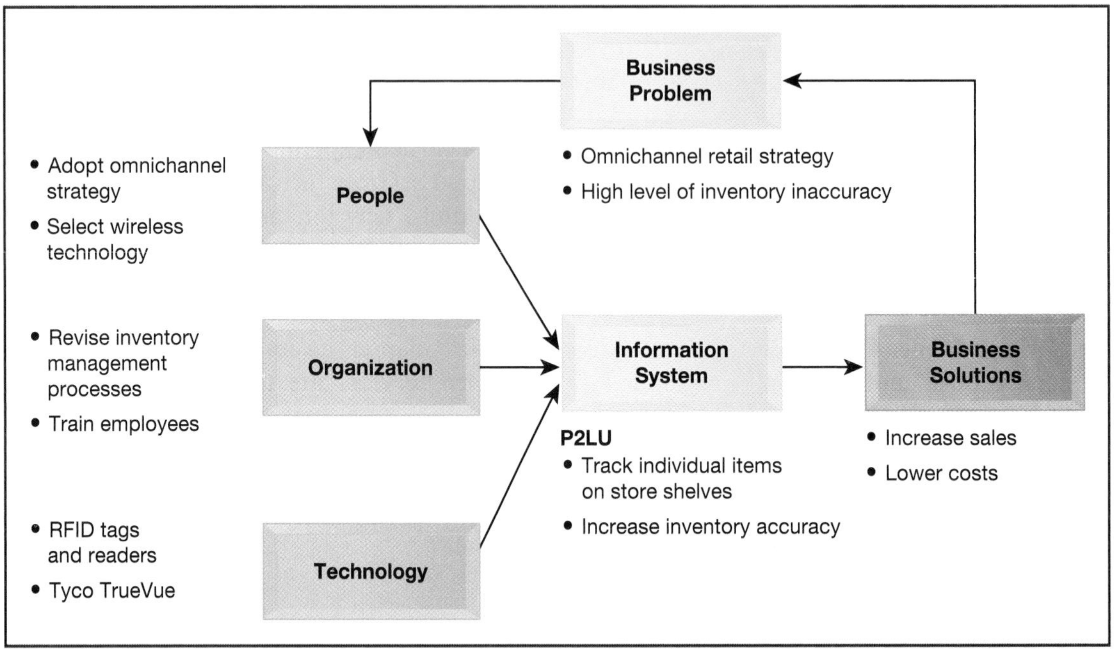

A diagram accompanying each chapter-opening case graphically illustrates how people, organization, and technology elements work together to create an information system solution to the business challenges discussed in the case.

Chapter Organization

Each chapter contains the following elements:

- A Chapter Outline based on Learning Objectives
- Lists of all the Case Studies and Video Cases for each chapter
- A chapter-opening case describing a real-world organization to establish the theme and importance of the chapter
- A diagram analyzing the opening case in terms of the people, organization, and technology model used throughout the text
- Two Interactive Sessions with Case Study Questions
- A Career Opportunities section showing students how to use the text for job hunting and career preparation
- A Review Summary keyed to the Student Learning Objectives
- A list of Key Terms that students can use to review concepts
- Review questions for students to test their comprehension of chapter material
- Discussion questions raised by the broader themes of the chapter
- A series of Hands-on MIS Projects consisting of two Management Decision Problems, a hands-on application software project, and a project to develop Internet skills
- A Collaboration and Teamwork Project to develop teamwork and presentation skills with options for using open source collaboration tools
- A chapter-ending case study for students to apply chapter concepts
- Two assisted-graded writing questions with prebuilt grading rubrics
- Chapter references

KEY FEATURES

We have enhanced the text to make it more interactive, leading edge, and appealing to both students and instructors. The features and learning tools are described in the following sections.

Business-Driven with Real-World Business Cases and Examples

The text helps students see the direct connection between information systems and business performance. It describes the main business objectives driving the use of information systems and technologies in corporations all over the world: operational excellence, new products and services, customer and supplier intimacy, improved decision making, competitive advantage, and survival. In-text examples and case studies show students how specific companies use information systems to achieve these objectives.

We use current (2017) examples from business and public organizations throughout the text to illustrate the important concepts in each chapter. All the case studies describe companies or organizations that are familiar to students, such as Uber, the NFL, Facebook, Crayola, Walmart, Amazon, Google, Macy's, and GE.

Interactivity

There's no better way to learn about MIS than by doing MIS! We provide different kinds of hands-on projects where students can work with real-world business scenarios and data and learn firsthand what MIS is all about. These projects heighten student involvement in this exciting subject.

- **Online Video Case Package.** Students can watch short videos online, either in-class or at home or work, and then apply the concepts of the book to the analysis of the video. Every chapter contains at least two business video cases that explain how business firms and managers are using information systems and explore concepts discussed in the chapter. Each video case consists of one or more videos about a real-world company, a background text case, and case study questions. These video cases enhance students' understanding of MIS topics and the relevance of MIS to the business world. In addition, there are 10 Instructional Videos that describe developments and concepts in MIS keyed to respective chapters.
- **Online Conceptual Videos [the digital edition only].** Forty-five video animations where the authors walk students through three concepts from each chapter.
- **Interactive Sessions.** Two short cases in each chapter have been redesigned as Interactive Sessions to be used in the classroom (or on Internet discussion boards) to stimulate student interest and active learning. Each case concludes with case study questions. The case study questions provide topics for class discussion, Internet discussion, or written assignments.
- **Hands-On MIS Projects.** Every chapter concludes with a Hands-On MIS Projects section containing three types of projects: two Management Decision Problems; a hands-on application software exercise using Microsoft Excel, Access, or web page and blog creation tools; and a project that develops Internet business skills. A Dirt Bikes USA running case in MyLabMIS provides additional hands-on projects for each chapter.

INTERACTIVE SESSION: PEOPLE — **"Socializing" with Customers**

More than 2 billion people worldwide use social media, making it an obvious platform for companies seeking to engage consumers, amplify product messages, discover trends and influencers, build brand awareness, and take action on customer requests and recommendations. More than 30 million businesses have active Facebook brand pages, enabling users to interact with the brand through blogs, comment pages, contests, and offerings on the brand page. The "like" button gives users a chance to share with their social network their feelings about content and other objects they are viewing and websites they are visiting. With like buttons on many millions of websites, Facebook can track user behavior on other sites and then sell

social campaigns are designed to teach first-time homeowners or young renters about home improvement, the company is also hoping they will encourage consumers to think differently about the brand beyond its products and services. Management believes millennials who are becoming first-time homeowners want to know the deeper meaning of what a company is trying to stand for, not just the products and services it offers.

An estimated 90 percent of customers are influenced by online reviews, and nearly half of U.S. social media users actively seek customer service through social media. As a result, marketing is now placing much more emphasis on customer satisfaction and service. Social media monitoring

Each chapter contains two Interactive Sessions on, People, Organizations, or Technology using real-world companies to illustrate chapter concepts and issues.

Case Study Questions encourage students to apply chapter concepts to real-world companies in class discussions, student presentations, or writing assignments.

CASE STUDY QUESTIONS

1. Assess the people, organization, and technology issues for using social media technology to engage with customers.
2. What are the advantages and disadvantages of using social media for advertising, brand building, market research, and customer service?
3. Give an example of a business decision in this case study that was facilitated by using social media to interact with customers.
4. Should all companies use social media technology for customer service and marketing? Why or why not? What kinds of companies are best suited to use these platforms?

Two real-world business scenarios per chapter provide opportunities for students to apply chapter concepts and practice management decision making.

Hands-On MIS Projects

MANAGEMENT DECISION PROBLEMS

The projects in this section give you hands-on experience in analyzing data quality problems, establishing companywide data standards, creating a database for inventory management, and using the web to search online databases for overseas business resources. Visit **MyLab MIS** to access this chapter's Hands-On MIS Projects.

6-8 Emerson Process Management, a global supplier of measurement, analytical, and monitoring instruments and services based in Austin, Texas, had a new data warehouse designed for analyzing customer activity to improve service and marketing. However, the data warehouse was full of inaccurate and redundant data. The data in the warehouse came from numerous transaction processing systems in Europe, Asia, and other locations around the world. The team that designed the warehouse had assumed that sales groups in all these areas would enter customer names and addresses the same way. In fact, companies in different countries were using multiple ways of entering quote, billing, shipping, and other data. Assess the potential business impact of these data quality problems. What decisions have to be made and steps taken to reach a solution?

Students practice using software in real-world settings for achieving operational excellence and enhancing decision making.

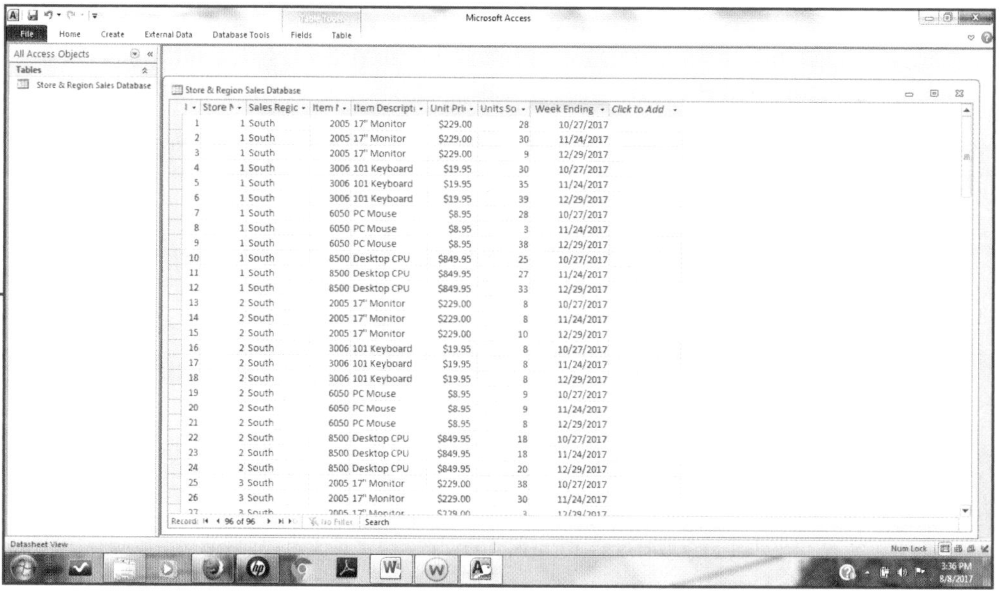

IMPROVING DECISION MAKING: USING WEB TOOLS TO CONFIGURE AND PRICE AN AUTOMOBILE

Software skills: Internet-based software
Business skills: Researching product information and pricing

3-11 In this exercise, you will use software at car-selling websites to find product information about a car of your choice and use that information to make an important purchase decision. You will also evaluate two of these sites as selling tools.

You are interested in purchasing a new Ford Escape (or some other car of your choice). Go to the website of CarsDirect (www.carsdirect.com) and begin your investigation. Locate the Ford Escape. Research the various Escape models; choose one you prefer in terms of price, features, and safety ratings. Locate and read at least two reviews. Surf the website of the manufacturer, in this case Ford (www.ford.com). Compare the information available on Ford's website with that of CarsDirect for the Ford Escape. Try to locate the lowest price for the car you want in a local dealer's inventory. Suggest improvements for CarsDirect.com and Ford.com.

Each chapter features a project to develop Internet skills for accessing information, conducting research, and performing online calculations and analysis.

- **Collaboration and Teamwork Projects.** Each chapter features a collaborative project that encourages students working in teams to use Google Drive, Google Docs, or other open source collaboration tools. The first team project in Chapter 1 asks students to build a collaborative Google site.

Career Opportunities and Resources

Every student who reads this text wants to know: How will this book help my career? Our new Career Opportunities feature shows you how to use this text as a tool for job-hunting and career-building. Job interviewers will typically ask about why you want the job, along with your ability to communicate, multitask, work in a team, show leadership, solve problems, and meet goals. These are general skills and behaviors you'll need to succeed in any job, and you should be prepared to provide examples from your course work and job experiences that demonstrate these skills. But there are also business knowledge and professional skills that employers will ask you about. Career Opportunities will show you how to use what you have learned in this text to demonstrate these skills.

The Career Opportunities section, identified by this icon is the last major section of each chapter under the heading "How will MIS help my career?". There you will find a description of an entry-level job for a recent college graduate based on a real-world job description from major online job sites related to the topics covered in that chapter. The name of the company offering the job and its location have been changed. Each chapter's job posting describes the required educational background and specific job skills, and suggests some of the business-related questions that might arise during the job interview. The authors provide tips for answering the questions and preparing for the interview. Career Opportunities also show where students can find out more information about the technical and business knowledge required for the job in this text and on the web and social media.

Below are the job descriptions used in this edition based on postings from both large and small businesses. A few of these jobs call for an MIS major, others for MIS course work, but many postings are not that specific. Some require some previous internship or job experience, but many are entry level positions suitable for new college graduates, and some of these positions provide on-the-job training. However, all require knowledge of business information systems and applications and the ability to work in a digital environment.

Chapter	Career Opportunity Job Description
1 Business Information Systems in Your Career	Financial Client Support and Sales Assistant
2 Global E-business and Collaboration	Entry Level Sales Support Specialist
3 Achieving Competitive Advantage with Information Systems	Entry Level Business Development Representative
4 Ethical and Social Issues in Information Systems	Junior Privacy Analyst
5 IT Infrastructure: Hardware and Software	Entry Level IT Consultant
6 Foundations of Business Intelligence: Databases and Information Management	Entry Level Data Analyst
7 Telecommunications , the Internet, and Wireless Technology	Automotive Digital Advisor
8 Securing Information Systems	Entry Level Identity Access and Management Support Specialist
9 Achieving Operational Excellence and Customer Intimacy: Enterprise Applications	Manufacturing Management Trainee
10 E-Commerce: Digital Markets, Digital Goods	Junior E-Commerce Data Analyst
11 Improving Decision Making and Managing Knowledge	Entry Level Data Analyst
12 Building Information Systems and Managing Projects	Entry Level Junior Business Systems Analyst

Students can use Career Opportunities to shape their resumes and career plans as well as to prepare for interviews. For instructors, Career Opportunities are potential projects for student research and in-class discussion.

Along with Career Opportunities, we have provided in MyLabMIS additional Career Resources, including job-hunting guides and instructions on how to build a Digital Portfolio demonstrating the business knowledge, application software proficiency, and Internet skills acquired from using the text. The portfolio can be included in a resume or job application or used as a learning assessment tool for instructors.

Assessment and AACSB Assessment Guidelines

The Association to Advance Collegiate Schools of Business (AACSB) is a not-for-profit corporation of educational institutions, corporations, and other organizations that seeks to improve business education primarily by accrediting university business programs. As a part of its accreditation activities, the AACSB has developed an Assurance of Learning Program designed to ensure that schools do in fact teach students what they promise. Schools are required to state a clear mission, develop a coherent business program, identify student learning objectives, and then prove that students do in fact achieve the objectives.

We have attempted in this book to support AACSB efforts to encourage assessment-based education. The front papers of this edition identify student learning objectives and anticipated outcomes for our Hands-On MIS projects. The authors will provide custom advice on how to use this text in colleges with different missions and assessment needs. Please e-mail the authors or contact your local Pearson representative for contact information.

Customization and Flexibility: Learning Track Modules

Our Learning Tracks feature gives instructors the flexibility to provide in-depth coverage of the topics they choose. There are 53 Learning Tracks in MyLabMIS available to instructors and students. This supplementary content takes students deeper into MIS topics, concepts, and debates and reviews basic technology concepts in hardware, software, database design, telecommunications, and other areas.

Author-Certified Test Bank and Supplements

- **Author-Certified Test Bank.** The authors have worked closely with skilled test item writers to ensure that higher-level cognitive skills are tested. Test bank multiple-choice questions include questions on content but also include many questions that require analysis, synthesis, and evaluation skills.
- **Annotated Slides.** The authors have prepared a comprehensive collection of 50 PowerPoint slides for each chapter to be used in your lectures. Many of these slides are the same as used by Ken Laudon in his MIS classes and executive education presentations. Each of the slides is annotated with teaching suggestions for asking students questions, developing in-class lists that illustrate key concepts, and recommending other firms as examples in addition to those provided in the text. The annotations are like an Instructor's Manual built into the slides and make it easier to teach the course effectively.

Student Learning-Focused

Student Learning Objectives are organized around a set of study questions to focus student attention. Each chapter concludes with a Review Summary and Review Questions organized around these study questions, and each major chapter section is based on a Learning Objective.

INSTRUCTOR RESOURCES

At the Instructor Resource Center, www.pearsonhighered.com/irc, instructors can easily register to gain access to a variety of instructor resources available with this text in downloadable format. If assistance is needed, our dedicated technical support team is ready to help with the media supplements that accompany this text. Visit support.pearson.com/getsupport for answers to frequently asked questions and user support.

The following supplements are available with this text:

- Instructor's Resource Manual
- Test Bank
- TestGen® Computerized Test Bank
- PowerPoint Presentation
- Image Library
- Lecture Notes

Video Cases and Instructional Videos

Instructors can download step-by-step instructions for accessing the video cases from the Instructor Resources Center. Video Cases and Instructional Videos are listed at the beginning of each chapter as well as in the Preface.

Learning Tracks Modules

There are 53 Learning Tracks in MyLabMIS providing additional coverage topics for students and instructors. See page xxvii for a list of the Learning Tracks available for this edition.

Video Cases and Instructional Videos

Chapter	Video
Chapter 1: Business Information Systems in Your Career	Business in the Cloud: Facebook, Google, and eBay Data Centers UPS Global Operations with the DIAD and Worldport Instructional Video: Tour IBM's Raleigh Data Center
Chapter 2: Global E-business and Collaboration	Walmart's Retail Link Supply Chain CEMEX: Becoming a Social Business Instructional Video: US Foodservice Grows Market with Oracle CRM on Demand
Chapter 3: Achieving Competititve Advantage with Information Systems,	GE Becomes a Digital Firm: The Emerging Industrial Internet National Basketball Association: Competing on Global Delivery with Akamai OS Streaming
Chapter 4: Ethical and Social Issues in Information Systems	What Net Neutrality Means for You Facebook and Google Privacy: What Privacy? The United States v. Terrorism: Data Mining for Terrorists and Innocents Instructional Video: Viktor Mayer Schönberger on the Right to Be Forgotten
Chapter 5: IT Infrastructure: Hardware and Software	Rockwell Automation Fuels the Oil and Gas Industry with the Internet of Things (IoT) ESPN.com: The Future of Sports Coverage in the Cloud Netflix: Building a Business in the Cloud
Chapter 6: Foundations of Business Intelligence: Databases and Information Management	Dubuque Uses Cloud Computing and Sensors to Build a Smarter City Brooks Brothers Closes in on Omnichannel Retail Maruti Suzuki Business Intelligence and Enterprise Databases
Chapter 7: Telecommunications, the Internet, and Wireless Technology	Telepresence Moves out of the Boardroom and into the Field Virtual Collaboration with IBM Sametime
Chapter 8: Securing Information Systems	Stuxnet and Cyberwarfare Cyberespionage: The Chinese Threat Instructional Video: Sony PlayStation Hacked; Data Stolen from 77 Million Users Instructional Video: Meet the Hackers: Anonymous Statement on Hacking SONY
Chapter 9: Achieving Operational Excellence and Customer Intimacy: Enterprise Applications	Life Time Fitness Gets in Shape with Salesforce CRM Evolution Homecare Manages Patients with Microsoft CRM Instructional Video: GSMS Protects Products and Patients by Serializing Every Bottle of Drugs
Chapter 10: E-commerce: Digital Markets, Digital Goods	Walmart Takes on Amazon: A Battle of IT and Management Systems Groupon: Deals Galore Etsy: A Marketplace and Community Instructional Video: Walmart's eCommerce Fulfillment Center Network Instructional Video: Behind the Scenes of an Amazon Warehouse
Chapter 11: Improving Decision Making and Managing Knowledge	How IBM's Watson Became a Jeopardy Champion Business Intelligence Helps the Cincinnati Zoo Work Smarter
Chapter 12: Building Information Systems and Managing Projects	IBM: Business Process Management in a SaaS Environment IBM Helps the City of Madrid with Real-Time BPM Software Instructional Video: What is PaaS? What is Predix? Instructional Video: BPM: Business Process Management Customer Story

Learning Tracks

Chapter	Learning Tracks
Chapter 1: Business Information Systems in Your Career	How Much Does IT Matter? The Changing Business Environment for IT The Business Information Value Chain The Mobile Digital Platform Occupational and Career Outlook for Information Systems Majors 2014–2020
Chapter 2: Global E-business and Collaboration	Systems From a Functional Perspective IT Enables Collaboration and Teamwork Challenges of Using Business Information Systems Organizing the Information Systems Function
Chapter 3: Achieving Competitive Advantage with Information Systems	Challenges of Using Information Systems for Competitive Advantage Primer on Business Process Design and Documentation Primer on Business Process Management
Chapter 4: Ethical and Social Issues in Information Systems	Developing a Corporate Code of Ethics for IT
Chapter 5: IT Infrastructure: Hardware and Software	How Computer Hardware and Software Work Service Level Agreements Cloud Computing The Open Source Software Initiative The Evolution of IT Infrastructure Technology Drivers of IT Infrastructure Fourth Generation Languages
Chapter 6: Foundations of Business Intelligence: Databases and Information Management	Database Design, Normalization, and Entity-Relationship Diagramming Introduction to SQL Hierarchical and Network Data Models
Chapter 7: Telecommunications, the Internet, and Wireless Technology	Broadband Network Services and Technologies Cellular System Generations Wireless Applications for Customer Relationship Management, Supply Chain Management, and Healthcare Introduction to Web 2.0 LAN Topologies
Chapter 8: Securing Information Systems	The Booming Job Market in IT Security The Sarbanes-Oxley Act Computer Forensics General and Application Controls for Information Systems Management Challenges of Security and Control Software Vulnerability and Reliability
Chapter 9: Achieving Operational Excellence and Customer Intimacy: Enterprise Applications	SAP Business Process Map Business Processes in Supply Chain Management and Supply Chain Metrics Best-Practice Business Processes in CRM Software
Chapter 10: E-commerce: Digital Markets, Digital Goods	E-Commerce Challenges: The Story of Online Groceries Build an E-commerce Business Plan Hot New Careers in E-Commerce E-commerce Payment Systems Building an E-commerce Web Site
Chapter 11: Improving Decision Making and Managing Knowledge	Building and Using Pivot Tables The Expert System Inference Engine Case-Based Reasoning Fuzzy Logic Challenges of Knowledge Management Systems
Chapter 12: Building Information Systems and Managing Projects	Capital Budgeting Methods for Information Systems Investments Enterprise Analysis: Business Systems Planning and Critical Success Factors Unified Modeling Language Information Technology Investments and Productivity

MyLabMIS

Available in MyLabMIS

- MIS Video Exercises – Videos illustrating MIS concepts, paired with brief quizzes
- MIS Decision Simulations – interactive exercises allowing students to play the role of a manager and make business decisions
- Auto-Graded writing exercises
- Assisted-Graded writing exercises – taken from the end of chapter, with a rubric provided
- Chapter Warm Ups, Chapter Quizzes – objective-based quizzing to test knowledge
- Discussion Questions – threaded discussion topics taken from the end of chapter
- Dynamic Study Modules – on the go adaptive quizzing, also available on a mobile phone
- Learning Catalytics – bring-your-own-device classroom response question banks of critical thinking and collaboration interactive quizzes
- Enhanced eText – an accessible, mobile-friendly eText with interactive elements, including Conceptual Animations, which walk students through key concepts in the chapter by making figures come to life
- Excel & Access Grader Projects – live in the application auto-graded Grader projects provided inside MyLabMIS to support classes covering Office tools

Acknowledgments

The production of any book involves valued contributions from a number of persons. We would like to thank all of our editors for encouragement, insight, and strong support for many years. We thank our editor Samantha McAfee Lewis and project manager Katrina Ostler for their role in managing the project.

Our special thanks go to our supplement authors for their work, including the following MyLabMIS content contributors: John Hupp, Columbus State University; Robert J. Mills, Utah State University; John P. Russo, Wentworth Institute of Technology; and Michael L. Smith, SUNY Oswego. We are indebted to Erica Laudon for her contributions to Career Opportunities and to Megan Miller for her help during production. We thank Diana R. Craig for her assistance with database and software topics.

Special thanks to colleagues at the Stern School of Business at New York University; to Professor Werner Schenk, Simon School of Business, University of Rochester; to Professor Mark Gillenson, Fogelman College of Business and Economics, University of Memphis; to Robert Kostrubanic, Indiana-Purdue University Fort Wayne; to Professor Lawrence Andrew of Western Illinois University; to Professor Detlef Schoder of the University of Cologne; to Professor Walter Brenner of the University of St. Gallen; to Professor Lutz Kolbe of the University of Gottingen; to Professor Donald Marchand of the International Institute for Management Development; and to Professor Daniel Botha of Stellenbosch University who provided additional suggestions for improvement. Thank you to Professor Ken Kraemer, University of California at Irvine, and Professor John King, University of Michigan, for more than a decade-long discussion of information systems and organizations. And a special remembrance and dedication to Professor Rob Kling, University of Indiana, for being our friend and colleague over so many years.

We also want to especially thank all our reviewers whose suggestions helped improve our texts. Reviewers for this edition include:

Brad Allen, Plymouth State University
Wanda Curtsinger, Texas A&M University
Dawit Demissie, University of Albany
Anne Formalarie, Plymouth State University
Bin Gu,University of Texas–Austin
Essia Hamouda, University of California–Riverside
Linda Lau, Longwood University
Kimberly L. Merritt, Oklahoma Christian University
James W. Miller, Dominican University
Fiona Nah, University of Nebraska–Lincoln
M. K. Raja, University of Texas Arlington
Thomas Schambach, Illinois State University
Shawn Weisfeld, Florida Institute of Technology

K.C.L.
J.P.L.

Essentials of Management Information Systems

PART I

Information Systems in the Digital Age

Part I introduces the major themes and the problem-solving approaches that are used throughout this book. While surveying the role of information systems in today's businesses, this part raises a series of major questions: What is an information system? Why are information systems so essential in businesses today? How can information systems help businesses become more competitive? What do I need to know about information systems to succeed in my business career? What ethical and social issues do widespread use of information systems raise?

CHAPTER

1 Business Information Systems in Your Career

LEARNING OBJECTIVES

After reading this chapter, you will be able to answer the following questions:

1-1 Why are information systems so essential for running and managing a business today?

1-2 What exactly is an information system? How does it work? What are its people, organizational, and technology components?

1-3 How will a four-step method for business problem solving help you solve information system–related problems?

1-4 What information systems skills and knowledge are essential for business careers?

1-5 How will MIS help my career?

CHAPTER CASES

- The Grocery Store of the Future: Look at Kroger
- Can You Run Your Company with Your iPhone?
- UPS Competes Globally with Information Technology
- Did Information Systems Cause Deutsche Bank to Stumble?

VIDEO CASES

- Business in the Cloud: Facebook, Google, and eBay Data Centers
- UPS Global Operations with the DIAD and Worldport

Instructional Video:

- Tour IBM's Raleigh Data Center

MyLab MIS

- Discussion questions: 1-5, 1-6, 1-7;
- Hands-on MIS Projects: 1-8, 1-9, 1-10, 1-11;
- Writing Assignments: 1-17, 1-18;
- eText with Conceptual Animations

THE GROCERY STORE OF THE FUTURE: LOOK AT KROGER

If you were to step into the grocery store of the future, what would it look like? Well, you can get a glimpse by visiting a Kroger supermarket. Kroger Company, headquartered in Cincinnati, Ohio, is the largest U.S. supermarket chain by revenue (with fiscal 2017 sales of $115.348 billion) and the second-largest general retailer (after Walmart). Kroger operates 2,778 supermarkets and multi-department stores in 34 states. It's also a leading-edge user of information systems.

Every time you walk into a Kroger store, infrared sensors note your arrival. Kroger uses its knowledge of how many customers are in that store to predict when long lines will pop up and where cashiers should be allocated to prevent pileups from happening. Data collected over time about customer shopping patterns, purchase transactions, staffing levels, and store layouts are fed into analytics software to help Kroger predict what is likely to happen on certain days of the week or month and how many registers should be open. For example, a Saturday afternoon shopper is likely to spend a longer amount of time in the store than someone shopping at 5:30 on a Wednesday evening. A screen at the front of the store lets employees know when to open up or close down an additional lane. This system, called QueVision, has cut the average wait time at a Kroger store from four minutes to less than 30 seconds. The sensors do not photograph or identify shoppers, and they are only located at checkout lines and store entrances—not throughout the entire store.

Kroger equipped refrigerated containers with sensors that check cold food storage temperatures every 30 minutes and alert store managers and facilities engineers if temperatures hit unsafe levels. A typical Kroger store temperature monitoring system has more than 220 radio frequency identification (RFID) tags connected to a wireless network. Before sensors were installed, Kroger employees had to manually check food storage thermometers twice a day. This process ran up costs if food spoiled or staff made measurement mistakes. The new sensor-based system for reporting temperature changes cuts down on the number of cold products that go bad and have to be thrown out, reduces labor, and saves energy.

©Turgaygundogdu/Shutterstock

Kroger started its own online ordering service called Click List, which allows customers to order groceries online and then pay for and collect their goods at a pickup window at an appointed time without having to leave their car. The fee for this service is $4.95. Traditional e-commerce services tend to attract shoppers purchasing just a few items, but Kroger's service appeals to convenience-minded customers purchasing many grocery items at once as a means of speeding up their regular shopping trips.

Kroger also found that customers wanted to integrate their mobile devices into their shopping experience to view store maps, create grocery lists, pay for goods, and earn loyalty points. Kroger developed a mobile app that features localized shopping lists, targeted ads, and, in select areas, the ability to scan and bag items while shopping.

Kroger surveys have found that what bothers people the most about grocery shopping is the dreaded wait at the checkout line. Technology is eliminating that problem at Kroger stores and providing customers with a better shopping experience. The grocery business is extremely competitive and low-margin, with profits of only a few cents per dollar. Customer loyalty is especially critical, and Kroger's systems for making shopping easier and more pleasant are a major source of competitive advantage.

Sources: Kim S. Nash, "At Kroger, Technology Is Changing the Grocery-Store Shopping Experience," *Wall Street Journal*, February 20, 2017; www.thekrogerco.com, accessed June 27, 2017; Demitrios Kalogeropoulos, "How Kroger Co. Plans to Spend $4 Billion This Year," *Fox Business*, March 10, 2016; Kate Taylor, "Kroger Is Building the Grocery Store of the Future," *Business Insider*, November 8, 2015; Tom Kaneshige, "The Internet of Things Now Includes the Grocer's Frozen Food Aisle," *CIO*, July 31, 2015; and Laurianne McLaughlin, "Kroger Solves Top Customer Issue: Long Lines," *Information Week*, April 2, 2014.

The challenges facing Kroger show why information systems are so essential today. Kroger operates in a highly competitive industry with ultra-thin profit margins of only 1 or 2 percent. There is a limit to the number of customers each Kroger store can handle at one time, and long checkout lines will appear if there are too many people and too few available registers. Surveys have shown that eliminating long checkout lines makes customers very happy and is the best predictor of whether they will return and purchase again. Kroger used leading-edge information systems to shorten checkout lines, reduce food spoilage costs, and make the customer buying experience more pleasant and convenient. The use of networked sensors linked to the Internet (known as the Internet of Things) and powerful analytics to drive business operations and management decisions are key topics today in the MIS world and will be discussed throughout this text.

The chapter-opening diagram calls attention to important points raised by this case and this chapter. To remain profitable in a hyper-competitive industry, Kroger management chose to use information technology to improve the customer experience. Kroger stores use infrared sensors, wireless networks, and powerful analytics software to predict customer levels, calculate checkout times, and provide information on when and where to open additional checkout stations to reduce waiting times and checkout lines. Kroger also uses wireless sensor systems to monitor the status of cold food storage devices as well as mobile technology to help customers plan for and expedite their shopping.

It is also important to note that deploying these new information systems has changed the way Kroger runs its business. To effectively use its sensor-driven and mobile systems, Kroger had to redesign jobs and procedures for allocating checkout lines, bagging groceries, and monitoring food temperatures. These changes had to be carefully planned to make sure they enhanced service, efficiency, and profitability.

Here are some questions to think about: How are information systems improving operations and customer service at Kroger stores? Give examples of two management decisions that are facilitated by Kroger's information systems. How much of an advantage does Kroger have over its competitors?

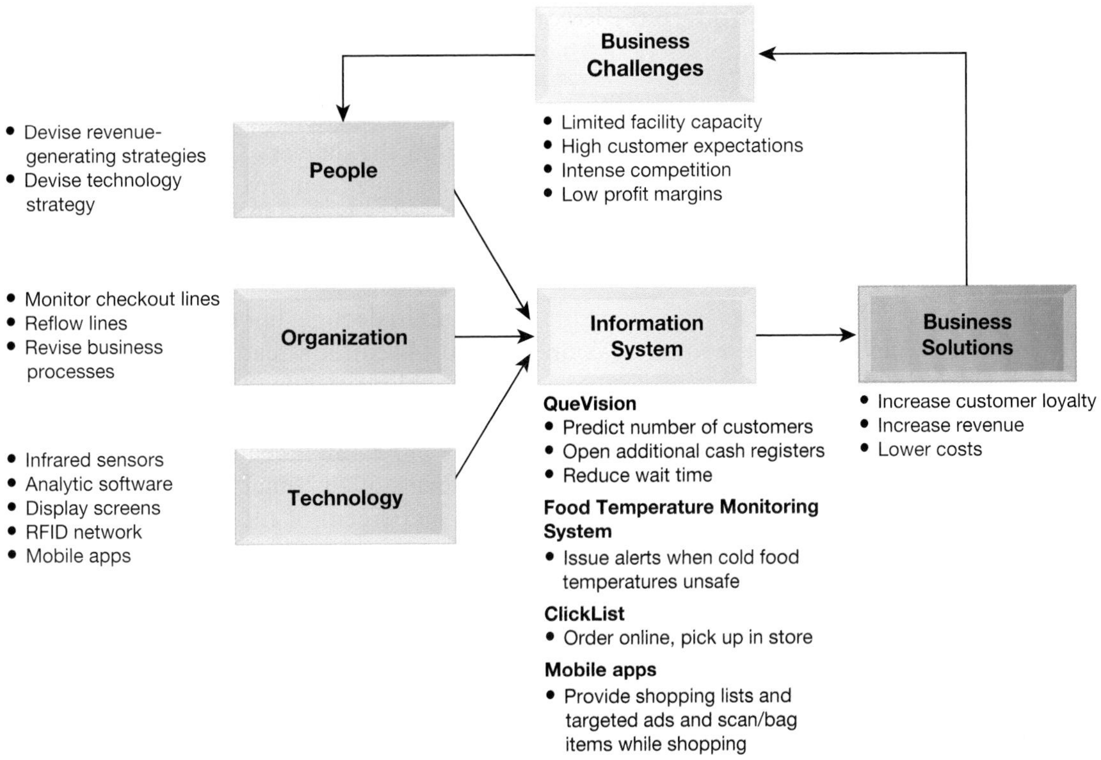

1-1 Why are information systems so essential for running and managing a business today?

It's not business as usual in America, or the rest of the global economy, anymore. In 2016, American businesses invested nearly $2.8 trillion in information systems hardware, software, and telecommunications equipment—about 32 percent of all capital investment in the United States. In addition, they spent another $800 billion on business and management consulting and information technology services, much of which involves redesigning firms' business operations to take advantage of these new technologies. Together, investments in technology and management consulting grew at around 3.5 percent in 2016, far faster than the economy as a whole (Bureau of Economic Analysis, 2017). Worldwide, non-U.S. expenditures for information technology exceeded $3.5 trillion (Gartner, Inc., 2017).

HOW INFORMATION SYSTEMS ARE TRANSFORMING BUSINESS

You can see the results of this spending around you every day. Cell phones, smartphones, tablet computers, email, and online conferencing over the Internet have all become essential tools of business. In 2016, more than 142 million businesses had registered .com or .net Internet sites. Approximately 273 million adult Americans were online, 183 million people bought something online, 214 million researched a product, 230 million used a search engine, and 177 million of these searchers used their mobile devices. What this means is that if you and your business aren't connected to the Internet and mobile apps, chances are you are not being as effective as you could be (eMarketer, 2017; Pew Internet and American Life, 2017).

In 2016 FedEx moved more than 1 billion packages worldwide, mostly overnight, and United Parcel Service (UPS) moved more than 5 billion packages as businesses sought to sense and respond to rapidly changing customer demand, reduce inventories to the lowest possible levels, and achieve higher levels of operational efficiency. The growth of e-commerce has had a significant impact on UPS's shipping volume; UPS delivers about 42 percent of all e-commerce shipments, representing about 25 percent of its revenue. Supply chains have become faster paced, with companies of all sizes depending on the delivery of just-in-time inventory to help them compete. Companies today manage their inventories in near real time to reduce their overhead costs and get to market faster. If you are not part of this new supply chain management economy, chances are your business is not as efficient as it could be.

Print newspaper readership continues to decline, but more than 200 million people read at least some news online, and 144 million read actual newspapers online, with digital newspaper subscriptions doubling in 2016. Two hundred twenty million used a social networking site such as Facebook, Tumblr, or Google+. More than 150 million banked online, and about 210 million read blogs, creating an explosion of new writers, readers, and new forms of customer feedback that did not exist before. At 39 of the top 50 news sites, 60 percent of the visitors came from mobile devices. Adding to this mix of new social media, about 310 million people worldwide used Twitter (about 115 million in the United States), including 80 percent of *Fortune* 500 firms communicating with their customers. This means your customers are empowered and able to talk to each other about your business products and services. Do you have a solid online customer relationship program in place? Do you know what your customers are saying about your firm? Is your marketing department listening?

E-commerce and Internet advertising spending reached $83 billion in 2017, growing at about 15 percent at a time when traditional advertising and commerce have been flat. Facebook's ad revenue hit $26 billion in 2016, and Google's online ad revenues surpassed $79 billion. Is your advertising department reaching this new web and mobile customer?

New federal security and accounting laws require many businesses to keep email messages for five years. Coupled with existing occupational and health laws requiring firms to store employee chemical exposure data for up to 60 years, these laws are spurring the growth of digital information now estimated to be 4.7 zettabytes (4.7 trillion gigabytes), equivalent to more than 60,000 Libraries of Congress. This trove of information is doubling every year thanks in part to more than 200 billion Internet sensors and data generators. Does your compliance department meet the minimal requirements for storing financial, health, and occupational information? If it doesn't, your entire business may be at risk.

Briefly, it's a new world of doing business, one that will greatly affect your future business career. Along with the changes in business come changes in jobs and careers. No matter whether you are a finance, accounting, management, marketing, operations management, or information systems major, how you work, where you work, and how well you are compensated will all be affected by business information systems. The purpose of this book is to help you understand and benefit from these new business realities and opportunities.

WHAT'S NEW IN MANAGEMENT INFORMATION SYSTEMS?

Lots! What makes management information systems the most exciting topic in business is the continual change in technology, management use of the technology, and the impact on business success. New businesses and industries appear, old ones decline, and successful firms are those that learn how to use the new technologies. Table 1.1 summarizes the major new themes in business uses of information systems. These themes will appear throughout the book in all the chapters, so it might be a good idea to take some time now to discuss these with your professor and classmates

TABLE 1.1

What's New in MIS

Change	Business Impact
TECHNOLOGY	
Cloud computing platform emerges as a major business area of innovation.	A flexible collection of computers on the Internet begins to perform tasks traditionally performed on corporate computers. Major business applications are delivered online as an Internet service (software as a service [SaaS]).
Big data and the Internet of Things (IoT)	Businesses look for insights in huge volumes of data from web traffic, email messages, social media content, and Internet-connected machines (sensors).
A mobile digital platform emerges to compete with the PC as a business system.	The Apple iPhone and Android mobile devices can download millions of applications to support collaboration, location-based services, and communication with colleagues. Small tablet computers, including the iPad, Samsung Galaxy, and Kindle Fire, challenge conventional laptops as platforms for consumer and corporate computing.
MANAGEMENT	
Managers adopt online collaboration and social networking software to improve coordination, collaboration, and knowledge sharing.	Millions of business professionals worldwide use Google Apps, Google Drive, Microsoft Office 365, Yammer, and IBM Connections to support blogs, project management, online meetings, personal profiles, and online communities.
Business intelligence applications accelerate.	More powerful data analytics and interactive dashboards provide real-time performance information to managers to enhance decision making.
Virtual meetings proliferate.	Managers adopt telepresence, video conferencing, and web conferencing technologies to reduce travel time and cost, improving collaboration and decision making.
ORGANIZATIONS	
Social business	Businesses use social networking platforms, including Facebook, Twitter, Instagram, and internal corporate social tools, to deepen interactions with employees, customers, and suppliers. Employees use blogs, wikis, email, texting, and messaging to interact in online communities.
Telework gains momentum in the workplace.	The Internet, wireless laptops, smartphones, and tablet computers make it possible for growing numbers of people to work away from the traditional office. Forty-three percent of employed Americans reported spending some time working remotely and doing so for longer times.
Co-creation of business value	Sources of business value shift from products to solutions and experiences and from internal sources to networks of suppliers and collaboration with customers. Supply chains and product development become more global and collaborative; customer interactions help firms define new products and services.

In the technology area are three interrelated changes: (1) the mobile digital platform composed of smartphones and tablet devices; (2) the growing business use of big data, including the Internet of Things (IoT) driven by billions of data-producing sensors; and (3) the growth in cloud computing, by which more and more business software runs over the Internet.

IPhones, Android phones, and high-definition tablet computers are not just gadgets or entertainment outlets. They represent new emerging computing and media platforms based on an array of new hardware and software technologies. More and more business computing is moving from PCs and desktop machines to these mobile devices. Managers are increasingly using these devices to coordinate work, communicate with employees, and provide information for decision making. Today more than 50 percent of Internet users access the web through mobile devices. To a large extent, these devices change the character of corporate computing.

iPhone and iPad Applications for Business

1. *Salesforce1*
2. *Cisco WebEx Meetings*
3. *SAP Business One*
4. *iWork*
5. *Evernote*
6. *Adobe Acrobat Reader*
7. *Oracle Business Intelligence Mobile*
8. *Dropbox*

STANCA SANDA/Alamy Stock Photo

Whether it's attending an online meeting, checking orders, working with files and documents, or obtaining business intelligence, Apple's iPhone and iPad offer unlimited possibilities for business users. A stunning multitouch display, full Internet browsing, and capabilities for messaging, video and audio transmission, and document management make each an all-purpose platform for mobile computing.

Managers routinely use online collaboration and social technologies to make better, faster decisions. As management behavior changes, how work is organized, coordinated, and measured also changes. By connecting employees working on teams and projects, the social network is where work is done, where plans are executed, and where managers manage. Collaboration spaces are where employees meet one another—even when they are separated by continents and time zones.

The strength of cloud computing and the growth of the mobile digital platform mean that organizations can rely more on telework, remote work, and distributed decision making. This same platform means firms can outsource more work and rely on markets (rather than employees) to build value. It also means that firms can collaborate with suppliers and customers to create new products or make existing products more efficiently.

You can see some of these trends at work in the Interactive Session on People. Millions of managers and employees rely heavily on the mobile digital platform to coordinate suppliers and shipments, satisfy customers, and organize work activities. A business day without these mobile devices or Internet access would be unthinkable. As you read the case, note how the mobile platform has changed the way people do their work and make decisions.

GLOBALIZATION CHALLENGES AND OPPORTUNITIES: A FLATTENED WORLD

Prior to AD 1500, there was no truly global economic system of trade that connected all the continents on earth. After the sixteenth century, a global trading system began to emerge based on global shipping and voyages of discovery and regular trade. The world trade that ensued after these voyages has brought the peoples and cultures of the world much closer together. The industrial revolution was really a worldwide phenomenon energized by expansion of trade among nations, making nations both competitors and collaborators in business. The Internet has greatly heightened the competitive tensions among nations as global trade expands and strengthened the benefits that flow from trade.

In 2005, journalist Thomas Friedman wrote an influential book declaring the world was now flat, by which he meant that the Internet and global communications

INTERACTIVE SESSION: PEOPLE — Can You Run Your Company with Your iPhone?

Can you run your company just by using your iPhone? Perhaps not entirely, but there are many business functions today that can be performed using an iPhone, iPad, or Android mobile device. Smartphones and tablets have become all-in-one tools that help managers and employees work more efficiently. With a tap or flick of a finger, they can access the Internet or serve as a telephone, a camera, a music or video player, an email and messaging machine, and, increasingly, a gateway into corporate systems. New software applications for document sharing, collaboration, sales, order processing, inventory management, scheduling, and production monitoring make these devices even more versatile business tools.

Network Rail runs, maintains, and develops the rail tracks, signaling, bridges, tunnels, level crossings, and many key stations for most of the rail network in England, Scotland, and Wales. Keeping trains running on time is one of its top priorities. To maintain 20,000 miles of track safely and efficiently, skilled workers must be equipped with appropriate tools and training so they can work across thousands of sites throughout the rail network 24 hours a day. Network Rail uses a group of custom apps for its 22,000 iPhone and iPad devices to streamline maintenance operations, capture incident data quickly, and immediately share critical information.

Several apps help Network Rail improve railway performance and safety. The Close Call app helps employees report hazards as they are found so problems can be addressed quickly. The MyWork app gives maintenance teams all the information they need to start and complete repair tasks. The Sentinel app allows field managers to electronically scan ID cards to verify that workers are qualified to perform specific tasks.

The iPhone and iPad apps provide maintenance technicians with current technical data, GPS locations, and streamlined reports, replacing cumbersome reference books and rain-soaked paperwork that slowed the repair process. Many service calls start with hazardous conditions reported by Network Rail employees themselves. Rather than waiting hours to fill out a report at the depot, workers can take pictures of dangerous situations right away, using the Close Call app to describe situations and upload photos to the call center. Once provided with the hazard's GPS coordinates, the call center will usually schedule repairs within 24 hours.

MyWork gives maintenance workers a simple overview of all of the jobs each team needs to complete during a specific shift. This mobile app clusters jobs by location, skills required, and opening and closing times. Using precise map coordinates, workers can find sites easily and finish jobs more quickly. By electronically delivering daily job schedules to more than 14,000 maintenance staff members, MyWork has enabled them to complete more than half a million work orders to date while minimizing interruptions.

British Airways is the largest airline in the United Kingdom, with operations in more than 200 airports worldwide. The airline has found many ways to use iPads to improve customer service and operational efficiency. The airline has created more than 40 custom apps for more than 17,000 iPads for its workforce, which have transformed the way it does business.

Unforeseen disruptions can create long lines of passengers seeking flight information and rebooking. British Airways' FlightReact app mobilizes agents to scan a boarding pass, review the customer's booking, look up alternate flight options, and rebook and reticket passengers—all within four minutes. iBanner allows agents to identify passengers transferring onto a specific flight, while iTranslate enables staff to communicate easily with travelers speaking any language, and BagReport helps customers find misplaced baggage in the event of a disruption.

Inside the airport, iPads and iPhones communicate with low-energy wireless Bluetooth signals from iBeacon, notifying customers of Wi-Fi access, gate locations, and flight updates. Beyond the terminal, mobile apps are helping British Airways to improve the aircraft turnaround process. British Airways has more than 70 planes at London Heathrow Terminal, five turning around at once and each requiring a team of about 30 people, so any way to shorten and streamline this process can generate huge business benefits.

Loading luggage and cargo onto an aircraft is one of the most complex parts of the turnaround process, requiring detailed communications between the turnaround manager (TRM), who coordinates and manages the services around the aircraft during departure and arrival; the offsite

Centralized Load Control (CLC) team; and the pilot. With iPads running the iLoad Direct app, turnaround managers are able to monitor the aircraft loading process and share data with pilots and back-office staff in real time. TRMs can receive and input real-time data about the aircraft load's contents, weight, and distribution. These data are essential to help the pilot calculate the right amount of fuel and position the plane for takeoff. By streamlining communications between the ground crew, the CLC team, and the pilot, iLoad Direct on the iPad speeds up the pace at which aircraft become airborne. These mobile tools have helped British Airways achieve an industry-leading benchmark for aircraft turnaround.

In addition to facilitating managerial work, mobile devices are helping rank-and-file employees manage their work lives more effectively. Shyft is one of several smartphone apps that allow workers to share information, make schedule changes, and report labor violations. Thousands of employees at chains like Starbucks and Old Navy are using these apps to view their schedules and swap shifts when they've got a scheduling conflict or need extra work.

Sources: "British Airways: Transforming the Travel Experience from Start to Finish" and "Network Rail, " iPhone in Business, www.apple.com, accessed January 4, 2017; and Lauren Weber, "Apps Empower Employees, Ease Scheduling," *Wall Street Journal*, January 3, 2017.

CASE STUDY QUESTIONS

1. What kinds of applications are described here? What business functions do they support? How do they improve operational efficiency and decision making?
2. Identify the problems in this case study that businesses solved by using mobile digital devices.
3. What kinds of businesses are most likely to benefit from equipping their employees with mobile devices such as iPhones and iPads?
4. One company deploying iPhones has said, "The iPhone is not a game changer, it's an industry changer. It changes the way that you can interact with your customers and with your suppliers." Discuss the implications of this statement.

had greatly expanded the opportunities for people to communicate with one another and reduced the economic and cultural advantages of developed countries. U.S. and European countries were in a fight for their economic lives, according to Friedman, competing for jobs, markets, resources, and even ideas with highly educated, motivated populations in low-wage areas in the less developed world (Friedman, 2007). In 2017 a new globalization driven largely by information technology has radically reduced the cost of moving goods and ideas to low-wage countries, leading to the deindustrialization of wealthy developed countries (Baldwin, 2016). This globalization presents you and your business with both challenges and opportunities.

A growing percentage of the economy of the United States and other advanced industrial countries in Europe and Asia depends on imports and exports. In 2016, more than 30 percent of the U.S. economy resulted from foreign trade of goods and services, both imports and exports. In Europe and Asia, the number exceeds 50 percent. Half of *Fortune* 500 U.S. firms obtain nearly 50 percent of their revenue from foreign operations. For instance, more than 50 percent of Intel's revenues in 2016 came from overseas sales of its microprocessors. Eighty percent of the toys sold in the United States are manufactured in China; about 90 percent of the PCs manufactured in China use American-made Intel or Advanced Micro Design (AMD) chips.

It's not just goods that move across borders. So too do jobs, some of them high-level jobs that pay well and require a college degree. In the past decade, the United States lost several million manufacturing jobs to offshore, low-wage producers, but manufacturing is now a very small part of U.S. employment (less than 12 percent). In a normal year, about 300,000 service jobs move offshore to lower-wage countries, many of them in less-skilled information system occupations but also in tradable service jobs in architecture, financial services, customer call centers, consulting, engineering, and even radiology.

On the plus side, the U.S. economy creates more than 2 million new jobs in a normal year, and there have been 75 months of positive job growth. Employment in information systems and the other service occupations listed previously has rapidly expanded in sheer numbers, wages, productivity, and quality of work. Outsourcing has actually accelerated the development of new systems in the United States and worldwide by reducing the cost of building and maintaining them. In 2017 job openings in information systems and technologies far exceeded the supply of applicants.

The challenge for you as a business student is to develop high-level skills through education and on-the-job experience that cannot be outsourced. The challenge for your business is to avoid markets for goods and services that can be produced offshore much less expensively. The opportunities are equally immense. You can learn how to profit from the lower costs available in world markets and the chance to serve a marketplace with billions of customers. You have the opportunity to develop higher-level and more profitable products and services. Throughout this book, you will find examples of companies and individuals who either failed or succeeded in using information systems to adapt to this new global environment.

What does globalization have to do with management information systems? The answer is simple: everything. The emergence of the Internet into a full-blown international communications system has drastically reduced the costs of operating and transacting on a global scale. Communication between a factory floor in Shanghai and a distribution center in Sioux Falls, South Dakota, is now instant and virtually free. Customers now can shop in a worldwide marketplace, obtaining price and quality information reliably 24 hours a day. Firms producing goods and services on a global scale achieve extraordinary cost reductions by finding low-cost suppliers and managing production facilities in other countries. Internet service firms, such as Google and eBay, can replicate their business models and services in multiple countries without having to redesign their expensive, fixed-cost information systems infrastructure.

BUSINESS DRIVERS OF INFORMATION SYSTEMS

What makes information systems so essential today? Why are businesses investing so much in information systems and technologies? They do so to achieve six important business objectives: operational excellence; new products, services, and business models; customer and supplier intimacy; improved decision making; competitive advantage; and survival.

Operational Excellence

Businesses continuously seek to improve the efficiency of their operations to achieve higher profitability. Information systems and technologies are some of the most important tools available to managers for achieving higher levels of efficiency and productivity in business operations, especially when coupled with changes in business practices and management behavior.

Walmart, the largest retailer on earth, exemplifies the power of information systems coupled with brilliant business practices and supportive management to achieve world-class operational efficiency. In 2016, Walmart achieved more than $485 billion in sales—nearly one-tenth of retail sales in the United States—in large part because of its Retail Link system, which digitally links its suppliers to every one of Walmart's 11,700 stores worldwide. As soon as a customer purchases an item, the supplier monitoring the item knows to ship a replacement to the shelf. Walmart is the most efficient retail store in the industry, achieving sales of more than $600 per square foot compared to its closest competitor, Target, at $425 a square foot, with other large general merchandise retail firms producing less than $200 a square foot.

Amazon, the largest online retailer on earth, generating more than $135 billion in sales in 2016, invested $2.1 billion in information systems so that when one of its estimated 170 million customers searches for a product, Amazon can respond in milliseconds with the correct product displayed (and recommendations for other products).

New Products, Services, and Business Models

Information systems and technologies are a major enabling tool for firms to create new products and services, as well as entirely new business models. A **business model** describes how a company produces, delivers, and sells a product or service to create wealth. Today's music industry is vastly different from the industry a decade ago. Apple Inc. transformed an old business model of music distribution based on vinyl records, tapes, and CDs into an online, legal download distribution model based on its own operating system and iTunes store. Apple has prospered from a continuing stream of innovations, including the original iPod, iPod nano, iTunes music service, iPhone, and iPad.

Customer and Supplier Intimacy

When a business really knows its customers and serves them well, the way they want to be served, the customers generally respond by returning and purchasing more. This raises revenues and profits. Likewise with suppliers: the more a business engages its suppliers, the better the suppliers can provide vital inputs. This lowers costs. How really to know your customers, or suppliers, is a central problem for businesses with millions of offline and online customers.

The Mandarin Oriental in Manhattan and other high-end hotels exemplify the use of information systems and technologies to achieve customer intimacy. These hotels use information systems to keep track of guests' preferences, such as their preferred room temperature, check-in time, frequently dialed telephone numbers, and television programs, and store these data in a giant data repository. Individual rooms in the hotels are networked to a central network server so that they can be remotely monitored or controlled. When a customer arrives at one of these hotels, the system automatically changes the room conditions, such as dimming the lights, setting the room temperature, or selecting appropriate music, based on the customer's digital profile. The hotels also analyze their customer data to identify their best customers and develop individualized marketing campaigns based on customers' preferences.

JCPenney exemplifies the benefits of information systems-enabled supplier intimacy. Every time a dress shirt is bought at a JCPenney store in the United States, the record of the sale appears immediately on computers in Hong Kong at TAL Apparel Ltd., a giant contract manufacturer that produces one in eight dress shirts sold in the United States. TAL runs the numbers through a computer model it developed and decides how many replacement shirts to make and in what styles, colors, and sizes. TAL then sends the shirts to each JCPenney store, completely bypassing the retailer's warehouses. In other words, JCPenney's surplus shirt inventory is near zero, as is the cost of storing it.

Improved Decision Making

Many business managers operate in an information fog bank, never really having the right information at the right time to make an informed decision. Instead, managers rely on forecasts, best guesses, and luck. The result is over- or underproduction of goods and services, misallocation of resources, and poor response times. These poor outcomes raise costs and lose customers. In the past 10 years, information systems and technologies have made it possible for managers to use real-time data from the marketplace when making decisions.

For instance, Verizon Corporation, one of the largest regional telecommunications operating companies in the United States, uses a web-based digital dashboard to provide managers with precise real-time information on customer complaints, network performance for each locality served, and line outages or storm-damaged lines. Using this information, managers can immediately allocate repair resources to affected areas, inform consumers of repair efforts, and restore service fast.

Competitive Advantage

When firms achieve one or more of these business objectives—operational excellence; new products, services, and business models; customer/supplier intimacy; and improved decision making—chances are they have already achieved a competitive advantage. Doing things better than your competitors, charging less for superior products, and responding to customers and suppliers in real time all add up to higher sales and higher profits that your competitors cannot match. Apple Inc., Walmart, and UPS are industry leaders because they know how to use information systems for this purpose.

Survival

Business firms also invest in information systems and technologies because they are necessities of doing business. Sometimes these necessities are driven by industry-level changes. For instance, after Citibank introduced the first automated teller machines (ATMs) in the New York region to attract customers through higher service levels, its competitors rushed to provide ATMs to their customers to keep up with Citibank. Today, virtually all banks in the United States have regional ATMs and link to national and international ATM networks, such as CIRRUS. Providing ATM services to retail banking customers is simply a requirement of being in and surviving in the retail banking business.

Many federal and state statutes and regulations create a legal duty for companies and their employees to retain records, including digital records. For instance, the Toxic Substances Control Act (1976), which regulates the exposure of U.S. workers to more than 75,000 toxic chemicals, requires firms to retain records on employee exposure for 30 years. The Sarbanes–Oxley Act (2002), which was intended to improve the accountability of public firms and their auditors, requires public companies to retain audit working papers and records, including all email messages, for five years. Firms turn to information systems and technologies to provide the capability to respond to these information retention and reporting requirements. The Dodd–Frank Act (2010) requires financial service firms to expand their public reporting greatly on derivatives and other financial instruments.

1-2 What exactly is an information system? How does it work? What are its people, organizational, and technology components?

So far we've used *information systems and technologies* informally without defining the terms. **Information technology (IT)** consists of all the hardware and software that a firm needs to use to achieve its business objectives. This includes not only computers, storage technology, and mobile handheld devices but also software, such as the Windows or Linux operating systems, the Microsoft Office desktop productivity suite, and the many thousands of computer programs that can be found in a typical large firm. Information systems are more complex and can be understood best by looking at them from both a technology and a business perspective.

WHAT IS AN INFORMATION SYSTEM?

An **information system (IS)** can be defined technically as a set of interrelated components that collect (or retrieve), process, store, and distribute information to support decision making, coordinating, and control in an organization. In addition,

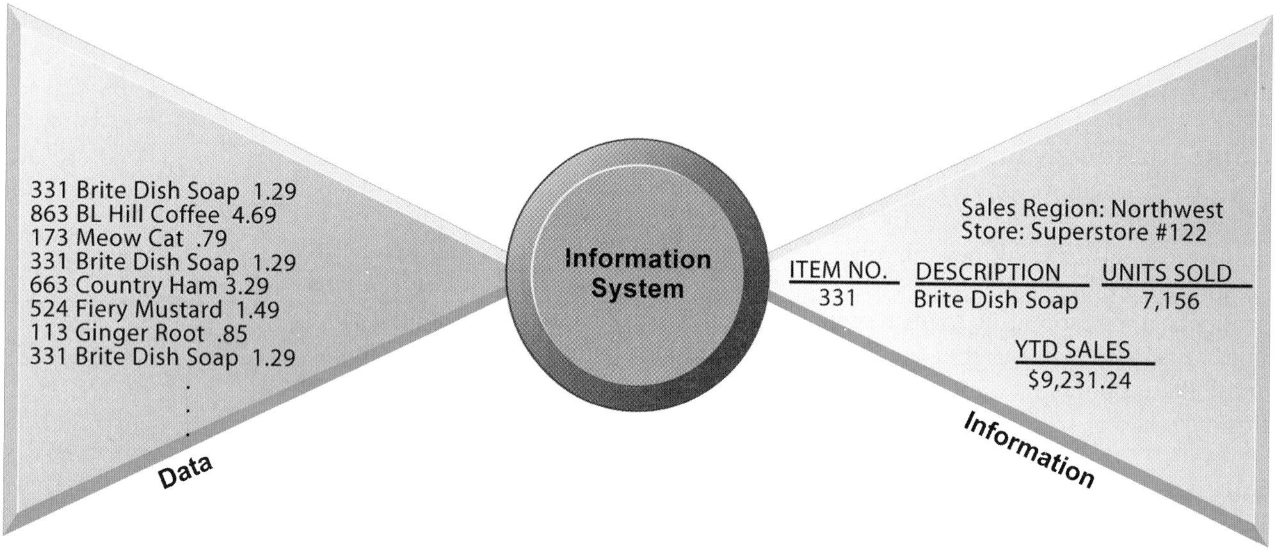

Figure 1.1
Data and Information
Raw data from a supermarket checkout counter can be processed and organized to produce meaningful information, such as the total unit sales of dish detergent or the total sales revenue from dish detergent for a specific store or sales territory.

information systems may also help managers and workers analyze problems, visualize complex subjects, and create new products.

Information systems contain information about significant people, places, and things within the organization or in the environment surrounding it. By **information**, we mean data that have been shaped into a form that is meaningful and useful to human beings. **Data**, in contrast, are streams of raw facts representing events occurring in organizations or the physical environment before they have been organized and arranged into a form that people can understand and use.

A brief example contrasting information and data may prove useful. Supermarket checkout counters scan millions of pieces of data, such as bar codes, that describe the product. Such pieces of data can be totaled and analyzed to provide meaningful information, such as the total number of bottles of dish detergent sold at a particular store, which brands of dish detergent were selling the most rapidly at that store or sales territory, or the total amount spent on that brand of dish detergent at that store or sales region (see Figure 1.1).

Three activities in an information system produce the information that organizations need to make decisions, control operations, analyze problems, and create new products or services. These activities are input, processing, and output (see Figure 1.2). **Input** captures or collects raw data from within the organization or from its external environment. **Processing** converts this raw input into a meaningful form. **Output** transfers the processed information to the people who will use it or to the activities for which it will be used. Information systems also require **feedback**, which is output that is returned to appropriate members of the organization to help them evaluate or correct the input stage.

In the Kroger system for monitoring cold food storage temperatures, the raw input consists of RFID sensor-generated data on stored food items, such as the item's identification number, item description, storage location, temperature, and time of day. Computers store these data and process them to calculate how much each food item registers above or below its ideal storage temperature. The system output consists of indicators flagging items not stored at the proper temperature that might spoil or be damaged. The system provides meaningful information, such as food items flagged for storage, total number of food items with storage temperature problems, and location of those items.

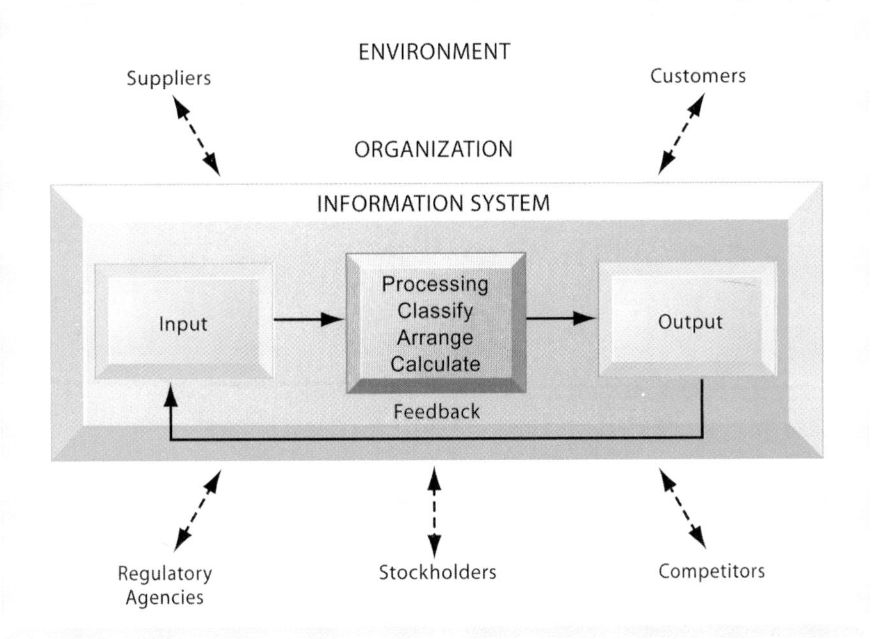

Figure 1.2
Functions of an Information System
An information system contains information about an organization and its surrounding environment. Three basic activities—input, processing, and output—produce the information organizations need. Feedback is output returned to appropriate people or activities in the organization to evaluate and refine the input. Environmental actors, such as customers, suppliers, competitors, stockholders, and regulatory agencies, interact with the organization and its information systems.

Although computer-based information systems use computer technology to process raw data into meaningful information, there is a sharp distinction between a computer and a computer program and an information system. Computers and related software programs are the technical foundation, the tools and materials, of modern information systems. Computers provide the equipment for storing and processing information. Computer programs, or software, are sets of operating instructions that direct and control computer processing. Knowing how computers and computer programs work is important in designing solutions to organizational problems, but computers are only part of an information system.

A house is an appropriate analogy. Houses are built with hammers, nails, and wood, but these alone do not make a house. The architecture, design, setting, landscaping, and all of the decisions that lead to the creation of these features are part of the house and are crucial for solving the problem of putting a roof over one's head. Computers and programs are the hammer, nails, and lumber of computer-based information systems, but alone they cannot produce the information a particular organization needs. To understand information systems, you must understand the problems they are designed to solve, their architectural and design elements, and the organizational processes that lead to these solutions.

IT ISN'T SIMPLY TECHNOLOGY: THE ROLE OF PEOPLE AND ORGANIZATIONS

To understand information systems fully, you will need to be aware of the broader organization, people, and information technology dimensions of systems (see Figure 1.3) and their power to provide solutions to challenges and problems in the business environment. We refer to this broader understanding of information systems, which encompasses an understanding of the people and organizational dimensions of systems as well as the technical dimensions of systems, as **information systems literacy**. Information systems literacy includes a behavioral as well as a technical approach to studying information systems. **Computer literacy**, in contrast, focuses primarily on knowledge of information technology.

The field of **management information systems (MIS)** tries to achieve this broader information systems literacy. MIS deals with behavioral issues as well as technical

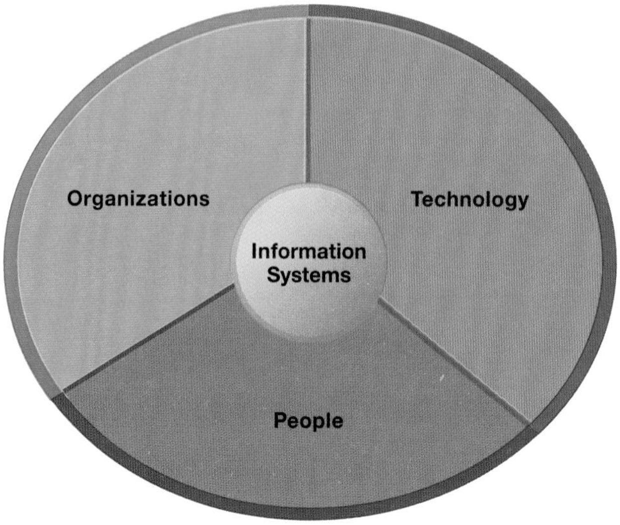

Figure 1.3
Information Systems Are More Than Computers
Using information systems effectively requires an understanding of the organization, people, and information technology shaping the systems. An information system provides a solution to important business problems or challenges facing the firm.

issues surrounding the development, use, and impact of information systems that managers and employees in the firm use.

DIMENSIONS OF INFORMATION SYSTEMS

Let's examine each of the dimensions of information systems—organizations, people, and information technology.

Organizations

Information systems are an integral part of organizations and, although we tend to think about information technology changing organizations and business firms, it is, in fact, a two-way street. The history and culture of business firms also affects how the technology is used and how it should be used. To understand how a specific business firm uses information systems, you need to know something about the structure, history, and culture of the company.

Organizations have a structure that is composed of different levels and specialties. Their structures reveal a clear-cut division of labor. A business firm is organized as a hierarchy, or a pyramid structure, of rising authority and responsibility. The upper levels of the hierarchy consist of managerial, professional, and technical employees, whereas the lower levels consist of operational personnel. Experts are employed and trained for different business functions, such as sales and marketing, manufacturing and production, finance and accounting, and human resources. The firm builds information systems to serve these different specialties and levels of the firm. Chapter 2 provides more detail on these business functions and organizational levels and the ways in which information systems support them.

An organization accomplishes and coordinates work through this structured hierarchy and through its **business processes**, which are logically related tasks and behaviors for accomplishing work. Developing a new product, fulfilling an order, and hiring a new employee are examples of business processes.

Most organizations' business processes include formal rules that it has developed over a long time for accomplishing tasks. These rules guide employees in a variety of procedures, from writing an invoice to responding to customer complaints. Some of these business processes have been written down, but others are informal work practices, such as a requirement to return telephone calls from coworkers or customers, that are not formally documented. Information systems automate many business processes. For instance, how a customer receives credit or how a customer is billed is often determined by an information system that incorporates a set of formal business processes.

Each organization has a unique **culture**, or fundamental set of assumptions, values, and ways of doing things, that has been accepted by most of its members. Parts of an organization's culture can always be found embedded in its information systems. For instance, the United Parcel Service's concern with placing service to the customer first is an aspect of its organizational culture that can be found in the company's package tracking systems.

Different levels and specialties in an organization create different interests and points of view. These views often conflict. Conflict is the basis for organizational politics. Information systems come out of this cauldron of differing perspectives, conflicts, compromises, and agreements that are a natural part of all organizations.

People

A business is only as good as the people who work there and run it. Likewise with information systems, they are useless without skilled people to build and maintain them or people who can understand how to use the information in a system to achieve business objectives.

For instance, a call center that provides help to customers by using an advanced customer relationship management system (described in later chapters) is useless if employees are not adequately trained to deal with customers, find solutions to their problems, and leave the customer feeling that the company cares for them. Likewise, employee attitudes about their jobs, employers, or technology can have a powerful effect on their abilities to use information systems productively.

Business firms require many kinds of skills and people, including managers as well as rank-and-file employees. The job of managers is to make sense out of the many situations organizations face, make decisions, and formulate action plans to solve organizational problems. Managers perceive business challenges in the environment, they set the organizational strategy for responding to those challenges, and they allocate the human and financial resources to coordinate the work and achieve success. Throughout, they must exercise responsible leadership.

However, managers must do more than manage what already exists. They must also create new products and services and even re-create the organization from time to time. A substantial part of management responsibility is creative work driven by new knowledge and information. Information technology can play a powerful role in helping managers develop novel solutions to a broad range of problems.

As you will learn throughout this text, technology is relatively inexpensive today, but people are very expensive. Because people are the only ones capable of business problem solving and converting information technology into useful business solutions, we spend considerable effort in this text looking at the people dimension of information systems.

Technology

Information technology is one of many tools managers use to cope with change and complexity. **Computer hardware** is the physical equipment used for input, processing, and output activities in an information system. It consists of the following: computers of various sizes and shapes; various input, output, and storage devices; and networking devices that link computers.

Computer software consists of the detailed, preprogrammed instructions that control and coordinate the computer hardware components in an information system. Chapter 5 describes the contemporary software and hardware platforms firms use today in greater detail.

Data management technology consists of the software governing the organization of data on physical storage media. More detail on data organization and access methods can be found in Chapter 6.

Networking and telecommunications technology, consisting of both physical devices and software, links the various pieces of hardware and transfers data from one physical location to another. Computers and communications equipment can be connected in networks for sharing voice, data, images, sound, and video. A **network** links two or more computers to share data or resources such as a printer.

The world's largest and most widely used network is the **Internet**, a global network of networks that uses universal standards (described in Chapter 7) to connect millions of networks in more than 230 countries around the world.

The Internet has created a new, universal technology platform on which to build new products, services, strategies, and business models. This same technology platform has internal uses, providing the connectivity to link different systems and networks within the firm. Internal corporate networks based on Internet technology are called **intranets**. Private intranets extended to authorized users outside the organization are called **extranets**, and firms use such networks to coordinate their activities with other firms for making purchases, collaborating on design, and performing other interorganizational work. For most business firms today, using Internet technology is a business necessity and a competitive advantage.

The **World Wide Web** is a service the Internet provides that uses universally accepted standards for storing, retrieving, formatting, and displaying information in a page format on the Internet. Web pages contain text, graphics, animations, sound, and video and are linked to other web pages. By clicking highlighted words or buttons on a web page, you can link to related pages to find additional information and links to other locations on the web. The web can serve as the foundation for new kinds of information systems such as UPS's web-based package tracking system.

All these technologies, along with the people required to run and manage them, represent resources that can be shared throughout the organization and constitute the firm's **information technology (IT) infrastructure**. The IT infrastructure provides the foundation, or *platform*, on which the firm can build its specific information systems. Each organization must carefully design and manage its information technology infrastructure so that it has the set of technology services it needs for the work it wants to accomplish with information systems. Chapters 5, 6, 7, and 8 of this text examine each major technology component of information technology infrastructure and show how they all work together to create the technology platform for the organization.

The Interactive Session on Technology describes some of the typical technologies used in computer-based information systems today. UPS invests heavily in information systems technology to make its business more efficient and customer oriented. It uses an array of information technologies, including bar code scanning systems, wireless networks, large mainframe computers, handheld computers, the Internet, and many pieces of software for tracking packages, calculating fees, maintaining customer accounts, and managing logistics. As you read this case, try to identify the problem this company was facing, what alternative solutions were available to management, and how well the chosen solution worked.

Let's identify the organization, people, and technology elements in the UPS package tracking system we have just described. The organization element anchors the package tracking system in UPS's sales and production functions (the main product of UPS is a service—package delivery). It specifies the required procedures for identifying packages with both sender and recipient information, taking inventory, tracking the packages en route, and providing package status reports for UPS customers and customer service representatives.

The system must also provide information to satisfy the needs of managers and workers. UPS drivers need to be trained in both package pickup and delivery procedures and in how to use the package tracking system so that they can work efficiently and effectively. UPS customers may need some training to use UPS in-house package tracking software or the UPS website.

UPS Competes Globally with Information Technology

United Parcel Service (UPS) started out in 1907 in a closet-sized basement office. Jim Casey and Claude Ryan—two teenagers from Seattle with two bicycles and one phone—promised the "best service and lowest rates." UPS has used this formula successfully for more than a century to become the world's largest ground and air package-delivery company. It's a global enterprise with more than 434,000 employees, 108,210 vehicles, and the world's ninth-largest airline.

Today UPS delivers 19.1 million packages and documents each day in the United States and more than 220 other countries and territories. The firm has been able to maintain leadership in small-package delivery services despite stiff competition from FedEx and the U.S. Postal Service by investing heavily in advanced information technology. UPS spends more than $1 billion each year to maintain a high level of customer service while keeping costs low and streamlining its overall operations.

It all starts with the scannable bar-coded label attached to a package, which contains detailed information about the sender, the destination, and when the package should arrive. Customers can download and print their own labels using special software provided by UPS or by accessing the UPS website. Before the package is even picked up, information from the "smart" label is transmitted to one of UPS's computer centers in Mahwah, New Jersey, or Alpharetta, Georgia, and sent to the distribution center nearest its final destination.

Dispatchers at this center download the label data and use special routing software called ORION to create the most efficient delivery route for each driver that considers traffic, weather conditions, and the location of each stop. Each UPS driver makes an average of 120 stops per day. In a network with 55,000 routes in the United States alone, shaving even one mile off each driver's daily route translates into big savings: $50 million per year. These savings are critical as UPS tries to boost earnings growth as more of its business shifts to less-profitable e-commerce deliveries. UPS drivers who used to drop off several heavy packages a day at one retailer now make several stops scattered across residential neighborhoods, delivering one lightweight package per household. The shift requires more fuel and more time, increasing the cost to deliver each package.

The first thing a UPS driver picks up each day is a handheld computer called a Delivery Information Acquisition Device (DIAD), which can access a wireless cell phone network. As soon as the driver logs on, his or her day's route is downloaded onto the handheld. The DIAD also automatically captures customers' signatures along with pickup and delivery information. Package tracking information is then transmitted to UPS's computer network for storage and processing. From there, the information can be accessed worldwide to provide proof of delivery to customers or to respond to customer queries. It usually takes less than 60 seconds from the time a driver presses "complete" on the DIAD for the new information to be available on the web.

Through its automated package tracking system, UPS can monitor and even reroute packages throughout the delivery process. At various points along the route from sender to receiver, bar code devices scan shipping information on the package label and feed data about the progress of the package into the central computer. Customer service representatives are able to check the status of any package from desktop computers linked to the central computers and respond immediately to inquiries from customers. UPS customers can also access this information from the company's website using their own computers or mobile phones. UPS now has mobile apps and a mobile website for iPhone, BlackBerry, and Android smartphone users.

Anyone with a package to ship can access the UPS website to track packages, check delivery routes, calculate shipping rates, determine time in transit, print labels, and schedule a pickup. The data collected at the UPS website are transmitted to the UPS central computer and then back to the customer after processing. UPS also provides tools that enable customers, such Cisco Systems, to embed UPS functions, such as tracking and cost calculations, into their own websites so that they can track shipments without visiting the UPS site.

A web-based Post Sales Order Management System (OMS) manages global service orders and inventory for critical parts fulfillment. The system enables high-tech electronics, aerospace, medical equipment, and other companies anywhere in the world that ship critical parts to quickly assess their critical parts inventory, determine the most optimal routing strategy to meet customer needs, place orders online, and track parts from the warehouse to the end user. An automated email or fax feature keeps customers informed of each shipping milestone and can provide notification of any changes to flight schedules for commercial airlines carrying their parts.

UPS is now leveraging its decades of expertise managing its own global delivery network to manage logistics and supply chain activities for other companies. It created a UPS Supply Chain Solutions division that provides a complete bundle of standardized services to subscribing companies at a fraction of what it would cost to build their own systems and infrastructure. These services include supply chain design and management, freight forwarding, customs brokerage, mail services, multimodal transportation, and financial services in addition to logistics services.

CandleScience, based in Durham, North Carolina, is an industry leader in the candle and soap supply industry, providing raw materials such as waxes, wicks, and fragrances to candle makers around the world. UPS worked with CandleScience to accurately model shipping rates for the company and its customers and to add a freight shipping option capability to its website. UPS also helped CandleScience identify the optimal location for a new warehouse for its West Coast customers. The new West Coast warehouse in Sparks, Nevada, lets the company reach some of its largest customers faster, more efficiently, and less expensively.

Sources: "Igniting Growth with CandleScience," UPS Compass, May 2017; www.ups.com, accessed June 25, 2017; and Steven Rosenbush and Laura Stevens, "At UPS, Algorithm Is the Driver," *Wall Street Journal*, February 16, 2015.

CASE STUDY QUESTIONS

1. What are the inputs, processing, and outputs of UPS's package tracking system?
2. What technologies are used by UPS? How are these technologies related to UPS's business strategy?
3. What strategic business objectives do UPS's information systems address?
4. What would happen if UPS's information systems were not available?

UPS's management is responsible for monitoring service levels and costs and for promoting the company's strategy of combining low cost and superior service. Management decided to use automation to increase the ease of sending a package via UPS and of checking its delivery status, thereby reducing delivery costs and increasing sales revenues.

The technology supporting this system consists of handheld computers, bar code scanners, wired and wireless communications networks, desktop computers, UPS's central computer, storage technology for the package delivery data, UPS in-house package tracking software, and software to access the World Wide Web. The result is an information system solution to the business challenge of providing a high level of service with low prices in the face of mounting competition.

1-3 How will a four-step method for business problem solving help you solve information system–related problems?

Our approach to understanding information systems is to consider information systems and technologies as solutions to a variety of business challenges and problems. We refer to this as a problem-solving approach. Businesses face many challenges and problems, and information systems are one major way of solving these problems. All the cases in this book illustrate how a company used information systems to solve a specific problem.

The problem-solving approach has direct relevance to your future career. Your future employers will hire you because you can solve business problems and achieve business objectives. Your knowledge of how information systems contribute to problem solving will be very helpful to both you and your employers.

THE PROBLEM-SOLVING APPROACH

At first glance, problem solving in daily life seems to be perfectly straightforward; a machine breaks down, parts and oil spill all over the floor, and, obviously, somebody has to do something about it. So, of course, you find a tool around the shop and start repairing the machine. After a cleanup and proper inspection of other parts, you start the machine, and production resumes.

No doubt, some problems in business are this straightforward, but few problems are this simple in the real world of business. In real-world business firms, a number of major factors are simultaneously involved in problems. These major factors can usefully be grouped into three categories: *organization, technology,* and *people.* In other words, a whole set of problems is usually involved.

A MODEL OF THE PROBLEM-SOLVING PROCESS

There is a simple model of problem solving that you can use to help you understand and solve business problems by using information systems. You can think of business problem-solving as a four-step process (see Figure 1.4). Most problem solvers work through this model on their way to finding a solution. Let's take a brief look at each step.

Problem Identification

The first step in the problem-solving process is to understand what kind of problem exists. Contrary to popular beliefs, problems are not like basketballs on a court simply waiting to be picked up by some objective problem solver. Before problems can be solved, there must be agreement in a business that a problem exists, about what the problem is, about its causes, and about what can be done about it, given the limited resources of the organization. Problems have to be properly defined by people in an organization before they can be solved.

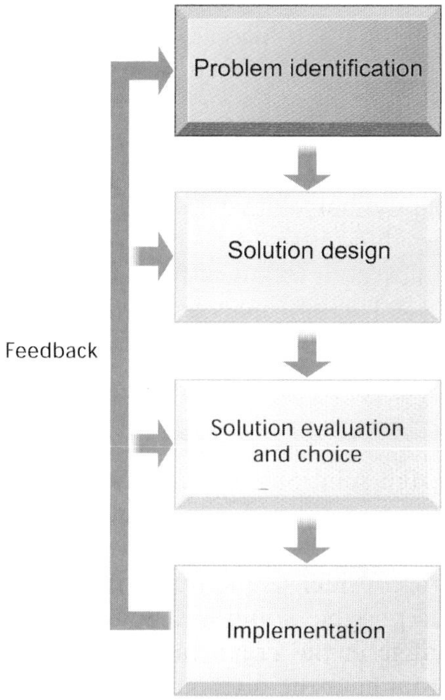

Figure 1.4
Problem Solving Is a Continuous Four-Step Process
During implementation and thereafter, the outcome must be continually measured, and the information about how well the solution is working is fed back to the problem solvers. In this way, the identification of the problem can change over time, solutions can be changed, and new choices can be made, all based on experience.

TABLE 1.2

Dimensions of Business Problems

Dimension	Description
Organizational dimensions	Outdated business processes
	Unsupportive culture and attitudes
	Political conflict
	Turbulent business environment, change
	Complexity of task
	Inadequate resources
Technology dimensions	Insufficient or aging hardware
	Outdated software
	Inadequate database capacity
	Insufficient network capacity
	Incompatibility of old systems with new technology
	Rapid technological change and failure to adopt new technology
People dimensions	Lack of employee training
	Difficulties of evaluating performance
	Legal and regulatory compliance
	Work environment
	Lack of employee support and participation
	Indecisive management
	Poor management
	Wrong incentives

For instance, what at first glance what might seem like a problem with employees not adequately responding to customers in a timely and accurate manner might in reality be a result of an older, out-of-date information system for keeping track of customers; or it might be a combination of both poor employee incentives for treating customers well and an outdated system. Once you understand this critical fact, you can start to solve problems creatively. Finding answers to these questions will require fact gathering, interviews with people involved in the problem, and analysis of documents and data.

In this text, we emphasize three different and typical dimensions of business problems: organizations, technology, and people (see Table 1.2). Typical organizational problems include poor business processes (usually inherited from the past), unsupportive culture, political infighting, and changes in the organization's surrounding environment. Typical technology problems include insufficient or aging hardware, outdated software, inadequate database capacity, insufficient network capacity, and the incompatibility of old systems with new technology. Typical people problems include employee training, difficulties of evaluating performance, legal and regulatory compliance, ergonomics, poor or indecisive management, and employee support and participation. When you begin to analyze a business problem, you will find these dimensions are helpful guides to understanding the kind of problem with which you are working.

Solution Design

The second step is to design solutions to the problem(s) you have identified. As it turns out, there are usually a great many solutions to any given problem, and the choice of solution often reflects the differing perspectives of people in an organization. You should try to consider as many solutions as possible so that you can understand the range of possible solutions. Some solutions emphasize technology; others focus on change in the organization and people aspects of the problem. As you will find throughout the text, most successful solutions result from an integrated approach in which changes in organization and people accompany new technologies.

Solution Evaluation and Choice

Choosing the best solution for your business firm is the next step in the process. Some of the factors to consider when trying to find the best single solution are the cost of the solution, the feasibility of the solution for your business given existing resources and skills, and the length of time required to build and implement the solution. Also very important at this point are the attitudes and support of your employees and managers. A solution that does not have the support of all the major interests in the business can quickly turn into a disaster.

Implementation

The best solution is one that can be implemented. Implementation of an information system solution involves building the solution and introducing it into the organization. This includes purchasing or building the software and hardware—the technology part of the equation. The software must be tested in a realistic business setting; then employees need to be trained, and documentation about how to use the new system needs to be written.

You will definitely need to think about change management. **Change management** refers to the many techniques used to bring about successful change in a business. Nearly all information systems require changes in the firm's business processes and, therefore, changes in what hundreds or even thousands of employees do every day. You will have to design new, more efficient business processes and then figure out how to encourage employees to adapt to these new ways of doing business. This may require meeting sessions to introduce the change to groups of employees, new training modules to bring employees quickly up to speed on the new information systems and processes, and, finally, some kind of rewards or incentives to encourage people to support the changes enthusiastically.

Implementation also includes the measurement of outcomes. After a solution has been implemented, it must be evaluated to determine how well it is working and whether any additional changes are required to meet the original objectives. This information is fed back to the problem solvers. In this way, the identification of the problem can change over time, solutions can be changed, and new choices made, all based on experience.

Problem Solving: A Process, Not an Event

It is easy to fall into the trap of thinking about problem solving as an event that is over at some point, like a relay race or a baseball game. Often in the real world, this does not happen. Sometimes the chosen solution does not work, and new solutions are required.

For instance, the U.S. National Aeronautics and Space Administration (NASA) spent more than $1 billion to fix a problem with shedding foam on the space shuttle. Experience proved the initial solution did not work. More often, the chosen solution partially works but needs a lot of continuous changes to fit the situation well. Sometimes, the nature of the problem changes in a way that makes the initial solution ineffective. For instance, hackers create new variations on computer viruses that require continually evolving antivirus programs to hold them in check. For all these reasons, problem solving is a continuous process rather than a single event.

THE ROLE OF CRITICAL THINKING IN PROBLEM SOLVING

It is amazingly easy to accept someone else's definition of a problem or to adopt the opinions of some authoritative group that has objectively analyzed the problem and offers quick solutions. You should try to resist this tendency to accept existing definitions of any problem. It is essential for you to try to maintain some distance from any specific solution until you are sure you have properly identified the problem, developed understanding, and analyzed alternatives. Otherwise, you may leap off in the wrong direction, solve the wrong problem, and waste resources. You will have to engage in some critical-thinking exercises.

Critical thinking can be briefly defined as the sustained suspension of judgment with an awareness of multiple perspectives and alternatives. It involves at least four elements as described below:

- Maintaining doubt and suspending judgment
- Being aware of different perspectives
- Testing alternatives and letting experience guide
- Being aware of organizational and personal limitations

Simply following a rote pattern of decision making, or a model, does not guarantee a correct solution. The best protection against incorrect results is to engage in critical thinking throughout the problem-solving process.

First, maintain doubt and suspend judgment. Perhaps the most frequent error in problem solving is to arrive prematurely at a judgment about the nature of the problem. By doubting all solutions at first and refusing to rush to a judgment, you create the necessary mental conditions to take a fresh, creative look at problems, and you keep open the chance to make a creative contribution.

Second, recognize that all interesting business problems have many dimensions and that the same problem can be viewed from different perspectives. In this text, we have emphasized the usefulness of three perspectives on business problems: technology, organizations, and people. Within each of these very broad perspectives are many subperspectives, or views. The *technology perspective*, for instance, includes a consideration of all the components in the firm's IT infrastructure and the way they work together. The *organization perspective* includes a consideration of a firm's business processes, structure, culture, and politics. The *people perspective* includes consideration of the firm's management as well as employees as individuals and their interrelationships in workgroups.

You will have to decide for yourself which major perspectives are useful for viewing a given problem. The ultimate criterion here is usefulness: Does adopting a certain perspective tell you something more about the problem that is useful for solving the problem? If not, reject that perspective as not meaningful in this situation and look for other perspectives.

The third element of critical thinking involves testing alternatives, or modeling solutions to problems, letting experience be the guide. Not all contingencies can be known in advance, and much can be learned through experience. Therefore, experiment, gather data, and reassess the problem periodically.

THE CONNECTIONS AMONG BUSINESS OBJECTIVES, PROBLEMS, AND SOLUTIONS

Now let's make the connection between business information systems and the problem-solving approach. At the beginning of this chapter, we identified six business objectives of information systems: operational excellence; new products, services, and business models; customer/supplier intimacy; improved decision making; strategic advantage; and survival. When firms cannot achieve these objectives, they become challenges or problems that receive attention. Managers and employees who are aware of these challenges often turn to information systems as one of the solutions or the entire solution.

Review the diagram at the beginning of this chapter. The diagram shows how Kroger's systems solved the business problem presented by the need to retain customers and generate revenue in a highly competitive industry with razor-thin profit margins. These systems created a solution that takes advantage of opportunities that new digital technology and the Internet provided. They opened up new channels for selling goods, increased quality, and improved the customer buying experience. These systems have been essential in improving Kroger's overall business performance. The diagram also illustrates how people, technology, and organizational elements work together to create the systems.

Each chapter of this text begins with a diagram similar to this one to help you analyze the chapter-opening case. You can use this diagram as a starting point for analyzing any information system or information system problem you encounter.

1-4 What information systems skills and knowledge are essential for business careers?

Looking out to 2024, the U.S. economy will create 9.8 million new jobs, and 34 million existing jobs will open up as their occupants retire. More than 95 percent of the new jobs will be created in the service sector. The vast majority of these new jobs and replacement jobs will require a college degree to perform (Dubina, 2015; U.S. Bureau of Labor Statistics, 2017; U.S. Census, 2017).

What this means is that U.S. business firms are looking for candidates who have a broad range of problem-solving skills—the ability to read, write, and present ideas—as well as the technical skills required for specific tasks. Regardless of your business school major, or your future occupation, information systems and technologies will play a major and expanding role in your day-to-day work and your career. Your career opportunities, and your compensation, will in part depend on your ability to help business firms use information systems to achieve their objectives.

HOW INFORMATION SYSTEMS WILL AFFECT BUSINESS CAREERS

In the following sections, we describe how specific occupations will be affected by information systems and what skills you should be building in order to benefit from this emerging labor market based on the research of the Bureau of Labor Statistics (Bureau of Labor Statistics, 2017).

Accounting

There are about 1.3 million accountants in the U.S. labor force today, and the field is expected to expand by 11 percent by the year 2024, adding 142,000 new jobs and twice as many to replace retirees. This above-average growth in accounting is driven in part by new accounting laws for public companies, greater scrutiny of public and private firms by government tax auditors, and a growing demand for management and operational advice.

Accountants rely heavily on information systems to summarize transactions, create financial records, organize data, and perform financial analysis. Because of new public laws, accountants require an intimate knowledge of databases, reporting systems, and networks to trace financial transactions. Because so many transactions are occurring over the Internet, accountants need to understand online transaction and reporting systems and how systems are used to achieve management accounting functions in an online and mobile business environment.

Finance

If you include financial analysts, stock analysts, brokers, loan officers, budget analysts, financial advisors, and related financial service occupations, there are currently about 2 million managers and employees in finance. These financial occupations are expected to grow on average by about 12 percent by the year 2024 and add more than 100,000 new jobs. Financial advisors will grow by 30 percent in this period

Financial managers play important roles in planning, organizing, and implementing information system strategies for their firms. Financial managers work directly with a firm's board of directors and senior management to ensure that investments in information systems help achieve corporate goals and high returns. The relationship between information systems and the practice of modern financial management and services is so strong that many advise finance majors to co-major in information systems (and vice versa).

Marketing

No field has undergone more technology-driven change in the past five years than marketing and advertising. The explosion in e-commerce activity described earlier means that eyeballs are moving rapidly to the Internet. Internet advertising is the fastest-growing form of advertising, reaching $83 billion in 2016. Product branding and customer communication are moving online at a fast pace.

There are about 1.5 million public relations, marketing analysts, and marketing and sales managers in the U.S. labor force. This field is growing faster than average, at about 8 percent, and is expected to add more than 300,000 jobs by 2024. There is a much larger group of 1.2 million nonmanagerial employees in marketing-related occupations (art, design, entertainment, sports, and media) and more than 15.9 million employees in sales. These occupations together are expected to create an additional 2 million jobs by 2024. Marketing and advertising managers deal with large databases of customer behavior both online and offline in the process of creating brands and selling products and services. They develop reports on product performance, retrieve feedback from customers, and manage product development. These managers need an understanding of how enterprise-wide systems for product management, sales force management, and customer relationship management are used to develop products that consumers want, to manage the customer relationship, and to manage an increasingly mobile sales force.

Operations Management in Services and Manufacturing

The growing size and complexity of modern industrial production and the emergence of huge global service companies have created a growing demand for employees who can coordinate and optimize the resources required to produce goods and services. Operations management as a discipline is directly relevant to three occupational categories: industrial production managers, administrative service managers, and operations analysts.

Production managers, administrative service managers, and operations analysts will be employing information systems and technologies every day to accomplish their jobs, with extensive use of database and analytical software.

Management

Management is the largest single group in the U.S. business labor force with more than 16 million members, not including an additional 627,000 management consultants. Overall, the management corps in the United States is expected to expand at an average pace of 5 percent, adding about 2.4 million new jobs by 2024. The Bureau of Labor Statistics tracks more than 20 types of managers, all the way from chief executive officer to human resource managers, production managers, project managers, lodging managers, medical managers, and community service managers.

Arguably, it would be impossible to manage business firms today, even very small firms, without the extensive use of information systems. Nearly all U.S. managers use information systems and technologies every day to accomplish their jobs, from desktop productivity tools to mobile applications coordinating the entire enterprise. Managers today manage through a variety of information technologies without which it would be impossible to control and lead the firm.

The job of management requires extensive use of information systems to support decision making and monitor the performance of the firm.

Information Systems

The information systems field is one of the fastest-changing and dynamic of all the business professions because information technologies are among the most important tools for achieving business firms' key objectives. The explosive growth of business information systems has generated a growing demand for information systems employees and managers who work with other business professionals to design and develop new hardware and software systems to serve the needs of business.

There are about 3.6 million information system managers and employees in the United States, with an estimated growth rate of 12 percent through 2024, expanding the number of new jobs by more than 500,000. As businesses and government agencies increasingly rely on the Internet for communication and computing resources, system and network security management positions are growing very rapidly. The fastest-growing occupations in this category are software developers (up 17 percent) and web developers (up 27 percent).

Outsourcing and Offshoring

The Internet has created new opportunities for outsourcing many information systems jobs, along with many other service sector and manufacturing jobs. There are two kinds of outsourcing: outsourcing to domestic U.S. firms and offshore outsourcing to low-wage countries such as India, China, and eastern European countries. Even this distinction blurs as domestic service providers, such as IBM, develop global outsourcing centers in India.

The most common and successful offshore outsourcing projects involve production programming and system maintenance programming work, along with call center work related to customer relationship management systems. However, inflation in Indian and Chinese wages for technology work, coupled with the additional management costs incurred in outsourcing projects, is leading to a counter movement of some IT jobs back to the United States. Moreover, although routine technical information systems (IS) jobs such as software maintenance can be outsourced easily, all those management and organizational tasks required in systems development—including business process design, user interface design, and supply chain management—often remain in the United States.

Innovative new products, services, and systems are rarely outsourced either domestically or globally. The advantage of low-wage countries is their low wages and ready availability of technical talent, not their keen sense of new products, services, and technologies for other countries' markets. Software outsourcing of routine IS work to low-wage countries lowers the cost of building and maintaining systems in the United States and other high-wage countries. As systems become less expensive, more are built. The net result is that offshore outsourcing likely increase demand domestically for managerial and employment in a wide variety of IS positions.

Given all these factors in the IT labor market, on what kinds of skills should information system majors focus? Following is a list of general skills we believe will optimize employment opportunities.

- An in-depth knowledge of how business firms can use new and emerging hardware and software to make them more efficient and effective, enhance customer and supplier intimacy, improve decision making, achieve competitive advantage, and ensure firm survival. This includes an in-depth understanding of cloud computing, databases, system implementation, and mobile application development.
- An ability to take a leadership role in the design and implementation of new information systems, work with other business professionals to ensure systems meet business objectives, and work with cloud computing services and software providing new system solutions

INFORMATION SYSTEMS AND BUSINESS CAREERS: WRAP-UP

Looking back at the information system skills and knowledge required for specific majors, there are some common themes that affect all business majors. Following is a list of these common requirements.

- All business students, regardless of major, should understand how information systems and technologies can help firms achieve business objectives such as attaining operational efficiency, developing new products and services, and maintaining customer intimacy.
- All business students need to develop skills in analysis of information and helping firms understand and make sense of their data. Business analytics and intelligence are important skill sets to analyze the mountains of big data the online business environment and Internet of Things (IoT) produce.
- All business majors need to be able to work with specialists and system designers who build and implement information systems. This is necessary to ensure that the systems that are built actually service business purposes and provide the information and understanding managers and employees require.
- Each of the business majors will be affected by changes in the ethical, social, and legal environment of business. Business school students need to understand how information systems can be used to meet business requirements for reporting to government regulators and the public and how information systems affect the ethical issues in their fields.

Regardless of your major, liberal arts skills are highly prized, including the ability to communicate verbally and in writing and to collaborate with others on a team.

HOW THIS BOOK PREPARES YOU FOR THE FUTURE

This book is explicitly designed to prepare you for your future business career. It provides you with the necessary knowledge and foundational concepts for understanding the role of information systems in business organizations. You will be able to use this knowledge to identify opportunities for increasing the effectiveness of your business. You will learn how to use information systems to improve operations, create new products and services, improve decision making, increase customer intimacy, and promote competitive advantage.

Equally important, this book develops your ability to use information systems to solve problems that you will encounter on the job. You will learn how to analyze and define a business problem and how to design an appropriate information system solution. You will deepen your critical-thinking and problem-solving skills. The following features of the text and the accompanying learning package reinforce this problem-solving and career orientation.

A Framework for Describing and Analyzing Information Systems

The text provides you with a framework for analyzing and solving problems by examining the people, organizational, and technology components of information systems. This framework is used repeatedly throughout the text to help you understand information systems in business and analyze information systems problems.

A Four-Step Model for Problem Solving

The text provides you with a four-step method for solving business problems, which we introduced in this chapter. You will learn how to identify a business problem, design alternative solutions, choose the correct solution, and implement the solution. You will be asked to use this problem-solving method to solve the case studies in each chapter. Chapter 12 will show you how to use this approach to design and build new information systems.

Hands-On MIS Projects for Stimulating Critical Thinking and Problem Solving

Each chapter concludes with a series of hands-on MIS projects to sharpen your critical-thinking and problem-solving skills. These projects include two Management Decision Problems, hands-on application software problems, and projects for building Internet skills. For each of these projects, we identify both the business skills and the software skills required for the solution.

Career Resources

To make sure you know how the text is directly useful in your future business career, we've added a full set of career resources to help you with career development and job hunting.

New Career Opportunities Feature To show you how this book can help you find a job and build your career, we have added a new "Career Opportunities" feature, identified by this icon, to each chapter. The last major section of each chapter, titled "How will MIS help my career?," presents a description of an entry-level job for a recent college graduate based on a real-world job description. The job requirements are related to the topics covered in that chapter. The job description shows the required educational background and skills, lists business-related questions that might arise during the job interview, and provides author tips for answering the questions and preparing for the interview. Students and instructors can find more detail about how to use this feature in the Preface and in MyLab MIS.

Digital Portfolio MyLab MIS includes a template for preparing a structured digital portfolio to demonstrate the business knowledge, application software skills, Internet skills, and analytical skills you have acquired in this course. You can include this portfolio in your résumé or job applications. Your professors can also use the portfolio to assess the skills you have learned.

Additional Career Resources A Career Resources section in MyLab MIS shows you how to integrate what you have learned in this course in your résumé, cover letter, and job interview to improve your chances for success in the job market.

1-5 How will MIS help my career?

Here is how Chapter 1 can help you find an entry-level job as a financial client support and sales assistant.

THE COMPANY

Power Financial Analytics Data Services, a data and software company serving the financial industry with offices in New York City, Atlanta, Los Angeles, and Chicago, is looking to fill an entry-level position for a financial client support and sales assistant. The company has 1,600 employees, many of whom are consultants showing clients how to work with its powerful financial analytics software and data products.

POSITION DESCRIPTION

The financial client support and sales assistant will be part of a team in the company's consulting services. Consulting teams combine a thorough understanding of finance and technology with specific expertise in Power Financial Analytics Data Services software and assist clients in a variety of ways. The company provides on-the-job training in its software and consulting methods. Job responsibilities include:

- Supporting Financial Analytics Data Services applications.
- Helping the team create custom models and screens.
- Training clients in their offices and at seminars.
- Providing expert consultation to clients by telephone and on site.

JOB REQUIREMENTS

- Recent college graduate or investment professional with one to two years of experience. Applicants with backgrounds in finance, MIS, economics, accounting, business administration, and mathematics are preferred.
- Knowledge of or interest in learning about financial markets
- Sound working knowledge of spreadsheets
- Very strong communication and interpersonal skills
- Strong desire to learn in rapidly changing environment

INTERVIEW QUESTIONS

1. What is your background in finance? What courses did you take? Have you ever worked in the financial industry? What did you do there?
2. What is your proficiency level with spreadsheet software? What work have you done with Excel spreadsheets? Can you show examples of your work?
3. Are you able to discuss current trends in the financial industry and how they impact Power Financial's business model and client base?
4. Did you ever work with clients? Can you give examples of how you provided client service or support?
5. Can you give us an example of a finance-related problem or other business problem that you helped solve? Did you do any writing and analysis? Can you provide examples?

AUTHOR TIPS

1. Use the web to learn about financial markets and the financial industry.
2. Use the web to research the company, its financial products, and the tools and services it offers customers. Learn what you can about its consulting services. Addtionally, examine the company's social medial channels, such as LinkedIn and Facebook, for trends and themes.

3. Inquire exactly how you would be using spreadsheets for this job. Provide examples of how you used spreadsheets to solve problems in the classroom or for a job assignment. Show the spreadsheet work you did in finance.
4. Bring examples of your writing (including some from your Digital Portfolio described in MyLab MIS) demonstrating your analytical skills and project experience. Be prepared to discuss how you helped customers solve a business problem or the business problem solving you did for your courses.

Review Summary

1-1 **Why are information systems so essential for running and managing a business today?** Information systems are a foundation for conducting business today. In many industries, survival and even existence is difficult without extensive use of information technology. Businesses use information systems to achieve six major objectives: operational excellence; new products, services, and business models; customer/supplier intimacy; improved decision making; competitive advantage; and day-to-day survival.

1-2 **What exactly is an information system? How does it work? What are its people, organization, and technology components?** From a technical perspective, an information system collects, stores, and disseminates information from an organization's environment and internal operations to support organizational functions and decision making, communication, coordination, control, analysis, and visualization. Information systems transform raw data into useful information through three basic activities: input, processing, and output. From a business perspective, an information system provides a solution to a problem or challenge facing a firm and represents a combination of people, organization, and technology elements.

The people dimension of information systems involves issues such as training, job attitudes, and management behavior. The technology dimension consists of computer hardware, software, data management technology, and networking/telecommunications technology, including the Internet. The organization dimension of information systems involves issues such as the organization's hierarchy, functional specialties, business processes, culture, and political interest groups.

1-3 **How will a four-step method for business problem solving help you solve information system–related problems?** Problem identification involves understanding what kind of problem is being presented and identifying people, organizational, and technology factors. Solution design involves designing several alternative solutions to the problem that has been identified. Evaluation and choice entail selecting the best solution, taking into account its cost and the available resources and skills in the business. Implementation of an information system solution entails purchasing or building hardware and software, testing the software, providing employees with training and documentation, managing change as the system is introduced into the organization, and measuring the outcome. Problem solving requires critical thinking in which one suspends judgment to consider multiple perspectives and alternatives.

1-4 **What information system skills and knowledge are essential for business careers?** Business careers in accounting, finance, marketing, operations management, management and human resources, and information systems all will need an understanding of how information systems help firms achieve major business objectives; an appreciation of the central role of databases; skills in information analysis and business intelligence; sensitivity to the ethical, social, and legal issues systems raise; and the ability to work with technology specialists and other business professionals in designing and building systems.

Key Terms

Business model, 12
Business processes, 16
Change management, 23
Computer hardware, 17
Computer literacy, 15
Computer software, 17
Critical thinking, 24
Culture, 17
Data, 14
Data management technology, 17
Extranets, 18
Feedback, 14
Information, 14
Information system (IS), 13
Information systems literacy, 15
Information technology (IT), 13
Information technology (IT) infrastructure, 18
Input, 14
Internet, 18
Intranets, 18
Management information systems (MIS), 15
Network, 18
Networking and telecommunications technology, 17
Output, 14
Processing, 14
World Wide Web, 18

MyLab MIS

To complete the problems with **MyLab MIS**, go to the EOC Discussion Questions in MyLab MIS.

Review Questions

1-1 Why are information systems so essential for running and managing a business today?

- List and describe the six reasons information systems are so important for business today.
- Describe the challenges and opportunities of globalization.

1-2 What exactly is an information system? How does it work? What are its people, organization, and technology components?

- List and describe the organizational, people, and technology dimensions of information systems.
- Define an information system and describe the activities it performs.
- Distinguish between data and information and between information systems literacy and computer literacy.
- Explain how the Internet and the World Wide Web are related to the other technology components of information systems.

1-3 How will a four-step method for business problem solving help you solve information system–related problems?

- List and describe each of the four steps for solving business problems.
- Give some examples of people, organizational, and technology problems found in businesses.
- Describe the relationship of critical thinking to problem solving.
- Describe the role of information systems in business problem solving.

1-4 What information system skills and knowledge are essential for business careers?

- Describe the role of information systems in careers in accounting, finance, marketing, management, and operations management and explain how careers in information systems have been affected by new technologies and outsourcing.
- List and describe the information system skills and knowledge that are essential for all business careers.

Discussion Questions

1-5 MyLab MIS What are the implications of globalization when you have to look for a job? What can you do to prepare yourself for competing in a globalized business environment? How would knowledge of information systems help you compete?

1-6 If you were setting up the website for a Major League Baseball team, what people, organizational, and technology issues might you encounter?
MyLab MIS

1-7 Identify some of the people, organizational, and technology issues that UPS had to address when creating its successful information systems.
MyLab MIS

Hands-On MIS Projects

The projects in this section give you hands-on experience in analyzing financial reporting and inventory management problems, using data management software to improve management decision making about increasing sales, and using Internet software for researching job requirements. Visit MyLab MIS to access this chapter's Hands-On MIS Projects

MANAGEMENT DECISION PROBLEMS

1-8 Snyders of Hanover, which sells about 80 million bags of pretzels, snack chips, and organic snack items each year, had its financial department use spreadsheets and manual processes for much of its data gathering and reporting. Hanover's financial analyst would spend the entire final week of every month collecting spreadsheets from the heads of more than 50 departments worldwide. She would then consolidate and reenter all the data into another spreadsheet, which would serve as the company's monthly profit-and-loss statement. If a department needed to update its data after submitting the spreadsheet to the main office, the analyst had to return the original spreadsheet and wait for the department to resubmit its data before finally submitting the updated data in the consolidated document. Assess the impact of this situation on business performance and management decision making.

1-9 Dollar General Corporation operates deep-discount stores offering housewares, cleaning supplies, clothing, health and beauty aids, and packaged food, with most items selling for $1. Its business model calls for keeping costs as low as possible. The company has no automated method for keeping track of inventory at each store. Managers know approximately how many cases of a particular product the store is supposed to receive when a delivery truck arrives, but the stores lack technology for scanning the cases or verifying the item count inside the cases. Merchandise losses from theft or other mishaps have been rising and now represent more than 3 percent of total sales. What decisions have to be made before investing in an information system solution?

IMPROVING DECISION MAKING: USING DATABASES TO ANALYZE SALES TRENDS

Software skills: Database querying and reporting
Business skills: Sales trend analysis

1-10 In this project, you will start out with raw transactional sales data and use Microsoft Access database software to develop queries and reports that help managers make better decisions about product pricing, sales promotions, and inventory replenishment. In MyLab MIS, you can find a Store and Regional Sales Database developed in Microsoft Access. The database contains raw data on weekly store sales of computer equipment in various sales regions. The database includes fields for store identification number, sales region, item number, item description, unit price, units sold, and the weekly sales period when the sales were made. Use Access to develop some reports and queries to make this information more useful for running the business. Sales and production managers want answers to the following questions:

- Which products should be restocked?
- Which stores and sales regions would benefit from a promotional campaign and additional marketing?
- When (what time of year) should products be offered at full price, and when should discounts be used?

Print your reports and results of queries.

IMPROVING DECISION MAKING: USING THE INTERNET TO LOCATE JOBS REQUIRING INFORMATION SYSTEMS KNOWLEDGE

Software skills: Internet-based software
Business skills: Job searching

1-11 Visit a job-posting website such as Monster.com. Spend some time at the site examining jobs for accounting, finance, sales, marketing, and human resources. Find two or three descriptions of jobs that require some information systems knowledge. What information systems knowledge do these jobs require? What do you need to do to prepare for these jobs? Write a one- to two-page report summarizing your findings.

Collaboration and Teamwork Project

Selecting Team Collaboration Tools

1-12 Form a team with three or four classmates and review the capabilities of Google Drive and Google Sites for your team collaboration work. Compare the capabilities of these two tools for storing team documents, project announcements, source materials, work assignments, illustrations, presentations, and web pages of interest. Learn how each works with Google Docs. Explain why Google Drive or Google Sites is more appropriate for your team. If possible, use Google Docs to brainstorm and develop a presentation of your findings for the class. Organize and store your presentation by using the Google tool you have selected.

BUSINESS PROBLEM-SOLVING CASE

Did Information Systems Cause Deutsche Bank to Stumble?

Deutsche Bank AG, founded in 1870, is one of the world's top financial companies, with 2,790 branches in 70 countries. It offers a range of financial products and services, including retail and commercial banking, foreign exchange, and services for mergers and acquisitions. The bank provides products for mortgages, consumer finance, credit cards, life insurance, and corporate pension plans; financing for international trade; and customized wealth management services for wealthy private clients. Deutsche Bank is also the largest bank in Germany, with 1,845 retail branch locations, and plays a central role in German economic life. In many ways, Deutsche Bank is the embodiment of the global financial system.

Deutsche Bank has the world's largest portfolio of derivatives, valued at about $46 trillion. A financial derivative is a contract between two or more parties whose value is dependent upon or derived from one or more underlying assets, such as stocks, bonds, commodities, currencies, and interest rates. Although Deutsche Bank had survived the 2008 banking crisis, which was partly triggered by flawed derivatives, it is now struggling with seismic changes in the banking industry, including recent regulatory change. The bank was forced to pay $7.2 billion to resolve U.S. regulator complaints about its sale of toxic mortgage securities that contributed to the 2008 financial crisis.

In addition, the Commodity Futures Trading Commission (CFTC) charged that Deutsche Bank submitted incomplete and untimely credit default swap data, failed to properly supervise employees responsible for swap data reporting, and lacked an adequate business continuity and disaster recovery plan. (A credit default swap is a type of credit insurance contract in which an insurer promises to compensate an insured party [such as a bank] for losses incurred when a debtor [such as a corporation] defaults on a debt and that can be purchased or sold by either party on the financial market. Credit default swaps are very complex financial instruments.)

The CFTC complained that on April 16, 2016, Deutsche Bank's swap data reporting system experienced a system outage that prevented Deutsche Bank from reporting any swap data for multiple asset classes for approximately five days. Deutsche Bank's subsequent efforts to end the system outage repeatedly exacerbated existing reporting problems and led to the discovery and creation of new reporting problems.

For example, Deutsche Bank's swap data reported before and after the system outage revealed persistent problems with the integrity of certain data fields, including numerous invalid legal entity identifiers. (A legal entity identifier [LEI] is an identification code to uniquely identify all legal entities that are parties to financial transactions.) The CFTC complaint alleged that a number of these reporting problems persist today, affecting market data that is made available to the public as well as data that is used by the CFTC to evaluate systemic risk throughout the swaps markets. The CFTC complaint also alleged that Deutsche Bank's system outage and subsequent reporting problems occurred in part because Deutsche Bank failed to have an adequate business continuity and disaster recovery plan and other appropriate supervisory systems in place.

In addition to incurring high costs associated with coping with regulators and paying fines, Deutsche Bank was a very unwieldy and expensive bank to operate. U.S. regulators have identified Deutsche Bank's antiquated technology as one reason why the bank was not always able to provide the correct information for running its business properly and responding to regulators. Poor information systems may have even contributed to the 2008 financial crisis. Banks often had trouble untangling the complex financial products they had bought and sold to determine their underlying value.

Banks, including Deutsche Bank, are intensive users of information technology, and they rely on technology to spot misconduct. If Deutsche Bank was such an important player in the German and world financial systems, why were its systems not up to the job?

It turns out that Deutsche Bank, like other leading global financial companies, had undergone decades of mergers and expansion. When these banks merged or acquired other financial companies, they often did not make the requisite (and often far-reaching) changes to integrate their information systems with those of their acquisitions. The effort and costs required for this integration, including coordination across many management teams, were too great. So the banks left many old systems in place to handle the workload for each of their businesses. This created what experts call "spaghetti balls" of overlapping and often incompatible technology platforms and software programs. These antiquated legacy systems were designed to handle large numbers of transactions and sums of money, but they were not well suited to managing large bank operations. They often did not allow information to be shared easily among departments or provide senior management with a coherent overview of bank operations.

Deutsche Bank had more than 100 different booking systems for trades in London alone and no common set of codes for identifying clients in each of these systems. Each of these systems might use a different number or code for identifying the same client, so it would be extremely difficult or impossible to show how the same client was treated in all of these systems. Individual teams and traders each had their own incompatible platforms. The bank had employed a deliberate strategy of pitting teams against each other to spur them on, but this further encouraged the use of different systems because competing traders and teams were reluctant to share their data. Yet the bank ultimately had to reconcile the data from these disparate systems, often by hand, before trades could be processed and recorded.

This situation has made it very difficult for banks to undertake ambitious technology projects for the systems that they need today or to comply with regulatory requirements. U.S. regulators criticized Deutsche Bank for its inability to provide essential information because of its antiquated technology. Regulators are demanding that financial institutions improve the way they manage risk. The banks are under pressure to make their aging computer systems comply, but the IT infrastructures at many traditional financial institutions are failing to keep up with these regulatory pressures as well as changing consumer expectations. Deutsche Bank and its peers must also adapt to new innovative technology competitors such as Apple that are muscling into banking services.

In July 2015, John Cryan became Deutsche Bank's CEO. He has been trying to reduce costs and improve efficiency, laying off thousands of employees. He is focusing on overhauling Deutsche Bank's fragmented, antiquated information systems, which are a major impediment to controlling costs and finding new sources of profit and growth. Cryan noted that the bank's cost base was swollen by poor and ineffective business processes, inadequate technology, and too many tasks being handled manually. He has called for standardizing the bank's systems and procedures, eliminating legacy software, standardizing and enhancing data, and improving reporting.

Cryan appointed technology specialist Kim Hammonds as chief operating officer to oversee reengineering the bank's information systems and operations. Hammonds had been Deutsche Bank's global chief information officer and before that chief information officer at Boeing. Hammonds observed that Deutsche Bank's information systems operated by trial and error, as if her former employer Boeing launched aircraft into the sky, watched them crash, and then tried to learn from the mistakes.

In February 2015, Deutsche Bank announced a 10-year, multibillion-dollar deal with Hewlett-Packard (HP) to standardize and simplify its IT infrastructure, reduce costs, and create a more modern and agile technology platform for launching new products and services. Deutsche Bank is migrating to a cloud computing infrastructure where it would run its information systems in HP's remote computer centers. HP will provide computing services, hosting, and storage. Deutsche Bank will still be in charge of application development and information security technologies, which it considers as proprietary and crucial for competitive differentiation.

Deutsche Bank is withdrawing from high-risk client relationships, improving its control framework, and automating manual reconciliations. To modernize its IT infrastructure, the bank will reduce the number of its individual operating systems that control the way a computer works from 45 to four, replace scores of outdated computers, and replace antiquated software applications. Thousands of applications and functions will be shifted from Deutsche Bank's mainframes to HP cloud computing services. Automating manual processes will promote efficiency and better control. These improvements are expected to reduce "run the bank" costs by 800 million euros. Eliminating 6,000 contractors will create total savings of 1 billion euros. Deutsche Bank has also opened four technology centers to work with financial technology startups. In March 2017, the bank opened a new center in New York to work with financial technology startups to improve its technology.

Deutsche Bank is not the only major bank to be hampered by system problems. IT shortcomings were one reason Banco Santander's U.S. unit in 2016 failed the U.S. Federal Reserve's annual "stress tests," which gauge how big banks would fare in a new financial crisis. According to Peter Roe, research director with TechMarketView LLP in the United Kingdom, banks now spend about 75 percent of their IT budgets on maintaining existing systems and operations and only 25 percent on innovation.

A 2015 Accenture consultants report found that only 6 percent of board of director members and 3 percent of CEOs at the world's largest banks had professional technology experience. Financial technology innovations, security, IT resilience, and technology implications of regulatory changes are now all critical issues for bank boards of directors, but many lack the knowledge to assess these issues and make informed decisions about strategy, investment, and how best to allocate technology resources.

Sources: Anna Irrera, "Deutsche Bank Launches Tech Startup Lab in New York City," Reuters, March 21, 2017; Geoffrey Smith, "Things You Should Know About the Deutsche Bank Train Wreck," *Fortune*, September 28, 2016; Hayley McDowell, "System Outage Sees Deutsche Bank Charged over Reporting Failures," *The Trade News*, August 19, 2016; Derek du Preez, "US Regulator Charges Deutsche Bank over Multiple Systems Failures," Diginomica, August 19, 2016; Kat Hall, "Deutsche Bank's Creaking IT Systems Nervously Eyeing Bins," *The Register*, October 27, 2015; Martin Arnold and Tom Braithwaite, "Banks' Ageing IT Systems Buckle Under Strain," *Financial Times*, June 18, 2015; Martin Arnold, "Deutsche Bank to Rip Out IT Systems Blamed for Problems," *Financial Times*, October 26, 2015; Ben Moshinsky, "Deutsche Bank Has a Technology Problem," *Business Insider*, October 20, 2015; Edward Robinson and Nicholas Comfort, "Cryan's Shakeup at Deutsche Bank Sees Tech Restart," Bloomberg, December 20, 2015; and Accenture, "Bank Boardrooms Lack Technology Experience, Accenture Global Research Finds," October 28, 2015.

CASE STUDY QUESTIONS

1-13 Identify the problem described in this case study. What people, organization, and technology factors contributed to this problem?

1-14 What was the role of information technology at Deutsche Bank? How was IT related to the bank's operational efficiency, decision-making capability, and business strategy?

1-15 Was Deutsche Bank using technology effectively to pursue its business strategy? Explain your answer.

1-16 What solution for Deutsche Bank was proposed? How effective do you think it will be? Explain your answer.

MyLab MIS

Go to the Assignments section of MyLab MIS to complete these writing exercises.

1-17 What are the strategic objectives that firms try to achieve by using information systems? For each strategic objective, give an example of how a firm could use information systems to achieve the objective.

1-18 Describe three ways in which information systems are transforming how business is conducted.

Chapter 1 References

Baldwin, Richard. *The Great Convergence: Information Technology and the New Globalization*. Cambridge, MA: Harvard University Press, 2016.

Brynjolfsson, Erik. "VII Pillars of IT Productivity." *Optimize* (May 2005).

Bureau of Economic Analysis. *National Income and Product Accounts*, www.bea.gov, accessed June 30, 2017.

Chae, Ho-Chang, Chang E. Koh, and Victor Prybutok. "Information Technology Capability and Firm Performance: Contradictory Findings and Their Possible Causes." *MIS Quarterly* 38, No. 1 (March 2014).

Chokshi, Niraj. "Out of the Office: More People Are Working Remotely, Survey Finds." *New York Times* (February 15, 2017).

Davidson, Kate. "The 'Soft Skills' Employers Are Looking For." *Wall Street Journal* (August 30, 2016).

Dubina, Kevin. "Job Openings Reach a New High, Hires and Quits Also Increase." *Bureau of Labor Statistics Monthly Labor Review* (June 2015).

eMarketer. "U.S. Digital Shoppers and Buyers (Millions and % of Internet Users)." (February 28, 2017).

FedEx Corporation. "SEC Form 10-K for the Fiscal Year Ended 2016." www.sec.gov, accessed June 28, 2017.

Friedman, Thomas. *The World Is Flat*. New York: Picador, 2007.

Gartner, Inc. "Gartner Says Worldwide IT Spending Forecast to Grow 2.7 Percent in 2017." (January 12, 2017).

Greenfield, Rebecca. "Forget Robots—People Skills Are the Future of American Jobs." *Bloomberg* (December 7, 2016).

Laudon, Kenneth C. *Computers and Bureaucratic Reform.* New York: Wiley, 1974.

Morris, Betsy. "From Music to Maps: How Apple's iPhone Changed Business." *Wall Street Journal* (June 23, 2017).

Pew Internet and American Life. "Internet Use Over Time." (January 11, 2017).

Ross, Jeanne W., and Peter Weill. "Four Questions Every CEO Should Ask About IT." *Wall Street Journal* (April 25, 2011).

U.S. Bureau of Labor Statistics. *Occupational Outlook Handbook,*www.bls.gov, accessed July 1, 2017.

U.S. Census. *Statistical Abstract of the United States.* www.census.gov, accessed June 29, 2017.

Wedell-Wedellsborg, Thomas. "Are You Solving the Right Problems?" *Harvard Business Review* (January–February 2017).

Weill, Peter, and Jeanne Ross. *IT Savvy: What Top Executives Must Know to Go from Pain to Gain.* Boston: Harvard Business School Press, 2009.

CHAPTER

2 Global E-business and Collaboration

LEARNING OBJECTIVES

After reading this chapter, you will be able to answer the following questions:

2-1 What major features of a business are important for understanding the role of information systems?

2-2 How do systems serve different management groups in a business, and how do systems that link the enterprise improve organizational performance?

2-3 Why are systems for collaboration and social business so important, and what technologies do they use?

2-4 What is the role of the information systems function in a business?

2-5 How will MIS help my career?

CHAPTER CASES

- Enterprise Social Networking Helps Sanofi Pasteur Innovate and Improve Quality
- Data Changes How NFL Teams Play the Game and How Fans See It
- Cisco IX5000: What State-of-the-Art Telepresence Can Do for Collaboration
- Social Business: Full Speed Ahead or Proceed with Caution?

VIDEO CASES

- Walmart's Retail Link Supply Chain
- CEMEX—Becoming a Social Business

Instructional Video:

- US Foodservice Grows Market with Oracle CRM on Demand

MyLab MIS

- Discussion questions: 2-5, 2-6, 2-7;
- Hands-on MIS Projects: 2-8, 2-9, 2-10, 2-11;
- Writing Assignments: 2-16, 2-17;
- eText with Conceptual Animations

ENTERPRISE SOCIAL NETWORKING HELPS SANOFI PASTEUR INNOVATE AND IMPROVE QUALITY

Sanofi Pasteur is the vaccines division of the multinational pharmaceutical company Sanofi and the largest company in the world devoted entirely to vaccines. It is headquartered in Lyon, France, has nearly 15,000 employees worldwide, and produces more than 1 billion doses of vaccine per year to inoculate more than 500 million people around the globe. Sanofi Pasteur's corporate vision is to work toward a world where no one suffers or dies from a vaccine-preventable disease. Every day the company invests more than €1 million in research and development. Collaboration, sharing information, ongoing innovation and rigorous pursuit of quality are essential for Sanofi Pasteur's business success and commitment to improving the health of the world's population.

Until recently, the company lacked appropriate tools to encourage staff to have dialogues, share ideas, and work with other members of the company, including people that they might not know. As a large, centralized firm with a traditional hierarchical culture, initiatives were primarily driven from the top down. The company wanted to give employees more opportunities to experiment and innovate on their own and adopted Microsoft Yammer as the platform for this change. Ideas for improvement can come from anywhere in the organization and through Yammer can be shared everywhere.

Microsoft Yammer is an enterprise social networking platform for internal business uses, although it can also create external networks linking to suppliers, customers, and others outside the organization. Yammer enables employees to create groups to collaborate on projects and share and edit documents and includes a news feed to find out what's happening within the company. A People Directory provides a searchable database of contact information, skills, and expertise. Yammer can be accessed through the web, desktop, and mobile devices and can be integrated with other Microsoft tools such as SharePoint and Office 365 to make other applications more "social." (SharePoint is Microsoft's platform for collaboration, document sharing, and document management. Office 365 is Microsoft's online service for its desktop productivity applications such as word processing, spreadsheet, electronic presentations, and data management.)

© Rawpixel.com/Shutterstock

How has Sanofi Pasteur benefited from becoming more "social"? Employees are using Yammer to share updates, ask for feedback, and connect volunteers around improvement initiatives. A recent project involving Yammer resulted in a 60 percent simplification of a key quality process at one manufacturing site, saving the company thousands of euros and reducing overall end-to-end process time. Through Yammer, employees spread the word about this improvement to other locations around the globe.

Using Yammer, Sanofi employees set up activist networks for change in large manufacturing sites. Each group has attracted more than 1,000 people. These networks help create a more collegial, personal culture that makes people more comfortable about making suggestions for improvements and working with other groups across the globe. The groups also provide management with observations about policies and procedures across departments and hierarchies that can be used to redesign the firm's manufacturing and business processes to increase quality and cost-effectiveness. For example, a building operator shared his ideas about how to reduce waste when managing a specific material in his production facility. The new procedure for handling the material saved his facility more than €100,000 per year and became a global best practice at all Sanofi Pasteur production sites. Yammer-powered communities raised awareness of health, safety, and attention to detail issues and helped reduce human errors by 91 percent.

Sources: "Yammer Collaboration Helps Sanofi Pasteur Improve Quality, Make More Life-Saving Vaccines," www.microsoft.com, January 24, 2017; www.sanofipasteur.us, accessed March 10, 2017; and Jacob Morgan, "Three Ways Sanofi Pasteur Encourages Collaboration," *Forbes*, October 20, 2015.

Sanofi Pasteur's experience illustrates how much organizations today rely on information systems to improve their performance and remain competitive. It also shows how much systems supporting collaboration and teamwork make a difference in an organization's ability to innovate, execute, grow profits, and, in this case, provide important social benefits.

The chapter-opening diagram calls attention to important points raised by this case and this chapter. Sanofi Pasteur is a knowledge-intensive company that prizes innovation, but it was hampered by hierarchical top-down processes that prevented employees and managers from freely sharing information and innovating. This impacted the company's ability to create and deliver new leading-edge products and maintain its high-quality standards.

Sanofi Pasteur management found that the best solution was to deploy new technology to move from a hierarchical corporate knowledge and work environment to one which actively engaged employees and enabled them to obtain more knowledge from colleagues. The company took advantage of Microsoft Yammer's social tools to increase employee collaboration and engagement. There is now more effective sharing of employee knowledge, and the company has become more innovative and cost-efficient.

New technology alone would not have solved Sanofi Pasteur's problem. To make the solution effective, Sanofi Pasteur had to change its organizational culture and business processes for knowledge dissemination and collaborative work, and the new technology made these changes possible.

Here are some questions to think about: How are collaboration and employee engagement keeping Sanofi Pasteur competitive and quality-conscious? How did using Yammer change the way work was performed at Sanofi Pasteur?

2-1 What major features of a business are important for understanding the role of information systems?

A **business** is a formal organization whose aim is to produce products or provide services for a profit—that is, to sell products or services at a price greater than the costs of production. Customers are willing to pay this price because they believe they

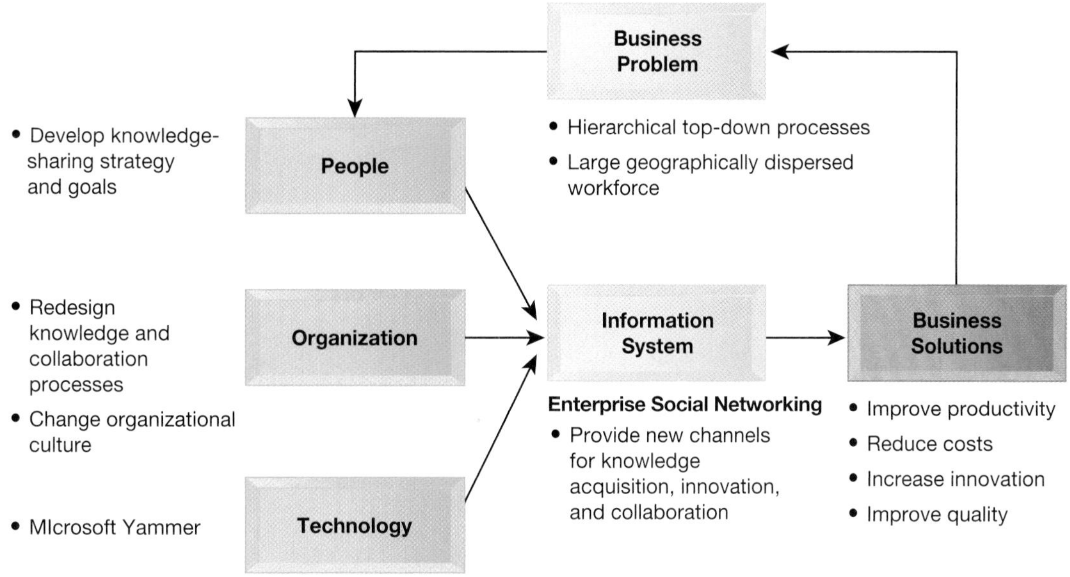

receive a value greater than or equal to the sale price. Business firms purchase inputs and resources from the larger environment (suppliers who are often other firms). Employees of the business firm transform these inputs by adding value to them in the production process.

There are, of course, nonprofit firms and government agencies that are complex formal organizations that produce services and products but do not operate to generate a profit. Nevertheless, even these organizations consume resources from their environments, add value to these inputs, and deliver their outputs to constituents and customers. In general, the information systems found in government and nonprofit organizations are remarkably similar to those found in private industry.

ORGANIZING A BUSINESS: BASIC BUSINESS FUNCTIONS

Imagine you want to set up your own business. Simply deciding to go into business is the most important decision, but next is the question of what product or service to produce (and hopefully sell). The decision of what to produce is called a *strategic choice* because it determines your likely customers, the kinds of employees you will need, the production methods and facilities needed, the marketing themes, and many other choices.

Once you decide what to produce, what kind of organization do you need? First, you need to develop a production division—an arrangement of people, machines, and business processes (procedures) that will produce the product. Second, you need a sales and marketing group who will attract customers, sell the product, and keep track of after-sales issues, such as warranties and maintenance. Third, once you generate sales, you will need a finance and accounting group to keep track of financial transactions, such as orders, invoices, disbursements, and payroll. In addition, this group will seek out sources of credit and finance. Finally, you will need a group of people to focus on recruiting, hiring, training, and retaining employees. Figure 2.1 summarizes the four basic functions found in every business.

If you were an entrepreneur or your business was very small with only a few employees, you would not need, and probably could not afford, all these separate groups of people. Instead, in small firms, you would be performing all these functions yourself or with a few others. In any event, even in small firms, the four basic functions of a firm are required. Larger firms often will have separate departments for each function: production and manufacturing, sales and marketing, finance and accounting, and human resources.

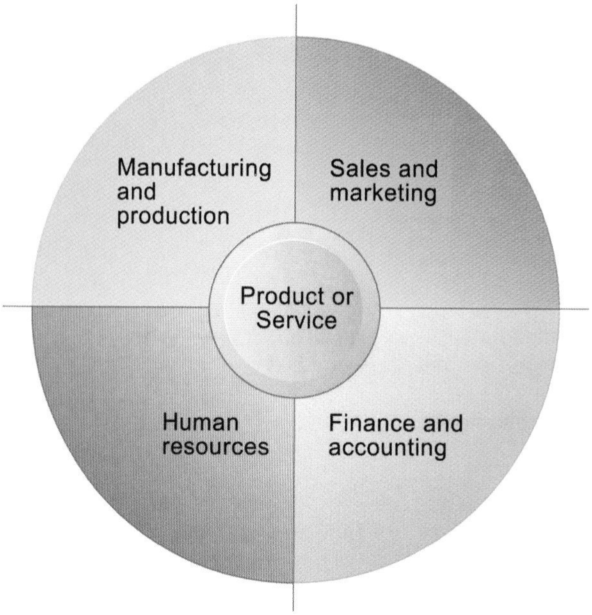

Figure 2.1
The Four Major Functions of a Business
Every business, regardless of its size, must perform four functions to succeed. It must produce the product or service; market and sell the product or service; keep track of accounting and financial transactions; and perform basic human resources tasks such as hiring and retaining employees.

Figure 2.1 is also useful for thinking about the basic entities that make up a business. The five basic entities in a business with which it must deal are: suppliers, customers, employees, invoices/payments, and, of course, products and services. A business must manage and monitor many other components, but these are the basic ones at the foundation of any business.

BUSINESS PROCESSES

Once you identify the basic business functions and entities for your business, your next job is to describe exactly how you want your employees to perform these functions. What specific tasks do you want your sales personnel to perform, in what order, and on what schedule? What steps do you want production employees to follow as they transform raw resources into finished products? How will customer orders be fulfilled? How will vendor bills be paid?

The actual steps and tasks that describe how work is organized in a business are called **business processes**. A business process is a logically related set of activities that defines how specific business tasks are performed. Business processes also refer to the unique ways in which work, information, and knowledge are coordinated in a specific organization.

Every business can be seen as a collection of business processes. Some of these processes are part of larger, encompassing processes. Many business processes are tied to a specific functional area. For example, the sales and marketing function would be responsible for identifying customers, and the human resources function would be responsible for hiring employees. Table 2.1 describes some typical business processes for each of the functional areas of business.

Other business processes cross many functional areas and require coordination across departments. Consider the seemingly simple business process of fulfilling a customer order (see Figure 2.2). Initially, the sales department receives a sales order. The order goes to accounting to ensure that the customer can pay for the order either by a credit verification or request for immediate payment prior to shipping. Once the customer credit is established, the production department has to pull the product from inventory or produce the product. Next, the product needs to be shipped (which may require working with a logistics firm such as UPS or FedEx). The accounting department then generates a bill or invoice and sends a notice to the customer, indicating that the product has shipped. Sales has to be notified of the shipment and prepare to support the customer by answering calls or fulfilling warranty claims.

TABLE 2.1
Examples of Functional Business Processes

Functional Area	Business Process
Manufacturing and production	Assembling the product Checking for quality Producing bills of materials
Sales and marketing	Identifying customers Making customers aware of the product Selling the product
Finance and accounting	Paying creditors Creating financial statements Managing cash accounts
Human resources	Hiring employees Evaluating employees' job performance Enrolling employees in benefits plans

What at first appears to be a simple process—fulfilling an order—turns out to be a very complicated series of business processes that require the close coordination of major functional groups in a firm. Moreover, to perform all these steps efficiently in the order fulfillment process requires the rapid flow of a great deal of information within the firm, with business partners such as delivery firms, and with the customer. The particular order fulfillment process we have just described is not only *cross-functional*, it is also *interorganizational* because it includes interactions with delivery firms and customers who are outside the boundaries of the organization. Ordering raw materials or components from suppliers would be another interorganizational business process.

To a large extent, the efficiency of a business firm depends on how well its internal and interorganizational business processes are designed and coordinated. A company's business processes can be a source of competitive strength if they enable the company to innovate or to execute better than its rivals. Business processes can also be liabilities if they are based on outdated ways of working that impede organizational responsiveness and efficiency.

How Information Technology Enhances Business Processes

Exactly how do information systems enhance business processes? Information systems automate many steps in business processes that were formerly performed manually, such as checking a client's credit or generating an invoice and shipping order.

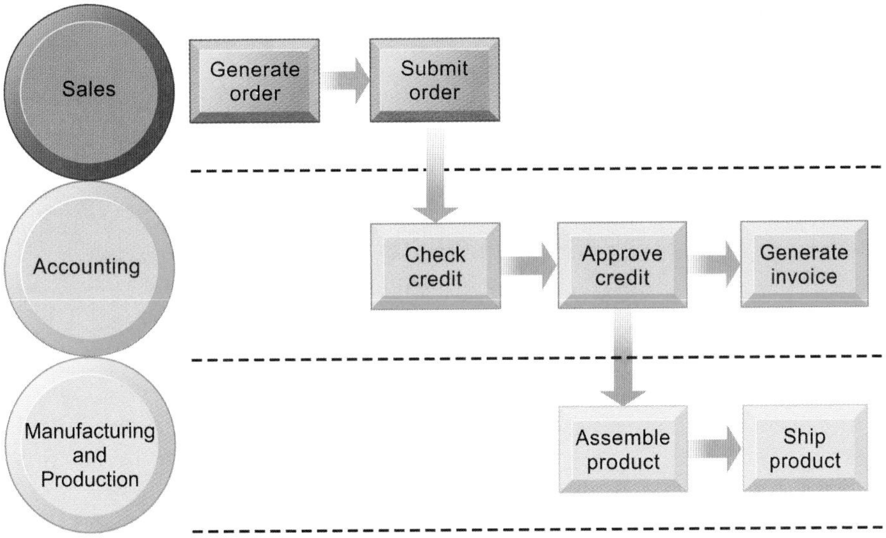

Figure 2.2
The Order Fulfillment Process
Fulfilling a customer order involves a complex set of steps that requires the close coordination of the sales, accounting, and manufacturing functions.

Today, however, information technology can do much more. New technology can actually change the flow of information, making it possible for many more people to access and share information, replacing sequential steps with tasks that can be performed simultaneously and eliminating delays in decision making. It can even transform the way the business works and drive new business models. Ordering a book online from Amazon.com and downloading a music track from iTunes are new business processes based on new business models that are inconceivable without information technology.

That's why it's so important to pay close attention to business processes, both in your information systems course and in your future career. By analyzing business processes, you can achieve a very clear understanding of how a business actually works. Moreover, by conducting a business process analysis, you will also begin to understand how to change the business to make it more efficient or effective. Throughout this book, we examine business processes with a view to understanding how they might be changed, or replaced, by using information technology to achieve greater efficiency, innovation, and customer service. Chapter 3 discusses the business impact of using information technology to redesign business processes, and MyLab MIS™ has a Learning Track with more detailed coverage of this topic.

MANAGING A BUSINESS AND FIRM HIERARCHIES

Each business function has its own goals and processes, and they obviously need to cooperate for the whole business to succeed. Business firms, like all organizations, achieve coordination by hiring managers whose responsibility is to ensure that all the various parts of an organization work together. Firms coordinate the work of employees in various divisions by developing a hierarchy in which authority (responsibility and accountability) is concentrated at the top.

The hierarchy of management is composed of **senior management**, which makes long-range strategic decisions about products and services and ensures financial performance of the firm; **middle management**, which carries out the programs and plans of senior management; and **operational management**, which is responsible for monitoring the daily activities of the business. **Knowledge workers**, such as engineers, scientists, or architects, design products or services and create new knowledge for the firm, whereas **data workers**, such as secretaries or clerks, assist with administrative work at all levels of the firm. **Production or service workers** actually produce the product and deliver the service (Figure 2.3).

Figure 2.3
Levels in a Firm
Business organizations are hierarchies consisting of three principal levels: senior management, middle management, and operational management. Information systems serve each of these levels. Scientists and knowledge workers often work with middle management.

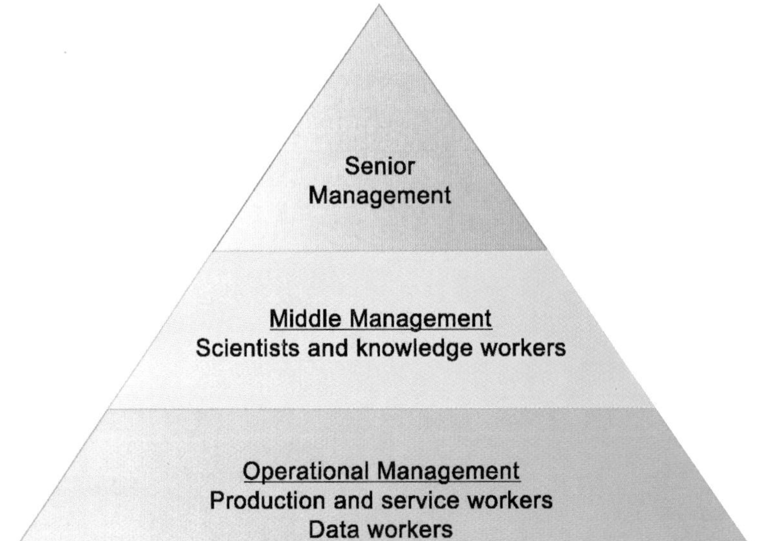

Each of these groups has different needs for information given their different responsibilities. Senior managers need summary information that can quickly inform them about the overall performance of the firm, such as gross sales revenues, sales by product group and region, and overall profitability. Middle managers need more specific information about the results of specific functional areas and departments of the firm such as sales contacts by the sales force, production statistics for specific factories or product lines, employment levels and costs, and sales revenues for each month or even each day. Operational managers need transaction-level information such as the number of parts in inventory each day or the number of hours logged on Tuesday by each employee. Knowledge workers may need access to external scientific databases or internal databases with organizational knowledge. Finally, production workers need access to information from production machines, and service workers need access to customer records to take orders and answer questions from customers.

THE BUSINESS ENVIRONMENT

So far, we have talked about business as if it operated in a vacuum, but nothing could be further from the truth. In fact, business firms depend heavily on their environments to supply capital, labor, customers, new technology, services and products, stable markets and legal systems, and general educational resources. Even a pizza parlor cannot survive long without a supportive environment that delivers the cheese, tomato sauce, and flour!

Figure 2.4 summarizes the key actors in the environment of every business. To stay in business, a firm must monitor changes in its environment and share information with the key entities in that environment. For instance, a firm must respond to political shifts, respond to changes in the overall economy (such as changes in labor rates and price inflation), keep track of new technologies, and respond to changes in the global business environment (such as foreign exchange rates). In their immediate environment, firms need to track and share information with suppliers, customers, stockholders, regulators, and logistic partners (such as shipping firms).

Business environments are constantly changing; new developments in technology, politics, customer preferences, and regulations happen all the time. In general, when businesses fail, it is often because they failed to respond adequately to changes in their environments.

Figure 2.4
The Business Environment
To be successful, an organization must constantly monitor and respond to—or even anticipate—developments in its environment. A firm's environment includes specific groups with which the business must deal directly, such as customers, suppliers, and competitors, as well as the broader general environment, including socioeconomic trends, political conditions, technological innovations, and global events.

Changes in technology, such as the Internet, are forcing entire industries and leading firms to change their business models or suffer failure. Apple's iTunes and other online music services have made the music industry's traditional business model based on distributing music on CDs obsolete. Traditional cameras with film have been largely supplanted by digital photography, and digital cameras themselves are losing ground to iPhones and other mobile devices with cameras.

THE ROLE OF INFORMATION SYSTEMS IN A BUSINESS

Until now, we have not mentioned information systems, but from the brief review of business functions, entities, and environments, you can see the critical role that information plays in the life of a business. Up until the mid-1950s, firms managed all this information and information flow with paper records. Since then, more and more business information, and the flow of information among key business actors in the environment, has been moved from manual to digital systems.

Businesses invest in information systems as a way to cope with and manage their internal production functions and cope with the demands of key actors in their environments. Specifically, as we noted in Chapter 1, firms invest in information systems for the following business objectives:

- To achieve operational excellence (productivity, efficiency, agility)
- To develop new products and services
- To attain customer intimacy and service (continuous marketing, sales, and service; customization and personalization)
- To improve decision making (accuracy and speed)
- To achieve competitive advantage
- To ensure survival

2-2 How do systems serve different management groups in a business, and how do systems that link the enterprise improve organizational performance?

Now it is time to look more closely at how businesses use information systems to achieve these goals. Because there are different interests, specialties, and levels in an organization, there are different kinds of systems. No single system can provide all the information an organization needs.

A typical business organization will have systems supporting processes for each of the major business functions—sales and marketing, manufacturing and production, finance and accounting, and human resources. You can find examples of systems for each of these business functions in the Learning Tracks for this chapter. Functional systems that operated independently of each other are becoming outdated because they cannot easily share information to support cross-functional business processes. They are being replaced with large-scale cross-functional systems that integrate the activities of related business processes and organizational units. We describe these integrated cross-functional applications later in this section.

A typical firm will also have different systems supporting the decision-making needs of each of the main management groups described earlier. Operational management, middle management, and senior management each use a specific type of system to support the decisions they must make to run the company. Let's look at these systems and the types of decisions they support.

SYSTEMS FOR DIFFERENT MANAGEMENT GROUPS

A business firm has systems to support decision making and work activities at different levels of the organization. They include transaction processing systems and systems for business intelligence.

Transaction Processing Systems

Operational managers need systems that keep track of the elementary activities and transactions of the organization, such as sales, receipts, cash deposits, payroll, credit decisions, and the flow of materials in a factory. **Transaction processing systems (TPS)** provide this kind of information. A transaction processing system is a computerized system that performs and records the daily routine transactions necessary to conduct business, such as sales order entry, hotel reservations, payroll, employee record keeping, and shipping.

The principal purpose of systems at this level is to answer routine questions and to track the flow of transactions through the organization. How many parts are in inventory? What happened to Mr. Williams's payment? To answer these kinds of questions, information generally must be easily available, current, and accurate.

At the operational level, tasks, resources, and goals are predefined and highly structured. The decision to grant credit to a customer, for instance, is made by a lower-level supervisor according to predefined criteria. All that must be determined is whether the customer meets the criteria.

Figure 2.5 illustrates a TPS for payroll processing. A payroll system keeps track of money paid to employees. An employee time sheet with the employee's name, identification number, and number of hours worked per week represents a single transaction for this system. Once this transaction is input in the system, it updates the system's file (or database—see Chapter 6) that permanently maintains employee information for the organization. The data in the system are combined in different ways to create reports of interest to management and government agencies and to send paychecks to employees.

Managers need TPS to monitor the status of internal operations and the firm's relations with the external environment. TPS are also major producers of information for the other systems and business functions. For example, the payroll system illustrated in Figure 2.5, along with other accounting TPS, supplies data to the company's general ledger system, which is responsible for maintaining records of the firm's income and expenses and for producing reports such as income statements and balance sheets. It also supplies employee payment history data for insurance, pension,

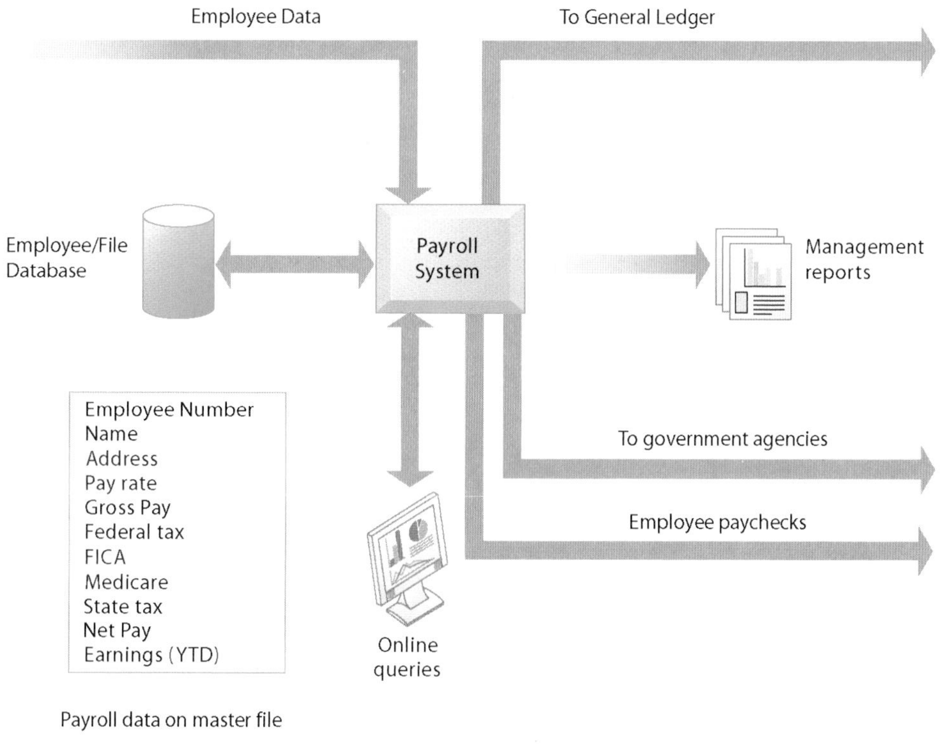

Figure 2.5
A Payroll TPS
A TPS for payroll processing captures employee payment transaction data (such as a timecard). System outputs include online and hard copy reports for management and employee paychecks.

and other benefits calculations to the firm's human resources function, and employee payment data to government agencies such as the U.S. Internal Revenue Service and Social Security Administration.

Transaction processing systems are often so central to a business that TPS failure for a few hours can lead to a firm's demise and perhaps that of other firms linked to it. Imagine what would happen to UPS if its package tracking system were not working! What would the airlines do without their computerized reservation systems?

Systems for Business Intelligence

Firms also have business intelligence systems that focus on delivering information to support management decision making. **Business intelligence** is a contemporary term for data and software tools for organizing, analyzing, and providing access to data to help managers and other enterprise users make more informed decisions. Business intelligence addresses the decision-making needs of all levels of management. This section provides a brief introduction to business intelligence. You'll learn more about this topic in Chapters 6 and 11.

Business intelligence systems for middle management help with monitoring, controlling, decision-making, and administrative activities. In Chapter 1, we defined management information systems as the study of information systems in business and management. The term **management information systems (MIS)** also designates a specific category of information systems serving middle management. MIS provide middle managers with reports about the organization's current performance. Managers use this information to monitor and control the business and predict future performance.

MIS summarize and report on the company's basic operations using data supplied by transaction processing systems. The basic transaction data from TPS are compressed and usually presented in reports that are produced on a regular schedule. Today, many of these reports are delivered online. Figure 2.6 shows how a typical MIS transforms transaction-level data from inventory, production, and accounting into MIS files that provide managers with reports. Figure 2.7 shows a sample report from this system.

MIS typically provide answers to routine questions that have been specified in advance and have a predefined procedure for answering them. For instance,

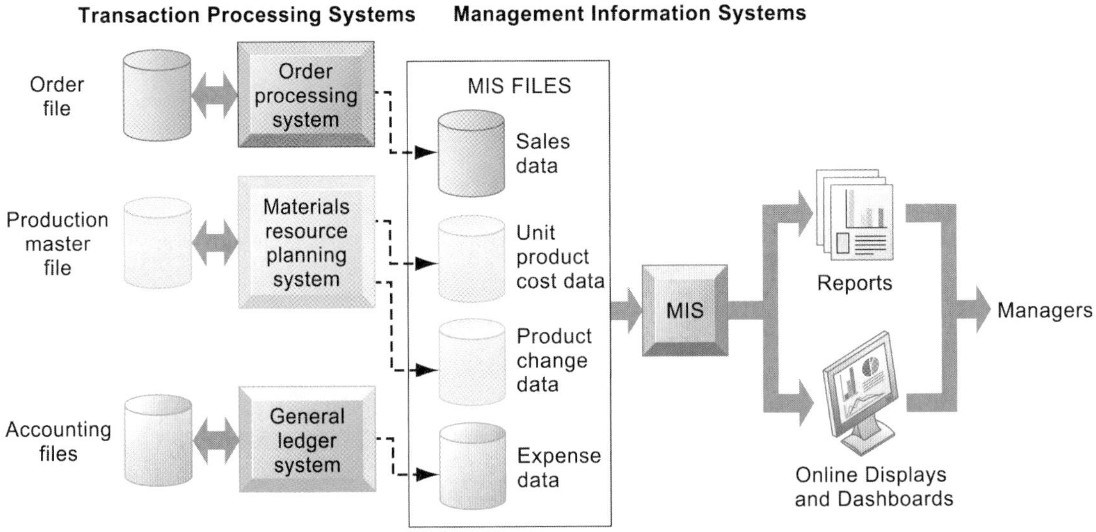

Figure 2.6
How Management Information Systems Obtain Their Data from the Organization's TPS
In the system illustrated by this diagram, three TPS supply summarized transaction data to the MIS reporting system at the end of the time period. Managers gain access to the organizational data through the MIS, which provides them with the appropriate reports.

Consolidated Consumer Products Corporation Sales by Product and Sales Region: 2018

PRODUCT CODE	PRODUCT DESCRIPTION	SALES REGION	ACTUAL SALES	PLANNED	ACTUAL versus PLANNED
4469	Carpet Cleaner	Northeast	4,066,700	4,800,000	0.85
		South	3,778,112	3,750,000	1.01
		Midwest	4,867,001	4,600,000	1.06
		West	4,003,440	4,400,000	0.91
	TOTAL		16,715,253	17,550,000	0.95
5674	Room Freshener	Northeast	3,676,700	3,900,000	0.94
		South	5,608,112	4,700,000	1.19
		Midwest	4,711,001	4,200,000	1.12
		West	4,563,440	4,900,000	0.93
	TOTAL		18,559,253	17,700,000	1.05

Figure 2.7
Sample MIS Report
This report, showing summarized annual sales data, was produced by the MIS in Figure 2.6.

MIS reports might list the total pounds of lettuce used this quarter by a fast-food chain or, as illustrated in Figure 2.7, compare total annual sales figures for specific products to planned targets. These systems generally are not flexible and have little analytical capability. Most MIS use simple routines, such as summaries and comparisons, as opposed to sophisticated mathematical models or statistical techniques.

Other types of business intelligence systems support more nonroutine decision making. **Decision-support systems (DSS)** focus on problems that are unique and rapidly changing, for which the procedure for arriving at a solution may not be fully predefined in advance. They try to answer questions such as these: What would be the impact on production schedules if we were to double sales in the month of December? What would happen to our return on investment if a factory schedule were delayed for six months?

Although DSS use internal information from TPS and MIS, they often bring in information from external sources, such as current stock prices or product prices of competitors. Super-user managers and business analysts who want to use sophisticated analytics and models to analyze data employ these systems.

An interesting, small but powerful DSS is the voyage-estimating system of a large global shipping company that exists primarily to carry bulk cargoes of coal, oil, ores, and finished products for its parent company. The firm owns some vessels, charters others, and bids for shipping contracts in the open market to carry general cargo. A voyage-estimating system calculates financial and technical voyage details. Financial calculations include ship/time costs (fuel, labor, capital), freight rates for various types of cargo, and port expenses. Technical details include a myriad of factors, such as ship cargo capacity, speed, port distances, fuel and water consumption, and loading patterns (location of cargo for different ports).

The system can answer questions such as the following: Given a customer delivery schedule and an offered freight rate, which vessel should be assigned at what rate to maximize profits? What is the optimal speed at which a particular vessel can optimize its profit and still meet its delivery schedule? What is the optimal loading pattern for a ship bound for the U.S. West Coast from Malaysia? Figure 2.8 illustrates the DSS built for this company. The system operates on a powerful desktop personal computer, providing a system of menus that makes it easy for users to enter data or obtain information.

The voyage-estimating DSS we have just described draws heavily on models. Other business intelligence systems are more data-driven, focusing instead on extracting useful information from massive quantities of data. For example, large ski resort companies such as Intrawest and Vail Resorts collect and store large amounts

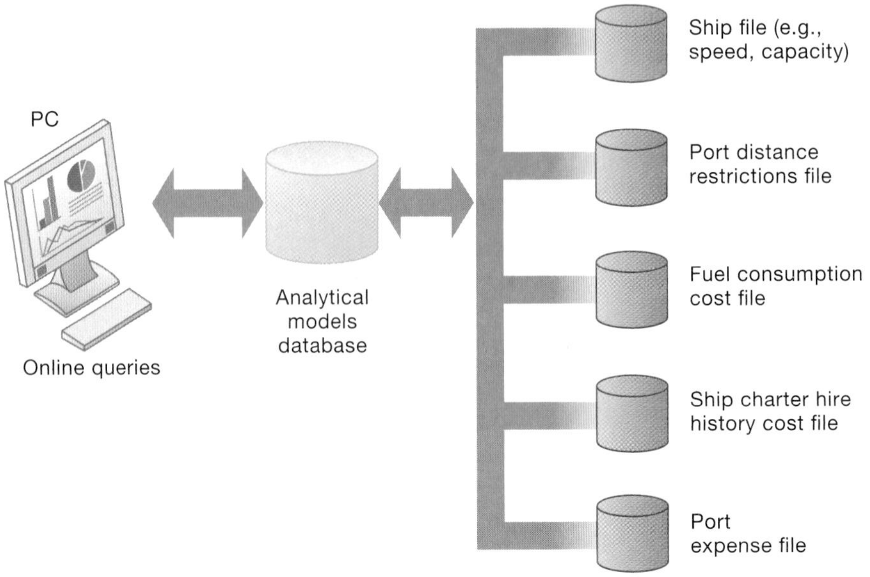

Figure 2.8 Voyage-Estimating Decision-Support System

This DSS operates on a powerful PC. Managers who must develop bids on shipping contracts use it daily.

of customer data from call centers, lift tickets, lodging and dining reservations, ski schools, and ski equipment rental stores. They use special software to analyze these data to determine the value, revenue potential, and loyalty of each customer to help managers make better decisions about how to target their marketing programs.

Business intelligence systems also address the decision-making needs of senior management. Senior managers need systems that focus on strategic issues and long-term trends, both in the firm and in the external environment. They are concerned with questions such as: What will employment levels be in five years? What are the long-term industry cost trends? What products should we be making in five years?

Executive support systems (ESS) help senior management make these decisions. They address nonroutine decisions requiring judgment, evaluation, and insight because there is no agreed-on procedure for arriving at a solution. ESS present graphs and data from many sources through an interface that is easy for senior managers to use. Often the information is delivered to senior executives through a **portal**, which uses a web interface to present integrated personalized business content.

ESS are designed to incorporate data about external events such as new tax laws or competitors, but they also draw summarized information from internal MIS and DSS. They filter, compress, and track critical data, displaying the data of greatest importance to senior managers. Increasingly, such systems include business intelligence analytics for analyzing trends, forecasting, and drilling down to data at greater levels of detail.

For example, the chief operating officer (COO) and plant managers at Valero, the world's largest independent petroleum refiner, use a Refining Dashboard to display real-time data related to plant and equipment reliability, inventory management, safety, and energy consumption. With the displayed information, management can review the performance of each Valero refinery in the United States and Canada in terms of how each plant is performing compared to the production plan of the firm. The headquarters group can drill down to from executive level to refinery level and individual system-operator level displays of performance. Valero's Refining Dashboard is an example of a **digital dashboard**, which displays on a single screen graphs and charts of key performance indicators for managing a company. Digital dashboards are becoming an increasingly popular tool for management decision makers.

The Interactive Session on People describes real-world examples of several of these types of systems that the National Football League (NFL) and its teams use.

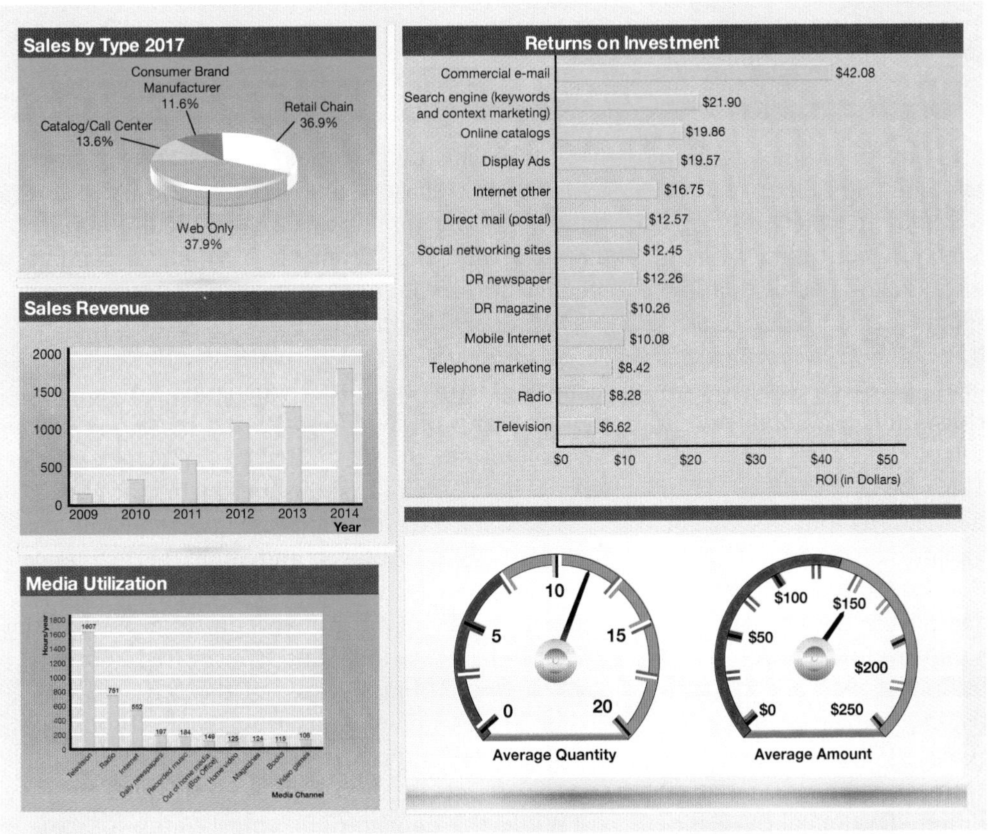

A digital dashboard delivers comprehensive and accurate information for decision making, often using a single screen. The graphical overview of key performance indicators helps managers quickly spot areas that need attention.

Note the types of systems this case illustrates and the role they play in improving both operations and decision making.

SYSTEMS FOR LINKING THE ENTERPRISE

Reviewing all the types of systems we have just described, you might wonder how a business can manage all the information in these differing systems. You might also wonder how costly it is to maintain so many systems. You might also wonder how all these systems can share information and how managers and employees can coordinate their work. In fact, these are all important questions for businesses today.

Enterprise Applications

Getting the different kinds of systems in a company to work together has proven a major challenge. Typically, corporations are put together both through normal organic growth and through acquisition of smaller firms. Over time, corporations end up with a collection of systems, most of them older, and face the challenge of getting them all to talk with one another and work together as one corporate system. There are several solutions to this problem.

One solution is to implement **enterprise applications**, which are systems that span functional areas, focus on executing business processes across the business firm, and include all levels of management. Enterprise applications help businesses become more flexible and productive by coordinating their business processes more closely and integrating groups of processes so they focus on efficient management of resources and customer service.

There are four major enterprise applications: enterprise systems, supply chain management systems, customer relationship management systems, and knowledge management systems. Each of these enterprise applications integrates a related set

INTERACTIVE SESSION: PEOPLE

Data Changes How NFL Teams Play the Game and How Fans See It

All professional sports teams today collect detailed data on player and team performance, fan behavior, and sales and increasingly use these data to drive decisions about every aspect of the business—marketing, ticketing, player evaluation, and TV and digital media deals. This includes the National Football League (NFL), which is increasingly turning to data to improve how its players and teams perform and how fans experience the game.

Since 2014 the NFL has been capturing player movement data on the field by putting nickel-sized radio frequency identification (RFID) tags beneath players' shoulder pads to track every move they make. The information the sensors gather is used by NFL teams to improve their training and strategy, by commentators on live game broadcasts, and by fans attending games or using the NFL app on the Xbox One.

The NFL's player tracking system is based on the Zebra Sports Solution developed by Zebra Technologies, a Chicago-based firm specializing in tracking technology that includes the bar codes on groceries and other consumer goods and RFID technology. The Zebra Sports Solution system records players' speed, direction, location on the field, how far they ran on a play, and how long they were sprinting, jogging, or walking. The system can also determine what formation a team was in and how players' speed or acceleration impacts their on-field performance. Want to know how hard Eli Manning is throwing passes or the force with which a ball arrives in the hands of receiver Odell Beckham? The system knows how to do all that.

NFL players have an RFID chip in their left and right shoulder pads that transmit data to 20 radio receivers strategically located in the lower and upper levels of stadiums to collect data about how each player moves, using metrics such as velocity, speed in miles per hour, and distance traveled. From there the data are transmitted to an on-site server computer, where Zebra's software matches an RFID tag to the correct player or official. The football also has a sensor transmitting location data. The data are generated in real time as the game is being played. Each sensor transmits its location about 25 times per player.

It takes just two seconds for data to be received by the motion sensors, analyzed, and pushed out to remote cloud computers run by Amazon Web Services for the NFL. From the NFL cloud computers, the data are shared with fans, broadcasters, and NFL teams. Once the data are stored by the NFL, Microsoft gathers and displays the data to fans using NFL.com, the NFL's social media outlet, and the NFL app on Windows 10 and the Xbox One. The data are also transmitted to the giant display screens in the arena to show fans during the game.

The data have multiple uses. NFL teams use them to evaluate player and team performance and to analyze tactics, such as whether it might be better to press forward or to punt in a particular fourth-down situation. Data transmitted to broadcasters, to stadium screens, to the NFL website, and to the NextGen Stats feature of Microsoft's Xbox One NFL app help create a deeper fan experience that gets fans more involved in the game.

While the data may be entertaining for fans, they could prove strategic for the teams. Data markers for each play are recorded, including type of offense, type of defense, whether there was a huddle, all movement during the play, and the yard line where the ball was stopped. The NFL runs custom-created analytics to deliver visualizations of the data to each team within 24 hours of the game via a custom-built web portal. The system displays charts and graphs as well as tabular data to let teams have more insight. Each NFL team may also hire its own data analyst to wring even more value from the data.

Zebra sees other potential uses for the data. For example, more analytics could identify when a player's performance is likely to flag late in the game and how to improve training to prevent such fatigue. Coaches could use that information to decide whether to pull out a certain receiver during the fourth quarter or to rely on that player less in a critical moment. Even now the data are giving NFL fans, teams, coaches, and players a deeper look into the game they love.

Sources: Brian McDonough, "How the NFL's Data Operation Tracks Every Move on the Field," *Information Management*, December 7, 2016; www.zebra.com, accessed March 15, 2017; Mark J. Burns, "Zebra Technologies, NFL Revamp Partnership for Third Season," SportTechie, September 6, 2016; and "Zebra Tracking Technology May Change How NFL Fans See the Game and Teams Play It, MarketWatch, September 15, 2015.

CASE STUDY QUESTIONS

1. What kinds of systems are illustrated in this case study? Where do they obtain their data? What do they do with the data? Describe some of the inputs and outputs of these systems.
2. What business functions do these systems support? Explain your answer.
3. How do the data about teams and players captured by the NFL help NFL football teams and the NFL itself make better decisions? Give examples of two decisions that were improved by the systems described in this case.
4. How did using data help the NFL and its teams improve the way they run their business?

of functions and business processes to enhance the performance of the organization as a whole. Figure 2.9 shows that the architecture for these enterprise applications encompasses processes spanning the entire organization and, in some cases, extending beyond the organization to customers, suppliers, and other key business partners.

Enterprise Systems Firms use **enterprise systems**, also known as *enterprise resource planning (ERP)* systems, to integrate business processes in manufacturing and production, finance and accounting, sales and marketing, and human resources into a single software system. Information that was previously fragmented in many systems is stored in a single comprehensive data repository where it can be used by many parts of the business.

For example, when a customer places an order, the order data flow automatically to other parts of the company that they affect. The order transaction triggers

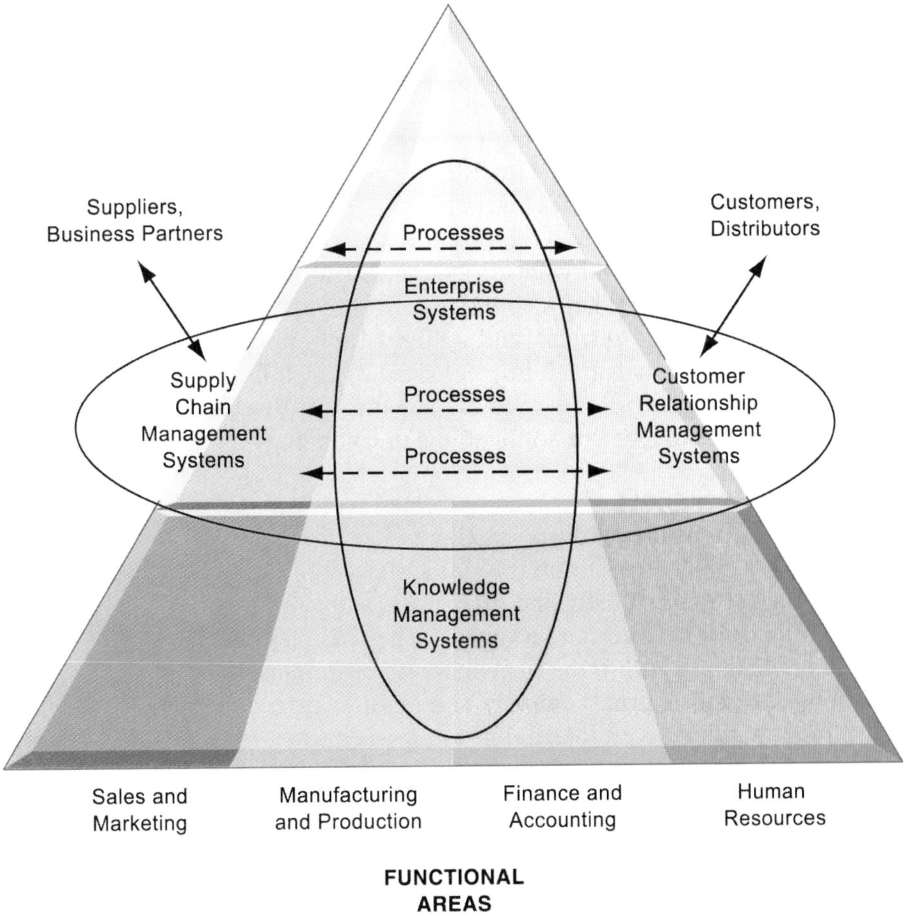

Figure 2.9
Enterprise Application Architecture
Enterprise applications automate processes that span multiple business functions and organizational levels and may extend outside the organization.

the warehouse to pick the ordered products and schedule shipment. The warehouse informs the factory to replenish whatever has been depleted. The accounting department is notified to send the customer an invoice. Customer service representatives track the progress of the order through every step to inform customers about the status of their orders. Managers can use firmwide information to make more precise and timely decisions about daily operations and longer-term planning.

Supply Chain Management Systems Firms use **supply chain management (SCM) systems** to help manage relationships with their suppliers. These systems help suppliers, purchasing firms, distributors, and logistics companies share information about orders, production, inventory levels, and delivery of products and services so that they can source, produce, and deliver goods and services efficiently. The ultimate objective is to get the right number of their products from their source to their point of consumption in the shortest time and at the lowest cost. These systems increase firm profitability by lowering the costs of moving and making products and by enabling managers to make better decisions about how to organize and schedule sourcing, production, and distribution.

Supply chain management systems are one type of **interorganizational system** because they automate the flow of information across organizational boundaries. You will find examples of other types of interorganizational information systems throughout this text because such systems make it possible for firms to link firms to customers and to outsource their work to other companies.

Customer Relationship Management Systems Firms use **customer relationship management (CRM) systems** to help manage their relationships with their customers. CRM systems provide information to coordinate all the business processes that deal with customers in sales, marketing, and service to optimize revenue, customer satisfaction, and customer retention. This information helps firms identify, attract, and retain the most profitable customers; provide better service to existing customers; and increase sales.

Knowledge Management Systems Some firms perform better than others do because they have better knowledge about how to create, produce, and deliver products and services. This firm knowledge is unique, difficult to imitate, and can be leveraged into long-term strategic benefits. **Knowledge management systems (KMS)** enable organizations to manage processes better for capturing and applying knowledge and expertise. These systems collect all relevant knowledge and experience in the firm and make it available wherever and whenever it is needed to improve business processes and management decisions. They also link the firm to external sources of knowledge.

We examine enterprise systems and systems for supply chain management and customer relationship management in greater detail in Chapter 9. We discuss collaboration systems that support knowledge management in this chapter and cover other types of knowledge management applications in Chapter 11.

Intranets and Extranets

Enterprise applications create deep-seated changes in the way the firm conducts its business, offering many opportunities to integrate important business data into a single system. They are often costly and difficult to implement. Intranets and extranets deserve mention here as alternative tools for increasing integration and expediting the flow of information within the firm and with customers and suppliers.

Intranets are simply internal company websites that are accessible only by employees. The term *intranet* refers to an internal network in contrast to the Internet, which is a public network linking organizations and other external networks. Intranets use the same technologies and techniques as the larger Internet, and they often are simply a private access area in a larger company website. Extranets are company websites that are accessible to authorized vendors and suppliers and often used to coordinate the movement of supplies to the firm's production apparatus.

For example, Bank of America North America maintains a Human Resources intranet that helps employees take advantage of all the benefits available to them. Employees can review benefit plans, track time worked and time off, and learn about the bank's employee career development and training resources. We describe the technology for intranets and extranets in more detail in Chapter 7.

E-BUSINESS, E-COMMERCE, AND E-GOVERNMENT

The systems and technologies we have just described are transforming firms' relationships with customers, employees, suppliers, and logistic partners into digital relationships by using networks and the Internet. So much business is now enabled by or based on digital networks that we use the terms *e-business* and *e-commerce* frequently throughout this text.

E-business, or **electronic business**, refers to the use of digital technology and the Internet to execute the major business processes in the enterprise. E-business includes activities for the internal management of the firm and for coordination with suppliers and other business partners. It also includes **e-commerce**, or **electronic commerce**. E-commerce is the part of e-business that deals with buying and selling goods and services over the Internet. It also encompasses activities supporting those market transactions, such as advertising, marketing, customer support, security, delivery, and payment.

The technologies associated with e-business have also brought about similar changes in the public sector. Governments on all levels are using Internet technology to deliver information and services to citizens, employees, and businesses with which they work. **E-government** refers to the application of the Internet and networking technologies to enable government and public sector agencies' relationships with citizens, businesses, and other arms of government digitally. In addition to improving delivery of government services, e-government can make government operations more efficient and empower citizens by giving them easier access to information and the ability to network with other citizens. For example, citizens in some states can renew their driver's licenses or apply for unemployment benefits online, and the Internet has become a powerful tool for instantly mobilizing interest groups for political action and fund-raising.

2-3 Why are systems for collaboration and social business so important, and what technologies do they use?

With all these systems and information, you might wonder how is it possible to make sense of them. How do people working in firms pull it all together, work toward common goals, and coordinate plans and actions? In addition to the types of systems we have just described, businesses need special systems to support collaboration and teamwork.

WHAT IS COLLABORATION?

Collaboration is working with others to achieve shared and explicit goals. Collaboration focuses on task or mission accomplishment and usually takes place within a business or other organization and between businesses. You collaborate with a colleague in Tokyo who has expertise in a topic about which you know nothing. You collaborate with many colleagues in publishing a company blog. If you're in a law firm, you collaborate with accountants in an accounting firm in servicing the needs of a client with tax problems.

Collaboration can be short-lived, lasting a few minutes, or longer term, depending on the nature of the task and the relationship among participants. Collaboration can be one-to-one or many-to-many.

Employees may collaborate in informal groups that are not a formal part of the business firm's organizational structure, or they may be organized into formal teams. **Teams** have a specific mission that someone in the business assigned to them. Team members need to collaborate on the accomplishment of specific tasks and collectively achieve the team mission. The team mission might be to win the game or increase online sales by 10 percent. Teams are often short-lived, depending on the problems they tackle and the length of time needed to find a solution and accomplish the mission.

Collaboration and teamwork are more important today than ever for a variety of reasons.

- *Changing nature of work.* The nature of work has changed from factory manufacturing and pre-computer office work, when each stage in the production process occurred independently of one another and was coordinated by supervisors. Work was organized into silos, and passed from one machine tool station to another, from one desktop to another, until the finished product was completed. Today, the kinds of jobs we have require much closer coordination and interaction among the parties involved in producing the service or product. A recent report from the consulting firm McKinsey and Company argued that 41 percent of the U.S. labor force is now composed of jobs in which interaction (talking, emailing, presenting, and persuading) is the primary value-adding activity. Even in factories, workers today often work in production groups, or pods.
- *Growth of professional work.* Interaction jobs tend to be professional jobs in the service sector that require close coordination and collaboration. Professional jobs require substantial education and sharing information and opinions to get work done. Each actor on the job brings specialized expertise to the problem, and all the actors need to consider one another to accomplish the job.
- *Changing organization of the firm.* For most of the industrial age, managers organized work in a hierarchical fashion. Orders came down the hierarchy, and responses moved back up the hierarchy. Today, work is organized into groups and teams, which are expected to develop their own methods for accomplishing the task. Senior managers observe and measure results but are much less likely to issue detailed orders or operating procedures. In part, this is because, expertise and decision making power have been pushed down in organizations.
- *Changing scope of the firm.* The work of the firm has spread from a single location to occupying multiple locations—offices or factories throughout a region, a nation, or even around the globe. For instance, Henry Ford developed the first mass-production automobile plant at a single Dearborn, Michigan, factory. In 2016, Ford employed 201,000 people at 67 plants worldwide. With this kind of global presence, the need for close coordination of design, production, marketing, distribution, and service obviously takes on new importance and scale. Large global companies need teams to work on a global basis.
- *Emphasis on innovation.* Although we tend to attribute innovations in business and science to great individuals, these great individuals are most likely working with a team of brilliant colleagues. Think of Bill Gates and Steve Jobs (founders of Microsoft and Apple, respectively), both of whom are highly regarded innovators, and both of whom built strong collaborative teams to nurture and support innovation in their firms. Their initial innovations derived from close collaboration with colleagues and partners. Innovation, in other words, is a group and social process, and most innovations derive from collaboration among individuals in a lab, a business, or government agencies. Strong collaborative practices and technologies are believed to increase the rate and quality of innovation.
- *Changing culture of work and business.* Most research on collaboration supports the notion that diverse teams produce better outputs faster than individuals working on their own. Popular notions of the crowd (crowdsourcing and the wisdom of crowds) also provide cultural support for collaboration and teamwork.

WHAT IS SOCIAL BUSINESS?

Today, many firms are enhancing collaboration by embracing **social business**, the use of social networking platforms, including Facebook, Twitter, and internal corporate social tools, to engage their employees, customers, and suppliers. These tools enable workers to set up profiles, form groups, and follow each other's status updates. The goal of social business is to deepen interactions with groups inside and outside the firm to expedite and enhance information sharing, innovation, and decision making.

A key word in social business is *conversations*. Customers, suppliers, employees, managers, and even oversight agencies continually have conversations about firms, often without the knowledge of the firm or its key actors (employees and managers). Supporters of social business argue that if firms could tune into these conversations, they will strengthen their bonds with consumers, suppliers, and employees, increasing their emotional involvement in the firm.

All of this requires a great deal of information transparency. People need to share opinions and facts with others quite directly, without intervention from executives or others. Employees get to know directly what customers and other employees think; suppliers will learn very directly the opinions of supply chain partners; and even managers presumably will learn more directly from their employees how well they are doing. Nearly everyone involved in the creation of value will know much more about everyone else.

If such an environment could be created, it is likely to drive operational efficiencies, spur innovation, and accelerate decision making. If product designers can learn directly about how their products are doing in the market in real time, based on consumer feedback, they can speed up the redesign process. If employees can use social connections inside and outside the company to capture new knowledge and insights, they will be able to work more efficiently and solve more business problems.

Table 2.2 describes important applications of social business inside and outside the firm. This chapter focuses on enterprise social business: its internal corporate uses. Chapter 10 will describe social business applications relating to customers and suppliers outside the company.

BUSINESS BENEFITS OF COLLABORATION AND SOCIAL BUSINESS

Although many articles and books have been written about collaboration, nearly all the research on this topic is anecdotal. Nevertheless, among both business and academic communities, there is a general belief that the more collaborative a business firm is, the more successful it will be and that collaboration within and among

TABLE 2.2

Applications of Social Business

Business Application	Description
Social networks	Connect through personal and business profiles
Crowdsourcing	Harness collective knowledge to generate new ideas and solutions
Shared workspaces	Coordinate projects and tasks, co-create content
Blogs and wikis	Publish and rapidly access knowledge; discuss opinions and experiences
Social commerce	Share opinions about purchasing or purchase on social platforms
File sharing	Upload, share, and comment on photos, videos, audio, text documents
Social marketing	Use social media to interact with customers, derive customer insights
Communities	Discuss topics in open forums, share expertise

TABLE 2.3

Business Benefits of Collaboration and Social Business

Benefit	Rationale
Productivity	People interacting and working together can capture expert knowledge and solve problems more rapidly than the same number of people working in isolation from one another. There will be fewer errors.
Quality	People working collaboratively can communicate errors and correct actions faster than if they work in isolation. Collaborative and social technologies help reduce time delays in design and production.
Innovation	People working collaboratively can come up with more innovative ideas for products, services, and administration than the same number working in isolation from one another. Advantages to diversity and the wisdom of crowds.
Customer service	People working together using collaboration and social tools can solve customer complaints and issues faster and more effectively than if they were working in isolation from one another.
Financial performance (profitability, sales, and sales growth)	As a result of all these factors, collaborative firms have superior sales, sales growth, and financial performance.

firms is more essential than in the past. A global survey of business and information systems managers found that investments in collaboration technology produced organizational improvements that returned more than four times the amount of the investment, with the greatest benefits for sales, marketing, and research and development functions (Frost and Sullivan, 2009). McKinsey & Company consultants predicted that social technologies used within and across enterprises could raise the productivity of interaction workers by 20 to 25 percent (McKinsey Global Institute, 2012).

Table 2.3 summarizes some of the benefits of collaboration and social business that have been identified. Figure 2.10 graphically illustrates how collaboration is believed to affect business performance.

Figure 2.10
Requirements for Collaboration
Successful collaboration requires an appropriate organizational structure and culture along with appropriate collaboration technology.

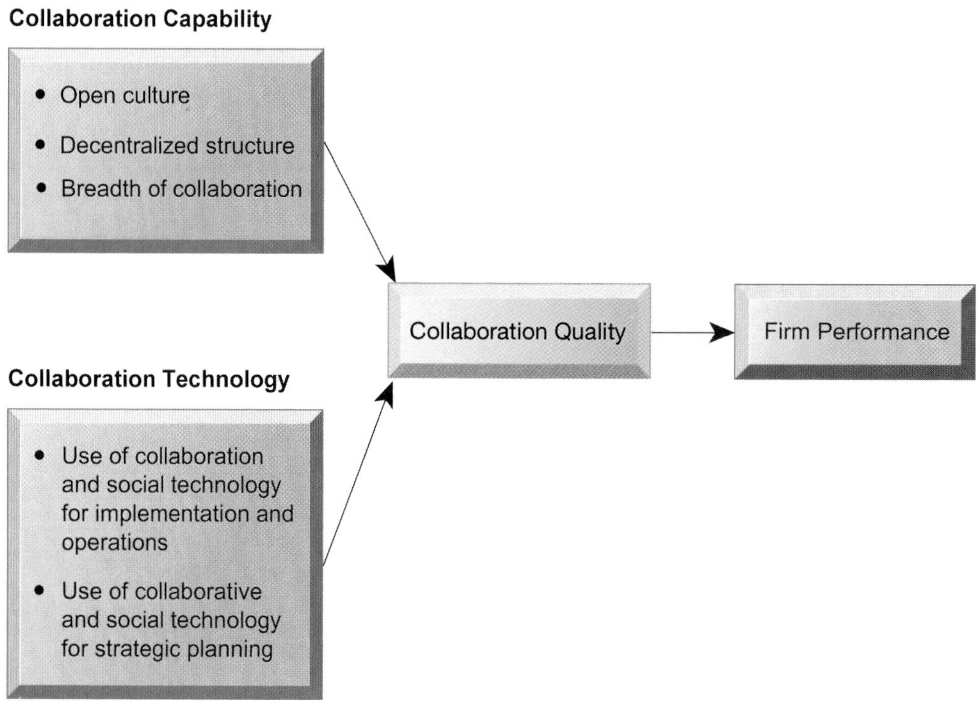

BUILDING A COLLABORATIVE CULTURE AND BUSINESS PROCESSES

Collaboration won't take place spontaneously in a business firm, especially if there is no supportive culture or business processes. Business firms, especially large firms, had in the past a reputation for being command-and-control organizations in which the top leaders thought up all the really important matters and then ordered lower-level employees to execute senior management plans. The job of middle management supposedly was to pass messages back and forth up and down the hierarchy.

Command-and-control firms required lower-level employees to carry out orders without asking too many questions, with no responsibility to improve processes, and with no rewards for teamwork or team performance. If your workgroup needed help from another work group, that was something for the bosses to figure out. You never communicated horizontally, always vertically, so management could control the process. Many business firms still operate this way.

A collaborative business culture and business processes are very different. Senior managers are responsible for achieving results but rely on teams of employees to achieve and implement the results. Policies, products, designs, processes, and systems are much more dependent on teams at all levels of the organization to devise, to create, and to build. Teams are rewarded for their performance, and individuals are rewarded for their performance in a team. The function of middle managers is to build the teams, coordinate their work, and monitor their performance. The business culture and business processes are more social. In a collaborative culture, senior management establishes collaboration and teamwork as vital to the organization, and it actually implements collaboration for the senior ranks of the business as well.

TOOLS AND TECHNOLOGIES FOR COLLABORATION AND SOCIAL BUSINESS

A collaborative, team-oriented culture won't produce benefits without information systems in place to enable collaboration and social business. Currently, hundreds of tools are designed for this purpose. Some of these tools are expensive, but others are available online for free (or with premium versions for a modest fee) and are suitable for small businesses. Let's look more closely at some of these tools.

Email and Instant Messaging (IM)

Email and instant messaging (including text messaging) have been major communication and collaboration tools for interaction jobs. Their software operates on computers and wireless mobile devices and includes features for sharing files as well as transmitting messages. Many instant messaging systems allow users to engage in real-time conversations with multiple participants simultaneously. In recent years, email use has declined, and messaging and social media have become preferred channels of communication.

Wikis

Wikis are a type of website that makes it easy for users to contribute and edit text content and graphics without any knowledge of web page development or programming techniques. The most well-known wiki is Wikipedia, the largest collaboratively edited reference project in the world. It relies on volunteers, makes no money, and accepts no advertising.

Wikis are very useful tools for storing and sharing corporate knowledge and insights. Enterprise software vendor SAP AG has a wiki that acts as a base of information for people outside the company, such as customers and software developers who build programs that interact with SAP software. In the past, those people asked and sometimes answered questions in an informal way on SAP online forums, but that was an inefficient system, with people asking and answering the same questions repeatedly.

Virtual Worlds

Virtual worlds, such as Second Life, are online 3-D environments populated by residents who have built graphical representations of themselves known as avatars. Companies such as IBM, Cisco, and Intel Corporation use this virtual world for online meetings, interviews, guest speaker events, and employee training. Real-world people represented by avatars meet, interact, and exchange ideas at these virtual locations using gestures, chat box conversations, and voice communication.

Collaboration and Social Business Platforms

There are now suites of software products providing multifunction platforms for collaboration and social business among teams of employees who work together from many locations. The most widely used are Internet-based audioconferencing and videoconferencing systems, cloud collaboration services such as Google's online services and tools, corporate collaboration systems such as IBM Notes and Microsoft SharePoint, and enterprise social networking tools such as Salesforce Chatter, Microsoft Yammer, Jive, Facebook Workplace, and IBM Connections.

Virtual Meeting Systems In an effort to reduce travel expenses, many companies, both large and small, are adopting videoconferencing and web conferencing technologies. Companies such as Heinz, General Electric, and PepsiCo are using virtual meeting systems for product briefings, training courses, strategy sessions, and even inspirational chats.

A videoconference allows individuals at two or more locations to communicate simultaneously through two-way video and audio transmissions. High-end videoconferencing systems feature **telepresence** technology, an integrated audio and visual environment that allows a person to give the appearance of being present at a location other than his or her true physical location (see the Interactive Session on Technology). Free or low-cost Internet-based systems such as Skype group videoconferencing, Google Hangouts, Amazon Chime, Zoom, and ooVoo are lower quality but still useful for smaller companies. Apple's FaceTime is useful for one-to-one videoconferencing. Some of these tools are available on mobile devices.

Companies of all sizes are finding web-based online meeting tools such as Cisco WebEx, Skype for Business, GoToMeeting, and Adobe Connect especially helpful for training and sales presentations. These products enable participants to share documents and presentations in conjunction with audioconferencing and live video.

Cloud Collaboration Services Google offers many online tools and services, and some are suitable for collaboration. They include Google Drive, Google Docs, G Suite, Google Sites, and Google+. Most are free of charge.

Google Drive is a web-based file storage and synchronization service for cloud storage, file sharing, and collaborative editing. Online file-sharing services allow users to upload files to secure online storage sites from which the files can be shared with others. Microsoft OneDrive and Dropbox are other leading cloud storage services. They feature both free and paid services, depending on the amount of storage space and administration required. Users can synchronize their files stored online with their local PCs and other kinds of devices, with options for making the files private or public and for sharing them with designated contacts.

Google Drive and Microsoft OneDrive are integrated with tools for document creation and sharing. OneDrive provides online storage for Microsoft Office documents and other files and works with Microsoft Office apps, both installed and on the web. It can share to Facebook as well. Google Drive is integrated with Google Docs, Sheets, and Slides (often called Google Docs), a suite of productivity applications that offer collaborative editing on documents, spreadsheets, and presentations. Google's cloud-based productivity suite for businesses called G Suite also works with Google Drive.

Google Sites allows users to quickly create online team-oriented sites where multiple people can collaborate and share files. Google+ is Google's effort to make these

INTERACTIVE SESSION: TECHNOLOGY

Cisco IX5000: What State-of-the-Art Telepresence Can Do for Collaboration

When it comes to collaboration, the fastest-growing requirement is for video-enabled business applications. In the past, videoconferencing was limited to the very largest companies that could afford dedicated videoconference rooms and expensive networking and software for this purpose. Today, videoconferencing has been democratized. There's something for everyone.

The cost of the technology has radically fallen, and global Internet and desktop transmission of video and audio data is inexpensive and available using standard corporate IT infrastructure. Videoconferencing can be integrated into mobile and desktop tools that are powerful, inexpensive, and ubiquitous. Now, for the first time, it's possible for most employees and professionals in a firm to use videoconferencing and telepresence tools to manage business processes and connect and collaborate with others, even customers, around the globe.

The current generation of telepresence platforms provide much more than video collaboration, with the ability coordinate multiple rich data streams that integrate mobile, desktop, and video streams of digital information, create a collaborative environment, and move the information to where managers and professionals are making decisions.

On the high end, let's look at Cisco's IX5000 immersive telepresence system. It offers leading-edge telepresence, but it's much more affordable and easier to use than in the past. It is sleekly sculpted, with three 4K ultra high-definition cameras clustered discreetly above three 70-inch LCD screens. The cameras provide crisp, high-definition video. Theater-quality sound emanates from 18 custom speakers and one powerful subwoofer, creating a high-quality lifelike collaboration experience for 8 to 18 people. Video and other content can move across any of the screens. The camera and graphic processors are able to capture the whole room in fine detail, so you can stand up and move around or go to the whiteboard. Using the 4K cameras, the IX 5000 creates an image four times larger than what's actually needed to fill the system's three screens. The images can be cropped down to show participants seated behind their tables, but when someone stands up, the crop is removed to show both standing and sitting participants.

The IX5000 is so intuitive that you can make that first call without looking at a manual or calling the information systems department. To install the IX500 system, no special changes to a room are required. And it needs only half the power, installation time, and data transmission capacity (bandwidth) as its previous telepresence systems. How much does all this cost? A six-seat IX5000 studio lists for $299,000, while the 18-seat studio costs $339,000.

The first company to deploy the IX5000 system was Produban, Grupo Santander's technology company specializing in the continuous design and operation of IT infrastructures. Grupo Santander is a Spanish banking group and one of the largest banks in the world in terms of market capitalization. It has 187,000 employees serving more than 100 million customers, 14,400 branches, and operations across Europe, Latin America, North America, Africa, and Asia. Grupo Santander is noted for innovation in its industry and has pioneered many new digital products and services for online banking, mobile banking, mobile wallet, and digital payments. Produban is responsible the entire IT infrastructure of this sprawling global company.

With more than 5,500 employees working in nine different countries, Produban services more than 120 companies in areas such as data center design and operation, IT infrastructure design and operation as a service, IT platform design and operation as a service, technology risk management and business continuity, and management of end user computing mobility and self-service management. The company is dedicated to technology innovation and continuous improvement.

Video collaboration helps Produban bring people together to make better decisions faster, which is why over the years it has invested in 76 Cisco TelePresence rooms worldwide. One reason this company is using IX500 technology is its lower total cost of ownership. As you will learn in Chapter 5, total cost of ownership (TCO) includes not only the purchase price of computer hardware, software, and networking equipment but also costs for ongoing maintenance, technical support, training, and utility and real estate costs for housing the technology. The IX5000 series can be installed into as little as a 19-by-4-foot space with 50 percent less power usage, 50 percent less data transmission capacity, and half the installation time than earlier systems (only eight hours); the IX5000 reduces TCO by 30 percent over three years.

Lower TCO will enable Produban to set up video rooms in more locations, so more teams can benefit. Produban is intent on using videoconferencing throughout the entire corporation. For locations where an IX5000 installation is not feasible, Cisco TelePresence meetings can be extended to users of Cisco WebEx, Cisco's low-cost web-based system for online meetings and application sharing. Remote attendees can join through the Cisco WebEx Meeting Center and receive video, audio and other digital content from the Cisco TelePresence system. Meetings become even easier to stage among different groups and locations and are more productive.

Sources: Snorre Kjesbu, "The Most Sophisticated Collaboration Experience on the Planet," "'Less Is More' as Cisco Completely Reimagines Flagship Three-Screen Video Conferencing Technology," and "Cisco TelePresence IX5000 Series," www.cisco.com, accessed March 11, 2017; www.produban.com, accessed March 13, 2017; www.pb-santander.com, accessed March 11, 2017.

CASE STUDY QUESTIONS

1. Describe the capabilities of Cisco's IX5000 telepresence system. How do they promote collaboration and innovation?
2. Why would a company like Produban want to invest in a telepresence system such as Cisco's IX5000? How is videoconferencing technology and telepresence related to Produban's business model and business strategy?
3. What kinds of other companies might benefit from a telepresence service such as IX5000? Why?

tools and other products and services it offers more social. Google+ users can create Circles for organizing people into specific groups for sharing and collaborating.

Microsoft SharePoint and IBM Notes Microsoft SharePoint is a browser-based collaboration and document management platform combined with a powerful search engine that is installed on corporate servers. SharePoint has a web-based interface and close integration with productivity tools such as Microsoft Office. SharePoint software makes it possible for employees to share their documents and collaborate on projects by using Office documents as the foundation.

SharePoint can be used to host internal websites that organize and store information in one central workspace to enable teams to coordinate work activities, collaborate on and publish documents, maintain task lists, implement workflows, and share information through wikis and blogs. Users are able to control versions of documents and document security. Because SharePoint stores and organizes information in one place, users can find relevant information quickly and efficiently while working together closely on tasks, projects, and documents. Enterprise search tools help locate people, expertise, and content. SharePoint now features social tools.

Southern Valve & Fitting USA (SVF) which provides wholesalers worldwide with plumbing, irrigation, and utility valves and fittings, uses Microsoft SharePoint online to provide a single platform for its documents and team sites. Employees can access documents from anywhere in the world using a standard Internet connection. An order placed in China is handled as a SharePoint project and all the sales order data and paperwork are shared throughout company (Microsoft, 2015).

IBM Notes (formerly Lotus Notes) is a collaborative software system with capabilities for sharing calendars, email, messaging, collective writing and editing, shared database access, and online meetings. Notes software installed on desktop or laptop computers obtains applications stored on an IBM Domino server. Notes is web-enabled and offers an application development environment so that users can build custom applications to suit their unique needs. Notes has also added capabilities for blogs, microblogs, wikis, online content aggregators, help-desk systems, voice and video conferencing, and online meetings. IBM Notes promises high levels of security and reliability and the ability to retain control over sensitive corporate information.

TABLE 2.4
Enterprise Social Networking Software Capabilities

Social Software Capability	Description
Profiles	Ability to set up member profiles describing who individuals are, educational background, interests. Includes work-related associations and expertise (skills, projects, teams).
Content sharing	Share, store, and manage content, including documents, presentations, images, and videos.
Feeds and notifications	Real-time information streams, status updates, and announcements from designated individuals and groups.
Groups and team workspaces	Establish groups to share information, collaborate on documents, and work on projects, with the ability to set up private and public groups and to archive conversations to preserve team knowledge.
Tagging and social bookmarking	Indicate preferences for specific pieces of content, similar to the Facebook Like button. Tagging lets people add keywords to identify content they like.
Permissions and privacy	Ability to make sure private information stays within the right circles as determined by the nature of relationships. In enterprise social networks, there is a need to establish who in the company has permission to see what information.

Enterprise Social Networking Tools The tools we have just described include capabilities for supporting social business, but there are also more specialized social tools for this purpose, such as Salesforce Chatter, Microsoft Yammer, Microsoft Teams, Jive, Facebook Workplace, and IBM Connections. Enterprise social networking tools create business value by connecting the members of an organization through profiles, updates, and notifications, similar to Facebook features but tailored to internal corporate uses. Table 2.4 provides more detail about these internal social capabilities.

Although many companies have benefited from enterprise social networking, internal social networking has not caught on as quickly as consumer uses of Facebook, Twitter, and other public social networking products. The chapter-ending case addresses this topic.

Checklist for Managers: Evaluating and Selecting Collaboration Software Tools

With so many collaboration tools and services available, how do you choose the right collaboration technology for your firm? You need a framework for understanding just what problems these tools are designed to solve. One framework that has been helpful for us in talking about collaboration tools is the time/space collaboration and social tool matrix developed by a number of collaborative-work scholars (Figure 2.11).

The time/space matrix focuses on two dimensions of the collaboration problem: time and space. For instance, you need to collaborate with people in different time zones and you cannot all meet at the same time. Midnight in New York is noon in Bombay, so this makes it difficult to have a video conference. Time is clearly an obstacle to collaboration on a global scale.

Place (location) also inhibits collaboration in large global or even national and regional firms. Assembling people for a physical meeting is made difficult by the physical dispersion of distributed firms (firms with more than one location), the cost of travel, and the time limitations of managers.

The collaboration technologies described previously are ways of overcoming the limitations of time and space. Using this time/space framework will help you choose the most appropriate collaboration and teamwork tools for your firm. Note that

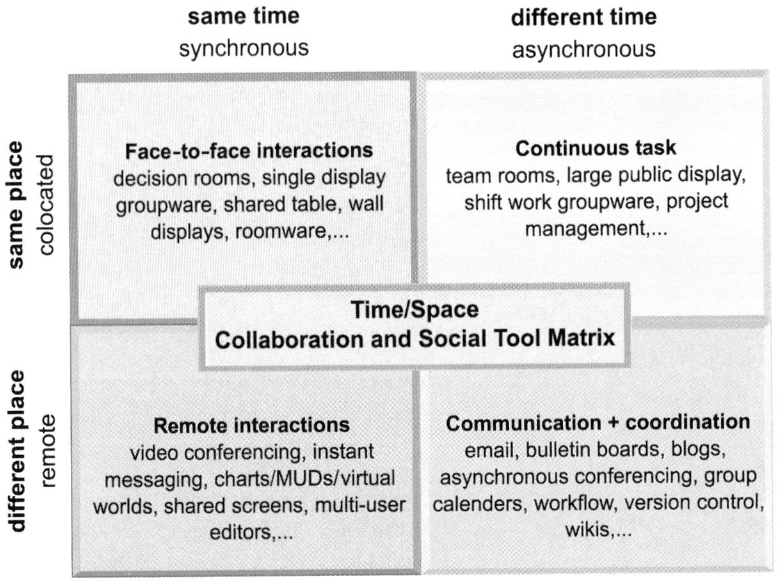

Figure 2.11
The Time/Space Collaboration and Social Tool Matrix
Collaboration technologies can be classified in terms of whether they support interactions at the same or different time or place and whether these interactions are remote or colocated.

some tools are applicable in more than one time/place scenario. For example, Internet collaboration suites such as IBM Notes have capabilities for both synchronous (instant messaging, meeting tools) and asynchronous (email, wikis, document editing) interactions.

Here's a to-do list to get started. If you follow these six steps, you should be led to investing in the correct collaboration software for your firm at a price you can afford and within your risk tolerance.

1. What are the collaboration challenges facing the firm in terms of time and space? Locate your firm in the time/space matrix. Your firm can occupy more than one cell in the matrix. Different collaboration tools will be needed for each situation.
2. Within each cell of the matrix where your firm faces challenges, exactly what kinds of solutions are available? Make a list of vendor products.
3. Analyze each of the products in terms of their cost and benefits to your firm. Be sure to include the costs of training and the costs of involving the information systems department in your cost estimates if needed.
4. Identify the risks to security and vulnerability involved with each of the products. Is your firm willing to put proprietary information into the hands of external service providers over the Internet? Is your firm willing to risk its important operations in systems other firms control? What are the financial risks facing your vendors? Will they be here in three to five years? What would be the cost of making a switch to another vendor in the event the vendor firm fails?
5. Seek the help of potential users to identify implementation and training issues. Some of these tools are easier to use than others are.
6. Make your selection of candidate tools, and invite the vendors to make presentations.

2-4 What is the role of the information systems function in a business?

We've seen that businesses need information systems to operate today and that they use many kinds of systems, but who is responsible for running these systems? Who is responsible for making sure the hardware, software, and other technologies these systems use are running properly and up to date? End users manage their systems from a business standpoint, but managing the technology requires a special information systems function.

In all but the smallest of firms, the **information systems department** is the formal organizational unit responsible for information technology services. The information systems department is responsible for maintaining the hardware, software, data storage, and networks that comprise the firm's IT infrastructure. We describe IT infrastructure in detail in Chapter 5.

THE INFORMATION SYSTEMS DEPARTMENT

The information systems department consists of specialists such as programmers, systems analysts, project leaders, and information systems managers. **Programmers** are highly trained technical specialists who write the software instructions for computers. **Systems analysts** constitute the principal liaisons between the information systems groups and the rest of the organization. It is the systems analyst's job to translate business problems and requirements into information requirements and systems. **Information systems managers** are leaders of teams of programmers and analysts, project managers, physical facility managers, telecommunications managers, or database specialists. They are also managers of computer operations and data entry staff. External specialists, such as hardware vendors and manufacturers, software firms, and consultants, also frequently participate in the day-to-day operations and long-term planning of information systems.

In many companies, the information systems department is headed by a **chief information officer (CIO)**. The CIO is a senior manager who oversees the use of information technology in the firm. Today's CIOs are expected to have a strong business background, as well as information systems expertise, and to play a leadership role in integrating technology with the firm's business strategy. Large firms today also have positions for a chief security officer, chief knowledge officer, chief data officer, and chief privacy officer, all of whom work closely with the CIO.

The **chief security officer (CSO)** is in charge of information systems security for the firm and is responsible for enforcing the firm's information security policy (see Chapter 8). (Where information systems security is separated from physical security, this position is sometimes called the chief information security officer [CISO]). The CSO is responsible for educating and training users and information systems specialists about security, keeping management aware of security threats and breakdowns, and maintaining the tools and policies chosen to implement security.

Information systems security and the need to safeguard personal data have become so important that corporations collecting vast quantities of personal data have established positions for a **chief privacy officer (CPO)**. The CPO is responsible for ensuring that the company complies with existing data privacy laws.

The **chief knowledge officer (CKO)** is responsible for the firm's knowledge management program. The CKO helps design programs and systems to find new sources of knowledge or to make better use of existing knowledge in organizational and management processes.

The **chief data officer (CDO)** is responsible for enterprise-wide governance and usage of information to maximize the value of the organization's data. The CDO ensures that the firm is collecting appropriate data to serve its needs, deploying appropriate technologies for analyzing the data, and using the results to support business decisions. This position arose to deal with the massive amounts of data organizations are now generating and collecting (see Chapter 6).

End users are representatives of departments outside of the information systems group for whom applications are developed. These users are playing an increasingly large role in the design and development of information systems.

In the early years of computing, the information systems group was composed mostly of programmers who performed highly specialized but limited technical functions. Today, a growing proportion of staff members are systems analysts and network specialists, with the information systems department acting as a powerful change agent in the organization. The information systems department suggests new business strategies and new information-based products and services and coordinates both the development of the technology and the planned changes in the organization.

INFORMATION SYSTEMS SERVICES

Services the information systems department provides include the following:

- Computing platforms provide computing services that connect employees, customers, and suppliers into a coherent digital environment, including large mainframes, desktop and laptop computers, and mobile handheld devices.
- Telecommunications services provide data, voice, and video connectivity to employees, customers, and suppliers.
- Data management services store and manage corporate data and provide capabilities for analyzing the data.
- Application software services provide development and support services for the firm's business systems, including enterprise-wide capabilities such as enterprise resource planning, customer relationship management, supply chain management, and knowledge management systems, that all business units share.
- Physical facilities management services develop and manage the physical installations required for computing, telecommunications, and data management services.
- IT management services plan and develop the infrastructure, coordinate with the business units for IT services, manage accounting for the IT expenditure, and provide project management services.
- IT standards services provide the firm and its business units with policies that determine not only which information technology will be used but when and how they are used.
- IT educational services provide training in system use to employees and offer managers training in how to plan for and manage IT investments.
- IT research and development services provide the firm with research on potential future information systems projects and investments that could help the firm differentiate itself in the marketplace.

In the past, firms generally built their own software and managed their own computing facilities. As our discussion of collaboration systems has shown, many firms are turning to external vendors and Internet-based services to provide these services (see also Chapters 5 and 12) and are using their information systems departments to manage these service providers.

2-5 How will MIS help my career?

Here is how Chapter 2 and this book can help you find a job as a sales support specialist.

THE COMPANY

Comprehensive Supplemental Insurance USA is a leading provider of individual supplemental accident, disability, health, and life insurance products headquartered in Minneapolis and has an open position for an entry-level sales support specialist. The company offers supplemental insurance to complement existing employer benefits programs, maintaining a field sales force and corporate staff of more than 5,000 people worldwide. It is known for investing in its employees and their career development.

POSITION DESCRIPTION

This position will provide overall systems, administrative and data management support to the national sales organization for the company's division that markets to small businesses. Job responsibilities include:

- Daily administration and support of the firm's Salesforce.com customer relationship management system, including managing user setup, profiles, and roles and validating data.
- Assisting with data management and providing system training and ongoing support to the field.
- Preparing routine weekly, monthly, and quarterly sales and key performance indicator reports for sales management.
- Preparing agent commission reports and creating new reports as requested.
- Supporting various projects related to agent licensing and agent compensation.

JOB REQUIREMENTS

- Strong Excel skills plus some knowledge of data management
- Strong customer service skills
- Strong analytical, critical thinking, and communication skills
- Ability to multitask in a fast-paced environment
- Bachelor's degree or two years' equivalent experience

INTERVIEW QUESTIONS

1. What do you know about our company? Our commitment to technology? Have you been following us on press releases, LinkedIn and our company Twitter account?
2. What do you know about customer relationship management? Have you ever worked with Salesforce.com? If so, what have you used the system for?
3. What do you know about data management? Have you ever worked with data management software? If so, what exactly have you done with it?
4. Tell us what you can do with Excel. What kinds of problems have you used Excel to solve? Did you take courses in Excel?
5. Have you ever worked in customer service? What exactly did you do? What do you think it takes to successfully take on a client-oriented role for this company's agents and customers?
6. Can you give an example of a client service challenge you had to face? How did you approach this challenge?

AUTHOR TIPS

1. Review the section of this chapter on enterprise applications, the Chapter 9 discussion of customer relationship management, and Chapter 6 on data management.
2. Use the web to research the company, its insurance products and services and the way it operates. Think about what it needs to do to support its agents and its customers and why customer relationship management and data management are so important at this firm. You might inquire about your responsibilities for data management in this job position.
3. Learn what you can about Salesforce.com, especially how to set up user profiles and roles and how to validate data. Indicate that you would like to learn more about Salesforce and work with this tool to support the sales function for the company.
4. Ask exactly how you would be using Excel, for example, calculating agent commissions. If you've never done that before, describe some of the Excel work you have done (and perhaps bring examples with you to the interview).

Review Summary

2-1 What major features of a business are important for understanding the role of information systems? A business is a formal, complex organization producing products or services for a profit. Businesses have specialized functions such as finance and accounting, human resources, manufacturing and production, and sales and marketing. Business organizations are arranged hierarchically into levels of management. A business process is a logically related set of activities that define how specific business tasks are performed. Business firms must monitor and respond to their surrounding environments.

2-2 How do systems serve different management groups in a business, and how do systems that link the enterprise improve organizational performance? Systems serving operational management are transaction processing systems (TPS), such as payroll or order processing, that track the flow of the daily routine transactions necessary to conduct business. Business intelligence systems serve multiple levels of management and help employees make more informed decisions. Management information systems (MIS) and decision-support systems (DSS) support middle management. Most MIS reports condense information from TPS and are not highly analytical. DSS support management decisions that are unique and rapidly changing, using advanced analytical models and data analysis capabilities. Executive support systems (ESS) support senior management by providing data that are often in the form of graphs and charts delivered in portals and dashboards using many sources of internal and external information.

Enterprise applications are designed to coordinate multiple functions and business processes. Enterprise systems integrate the key internal business processes of a firm into a single software system to improve coordination and decision making. Supply chain management (SCM) systems help the firm manage its relationship with suppliers to optimize the planning, sourcing, manufacturing, and delivery of products and services. Customer relationship management (CRM) systems coordinate the business processes surrounding the firm's customers. Knowledge management systems enable firms to optimize the creation, sharing, and distribution of knowledge. Intranets and extranets are private corporate networks based on Internet technology. Extranets make portions of private corporate intranets available to outsiders.

2-3 Why are systems for collaboration and social business so important, and what technologies do they use? Collaboration means working with others to achieve shared and explicit goals. Social business is the use of internal and external social networking platforms to engage employees, customers, and suppliers, and it can enhance collaborative work. Collaboration and social business have become increasingly important in business because of globalization, the decentralization of decision making, and growth in jobs where interaction is the primary value-adding activity. Collaboration and social business enhance innovation, productivity, quality, and customer service. Tools for collaboration and social business include email and instant messaging, wikis, virtual meeting systems, virtual worlds, cloud-based file-sharing services, corporate collaboration platforms such Microsoft SharePoint and IBM Notes, and enterprise social networking tools such as Chatter, Yammer, Jive, and IBM Connections.

2-4 What is the role of the information systems function in a business? The information systems department is the formal organizational unit responsible for information technology services. It is responsible for maintaining the hardware, software, data storage, and networks that comprise the firm's IT infrastructure. The department consists of specialists, such as programmers, systems analysts, project leaders, and information systems managers, and is often headed by a chief information officer (CIO).

Key Terms

Business, 42
Business intelligence, 50
Business processes, 44
Chief data officer (CDO), 67
Chief information officer (CIO), 67
Chief knowledge officer (CKO), 67
Chief privacy officer (CPO), 67
Chief security officer (CSO), 67
Collaboration, 57
Customer relationship management (CRM) systems, 56
Data workers, 46
Decision-support systems (DSS), 51
Digital dashboard, 52
E-government, 57
Electronic business (e-business), 57
Electronic commerce (e-commerce), 57
End users, 67
Enterprise applications, 53
Enterprise systems, 55
Executive support systems (ESS), 52
Information systems department, 67
Information systems managers, 67
Interorganizational system, 56
Knowledge management systems (KMS), 56
Knowledge workers, 46
Management information systems (MIS), 50
Middle management, 46
Operational management, 46
Portal, 52
Production or service workers, 46
Programmers, 67
Senior management, 46
Social business, 59
Supply chain management (SCM) systems, 56
Systems analysts, 67
Teams, 58
Telepresence, 62
Transaction processing systems (TPS), 49

MyLab MIS™

To complete the problems with **MyLab MIS**, go to EOC Discussion Questions in MyLab MIS.

Review Questions

2-1 What major features of a business are important for understanding the role of information systems?

- Define a business and describe the major business functions.
- Define business processes and describe the role they play in organizations.
- Identify and describe the different levels in a business firm and their information needs.
- Explain why environments are important for understanding a business.

2-2 How do systems serve different management groups in a business, and how do systems that link the enterprise improve organizational performance?

- Define business intelligence systems.
- Describe the characteristics of transaction processing systems (TPS) and the role they play in a business.
- Describe the characteristics of management information systems (MIS), decision support systems (DSS), and executive support systems (ESS) and explain how each type of system helps managers make decisions.
- Explain how enterprise applications improve organizational performance.
- Define enterprise systems, supply chain management systems, customer relationship management systems, and knowledge management systems and describe their business benefits.
- Explain how intranets and extranets help firms improve business performance.

2-3 Why are systems for collaboration and social business so important, and what technologies do they use?

- Define collaboration and social business and explain why they have become so important in business today.
- List and describe the business benefits of collaboration and social business.
- Describe a supportive organizational culture for collaboration.
- List and describe the various types of collaboration and social business tools.

2-4 What is the role of the information systems function in a business?

- Describe how the information systems function supports a business.
- Compare the roles programmers, systems analysts, information systems managers, the chief information officer (CIO), chief security officer (CSO), chief data officer (CDO), chief privacy officer (CPO), and chief knowledge officer (CKO) play.

Discussion Questions

2-5 MyLab MIS How could information systems be used to support the order fulfillment process illustrated in Figure 2.2? What are the most important pieces of information these systems should capture? Explain your answer.

2-6 MyLab MIS Identify the steps that are performed in the process of selecting and checking out a book from your college library and the information that flows among these activities. Diagram the process. Are there any ways this process could be adjusted to improve the performance of your library or your school? Diagram the improved process.

2-7 MyLab MIS Use the Time/Space Collaboration and Social Tool Matrix to classify the collaboration and social technologies Sanofi Pasteur uses.

Hands-On MIS Projects

The projects in this section give you hands-on experience analyzing opportunities to improve business processes with new information system applications, using a spreadsheet to improve decision making about suppliers and using Internet software to plan efficient transportation routes. Visit **MyLab MIS** to access this chapter's Hands-On MIS Projects.

MANAGEMENT DECISION PROBLEMS

2-8 Don's Lumber Company on the Hudson River features a large selection of materials for flooring, decks, moldings, windows, siding, and roofing. The prices of lumber and other building materials are constantly changing. When a customer inquires about the price on prefinished wood flooring, sales representatives consult a manual price sheet and then call the supplier for the most recent price. The supplier in turn uses a manual price sheet, which has been updated each day. Often, the supplier must call Don's sales reps back because the company does not have the newest pricing information immediately on hand. Assess the business impact of this situation, describe how this process could be improved with information technology, and identify the decisions that would have to be made to implement a solution.

2-9 Henry's Hardware is a small family business in Sacramento, California. The owners must use every square foot of store space as profitably as possible. They have never kept detailed inventory or sales records. As soon as a shipment of goods arrives, the items are immediately placed on store shelves. Invoices from suppliers are kept only for tax purposes. When an item is sold, the item number and price are rung up at the cash register. The owners use their own judgment in identifying items that need to be reordered. What is the business impact of this situation? How could information systems help the owners run their business? What data should these systems capture? What decisions could the systems improve?

IMPROVING DECISION MAKING: USE A SPREADSHEET TO SELECT SUPPLIERS

Software skills: Spreadsheet date functions, data filtering, DAVERAGE function
Business skills: Analyzing supplier performance and pricing

2-10 In this exercise, you will learn how to use spreadsheet software to improve management decisions about selecting suppliers. You will filter transactional data about suppliers based on several criteria to select the best suppliers for your company.

You run a company that manufactures aircraft components. You have many competitors who are trying to offer lower prices and better service to customers, and you are trying to determine whether you can benefit from better supply chain management. In MyLab MIS, you will find a spreadsheet file that contains a list of all the items your firm has ordered from its suppliers during the past three months. The fields in the spreadsheet file include vendor name, vendor identification number, purchaser's order number, item identification number and item description (for each item ordered from the vendor), cost per item, number of units of the item ordered (quantity), total cost of each order, vendor's accounts payable terms, order date, and actual arrival date for each order.

Prepare a recommendation of how you can use the data in this spreadsheet database to improve your decisions about selecting suppliers. Some criteria to consider for identifying preferred suppliers include the supplier's track record for on-time deliveries, suppliers offering the best accounts payable terms, and suppliers offering lower pricing when the same item can be provided by multiple suppliers. Use your spreadsheet software to prepare reports to support your recommendations.

ACHIEVING OPERATIONAL EXCELLENCE: USING INTERNET SOFTWARE TO PLAN EFFICIENT TRANSPORTATION ROUTES

2-11 In this exercise, you will use MapQuest software to map out transportation routes for a business and select the most efficient route.

You have just started working as a dispatcher for Cross-Country Transport, a new trucking and delivery service based in Cleveland, Ohio. Your first assignment is to plan a delivery of office equipment and furniture from Elkhart, Indiana (at the corner of E. Indiana Ave. and Prairie Street), to Hagerstown, Maryland (corner of Eastern Blvd. N. and Potomac Ave.). To guide your trucker, you need to know the most efficient route between the two cities. Use MapQuest to find the route that is the shortest distance between the two cities. Use MapQuest again to find the route that takes the least time. Compare the results. Which route should Cross-Country use?

Collaboration and Teamwork Project

Identifying Management Decisions and Systems

2-12 With a team of three or four other students, find a description of a manager in a corporation in *Business Week*, *Forbes*, *Fortune*, *Wall Street Journal*, or another business publication or do your research on the web. Gather information about what the manager does and the role he or she plays in the company. Identify the organizational level and business function where this manager works. Make a list of the kinds of decisions this manager has to make and the kind of information that manager would need for those decisions. Suggest how information systems could supply this information. If possible, use Google Docs and Google Drive or Google Sites to brainstorm, organize, and develop a presentation of your findings for the class.

BUSINESS PROBLEM-SOLVING CASE

Social Business: Full Speed Ahead or Proceed with Caution?

As companies become more dispersed in the global marketplace, employees are turning increasingly to workplace collaboration technology, including tools for internal social networking. According to Craig Le Clair, principal analyst for enterprise architecture at Forrester Research, 50 percent of global workers by 2020 will be between 20 and 35 years old. These employees are experienced users of texting, messaging, wikis, and Facebook and appreciate work tools like the social media and chat apps used in their private lives.

Adoption of internal social networking inside the company, often referred to as enterprise social networking, is also being driven by the flood of email that employees typically receive each day and are increasingly unable to handle. Hundreds of email messages must be opened, read, answered, forwarded, or deleted. For example, too much email is what drove Hawk Ridge Systems to adopt Glip, a cloud-based social tool for its 200 employees located in 15 offices in the United States and Canada. Glip features real-time messaging, group chat, videoconferencing, shared calendars, task management, and file sharing all in one place. Glip helped Hawk Ridge operations manager Samuel Eakin go from 200 to around 30 emails per day. Another driver of enterprise social networking is "app fatigue." In order to collaborate, many employees have to log on to numerous apps, creating additional work. Contemporary enterprise social networking systems often integrate multiple capabilities in one place.

A recent survey of 421 professionals conducted by Harvard Business Review Analytics Services found that collaboration tools could be effective in boosting efficiency and productivity while enabling users to make better business decisions. The products also expanded the potential for innovation. However, not all companies are successfully using them. Implementation and adoption of enterprise social networking depends not only on the capabilities of the technology but on the organization's culture and the compatibility of these tools with the firm's business processes.

When firms introduce new social media technology (as well as other technologies), a sizable number of employees resist the new tools, clinging to old ways of working, including email, because they are more familiar and comfortable. There are companies where employees have duplicated communication on both social media and email, increasing the time and cost of performing their jobs. BASF, the world's largest chemical producer with subsidiaries and joint ventures in more than 80 countries, prohibited some project teams from using email to encourage employees to use new social media tools.

Social business requires a change in thinking, including the ability to view the organization more democratically in a flatter and more horizontal way. A social business is much more open to everyone's ideas. A secretary, assembly line worker, or sales clerk might be the source of the next big idea. As a result, getting people to espouse social business tools requires more of a "pull" approach, one that engages workers and offers them a significantly better way to work. In most cases, they can't be forced to use social apps.

Enterprise capabilities for managing social networks and sharing digital content can help or hurt an organization. Social networks can provide rich and diverse sources of information that enhance organizational productivity, efficiency, and innovation, or they can be used to support preexisting groups of like-minded people who are reluctant to communicate and exchange knowledge with outsiders. Productivity and morale will fall if employees use internal social networks to criticize others or pursue personal agendas.

Social business applications modeled on consumer-facing platforms such as Facebook and Twitter will not necessarily work well in an organization or organizational department that has incompatible objectives. Will the firm use social business for operations, human resources, or innovation? The social media platform that will work best depends on its specific business purpose.

This means that instead of focusing on the technology, businesses should first identify how social initiatives will actually improve work practices for employees and managers. They need a detailed understanding of social networks: how people are currently working, with whom they are working, what their needs are, and measures for overcoming employee biases and resistance.

A successful social business strategy requires leadership and behavioral changes. Just sponsoring a social project is not enough—managers need to demonstrate their commitment to a more open, transparent work style. Employees who are used to collaborating and doing business in more traditional ways need an incentive to use social software. Changing an organization to work in a different way requires enlisting those most engaged and interested in designing and building the right workplace environment for using social technologies

Management needs to ensure that the internal and external social networking efforts of the company are providing genuine value to the business. Content on the networks needs to be relevant, up to date, and easy to access; users need to be able to connect to people who have the information they need and who would otherwise be out of reach or difficult to reach. Social business tools should be appropriate for the tasks on hand and the organization's business processes, and users need to understand how and why to use them.

For example, NASA's Goddard Space Flight Center had to abandon a custom-built enterprise social network called Spacebook because no one knew how its social tools would help people do their jobs. Spacebook was launched in 2009 to help small teams collaborate without emailing larger groups. Spacebook featured user profiles, group workspaces (wikis, file sharing, discussion forums, groups), and social bookmarks. Very few users adopted it, and Spacebook was decommissioned on June 1, 2012. According to Kevin Jones, a consulting social and organizational strategist at NASA's Marshall and Goddard Space Flight Centers, Spacebook failed because it didn't focus enough on people. It had been designed and developed without taking into consideration the organization's culture and politics. No one knew how Spacebook would help them do their jobs as opposed to an existing method of collaboration such as email. This is not an isolated phenomenon. Dimension Data found that one-fourth of the 900 enterprises it surveyed focused more on the successful implementation of collaboration technology than how it's used and adopted.

Despite the challenges associated with launching an internal social network, there are companies using these networks successfully. For example, Covestro, a leading global supplier of coatings and adhesives, polyurethanes, and highly impact-resistant plastics, made social collaboration a success by making the tools more accessible, demonstrating the value of these tools in pilot projects, employing a reverse mentoring program for senior executives, and training employee experts to spread know-how of the new social tools and approaches within the company and demonstrate their usefulness. Using IBM Connections as the social business toolset, Covestro's efforts are now paying off: 50 percent of employees are now routinely active in the company's enterprise social network. Although ROI on social business initiatives has been difficult to measure, Covestro has benefited from faster knowledge flows, increased efficiency, and lower operating costs.

Another company that has made social business work is Carlo's Bake Shop, an old family-owned business that is the star of the *Cake Boss* reality television series on the cable television network TLC. The company has 10 locations in New Jersey, New York, and Las Vegas, and people can order custom cakes from its website. Thanks to the popularity of *Cake Boss*, which created a huge upsurge in demand for Carlo's products, the firm is looking to create a national presence over the next few years.

However, store operations were holding the company back. Carlo's was heavily paper-based, and the mountain of paperwork wasted employee time and led to errors, which sometimes resulted in a need to fix or remake cakes or offer partial or total refunds to customers. Custom orders were on paper and carbon paper, order forms were misplaced or lost, and people couldn't read the handwriting from the order taker.

In the latter half of 2012, Carlo's implemented Salesforce CRM with the Salesforce social networking tool Chatter as a solution. Some employees and members of Carlo's management team initially resisted the new system. They believed that since they already used email, Facebook, and Twitter, they didn't need another social tool. The company was able to demonstrate the benefits of social business to bakers and store sales teams, and using Chatter changed the way they worked.

Carlo's produces a very large volume of custom cakes from a 75,000-square-foot commissary in Jersey City operating around the clock. Chatter is now the de facto standard for internal communication, from order to delivery. If a key cake decorator is away, that person is still included in the communication and discussion process. Upon returning, the decorator can view any changes in color, shape, or design.

Because Carlo's employees now work more socially, errors are down by more than 30 percent, and crews are able to produce cakes and other custom products more rapidly and efficiently. Managers have access to a data and analytics dashboard that allows them to instantly view store performance and which products are hot and which are not. They can see sales and transaction patterns in depth. As Carlo's expands nationally and perhaps globally, the ability to connect people and view order streams is critical. Social business tools have transformed an organization that was gradually sinking under the weight of paper into a highly efficient digital business.

Sources: Sue Hildreth, "What's Next for Workplace Collaboration?" searchcontentmanagement.com, March 2, 2017; Arunima Majumdar, "3 Reasons Why Collaboration Tools Fail to Make the Indented Impact," eLearning Industry, January 20, 2017; Margaret Jones, "Top Four Social Collaboration Software Fails," searchmobilecoputing.techtarget.com, accessed March 14, 2017; Cordelia Kroob, "The Growth of an Enterprise Social Network at BASF," www.simply-communicate.com, accessed March 12, 2017; Insight Enterprises Inc., "Collaboration Technology Boosts Organizations, According to an Insight-Sponsored Report by Harvard Business Review Analytic Services," February 13, 2017; Dimension Data, "2016 Connected Enterprise Report," 2016; Gerald C. Kane, "Enterprise Social Media: Current Capabilities and Future Possibilities," *MIS Quarterly Executive*, March 2015; and Dion Hinchcliffe, "In Europe's Biggest Firms, Social Business Is All Grown Up," Enterprise Web 2.0, February 12, 2015.

CASE STUDY QUESTIONS

2-13 Identify the people, organization, and technology factors responsible for impeding adoption of internal corporate social networks.

2-14 Compare the experiences implementing internal social networks of the organizations described in this case. Why were some successful? What role did management play in this process?

2-15 Should all companies implement internal enterprise social networks? Why or why not?

MyLab MIS

Go to the Assignments section of MyLab MIS to complete these writing exercises.

2-16 Identify and describe the capabilities of enterprise social networking software.

2-17 Describe the systems various management groups use within the firm in terms of the information they use, their outputs, and groups served.

Chapter 2 References

Banker, Rajiv D., Nan Hu, Paul A. Pavlou, and Jerry Luftman. "CIO Reporting Structure, Strategic Positioning, and Firm Performance." *MIS Quarterly* 35, No. 2 (June 2011).

Bernoff, Josh, and Charlene Li. "Harnessing the Power of Social Applications." *MIT Sloan Management Review* (Spring 2008).

Boughzala, Imed, and Gert-Jan De Vreede. "Evaluating Team Collaboration Quality: The Development and Field Application of a Collaboration Maturity Model." *Journal of Management Information Systems* 32, No. 3 (2015).

Bughin, Jacques, Michael Chui, and Martin Harrysson. "How Social Tools Can Reshape the Organization." McKinsey Global Institute (May 2016).

Bureau of Labor Statistics. "Occupational Outlook Handbook." Bureau of Labor Statistics (December 2015).

Compare Products. "Videoconferencing Trends of 2016" (2015).

Dawson, Gregory S., James S. Denford, Clay K. Williams, David Preston, and Kevin C. Desouza. "An Examination of Effective IT Governance in the Public Sector Using the Legal View of Agency Theory." *Journal of Management Information Systems* 33, No. 4 (2016).

Deloitte University Press. "Navigating Legacy: Charting the Course to Business Value: 2016–2017 Global CIO Survey." Deloitte Development LLC (2016).

Dimension Data. "2016 Connected Enterprise Report" (2016).

Forrester Research. "Social Business: Delivering Critical Business Value" (April 2012).

Frost and Sullivan. "Meetings Around the World II: Charting the Course of Advanced Collaboration." (October 14, 2009).

Gast, Arne, and Raul Lansink. "Digital Hives: Creating a Surge Around Change." *McKinsey Quarterly* (April 2015).

Greengard, Samuel. "Collaboration: At the Center of Effective Business." *Baseline* (January 24, 2014).

Guillemette, Manon G., and Guy Pare. "Toward a New Theory of the Contribution of the IT Function in Organizations." *MIS Quarterly* 36, No. 2 (June 2012).

Harvard Business Review Analytic Services. "Collaboration Technology Boosts Organizations." Insight Enterprises Inc. (February 13, 2017).

Hinchcliffe, Dion. "A New Generation of CIO Thinking Emerges." Enterprise Web 2.0 (September 30, 2016).

Johnson, Bradford, James Manyika, and Lareina Yee. "The Next Revolution in Interactions." *McKinsey Quarterly* No. 4 (2005).

Kane, Gerald C. "Enterprise Social Media: Current Capabilities and Future Possibilities." *MIS Quarterly Executive* 14, No. 1 (2015).

Kane, Gerald C., Doug Palmer, Anh Nguyen Phillips, and David Kiron. "Finding the Value in Social Business." *MIT Sloan Management Review* 55, No. 3 (Spring 2014).

Kiron, David, Doug Palmer, Anh Nguyen Phillips, and Nina Kruschwitz. "What Managers Really Think About Social Business." *MIT Sloan Management Review* 53, No. 4 (Summer 2012).

Kolfschoten, Gwendolyn L., Fred Niederman, Robert O. Briggs, and Gert-Jan De Vreede. "Facilitation Roles and Responsibilities for Sustained Collaboration Support in Organizations." *Journal of Management Information Systems* 28, No. 4 (Spring 2012).

Li, Charlene. "Making the Business Case for Enterprise Social Networks." Altimeter Group (February 22, 2012).

Malone, Thomas M., Kevin Crowston, Jintae Lee, and Brian Pentland. "Tools for Inventing Organizations: Toward a Handbook of Organizational Processes." *Management Science* 45, No. 3 (March 1999).

Maruping, Likoebe M., and Massimo Magni. "Motivating Employees to Explore Collaboration Technology in Team Contexts." *MIS Quarterly* 39, No.1 (March 2015).

McKinsey & Company. "Transforming the Business Through Social Tools" (2015).

McKinsey Global Institute. "The Social Economy: Unlocking Value and Productivity Through Social Technologies." McKinsey & Company (July 2012).

Microsoft Corporation. "Customer Stories: Southern Valve" (January 18, 2015).

Mortensen, Mark. "Technology Alone Won't Solve Our Collaboration Problems." *Harvard Business Review* (March 26, 2015).

Poltrock, Steven, and Mark Handel. "Models of Collaboration as the Foundation for Collaboration Technologies." *Journal of Management Information Systems* 27, No. 1 (Summer 2010).

Ricards, Tuck, Kate Smaje, and Vik Sohoni. "'Transformer in Chief': The New Chief Digital Officer." *McKinsey Digital* (September 2015).

Saunders, Carol, A. F. Rutkowski, Michiel van Genuchten, Doug Vogel, and Julio Molina Orrego. "Virtual Space and Place: Theory and Test." *MIS Quarterly* 35, No. 4 (December 2011).

Tallon, Paul P., Ronald V. Ramirez, and James E. Short. "The Information Artifact in IT Governance: Toward a Theory of Information Governance." *Journal of Management Information Systems* 30, No. 3 (Winter 2014).

Violino, Bob. "What Is Driving the Need for Chief Data Officers?" *Information Management* (February 3, 2014).

Weill, Peter, and Jeanne W. Ross. *IT Governance*. Boston: Harvard Business School Press (2004).

CHAPTER

3

Achieving Competitive Advantage with Information Systems

LEARNING OBJECTIVES

After reading this chapter, you will be able to answer the following questions:

3-1 How do Porter's competitive forces model, the value chain model, synergies, core competencies, and network-based strategies help companies use information systems for competitive advantage?

3-2 How do information systems help businesses compete globally?

3-3 How do information systems help businesses compete using quality and design?

3-4 What is the role of business process management (BPM) in enhancing competitiveness?

3-5 How will MIS help my career?

CHAPTER CASES

- Verizon or AT&T: Which Company Has the Best Digital Strategy?
- Digital Technology Helps Crayola Brighten Its Brand
- Carter's Redesigns Its Business Processes
- Walmart Versus Amazon and the Future of Retail

VIDEO CASES

- GE Becomes a Digital Firm: The Emerging Industrial Internet
- National Basketball Association: Competing on Global Delivery with Akamai OS Streaming

MyLab MIS

- Discussion Questions: 3-5, 3-6, 3-7;
- Hands-on MIS Projects 3-8, 3-9, 3-10, 3-11;
- Writing Assignments: 3-17, 3-18;
- eText with Conceptual Animations

VERIZON OR AT&T: WHICH COMPANY HAS THE BEST DIGITAL STRATEGY?

Verizon and AT&T are the two largest telecommunications companies in the United States. Today their customers do much more than make phone calls. They use their wireless and landline networks to watch high-definition (HD) TV; surf the Internet; send email, text, and video messages; share photos; listen to music, watch videos; and conduct videoconferences around the globe. All of these products and services are digital.

Competition in this industry is unusually intense. T-Mobile and Sprint have lured away many customers with their low prices and unlimited data plans. Both Verizon and AT&T are trying to outflank competitors by expanding the range of digital products and services they offer. But there are differences. AT&T is making a bet on content and media, having purchased DirecTV in July 2015. Verizon is focusing more on wireless and its wireless video service.

AT&T hopes to profit by merging its U-verse suite of TV, Internet, and phone service based on a high-speed network into a common service and offering bundled satellite-cable TV and wireless services that rivals won't be able to match. It also hopes to work out good deals with content companies, such as its multiyear agreement with Viacom for providing U-Verse and DirecTV programming content and the purchase of multinational media nd entertainment conglomerate Time Warner. AT&T still needs its consumer wireless business (and is investing in upgrading its high-speed networks), but this part of the business is sagging because of increased competition from lower-cost services. If AT&T's strategy works, it will become a computing company that manages all sorts of digital things: wireless phones, satellite television, and huge volumes of data, using software in remote online cloud computing centers.

Verizon is continuing to focus on its wireless business, in which it has been a leader for a number of years. To stem losses from lower-cost competitors, however, Verizon is trying to generate revenue from mobile ads and video on its own wireless video service. Although the number of smartphone users is peaking, users are spending more time on these mobile devices—about three hours per day for U.S. adults, according to eMarketer. Verizon bought AOL, which has a digital ad business, as well as web content sites such

© Gajus/Shutterstock

as Huffington Post, and it purchased Yahoo for similar reasons. Verizon plans to fold Yahoo's digital advertising technology and portfolio of websites like Yahoo News, Sports, and Finance into AOL while keeping the Yahoo brand.

Verizon hopes to generate revenue by selling customers larger data packages to handle the data-intensive video from its mobile streaming video service, which offers live sports, TV, and movies. Verizon will also be able to capitalize on "pay-per-view" opportunities such as sports events and concerts and on targeted advertising using its ability to track what customers watch and read on their smartphones. By combining customer data from smartphones with advertising on AOL and Yahoo, Verizon may even be able to assemble an online advertising technology platform that competes with web giants such as Google and Facebook.

Sources: Drew FitzGerald, "Spotlight on AT&T's Media Strategy as Wireless Loses Luster," *Wall Street Journal*, April 22, 2017; Eric Jackson, "Verizon Needs a Content Strategy," *Forbes*, January 31, 2017; Ryan Knutson and Joshua Jamerson, "Verizon Customers Defect as Competition Ramps Up," *Wall Street Journal*, April 20, 2017; Thomas Gryta, "AT&T to Sell Unlimited Wireless Data Plan Without Pay TV," *Wall Street Journal*, February 16, 2007; and "Verizon, AT&T Chart Different Paths," *Wall Street Journal*, October 19, 2015; and eMarketer, "Growth of Time Spent on Mobile Devices Slows," October 7, 2015.

The story of Verizon and AT&T illustrates some of the ways that information systems help businesses compete and also the challenges of sustaining a competitive advantage. The industry in which both companies operate is extremely crowded and competitive, with traditional telecommunications companies vying with cable companies, Internet services, mobile services, and each other to provide a wide array of digital services and content and low-cost competitors luring away customers. To meet the challenges of surviving and prospering in this environment, each of these companies has adopted a different competitive strategy using information technology.

The chapter-opening diagram calls attention to important points raised by this case and this chapter. Both companies saw that there were opportunities to use information technology to offer new products and services. AT&T forged a strategy based on combining satellite, high-speed cable TV, Internet, and wireless services and providing a superior package of services and content. Verizon is putting its money on mobile ads and video, with more emphasis on mining its customer data.

This case study also shows that it is difficult to sustain a competitive advantage. The market for online video is close to saturation, and Verizon's plan to track customers has been criticized by privacy advocates for its use of personal customer data. It is unclear how much low-cost rivals in the wireless market will continue to lure away AT&T's and Verizon's customers.

Here are some questions to think about: How do the competitive forces and value chain models apply to Verizon and AT&T? Which company has the better digital strategy? Why?

3-1 How do Porter's competitive forces model, the value chain model, synergies, core competencies, and network-based strategies help companies use information systems for competitive advantage?

In almost every industry you examine, you will find that some firms do better than most others do. There's almost always a standout firm. In pure online retail, Amazon is the leader; in offline retail, Walmart, the largest retailer on earth, has been the leader. In web search, Google is considered the leader.

Firms that do better than others are said to have a competitive advantage. They either have access to special resources that others do not, or they use commonly

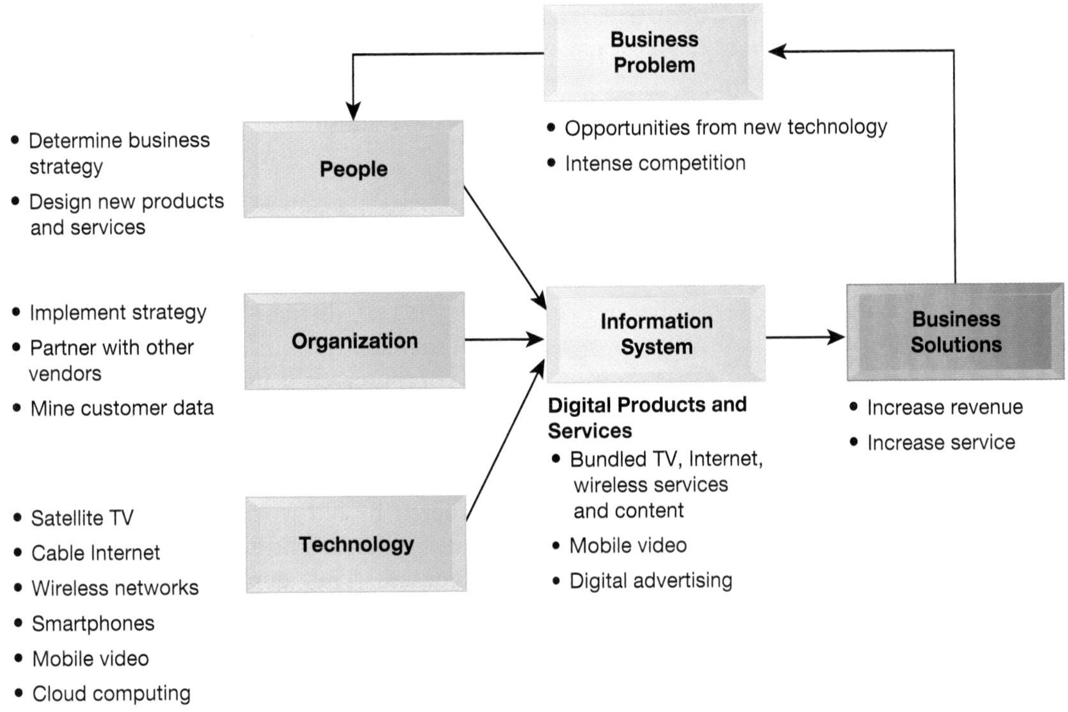

available resources more efficiently—usually because of superior knowledge and information assets. In any event, they do better in terms of revenue growth, profitability, or productivity growth (efficiency), all of which ultimately translate into higher stock market valuations than their competitors.

But why do some firms do better than others and how do they achieve competitive advantage? How can you analyze a business and identify its strategic advantages? How can you develop a strategic advantage for your own business? How do information systems contribute to strategic advantages? One answer to these questions is Michael Porter's competitive forces model.

PORTER'S COMPETITIVE FORCES MODEL

Arguably, the most widely used model for understanding competitive advantage is Michael Porter's **competitive forces model** (see Figure 3.1). This model provides a general view of the firm, its competitors, and the firm's environment. Recall that in Chapter 2 we described the importance of a firm's environment and the dependence of firms on environments. Porter's model is all about the firm's general business environment. In this model, five competitive forces shape the fate of the firm.

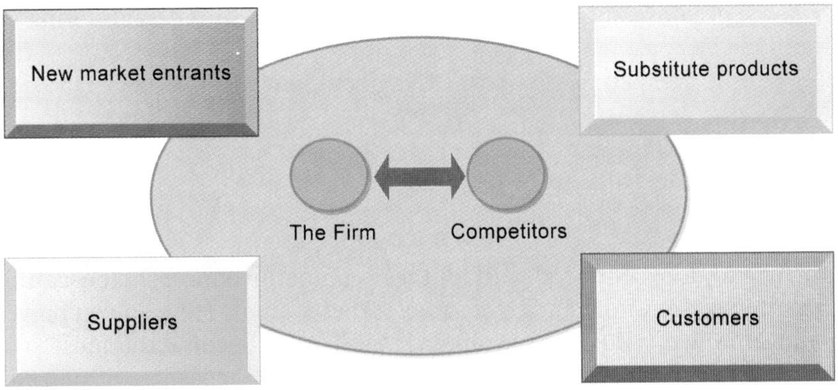

Figure 3.1
Porter's Competitive Forces Model
In Porter's competitive forces model, the strategic position of the firm and its strategies are determined not only by competition with its traditional direct competitors but also by four forces in the industry's environment: new market entrants, substitute products, customers, and suppliers.

Traditional Competitors

All firms share market space with other competitors who are continuously devising new, more efficient ways to produce by introducing new products and services and attempting to attract customers by developing their brands and imposing switching costs on their customers.

New Market Entrants

In a free economy with mobile labor and financial resources, new companies are always entering the marketplace. In some industries, there are very low barriers to entry, whereas in other industries, entry is very difficult. For instance, it is fairly easy to start a pizza business or just about any small retail business, but it is much more expensive and difficult to enter the computer chip business, which has very high capital costs and requires significant expertise and knowledge that is hard to obtain. New companies have several possible advantages. They are not locked into old plants and equipment, they often hire younger workers who are less expensive and perhaps more innovative, they are not encumbered by old worn-out brand names, and they are more hungry (more highly motivated) than traditional occupants of an industry. These advantages are also their weaknesses. They depend on outside financing for new plants and equipment, which can be expensive; they have a less-experienced workforce; and they have little brand recognition.

Substitute Products and Services

In just about every industry, there are substitutes that your customers might use if your prices become too high. New technologies create new substitutes all the time. Ethanol can substitute for gasoline in cars; vegetable oil for diesel fuel in trucks; and wind, solar, and hydropower for coal, oil, and gas electricity generation. Likewise, Internet telephone service has substituted for traditional telephone service, and streaming Internet music services for CDs, music stores, and digital download sites like iTunes. The more substitute products and services in your industry, the less you can control pricing and the lower your profit margins.

Customers

A profitable company depends in large measure on its ability to attract and retain customers (while denying them to competitors) and charge high prices. The power of customers grows if they can easily switch to a competitor's products and services or if they can force a business and its competitors to compete on price alone in a transparent marketplace where there is little product differentiation, and all prices are known instantly (such as on the Internet). For instance, in the used–college textbook market on the Internet, students (customers) can find multiple suppliers of just about any current college textbook. In this case, online customers have extraordinary power over used-book firms.

Suppliers

The market power of suppliers can have a significant impact on firm profits, especially when the firm cannot raise prices as fast as suppliers can. The more suppliers a firm has, the greater control it can exercise over those suppliers in terms of price, quality, and delivery schedules. For instance, manufacturers of laptop PCs usually have multiple competing suppliers of key components, such as keyboards, hard drives, and display screens.

INFORMATION SYSTEM STRATEGIES FOR DEALING WITH COMPETITIVE FORCES

What is a firm to do when faced with all these competitive forces? How can the firm use information systems to counteract some of these forces? How do you prevent substitutes and inhibit new market entrants? How do you become the most successful firm in an industry in terms of profit and share price (two measures of success)?

Basic Strategy 101: Align the IT with the Business Objectives

The basic principle of IT strategy for a business is to ensure that the technology serves the business and not the other way around. The research on IT and business performance has found that (a) the more successfully a firm can align its IT with its business goals, the more profitable it will be, and (b) only about one-quarter of firms achieve alignment of IT with business. About half of a business firm's profits can be explained by alignment of IT with business (Luftman, 2003). Most businesses get it wrong; instead of business people taking an active role in shaping IT to the enterprise, they ignore it, claim not to understand IT, and tolerate failure in the IT area as just a nuisance to work around. Such firms pay a hefty price in poor performance. Successful firms and managers understand what IT can do and how it works, take an active role in shaping its use, and measure its impact on revenues and profits.

So how do you as a manager achieve this alignment of IT with business? In the following sections, we discuss some basic ways to do this, but here's a summary:

- Identify your business strategy and goals.
- Break these strategic goals down into concrete activities and processes.
- Identify how you will measure progress toward the business goals (e.g., by using metrics).
- Ask yourself, "How can information technology help me achieve progress toward our business goals, and how will it improve our business processes and activities?"
- Measure actual performance. Let the numbers speak.

Let's see how this works out in practice. There are four generic strategies, each of which often is enabled by using information technology and systems: low-cost leadership, product differentiation, focus on market niche, and strengthening customer and supplier intimacy.

Low-Cost Leadership

Use information systems to achieve the lowest operational costs and the lowest prices. The classic example is Walmart. By keeping prices low and shelves well stocked using a legendary inventory replenishment system, Walmart became the leading retail

© Betty LaRue/Alamy Stock Photo

Supermarkets and large retail stores such as Walmart use sales data captured at the checkout counter to determine which items have sold and need to be reordered. Walmart's continuous replenishment system transmits orders to restock directly to its suppliers. The system enables Walmart to keep costs low while fine-tuning its merchandise availability to meet customer demands.

business in the United States. Point-of-sale terminals record the bar code of each item passing the checkout counter and send a purchase transaction directly to a central computer at Walmart headquarters. The computer collects the orders from all Walmart stores and transmits them to suppliers. Suppliers can also access Walmart's sales and inventory data by using web technology.

Because the system replenishes inventory with lightning speed, Walmart does not need to spend much money on maintaining large inventories of goods in its own warehouses. The system also enables Walmart to adjust the items stocked in its stores to meet customer demands. By using systems to keep operating costs low, Walmart can charge less for its products than competitors yet reap higher profits.

Walmart's continuous replenishment system is also an example of an **efficient customer response system**. An efficient customer response system directly links consumer behavior to distribution and production and supply chains. Walmart's continuous replenishment system provides such an efficient customer response.

Product Differentiation

Use information systems to provide new products and services or greatly change the customer convenience in using your existing products and services. For instance, Google continuously introduces new and unique search services, such as Google Pay peer payments in 2014, and improvements in Google Docs and Google Drive. Apple has continued to differentiate its hand held computing products with nearly annual introductions of new iPhone and iPad models. Crayola is creating new technology-based products and services to inspire children, parents, and educators (see the Interactive Session on People).

Manufacturers and retailers are using information systems to create products and services that are customized and personalized to fit the precise specifications of individual customers. For example, Nike sells customized sneakers through its NIKEiD program on its website. Customers can select the type of shoe, colors, material, outsoles, and even a logo of up to eight characters. Nike transmits the orders by computers to specially equipped plants in China and Korea. The sneakers cost only about $10 extra and take about three weeks to reach the customer. This ability to offer individually tailored products or services using the same production resources as mass production is called **mass customization**.

Table 3.1 lists a number of companies that have developed IS-based products and services that other firms have found difficult to copy.

Focus on Market Niche

Use information systems to enable a specific market focus and serve this narrow target market better than competitors. Information systems support this strategy by producing and analyzing data for finely tuned sales and marketing techniques. Information systems enable companies to analyze customer buying patterns, tastes, and preferences closely so that they efficiently pitch advertising and marketing campaigns to smaller and smaller target markets.

TABLE 3.1

IS-Enabled New Products and Services Providing Competitive Advantage

Amazon: One-click shopping	Amazon holds a patent on one-click shopping that it licenses to other online retailers.
Online music: Apple iPod and iTunes	Apple's integrated, handheld player is backed up with an online library of more than 40 million songs.
Golf club customization: Ping	Customers can select from more than 1 million golf club options; a build-to-order system ships their customized clubs within 48 hours.
Online person-to-person payment: PayPal.com	PayPal enables transfer of money between individual bank accounts and between bank accounts and credit card accounts.

Digital Technology Helps Crayola Brighten Its Brand

Crayola is one of the world's most beloved brands for children and their parents. The Easton, Pennsylvania-based company has been noted for high-quality, nontoxic crayons, markers, pencils, modeling clay, creative toys, and innovative art tools that have inspired artistic creativity in children for more than 100 years. You can find Crayola products nearly everywhere, including schools, offices, supermarkets, drug stores, hospitals, schools, theme parks, airports, gas stations, and restaurants.

The Crayola crayon box became part of the collective history and experiences of generations of Americans and a symbol of the color and fun of childhood. But today, that Crayola crayon box is not as iconic as in the past. The popularity of Crayola crayons is under assault—not by Crayola's traditional competitors (Faber-Castell, DixonTiconderoga, and MEGA Brands) but by changing times.

There has been a profound technological and cultural shift in how children play. Children and their families are being bombarded with increasingly sophisticated forms of entertainment, many of them digitally based. Digital products are starting to supplant physical ones in the world of children's play as well as in other areas of work and everyday life. With the advent of computers and web-based learning, children are leaving behind handheld art supplies at an increasingly younger age. The phenomenon is called KGOY: Kids Growing Older Younger. As children reach the age of four or five, when they become old enough to play with a computer, they become less interested in toys and crayons in favor of electronics such as video games, digital tablets, and smartphones. Crayola is not immune to this problem.

Will Crayola become a dinosaur from a different era? Not likely, thanks to the company's forward-looking management, which embarked more than a decade ago on far-reaching changes in leadership, organizational culture, and the product development function. The organization restructured around consumer insights and needs rather than specific product lines.

Vicky Lozano, Crayola's VP of Corporate Strategy, and her team recognized that Crayola's purpose has always been to nourish originality and to help parents and teachers raise creative and inspired children. Crayola's broader mission is not just to put crayons and art materials in children's hands but to help children learn and play in colorful ways. The question they asked was not how can we sell more crayons but what kinds of experiences and technologies should Crayola embrace? Crayola has reframed its business model, introduced a new innovation process for product development, and created new products and revenue streams. The company has been transformed from a manufacturer of crayons and art tools into to a trusted source of tools and experiences for creative play.

Crayola is using digital technology, but not to replace its core crayon business. Instead, it's integrating the old and the new. The company now offers a new range of products like the iMarker, an all-in-one digital pen, crayon, and pencil, designed for use with the Color Studio HD iPad app. It's like a traditional coloring book but includes new interactive sounds and motion. Lights, Camera, Color! is another digital application that allows kids to turn their favorite photos into digital coloring book pages. Tech toys such as the Digital Light Designer, a 360-degree domed drawing surface, encourage imaginations to run wild with colored LED lights. Children can play updated versions of their favorite games or animate and save up to 50 pieces of their own artwork. Crayola found that parents are looking for toys that are less messy than traditional markers or fingerpaints. These digital toys are "100 percent mess-proof," and technology has helped Crayola make its other products less messy as well.

In designing new digital products and experiences, Crayola has drawn on its extensive knowledge of child development. It understands how digital technology can play a part at different ages. For instance, the My First Crayola line is targeted specifically at one-year-olds, while Crayola Catwalk Creations is designed for tween girls who like expressing themselves through fashion.

Crayola also understood that it had to change the way it markets its products as well as the products themselves and has been investing more and more in digital marketing. These initiatives include online advertising, promotions, social media pushes, and other digital activation programs that allow Crayola to connect with parents and educators invested in raising children's creativity level. Social media has proven especially effective, and Crayola has a presence on Facebook, YouTube, Pinterest, Twitter, and Instagram. Crayola's YouTube channel features colorful videos on Crayola products and instructions for creative projects where they can be used. The company's Facebook presence features a live chat series with experts and creative celebrities called Inside the Crayon Box. Crayola wants to stimulate conversations around creativity so parents can learn from each other and understand how to build creativity in their children.

Crayola's core "mom" audience is turning to the web for gift and usage ideas, comparing prices, and reading reviews before making purchases. Crayola wants to be first in mind as a source of $20 artsy toys and mess-proof gifts. The company focuses heavily on search, social media, and digital display to help moms find the Crayola products needed for their children's school supplies or gifts. Crayola closely tracks activity on its online channels through Google Analytics to make sure it is getting the most out of its marketing and ad campaigns.

Crayola's website has been thoughtfully designed for children, parents, and educators. It features free ideas for crafts, printable coloring pages, and even advice on how to remove stains. The website also can be used for ordering Crayola products online. Thanks to its new array of products and services, Crayola has experienced better growth, and its future looks as bright as the vibrant colors of its iconic crayons.

Sources: www.crayola.com, accessed April 23, 2017; "Crayola SWOTA," www.marketingteacher.com, accessed December 18, 2016; and Jon Coen, "Crayola's Colorful Evolution," Think Play, July 2012.

CASE STUDY QUESTIONS

1. Analyze Crayola's problem. What people, organization, and technology factors contributed to the problem?
2. What competitive strategy is Crayola pursuing? How does digital technology support this strategy?
3. What people issues did Crayola have to address in designing its new technology-based products?
4. How has digital technology changed Crayola's business model and the way it runs its business?

The data come from a range of sources—credit card transactions, demographic data, purchase data from checkout counter scanners at supermarkets and retail stores, and data collected when people access and interact with websites. Sophisticated software tools find patterns in these large pools of data and infer rules from them that can be used to guide decision making. Analysis of such data drives one-to-one marketing by which personal messages can be created based on individualized preferences. For example, Hilton Hotels' OnQ system analyzes detailed data collected on active guests in all of its properties to determine the preferences of each guest and each guest's profitability. Hilton uses this information to give its most profitable customers additional privileges, such as late checkouts. Contemporary customer relationship management (CRM) systems feature analytical capabilities for this type of intensive data analysis (see Chapters 2 and 9).

Strengthen Customer and Supplier Intimacy

Use information systems to tighten linkages with suppliers and develop intimacy with customers. Toyota, Ford, and other automobile manufacturers have information systems that give their suppliers direct access to their production schedules, enabling suppliers to decide how and when to ship supplies to the plants where cars are assembled. This allows suppliers more lead time in producing goods. On the customer side, Amazon.com keeps track of user preferences for book and music purchases and can recommend titles purchased by others to its customers. Strong linkages to customers and suppliers increase **switching costs** (the cost of switching from one product or service to a competitor) and loyalty to your firm. Table 3.2 summarizes the competitive strategies we have just described.

As shown by the cases throughout this book, successfully using information systems to achieve a competitive advantage requires a precise coordination of technology,

TABLE 3.2

Four Basic Competitive Strategies

Strategy	Description	Example
Low-cost leadership	Use information systems to produce products and services at a lower price than competitors while enhancing quality and level of service.	Walmart
Product differentiation	Use information systems to differentiate products and provide new services and products.	Uber, Nike, Apple, Starbucks
Focus on market niche	Use information systems to enable a focused strategy on a single market niche; specialize.	Hilton Hotels, Harrah's
Customer and supplier intimacy	Use information systems to develop strong ties and loyalty with customers and suppliers.	Toyota Corporation, Amazon

organizations, and people. Indeed, as many have noted with regard to Walmart, Apple, and Amazon, the ability to implement information systems successfully is not equally distributed, and some firms are much better at it than others are.

THE INTERNET'S IMPACT ON COMPETITIVE ADVANTAGE

Because of the Internet, the traditional competitive forces are still at work, but competitive rivalry has become much more intense (Porter, 2001). Internet technology is based on universal standards that any company can use, making it easier for rivals to compete on price alone and for new competitors to enter the market. Because information is available to everyone, the Internet raises the bargaining power of customers, who can quickly find the lowest-cost provider on the web. Profits have often been dampened as a result of increased competition. Table 3.3 summarizes some of the potentially negative impacts of the Internet on business firms Porter has identified.

The Internet has nearly destroyed some industries and has severely threatened others. For instance, the printed encyclopedia industry and the travel agency industry have been nearly decimated by the availability of substitutes over the Internet. Likewise, the Internet has had a significant impact on the retail, music, book, retail brokerage, software, and telecommunications industries. However, the Internet has also created entirely new markets, formed the basis for thousands of new products,

TABLE 3.3

Impact of the Internet on Competitive Forces and Industry Structure

Competitive Force	Impact of the Internet
Substitute products or services	Enables new substitutes to emerge with new approaches to meeting needs and performing functions
Customers' bargaining power	Shifts bargaining power to customers due to the availability of global price and product information
Suppliers' bargaining power	Tends to raise bargaining power over suppliers in procuring products and services; however, suppliers can benefit from reduced barriers to entry and from the elimination of distributors and other intermediaries standing between them and their users
Threat of new entrants	Reduces barriers to entry, such as the need for a sales force, access to channels, and physical assets; provides a technology for driving business processes that makes other things easier to do
Positioning and rivalry among existing competitors	Widens the geographic market, increasing the number of competitors and reducing differences among competitors; makes it more difficult to sustain operational advantages; puts pressure to compete on price

services, and business models, and provided new opportunities for building brands with very large and loyal customer bases. Amazon, eBay, iTunes, YouTube, Facebook, Uber, and Google are examples. In this sense, the Internet is transforming entire industries, forcing firms to change how they do business.

Smart Products and the Internet of Things

The growing use of sensors in industrial and consumer products, often called the Internet of Things (IoT), is an excellent example of how the Internet is changing competition within industries and creating new products and services. Nike, Under Armour, Gatorade, and many other sports and fitness companies are pouring money into wearable health trackers and fitness equipment that use sensors to report users' activities to remote computing centers where the data can be analyzed. John Deere tractors are loaded with field radar, GPS transceivers, and hundreds of sensors keeping track of the equipment. GE is creating a new business out of helping its aircraft and wind turbine clients improve operations by examining the data generated from the many thousands of sensors in the equipment (see the Chapter 11 ending case). The result is what's referred to as smart products—products that are a part of a larger set of information services sold by firms (Gandhi and Gervet, 2016; Porter and Heppelmann, 2014; Iansiti and Lakhani, 2014).

The impact of smart, Internet-connected products is just now being understood. Smart products offer new functionality, greater reliability, and more intense use of products. They expand opportunities for product and service differentiation. When you buy a wearable digital health product, you not only get the product itself, you also get a host of services available from the manufacturer's cloud servers. Smart products increase rivalry among firms that will either innovate or lose customers to competitors. Smart products generally inhibit new entrants to a market simply because existing customers are enmeshed in the dominant firm's software environment. Finally, smart products may decrease the power of suppliers of industrial components if, as many believe, the physical product becomes less important than the software and hardware that makes it run.

THE BUSINESS VALUE CHAIN MODEL

Although the Porter model is very helpful for identifying competitive forces and suggesting generic strategies, it is not very specific about what exactly to do, and it does not provide a methodology to follow for achieving competitive advantages. If your goal is to achieve operational excellence, where do you start? Here's where the business value chain model is helpful.

The **value chain model** highlights specific activities in the business where competitive strategies can best be applied (Porter, 1985) and where information systems are most likely to have a strategic impact. This model identifies specific, critical advantage points at which a firm can use information technology most effectively to enhance its competitive position. The value chain model views the firm as a series or chain of basic activities that add a margin of value to a firm's products or services. These activities can be categorized as either primary activities or support activities (see Figure 3.2).

Primary activities are most directly related to the production and distribution of the firm's products and services, which create value for the customer. Primary activities include inbound logistics, operations, outbound logistics, sales and marketing, and service. Inbound logistics includes receiving and storing materials for distribution to production. Operations transforms inputs into finished products. Outbound logistics entails storing and distributing finished products. Sales and marketing includes promoting and selling the firm's products. The service activity includes maintenance and repair of the firm's goods and services.

Support activities make the delivery of the primary activities possible and consist of organization infrastructure (administration and management), human resources

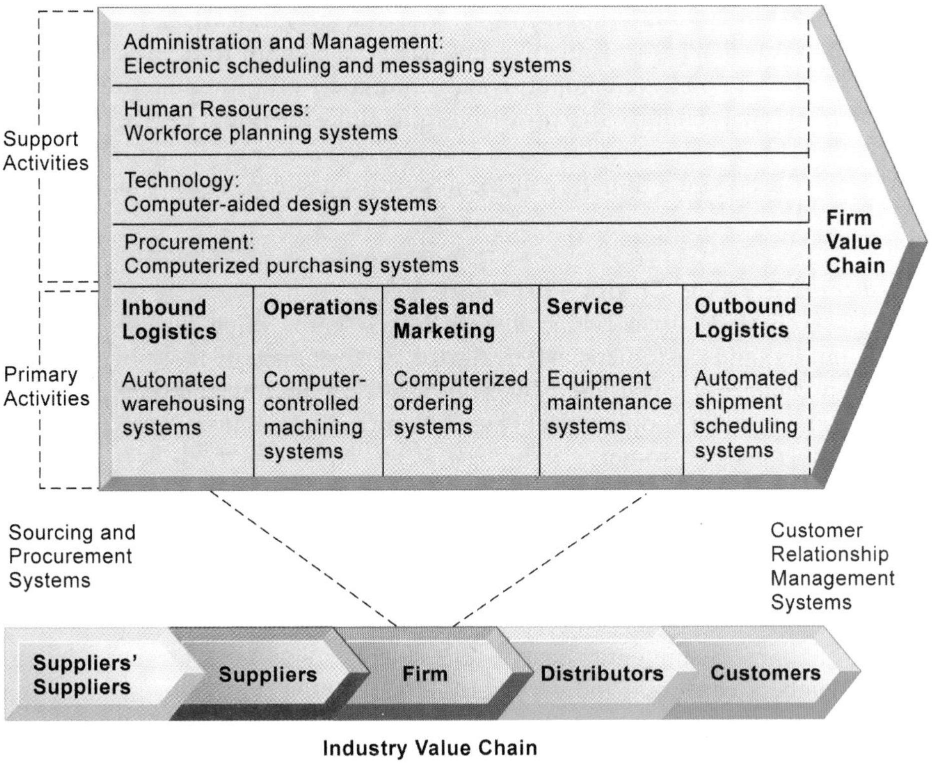

Figure 3.2
The Value Chain Model
This figure provides examples of systems for both primary and support activities of a firm and of its value partners that would add a margin of value to a firm's products or services.

(employee recruiting, hiring, and training), technology (improving products and the production process), and procurement (purchasing input).

You can ask at each stage of the value chain, "How can we use information systems to improve operational efficiency and improve customer and supplier intimacy?" This will force you to examine critically how you perform value-adding activities at each stage and how the business processes might be improved. For example, value chain analysis would indicate that Crayola, described in the Interactive Session on People, should use technology to improve its processes for sales and marketing and for differentiating its products. Crayola created technology-based products that provide additional value to customers because they take advantage of complementary existing technologies (such as the Internet and the iPad) that customers already own and are familiar with.

You can also begin to ask how information systems can be used to improve the relationship with customers and with suppliers who lie outside the firm's value chain but belong to the firm's extended value chain where they are absolutely critical to your success. Here, supply chain management systems that coordinate the flow of resources into your firm, and customer relationship management systems that coordinate your sales and support employees with customers, are two of the most common system applications that result from a business value chain analysis. We discuss these enterprise applications in detail in Chapter 9.

Using the business value chain model will also encourage you to consider benchmarking your business processes against your competitors or others in related industries and identifying industry best practices. **Benchmarking** involves comparing the efficiency and effectiveness of your business processes against strict standards and then measuring performance against those standards. Industry **best practices** are usually identified by consulting companies, research organizations, government agencies, and industry associations as the most successful solutions or problem-solving methods for consistently and effectively achieving a business objective.

Once you have analyzed the various stages in the value chain at your business, you can come up with candidate applications of information systems. Then, when you have a list of candidate applications, you can decide which to develop first. By making improvements in your own business value chain that your competitors might miss, you can achieve competitive advantage by attaining operational excellence, lowering costs, improving profit margins, and forging a closer relationship with customers and suppliers. If your competitors are making similar improvements, then at least you will not be at a competitive disadvantage—the worst of all cases!

Extending the Value Chain: The Value Web

Figure 3.2 shows that a firm's value chain is linked to the value chains of its suppliers, distributors, and customers. After all, the performance of most firms depends not only on what goes on inside a firm but also on how well the firm coordinates with direct and indirect suppliers, delivery firms (logistics partners, such as FedEx or UPS), and, of course, customers.

How can information systems be used to achieve strategic advantage at the industry level? By working with other firms, industry participants can use information technology to develop industry-wide standards for exchanging information or business transactions electronically, which force all market participants to subscribe to similar standards. Such efforts increase efficiency, making product substitution less likely and perhaps raising entry costs—thus discouraging new entrants. Moreover, industry members can build industrywide, IT-supported consortia, symposia, and communications networks to coordinate activities concerning government agencies, foreign competition, and competing industries.

Looking at the industry value chain encourages you to think about how to use information systems to link up more efficiently with your suppliers, strategic partners, and customers. Strategic advantage derives from your ability to relate your value chain to the value chains of other partners in the process. For instance, if you were Amazon.com, you would want to build systems that

- make it easy for suppliers to display goods and open stores on the Amazon site.
- make it easy for customers to search for goods.
- make it easy for customers to order and pay for goods.
- track and coordinate the shipment of goods to customers.

In fact, this is exactly what Amazon has done to make it one of the web's most satisfying online retail shopping sites.

Internet technology has made it possible to create highly synchronized industry value chains called value webs. A **value web** is a collection of independent firms that use information technology to coordinate their value chains to produce a product or service for a market collectively. It is more customer driven and operates in a less linear fashion than the traditional value chain.

Figure 3.3 shows that this value web synchronizes the business processes of customers, suppliers, and trading partners among different companies in an industry or in related industries. These value webs are flexible and adaptive to changes in supply and demand. Relationships can be bundled or unbundled in response to changing market conditions. Firms will accelerate time to market and to customers by optimizing their value web relationships to make quick decisions on who can deliver the required products or services at the right price and location.

SYNERGIES, CORE COMPETENCIES, AND NETWORK-BASED STRATEGIES

A large corporation is typically a collection of businesses. Often, the firm is organized financially as a collection of strategic business units, and the returns to the firm are directly tied to the performance of all the units. For instance, General Electric—one of the largest industrial firms in the world—is a collection of aerospace, heavy

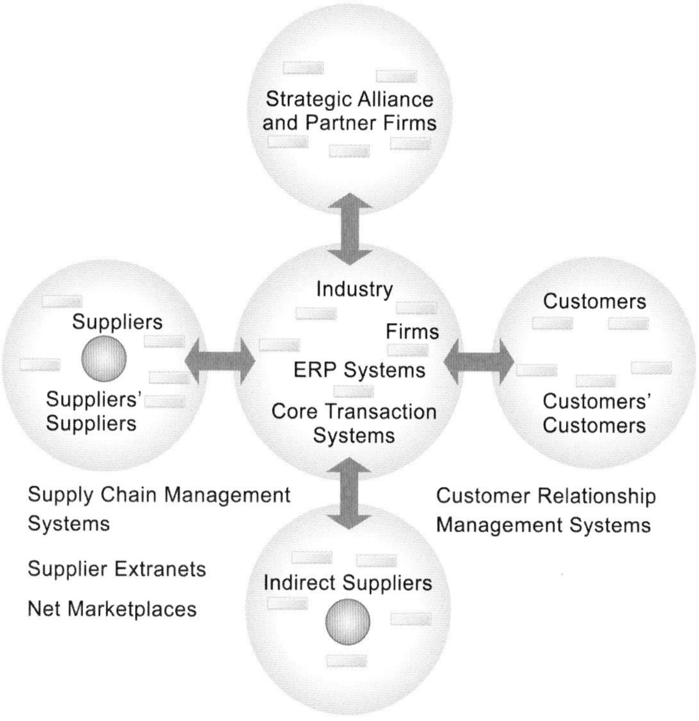

Figure 3.3
The Value Web
The value web is a networked system that can synchronize the value chains of business partners within an industry to respond rapidly to changes in supply and demand.

manufacturing, energy management, medical imaging, electronics, and software services firms called *business units*. Information systems can improve the overall performance of these business units by promoting communication, synergies, and core competencies among the units.

Synergies

Synergies develop when the output of some units can be used as inputs to other units, or two organizations can pool markets and expertise, and these relationships lower costs and generate profits. Information technology in these synergy situations can help tie together the operations of disparate business units so that they can act as a whole. For example, acquiring Countrywide Financial enabled Bank of America to expand its mortgage lending business and acquire a large pool of new customers that might be interested in its credit cards, consumer banking, and other financial products. Information systems would help the merged companies consolidate operations, lower retailing costs, and increase cross-marketing of financial products.

Enhancing Core Competencies

Another use of information systems for competitive advantage is to think about ways that systems can enhance core competencies. The argument is that the performance of all business units can increase insofar as these business units develop, or create, a central core of competencies. A **core competency** is an activity for which a firm is an industry leader, best in class leader. Core competencies may involve being the best miniature parts designer, the best package delivery service, or the best thin-film manufacturer. In general, a core competency relies on knowledge that is gained over many years of experience and a first-class research organization or, simply, key people who follow the literature and stay abreast of new external knowledge.

Any information system that encourages the sharing of knowledge across business units enhances competency. Such systems might encourage or enhance existing competencies and help employees become aware of new external knowledge; such systems might also help a business take advantage of existing competencies to related markets.

For example, Procter & Gamble, a world leader in brand management and consumer product innovation, uses a series of systems to enhance its core competencies. An intranet called InnovationNet helps people working on similar problems share ideas and expertise. InnovationNet connects those working in research and development (R&D), engineering, purchasing, marketing, legal affairs, and business information systems around the world, using a portal to provide browser-based access to documents, reports, charts, videos, and other data from various sources. It includes a directory of subject matter experts who can be tapped to give advice or collaborate on problem solving and product development and links to outside research scientists and entrepreneurs who are searching for new, innovative products worldwide.

Network-Based Strategies

Internet and networking technology have spawned strategies that take advantage of firms' abilities to create networks or network with each other. Network-based strategies include the use of a virtual company model, network economics, and business ecosystems.

A **virtual company** uses networks to link people, assets, and ideas, enabling it to ally with other companies to create and distribute products and services without being limited by traditional organizational boundaries or physical locations. The virtual company model is useful when a company finds it cheaper to acquire products, services, or capabilities from an external vendor or when it needs to move quickly to exploit new market opportunities and lacks the time and resources to respond on its own.

Fashion companies, such as GUESS, Ann Taylor, Levi Strauss, and Reebok, enlist Hong Kong-based Li & Fung to manage product design, raw material sourcing, manufacturing, quality assurance, and shipping for their garments. Li & Fung does not own any fabric, factories, or machines, outsourcing all of its work to a network of more than 15,000 suppliers in 40 countries all over the world. Customers place orders to Li & Fung over its private extranet. Li & Fung then sends instructions to appropriate raw material suppliers and factories where the clothing is produced. The Li & Fung extranet tracks the entire production process for each order. Working as a virtual company keeps Li & Fung flexible and adaptable so that it can design and produce quickly its clients' products to keep pace with rapidly changing fashion trends.

Business models based on a network may help firms strategically by taking advantage of **network economics**. In traditional economics—the economics of factories and agriculture—production experiences diminishing returns. The more any given resource is applied to production, the lower the marginal gain in output, until a point is reached when the additional inputs produce no additional outputs. This is the law of diminishing returns, and it is one foundation of modern economics.

In some situations, the law of diminishing returns does not work. For instance, in a network, the marginal costs of adding another participant are about zero, whereas the marginal gain is much larger. The larger the number of subscribers in a telephone system or the Internet, the greater the value to all participants because each user can interact with more people. It is no more expensive to operate a television station with 1,000 subscribers than with 10 million subscribers. The value of a community of people grows as the number of participants increases, whereas the cost of adding new members is inconsequential. This is referred to as a "network effect."

From this network economics perspective, information technology can be strategically useful. Firms can use Internet sites to build *communities of* like-minded customers who want to share their experiences. EBay, the giant online auction and retail site is an example. This business is based on a network of millions of users and has built an online community by using the Internet. The more people offering products on eBay, the more valuable the eBay site is to everyone because more products are listed, and more competition among suppliers lowers prices. Network economics also provide strategic benefits to commercial software vendors such as Microsoft. The value of their software and complementary software products increases as more people use them, and there is a larger installed base to justify continued use of the product and vendor support.

Business Ecosystems and Platforms Instead of participating in a single industry, some of today's firms participate in industry sets—collections of industries that provide related services and products that deliver value to the customer. **Business ecosystem** is another term for these loosely coupled but interdependent networks of suppliers, distributors, outsourcing firms, transportation service firms, and technology manufacturers (Iansiti and Levien, 2004). Information technology plays an important role in enabling a dense network of interactions among the participating firms.

Business ecosystems typically have one or a few keystone firms that dominate the ecosystem and create the **platforms** used by other niche firms. For instance, both Microsoft and Facebook provide platforms composed of information systems, technologies, and services that thousands of other firms in different industries use to enhance their own capabilities (Van Alstyne et. al, 2016). Facebook is a platform used by billions of people and millions of businesses to interact and share information as well as to buy, market, and sell numerous products and services. More firms are trying to use information systems to develop into keystone firms by building IT-based platforms that other firms can use. Alternatively, firms should consider how their information systems will enable them to become profitable niche players in the larger ecosystems created by keystone firms.

DISRUPTIVE TECHNOLOGIES: RIDING THE WAVE

Sometimes a technology and resulting business innovation comes along to change the business landscape and environment radically. These innovations are loosely called *disruptive* (Christensen, 2003). In some cases, **disruptive technologies** are substitute products that perform as well or better than anything currently produced. The automobile substituted for the horse-drawn carriage, the Apple iPod for portable CD players, digital photography for process film photography, and on-demand services like Uber for dispatched taxis. In these cases, entire industries are put out of business or significantly challenged.

In other cases, disruptive technologies simply extend the market, usually with less functionality and much less cost, than existing products. Eventually they turn into low-cost competitors for whatever was sold before. Disk drives are an example. Small hard-disk drives used in PCs extended the market for computer disk drives by offering cheap digital storage for small files on small computers. Eventually, small PC hard-disk drives became the largest segment of the disk drive marketplace.

Some firms can create these technologies and ride the wave to profits, whereas others learn quickly and adapt their business; still others are obliterated because their products, services, and business models become obsolete. There are also cases when no firms benefit, and all gains go to consumers (firms fail to capture any profits). Table 3.4 provides examples of some disruptive technologies.

Disruptive technologies are tricky. Firms that invent disruptive technologies as first movers do not always benefit if they lack the resources to exploit the technology or fail to see the opportunity. The MITS Altair 8800 is widely regarded as the first PC, but its inventors did not take advantage of their first-mover status. Second movers, so-called fast followers such as IBM and Microsoft, reaped the rewards. Citibank's ATMs revolutionized retail banking, but other banks copied them. Now all banks use ATMs, and the benefits go mostly to the consumers.

TABLE 3.4
Disruptive Technologies: Winners and Losers

Technology	Description	Winners and Losers
Microprocessor chips (1971)	Thousands and eventually millions of transistors on a silicon chip	Microprocessor firms win (Intel, Texas Instruments); transistor firms (GE) decline
Personal computers (1975)	Small, inexpensive, but fully functional desktop computers	PC manufacturers (HP, Apple, IBM) and chip manufacturers prosper (Intel); mainframe (IBM) and minicomputer (DEC) firms lose
Digital photography 1975	Using charge-coupled device (CCD) image sensor chips to record images	CCD manufacturers and smartphone companies win, manufacturers of film products lose
World Wide Web (1989)	A global database of digital files and pages instantly available	E-commerce online stores benefit; small retailers and shopping malls lose
Internet music, video, TV services	Repositories of downloadable music, video, TV broadcasts on the web	Owners of Internet platforms, telecommunications providers owning Internet backbone (AT&T, Verizon), local Internet service providers win; content owners and physical retailers lose (Tower Records, Blockbuster)
PageRank algorithm	A method for ranking web pages in terms of their popularity to supplement web search by key terms	Google is the winner (it owns the patent); traditional keyword search engines (Alta Vista) lose
Software as web service	Using the Internet to provide remote access to online software	Online software services companies (Salesforce.com) win; traditional boxed software companies (Microsoft, SAP, Oracle) lose

3-2 How do information systems help businesses compete globally?

Look closely at your jeans or sneakers. Even if they have a U.S. label, they were probably designed in California and stitched together in Hong Kong or Guatemala, using materials from China or India. Call Microsoft Support, or Verizon Support, and chances are good you will be speaking to a customer service representative located in India.

Consider the path to market for an iPhone, which is illustrated in Figure 3.4. The iPhone was designed by Apple engineers in the United States, sourced with more than 200 high-tech components from around the world, and assembled in China. Companies in Taiwan, South Korea, Japan, France, Italy, Germany, and the United States provided components such as the case, camera, processor, accelerator, gyroscope,

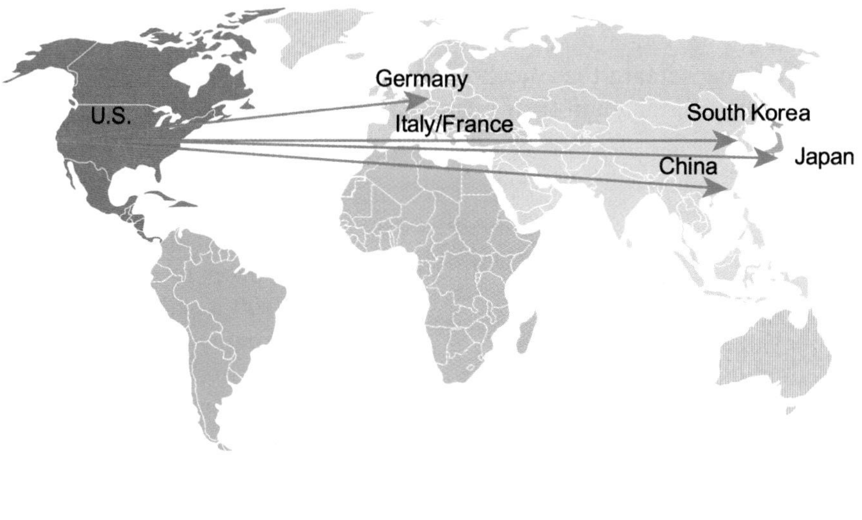

Figure 3.4
Apple iPhone's Global Supply Chain
Apple designs the iPhone in the United States and relies on suppliers in the United States, Germany, Italy, France, and South Korea for parts. Final assembly occurs in China.

electronic compass, power management chip, touch screen controller, and high-definition display screen. Foxconn, a Chinese division of Taiwan's Hon Hai Group, is in charge of manufacturing and assembly.

Firms pursuing a global strategy benefit from economies of scale and resource cost reduction (usually wage cost reduction). For example, Apple spread design, sourcing, and production for its iPhone over multiple countries overseas to reduce tariffs and labor costs.

THE INTERNET AND GLOBALIZATION

Until the mid-1990s, huge multinational firms, such as General Electric, General Motors, Toyota, and IBM, dominated competion on a global scale. These large firms could afford huge investments in factories, warehouses, and distribution centers in foreign countries and proprietary networks and systems that could operate on a global scale. The emergence of the Internet into a full-blown international communications system has drastically reduced the costs of operating on a global scale, deepening the possibilities for large companies but simultaneously creating many opportunities for small and medium-sized firms.

The global Internet, along with internal information systems, puts manufacturing firms in nearly instant contact with their suppliers. Internet telephony (see Chapter 7) permits millions of service calls to U.S. companies to be answered in India and Jamaica just as easily and cheaply as if the help desk were in New Jersey or California. Likewise, the Internet makes it possible to move very large computer files with hundreds of graphics, or complex industrial designs, across the globe in seconds.

GLOBAL BUSINESS AND SYSTEM STRATEGIES

There are four main ways of organizing businesses internationally: domestic exporter, multinational, franchiser, and transnational, each with different patterns of organizational structure or governance. In each type of global business organization, business functions may be centralized (in the home country), decentralized (to local foreign units), and coordinated (all units participate as equals).

The **domestic exporter** strategy is characterized by heavy centralization of corporate activities in the home country of origin. Production, finance/accounting, sales/marketing, human resources, and strategic management are set up to optimize resources in the home country. International sales are sometimes dispersed using agency agreements or subsidiaries, but foreign marketing still relies completely on the domestic home base for marketing themes and strategies. Caterpillar Corporation and other heavy capital equipment manufacturers fall into this category of firm.

A **multinational** strategy concentrates financial management and control out of a central home base while decentralizing production, sales, and marketing operations to units in other countries. The products and services on sale in different countries are adapted to suit local market conditions. The organization becomes a far-flung confederation of production and marketing facilities operating in different countries. Many financial service firms, along with a host of manufacturers, such as Ford Motor Co. and Intel Corporation, fit this pattern.

Franchisers have the product created, designed, financed, and initially produced in the home country but rely heavily on foreign personnel for further production, marketing, and human resources. Food franchisers, such as McDonald's and Starbucks, fit this pattern. McDonald's created a new form of fast-food chain in the United States and continues to rely largely on the United States for inspiration of new products, strategic management, and financing. Nevertheless, local production of some items, local marketing, and local recruitment of personnel are required.

Transnational firms have no single national headquarters but instead have many regional headquarters and perhaps a world headquarters. In a **transnational** strategy, nearly all the value-adding activities are managed from a global perspective without

Figure 3.5
Global Business Organization and Systems Configurations
The large Xs show the dominant patterns, and the small Xs show the emerging patterns. For instance, domestic exporters rely predominantly on centralized systems, but there is continual pressure and some development of decentralized systems in local marketing regions.

SYSTEM CONFIGURATION	Strategy			
	Domestic Exporter	Multinational	Franchiser	Transnational
Centralized	X			
Duplicated			X	
Decentralized	x	X	x	
Networked		x		X

reference to national borders, optimizing sources of supply and demand wherever they appear and taking advantage of any local competitive advantages. There is a strong central management core of decision making but considerable dispersal of power and financial muscle throughout the global divisions. Many *Fortune* 500 companies are transnational.

Nestlé S.A., the largest food and beverage company in the world, is one of the world's most globalized companies, with 335,000 employees at 418 facilities in 86 countries. Nestlé launched a $2.4 billion initiative to adopt a single set of business processes and systems for procurement, distribution, and sales management using SAP enterprise software. All of Nestlé's worldwide business units use the same processes and systems for making sales commitments, establishing factory production schedules, billing customers, compiling management reports, and reporting financial results. Nestlé has learned how to operate as a single unit on a global scale.

GLOBAL SYSTEM CONFIGURATION

Figure 3.5 depicts four types of systems configurations for global business organizations. *Centralized systems* are those in which systems development and operation occur totally at the domestic home base. *Duplicated systems* are those in which development occurs at the home base, but operations are handed over to autonomous units in foreign locations. *Decentralized systems* are those in which each foreign unit designs its own unique solutions and systems. *Networked systems* are those in which systems development and operations occur in an integrated and coordinated fashion across all units.

As can be seen in Figure 3.5, domestic exporters tend to have highly centralized systems in which a single domestic systems development staff develops worldwide applications. Multinationals allow foreign units to devise their own systems solutions based on local needs with few, if any, applications in common with headquarters (the exceptions being financial reporting and some telecommunications applications). Franchisers typically develop a single system, usually at the home base, and then replicate it around the world. Each unit, no matter where it is located, has identical applications. Firms such as Nestlé, organized along transnational lines, use networked systems that span multiple countries, using powerful telecommunications networks and a shared management culture that crosses cultural barriers.

3-3 How do information systems help businesses compete using quality and design?

Quality has developed from a business buzzword into a very serious goal for many companies. Quality is a form of differentiation. Companies with reputations for high quality, such as Lexus or Nordstrom, can charge premium prices for their products and services. Information systems have a major contribution to make in this drive for quality. In the services industries in particular, superior information systems and services generally enable quality strategies.

WHAT IS QUALITY?

Quality can be defined from both producer and customer perspectives. From the perspective of the producer, quality signifies conformance to specifications or the absence of variation from those specifications. The specifications for a telephone might include one that states the strength of the phone should not be weakened if the phone is dented or otherwise damaged by a drop from a four-foot height onto a wooden floor.

A customer definition of quality is much broader. First, customers are concerned with the quality of the physical product—its durability, safety, ease of use, installation. Second, customers are concerned with the quality of service, by which they mean the accuracy and truthfulness of advertising, responsiveness to warranties, and ongoing product support. Finally, customer concepts of quality include psychological aspects: the company's knowledge of its products, the courtesy and sensitivity of sales and support staff, and the reputation of the product. Today, as the quality movement in business progresses, the definition of quality is increasingly from the perspective of the customer.

Many companies have embraced the concept of **total quality management (TQM)**. TQM makes quality the responsibility of all people and functions within an organization. TQM holds that the achievement of quality control is an end in itself. Everyone is expected to contribute to the overall improvement of quality—the engineer who avoids design errors, the production worker who spots defects, the sales representative who presents the product properly to potential customers, and even the secretary who avoids typing mistakes. TQM derives from quality management concepts that American quality experts such as W. Edwards Deming and Joseph Juran developed, but the Japanese popularized it.

Another quality concept that is widely implemented today is Six Sigma, which Amazon.com used to reduce errors in order fulfillment. **Six Sigma** is a specific measure of quality, representing 3.4 defects per million opportunities. Most companies cannot achieve this level of quality but use Six Sigma as a goal to implement a set of methodologies and techniques for improving quality and reducing costs. Studies have repeatedly shown that the earlier in the business cycle a problem is eliminated, the less it costs the company. Thus, quality improvements not only raise the level of product and service quality but can also lower costs.

HOW INFORMATION SYSTEMS IMPROVE QUALITY

Let's examine some of the ways companies face the challenge of improving quality to see how information systems can be part of the process.

Reduce Cycle Time and Simplify the Production Process

Studies have shown that one of the best ways to reduce quality problems is to reduce **cycle time**, which refers to the total elapsed time from the beginning of a process to its end. Shorter cycle times mean that problems are caught earlier in the process, often before the production of a defective product is completed, saving some of the hidden production costs. Finally, finding ways to reduce cycle time often means finding ways to simplify production steps. The fewer steps in a process, the less time and opportunity for an error to occur. Information systems help eliminate steps in a process and critical time delays.

1-800-Flowers, a multimillion-dollar company selling flowers by telephone or over the web, used to be a much smaller company that had difficulty retaining its customers. It had poor service, inconsistent quality, and a cumbersome manual order-taking process. Telephone representatives had to write each order, obtain credit card approval, determine which participating florist was closest to the delivery location, select a floral arrangement, and forward the order to the florist. Each step in the manual process increased the chance of human error, and the whole process took at least half an hour. A new information system now downloads orders taken in telecenters or over the web to a central computer and electronically transmits them to local florists. Orders are more accurate and arrive at the florist within two minutes.

Benchmark

Companies achieve quality by using benchmarking to set standards for products, services, and other activities and then measuring performance against those standards. Companies may use external industry standards, standards other companies set, internally developed standards, or some combination of the three. L.L. Bean, the Freeport, Maine, clothing company, used benchmarking to achieve an order-shipping accuracy of 99.9 percent. Its old batch order fulfillment system could not handle the surging volume and variety of items to be shipped. After studying German and Scandinavian companies with leading-edge order fulfillment operations, L.L. Bean carefully redesigned its order fulfillment process and information systems so that orders could be processed as soon as they were received and shipped within 24 hours.

Use Customer Demands to Improve Products and Services

Improving customer service, and making customer service the number-one priority, will improve the quality of the product itself. Delta Airlines decided to focus on its customers, installing a customer care system at its airport gates. For each flight, the airplane seating chart, reservations, check-in information, and boarding data are linked in a central database. Airline personnel can track which passengers are on board regardless of where they checked in and use this information to help passengers reach their destination quickly, even if delays cause them to miss connecting flights.

Improve Design Quality and Precision

Computer-aided design software has made a major contribution to quality improvements in many companies, from producers of automobiles to producers of razor blades. A **computer-aided design (CAD) system** automates the creation and revision of designs, using computers and sophisticated graphics software. The software enables users to create a digital model of a part, a product, or a structure and make changes to the design on the computer without having to build physical prototypes.

For example, Ford Motor Company used a computer simulation that came up with the most efficient design possible for an engine cylinder. Engineers altered that

Computer-aided design (CAD) systems improve the quality and precision of product design by performing much of the design and testing work on the computer.

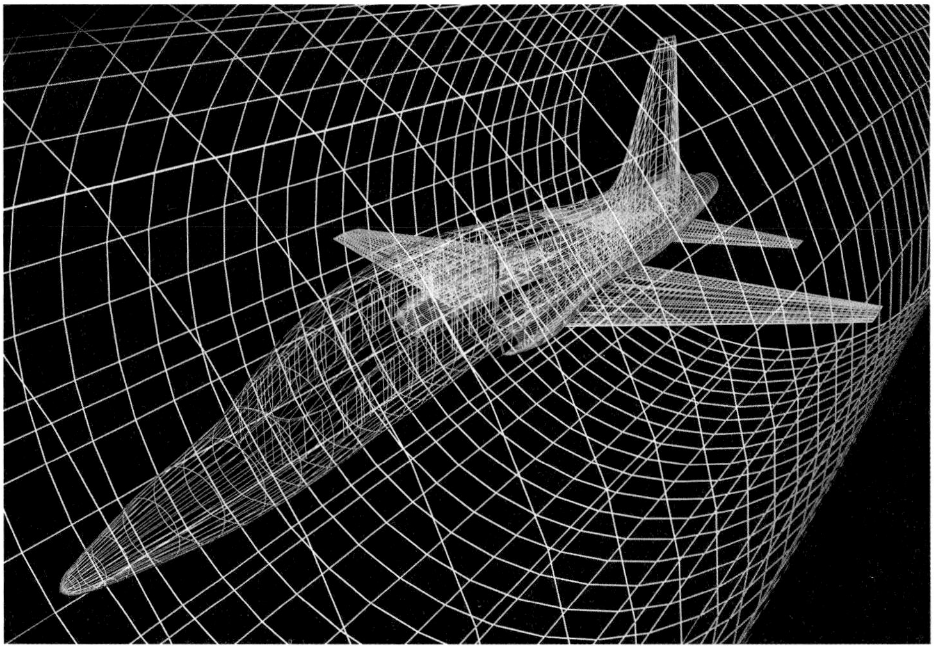

design to account for manufacturing constraints and tested the revised design on the computer, using models with decades of data on material properties and engine performance. Ford then created the physical mold to make a real part that could be bolted onto an engine for further testing. The entire process took days instead of months and cost thousands of dollars instead of millions.

CAD systems can supply data for **3-D printing**, also known as additive manufacturing, which uses machines to make solid objects, layer by layer, from specifications in a digital file. Unlike traditional techniques, by which objects are cut or drilled from molds, resulting in some wasted materials, 3-D printing lets workers model an object on a computer and print it out with plastic, metal, or composite materials. 3-D printing is currently being used for prototyping, custom manufacturing, and fashioning items with small production runs. Today's 3-D printers can handle materials including plastic, titanium, and human cartilage and produce fully functional components, including batteries, transistors, prosthetic devices, LEDs, and other complex mechanisms, and there are now 3-D printing services that run over the Internet, such as that offered by Staples.

Improve Production Precision and Tighten Production Tolerances

For many products, quality can be enhanced by making the production process more precise, thereby decreasing the amount of variation from one part to another. CAD software often produces design specifications for tooling and manufacturing processes, saving additional time and money while producing a manufacturing process with far fewer problems. The user of this software can design a more precise production system, a system with tighter tolerances, than could ever be done manually.

3-4 What is the role of business process management (BPM) in enhancing competitiveness?

Technology alone is often not enough to make organizations more competitive, efficient, or quality-oriented. The organization itself needs to be changed to take advantage of the power of information technology. These changes may require minor adjustments in work activities, but, often, entire business processes will need to be redesigned. Business process management (BPM) addresses these needs.

WHAT IS BUSINESS PROCESS MANAGEMENT?

Business process management (BPM) is an approach to business that aims to improve business processes continuously. BPM uses a variety of tools and methodologies to understand existing processes, design new processes, and optimize those processes. BPM is never concluded because continuous improvement requires continual change. Companies practicing business process management need to go through the following steps.

1. **Identify processes for change:** One of the most important strategic decisions that a firm can make is not deciding how to use computers to improve business processes but, rather, understanding which business processes need improvement. When systems are used to strengthen the wrong business model or business processes, the business can become more efficient at doing what it should not do. As a result, the firm becomes vulnerable to competitors who may have discovered the right business model. Considerable time and cost may also be spent improving business processes that have little impact on overall firm performance and revenue. Managers need to determine which business processes are the most important and how improving these processes will help business performance.
2. **Analyze existing processes:** Existing business processes should be modeled and documented, noting inputs, outputs, resources, and the sequence of activities. The process design team identifies redundant steps, paper-intensive tasks, bottlenecks, and other inefficiencies.

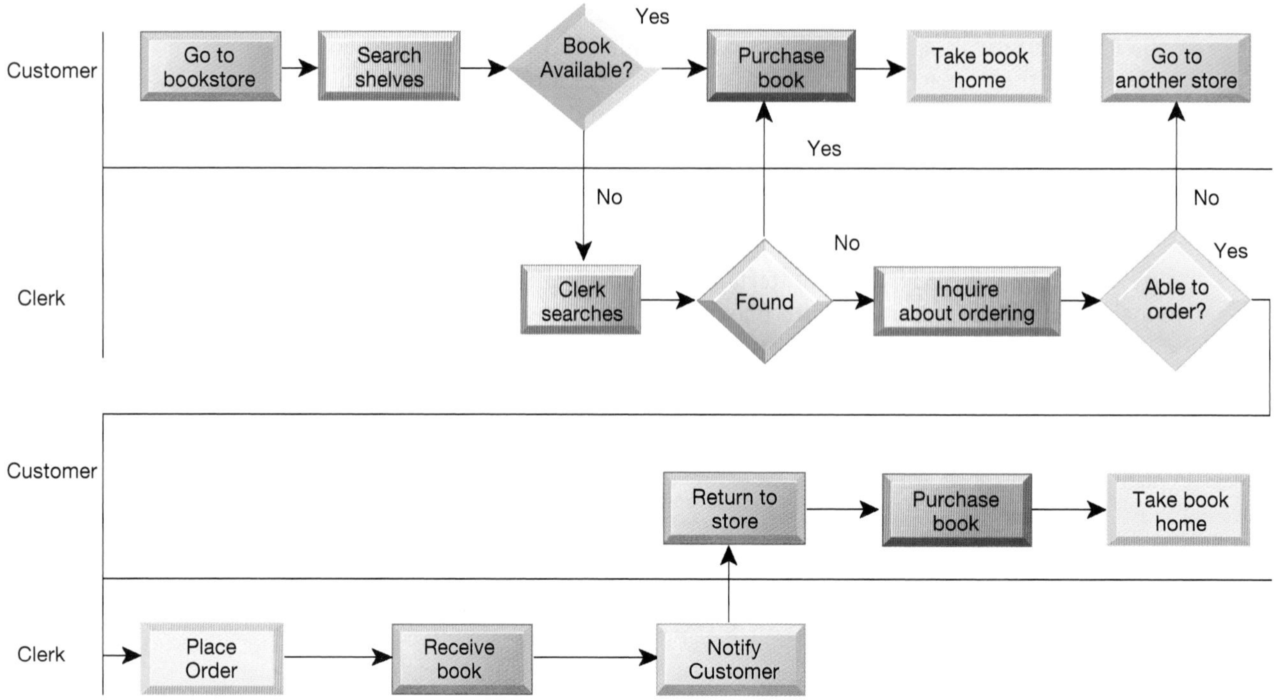

Figure 3.6
As-Is Business Process for Purchasing a Book from a Physical Bookstore
Purchasing a book from a physical bookstore requires both the seller and the customer to perform many steps.

Figure 3.6 illustrates the as-is process for purchasing a book from a physical bookstore. A customer would visit a physical bookstore and search its shelves for a book. If he or she finds the book, that person takes it to the checkout counter and pays for it by credit card, cash, or check. If the customer cannot locate the book, he or she must ask a bookstore clerk to search the shelves or check the bookstore's inventory records to see whether it is in stock. If the clerk finds the book, the customer purchases it and leaves. If the book is not available locally, the clerk inquires about ordering it for the customer, either from the bookstore's warehouse or from the book's distributor or publisher. Once the ordered book arrives at the bookstore, a bookstore employee telephones the customer with this information. The customer would have to go to the bookstore again to pick up the book and pay for it. If the bookstore cannot order the book for the customer, the customer would have to try another bookstore. You can see that this process has many steps and might require the customer to make multiple trips to the bookstore.

3. **Design the new process:** Once the existing process is mapped and measured in terms of time and cost, the process design team will try to improve the process by designing a new one. A new, streamlined to-be process will be documented and modeled for comparison with the old process.

Figure 3.7 illustrates how the book purchasing process can be redesigned by taking advantage of the Internet. The customer accesses an online bookstore over the Internet from his or her computer. He or she searches the bookstore's online catalog for the book he or she wants. If the book is available, the customer orders the book online, supplying credit card and shipping address information, and the book is delivered to the customer's home. If the online bookstore does not carry the book, the customer selects another online bookstore and searches for the book again. This process has far fewer steps than that for purchasing the book in a physical bookstore, requires much less effort from the customer, and requires fewer sales staff for customer service. The new process is therefore much more efficient and timesaving.

The new process design needs to be justified by showing how much it reduces time and cost or enhances customer service and value. Management first measures the

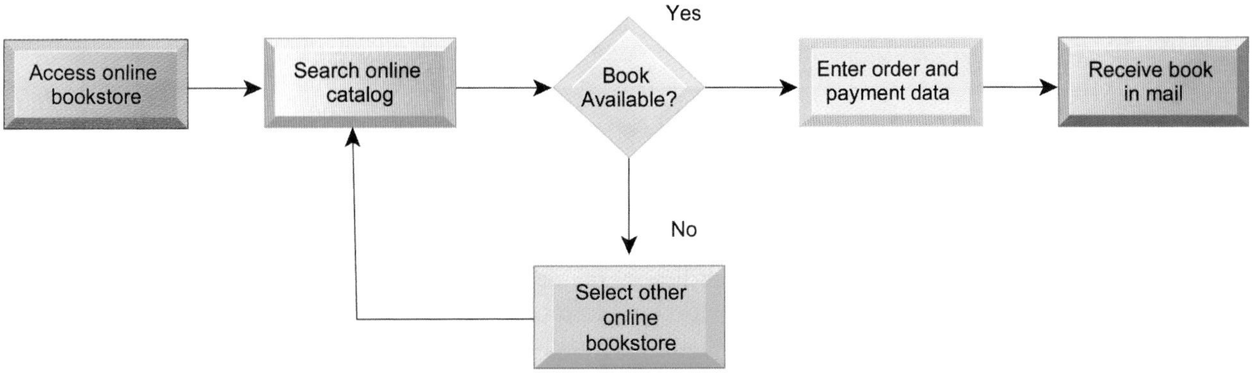

Figure 3.7
Redesigned Process for Purchasing a Book Online
Using Internet technology makes it possible to redesign the process for purchasing a book so that it only has a few steps and consumes fewer resources.

time and cost of the existing process as a baseline. In our example, the time required for purchasing a book from a physical bookstore might range from 15 minutes (if the customer immediately finds what he or she wants) to 30 minutes if the book is in stock but sales staff has to locate it. If the book has to be ordered from another source, the process might take one or two weeks and another trip to the bookstore for the customer. If the customer lives far away from the bookstore, the time to travel to the bookstore would have to be factored in. The bookstore will have to pay the costs for maintaining a physical store and keeping the book in stock, for sales staff on site, and for shipment costs if the book has to be obtained from another location.

The new process for purchasing a book online might only take several minutes, although the customer might have to wait several days or weeks to receive the book in the mail and will have to pay a small shipping charge. Nevertheless, the customer saves time and money by not having to travel to the bookstore or make additional visits to pick up the book. Booksellers' costs are lower because they do not have to pay for a physical store location or for local inventory.

4. **Implement the new process:** After the new process has been thoroughly modeled and analyzed, it must be translated into a new set of procedures and work rules. New information systems or enhancements to existing systems may have to be implemented to support the redesigned process. The new process and supporting systems are rolled out into the business organization. As the business starts using this process, problems are uncovered and addressed. Employees working with the process may recommend improvements.
5. **Continuous measurement:** After a process has been implemented and optimized, it needs to be measured continually. Why? Processes may deteriorate over time as employees fall back on old methods, or they may lose their effectiveness if the business experiences other changes.

Many software tools are available to facilitate various aspects of BPM. These tools help businesses identify and document processes requiring improvement, create models of improved processes, capture and enforce business rules for performing processes, and integrate existing systems to support new or redesigned processes. BPM software tools also provide analytics for verifying that process performance has been improved and for measuring the impact of process changes on key business performance indicators.

The Interactive Session on Organizations illustrates how a company can benefit from business process management. As you read this case, try to find out how changing business processes and their underlying technology improved Carter's business performance.

Carter's Redesigns Its Business Processes

Carter's has built a big business dressing little ones, and you probably wore some of its products when you were growing up. This company is the largest U.S. branded marketer of apparel exclusively for babies and young children and includes the OshKosh B'gosh brand. Carter's merchandise is sold online, in more than 1,000 company stores in the United States and Canada, and in 17,400 department and specialty stores. The company has annual revenue of $3 billion and 16,800 employees and is based in Atlanta, Georgia. Carter's financial systems handle hundreds of thousands of transactions each day.

Until recently, the systems Carter's used to process these transactions were heavily manual and paper-based and could no longer keep pace with the company's growth or the increasingly digital business environment. For many years that company had relied on more than 20 legacy financial systems, some of which were homegrown and antiquated. If the systems did not integrate with each other as they should, Carter's used manual processes to keep everything working together. This created bottlenecks that slowed down processing and also increased the chances of human error. For example, managing chargebacks required a great deal of manual data entry and tracking down spreadsheets, emails, folders, and faxes from various systems in order to reconcile a specific chargeback to the appropriate ledger. (A chargeback is the return of funds used to make a purchase to the buyer if the buyer disputes the purchase.)

Carter's management wanted to transform the role of the finance function from preoccupation with transaction processing to focusing more on analyzing financial data and guiding decision making. To accomplish this goal, the company needed to improve both the business's finance processes and technology. This meant streamlining and simplifying financial processes so the finance department had more time for analysis and reporting work. In 2015 Carter's launched a "Vision to Value" initiative to achieve this goal.

In addition to replacing outdated systems with more up-to-date technology, including a centralized enterprise resource planning (ERP) system, the project provided an opportunity to modernize financial processes. Carter's selected SAP Business Suite 4 SAP HANA (also known as SAP S/4HANA) software for this purpose and worked with Deloitte Consultants for assistance with systems integration and implementation. SAP S/4HANA is a business software suite based on SAP's proprietary HANA ultra-high-speed data management and computing platform and is designed to support the day-to-day processes of an enterprise. The new software solution had to interact well with other related systems beyond financials such as order management systems and point-of-sale systems. SAP S/4HANA offers integration to multiple data sources from many different SAP and non-SAP applications, financial and otherwise.

Business process redesign was as crucial to the success of the project as new technology. Implementing SAP software helped Carter's transform older and inefficient processes into modern processes reflecting best practices for its line of business and its industry. Carter's had to benchmark its financial processes against these best practices, many of which were incorporated in the SAP software. Thorough benchmarking required questioning the rationale behind every core financial process. For each process based on existing technology, the implementation had to ask whether it could be redesigned on a new technology platform to be more efficient. Carter's also examined whether the process would be better served by remaining on a legacy system rather than migrating to SAP S/4HANA. Carter's decided to keep a process on its existing system unless migrating to SAP S/4HANA provided clear benefits. For the systems that ran core financial processes, SAP S/4HANA was superior.

In July 2016 Carter's went live with SAP S/4HANA Finance with the procure-to-pay, invoice-to-cash, fixed assets, and record-to-report processes among the processes supported by the new system. Moving the procure-to-pay process to SAP S/4HANA increased efficiency by eliminating manual data entry and increasing the visibility of a transaction as it flows through the system. (Procure-to-pay is the process of buying goods and includes the initial decision to make the purchase, the process of selecting the goods, and the transaction to pay for the goods purchased.) Instead of requiring various phone calls, emails, and paper copies of supporting documentation, the software guides the process. The SAP Invoice Management application enables centralized invoicing process by scanning, reading, and filing invoices via optical character recognition (OCR), which kicks off an invoice workflow through a preset list of coders and approvers all the way to invoice payment. Once invoice information has been entered, it can be accessed automatically anywhere along the process life cycle, and users can view all information related to the invoice transaction on a single screen. For example, when approving an invoice, the system makes it possible for Carter's staff to see the invoice data flowing to accounts payable to start the payment process.

System-generated tracking of chargebacks and an improved capability to monitor chargeback status in the system have created significant time savings and efficiencies in billing and collections. All the information is in the SAP system, so whoever is approving the chargeback can see all the history in one place. In addition to chargeback history, once a chargeback is approved, the system sends a specific chargeback to a specific general ledger. The system has also made processes for fixed assets more efficient by eliminating manual routing and spreadsheet dependence.

Sources: "Carter's at SAPPHIRE 2016: Why SAP S/4HANA Finance?" and "Carter's at SAPPHIRE 2016: Implementing SAP S/4HANA Finance," www.sap.com, accessed February 24, 2017; Ken Murphy, "A Next-Generation Finance Platform at Carter's," SAP InsiderProfiles, December 19, 2016; and www.carters.com, accessed February 26, 2017.

CASE STUDY QUESTIONS

1. How did Carter's previous business processes affect its business performance?
2. What people, organization, and technology factors contributed to Carter's problems with its business processes?
3. Diagram Carter's old and redesigned business process for paying an invoice.
4. Describe the role of technology in Carter's business process changes.
5. How did Carter's redesigned business processes change the way the company worked? What was the business impact? Explain.

Business Process Reengineering

Many business process improvements are incremental and ongoing, but occasionally, more radical change is required. Our example of a physical bookstore redesigning the book purchasing process so that it can be carried out online is an example of this type of radical, far-reaching change. This radical rethinking and redesign of business processes is called **business process reengineering (BPR)**.

When properly implemented, BPR can lead to dramatic gains in productivity and efficiency, even changing the way the business is run. In some instances, it drives a paradigm shift that transforms the nature of the business itself. This actually happened in book retailing when Amazon challenged traditional physical bookstores with its online retail model. By radically rethinking the way a book can be purchased and sold, Amazon and other online bookstores have achieved remarkable efficiencies, cost reductions, and a whole new way of doing business.

BPM poses challenges. Executives report that the most significant barrier to successful business process change is organizational culture. Employees do not like unfamiliar routines and often resist change. This is especially true of business process reengineering projects because the organizational changes are so far-reaching. Managing change is neither simple nor intuitive, and companies committed to extensive process improvement need a good change management strategy (see Chapter 12).

3-5 How will MIS help my career?

Here is how Chapter 3 and this book can help you find a job as an entry-level business development representative.

THE COMPANY

A+ Superior Data Quality, a fast-growing Los Angeles-based company providing software and services to help large companies manage their data and data quality, is looking for an entry-level business development representative. The company's data quality and data management tools and services help firms correct, standardize, and enhance customer data by capturing accurate address, email, and phone information; removing duplicate data in corporate systems; analyzing data to discover relationships; restructuring and standardizing data; and monitoring data to ensure ongoing quality control and standardization. The company has 12,000 clients worldwide, 450 employees, and offices throughout the United States, Europe, and Asia,

POSITION DESCRIPTION

The business development representative will help the company's sales team meet aggressive growth targets. The company provides classroom and on-the-job training on how to communicate with prospects and customers, how to identify appropriate markets for its solutions, how to write a sales plan, and how to use tools such as Salesforce.com. Job responsibilities include:

- Researching targeted accounts to generate potential business opportunities.
- Supporting customer acquisition and sales strategies.
- Implementing tactics for successful execution of marketing campaigns.
- Building and managing a pipeline of sales leads through prospecting and qualifying marketing-generated leads.
- Reporting on the success of campaigns and lead generation activities.

JOB REQUIREMENTS

- Bachelor's degree
- Strong interest in a sales career
- Exceptional communication, interpersonal, analytical, and problem-solving skills
- Ability to multitask in fast-paced environment

INTERVIEW QUESTIONS

1. What do you know about data quality and data management? Have you any work experience in these areas? Have you ever encountered a data quality problem? If so, can you describe how the problem was solved?
2. Have you ever worked with Salesforce.com? What do you know about it? How have you used the software?
3. Can you give us an example of a marketing or sales-related problem or other business problem that you helped solve? Do you have any examples of your writing and analysis work?
4. Have you had much face-to-face contact with customers? Can you describe what work you did with customers?

AUTHOR TIPS

1. Review this chapter's discussion of IT and business strategy and also Chapter 6 on data management, including the section on data quality.
2. Use the web to find out more about tools and services for promoting data quality and data management and research the company's specific offerings in this area.

3. Review the company's LinkedIn profile and posts in addition to other social media channels. Are there consistent themes across these channels the company seems to be focused on? Be prepared to show you understand the kinds of business challenges and opportunities facing this company.
4. Learn what you can about Salesforce.com related to the responsibilities outlined for this job. Inquire about exactly how you would be using Salesforce.com in your work.
5. Consider inquiring what kinds of problems with customers' data quality you would be most likely encounter on the job.

Review Summary

3-1 How do Porter's competitive forces model, the value chain model, synergies, core competencies, and network-based strategies help companies use information systems for competitive advantage? In Porter's competitive forces model, the strategic position of the firm, and its strategies, are determined by competition with its traditional direct competitors. They are also greatly affected by new market entrants, substitute products and services, suppliers, and customers. Information systems help companies compete by maintaining low costs, differentiating products or services, focusing on market niche, strengthening ties with customers and suppliers, and increasing barriers to market entry with high levels of operational excellence. Information systems are most successful when the technology is aligned with business objectives.

The value chain model highlights specific activities in the business where competitive strategies and information systems will have the greatest impact. The model views the firm as a series of primary and support activities that add value to a firm's products or services. Primary activities are directly related to production and distribution, whereas support activities make the delivery of primary activities possible. A firm's value chain can be linked to the value chains of its suppliers, distributors, and customers. A value web consists of information systems that enhance competitiveness at the industry level by promoting the use of standards and industry-wide consortia and by enabling businesses to work more efficiently with their value partners.

Information systems achieve additional efficiencies or enhanced services by tying together the operations of disparate business units. Information systems help businesses use their core competencies by promoting the sharing of knowledge across business units. Information systems facilitate business models based on large networks of users or subscribers that take advantage of network economics. A virtual company strategy uses networks to link to other firms so that a company can use the capabilities of other companies to build, market, and distribute products and services. Firms can also redefine their businesses to become niche players or keystone firms in platform-based business ecosystems where multiple industries work together to deliver value to the customer. Disruptive technologies provide strategic opportunities, although first movers do not necessarily obtain long-term benefit.

3-2 How do information systems help businesses compete globally? Information systems and the Internet help companies operate internationally by facilitating coordination of geographically dispersed units of the company and communication with faraway customers and suppliers. There are four main strategies for organizing businesses internationally: domestic exporter, multinational, franchiser, and transnational.

3-3 How do information systems help businesses compete using quality and design? Information systems can enhance quality by simplifying a product or service, facilitating benchmarking, reducing product development cycle time, and increasing quality and precision in design and production.

3-4 What is the role of business process management (BPM) in enhancing competitiveness? Organizations often have to change their business processes to execute their business strategies successfully. If these business processes use technology, they can be redesigned to make the technology more effective. BPM combines and streamlines the steps in a business process to eliminate repetitive and redundant work and to achieve dramatic improvements in quality, service, and speed. BPM is most effective when it is used to strengthen a good business model and when it strengthens processes that have a major impact on firm performance.

Key Terms

3-D printing, 99
Benchmarking, 89
Best practices, 89
Business ecosystem, 93
Business process management (BPM), 99
Business process reengineering (BPR), 103
Competitive forces model, 81
Computer-aided design (CAD) system, 98
Core competency, 91
Cycle time, 97
Disruptive technologies, 93
Domestic exporter, 95
Efficient customer response system, 84
Franchiser, 95
Mass customization, 84
Multinational, 95
Network economics, 92
Platforms, 93
Primary activities, 88
Quality, 97
Six Sigma, 97
Support activities, 88
Switching costs, 86
Total quality management (TQM), 97
Transnational, 95
Value chain model, 88
Value web, 90
Virtual company, 92

MyLab MIS
To complete the problems with **MyLab MIS**, go to EOC Discussion Questions in MyLab MIS.

Review Questions

3-1 How do Porter's competitive forces model, the value chain model, synergies, core competencies, and network-based strategies help companies use information systems for competitive advantage?

- Define Porter's competitive forces model and explain how it works.
- List and describe four competitive strategies enabled by information systems that firms can pursue.
- Describe how information systems can support each of these competitive strategies and give examples.
- Explain why aligning IT with business objectives is essential for strategic use of systems.
- Define and describe the value chain model.
- Explain how the value chain model can be used to identify opportunities for information systems.
- Define the value web and show how it is related to the value chain.
- Describe how the Internet has changed competitive forces and competitive advantage.
- Explain how information systems promote synergies and core competencies that enhance competitive advantage.
- Explain how businesses benefit by using network economics.
- Define and describe a virtual company and the benefits of pursuing a virtual company strategy.

- Define and describe a business ecosystem and how it can provide competitive advantage.
- Explain how disruptive technologies create strategic opportunities.

3-2 How do information systems help businesses compete globally?

- Describe how globalization has increased opportunities for businesses.
- List and describe the four main ways of organizing a business internationally and the types of systems configuration for global business organizations.

3-3 How do information systems help businesses compete using quality and design?

- Define quality and compare the producer and consumer definitions of quality.
- Describe the various ways in which information systems can improve quality.

3-4 What is the role of business process management (BPM) in enhancing competitiveness?

- Define BPM and explain how it helps firms become more competitive.
- Distinguish between BPM and business process reengineering (BPR).
- List and describe the steps companies should take to make sure BPM is successful.

Discussion Questions

3-5 MyLab MIS It has been said that there is no such thing as a sustainable competitive advantage. Do you agree? Why or why not?

3-6 MyLab MIS What are some of the issues to consider in determining whether the Internet would provide your business with a competitive advantage?

3-7 MyLab MIS It has been said that the advantage that leading-edge retailers such as Walmart have over competitors isn't technology—it's their management. Do you agree? Why or why not?

Hands-On MIS Projects

The projects in this section give you hands-on experience identifying information systems to support a business strategy and solve a customer retention problem, using a database to improve decision making about business strategy, and using web tools to configure and price an automobile. Visit **MyLab MIS's** Multimedia Library to access this chapter's Hands-On MIS Projects.

MANAGEMENT DECISION PROBLEMS

3-8 Macy's, Inc., operates approximately 700 department stores in the United States. Its retail stores sell a range of merchandise, including apparel, home furnishings, and housewares. Senior management has decided that Macy's needs to tailor merchandise more to local tastes and that the colors, sizes, brands, and styles of clothing and other merchandise should be based on the sales patterns in each Macy's store. How could information systems help Macy's management implement this new strategy? What pieces of data should these systems collect to help management make merchandising decisions that support this strategy?

3-9 Tracfone Wireless is a leading prepaid wireless service in the United States, Puerto Rico, and the US Virgin Islands, offering products and services under brands such as TracFone, NET10 Wireless, Total Wireless, Straight Talk, SafeLink Wireless, Simple Mobile, and Page Plus Cellular. Despite its rock-bottom rates for mobile voice and data services, Tracfone's growth has been slowing. Management wants to know why this is happening and what can be done to attract more customers. Are customers rejecting Tracfone because of poor customer service, uneven network coverage, or low-cost wireless service charges offered by competitors such as Sprint and T-Mobile? How can the company use information systems to help find the answer? What management decisions could be made using information from these systems?

IMPROVING DECISION MAKING: USING A DATABASE TO CLARIFY BUSINESS STRATEGY

Software skills: Database querying and reporting; database design
Business skills: Reservation systems; customer analysis

3-10 In this exercise, you'll use database software to analyze the reservation transactions for a hotel and use that information to fine-tune the hotel's business strategy and marketing activities.

In MyLab MIS, you'll find a database for hotel reservation transactions developed in Microsoft Access with information about The President's Inn hotel in Cape May, New Jersey. At the Inn, 10 rooms overlook side streets, 10 rooms have bay windows with limited views of the ocean, and the remaining 10 rooms in the front of the hotel face the ocean. Room rates are based on room choice, length of stay, and number of guests per room. Room rates are the same for one to four guests. Fifth and sixth guests must pay an additional $20 per person per day. Guests staying for seven days or more receive a 10 percent discount on their daily room rates.

The owners currently use a manual reservation and bookkeeping system, which cannot provide management with immediate data about the hotel's daily operations and revenue. Use the database to develop reports on average length of stay per room type, average visitors per room type, base revenue per room (i.e., length of visit multiplied by the daily rate) during a specified period of time, and strongest customer base. After answering these questions, write a brief report about the Inn's current business situation and suggest future strategies.

IMPROVING DECISION MAKING: USING WEB TOOLS TO CONFIGURE AND PRICE AN AUTOMOBILE

Software skills: Internet-based software
Business skills: Researching product information and pricing

3-11 In this exercise, you will use software at car-selling websites to find product information about a car of your choice and use that information to make an important purchase decision. You will also evaluate two of these sites as selling tools.

You are interested in purchasing a new Ford Escape (or some other car of your choice). Go to the website of CarsDirect (www.carsdirect.com) and begin your investigation. Locate the Ford Escape. Research the various Escape models; choose one you prefer in terms of price, features, and safety ratings. Locate and read at least two reviews. Surf the website of the manufacturer, in this case Ford (www.ford.com). Compare the information available on Ford's website with that of CarsDirect for the Ford Escape. Try to locate the lowest price for the car you want in a local dealer's inventory. Suggest improvements for CarsDirect.com and Ford.com.

Collaboration and Teamwork Project

Identifying Opportunities for Strategic Information Systems

3-12 With your team of three or four students, select a company described in the *Wall Street Journal, Fortune, Forbes,* or another business publication. Visit the company's website to find additional information about that company and to see how the firm is using the web. On the basis of this information, analyze the business. Include a description of the organization's features, such as important business processes, culture, structure, and environment, as well as its business strategy. Suggest strategic information systems appropriate for that particular business, including those based on Internet technology, if appropriate. If possible, use Google Docs and Google Drive or Google Sites to brainstorm, organize, and develop a presentation of your findings for the class.

BUSINESS PROBLEM-SOLVING CASE

Walmart Versus Amazon and the Future of Retail

Walmart is the world's largest and most successful retailer, with more than $485 billion in 2016 sales and nearly 11,700 stores worldwide, including more than 4,600 in the United States. Walmart has 2.3 million employees and ranks number one on the *Fortune* 500 list of companies. Walmart had such a large and powerful selling machine that it really didn't have any serious competitors—until now.

Today Walmart's greatest threat is Amazon.com, often called the "Walmart of the Web." Amazon sells not only books but just about everything else people want to buy—DVDs, video and music streaming downloads, software, video games, electronics, apparel, furniture, food, toys, and jewelry. The company also produces consumer electronics—notably the Amazon Kindle e-book reader, Fire tablet, Echo and Tap speakers, and Fire TV streaming media player. No other online retailer can match Amazon's breadth of selection, low prices, and fast, reliable shipping. For many years, Amazon has been the world's largest e-commerce retailer with the world's largest and most powerful online selling machine. Moreover, Amazon has changed the habits and expectations of consumers in ways to which Walmart and other retailers must adapt. According to Brian Yarbrough, a retail analyst at Edward Jones in St. Louis, Amazon and online retailing is probably the biggest disrupter of retail since Walmart itself.

Walmart was founded as a traditional, offline, physical store in 1962, and that's still what it does best. But it is being forced to compete in e-commerce as well. Eight years ago, only one-fourth of all Walmart customers shopped at Amazon.com, according to data from researcher Kantar Retail. Today, however, half of Walmart customers say they've shopped at both retailers. Online competition and the profits to be reaped from e-commerce have become too important to ignore.

Walmart's traditional customers—who are primarily bargain hunters making less than $50,000 per year—are becoming more comfortable using technology. More affluent customers who started shopping at Walmart during the recession are returning to Amazon as their finances improve. Amazon has started stocking merchandise categories that Walmart traditionally sold, such as vacuum bags, diapers, and apparel, and its revenue is growing much faster than Walmart's. In 2016, Amazon had sales of nearly $136 billion.

For online shopping, Amazon has some clear-cut advantages. Amazon has created a recognizable and highly successful brand in online retailing. The company has developed extensive warehousing facilities and an extremely efficient distribution network specifically designed for web shopping. Its premium shipping service, Amazon Prime, provides fast "free" two-day shipping at an affordable fixed annual subscription price ($99 per year), often considered to be a weak point for online retailers. According to the *Wall Street Journal*, Amazon's shipping costs are lower than Walmart's, ranging from $3 to $4 per package, while Walmart's online shipping can run $5 to $7 per parcel. Shipping costs can make a big difference for a store like Walmart where popular purchases tend to be low-cost items like $10 packs of underwear. It makes no sense for Walmart to create a duplicate supply chain for e-commerce.

However, Walmart is no pushover. It is an even larger and more recognizable retail brand than Amazon. Consumers associate Walmart with the lowest price, which Walmart has the flexibility to offer on any given item because of its size. The company can lose money selling a hot product at extremely low margins and expect to make money on the strength of the large quantities of other items it sells. Walmart also has a significant physical presence, and its stores provide the instant gratification of shopping, buying an item, and taking it home immediately as opposed to waiting when ordering from Amazon. Seventy percent of the U.S. population is within five miles of a Walmart store, according to company management.

Walmart has steadily increased its investment in its online business, spending between $1.2 billion and $1.5 billion annually in 2015 and the next few years on e-commerce. This includes fulfillment centers and technology and purchases such as $3 billion for Jet.com to secure expertise for delivering the lowest-cost basket of goods online. Walmart.com is now the second-most visited e-commerce site in the United States with 88 million unique visitors per month. Walmart has constructed one of the world's largest private cloud computing centers, which provides the computing horsepower for Walmart to increase the number of items available for sale on Walmart.com from 1 million three years ago to more than 50 million today. In the spring of 2015 the company opened four new fulfillment centers around the country, each of which is more than 1 million square feet. To further counter Amazon,

Walmart introduced its own free two-day shipping program for orders totaling more than $35.

New technology will also give Walmart more expertise in improving the product recommendations for web visitors to Walmart.com, using smartphones as a marketing channel, and personalizing the shopping experience. Walmart has been steadily adding new applications to its mobile and online shopping channels and is expanding its integration with social networks such as Pinterest.

More than half of Walmart customers own smartphones. Walmart has designed its mobile app to maximize Walmart's advantage over Amazon: its physical locations. About 140 million people visit a Walmart store each week. The app's Walmart Pay feature enables users to quickly, easily and securely pay with their smartphones in all Walmart stores. Users link a credit card or bank account to the app. At checkout, they can just scan the phone to pay rather than pulling out their wallets. The app can also store shopping lists, save wish lists, and arrange online orders. About 22 million people now use the app as they shop.

The Walmart website uses software to monitor prices at competing retailers in real time and lower its online prices if necessary. The company is also doubling inventory sold from third-party retailers in its online marketplace and tracking patterns in search and social media data to help it select more trendy products. This strikes directly at Amazon's third-party marketplace, which accounts for a significant revenue stream for Amazon. Additionally, Walmart is expanding its online offerings to include upscale items like $146 Nike sunglasses and wine refrigerators costing more than $2,500 to attract customers who never set foot in a Walmart store. A new Product Content Collection System will facilitate vendors sending their product catalogs to Walmart, and the product information will then be available online.

Walmart's commitment to e-commerce is not designed to replicate Amazon's business model. Instead, CEO Doug McMillon is crafting a strategy that gives consumers the best of both worlds—what is called an omnichannel approach to retailing. Walmart's management believes the company's advantage is that it is not a pure-play e-commerce retailer and that customers want some real interaction with physical stores as well as digital. Walmart will sell vigorously through the web and also in its physical stores, retaining its hallmark everyday low prices and wide product assortment in both channels and using its large network of stores as distribution points. Walmart will closely integrate online shopping and fulfillment with its physical stores so that customers can shop however they want, whether it's ordering on their mobile phones for home delivery, through in-store pickup, or by wandering down the aisles of a Walmart superstore. Walmart is aiming to be the world's biggest omnichannel retailer.

Amazon is working on expanding its selection of goods to be as exhaustive as Walmart's. Amazon has allowed third-party sellers to sell goods through its website for a number of years, and it has dramatically expanded product selection via acquisitions such as its 2009 purchase of online shoe shopping site Zappos.com to give the company an edge in footwear. Amazon has been building its grocery offerings, with Amazon Prime, Prime Now, Prime Pantry, and Amazon Fresh offering delivery times as short as an hour in some cases.

It looks like Amazon is trying to innovate in physical retail store sales as well as online. Amazon has opened retail bookstores in Seattle, Chicago, San Diego, and other U.S. locations featuring Amazon electronic devices as well as books. It is thinking about moving into the grocery business as well as retail stores for furniture and appliances. These are retail experiences that lend themselves less easily to online purchasing because customers like to see and feel these types of goods in person. Amazon set up a physical grocery store in downtown Seattle called Amazon Go that is designed around an app that is able to place the items customers buy in a digital shopping cart so they can leave the store without waiting in a checkout line. The system automatically charges the credit card linked to the customer's Amazon account and even knows when that person puts something back.

Amazon continues to build more fulfillment centers closer to urban centers and expand its same-day delivery services, and it has a supply chain optimized for online commerce that Walmart just can't match. It now has more than 100 warehouses from which to package and ship goods. Warehouses speed up Amazon's shipping, encouraging users to shop more at Amazon, and the cost of these centers as a portion of Amazon's operations is decreasing. Amazon is building up its own delivery operation to compete with UPS, FedEx, and the U.S. Postal Service by offering better delivery and lower costs for both its own customers and possibly those of other retailers. Both Amazon and Walmart are experimenting with drones to accelerate fulfillment and delivery. But Walmart has thousands of stores, one in almost every neighborhood, which Amazon won't ever be able to replicate.

The winner of this epic struggle will be the company that leverages its advantage better. Walmart's technology initiative looks promising, but it still has work to do before its local stores are anything more than local stores. Can Walmart successfully move to an omnichannel strategy? Can Amazon's business model work for physical retail store sales? Which giant will dominate future retailing?

Sources: Rachel Abrams, "Walmart, with Amazon in Its Cross Hairs, Posts E-Commerce Gains," New York Times, May 18, 2017; William White, "Walmart ShippingPass to Be Replaced by Free Two-Day Shipping," InvestorPlace, January 31, 2017; Nick Wingfield, "Amazon's Ambitions Unboxed: Stores for Furniture, Appliances and More," *New York Times*, March 25, 2017, and "Amazon's Living Lab: Reimagining Retail on Seattle Streets," *New York Times*, February 12, 2017; Tim Denman, "Walmart's Plan for Worldwide E-Commerce Domination," *Info Systems News*, November 21, 2016; Greg Bensinger and Laura Stevens, "Amazon's Newest Ambition: Competing Directly with UPS and FedEx," *Wall Street Journal*, September 27, 2016; Rachel Abrams, "Walmart Outperforms Estimates, but Online Retail Lags," *New York Times*, May 19, 2016; Nathan Olivarez-Giles, "Amazon's Alexa Now Lets You Order Tens of Millions of Products with Your Voice," *Wall Street Journal*, July 1, 2016; Farhad Manjoo, "How Amazon's Long Game Yielded a Retail Juggernaut," *New York Times*, November 19, 2015; Brian O'Keefe, "The Man Who's Reinventing Walmart," *Fortune*, June 4, 2015; and Nathan Layne, "Wal-Mart Eyes Amazon in Potentially Costly E-commerce Battle," *Reuters*, May 20, 2015.

CASE STUDY QUESTIONS

3-13 Analyze Walmart and Amazon.com using the competitive forces and value chain models.

3-14 Compare Walmart and Amazon's business models and business strategies.

3-15 What role does information technology play in each of these businesses? How is it helping them refine their business strategies?

3-16 Which company will dominate retailing? Explain your answer.

MyLab MIS

Go to the Assignments section of MyLab MIS to complete these writing exercises.

3-17 Describe the impact of the Internet on each of the five competitive forces.

3-18 Describe how computer-aided design (CAD) systems improve quality and operational efficiency.

Chapter 3 References

Andriole, Stephen J. "Five Myths About Digital Transformation." *MIT Sloan Management Review* (Spring 2017).

Amladi, Pradip. "The Digital Economy: How It Will Transform Your Products and Your Future." *Big Data Quarterly* (March 25, 2016).

Chen, Daniel Q., Martin Mocker, David S. Preston, and Alexander Teubner. "Information Systems Strategy: Reconceptualization, Measurement, and Implications." *MIS Quarterly* 34, No. 2 (June 2010).

Christensen, Clayton. *Competitive Advantage: The Revolutionary Book That Will Change the Way You Do Business* (New York: HarperCollins, 2003).

Christensen, Clayton M., Michael E. Raynor, and Rory McDonald. "What Is Disruptive Innovation?" *Harvard Business Review* (December 2015).

Cohen, Daniel, and Joshua S. Gans. "Warding Off the Threat of Digital Disruption." *MIT Sloan Management Review* 58, no. 2 (Winter 2017).

Davenport, Thomas H., and Jeanne G. Harris. *Competing on Analytics: The New Science of Winning* (Boston: Harvard Business School Press, 2007).

Davenport, Thomas H., and Stephan Kudyba. "Designing and Developing Analytics-Based Data Products." *MIT Sloan Management Review* 58, No. 1 (Winter 2016).

Dedrick, Jason, Kenneth L. Kraemer, and Eric Shih. "Information Technology and Productivity in Developed and Developing Countries." *Journal of Management Information Systems* 30, No. 1 (Summer 2013).

Drnevich, Paul L., and David C. Croson. "Information Technology and Business-Level Strategy: Toward an Integrated Theoretical Perspective." *MIS Quarterly* 37, No. 2 (June 2013).

El Sawy, Omar A. *Redesigning Enterprise Processes for E-Business* (New York: McGraw-Hill, 2001).

Gandhi, Suketo, and Eric Gervet. "Now That Your Products Can Talk, What Will They Tell You?" Special Collection Getting Product Development Right. *MIT Sloan Management Review* (Spring 2016).

Gerow, Jennifer E., Varun Grover, Jason Thatcher, and Philip L. Roth. "Looking Toward the Future of IT–Business Strategic Alignment Through the Past: A Meta-Analysis." *MIS Quarterly* 38, No. 4 (December 2014).

Hagiu, Andrei, and Simon Rothman. "Network Effects Aren't Enough." *Harvard Business Review* (April 2016).

Hammer, Michael, and James Champy. *Reengineering the Corporation* (New York: HarperCollins, 1993).

Hirt, Martin, and Paul Willmott. "Strategic Principles for Competing in the Digital Age." *McKinsey Quarterly* (May 2014).

Iansiti, Marco, and Karim R. Lakhani. "Digital Ubiquity: How Connections, Sensors, and Data Are Revolutionizing Business." *Harvard Business Review* (November 2014).

Iansiti, Marco, and Roy Levien. "Strategy as Ecology." *Harvard Business Review* (March 2004).

Kapur, Rahul, and Thomas Klueter. "Organizing for New Technologies." *MIT Sloan Management Review* 58, No. 2 (Winter 2017).

Kauffman, Robert J., and Yu-Ming Wang. "The Network Externalities Hypothesis and Competitive Network Growth." *Journal of Organizational Computing and Electronic Commerce* 12, No. 1 (2002).

King, Andrew A., and Baljir Baatartogtokh. "How Useful Is the Theory of Disruptive Innovation?" *MIT Sloan Management Review* (Fall 2015).

Luftman, Jerry. *Competing in the Information Age: Align in the Sand*, 2nd ed. (New York: Oxford University Press, 2003).

Mithas, Sunil, Ali Tafti, and Will Mitchell. "How a Firm's Competitive Environment and Digital Strategic Posture Influence Digital Business Strategy." *MIS Quarterly* 37, No. 2 (June 2013).

Parker, Geoffrey, Marshall Van Alstyne, and Xiaoyue Jiang. "Platform Ecosystems: How Developers Invert the Firm." *MIS Quarterly* 41, No. 1 (March 2017).

Porter, Michael. *Competitive Advantage* (New York: Free Press, 1985).

________. "Strategy and the Internet." *Harvard Business Review* (March 2001).

Porter, Michael E., and James E. Heppelmann. "How Smart, Connected Products Are Transforming Competition." *Harvard Business Review* (November 2014).

Porter, Michael E., and Scott Stern. "Location Matters." *MIT Sloan Management Review* 42, No. 4 (Summer 2001).

Rigby, Darrell. "Digital-Physical Mashups." *Harvard Business Review* (September 2014).

Roca, Jaime Bonnin, Parth Vaishnav, Joana Mendonça, and M. Granger Morgan. "Getting Past the Hype About 3-D Printing." *MIT Sloan Management Review* (Spring 2017).

Ross, Jeanne W., Ina M. Sebastian, and Cynthia M. Beath. "How to Develop a Great Digital Strategy." MIT Sloan Management Review 58, No. 2 (Winter 2017).

Shapiro, Carl, and Hal R. Varian. *Information Rules* (Boston: Harvard Business School Press, 1999).

Svahn, Fredrik, Lars Mathiassen, and Rikard Lindgren. "Embracing Digital Innovation in Incumbent Firms: How Volvo Cars Managed Competing Concerns." *MIS Quarterly* 41, No. 1 (March 2017).

Weill, Peter, and Stephen L. Weorner. "Thriving in an Increasingly Digital Ecosystem." *MIT Sloan Management Review* 56, No. 4 (Summer 2014).

Wixom, Barbara H., and Jeanne W. Ross. "How to Monetize Your Data." *MIT Sloan Management Review* (Spring 2017).

Van Alstyne, Marshall W., Geoffrey G. Parer, and Sangeet Paul Choudary. "Pipelines, Platforms, and the New Rules of Strategy." *Harvard Business Review* (April 2016).

Zhu, Feng, and Nathan Furr. "Products to Platforms: Making the Leap." *Harvard Business Review* (April 2016).

CHAPTER 4

Ethical and Social Issues in Information Systems

LEARNING OBJECTIVES

After reading this chapter, you will be able to answer the following questions:

4-1 What ethical, social, and political issues are raised by information systems?

4-2 What specific principles for conduct can be used to guide ethical decisions?

4-3 Why do contemporary information systems technology and the Internet pose challenges to the protection of individual privacy and intellectual property?

4-4 How have information systems affected laws for establishing accountability and liability and the quality of everyday life?

4-5 How will MIS help my career?

CHAPTER CASES

- The Dark Side of Big Data
- Volkswagen Pollutes Its Reputation with Software to Evade Emissions Testing
- Will Automation Kill Jobs?
- Facebook Privacy: Your Life for Sale

VIDEO CASES

- What Net Neutrality Means for You
- Facebook and Google Privacy: What Privacy?
- United States v. Terrorism: Data Mining for Terrorists and Innocents

Instructional Video:

- Viktor Mayer-Schönberger on the Right to Be Forgotten

MyLab MIS

- Discussion Questions: 4-5, 4-6, 4-7;
- Hands-on MIS Projects: 4-8, 4-9, 4-10, 4-11;
- Writing Assignments: 4-17, 4-18;
- eText with Conceptual Animations

THE DARK SIDE OF BIG DATA

Organizations today are furiously mining big data, looking for ways to benefit from this technology. There are many big data success stories. For example big data is being used to detect suspicious transactions indicating healthcare fraud that bilks as much as $100 billion annually from Medicare and Medicaid. Big data analytics saves UPS $50 million per year by determining the most efficient daily delivery route for each of its drivers.

But there's a dark side to big data, and it has to do with privacy. We can now collect or analyze data on a much larger scale than ever before and use what we have learned about individuals in ways that may be harmful to them. The following are some examples.

Insurance rates Auto insurance companies such as Progressive offer a small device to install in your car to analyze your driving habits, ostensibly to give you a better insurance rate. However, some of the criteria for lower auto insurance rates are considered discriminatory. For example, insurance companies like people who don't drive late at night and don't spend much time in their cars. However, poorer people are more likely to work a late shift and to have longer commutes to work, which would increase their auto insurance rates.

Deloitte Consulting LLP developed a predictive modeling system for insurance applicants that predicts life expectancy by using data about individual consumers' buying habits as well as their personal and family medical histories. The company claims it can accurately predict whether people have any of 17 diseases, including diabetes, tobacco-related cancer, cardiovascular disease, and depression, by analyzing their buying habits. What you pick up at the drugstore might increase your health insurance rates.

Computerized hiring More and more companies are turning to computerized systems to filter and hire job applicants, especially for lower-wage, service-sector jobs. The algorithms these systems use to evaluate job candidates may be preventing qualified applicants from obtaining these jobs. For example, some of these algorithms have determined that,

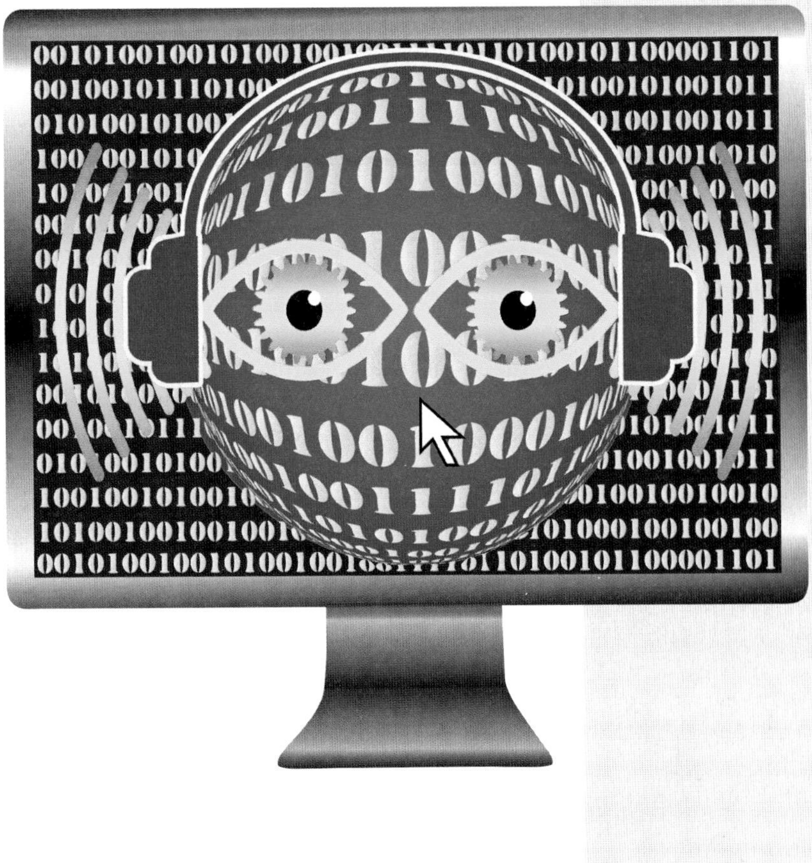

© sangoiri/123RF

statistically, people with shorter commutes are more likely to stay in a job longer than those with longer commutes or less reliable transportation or those who haven't been at their address for very long. If asked, "How long is your commute?" applicants with long commuting times will be scored lower for the job. Although such considerations may be statistically accurate, is it fair to screen job applicants this way?

Targeting financially vulnerable individuals Data brokers have been around for decades, but their tools for collecting and finely analyzing huge quantities of personal data grow ever more powerful. These data brokers now sell reports that specifically highlight and target financially vulnerable individuals. For example, a data broker might provide a report on retirees with little or no savings to a company offering reverse mortgages, high-cost loans, or other financially risky products. Very few rules or regulations exist to prevent targeting of vulnerable groups. Privacy laws and regulations haven't caught up with big data technology.

Revealing information about predicted life events without people's knowledge or consent Retailer Target developed a giant database of detailed customer data obtained from internal and external sources to predict what kinds of purchases customers were likely to make. It included data on purchase history, age, ethnicity, education, marital status, number of children, estimated income, job history, and life events such as when you last moved or if you have been divorced or declared bankruptcy. Analyzing these data helped Target identify women who were pregnant, even though these women had not notified Target—or often anybody else—they were expecting. In one glaring instance, Target sent promotional mail to the home of a pregnant teenager who had not yet informed her parents of her condition. More precise knowledge of how significant life events change a consumer's overall shopping habits gave a big boost to Target sales, but it also could lead to unwanted disclosures of highly sensitive personal information.

Sources: Warren Richey, "How Data-Crunching Is Cutting Down on Massive Health-care Fraud," *Christian Science Monitor,* May 30, 2017; Chuck Schaeffer, "5 Retail Big Data Examples with Big Paybacks," crmsearch.com, accessed June 1, 2017; Brian Brinkmann, "Big Data Privacy: What Privacy?" Business2Community, March 2, 2016; and Bernard Marr, "The 5 Scariest Ways Big Data Is Used Today," *DataInformed*, May 20, 2015.

The challenges of big data to privacy described in the chapter-opening case show that technology can be a double-edged sword. It can be the source of many benefits, including the ability to combat disease and crime and to achieve major cost savings and efficiencies for business. At the same time, digital technology creates new opportunities for invading your privacy and using information that could cause you harm.

The chapter-opening diagram calls attention to important points this case and this chapter raise. Developments in data management technology and analytics have created opportunities for organizations to use big data to improve operations and decision making. One popular use of big data analysis is for predictive modeling—sifting through data to identify how specific individuals will behave and react in the future. The organizations described here are benefiting from using predictive modeling to fight fraud, increase retail sales, select the best employees, and lower insurance and credit lending risks. However, their use of big data is also taking benefits away from individuals. Individuals might be subject to job discrimination, socioeconomic profiling, higher insurance rates, or unwanted disclosures of personal information because organizations have new tools to assemble and analyze huge quantities of data about them. New privacy protection laws and policies need to be developed to keep up with the technologies for assembling and analyzing big data.

This case illustrates an ethical dilemma because it shows two sets of interests at work: the interests of organizations that have raised profits or even helped many people with medical breakthroughs and those who fervently believe that businesses and public organizations should not use big data analysis to invade privacy or harm

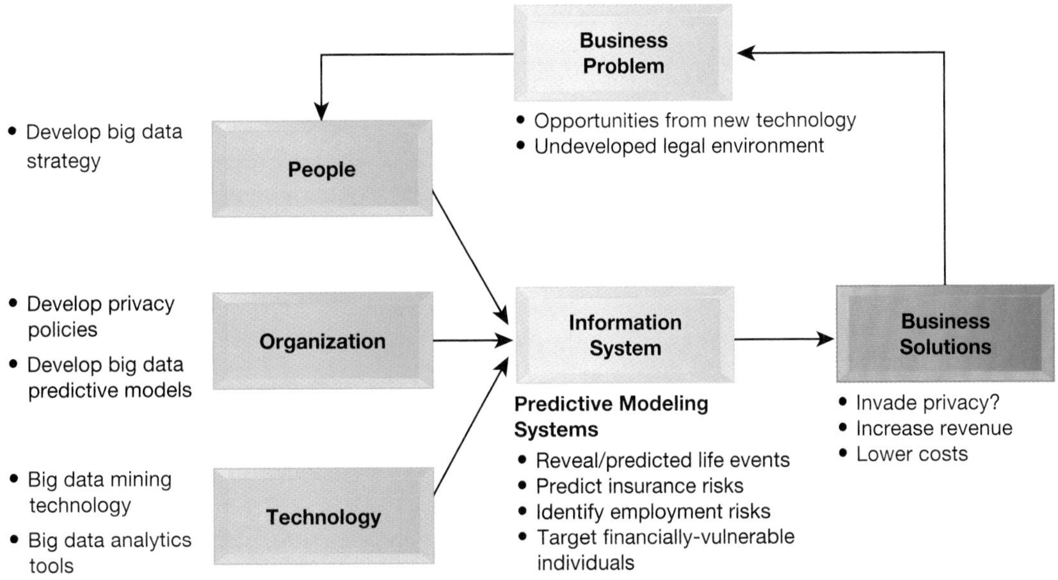

individuals. As a manager, you will need to be sensitive to both the positive and negative impacts of information systems for your firm, employees, and customers. You will need to learn how to resolve ethical dilemmas involving information systems.

Here are some questions to think about: Does analyzing big data about people create an ethical dilemma? Why or why not? Should there be new privacy laws to protect individuals from being targeted by companies analyzing big data? Why or why not?

4-1 What ethical, social, and political issues are raised by information systems?

In the past 20 years, we have witnessed, arguably, one of the most ethically challenging periods for U.S. and global business. Table 4.1 provides a small sample of recent cases demonstrating failed ethical judgment by senior and middle managers. These lapses in ethical and business judgment occurred across a broad spectrum of industries.

In today's new legal environment, managers who violate the law and are convicted will most likely spend time in prison. U.S. federal sentencing guidelines adopted in 1987 mandate that federal judges impose stiff sentences on business executives based on the monetary value of the crime, the presence of a conspiracy to prevent discovery of the crime, the use of structured financial transactions to hide the crime, and failure to cooperate with prosecutors (U.S. Sentencing Commission, 2004).

Although business firms would, in the past, often pay for the legal defense of their employees enmeshed in civil charges and criminal investigations, firms are now encouraged to cooperate with prosecutors to reduce charges against the entire firm for obstructing investigations. More than ever, as a manager or an employee, you will have to decide for yourself what constitutes proper legal and ethical conduct.

These major instances of failed ethical and legal judgment were not masterminded by information systems departments, but information systems were instrumental in many of these frauds. In many cases, the perpetrators of these crimes artfully used financial reporting information systems to bury their decisions from public scrutiny.

We deal with the issue of control in information systems in Chapter 8. In this chapter, we will talk about the ethical dimensions of these and other actions based on the use of information systems.

TABLE 4.1

Recent Examples of Failed Ethical Judgment by Senior Managers

Deerfield Management (2017)	Washington, D.C., hedge fund indicted for using confidential information about government financing to trade shares in healthcare companies that would be affected by the changes.
Teva Pharmaceutical Industries Ltd. (2016)	Teva executives admitted to paying to paying bribes to high-ranking officials in Russia, Ukraine, and Mexico to boost sales. Teva is the world's largest maker of generic medicines.
General Motors Inc. (2015)	General Motors CEO admitted the firm covered up faulty ignition switches for more than a decade, resulting in the deaths of at least 114 customers. More than 100 million vehicles worldwide needed to be replaced.
Takata Corporation (2015)	Takata executives admitted they covered up faulty airbags used in millions of cars over many years. Three executives indicted on criminal charges and Takata fined $1 billion. Takata filed for bankruptcy in June 2017.
Citigroup, JPMorgan Chase, Barclays, UBS (2012)	Four of the largest money center banks in the world pleaded guilty to criminal charges that they manipulated the LIBOR interest rate used to establish loan rates throughout the world.
GlaxoSmithKline LLC (2012)	The global healthcare giant admitted to unlawful and criminal promotion of certain prescription drugs, its failure to report certain safety data, and its civil liability for alleged false price reporting practices. Fined $3 billion, the largest healthcare fraud settlement in U.S. history.
Bank of America (2012)	Federal prosecutors charged Bank of America and its affiliate, Countrywide Financial, of defrauding government-backed mortgage agencies by churning out loans at a rapid pace without proper controls. Prosecutors sought $1 billion in penalties from the bank.

Ethics refers to the principles of right and wrong that individuals, acting as free moral agents, use to make choices to guide their behaviors. Information systems raise new ethical questions for both individuals and societies because they create opportunities for intense social change and, thus, threaten existing distributions of power, money, rights, and obligations. Like other technologies, such as steam engines, electricity, and the telephone, information technology can be used to achieve social progress, but it can also be used to commit crimes and threaten cherished social values. The development of information technology will produce benefits for many and costs for others.

Ethical issues in information systems have been given new urgency by the rise of the Internet and e-commerce. Internet and digital firm technologies make it easier than ever to assemble, integrate, and distribute information, unleashing new concerns about the appropriate use of customer information, the protection of personal privacy, and the protection of intellectual property.

Other pressing ethical issues that information systems raise include establishing accountability for the consequences of information systems, setting standards to safeguard system quality that protects the safety of the individual and society, and preserving values and institutions considered essential to the quality of life in an information society. When using information systems, it is essential to ask, "What is the ethical and socially responsible course of action?"

A MODEL FOR THINKING ABOUT ETHICAL, SOCIAL, AND POLITICAL ISSUES

Ethical, social, and political issues are closely linked. The ethical dilemma you may face as a manager of information systems typically is reflected in social and political debate. One way to think about these relationships is shown in Figure 4.1. Imagine

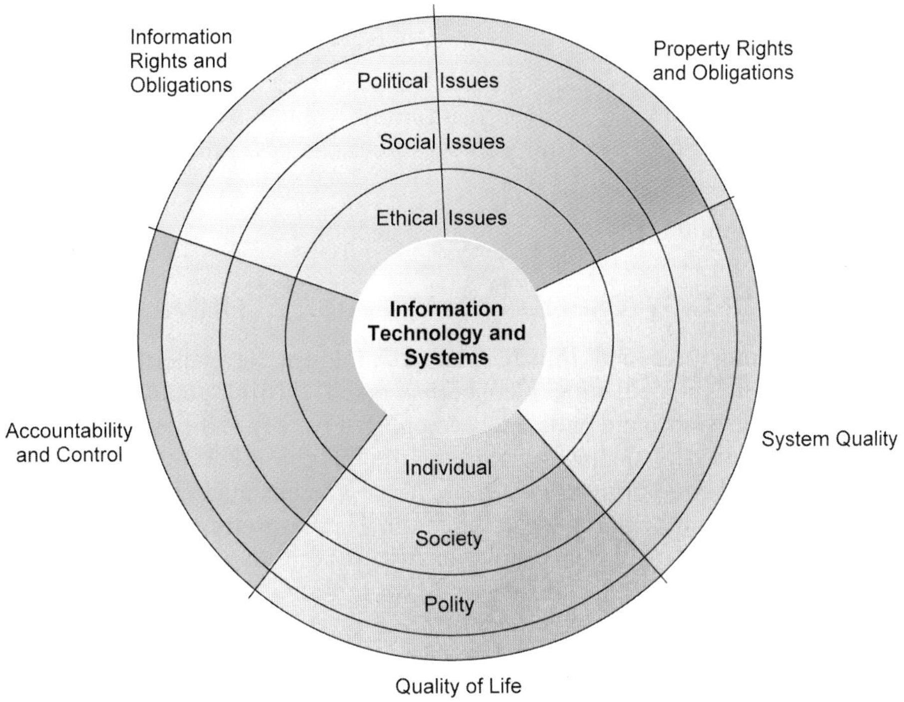

Figure 4.1
The Relationship Between Ethical, Social, and Political Issues in an Information Society
The introduction of new information technology has a ripple effect, raising new ethical, social, and political issues that must be dealt with on the individual, social, and political levels. These issues have five moral dimensions: information rights and obligations, property rights and obligations, system quality, quality of life, and accountability and control.

society as a more or less calm pond on a summer day, a delicate ecosystem in partial equilibrium with individuals and with social and political institutions. Individuals know how to act in this pond because social institutions (family, education, organizations) have developed well-honed rules of behavior, and these are supported by laws developed in the political sector that prescribe behavior and promise sanctions for violations. Now toss a rock into the center of the pond. What happens? Ripples, of course.

Imagine instead that the disturbing force is a powerful shock of new information technology and systems hitting a society more or less at rest. Suddenly, individual actors are confronted with new situations often not covered by the old rules. Social institutions cannot respond overnight to these ripples—it may take years to develop etiquette, expectations, social responsibility, politically correct attitudes, or approved rules. Political institutions also require time before developing new laws and often require the demonstration of real harm before they act. In the meantime, you may have to act. You may be forced to act in a legal gray area.

We can use this model to illustrate the dynamics that connect ethical, social, and political issues. This model is also useful for identifying the main moral dimensions of the information society, which cut across various levels of action—individual, social, and political.

FIVE MORAL DIMENSIONS OF THE INFORMATION AGE

The major ethical, social, and political issues that information systems raise include the following moral dimensions.

- *Information rights and obligations* What **information rights** do individuals and organizations possess with respect to themselves? What can they protect?
- *Property rights and obligations* How will traditional intellectual property rights be protected in a digital society in which tracing and accounting for ownership are difficult and ignoring such property rights is so easy?
- *Accountability and control* Who can and will be held accountable and liable for the harm done to individual and collective information and property rights?

- *System quality* What standards of data and system quality should we demand to protect individual rights and the safety of society?
- *Quality of life* What values should be preserved in an information- and knowledge-based society? Which institutions should we protect from violation? Which cultural values and practices does the new information technology support?

We explore these moral dimensions in detail in Section 4-3.

KEY TECHNOLOGY TRENDS THAT RAISE ETHICAL ISSUES

Ethical issues long preceded information technology. Nevertheless, information technology has heightened ethical concerns, taxed existing social arrangements, and made some laws obsolete or severely crippled. Five key technological trends are responsible for these ethical stresses, summarized in Table 4.2.

The doubling of computing power every 18 months has made it possible for most organizations to use information systems for their core production processes. As a result, our dependence on systems and our vulnerability to system errors and poor data quality have increased. Social rules and laws have not yet adjusted to this dependence. Standards for ensuring the accuracy and reliability of information systems (see Chapter 8) are not universally accepted or enforced.

Advances in data storage techniques and rapidly declining storage costs have been responsible for the multiplying databases on individuals—employees, customers, and potential customers—maintained by private and public organizations. These advances in data storage have made the routine violation of individual privacy both inexpensive and effective. Enormous data storage systems for terabytes and petabytes of data are now available on-site or as online services for firms of all sizes to use in identifying customers.

Advances in data analysis techniques for large pools of data are another technological trend that heightens ethical concerns because companies and government agencies can find out highly detailed personal information about individuals. With contemporary data management tools (see Chapter 6), companies can assemble and combine the myriad pieces of information about you stored on computers much more easily than in the past.

Think of all the ways you generate digital information about yourself—credit card purchases; telephone calls; magazine subscriptions; video rentals; mail-order purchases; banking records; local, state, and federal government records (including court and police records); and visits to websites. Put together and mined properly, this information could reveal not only your credit information but also your driving

TABLE 4.2

Technology Trends That Raise Ethical Issues

Trend	Impact
Computing power doubles every 18 months	More organizations depend on computer systems for critical operations and become more vulnerable to system failures.
Data storage costs rapidly decline	Organizations can easily maintain detailed databases on individuals. There are no limits on the data collected about you.
Data analysis advances	Companies can analyze vast quantities of data gathered on individuals to develop detailed profiles of individual behavior. Large-scale population surveillance is enabled.
Networking advances	The cost of moving data and making it accessible from anywhere falls exponentially. Access to data becomes more difficult to control.
Mobile device growth impact	Individual cell phones may be tracked without user consent or knowledge. The always-on device becomes a tether.

© Ivan Kruk/123RF

Credit card purchases can make personal information available to market researchers, telemarketers, and direct mail companies. Advances in information technology facilitate the invasion of privacy.

habits, your tastes, your associations, what you read and watch, and your political interests.

Companies purchase relevant personal information from these sources to help them more finely target their marketing campaigns. Chapters 6 and 11 describe how companies can analyze large pools of data from multiple sources to identify buying patterns of customers rapidly and suggest individual responses. The use of computers to combine data from multiple sources and create digital dossiers of detailed information on individuals is called **profiling**.

For example, several thousand of the most popular websites allow DoubleClick (owned by Google), an Internet advertising broker, to track the activities of their visitors in exchange for revenue from advertisements based on visitor information DoubleClick gathers. DoubleClick uses this information to create a profile of each online visitor, adding more detail to the profile as the visitor accesses an associated DoubleClick site. Over time, DoubleClick can create a detailed dossier of a person's spending and computing habits on the web that is sold to companies to help them target their web ads more precisely.

LexisNexis Risk Solutions (formerly ChoicePoint) gathers data from police, criminal, and motor vehicle records, credit and employment histories, current and previous addresses, professional licenses, and insurance claims to assemble and maintain dossiers on almost every adult in the United States. The company sells this personal information to businesses and government agencies. Demand for personal data is so enormous that data broker businesses such as Risk Solutions are flourishing. The two largest credit card networks, Visa Inc. and MasterCard Inc., have agreed to link credit card purchase information with consumer social network and other information to create customer profiles that could be sold to advertising firms.

A data analysis technology called **nonobvious relationship awareness (NORA)** has given both the government and the private sector even more powerful profiling capabilities. NORA can take information about people from many disparate sources, such as employment applications, telephone records, customer listings, and wanted lists, and correlate relationships to find obscure connections that might help identify criminals or terrorists (see Figure 4.2).

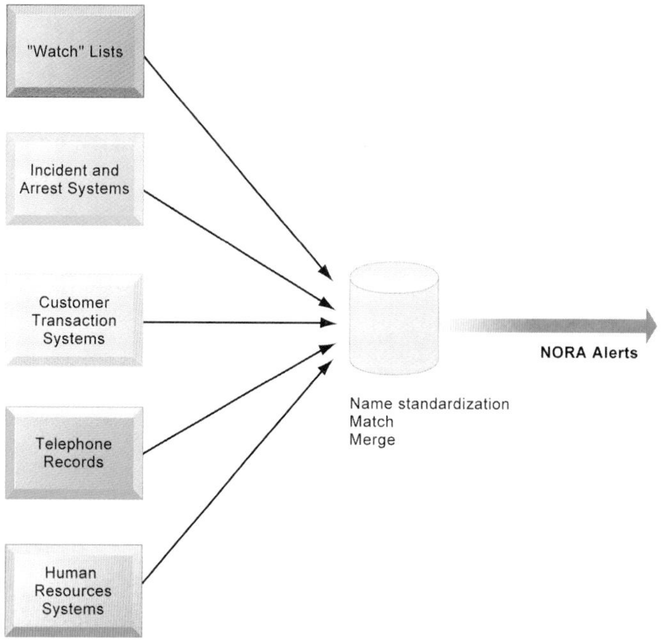

Figure 4.2 Nonobvious Relationship Awareness (NORA)
NORA technology can take information about people from disparate sources and find obscure, nonobvious relationships. It might discover, for example, that an applicant for a job at a casino shares a telephone number with a known criminal and issue an alert to the hiring manager.

NORA technology scans data and extracts information as the data are being generated so that it could, for example, instantly discover a man at an airline ticket counter who shares a phone number with a known terrorist before that person boards an airplane. The technology is considered a valuable tool for homeland security but does have privacy implications because it can provide such a detailed picture of the activities and associations of a single individual.

Finally, advances in networking, including the Internet, promise to reduce greatly the costs of moving and accessing large quantities of data and open the possibility of mining large pools of data remotely by using small desktop machines, mobile devices, and cloud servers, permitting an invasion of privacy on a scale and with a precision heretofore unimaginable.

4-2 What specific principles for conduct can be used to guide ethical decisions?

Ethics is a concern of humans who have freedom of choice. Ethics is about individual choice: When faced with alternative courses of action, what is the correct moral choice? What are the main features of ethical choice?

BASIC CONCEPTS: RESPONSIBILITY, ACCOUNTABILITY, AND LIABILITY

Ethical choices are decisions made by individuals who are responsible for the consequences of their actions. **Responsibility** is a key element of ethical action. Responsibility means that you accept the potential costs, duties, and obligations for the decisions you make. **Accountability** is a feature of systems and social institutions; it means that mechanisms are in place to determine who took action and who is responsible. Systems and institutions in which it is impossible to find out who took what action are inherently incapable of ethical analysis or ethical action. **Liability** extends the concept of responsibility further to the area of laws. Liability is a feature of political systems in which a body of laws is in place that permits individuals to recover the damages done to them by other actors, systems, or organizations. **Due process** is a related feature of law-governed societies and is a process in which laws are known and understood, and ability exists to appeal to higher authorities to ensure that the laws are applied correctly.

These basic concepts form the underpinning of an ethical analysis of information systems and those who manage them. First, information technologies are filtered through social institutions, organizations, and individuals. Systems do not have impacts by themselves. Whatever information system effects exist are products of institutional, organizational, and individual actions and behaviors. Second, responsibility for the consequences of technology falls clearly on the institutions, organizations, and individual managers who choose to use the technology. Using information technology in a socially responsible manner means that you can and will be held accountable for the consequences of your actions. Third, in an ethical, political society, individuals and others can recover damages done to them through a set of laws characterized by due process.

ETHICAL ANALYSIS

When confronted with a situation that seems to present ethical issues, how should you analyze it? The following five-step process should help:

1. *Identify and describe the facts clearly* Find out who did what to whom and where, when, and how. In many instances, you will be surprised at the errors in the initially reported facts, and often you will find that simply getting the facts straight helps define the solution. It also helps to get the opposing parties involved in an ethical dilemma to agree on the facts.
2. *Define the conflict or dilemma and identify the higher-order values involved* Ethical, social, and political issues always reference higher values. The parties to a dispute all claim to be pursuing higher values (e.g., freedom, privacy, protection of property, and the free enterprise system). Typically, an ethical issue involves a dilemma: two diametrically opposed courses of action that support worthwhile values. For example, the chapter-opening case study illustrates two competing values: the need to make organizations more efficient and cost-effective and the need to respect individual privacy.
3. *Identify the stakeholders* Every ethical, social, and political issue has stakeholders: players in the game who have an interest in the outcome, who have invested in the situation, and usually who have vocal opinions. Find out the identity of these groups and what they want. This will be useful later when designing a solution.
4. *Identify the options that you can reasonably take* You may find that none of the options satisfy all the interests involved but that some options do a better job than others. Sometimes arriving at a good or ethical solution may not always be a balancing of consequences to stakeholders.
5. *Identify the potential consequences of your options* Some options may be ethically correct but disastrous from other points of view. Other options may work in one instance but not in similar instances. Always ask yourself, "What if I choose this option consistently over time?"

CANDIDATE ETHICAL PRINCIPLES

Once your analysis is complete, what ethical principles or rules should you use to make a decision? What higher-order values should inform your judgment? Although you are the only one who can decide which among many ethical principles you will follow, and how you will prioritize them, it is helpful to consider some ethical principles with deep roots in many cultures that have survived throughout recorded history:

1. Do unto others as you would have them do unto you (the **Golden Rule**). Putting yourself in the place of others, and thinking of yourself as the object of the decision, can help you think about fairness in decision making.

2. If an action is not right for everyone to take, it is not right for anyone (**Immanuel Kant's categorical imperative**). Ask yourself, "If everyone did this, could the organization, or society, survive?"
3. If an action cannot be taken repeatedly, it is not right to take at all. This is the **slippery slope rule**: An action may bring about a small change now that is acceptable, but if it is repeated, it would bring unacceptable changes in the long run. In the vernacular, it might be stated as "once started down a slippery path, you may not be able to stop."
4. Take the action that achieves the higher or greater value (**utilitarian principle**). This rule assumes you can prioritize values in a rank order and understand the consequences of various courses of action.
5. Take the action that produces the least harm or the least potential cost (**risk aversion principle**). Some actions have extremely high failure costs of very low probability (e.g., building a nuclear generating facility in an urban area) or extremely high failure costs of moderate probability (speeding and automobile accidents). Avoid actions which have extremely high failure costs; focus on reducing the probability of accidents occurring.
6. Assume that virtually all tangible and intangible objects are owned by someone else unless there is a specific declaration otherwise. (This is the **ethical no-free-lunch rule**.) If something someone else has created is useful to you, it has value, and you should assume the creator wants compensation for this work.

Actions that do not easily pass these rules deserve close attention and a great deal of caution. The appearance of unethical behavior may do as much harm to you and your company as actual unethical behavior.

PROFESSIONAL CODES OF CONDUCT

When groups of people claim to be professionals, they take on special rights and obligations because of their special claims to knowledge, wisdom, and respect. Professional codes of conduct are promulgated by associations of professionals such as the American Medical Association (AMA), the American Bar Association (ABA), the Association of Information Technology Professionals (AITP), and the Association for Computing Machinery (ACM). These professional groups take responsibility for the partial regulation of their professions by determining entrance qualifications and competence. Codes of ethics are promises by professions to regulate themselves in the general interest of society. For example, avoiding harm to others, honoring property rights (including intellectual property), and respecting privacy are among the General Moral Imperatives of the ACM's Code of Ethics and Professional Conduct.

SOME REAL-WORLD ETHICAL DILEMMAS

Information systems have created new ethical dilemmas in which one set of interests is pitted against another. For example, many companies use voice recognition software to reduce the size of their customer support staff by enabling computers to recognize a customer's responses to a series of computerized questions. Many companies monitor what their employees are doing on the Internet to prevent them from wasting company resources on nonbusiness activities (see the Chapter 7 Interactive Session on People).

In each instance, you can find competing values at work, with groups lined up on either side of a debate. A company may argue, for example, that it has a right to use information systems to increase productivity and reduce the size of its workforce to lower costs and stay in business. Employees displaced by information systems may argue that employers have some responsibility for their welfare. Business owners might feel obligated to monitor employee email and Internet use to minimize drains on productivity. Employees might believe they should be able to use the Internet for short personal tasks in place of the telephone. A close analysis of the facts can sometimes produce compromised solutions that give each side half a loaf. Try to apply some of the principles of ethical analysis described to each of these cases. What is the right thing to do?

4-3 Why do contemporary information systems technology and the Internet pose challenges to the protection of individual privacy and intellectual property?

In this section, we take a closer look at the five moral dimensions of information systems first described in Figure 4.1. In each dimension, we identify the ethical, social, and political levels of analysis and use real-world examples to illustrate the values involved, the stakeholders, and the options chosen.

INFORMATION RIGHTS: PRIVACY AND FREEDOM IN THE INTERNET AGE

Privacy is the claim of individuals to be left alone, free from surveillance or interference from other individuals or organizations, including the state. Claims to privacy are also involved at the workplace. Millions of employees are subject to digital and other forms of high-tech surveillance. Information technology and systems threaten individual claims to privacy by making the invasion of privacy cheap, profitable, and effective.

The claim to privacy is protected in the United States, Canadian, and German constitutions in a variety of ways and in other countries through various statutes. In the United States, the claim to privacy is protected primarily by the First Amendment guarantees of freedom of speech and association, the Fourth Amendment protections against unreasonable search and seizure of one's personal documents or home, and the guarantee of due process.

Table 4.3 describes the major U.S. federal statutes that set forth the conditions for handling information about individuals in such areas as credit reporting, education,

TABLE 4.3

Federal Privacy Laws In The United States

General Federal Privacy Laws	Privacy Laws Affecting Private Institutions
Freedom of Information Act of 1966 as Amended (5 USC 552)	Fair Credit Reporting Act of 1970
Privacy Act of 1974 as Amended (5 USC 552a)	Family Educational Rights and Privacy Act of 1974
Electronic Communications Privacy Act of 1986	Right to Financial Privacy Act of 1978
Computer Matching and Privacy Protection Act of 1988	Privacy Protection Act of 1980
Computer Security Act of 1987	Cable Communications Policy Act of 1984
Federal Managers Financial Integrity Act of 1982	Electronic Communications Privacy Act of 1986
Driver's Privacy Protection Act of 1994	Video Privacy Protection Act of 1988
E-Government Act of 2002	The Health Insurance Portability and Accountability Act (HIPAA) of 1996
	Children's Online Privacy Protection Act (COPPA) of 1998
	Financial Modernization Act (Gramm-Leach-Bliley Act) of 1999

financial records, newspaper records, and electronic and digital communications. The Privacy Act of 1974 has been the most important of these laws, regulating the federal government's collection, use, and disclosure of information. At present, most U.S. federal privacy laws apply only to the federal government and regulate very few areas of the private sector.

Most American and European privacy law is based on a regime called **Fair Information Practices (FIP)** first set forth in a report written in 1973 by a federal government advisory committee and updated in 2010 to take into account new privacy-invading technology (U.S. Department of Health, Education, and Welfare, 1973). FIP is a set of principles governing the collection and use of information about individuals. FIP principles are based on the notion of a mutuality of interest between the record holder and the individual. The individual has an interest in engaging in a transaction, and the record keeper—usually a business or government agency—requires information about the individual to support the transaction. After information is gathered, the individual maintains an interest in the record, and the record may not be used to support other activities without the individual's consent. In 1998, the Federal Trade Commission (FTC) restated and extended the original FIP to provide guidelines for protecting online privacy. Table 4.4 describes the FTC's FIP principles.

The FTC's FIP principles are being used as guidelines to drive changes in privacy legislation. In July 1998, the U.S. Congress passed the Children's Online Privacy Protection Act (COPPA), requiring websites to obtain parental permission before collecting information on children under the age of 13. The FTC has recommended additional legislation to protect online consumer privacy in advertising networks that collect records of consumer web activity to develop detailed profiles, which other companies then use to target online ads. In 2010, the FTC added three practices to its framework for privacy. Firms should adopt privacy by design, building products and services that protect privacy, firms should increase the transparency of their data practices, and firms should require consumer consent and provide clear options to opt out of data collection schemes (FTC, 2012). Other proposed Internet privacy legislation focuses on protecting the online use of personal identification numbers, such as social security numbers; protecting personal information collected on the Internet that deals with individuals not covered by COPPA; and limiting the use of data mining for homeland security. In 2015 the FTC was researching new guidance for the protection of privacy and the Internet of Things (IoT), and mobile health apps. (Federal Trade Commission, 2015).

TABLE 4.4

Federal Trade Commission Fair Information Practice Principles

Notice/awareness (core principle). Websites must disclose their information practices before collecting data. Includes identification of collector; uses of data; other recipients of data; nature of collection (active/inactive); voluntary or required status; consequences of refusal; and steps taken to protect confidentiality, integrity, and quality of the data.
Choice/consent (core principle). A choice regime must be in place allowing consumers to choose how their information will be used for secondary purposes other than supporting the transaction, including internal use and transfer to third parties.
Access/participation. Consumers should be able to review and contest the accuracy and completeness of data collected about them in a timely, inexpensive process.
Security. Data collectors must take responsible steps to ensure that consumer information is accurate and secure from unauthorized use.
Enforcement. A mechanism must be in place to enforce FIP principles. This can involve self-regulation, legislation giving consumers legal remedies for violations, or federal statutes and regulations.

In 2012, the FTC extended its FIP doctrine to address the issue of behavioral targeting. The online advertising trade group Network Advertising Initiative (discussed later in this section) published its own self-regulatory principles that largely agreed with the FTC. Nevertheless, the government, privacy groups, and the online ad industry are still at loggerheads over two issues. Privacy advocates want both an opt-in policy at all sites and a national Do Not Track list. The industry opposes these moves and continues to insist that an opt-out capability is the only way to avoid tracking. Nevertheless, there is an emerging consensus among all parties that greater transparency and user control (especially making opting out of tracking the default option) is required to deal with behavioral tracking. Public opinion polls show an ongoing distrust of online marketers. Although there are many studies of privacy issues at the federal level, there has been no significant legislation in recent years. A 2016 survey by the Pew Research Center found that 91 percent of Americans feel consumers have lost control of their personal information online and 86 percent have taken steps to protect their information online.

Privacy protections have also been added to recent laws deregulating financial services and safeguarding the maintenance and transmission of health information about individuals. The Gramm-Leach-Bliley Act of 1999, which repeals earlier restrictions on affiliations among banks, securities firms, and insurance companies, includes some privacy protection for consumers of financial services. All financial institutions are required to disclose their policies and practices for protecting the privacy of nonpublic personal information and to allow customers to opt out of information-sharing arrangements with nonaffiliated third parties.

The Health Insurance Portability and Accountability Act (HIPAA) of 1996, which took effect on April 14, 2003, includes privacy protection for medical records. The law gives patients access to their personal medical records that healthcare providers, hospitals, and health insurers maintain and the right to authorize how protected information about themselves can be used or disclosed. Doctors, hospitals, and other healthcare providers must limit the disclosure of personal information about patients to the minimum amount necessary to achieve a given purpose.

The European Directive on Data Protection

In Europe, privacy protection is much more stringent than in the United States. Unlike the United States, European countries do not allow businesses to use personally identifiable information without consumer's prior consent. On October 25, 1998, the European Commission's Directive on Data Protection went into effect, requiring companies in European Union (EU) nations to inform people when they collect information about them and disclose how it will be stored and used. Customers must provide their **informed consent** before any company can legally use data about them, and they have the right to access that information, correct it, and request that no further data be collected. Informed consent can be defined as consent given with knowledge of all the facts needed to make a rational decision. EU member nations must translate these principles into their own laws and cannot transfer personal data to countries, such as the United States, that do not have similar privacy protection regulations. In 2009, the European Parliament passed new rules governing the use of third-party cookies for behavioral tracking purposes. These new rules require website visitors to give explicit consent to be tracked by cookies and websites to have highly visible warnings on their pages if third-party cookies are being used (European Parliament, 2009).

In January 2012, the EU issued changed its data protection rules to apply to all companies providing services in Europe and require Internet companies such as Amazon, Facebook, Apple, Google, and others to obtain explicit consent from consumers about the use of their personal data, delete information at the user's request, and retain information only as long as absolutely necessary. In 2014, the European

Parliament extended greater control to Internet users by establishing the "right to be forgotten," which gives EU citizens the right to ask Google and social network sites to remove their personal information. Although the privacy policies of U.S. firms (in contrast to the government's) are largely voluntary, in Europe, corporate privacy policies are mandated and more consistent across jurisdictions.

Working with the European Commission, the U.S. Department of Commerce developed a safe harbor framework for U.S. firms. A **safe harbor** is a private, self-regulating policy and enforcement mechanism that meets the objectives of government regulators and legislation but does not involve government regulation or enforcement. U.S. businesses would be allowed to use personal data from EU countries if they develop privacy protection policies that meet EU standards. Enforcement would occur in the United States by using self-policing, regulation, and government enforcement of fair trade statutes.

In June 2015, the European Council approved a new EU General Data Protection Regulation (GDPR) to replace the existing Data Protection Directive. The concept of safe harbor was replaced by a policy called **Privacy Shield**. When it takes effect, the GDPR will apply across all EU countries, rather than the current situation where each member-state regulates privacy matters within its own borders. The GDPR will apply to any firm operating in any EU country, require unambiguous consent to use personal data for purposes like tracking individuals across the web, and limit the ability to use data for purposes other than those for which it was collected (such as constructing user profiles). It will also strengthen the right to be forgotten by allowing individuals to remove personal data from social platforms like Facebook and prevent such companies from collecting any new information. Companies operating in the EU will have to delete personal information once it no longer serves the purpose for which it was collected (European Commission, 2016).

In the end, the Privacy Shield places stronger obligations on U.S. companies to comply with EU privacy protections while still allowing data on EU citizens to be processed and used in the United States.

The current privacy environment has turned decidedly against American firms like Facebook, Google, and others whose business model requires nearly unfettered use of personal information to support advertising revenues. Five EU nations—the Netherlands, Germany, France, Spain, and Belgium—have initiated a series of coordinated investigations into these firms' privacy and data policies.

Internet Challenges to Privacy

Internet technology has posed new challenges for the protection of individual privacy. Websites track searches that have been conducted, the websites and web pages visited, the online content a person has accessed, and what items that person has inspected or purchased over the web. This monitoring and tracking of website visitors occurs in the background without the visitor's knowledge. It is conducted not just by individual websites but by advertising networks such as Microsoft Advertising, Yahoo, and Google's DoubleClick that are capable of tracking personal browsing behavior across thousands of websites. Both website publishers and the advertising industry defend tracking of individuals across the web because doing so allows more relevant ads to be targeted to users, and it pays for the cost of publishing websites. In this sense, it's like broadcast television: advertiser-supported content that is free to the user. The commercial demand for this personal information is virtually insatiable. However, these practices also impinge on individual privacy.

Cookies are small text files deposited on a computer hard drive when a user visits websites. Cookies identify the visitor's web browser software and track visits to the website. When the visitor returns to a site that has stored a cookie, the website software searches the visitor's computer, finds the cookie, and knows what that person has done in the past. It may also update the cookie, depending on the activity

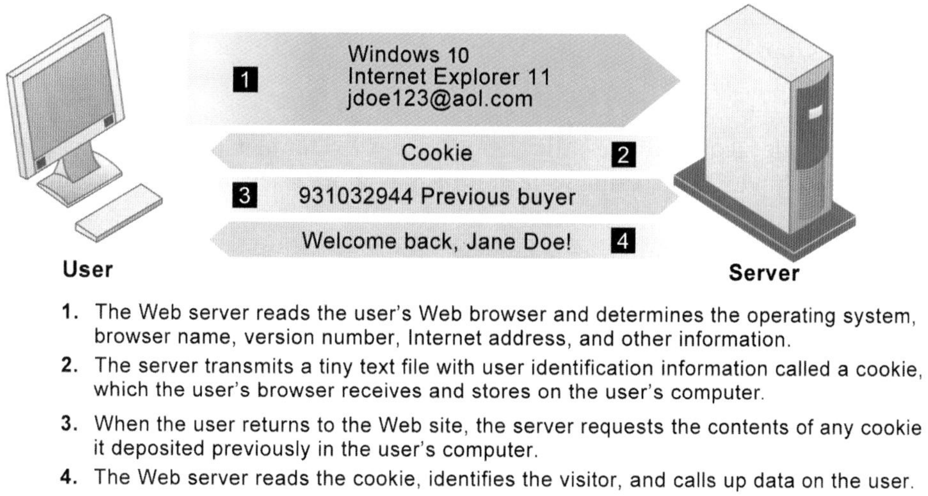

Windows 10
Internet Explorer 11
jdoe123@aol.com
1
Cookie
2
3
931032944 Previous buyer
Welcome back, Jane Doe!
4
User
Server
1. The Web server reads the user's Web browser and determines the operating system, browser name, version number, Internet address, and other information.
2. The server transmits a tiny text file with user identification information called a cookie, which the user's browser receives and stores on the user's computer.
3. When the user returns to the Web site, the server requests the contents of any cookie it deposited previously in the user's computer.
4. The Web server reads the cookie, identifies the visitor, and calls up data on the user.

Figure 4.3
How Cookies Identify Web Visitors
Cookies are written by a website on a visitor's computer. When the visitor returns to that website, the web server requests the ID number from the cookie and uses it to access the data stored by that server on that visitor. The website can then use these data to display personalized information.

during the visit. In this way, the site can customize its content for each visitor's interests. For example, if you purchase a book on Amazon.com and return later from the same browser, the site will welcome you by name and recommend other books of interest based on your past purchases. DoubleClick, described earlier in this chapter, uses cookies to build its dossiers with details of online purchases and examine the behavior of website visitors. Figure 4.3 illustrates how cookies work.

Websites using cookie technology cannot directly obtain visitors' names and addresses. However, if a person has registered at a site, that information can be combined with cookie data to identify the visitor. Website owners can also combine the data they have gathered from cookies and other website monitoring tools with personal data from other sources, such as offline data collected from surveys or paper catalog purchases, to develop very detailed profiles of their visitors.

There are now even more subtle and surreptitious tools for surveillance of Internet users. **Web beacons**, also called *web bugs* (or simply tracking files), are tiny software programs that keep a record of users' online clickstreams. They report this data back to whomever owns the tracking file invisibly embedded in email messages and web pages that are designed to monitor the behavior of the user visiting a website or sending email. Web beacons are placed on popular websites by third-party firms who pay the websites a fee for access to their audience. So how common is web tracking? In a path-breaking series of articles in the *Wall Street Journal*, researchers examined the tracking files on 50 of the most popular U.S websites. What they found revealed a very widespread surveillance system. On the 50 sites, they discovered 3,180 tracking files installed on visitor computers. Only one site, Wikipedia, had no tracking files. Two-thirds of the tracking files came from 131 companies whose primary business is identifying and tracking Internet users to create consumer profiles that can be sold to advertising firms looking for specific types of customers. The biggest trackers were Google, Microsoft, and Quantcast, all of whom are in the business of selling ads to advertising firms and marketers. A follow-up study found tracking on the 50 most popular sites had risen nearly fivefold due to the growth of online ad auctions where advertisers buy the data about users' web-browsing behavior.

Other **spyware** can secretly install itself on an Internet user's computer by piggybacking on larger applications. Once installed, the spyware calls out to websites to send banner ads and other unsolicited material to the user, and it can report the user's movements on the Internet to other computers. More information is available about intrusive software in Chapter 8.

Nearly 80 percent of global Internet users use Google Search and other Google services, making Google the world's largest collector of online user data. Whatever

Google does with its data has an enormous impact on online privacy. Most experts believe that Google possesses the largest collection of personal information in the world—more data on more people than any government agency. The nearest competitor is Facebook.

After Google acquired the advertising network DoubleClick in 2007, Google began using behavioral targeting to help it display more relevant ads based on users' search activities and to target individuals as they move from one site to another to show them display or banner ads. Google allows tracking software on its search pages, and using DoubleClick, it can track users across the Internet. One of its programs enables advertisers to target ads based on the search histories of Google users, along with any other information the user submits to Google such as age, demographics, region, and other web activities (such as blogging). Google's AdSense program enables Google to help advertisers select keywords and design ads for various market segments based on search histories such as helping a clothing website create and test ads targeted at teenage females. Google now displays targeted ads on YouTube and Google mobile applications, and its DoubleClick ad network serves up targeted banner ads.

The United States has allowed businesses to gather transaction information generated in the marketplace and then use that information for other marketing purposes without obtaining the informed consent of the individual whose information is being used. These firms argue that when users agree to the sites' terms of service, they are also agreeing to allow the site to collect information about their online activities. An **opt-out** model of informed consent permits the collection of personal information until the consumer specifically requests the data not to be collected. Privacy advocates would like to see wider use of an **opt-in** model of informed consent in which a business is prohibited from collecting any personal information unless the consumer specifically takes action to approve information collection and use. Here, the default option is no collection of user information.

The online industry has preferred self-regulation to privacy legislation for protecting consumers. The online advertising industry formed the Online Privacy Alliance to encourage self-regulation to develop a set of privacy guidelines for its members. Members of the advertising network industry, including Google's DoubleClick, have created an additional industry association called the Network Advertising Initiative (NAI) to develop its own privacy policies to help consumers opt out of advertising network programs and provide consumers redress from abuses.

Individual firms such as Microsoft, Mozilla Foundation, Yahoo, and Google have recently adopted policies on their own in an effort to address public concern about tracking people online. Microsoft's Internet Explorer 11 web browser was released in 2015 with the opt-out option as the default, but by 2016 Microsoft removed this feature in large part because most websites ignore the request to opt out. Other browsers have opt-out options, but users need to turn them on, and most users fail to do this. AOL established an opt-out policy that allows users of its site to choose not to be tracked. Yahoo follows NAI guidelines and allows opt-out for tracking and web beacons (web bugs). Google has reduced retention time for tracking data.

In general, most Internet businesses do little to protect the privacy of their customers, and consumers do not do as much as they should to protect themselves. For commercial websites that depend on advertising to support themselves, most revenue derives from selling customer information. Of the companies that do post privacy policies on their websites, about half do not monitor their sites to ensure that they adhere to these policies. The vast majority of online customers claim they are concerned about online privacy, but fewer than half read the privacy statements on websites. In general, website privacy policies require a law degree to understand and are ambiguous about key terms (Laudon and Traver, 2018). Today, what firms such as Facebook and Google call a privacy policy is in fact a data use policy. The concept of privacy is associated with consumer rights, which firms do not wish to recognize.

A data use policy simply tells customers how the information will be used without any mention of rights.

A group of students at the University of California at Berkeley conducted surveys of online users and of complaints filed with the FTC involving privacy issues. Some of their results show that people feel they have no control over the information collected about them, and they don't know to whom to complain. Websites collect all this information but do not let users have access, the website policies are unclear, and they share data with affiliates but never identify who the affiliates are and how many there are. Web bug trackers are ubiquitous, and users are not informed of trackers on the pages they visit. The results of this study and others suggest that consumers want some controls on what personal information can be collected, what is done with the information, and the ability to opt out of the entire tracking enterprise. (The full report is available at knowprivacy.org.)

Technical Solutions

In addition to legislation, there are a few technologies that can protect user privacy during interactions with websites. Many of these tools are used for encrypting email, for making email or surfing activities appear anonymous, for preventing client computers from accepting cookies, or for detecting and eliminating spyware. For the most part, technical solutions have failed to protect users from being tracked as they move from one site to another.

Many browsers have Do Not Track options. For users who have selected the Do Not Track browser option, their browser will send a request to websites requesting the user's behavior not be tracked, but websites are not obligated to honor their visitors' requests not to be tracked. There is no online advertising industry agreement on how to respond to Do Not Track requests nor, currently, any legislation requiring websites to stop tracking. Private browser encryption software or apps on mobile devices provide consumers a powerful opportunity to at least keep their messages private.

PROPERTY RIGHTS: INTELLECTUAL PROPERTY

Contemporary information systems have severely challenged existing laws and social practices that protect **intellectual property**. Intellectual property is considered to be tangible and intangible products of the mind created by individuals or corporations. Information technology has made it difficult to protect intellectual property because computerized information can be so easily copied or distributed on networks. Intellectual property is subject to a variety of protections under four legal traditions: copyright, patents, trademarks, and trade secrets.

Copyright

Copyright is a statutory grant that protects creators of intellectual property from having their work copied by others for any purpose during the life of the author plus an additional 70 years after the author's death. For corporate-owned works, copyright protection lasts for 95 years after their initial creation. Congress has extended copyright protection to books, periodicals, lectures, dramas, musical compositions, maps, drawings, artwork of any kind, and motion pictures. The intent behind copyright laws has been to encourage creativity and authorship by ensuring that creative people receive the financial and other benefits of their work. Most industrial nations have their own copyright laws, and there are several international conventions and bilateral agreements through which nations coordinate and enforce their laws.

In the mid-1960s, the Copyright Office began registering software programs, and in 1980, Congress passed the Computer Software Copyright Act, which clearly provides protection for software program code and copies of the original sold in commerce; it sets forth the rights of the purchaser to use the software while the creator retains legal title.

Copyright protects against copying entire programs or their parts. Damages and relief are readily obtained for infringement. The drawback to copyright protection is that the underlying ideas behind a work are not protected, only their manifestation in a work. A competitor can use your software, understand how it works, and build new software that follows the same concepts without infringing on a copyright.

Look-and-feel copyright infringement lawsuits are precisely about the distinction between an idea and its expression. For instance, in the early 1990s, Apple Computer sued Microsoft Corporation and Hewlett-Packard for infringement of the expression of Apple's Macintosh interface, claiming that the defendants copied the expression of overlapping windows. The defendants countered that the idea of overlapping windows can be expressed only in a single way and, therefore, was not protectable under the merger doctrine of copyright law. When ideas and their expression merge, the expression cannot be copyrighted.

In general, courts appear to be following the reasoning of a 1989 case—*Brown Bag Software v. Symantec Corp*—in which the court dissected the elements of software alleged to be infringing. The court found that similar concept, function, general functional features (e.g., drop-down menus), and colors are not protectable by copyright law (*Brown Bag Software v. Symantec Corp.,* 1992).

Patents

A **patent** grants the owner an exclusive monopoly on the ideas behind an invention for 20 years. The congressional intent behind patent law was to ensure that inventors of new machines, devices, or methods receive the full financial and other rewards of their labor and yet make widespread use of the invention possible by providing detailed diagrams for those wishing to use the idea under license from the patent's owner. The granting of a patent is determined by the United States Patent and Trademark Office and relies on court rulings.

The key concepts in patent law are originality, novelty, and invention. The Patent Office did not accept applications for software patents routinely until a 1981 Supreme Court decision that held that computer programs could be part of a patentable process. Since that time, hundreds of patents have been granted, and thousands await consideration.

The strength of patent protection is that it grants a monopoly on the underlying concepts and ideas of software. The difficulty is passing stringent criteria of nonobviousness (e.g., the work must reflect some special understanding and contribution), originality, and novelty as well as years of waiting to receive protection.

In what some call the patent trial of the century, in 2011, Apple sued Samsung for violating its patents for iPhones, iPads, and iPods. On August 24, 2012, a California jury in federal district court delivered a decisive victory to Apple and a stunning defeat to Samsung. The jury awarded Apple $1 billion in damages. The decision established criteria for determining just how close a competitor can come to an industry-leading and standard-setting product like Apple's iPhone before it violates the design and utility patents of the leading firm. The same court ruled that Samsung could not sell its new tablet computer (Galaxy 10.1) in the United States. In a later patent dispute, Samsung won an infringement case against Apple. In June 2013, the United States International Trade Commission issued a ban for a handful of older iPhone and iPad devices because they violated Samsung patents from years ago. In 2014, Apple sued Samsung again, claiming infringement of five patents. The patents cover hardware and software techniques for handling photos, videos, and lists used on the popular Galaxy 5. Apple sought $2 billion in damages. In 2015, the U.S. Court of Appeals reaffirmed that Samsung had copied specific design patents, but dropped the damages Apple was granted to $930 million.

To make matters more complicated, Apple has been one of Samsung's largest customers for flash memory processors, graphic chips, solid-state drives, and display parts that are used in Apple's iPhones, iPads, iPod Touch devices, and MacBooks. The Samsung and Apple patent cases are indicative of the complex relationships among the leading computer firms.

Trademarks

Trademarks are the marks, symbols, and images used to distinguish products in the marketplace. Trademark laws protect consumers in the marketplace by ensuring they receive what they paid for. These laws also protect the investments that firms have made to bring products to market. Typical trademark infringement violations occur when one firm appropriates or pirates the marks of a competing firm. Infringement also occurs when firms dilute the value of another firm's marks by weakening the connection between a mark and the product. For instance, if a search engine firm copies the trademarked Google icon, colors, and images, it would be infringing on Google's trademarks. It would also be diluting the connection between the Google search service, and its trademarks, potentially creating confusion in the marketplace.

Trade Secrets

Any intellectual work product—a formula, device, pattern, or compilation of data—used for a business purpose can be classified as a **trade secret**, provided it is not based on information in the public domain. Protections for trade secrets vary from state to state. In general, trade secret laws grant a monopoly on the ideas behind a work product, but it can be a very tenuous monopoly.

Software that contains novel or unique elements, procedures, or compilations can be included as a trade secret. Trade secret law protects the actual ideas in a work product, not only their manifestation. To make this claim, the creator or owner must take care to bind employees and customers with nondisclosure agreements and prevent the secret from falling into the public domain.

The limitation of trade secret protection is that, although virtually all software programs of any complexity contain unique elements of some sort, it is difficult to prevent the ideas in the work from falling into the public domain when the software is widely distributed.

Challenges to Intellectual Property Rights

Contemporary information technologies, especially software, pose severe challenges to existing intellectual property regimes and, therefore, create significant ethical, social, and political issues. Digital media differ from books, periodicals, and other media in terms of ease of replication; ease of transmission; ease of alteration; compactness—making theft easy; and difficulties in establishing uniqueness.

The proliferation of digital networks, including the Internet, has made it even more difficult to protect intellectual property. Before widespread use of networks, copies of software, books, magazine articles, or films had to be stored on physical media, such as paper, computer disks, or videotape, creating some hurdles to distribution. Using networks, information can be more widely reproduced and distributed. The BSA Global Software Survey conducted by International Data Corporation and The Software Alliance (also known as BSA) reported that the rate of global software piracy was 39 percent in 2016 (The Software Alliance, 2017).

The Internet was designed to transmit information freely around the world, including copyrighted information. You can easily copy and distribute virtually anything to millions of people worldwide, even if they are using different types of computer systems. Information can be illicitly copied from one place and distributed through other systems and networks even though these parties do not willingly participate in the infringement.

Individuals have been illegally copying and distributing digitized music files on the Internet for several decades. File-sharing services such as Napster and, later, Grokster, Kazaa, Morpheus, Megaupload, and The Pirate Bay sprang up to help users locate and swap digital music and video files, including those protected by copyright. Illegal file sharing became so widespread that it threatened the viability of the music recording industry and, at one point, consumed 20 percent of Internet bandwidth. The recording industry won several legal battles for shutting these services down, but it has not been able to halt illegal file sharing entirely. The motion picture and cable television industries are waging similar battles. Several European nations have worked with U.S. authorities to shut down illegal sharing sites, with mixed results.

As legitimate online music stores such as iTunes and streaming services such as Pandora expanded, illegal file sharing significantly declined. The Apple iTunes Store legitimated paying for music and entertainment and created a closed environment from which music and videos could not be easily copied and widely distributed unless played on Apple devices. Amazon's Kindle also protects the rights of publishers and writers because its books cannot be copied to the Internet and distributed. Streaming of Internet radio, on services such as Pandora and Spotify, and Hollywood movies (at sites such as Hulu and Netflix) also inhibits piracy because the streams cannot be easily recorded on separate devices and videos can be downloaded so easily. Despite these gains in legitimate online music platforms, artists and record labels have experienced a 50 percent decline in revenues and the loss of thousands of jobs since 2000.

The **Digital Millennium Copyright Act (DMCA)** of 1998 also provides some copyright protection. The DMCA implemented a World Intellectual Property Organization Treaty that makes it illegal to circumvent technology-based protections of copyrighted materials. Internet service providers (ISPs) are required to take down sites of copyright infringers they are hosting when the ISPs are notified of the problem. Microsoft and other major software and information content firms are represented by the Software and Information Industry Association (SIIA), which lobbies for new laws and enforcement of existing laws to protect intellectual property around the world. The SIIA runs an antipiracy hotline for individuals to report piracy activities, offers educational programs to help organizations combat software piracy, and has published guidelines for employee use of software.

4-4 How have information systems affected laws for establishing accountability and liability and the quality of everyday life?

Along with privacy and property laws, new information technologies are challenging existing liability laws and social practices for holding individuals and institutions accountable. If a person is injured by a machine controlled, in part, by software, who should be held accountable and, therefore, held liable? Should a social network site like Facebook or Twitter be held liable and accountable for the posting of pornographic material or racial insults, or should it be held harmless against any liability for what users post (as is true of common carriers, such as the telephone system)? What about the Internet? If you outsource your information processing to the cloud, and the cloud provider fails to provide adequate service, what can you do? Cloud providers often claim the software you are using is the problem, not the cloud servers.

COMPUTER-RELATED LIABILITY PROBLEMS

In late 2013 hackers obtained credit card, debit card, and additional personal information about 70 to 110 million customers of Target, one of the largest U.S. retailers. Target's sales and reputation took an immediate hit from which it has still not completely recovered. Target says it has spent over $60 million to strengthen its systems. In 2015, Target agreed to pay $10 million to customers and $19 million to MasterCard. It has paid an even greater price through the loss of sales and trust.

Who is liable for any economic harm caused to individuals or businesses whose credit cards were compromised? Is Target responsible for allowing the breach to occur despite efforts it did make to secure the information? Or is this just a cost of doing business in a credit card world where customers and businesses have insurance policies to protect them against losses? Customers, for instance, have a maximum liability of $50 for credit card theft under federal banking law.

Are information system managers responsible for the harm that corporate systems can do? Beyond IT managers, insofar as computer software is part of a machine, and the machine injures someone physically or economically, the producer of the software and the operator can be held liable for damages. Insofar as the software acts like a book, storing and displaying information, courts have been reluctant to hold authors, publishers, and booksellers liable for contents (the exception being instances of fraud or defamation); hence, courts have been wary of holding software authors liable for software.

In general, it is very difficult (if not impossible) to hold software producers liable for their software products that are considered to be like books, regardless of the physical or economic harm that results. Historically, print publishers of books and periodicals have not been held liable because of fears that liability claims would interfere with First Amendment rights guaranteeing freedom of expression. The kind of harm software failures cause is rarely fatal and typically inconveniences users but does not physically harm them (the exception being medical devices).

What about software as a service? ATMs are a service provided to bank customers. If this service fails, customers will be inconvenienced and perhaps harmed economically if they cannot access their funds in a timely manner. Should liability protections be extended to software publishers and operators of defective financial, accounting, simulation, or marketing systems?

Software is very different from books. Software users may develop expectations of infallibility about software; software is less easily inspected than a book, and it is more difficult to compare with other software products for quality; software claims to perform a task rather than describe a task, as a book does; and people come to depend on services essentially based on software. Given the centrality of software to everyday life, the chances are excellent that liability law will extend its reach to include software even when the software merely provides an information service.

Telephone systems have not been held liable for the messages transmitted because they are regulated common carriers. In return for their right to provide telephone service, they must provide access to all, at reasonable rates, and achieve acceptable reliability. Likewise, cable networks are considered private networks not subject to regulation, but broadcasters using the public airwaves are subject to a wide variety of federal and local constraints on content and facilities. In the United States, with few exceptions, websites are not held liable for content posted on their sites regardless of whether it was placed there by the website owners or users.

SYSTEM QUALITY: DATA QUALITY AND SYSTEM ERRORS

White Christmas turned into a blackout for millions of Netflix customers and social network users on December 24, 2012. The blackout was caused by the failure of Amazon's cloud computing service (AWS), which provides storage and computing power for all kinds of websites and services, including Netflix. The loss of service lasted for a day. Amazon blamed it on elastic load balancing, a software program that balances the loads on all its cloud servers to prevent overload. Amazon's cloud computing services have had several subsequent outages, although not as long-lasting as the Christmas Eve outage. In September 2016 AWS experienced a major five-hour outage again. Outages at cloud computing services are rare but recurring. These outages have called into question the reliability and quality of cloud services. Are these outages acceptable?

The debate over liability and accountability for unintentional consequences of system use raises a related but independent moral dimension: What is an acceptable, technologically feasible level of system quality? At what point should system managers say, "Stop testing, we've done all we can to perfect this software. Ship it!" Individuals and organizations may be held responsible for avoidable and foreseeable consequences, which they have a duty to perceive and correct. The gray area is that some system errors are foreseeable and correctable only at very great expense, expense so great that pursuing this level of perfection is not feasible economically—no one could afford the product.

For example, although software companies try to debug their products before releasing them to the marketplace, they knowingly ship buggy products because the time and cost of fixing all minor errors would prevent these products from ever being released. What if the product was not offered on the marketplace? Would social welfare as a whole falter and perhaps even decline? Carrying this further, just what is the responsibility of a producer of computer services—should it withdraw the product that can never be perfect, warn the user, or forget about the risk (let the buyer beware)?

Three principal sources of poor system performance are (1) software bugs and errors, (2) hardware or facility failures caused by natural or other causes, and (3) poor input data quality. The Chapter 8 Learning Track discusses why zero defects in software code of any complexity cannot be achieved and why the seriousness of remaining bugs cannot be estimated. Hence, there is a technological barrier to perfect software, and users must be aware of the potential for catastrophic failure. The software industry has not yet arrived at testing standards for producing software of acceptable but imperfect performance.

Although software bugs and facility catastrophes are likely to be widely reported in the press, by far the most common source of business system failure is data quality (see Chapter 6). Few companies routinely measure the quality of their data, but individual organizations report data error rates ranging from 0.5 to 30 percent.

QUALITY OF LIFE: EQUITY, ACCESS, AND BOUNDARIES

The negative social costs of introducing information technologies and systems are beginning to mount along with the power of the technology. Many of these negative social consequences are not violations of individual rights or property crimes. Nevertheless, they can be extremely harmful to individuals, societies, and political institutions. Computers and information technologies potentially can destroy valuable elements of our culture and society even while they bring us benefits. If there is a balance of good and bad consequences of using information systems, who do we hold responsible for the bad consequences? Next, we briefly examine some of the negative social consequences of systems, considering individual, social, and political responses.

Balancing Power: Center Versus Periphery

An early fear of the computer age was that huge, centralized mainframe computers would centralize power in the nation's capital, resulting in a Big Brother society, as was suggested in George Orwell's novel *1984*. The shift toward highly decentralized client–server computing, coupled with an ideology of empowerment of Twitter and social media users, and the decentralization of decision making to lower organizational levels, up until recently reduced the fears of power centralization in government institutions. Yet much of the empowerment described in popular business magazines is trivial. Lower-level employees may be empowered to make minor decisions, but the key policy decisions may be as centralized as in the past. At the same time, corporate Internet behemoths such as Google, Apple, Yahoo, Amazon, and Microsoft have come to dominate the collection and analysis of personal private information of all citizens. Since the terrorist attacks against the United States on September 11, 2001, the federal government has greatly expanded its use of this private sector information under the authority of the Patriot Act of 2001 and subsequent and secret executive orders. In this sense, the power of information has become more centralized in the hands of a few private oligopolies and large government agencies.

Rapidity of Change: Reduced Response Time to Competition

Information systems have helped to create much more efficient national and international markets. Today's more efficient global marketplace has reduced the normal social buffers that permitted businesses many years to adjust to competition. Time-based competition has an ugly side; the business you work for may not have enough time to respond to global competitors and may be wiped out in a year along with your job. We stand the risk of developing a just-in-time society with just-in-time jobs and just-in-time workplaces, families, and vacations. One impact of Uber (see Chapter 10) and other on-demand services firms is to create just-in-time jobs with no benefits or insurance for employees.

Maintaining Boundaries: Family, Work, and Leisure

The danger of ubiquitous computing, telecommuting, nomad computing, mobile computing, and the do-anything-anywhere computing environment is that it is actually coming true. The traditional boundaries that separate work from family and just plain leisure have been weakened.

Although writers have traditionally worked just about anywhere, the advent of information systems, coupled with the growth of knowledge-work occupations, means that more and more people are working when traditionally they would have been playing or communicating with family and friends. The work umbrella now extends far beyond the eight-hour day into commuting time, vacation time, and leisure time. The explosive growth and use of smartphones have only heightened the sense of many employees that they are never away from work.

Although some people enjoy the convenience of working at home, the do-anything-anywhere computing environment can blur the traditional boundaries between work and family time.

Even leisure time spent on the computer threatens these close social relationships. Extensive Internet and cell phone use, even for entertainment or recreational purposes, takes people away from their family and friends. Among middle school and teenage children, it can lead to harmful antisocial behavior, such as the recent upsurge in cyberbullying.

Weakening these institutions poses clear-cut risks. Family and friends historically have provided powerful support mechanisms for individuals, and they act as balance points in a society by preserving private life, providing a place for people to collect their thoughts, think in ways contrary to their employer, and dream.

Dependence and Vulnerability

Today, our businesses, governments, schools, and private associations, such as churches, are incredibly dependent on information systems and are, therefore, highly vulnerable if these systems fail. Think of what would happen if the nation's electric power grid shut down, with no backup structure to make up for the loss of the system. With systems now as ubiquitous as the telephone system, it is startling to remember that there are no regulatory or standard-setting forces in place that are similar to telephone, electrical, radio, television, or other public utility technologies. The absence of standards and the criticality of some system applications will probably call forth demands for national standards and perhaps regulatory oversight.

Computer Crime and Abuse

New technologies, including computers, create new opportunities for committing crime by creating new, valuable items to steal, new ways to steal them, and new ways to harm others. **Computer crime** is the commission of illegal acts by using a computer or against a computer system. Simply accessing a computer system without authorization or with intent to do harm, even by accident, is now a federal crime. The most frequent types of incidents comprise a greatest hits list of cybercrime: malware, phishing, network interruption, spyware, and denial of service attacks (PwC, 2016). The true cost of all computer crime is unknown, but it is estimated to be in the billions of dollars. You can find a more detailed discussion of computer crime in Chapter 8.

Computer abuse is the commission of acts involving a computer that may not be illegal but are considered unethical. The popularity of the Internet. email, and mobile phones has turned one form of computer abuse—spamming—into a serious problem for both individuals and businesses. Originally, **spam** was junk email an organization or individual sent to a mass audience of Internet users who had expressed no interest in the product or service being marketed. Spammers tend to market pornography, fraudulent deals and services, outright scams, and other products not widely approved in most civilized societies. Some countries have passed laws to outlaw spamming or restrict its use. In the United States, it is still legal if it does not involve fraud and the sender and subject of the email are properly identified.

Spamming has mushroomed because it costs only a few cents to send thousands of messages advertising wares to Internet users. The percentage of all email that is spam was estimated at around 58 percent in 2016 (Kaspersky Lab, 2017). About 20 percent of spam is made up of phishing attacks on firms and individuals. Most spam originates from bot networks, which consist of thousands of captured PCs that can initiate and relay spam messages. Spam costs for businesses are very high (estimated at more than $50 billion per year) because of the computing and network resources billions of unwanted email messages and the time required to deal with them consume.

Identity and financial-theft cybercriminals are targeting smartphones as users check email, do online banking, pay bills, and reveal personal information. Cell phone spam usually comes in the form of SMS text messages, but increasingly, users are receiving spam in their Facebook Newsfeed and messaging service as well.

ISPs and individuals can combat spam by using spam filtering software to block suspicious email before it enters a recipient's email inbox. However, spam filters may block legitimate messages. Spammers know how to skirt filters by continually changing their email accounts, by incorporating spam messages in images, by embedding spam in email attachments and digital greeting cards, and by using other people's computers that have been hijacked by botnets (see Chapter 8). Many spam messages are sent from one country although another country hosts the spam website.

Spamming is more tightly regulated in Europe than in the United States. In 2002, the European Parliament passed a ban on unsolicited commercial messaging. Digital marketing can be targeted only to people who have given prior consent.

The U.S. CAN-SPAM Act of 2003, which went into effect in 2004, does not outlaw spamming but does ban deceptive email practices by requiring commercial email messages to display accurate subject lines, identify the true senders, and offer recipients an easy way to remove their names from email lists. It also prohibits the use of fake return addresses. A few people have been prosecuted under the law, but it has had a negligible impact on spamming in large part because of the Internet's exceptionally poor security and the use of offshore servers and botnets. Most large-scale spamming has moved offshore to Russia and Eastern Europe where hackers control global botnets capable of generating billions of spam messages. The largest spam network in recent years was the Russian network Festi based in St. Petersburg. Festi is best known as the spam generator behind the global Viagra-spam industry, which stretches from Russia to Indian pharmaceutical firms selling counterfeit Viagra.

For a many years automobile manufacturers around the globe have tried to find ways of manipulating mileage and emissions tests to produce more favorable results on paper than what actually takes place on the road. The use of software for this purpose recently came to light with revelations that Volkswagen Group installed "cheating" software in some of its car models to violate the U.S. Clean Air Act, as described in the Interactive Session on Technology.

Employment: Trickle-Down Technology and Reengineering Job Loss

Reengineering work is typically hailed in the information systems community as a major benefit of new information technology. It is much less frequently noted that redesigning business processes has caused millions of mid-level factory managers and clerical workers to lose their jobs. Some economists have sounded new alarms about information and computer technology threatening middle-class, white-collar jobs (in addition to blue-collar factory jobs). Erik Brynjolfsson and Andrew P. McAfee argue that the pace of automation has picked up in recent years because of a combination of technologies, including robotics, numerically controlled machines, computerized inventory control, pattern recognition, voice recognition, and online commerce. One result is that machines can now do a great many jobs heretofore reserved for humans, including tech support, call center work, X-ray examination, and even legal document review (Brynjolfsson and McAfee, 2011).

These views contrast with other economists' assessments that new technologies created as many or more new jobs as they destroyed. In some cases, employment has grown or remained unchanged in industries where investment in IT capital is highest. These economists also believe that bright, educated workers who are displaced by technology will move to better jobs in fast-growth industries. Missing from this equation are unskilled, blue-collar workers and older, less well-educated middle managers. It is not clear that these groups can be retrained easily for high-quality, high-paying jobs. The Interactive Session on People explores this issue.

INTERACTIVE SESSION: TECHNOLOGY

Volkswagen Pollutes Its Reputation with Software to Evade Emissions Testing

Volkswagen Group AG tried to bypass Toyota as the world's largest automaker. One part of its strategy called for tripling U.S. sales in a decade by promoting "clean" diesel-powered cars promising low emissions and high mileage without sacrificing performance. It turned out that about 580,000 cars in the United States and almost 10.5 million more "clean" diesel models sold worldwide by VW under its VW, Audi, and Porsche brands weren't really "green" at all.

On September 18, 2015, the U.S. Environmental Protection Agency (EPA) issued a notice of violation of the Clean Air Act to the Volkswagen Group after finding that Volkswagen had intentionally programmed turbocharged direct injection diesel engines to activate certain emissions controls only during laboratory emissions testing. The programming caused the vehicle's nitrogen oxide (NOx) output to meet U.S. standards during regulatory testing but emit up to 40 times more NOx when the cars were actually driven on the road. Volkswagen put this software in about 11 million cars worldwide, and in 580,000 in the United States, during model years 2009 through 2015.

Volkswagen was able to get away with cheating on emissions tests for years because it was hidden in lines of software code. Many functions in today's automobiles are controlled by millions of lines of software program code, including monitoring carbon monoxide and nitrogen oxide levels to help a car control the amount of pollutants it emits. Diesel engines don't emit much carbon monoxide, but they generally emit a greater amount of nitrogen oxide (NOx), a component in low-atmosphere ozone and acid rain. The United States has tougher NOx standards than Europe, where diesel cars are more common.

Diesel-powered cars use sensors and engine-management software to monitor and limit emission levels. The software can control how much NOx is produced during combustion by regulating the car's mix of diesel fuel and oxygen or by deploying NOx traps to capture the pollutant and catalysts to clean emissions. However, these pollution-reducing measures also reduce fuel economy. Experts believe that by examining data on steering, tire rotation, and accelerator use, a software program would be able to determine whether a car was being actually driven on the road or on an emissions-testing bed and adjust engine performance and emissions to pass the test.

Around 2007 VW's hard-driving chief executive Martin Winterkorn started pressuring his managers with much higher growth targets for the U.S. car market. In order to increase market share, VW needed to build the larger cars favored by Americans—and it also had to comply with the Obama administration's toughening standards on mileage. All automakers developed strategies to meet the new mileage rules, and VW's focused on diesel. However, diesel engines, while offering better mileage, also emit more smog-forming pollutants than conventional engines. American air pollution standards are stricter than those in Europe. Cheating on emissions tests solved multiple problems. Cars equipped with the "cheating" software were able to deliver better mileage and performance while VW avoided having to pay for expensive and cumbersome pollution-control systems.

VW started installing the software to cheat emissions tests in 2008 after learning that its new diesel engine, developed at great expense for its growth strategy, could not meet pollution standards in the U.S. and other countries. Rather than halt production, VW decided the best course of action was to game the system. It is unclear who in VW management was responsible for this decision. Lawsuits by New York, Maryland, and Massachusetts have charged that dozens of engineers and managers, including VW's chief executive, were involved. German parts supplier Robert Bosch was alleged to have developed the software code that instructed computers in diesel engines to fully deploy pollution controls only when the cars were being tested in laboratories, using VW-supplied specifications.

Volkswagen's cheating on auto emissions tests is not an isolated incident. The entire automobile industry has a history of trying to rig emissions and mileage data, which began as soon as governments began regulating automotive emissions in the early 1970s. Ford, GM, Caterpillar, Volvo, Renault, and other manufacturers have been fined for using defeat devices. Auto manufacturers have also used other ploys to demonstrate better performance and gas mileage, such as taping cars doors and grilles to improve aerodynamics or making test vehicles lighter by removing the back seats.

The emissions scandal has shaken the entire auto industry. Volkswagen became the target of regulatory investigations in multiple countries, and Volkswagen's stock price fell in value by a third in the days immediately following the cheating revelation. Chief executive Winterkorn resigned, and the head of brand development Heinz-Jakob Neusser, Audi research and development head Ulrich Hackenberg, and Porsche research and development head Wolfgang Hatz were suspended. In early 2017 criminal charges were brought against six other ranking VW executives. The cost to Volkswagen for compensating U.S. vehicle owners affected by the emissions scandal and paying criminal and civil penalties could top $30 billion. The scandal raised awareness of the higher levels of pollution being emitted by all vehicles built by a wide range of car makers

The emissions crisis has also sparked discussions about how to deal with other kinds of software-controlled machinery besides automobiles. It is believed that such machines will generally be prone to cheating and that their software source code should be made accessible to the public.

Sources: William Wilkes, "Volkswagen's Emissions Bill Could Top $25 Billion," *Wall Street Journal*, February 1, 2017; Jack Ewing, "Supplier's Role Shows Breadth of VW's Deceit," *New York Times*, February 1, 2017; Hiroko Tabuchi, Jack Ewing, and Matt Apuzzo, "6 Volkswagen Executives Charged as Company Pleads Guilty in Emissions Case," *New York Times*, January 11, 2017; Jack Ewing and Hiroko Tabuchi, "Volkswagen Scandal Reaches All the Way to the Top, Lawsuits Say," *New York Times*, July 19, 2016; Geoffrey Smith and Roger Parloff. "Hoaxwagen," *Fortune*, March 15 2016; Danny Hakim and Hiroko Tabuchi, "Volkswagen Test Rigging Follows a Long Auto Industry Pattern," *New York Times*, September 23, 2015; and Danny Hakim, Aaron M. Kessler, and Jack Ewing, "As Volkswagen Pushed to Be No. 1, Ambitions Fueled a Scandal," *New York Times*, September 26, 2015.

CASE STUDY QUESTIONS

1. Does the Volkswagen emission cheating crisis pose an ethical dilemma? Why or why not? If so, who are the stakeholders?
2. Describe the role of people, organization, and technology factors in creating VW's software cheating problem. To what extent was management responsible? Explain your answer.
3. Should all software-controlling machines be available for public inspection? Why or why not?

Equity and Access: Increasing Racial and Social Class Cleavages

Does everyone have an equal opportunity to participate in the digital age? Will the social, economic, and cultural gaps that exist in the United States and other societies be reduced by information systems technology? Or will the cleavages be increased, permitting the better off to become even more better off relative to others?

These questions have not yet been fully answered because the impact of systems technology on various groups in society has not been thoroughly studied. What is known is that information, knowledge, computers, and access to these resources through educational institutions and public libraries are inequitably distributed along ethnic and social class lines, as are many other information resources. Several studies have found that poor and minority groups in the United States are less likely to have computers or online Internet access even though computer ownership and Internet access have soared in the past five years. Although the gap in computer access is narrowing, higher-income families in each ethnic group are still more likely to have home computers and broadband Internet access than lower-income families in the same group. Moreover, the children of higher-income families are far more likely to use their Internet access to pursue educational goals, whereas lower-income children are much more likely to spend time on entertainment and games. This is called the "time-wasting" gap.

Left uncorrected, this **digital divide** could lead to a society of information haves, computer literate and skilled, versus a large group of information have-nots, computer illiterate and unskilled. Public interest groups want to narrow this digital divide by making digital information services—including the Internet—available to virtually everyone, just as basic telephone service is now.

INTERACTIVE SESSION: PEOPLE

Will Automation Kill Jobs?

Dennis Kriebal of Youngstown, Ohio, had been a supervisor at an aluminum extrusion factory, where he punched out parts for cars and tractors. Six years ago, he lost his job to a robot, and since then has been doing odd jobs to keep afloat. Sherry Johnson used to work for the local newspaper in Marietta, Georgia, feeding paper into printing machines and laying out pages. She lost this job as well as others making medical equipment and working in inventory and filing to automation. Customers at Fatsa, an automated restaurant chain, do all their ordering on iPads and fetch their food from cubbies. There are no waiters or waitresses.

All of these situations illustrate the negative impact of computer technology on jobs. Far more U.S. jobs have been lost to robots and automation than to trade with China, Mexico, or any other country. According to a study by the Center for Business and Economic Research at Ball State University, about 87 percent of manufacturing job losses between 2000 and 2010 stemmed from factories becoming more efficient through automation and better technology. Only 13 percent of job losses were due to trade. For example, the U.S. steel industry lost 400,000 jobs between 1962 and 2005. A study by the American Economic Review found that steel shipments did not decline, but fewer people were needed to do the same amount of work as before, with major productivity gains from using mini mills (small plants that make specialty steel from scrap iron).

A November 2015 McKinsey Global Institute report by Michael Chui, James Manyika, and Mehdi Miremadi examined 2,000 distinct types of work activities in 800 occupations. The authors found that 45 percent of these work activities could be automated by 2055 using technologies that currently exist. About 51 percent of the work activities Americans perform involve predictable and routine physical work, data collection, and data processing. All of these tasks are ripe for some degree of automation. No one knows exactly how many U.S. jobs will be lost or how soon, but the researchers estimate that from 9 to 47 percent of jobs could eventually be affected and perhaps 5 percent of jobs eliminated entirely. These changes shouldn't lead to mass unemployment because automation could increase global productivity by 0.8 percent to 1.4 percent annually over the next 50 years and create many new jobs.

According to a study by MIT labor economist David Autor, automation advances up to this point have not eliminated most jobs. Sometimes machines do replace humans, as in agriculture and manufacturing, but not across an entire economy. Productivity gains from workforce automation have increased the demand for goods and services, in turn increasing the demand for new forms of labor. Jobs that have not been eliminated by automation are often enhanced by it. For example, the number of ATMs in the United States quadrupled between 1980 and 2010, but the number of bank employees increased during this period. ATMs reduced the number of cash-handling tasks, but technology provided new data on customers and thus new opportunities for banks to become more involved in relationship banking. Tellers became more like sales representatives.

The positive and negative impacts of technology are not delivered in an equal way. All the new jobs created by automation are not necessarily better jobs. There have been increases in high-paying jobs (such as accountants) but also in low-paying jobs such as food service workers and home health aides. Disappearing factory jobs have been largely replaced by new jobs in the service sector.

Manufacturing jobs have been the hardest hit by robots and automation. There are more than 5 million fewer jobs in manufacturing today than in 2000. According to a study by economists Daron Acemoglu of MIT and Pascual Restrepo of Boston University, for every robot per thousand workers, up to six workers lost their jobs and wages fell as much as 0.75 percent. Acemoglu and Restrepo found very little employment increase in other occupations to offset job losses in manufacturing. That increase could eventually happen, but right now there are large numbers of people out of work in the United States, especially blue-collar men and women without college degrees. These researchers also found industrial robots were to blame for as many as 670,000 lost manufacturing jobs lost between 1990 and 2007, and this number will rise going forward because the number of industrial robots is predicted to quadruple. Acemoglu and Restrepo noted that a specific local economy, such as Detroit, could be especially hard-hit, although nationally the effects of robots were smaller because jobs were created in other places. The new jobs created by technology are not necessarily in the places losing jobs, such as the Rust Belt. Those forced out of a job by robots generally do not have the skills or mobility to assume the new jobs created by automation.

Automation is not just affecting manual labor and factory jobs. Computers are now capable of taking over certain kinds of white collar and service-sector work, including X-ray analysis and sifting through documents. Job opportunities are shrinking slightly for medical technicians, supervisors, and even lawyers. Work that requires creativity, management, information technology skills, or personal caregiving is least at risk.

According to Boston University economist James Bessen, the problem is not mass unemployment; it's transitioning people from one job to another. People need to learn new skills to work in the new economy. When the United States moved from an agrarian to an industrialized economy, high school education expanded rapidly. By 1951 the average American had 6.2 more years of education than someone born 75 years earlier. Additional education enabled people to do new kinds of jobs in factories, hospitals, and schools.

Sources: Patrick Gillespoe, "Rise of the Machines: Fear Robots, Not China or Mexico," *CNN Money*, January 30, 2017; Claire Cain Miller, "Evidence That Robots Are Winning the Race for American Jobs," *New York Times*, March 28, 2017, "The Long-Term Jobs Killer Is Not China, It's Automation," *New York Times*, December 21, 2016, "A Darker Theme in Obama's Farewell: Automation Can Divide Us," *New York Times*, January 12, 2017; Steve Lohr, "Robots Will Take Jobs, but Not as Fast as Some Fear," *New York Times*, January 12, 2017; Michael Chui, James Manyika, and Mehdi Miremadi, "Where Machines Could Replace Humans—and Where They Can't (Yet)," *McKinsey Quarterly*, July 2016; Stephen Gold, "The Future of Automation—and Your Job," *Industry Week*, January 18, 2016; and Christopher Mims, "Automation Can Actually Create More Jobs," *Wall Street Journal*, December 11, 2016.

CASE STUDY QUESTIONS

1. How does automating jobs pose an ethical dilemma? Who are the stakeholders? Identify the options that can be taken and the potential consequences of each.
2. If you were the owner of a factory deciding on whether to acquire robots to perform certain tasks, what people, organization, and technology factors would you consider?

HEALTH RISKS: RSI, CVS, AND COGNITIVE DECLINE

A common occupational disease today is **repetitive stress injury (RSI)**. RSI occurs when muscle groups are forced through repetitive actions often with high-impact loads (such as tennis) or tens of thousands of repetitions under low-impact loads (such as working at a computer keyboard). The incidence of RSI is estimated to be as much as one-third of the labor force and accounts for one-third of all disability cases.

The single largest source of RSI is computer keyboards. The most common kind of computer-related RSI is **carpal tunnel syndrome (CTS)**, in which pressure on the median nerve through the wrist's bony structure, called a carpal tunnel, produces pain. The pressure is caused by constant repetition of keystrokes: in a single shift, a word processor may perform 23,000 keystrokes. Symptoms of CTS include numbness, shooting pain, inability to grasp objects, and tingling. Millions of workers have been diagnosed with CTS. It affects an estimated 3 percent to 6 percent of the workforce (LeBlanc and Cestia, 2011).

RSI is avoidable. Designing workstations for a neutral wrist position (using a wrist rest to support the wrist), proper monitor stands, and footrests all contribute to proper posture and reduced RSI. Ergonomically correct keyboards are also an option. These measures should be supported by frequent rest breaks and rotation of employees to different jobs.

RSI is not the only occupational illness computers cause. Back and neck pain, leg stress, and foot pain also result from poor ergonomic designs of workstations. **Computer vision syndrome (CVS)** refers to any eyestrain condition related to display screen use in desktop computers, laptops, e-readers, smartphones, and handheld video games. CVS affects about 90 percent of people who spend three hours or more per day at a computer. Its symptoms, which are usually temporary, include headaches, blurred vision, and dry and irritated eyes.

In addition to these maladies, computer technology may be harming our cognitive functions or at least changing how we think and solve problems. Although the

Repetitive stress injury (RSI) is a leading occupational disease today. The single largest cause of RSI is computer keyboard work.

© Ian Allenden/123RF

Internet has made it much easier for people to access, create, and use information, some experts believe that it is also preventing people from focusing and thinking clearly on their own. They argue that exposure to computers reduces intelligence. One MIT scholar believes exposure to computers encourages looking up answers rather than engaging in real problem solving. Students, in this view, don't learn much surfing the web or answering email when compared to listening, drawing, arguing, looking, and exploring (Henry, 2011).

The computer has become part of our lives—personally as well as socially, culturally, and politically. It is unlikely that the issues and our choices will become easier as information technology continues to transform our world. The growth of the Internet and the information economy suggests that all the ethical and social issues we have described will be heightened further as we move further into the first digital century.

4-5 How will MIS help my career?

Here is how Chapter 4 and this book can help you find a job as a junior privacy analyst.

THE COMPANY

Pinnacle Air Force Base in Texas has an open entry-level position for a junior privacy analyst in its human resources office. The office maintains detailed personnel records, including work history, compensation, healthcare, and retirement benefits, on more than 6,800 military members and their families and 1,250 civilian employees.

POSITION DESCRIPTION

The junior privacy analyst will assist with employee recordkeeping and help ensure compliance with all federal and state privacy regulations. Job responsibilities include:

- Analyzing and developing policy and procedures related to privacy office functions.
- Logging and tracking Privacy Act requests, assistance with review, redaction and preparation of responsive records, and tracking all privacy office correspondence.

- Monitoring and responding to written, verbal, and electronic correspondence and inquiries directed to the government privacy office, including sensitive beneficiary/personnel correspondence.
- Coordinating privacy office meetings.
- Reviewing and analyzing data and documents and assessing options, issues, and positions for a variety of program planning, reporting, and execution activities.

JOB REQUIREMENTS

- Bachelor's degree in liberal arts or business
- Strong communication and organizational skills
- Experience with recordkeeping and file systems desirable

INTERVIEW QUESTIONS

1. What background or job experience do you have in the privacy protection field?
2. What do you know about the Privacy Act?
3. What do you know about privacy protection practices for both written and electronic correspondence?
4. If you were asked to improve privacy protection for our organization, how would you proceed?
5. Have you ever dealt with a problem involving privacy protection? What role did you play in its solution?

AUTHOR TIPS

1. Review this chapter, with special attention to the sections dealing with information systems and privacy.
2. Use the web to find out more about the Privacy Act and privacy protection procedures and policies for personnel records.
3. Try to find out more about employee recordkeeping and privacy protection at U.S. military bases or other organizations.
4. If you do not have any hands-on experience in the privacy area, explain what you do know about privacy and why it is so important to protect sensitive personal data, and indicate you would be very interested in learning more and doing privacy-related work.

Review Summary

4-1 **What ethical, social, and political issues are raised by information systems?** Information technology is introducing changes for which laws and rules of acceptable conduct have not yet been developed. Increasing computing power, storage, and networking capabilities—including the Internet—expand the reach of individual and organizational actions and magnify their impacts. The ease and anonymity with which information is now communicated, copied, and manipulated in online environments pose new challenges to the protection of privacy and intellectual property. The main ethical, social, and political issues information systems raise center on information rights and obligations, property rights and obligations, accountability and control, system quality, and quality of life.

4-2 **What specific principles for conduct can be used to guide ethical decisions?** Six ethical principles for judging conduct include the Golden Rule, Immanuel Kant's categorical imperative, the slippery slope rule, the utilitarian principle, the risk aversion principle, and the ethical no-free-lunch rule. These principles should be used in conjunction with an ethical analysis.

4-3 Why do contemporary information systems technology and the Internet pose challenges to the protection of individual privacy and intellectual property? Contemporary data storage and data analysis technology enable companies to gather personal data from many sources easily about individuals and analyze these data to create detailed digital profiles about individuals and their behaviors. Data flowing over the Internet can be monitored at many points. Cookies and other web monitoring tools closely track the activities of website visitors. Not all websites have strong privacy protection policies, and they do not always allow for informed consent regarding the use of personal information. Traditional copyright laws are insufficient to protect against software piracy because digital material can be copied so easily and transmitted to many locations simultaneously over the Internet.

4-4 How have information systems affected laws for establishing accountability and liability and the quality of everyday life? New information technologies are challenging existing liability laws and social practices for holding individuals and institutions accountable for harm done to others. Although computer systems have been sources of efficiency and wealth, they have some negative impacts. Computer errors can cause serious harm to individuals and organizations. Poor data quality is also responsible for disruptions and losses for businesses. Jobs can be lost when computers replace workers or tasks become unnecessary in reengineered business processes. The ability to own and use a computer may be exacerbating socioeconomic disparities among different racial groups and social classes. Widespread use of computers increases opportunities for computer crime and computer abuse. Computers can also create health and cognitive problems such as repetitive stress injury, computer vision syndrome, and the inability to think clearly and perform complex tasks.

Key Terms

Accountability, 122
Carpal tunnel syndrome (CTS), 143
Computer abuse, 138
Computer crime, 138
Computer vision syndrome (CVS), 143
Cookies, 128
Copyright, 131
Digital divide, 141
Digital Millennium Copyright Act (DMCA), 134
Due process, 122
Ethical no-free-lunch rule, 124
Ethics, 118
Fair Information Practices (FIP), 126
Golden Rule, 123
Immanuel Kant's categorical imperative, 124
Information rights, 119
Informed consent, 127
Intellectual property, 131
Liability, 122
Nonobvious relationship awareness (NORA), 121
Opt-in, 130
Opt-out, 130
Patent, 132
Privacy, 125
Privacy Shield, 128
Profiling, 121
Repetitive stress injury (RSI), 143
Responsibility, 122
Risk aversion principle, 124
Safe harbor, 128
Slippery slope rule, 124
Spam, 138
Spyware, 129
Trade secret, 133
Trademark, 133
Utilitarian principle, 124
Web beacons, 129

MyLab MIS

To complete the problems with **MyLab MIS**, go to the EOC Discussion Questions in MyLab MIS.

Review Questions

4-1 What ethical, social, and political issues are raised by information systems?

- Explain how ethical, social, and political issues are connected and give some examples.
- List and describe the key technological trends that heighten ethical concerns.
- Differentiate between responsibility, accountability, and liability.

4-2 What specific principles for conduct can be used to guide ethical decisions?
- List and describe the five steps in an ethical analysis.
- Identify and describe six ethical principles.

4-3 Why do contemporary information systems technology and the Internet pose challenges to the protection of individual privacy and intellectual property?
- Define privacy and Fair Information Practices.
- Explain how the Internet challenges the protection of individual privacy and intellectual property.
- Explain how informed consent, legislation, industry self-regulation, and technology tools help protect the individual privacy of Internet users.
- List and define the three regimes that protect intellectual property rights.

4-4 How have information systems affected laws for establishing accountability and liability and the quality of everyday life?
- Explain why it is so difficult to hold software services liable for failure or injury.
- List and describe the principal causes of system quality problems.
- Name and describe four quality of life impacts of computers and information systems.
- Define and describe computer vision syndrome and repetitive stress injury (RSI) and explain their relationship to information technology.

Discussion Questions

4-5 MyLab MIS Should producers of software-based services, such as ATMs, be held liable for economic injuries suffered when their systems fail?

4-6 MyLab MIS Should companies be responsible for unemployment their information systems cause? Why or why not?

4-7 MyLab MIS Discuss the pros and cons of allowing companies to amass personal data for behavioral targeting.

Hands-On MIS Projects

The projects in this section give you hands-on experience in analyzing the privacy implications of using online data brokers, developing a corporate policy for employee web usage, using blog creation tools to create a simple blog, and analyzing web browser privacy. Visit **MyLab MIS** to access this chapter's Hands-On MIS Projects.

MANAGEMENT DECISION PROBLEMS

4-8 InfoFree's website is linked to massive databases that consolidate personal data on millions of people. Users can purchase marketing lists of consumers broken down by location, age, gender, income level, home value, and interests. One could use this capability to obtain a list, for example, of everyone in Peekskill, New York, making $150,000 or more per year. Do data brokers such as InfoFree raise privacy issues? Why or why not? If your name and other personal information were in this database, what limitations on access would you want to preserve your privacy? Consider the following data users: government agencies, your employer, private business firms, other individuals.

4-9 As the head of a small insurance company with six employees, you are concerned about how effectively your company is using its networking and human resources. Budgets are tight, and you are struggling to meet payrolls because employees are reporting many overtime hours. You do not believe that the employees have a sufficiently heavy workload to warrant working longer hours and are looking into the amount of time they spend on the Internet.

Each employee uses a computer with Internet access on the job. Review a sample of your company's weekly report of employee web usage, which can be found in MyLab MIS.

- Calculate the total amount of time each employee spent on the web for the week and the total amount of time that company computers were used for this purpose. Rank the employees in the order of the amount of time each spent online.
- Do your findings and the contents of the report indicate any ethical problems employees are creating? Is the company creating an ethical problem by monitoring its employees' use of the Internet?
- Use the guidelines for ethical analysis presented in this chapter to develop a solution to the problems you have identified.

ACHIEVING OPERATIONAL EXCELLENCE: CREATING A SIMPLE BLOG

Software skills: Blog creation
Business skills: Blog and web page design

4-10 In this project, you'll learn how to build a simple blog of your own design using the online blog creation software available at Blogger.com. Pick a sport, hobby, or topic of interest as the theme for your blog. Name the blog, give it a title, and choose a template for the blog. Post at least four entries to the blog, adding a label for each posting. Edit your posts if necessary. Upload an image, such as a photo from your computer, or the web, to your blog. Add capabilities for other registered users, such as team members, to comment on your blog. Briefly describe how your blog could be useful to a company selling products or services related to the theme of your blog. List the tools available to Blogger that would make your blog more useful for business and describe the business uses of each. Save your blog and show it to your instructor.

IMPROVING DECISION MAKING: ANALYZING WEB BROWSER PRIVACY

Software Skills: Web browser software
Business Skills: Analyzing web browser privacy protection features

4-11 This project will help develop your Internet skills for using the privacy protection features of leading web browser software.

Examine the privacy protection features and settings for two leading web browsers such as Internet Explorer, Mozilla Firefox, or Google Chrome. Make a table comparing the features of two of these browsers in terms of functions provided and ease of use.

- How do these privacy protection features protect individuals?
- How do these privacy protection features affect what businesses can do on the Internet?
- Which browser does the best job of protecting privacy? Why?

Collaboration and Teamwork Project

Developing a Corporate Code of Ethics

4-12 With three or four of your classmates, develop a corporate ethics code on privacy that addresses both employee privacy and the privacy of customers and users of the corporate website. Be sure to consider email privacy and employer monitoring of worksites as well as corporate use of information about employees concerning their off-the-job behavior (e.g., lifestyle, marital arrangements, and so forth). If possible, use Google Docs and Google Drive or Google Sites to brainstorm, organize, and develop a presentation of your findings for the class.

BUSINESS PROBLEM-SOLVING CASE

Facebook Privacy: Your Life for Sale

Facebook has quickly morphed from a small, niche networking site for mostly Ivy League college students into a publicly traded company with a market worth of $434 billion in 2017. Facebook boasts that it is free to join and always will be, so where's the money coming from to service 1.9 billion worldwide subscribers? Just like its fellow tech titan and rival Google, Facebook's revenue comes almost entirely from advertising. All Facebook has to sell is your personal information and the information of hundreds of millions of others with Facebook accounts.

Advertisers have long understood the value of Facebook's unprecedented trove of personal information. They can serve ads using highly specific details such as relationship status, location, employment status, favorite books, movies, or TV shows and a host of other categories. For example, an Atlanta woman who posts that she has become engaged might be offered an ad for a wedding photographer on her Facebook page. When advertisements are served to finely targeted subsets of users, the response is much more successful than traditional types of advertising.

In 2016 Facebook generated $27.6 billion in revenue, 97 percent of which ($26.7 billion) was from selling ads and the remaining 3 percent from selling games and virtual goods. Facebook's revenues in 2016 grew by 54 percent over the previous year, driven mostly by adding new users and showing 40 percent more ads than a year earlier. A major contributor to revenue growth in 2016 was ads sold in the mobile news feed.

That was good news for Facebook, but is it good news for you, the Facebook user? More than ever, companies such as Facebook and Google, which made approximately $90 billion in advertising revenue in 2016, are using your online activity to develop a frighteningly accurate digital picture of your life. Facebook's goal is to serve advertisements that are more relevant to you than anywhere else on the web, but the personal information it gathers about you both with and without your consent can also be used against you in other ways.

Facebook has a diverse array of compelling and useful features. Facebook's partnership with the Department of Labor helps connect job seekers and employers; Facebook has helped families find lost pets; Facebook allows active-duty soldiers to stay in touch with their families; it gives smaller companies a chance to further their e-commerce efforts and larger companies a chance to solidify their brands; and, perhaps most obviously, Facebook allows you to keep in touch with your friends, relatives, local restaurants, and, in short, just about all things you are interested in more easily. These are the reasons so many people use Facebook—it provides value to users.

However, Facebook's goal is to get its users to share as much data as possible because the more Facebook knows about you, the more accurately it can serve relevant advertisements to you. Critics of Facebook are concerned that the existence of a repository of personal data of the size that Facebook has amassed requires protections and privacy controls that extend far beyond those that Facebook currently offers.

Facebook wanting to make more money is understandable, but the company has a checkered past of privacy violations and missteps that raise doubts about whether it should be responsible for the personal data of billions of people. There are no laws in the United States that give consumers the right to know what data companies like Facebook have compiled. You can challenge information in credit reports, but you can't even see what data Facebook has gathered about you. It's different in Europe: you can request Facebook to turn over a report of all the information it has about you.

Think you own your face? Not on Facebook, thanks to its facial recognition software for photo tagging of users. This "tag suggestions" feature is automatically on when you sign up, and there is no user consent. A federal court in 2016 allowed a lawsuit to go forward contesting Facebook's right to photo tag without user consent. This feature is in violation of several state laws that seek to secure the privacy of biometric data.

A recent *Consumer Reports* study found that of 150 million Americans on Facebook, every day, at least 4.8 million are willingly sharing information that could be used against them in some way. That includes plans to travel on a particular day, which burglars could use to time robberies, or Liking a page about a particular health condition or treatment, which might prompt insurers to deny coverage. Credit card companies and similar organizations have begun engaging in weblining, taken from the term *redlining*, by altering their treatment of you based on the actions of other people with profiles similar to yours. Employers can assess your personality and behavior by using your Facebook Likes. Thirteen million users have never adjusted Facebook's privacy controls, which allow friends using Facebook applications to transfer your data unwittingly to a third party without your knowledge.

Why, then, do so many people share sensitive details of their life on Facebook? Often it's because users do not realize that their data are being collected and transmitted in this way. A Facebook user's friends are not notified if information about them is collected by that user's applications. Many of Facebook's features and services are enabled by default when they are launched without notifying users, and a study by Siegel+Gale found that Facebook's privacy policy is more difficult to comprehend than government notices or typical bank credit card agreements, which are notoriously dense. Did you know that whenever you log into a website using Facebook, Facebook shares some personal information with that site and can track your movements in that site? Next time you visit Facebook, click Privacy Settings and see whether you can understand your options.

Facebook's value and growth potential are determined by how effectively it can leverage the personal data it aggregates about its users to attract advertisers. Facebook thus stands to gain from managing and avoiding the privacy concerns its users and government regulators raise. However, there are some signs that Facebook might become more responsible with its data collection processes, whether by its own volition or because it is forced to do so. As a publicly traded company, Facebook now invites more scrutiny from investors and regulators because, unlike in the past, its balance sheets, assets, and financial reporting documents are readily available.

In August 2012, Facebook settled a lawsuit with the Federal Trade Commission (FTC) in which it was barred from misrepresenting the privacy or security of users' personal information. Facebook was charged with deceiving its users by telling them they could keep their information on Facebook private but then repeatedly allowing it to be shared and made public. Facebook agreed to obtain user consent before making any change to that user's privacy preferences and to submit to biannual privacy audits by an independent firm for the next 20 years.

Privacy advocate groups such as the Electronic Privacy Information Center (EPIC) want Facebook to restore its more robust privacy settings from 2009 as well as to offer complete access to all data it keeps about its users. Facebook has also come under fire from EPIC for collecting information about users who are not even logged on to Facebook or may not even have accounts on Facebook. Facebook keeps track of activity on other sites that have Like buttons or recommendations widgets and records the time of your visit and your IP address when you visit a site with those features, regardless of whether you click them.

Although U.S. Facebook users have little recourse to access data that Facebook has collected on them, users from other countries have done better. In Europe, over 100,000 Facebook users have already requested their data, and European law requires Facebook to respond to these requests within 40 days. Government privacy regulators from France, Spain, Italy, Germany, Belgium, and the Netherlands have been actively investigating Facebook's privacy controls as the European Union pursues more stringent privacy protection legislation, In June 2015, Belgium's data-protection watchdog sued Facebook over privacy practices such as how Facebook tracks users across the web through Like and Share buttons on external websites. In 2016 European privacy authorities ordered Facebook to stop harvesting personal data from users of its texting platform WhatsApp, and in 2017 Facebook was fined $122 million for harvesting WhatsApp user data without permission.

In January 2014, Facebook shut down its Sponsored Stories feature, which served advertisements in the user's news feed highlighting products and businesses that Facebook friends were using. Sponsored Stories had been one of the most effective forms of advertising on Facebook because they don't seem like advertisements at all to most users. However, this feature triggered many lawsuits, attempted settlements, and criticism from privacy groups, the FTC, and annoyed parents whose children's photos were being used throughout Facebook to sell products.

Although Facebook has shut down one of its more egregious privacy-invading features, the company's data use policies make it very clear that, as a condition of using the service, users grant the company wide latitude in using their personal information in advertising. This includes a person's name, photo, comments, and social advertising. by which your personal information is broadcast to your friends and, indeed, the entire Facebook service if the company sees fit. Although users can limit some uses, an advanced degree in Facebook data features is required. Facebook shows you ads not only on Facebook but across the web through its Facebook Audience Network, which keeps track of what users do on other websites and then targets ads to those users on those websites. Ad-based firms like Facebook and hundreds of others, including Google, justify their collection of personal information by arguing that consumers, by virtue of using the service, implicitly know about the data collection efforts and the role of advertisers in paying for the service and must, therefore, believe they are receiving real economic value from ads. This line of reasoning received a blow when in June 2015, researchers at the Annenberg School of Communication at the University of Pennsylvania found that 65 percent of Americans feel they have lost control over their information to advertisers, 84 percent want to control their information, and

91 percent do not believe it is fair for companies to offer discounts or coupons in exchange for their personal information without their knowledge.

Critics have asked Facebook why it doesn't offer an ad-free service—like music streaming sites—for a monthly fee. Others wanted to know why Facebook does not allow users just to opt out of tracking. But these kinds of changes would be very difficult for Facebook because its business model depends entirely on the unfettered use of its users' personal private information, just like it declares in its data use policy. That policy declares very openly that if you use Facebook, you don't have any privacy with respect to any data you provide to it.

Sources: Aria Bendix, "EU Fines Facebook $122 Million," *The Atlantic*, May 18, 2017; Mark Scottmay, "E.U. Fines Facebook $122 Million over Disclosures in WhatsApp Deal," *New York Times*, May 18, 2017; Samuel Gibbs, "Facebook Facing Privacy Actions Across Europe as France Fines Firm €150k," *The Guardian*, May 16, 2017; Facebook, Inc., SEC Form 10K filed with the Securities and Exchange Commission for the fiscal year ending December 31, 2016, January 29, 2017; "'Privacy Shield,' the New Deal Governing How Europe's User Data Is Sent to the US," *Reuters*, February 29, 2016; Katie Collins, "Facebook's Newest Privacy Problem: 'Faceprint' Data," *CNET*, May 16, 2016; United States District Court Northern District of California in Re Facebook Biometric Information Privacy Litigation. Case No. 15-cv-03747-JD Order Re Motion to Dismiss and Summary Judgment, May 6, 2016; Jessica Guynn, "Facebook to Face Privacy Lawsuit over Photo Tagging," *USA Today*, May 6, 2016; Natasha Singer, "Sharing Data, but Not Happily," *New York Times*, June 4, 2015; 2015; Zeynep Tufecki, "Let Me Pay for Facebook," *New York Times*, June, 4, 2015; Lisa Fleisher, "Admitting Tracking Bug, Facebook Defends European Privacy Practices," *Wall Street Journal*, April 9, 2015; and Natasha Singer, "Didn't Read Those Terms of Service? Here's What You Agreed to Give Up," *New York Times*, April 28, 2014.

CASE STUDY QUESTIONS

4-13 Perform an ethical analysis of Facebook. What is the ethical dilemma presented by this case?

4-14 What is the relationship of privacy to Facebook's business model?

4-15 Describe the weaknesses of Facebook's privacy policies and features. What people, organization, and technology factors have contributed to those weaknesses?

4-16 Will Facebook be able to have a successful business model without invading privacy? Explain your answer. Could Facebook take any measures to make this possible?

MyLab MIS

Go to the Assignments section of MyLab MIS to complete these writing exercises.

4-17 What are the five principles of Fair Information Practices? For each principle, describe a business situation in which the principle comes into play and how you think managers should react.

4-18 What are five digital technology trends in business today that raise ethical issues for business firms and managers? Provide an example from business or personal experience when an ethical issue resulted from each of these trends.

Chapter 4 References

Aeppel, Timothy. "What Clever Robots Mean for Jobs." *Wall Street Journal* (February 24, 2015).

Belanger, France, and Robert E. Crossler. "Privacy in the Digital Age: A Review of Information Privacy Research in Information Systems." *MIS Quarterly* 35, No. 4 (December 2011).

Bernstein, Amy, and Anand Raman. "The Great Decoupling: An Interview with Erik Brynjolfsson and Andrew McAfee." *Harvard Business Review* (June 2015).

Bernstein, Ethan, Saravanan Kesavan, and Bradley Staats. "How to Manage Scheduling Software Fairly." *Harvard Business Review* (December 2014).

Bertolucci, Jeff. "Big Data Firm Chronicles Your Online, Offline Lives." *Information Week* (May 7, 2013).

Bilski v. Kappos, 561 US (2010).

Brown Bag Software vs. Symantec Corp. 960 F2D 1465 (Ninth Circuit, 1992).

Brynjolfsson, Erik, and Andrew McAfee. *Race Against the Machine*. (Digital Frontier Press, 2011).

Chan, Jason, Anindya Ghose, and Robert Seamans. "The Internet and Racial Hate Crimes: Offline Spillovers from Online Access." *MIS Quarterly* 40, No. 2 (June 2016).

Clemons, Eric K., and Joshua S. Wilson. "Family Preferences Concerning Online Privacy, Data Mining, and Targeted Ads: Regulatory Implications." *Journal of Management Information Systems* 32, No. 2 (2015).

Culnan, Mary J., and Cynthia Clark Williams. "How Ethics Can Enhance Organizational Privacy." *MIS Quarterly* 33, No. 4 (December 2009).

Davenport, Thomas H., and Julia Kirby. "Beyond Automation." *Harvard Business Review* (June 2015).

European Commission. "The EU-U.S. Privacy Shield Factsheet." July 2016. http://ec.europa.eu, accessed June 15, 2017.

European Parliament. "Directive 2009/136/EC of the European Parliament and of the Council of November 25, 2009." European Parliament (2009).

Federal Trade Commission, "Internet of Things (IoT): Privacy & Security in a Connected World." (January 2015).

Federal Trade Commission. "Protecting Consumer Privacy in an Era of Rapid Change." (Washington, DC, 2012).

Goelmarch, Vindu. "One Billion Yahoo Accounts Still for Sale, Despite Hacking Indictments." *New York Times* (March 17, 2017).

Goldfarb, Avi, and Catherine Tucker. "Why Managing Consumer Privacy Can Be an Opportunity." *MIT Sloan Management Review* 54, No. 3 (Spring 2013).

Groysberg, Boris, Eric Lin, George Serafeim, and Robin Abrahams. "The Scandal Effect." *Harvard Business Review* (September 2016).

Henry, Patrick. "Why Computers Make Us Stupid." *Slice of MIT* (March 6, 2011).

Hsieh, J. J. Po-An, Arun Rai, and Mark Keil. "Understanding Digital Inequality: Comparing Continued Use Behavioral Models of the Socio-Economically Advantaged and Disadvantaged." *MIS Quarterly* 32, No. 1 (March 2008).

Hutter, Katja, Johann Fuller, Julia Hautz, Volker Bilgram, and Kurt Matzler. "Machiavellianism or Morality: Which Behavior Pays Off In Online Innovation Contests?" *Journal of Management Information Systems* 32, No. 3 (2015).

Kaspersky Lab. "Spam and Phishing Report 2016." (February 2017).

Laudon, Kenneth C. *Dossier Society: Value Choices in the Design of National Information Systems.* (New York: Columbia University Press, 1986).

Laudon, Kenneth C., and Carol Guercio Traver. *E-Commerce 2017: Business, Technology, Society*, 13th ed. (Upper Saddle River, NJ: Prentice-Hall, 2018).

LeBlanc, K. E., and W. Cestia. "Carpal Tunnel Syndrome." *American Family Physician* 83, No. 8 (2011).

Lee, Dong-Joo, Jae-Hyeon Ahn, and Youngsok Bang. "Managing Consumer Privacy Concerns in Personalization: A Strategic Analysis of Privacy Protection." *MIS Quarterly* 35, No. 2 (June 2011).

MacCrory, Frank, George Westerman, Erik Brynjolfsson, and Yousef Alhammadi. "Racing with and Against the Machine: Changes in Occupational Skill Composition in an Era of Rapid Technological Advance." (2014).

Pew Research Center. "The State of Privacy in America." (January 20, 2016).

PwC. "US State of Cybercrime Survey 2015." (June 2016).

Robinson, Francis. "EU Unveils Web-Privacy Rules." *Wall Street Journal* (January 26, 2012).

Smith, H. Jeff. "The Shareholders vs. Stakeholders Debate." *MIS Sloan Management Review* 44, No. 4 (Summer 2003).

The Software Alliance. "BSA Global Software Survey 2016." (May 2016).

Sojer, Manuel, Oliver Alexy, Sven Kleinknecht, and Joachim Henkel. "Understanding the Drivers of Unethical Programming Behavior: The Inappropriate Reuse of Internet-Accessible Code." *Journal of Management Information Systems* 31, No. 3 (Winter 2014).

Tarafdar, Monideepa, John D'Arcy, Ofir Turel, and Ashish Gupta. "The Dark Side of Information Technology." *MIT Sloan Management Review* 56, No. 2 (Winter 2015).

U.S. Department of Health, Education, and Welfare. *Records, Computers, and the Rights of Citizens.* (Cambridge: MIT Press, 1973).

U.S. Senate. "Do-Not-Track Online Act of 2011." Senate 913 (May 9, 2011).

U.S. Sentencing Commission. "Sentencing Commission Toughens Requirements for Corporate Compliance Programs." (April 13, 2004).

PART II

Information Technology Infrastructure

Part II provides the technical knowledge foundation for understanding information systems by examining hardware, software, databases, networking technologies, and tools and techniques for security and control. This part answers questions such as these: What technologies and tools do businesses today need to accomplish their work? What do I need to know about these technologies to make sure they enhance the performance of my firm? How are these technologies likely to change in the future?

CHAPTER

5 IT Infrastructure: Hardware and Software

LEARNING OBJECTIVES

After reading this chapter, you will be able to answer the following questions:

5-1 What are the components of IT infrastructure?

5-2 What are the major computer hardware, data storage, input, and output technologies used in business and the major hardware trends?

5-3 What are the major types of computer software used in business and the major software trends?

5-4 What are the principal issues in managing hardware and software technology?

5-5 How will MIS help my career?

CHAPTER CASES

- PeroxyChem's Cloud Computing Formula for Success
- Wearable Computers Change How We Work
- Computing Takes Off in the Cloud
- Is BYOD Good for Business?

VIDEO CASES

- Rockwell Automation Fuels the Oil and Gas Industry with the Internet of Things (IoT)
- ESPN.com: The Future of Sports Coverage in the Cloud
- Netflix: Building a Business in the Cloud

MyLab MIS

- Discussion Questions: 5-5, 5-6, 5-7;
- Hands-on MIS Projects: 5-8, 5-9, 5-10, 5-11
- Writing Assignments: 5-17, 5-18
- eText with Conceptual Animations

PEROXYCHEM'S CLOUD COMPUTING FORMULA FOR SUCCESS

PeroxyChem is a leading global supplier of hydrogen peroxide and related substances for electronics, paper production, and household medical products. The company is headquartered in Philadelphia, Pennsylvania; has about 550 employees and more than $340 million in revenue; and operates manufacturing facilities in North America, Europe, and Asia.

In February 2014 PeroxyChem was divested from its parent company and had just one year to take over management of its business systems. It would have to create its own IT infrastructure and IT department, all while keeping day-to-day business systems and operations running smoothly. As part of a large corporation, PeroxyChem had not been responsible for maintaining and managing its own IT systems but suddenly had to become self-sufficient. The company was understandably reluctant at that point to take on the cost or risk of procuring its own hardware, setting up a data center on premises, and maintaining a large in-house IT department, nor did it have the in-house expertise to do so.

According to PeroxyChem CIO Jim Curley, management didn't want to change any of its applications, but it did want to transition to a cloud infrastructure where the computer hardware and software for running a firm's systems are available as on-demand services in remote computing centers accessed via the Internet. The goal was for PeroxyChem IT personnel to spend only 40 percent of their time on operational tasks to keep the company running and 60 percent on strategic projects designed to grow the business. PeroxyChem also lacked the time and resources to hire and train new personnel to run day-to-day operations.

PeroxyChem worked with IBM to migrate its existing systems to IBM's SoftLayer cloud computing infrastructure. This is a managed cloud infrastructure in which a trusted and experienced third party (IBM in this instance) manages the organization's cloud computing activities, freeing the organization to focus on its core competencies. IBM also helped implement enterprise and business intelligence applications from SAP, configuring the systems to meet PeroxyChem's business requirements. The new infrastructure was rigorously tested and was able to go live in four and a half months with no disruptions to PeroxyChem's existing IT operations.

© olegdudko/123RF

PeroxyChem can run and extend its enterprise business systems with a lean in-house team. The managed IBM Cloud hosting solution has made it possible for PeroxyChem's IT staff to spend less time on routine maintenance and more time on leveraging its core competencies and developing innovative products for specialty industries such as food safety and electronics.

Using a cloud infrastructure has reduced costs and risk by avoiding large up-front capital investment for new hardware, software, and a data center as well as the expense of maintaining a large in-house IT team. The infrastructure is scalable and can expand computing capacity if the company grows or has peaking workloads or reduce computing resources (and expenses) if the company has fewer users or less computing work. The company can easily add more users without purchasing additional computing, storage, and networking resources of its own. PeroxyChem's cloud infrastructure is operational around the clock, making it easier to for this global company to do business.

Sources: David Slovensky, "PeroxyChem Builds a Whole New IT Infrastructure in Less Than Five Months," www.ibm.com, January 17, 2017; "PeroxyChem LLC." www.03-ibm.com, accessed January 31, 2017; Ken Murphy, "PeroxyChem Starts a Cloud Reaction," SAP Insider Profiles, December 12, 2016; and www.peroxychem.com, accessed May 15, 2017.

The experience of PeroxyChem illustrates the importance of information technology infrastructure in running a business today. The right technology at the right price will improve organizational performance. After divestiture from its parent corporation, PeroxyChem was left on its own to manage its own information systems. The company would have been overwhelmed with setting up its own IT department and learning how to run its own systems, with no time for developing systems to support its strategy and future growth. PeroxyChem would be prevented from operating as efficiently and effectively as it could have.

The chapter-opening case diagram calls attention to important points raised by this case and this chapter. Divestiture left PeroxyChem with limited resources and time frame to set up and run its essential business information systems and data center. Using cloud computing for its IT infrastructure enables PeroxyChem to quickly delegate the operation and management of its IT systems to outside specialists, to maintain a very small in-house IT staff, and to use that staff to support innovation rather than day-to-day operations. The company pays for only the computing capacity it actually uses on an as-needed basis and did not have to make extensive and costly up-front IT investments.

Here are some questions to think about: What were the business benefits for PeroxyChem of using a cloud computing infrastructure? What role did divestiture play in PeroxyChem's choice of a solution?

5-1 What are the components of IT infrastructure?

If you want to know why businesses worldwide spend about $3.5 trillion annually on computing and information systems, just consider what it would take for you personally to set up a business or manage a business today. Businesses require a wide variety of computing equipment, software, and communications capabilities simply to operate and solve basic business problems.

Do your employees travel or do some work from home? You will want to equip them with laptop computers, tablets, or smartphones. If you are employed by a medium or large business, you will also need larger server computers, perhaps an entire data center or server farm with hundreds or even thousands of servers. A **data center** is a facility housing computer systems and associated components such as telecommunications, storage, security systems, and backup power supplies.

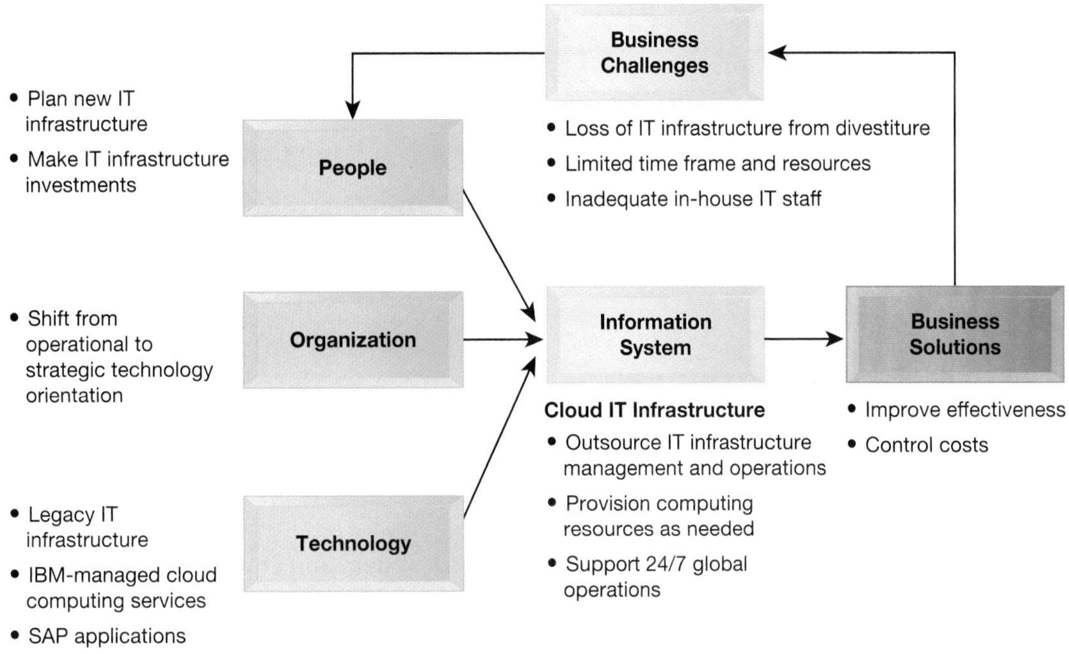

You will also need plenty of software. Each computer will require an operating system and a wide range of application software capable of dealing with spreadsheets, documents, and data files. Unless you are a single-person business, you will most likely want to have a network to link all the people in your business and perhaps your customers and suppliers. In fact, you will probably want several networks: a local area network connecting employees in your office and remote access capabilities so employees can share email and computer files while they are out of the office. You will also want all your employees to have access to landline phone systems, mobile phone networks, and the Internet. Finally, to make all this equipment and software work harmoniously, you will also need the services of trained people to help you run and manage this technology.

All the elements we have just described combine to make up the firm's *information technology (IT) infrastructure*, which we first defined in Chapter 1. A firm's IT infrastructure provides the foundation, or platform, for supporting all the information systems in the business.

IT INFRASTRUCTURE COMPONENTS

Today's IT infrastructure is composed of five major components: computer hardware, computer software, data management technology, networking and telecommunications technology, and technology services (see Figure 5.1). These components must be coordinated with each other.

Computer Hardware

Computer hardware consists of technology for computer processing, data storage, input, and output. This component includes large mainframes, servers, desktop and laptop computers, and mobile devices for accessing corporate data and the Internet. It also includes equipment for gathering and inputting data, physical media for storing the data, and devices for delivering the processed information as output.

Computer Software

Computer software includes both system software and application software. **System software** manages the resources and activities of the computer. **Application software** applies the computer to a specific task for an end user, such as processing an order

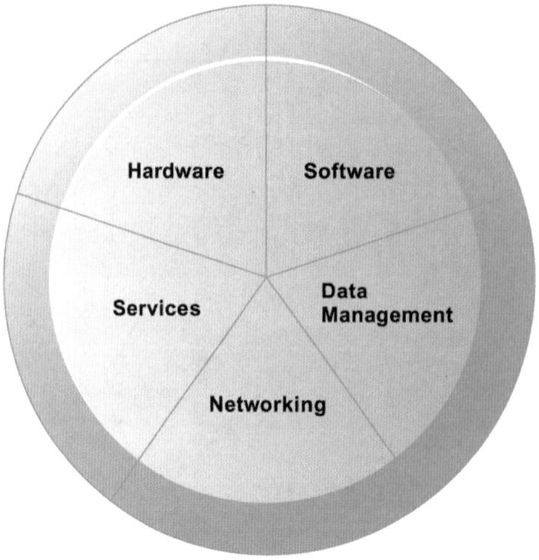

Figure 5.1
IT Infrastructure Components
A firm's IT infrastructure is composed of hardware, software, data management technology, networking technology, and technology services.

or generating a mailing list. Today, most system and application software is no longer custom programmed but rather is purchased from outside vendors. We describe these types of software in detail in Section 5-2.

Data Management Technology

In addition to physical media for storing the firm's data, businesses need specialized software to organize the data and make them available to business users. **Data management software** organizes, manages, and processes business data concerned with inventory, customers, and vendors. Chapter 6 describes data management software in detail.

Networking and Telecommunications Technology

Networking and telecommunications technology provides data, voice, and video connectivity to employees, customers, and suppliers. It includes technology for running a company's internal networks, telecommunications/telephone services, and technology for running websites and linking to other computer systems through the Internet. Chapter 7 provides an in-depth description of these technologies.

Technology Services

Businesses need people to run and manage the infrastructure components we have just described and to train employees in how to use these technologies for their work. Chapter 2 described the role of the information systems department, which is the firm's internal business unit set up for this purpose. Today, many businesses supplement their in-house information systems staff with external technology consultants to provide expertise that is not available internally. When businesses need to make major system changes or implement an entirely new IT infrastructure, they typically turn to external consultants to help them with systems integration.

Systems integration means ensuring that the new infrastructure works with the firm's legacy systems and that the new elements of the infrastructure work with one another. **Legacy systems** are generally older transaction-processing systems created for older computers that continue in use to avoid the high cost of replacing or redesigning them.

Thousands of technology vendors supply IT infrastructure components and services, and an equally large number of ways of putting them together exists. This chapter is about the hardware and software components of infrastructure you will need to run a business. Chapter 6 describes the data management component, and Chapter 7 is devoted to the networking and telecommunications technology component. Chapter 8 deals with hardware and software for ensuring that information systems are reliable and secure, and Chapter 9 discusses software for enterprise applications.

5-2 What are the major computer hardware, data storage, input, and output technologies used in business and the major hardware trends?

Business firms face many challenges and problems that computers and information systems can solve. To be efficient, firms need to match the right computer hardware to the nature of the business challenge, neither overspending nor underspending for the technology.

TYPES OF COMPUTERS

Computers come in an array of sizes with differing capabilities for processing information, from the smallest handheld devices to the largest mainframes and supercomputers. If you're working alone or with a few other people in a small business, you'll probably be using a desktop or laptop **personal computer (PC)**. You will likely have a mobile device with substantial computing capability, such as an iPhone, iPad, or Android mobile device. If you're doing advanced design or engineering work requiring powerful graphics or computational capabilities, you might use a **workstation**, which fits on a desktop but has more powerful mathematical and graphics-processing capabilities than a PC.

If your business has a number of networked computers or maintains a website, it will need a **server**. Server computers are specifically optimized to support a computer network, enabling users to share files, software, peripheral devices (such as printers), or other network resources.

Servers provide the hardware platform for electronic commerce. By adding special software, they can be customized to deliver web pages, process purchase and sale transactions, or exchange data with systems inside the company. You will sometimes find many servers linked to provide all the processing needs for large companies. If your company has to process millions of financial transactions or customer records, you will need multiple servers or a single large mainframe to solve these challenges.

Mainframe computers first appeared in the mid-1960s, and large banks, insurance companies, stock brokerages, airline reservation systems, and government agencies still use them to keep track of hundreds of thousands or even millions of records and transactions. A **mainframe** is a large-capacity, high-performance computer that can process large amounts of data very rapidly. For example, the IBM Z13 mainframe can process 2.5 billion transactions per day, the equivalent of 100 Cyber Mondays. IBM has repurposed its mainframe systems so they can be used as giant servers for large-scale enterprise networks and corporate websites. A single IBM mainframe can run enough instances of Linux or Windows server software to replace thousands of smaller Windows-based servers. A **supercomputer** is a specially designed and more sophisticated computer that is used for tasks requiring extremely rapid and complex calculations with thousands of variables, millions of measurements, and thousands of equations. Supercomputers traditionally have been used in engineering analysis of structures, scientific exploration and simulations, and military work such as classified weapons research. Some private business firms also use supercomputers. For instance, Volvo and most other automobile manufacturers use supercomputers to simulate vehicle crash tests.

If you are a long-term weather forecaster, such as the National Oceanic and Atmospheric Administration (NOAA) or the National Hurricane Center, and your challenge is to predict the movement of weather systems based on hundreds of thousands of measurements and thousands of equations, you would want access to a supercomputer or a distributed network of computers called a grid.

Grid computing involves connecting geographically remote computers into a single network and combining the computational power of all computers on the grid. Grid computing takes advantage of the fact that most computers in the United States use their central processing units on average only 25 percent of the time, leaving 75 percent of their capacity available for other tasks. By using the combined power of thousands of PCs and other computers networked together, the grid can solve complicated problems at supercomputer speeds at far lower cost.

For example, Royal Dutch/Shell Group is using a scalable grid computing platform that improves the accuracy and speed of its scientific modeling applications to find the best oil reservoirs. This platform, which links 1,024 IBM servers running Linux, in effect creates one of the largest commercial Linux supercomputers in the world. The grid adjusts to accommodate the fluctuating data volumes that are typical in this seasonal business.

Computer Networks and Client/Server Computing

Unless you are in a small business with a stand-alone computer, you'll be using networked computers for most processing tasks. The use of multiple computers linked by a communications network for processing is called **distributed processing**. **Centralized processing**, in which all processing is accomplished by one large central computer, is much less common.

One widely used form of distributed processing is **client/server computing**. Client/server computing splits processing between clients and servers. Both are on the network, but each machine is assigned functions it is best suited to perform. The **client** is the user point of entry for the required function and is normally a desktop or laptop computer. The user generally interacts directly only with the client portion of the application. The server provides the client with services. Servers store and process shared data and perform such functions as printer management and backup storage and network activities such as security, remote access, and user authentication. Figure 5.2 illustrates the client/server computing concept. Computing on the Internet uses the client/server model (see Chapter 7).

Figure 5.2 illustrates the simplest client/server network, consisting of a client computer networked to a server computer, with processing split between the two types of machines. This is called a *two-tiered client/server architecture*. Whereas simple client/server networks can be found in small businesses, most corporations have more complex, multitiered (often called **N-tier) client/server architectures**, in which the work of the entire network is balanced over several levels of servers, depending on the kind of service being requested (see Figure 5.3).

For instance, at the first level a **web server** will serve a web page to a client in response to a request for service. Web server software is responsible for locating and managing stored web pages. If the client requests access to a corporate system (a product list or price information, for instance), the request is passed along to an **application server**. Application server software handles all application operations between a user and an organization's back-end business systems. The application server may reside on the same computer as the web server or on its own dedicated computer. Chapters 6 and 7 provide more detail about other pieces of software that are used in multitiered client/server architectures for e-commerce and e-business.

Figure 5.2
Client/Server Computing
In client/server computing, computer processing is split between client machines and server machines linked by a network. Users interface with the client machines.

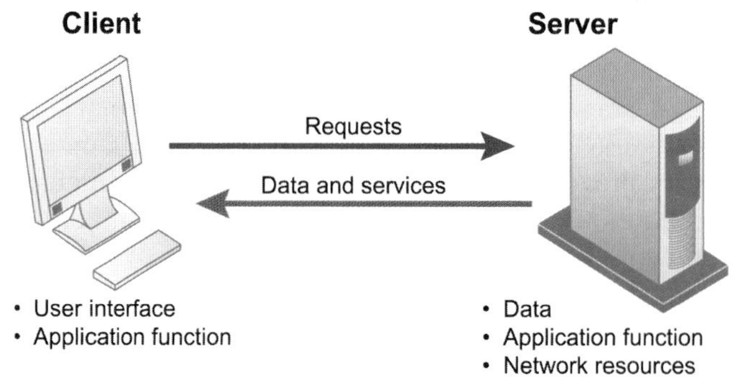

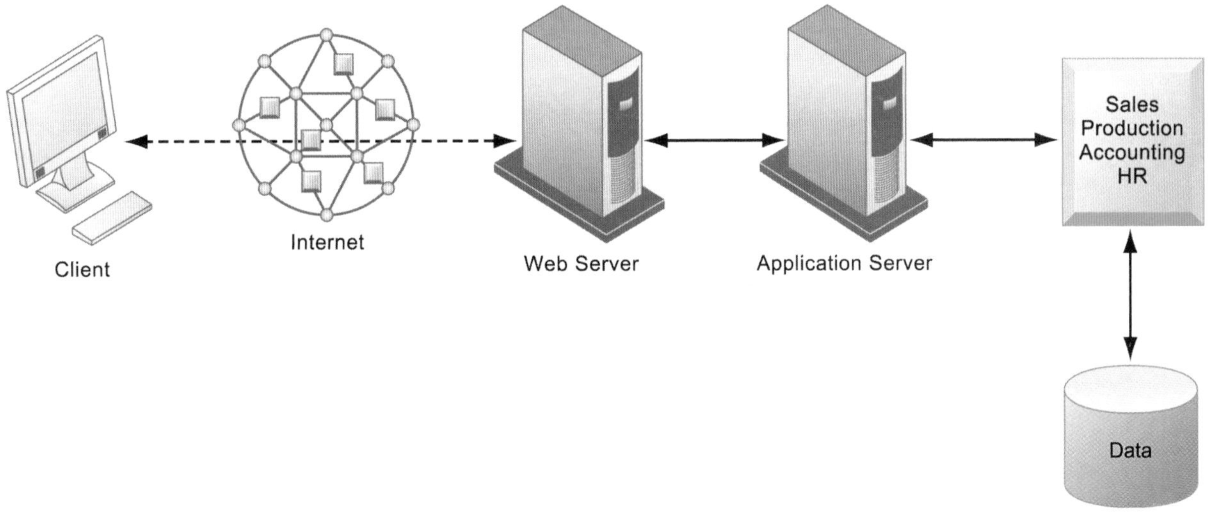

Figure 5.3
A Multitiered Client/Server Network (N-Tier)
In a multitiered client/server network, client requests for service are handled by different levels of servers.

STORAGE, INPUT, AND OUTPUT TECHNOLOGY

In addition to hardware for processing data, you will need technologies for data storage and input and output. Storage and input and output devices are called *peripheral devices* because they are outside the main computer system unit.

Secondary Storage Technology

Electronic commerce and electronic business, and regulations such as the Sarbanes-Oxley Act of 2002 and the Dodd Frank Act of 2010 have made storage a strategic technology. The amount of data that companies now need to store is doubling every 12 to 18 months. Traditional storage technologies include magnetic disks, optical drives, magnetic tape, and storage networks, which connect multiple storage devices on a separate high-speed network dedicated to storage.

Magnetic disk drives are still used for secondary storage in large and midrange computers and in some PCs. However, in lightweight PCs, such as the MacBook Air, smartphones, and tablets, hard drives have been replaced by **solid state drives (SSDs)**, which use an array of semiconductors organized as a very fast internal disk drive. Portable USB flash drives use similar technology for external storage. Optical drives (CD, DVD, and Blu-ray) use laser beaming technology to store very large quantities of data, including sound and images, in compact form. Firms also use cloud computing services for large scale data storage. We discuss cloud computing later in this chapter.

Input and Output Devices

Human beings interact with computer systems largely through input and output devices. **Input devices** gather data and convert them into electronic form for use by the computer, whereas **output devices** display data after they have been processed. Table 5.1 describes the principal input and output devices.

CONTEMPORARY HARDWARE TRENDS

The exploding power of computer hardware and networking technology has dramatically changed how businesses organize their computing power, putting more of this power on networks and mobile handheld devices. Let's look at seven hardware trends: the mobile digital platform, consumerization of IT, nanotechnology and quantum computing, virtualization, cloud computing, green computing, and high-performance/power-saving processors.

TABLE 5.1

Input and Output Devices

Input Device	Description
Keyboard	Principal method of data entry for text and numerical data.
Computer mouse	Handheld device with point-and-click capabilities for controlling a cursor's position on a computer display screen and selecting commands. Trackballs and touch pads often are used in place of the mouse as pointing devices on laptop PCs.
Touch screen	Device that allows users to interact with a computer by touching the surface of a sensitized display screen. Used in kiosks in airports, retail stores, and restaurants and in multitouch devices such as the iPhone, iPad, and multitouch PCs.
Optical character recognition	Device that can translate specially designed marks, characters, and codes into digital form. The most widely used optical code is the bar code.
Magnetic ink character recognition (MICR)	Technology used primarily in check processing for the banking industry. Characters on the bottom of a check identify the bank, checking account, and check number and are preprinted using special magnetic ink for translation into digital form for the computer.
Pen-based input	Handwriting-recognition devices that convert the motion made by an electronic stylus pressing on a touch-sensitive tablet screen into digital form.
Digital scanner	Device that translates images, such as pictures or documents, into digital form.
Audio input	Input devices that convert voice, music, or other sounds into digital form for processing by the computer.
Sensors	Devices that collect data directly from the environment for input into a computer system. For instance, farmers can use sensors to monitor the moisture of the soil in their fields.
Output Device	**Description**
Display	Often a flat-panel (LCD) display screen.
Printers	Devices that produce a printed hard copy of information output. They include impact printers (such as dot matrix printers) and nonimpact printers (such as laser, inkjet, and thermal transfer printers).
Audio output	Output devices that convert digital output data back into intelligible speech, music, or other sounds.

The Mobile Digital Platform

Chapter 1 pointed out that new mobile digital computing platforms have emerged as alternatives to PCs and larger computers. Mobile devices such as the iPhone and Android smartphones have taken on many functions of PCs, including transmitting data, surfing the web, transmitting email and instant messages, displaying digital content, and exchanging data with internal corporate systems. The new mobile platform also includes small, lightweight subnotebooks called *netbooks* optimized for wireless communication and Internet access, **tablet computers** such as the iPad, and digital e-book readers such as Amazon's Kindle with some web access capabilities.

Smartphones and tablet computers are becoming the primary means of accessing the Internet. These devices are increasingly used for business computing as well as for consumer applications. For example, senior executives at General Motors are using smartphone applications that drill down into vehicle sales information, financial performance, manufacturing metrics, and project management status.

Wearable computing devices are a recent addition to the mobile digital platform. These include smartwatches, smart glasses, smart badges, and activity trackers. Wearable computing technology is still in its infancy, but it already has business uses, as described in the Interactive Session on Technology.

Wearable Computers Change How We Work

It looks like wearable computing is taking off. Smartwatches, smart glasses, smart ID badges, head-mounted displays, and activity trackers promise to change how we go about each day and the way we do our jobs. According to Gartner, Inc., sales of wearables will increase from 275 million units in 2016 to 477 million units in 2020.

In some industries, wearable devices will become common workplace tools. Doctors and nurses are using smart eyewear for hands-free access to patients' medical records. Oil rig workers sport smart helmets to connect with land-based experts, who can view their work remotely and communicate instructions. Warehouse managers are able to capture real-time performance data using a smartwatch to better manage distribution and fulfillment operations. Wearable computing devices improve productivity by delivering information to workers without requiring them to interrupt their tasks, which in turn empowers employees to make more informed decisions more quickly.

Although primarily consumer devices, smartwatches are being used for business. The Apple Watch, for example, has a number of features to make employees more productive. It can take phone calls and accept voice commands. It will display an important message, email, or calendar appointment on your wrist. Instead of buzzing loudly and with every email, text message, and calendar alert you receive, the watch uses subtle, discreet vibrations that won't be a distraction in the middle of a meeting. There are Apple Watch versions of Evernote (note taking), PowerPoint (electronic presentations), and Invoice2go, which will automatically prompt you to start logging your work time as soon as you arrive at a job site, send basic invoices, and receive alerts when they're paid.

Salesforce.com has developed several enterprise applications for the Apple Watch. Salesforce1 for Apple Watch delivers instant notifications to salespeople, service agents, and other business users to help speed up their work. For example, sales managers can receive a discount approval request and take action right from the watch. Customer service managers can receive alerts if a critical case requires immediate attention or call wait times are about to exceed thresholds. Digital marketers can be alerted when a marketing campaign surpasses a goal. Salesforce Analytics for Apple Watch enables Salesforce customers to use analytics data delivered to their smartwatches to view performance metrics, uncover new insights, and take action with dashboards. Users will also be able to query via Voice Search to access a report, view a dashboard, or find other information.

Global logistics company DHL worked with Ricoh, the imaging and electronics company, and Ubimax, a wearable computing services and solutions company, to implement "vision picking" in its warehouse operations. Location graphics are displayed on smart glasses guiding staffers through the warehouse to both speed the process of finding items and reduce errors. The company says the technology delivered a 25 percent increase in efficiency.

Right now, vision picking gives workers locational information about the items they need to retrieve and allows them to automatically scan retrieved items. Future enhancements will enable the system to plot optimal routes through the warehouse, provide pictures of items to be retrieved (a key aid in case an item has been misplaced on the warehouse shelves), and instruct workers on loading carts and pallets more efficiently.

Southern Co., an Atlanta-based energy company, is experimenting with several different wearables in its power plants and its power distribution and transmission pipeline. Southern recently deployed both head-mounted and wrist-mounted computers and performed several "proofs of concept" with Google Glass, Apple Watch, and the Moto 360 Android Wear device. The proofs of concept focused on enhancing plant workers' ability to follow documented procedures more accurately and to document adherence to those procedures. The company also piloted Bluetooth video cameras worn on the head for documenting work processes and for videoconferencing between field personnel and central office personnel. Southern Co. now uses head-worn cameras in some plants and field locations.

The value of wearable computing devices isn't from transferring the same information from a laptop or smartphone to a smartwatch or eyeglass display. Rather, it's about finding ways to use wearables to augment and enhance business processes. Successful adoption of wearable computing depends not only on cost effectiveness but on the development of new and better apps and integration with existing IT infrastructure and the organization's tools for managing and securing mobile devices (see the chapter-ending case study).

Sources: "How Wearable Devices Are Creating Innovation in the Workplace," ITBusinessedge.com, accessed April 13, 2017; www.salesforce.com, accessed May 10, 2017; Linda Rosencrance, "Mobile Logistics Technology Takes Long Route to Consumer-Grade Devices," SearchMannufacturingERP.com, February 24, 2017; "Gartner: Wearables a $61.7 Billion Revenue Opportunity," BizTech Africa, April 12, 2016; Mary K. Pratt, "Wearables in the Enterprise? Yes, Really!" *Computerworld*, February 24, 2016; Bob Violino, "Wearables in the Workplace: Potential and Pitfalls," *Baseline*, September 9, 2015; and Brett Nuckles, "Apple Watch: Is It Good for Business?" *Business News Daily*, May 12, 2015.

CASE STUDY QUESTIONS

1. Wearables have the potential to change the way organizations and workers conduct business. Discuss the implications of this statement.
2. How would a business process such as ordering a product for a customer in the field be changed if the salesperson was wearing a smartwatch equipped with Salesforce software?
3. What people, organization, and technology issues would have to be addressed if a company was thinking of equipping its workers with a wearable computing device?
4. What kinds of businesses are most likely to benefit from wearable computers? Select a business and describe how a wearable computing device could help that business improve operations or decision making.

Consumerization of IT and BYOD

The popularity, ease of use, and rich array of useful applications for smartphones and tablet computers have created a groundswell of interest in allowing employees to use their personal mobile devices in the workplace, a phenomenon popularly called *bring your own device* (*BYOD*). **BYOD** is one aspect of the **consumerization of IT**, in which new information technology that first emerges in the consumer market spreads into business organizations. Consumerization of IT includes not only mobile personal devices but also business uses of software services that originated in the consumer marketplace as well, such as Google and Yahoo search, Gmail, Google's G Suite, and even Facebook and Twitter.

Consumerization of IT is forcing businesses to rethink the way they obtain and manage information technology equipment and services. Historically, at least in large firms, the IT department controlled selection and management of the firm's hardware and software. This ensured that information systems were protected and served the purposes of the firm. Today, employees and business departments are playing a much larger role in technology selection, in many cases demanding that employees be able to use their own personal mobile devices to access the corporate network. Although consumer technologies provide new tools to foster creativity, collaboration, and productivity, they are more difficult for firms to manage and control. We provide more detail on this topic in Section 5-3 and in the chapter-ending case study.

Nanotechnology and Quantum Computing

Over the years, microprocessor manufacturers have been able to increase processing power exponentially while shrinking chip size by finding ways to pack more transistors into less space. They are now turning to nanotechnology to shrink the size of transistors to the width of several atoms. **Nanotechnology** uses individual atoms and molecules to create computer chips and other devices that are thousands of times smaller than current technologies permit. IBM and other research labs have created transistors from nanotubes.

Another new way of enhancing computer processing power is to use quantum computing. **Quantum computing** uses the principles of quantum physics to represent data and perform operations on these data. While conventional computers handle bits of data either as 0 or 1 but not both, quantum computing can process bits as

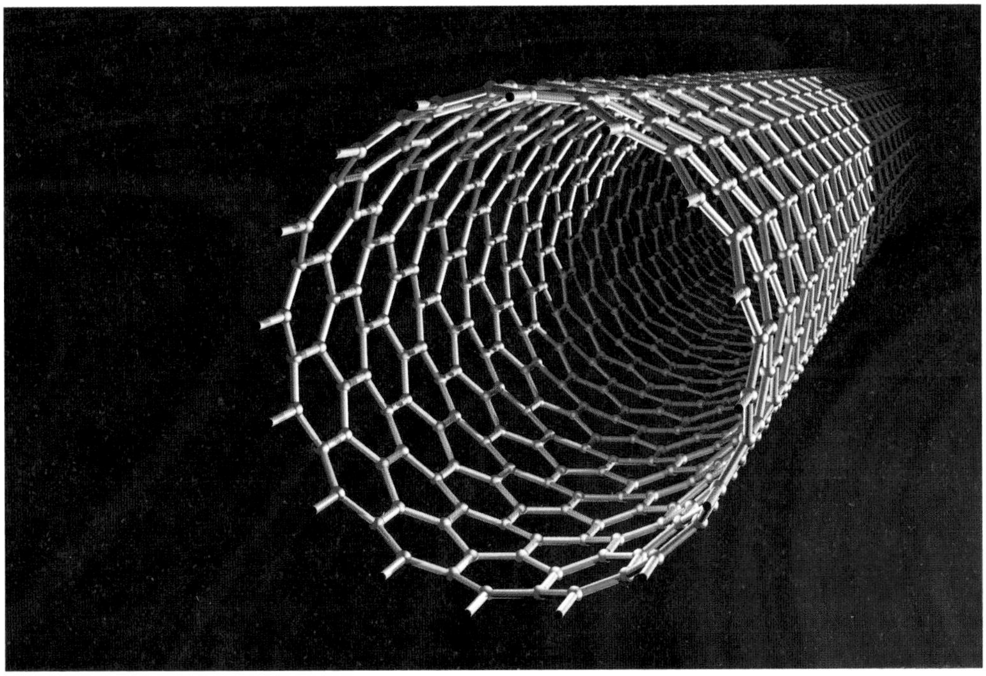

© forance/123RF

Nanotubes are tiny tubes about 10,000 times thinner than a human hair. They consist of rolled-up sheets of carbon hexagons and have potential uses as minuscule wires or in ultrasmall electronic devices and are very powerful conductors of electrical current.

0, 1, or both simultaneously. A quantum computer would gain enormous processing power through this ability to be in multiple states at once, allowing it to solve some scientific and business problems millions of times faster than can be done today. IBM has made quantum computing available to the general public through IBM Cloud. Google's Alphabet, Volkswagen, and Lockheed Martin are experimenting with quantum technology (Castellanos, 2017; Follow, 2016).

Virtualization

Virtualization is the process of presenting a set of computing resources (such as computing power or data storage) so that they can all be accessed in ways that are not restricted by physical configuration or geographic location. Virtualization enables a single physical resource (such as a server or a storage device) to appear to the user as multiple logical resources. For example, a server or mainframe can be configured to run many instances of an operating system (or different operating systems) so that it acts like many different machines. Each virtual server "looks" like a real physical server to software programs, and multiple virtual servers can run in parallel on a single machine. VMware is the leading virtualization software vendor for Windows and Linux servers.

Server virtualization is a common method of reducing technology costs by providing the ability to host multiple systems on a single physical machine. Most servers run at just 15 to 20 percent of capacity, and virtualization can boost server utilization rates to 70 percent or higher. Higher utilization rates translate into fewer computers required to process the same amount of work, reduced data center space to house machines, and lower energy usage. Virtualization also facilitates centralization and consolidation of hardware administration.

Virtualization also enables multiple physical resources (such as storage devices or servers) to appear as a single logical resource, as in **software-defined storage (SDS)**, which separates the software for managing data storage from storage hardware. Using software, firms can pool and arrange multiple storage infrastructure resources and efficiently allocate them to meet specific application needs. SDS enables firms to replace expensive storage hardware with lower-cost commodity hardware and cloud storage hardware. There is less under- or over-utilization of storage resources (Letschin, 2016).

Cloud Computing

Cloud computing is a model of computing in which computer processing, storage, software, and other services are provided as a shared pool of virtualized resources over a network, primarily the Internet. These clouds of computing resources can be accessed on an as-needed basis from any connected device and location. Currently, cloud computing is the fastest-growing form of computing, with cloud computing expenditures growing to $216 billion by 2020. Within five years, 50 percent of information technology will be in the cloud (Gartner, 2016; Walden, 2015). Figure 5.4 illustrates the cloud computing concept.

Consumers use cloud services such as Apple's iCloud or Google Drive to store documents, photos, videos, and email. Cloud-based software powers social networks, streamed video and music, and online games. Private and public organizations are turning to cloud services to replace internally run data centers and software applications. Amazon, Google, IBM, and Microsoft operate huge, scalable cloud computing centers offering computing power, data storage, and high-speed Internet connections to firms that want to maintain their IT infrastructures remotely. Google, Microsoft, SAP, Oracle, and Salesforce.com sell software applications as cloud services delivered over the Internet.

The U.S. National Institute of Standards and Technology (NIST) defines cloud computing as having the following essential characteristics:

- **On-demand self-service:** Consumers can obtain computing capabilities such as server time or network storage as needed automatically on their own.
- **Ubiquitous network access:** Cloud resources can be accessed using standard network and Internet devices, including mobile platforms.
- **Location-independent resource pooling:** Computing resources are pooled to serve multiple users, with different virtual resources dynamically assigned according to user demand. The user generally does not know where the computing resources are located.

Figure 5.4
Cloud Computing Platform
In cloud computing, hardware and software capabilities are a pool of virtualized resources provided over a network, often the Internet. Businesses and employees have access to applications and IT infrastructure anywhere and at any time.

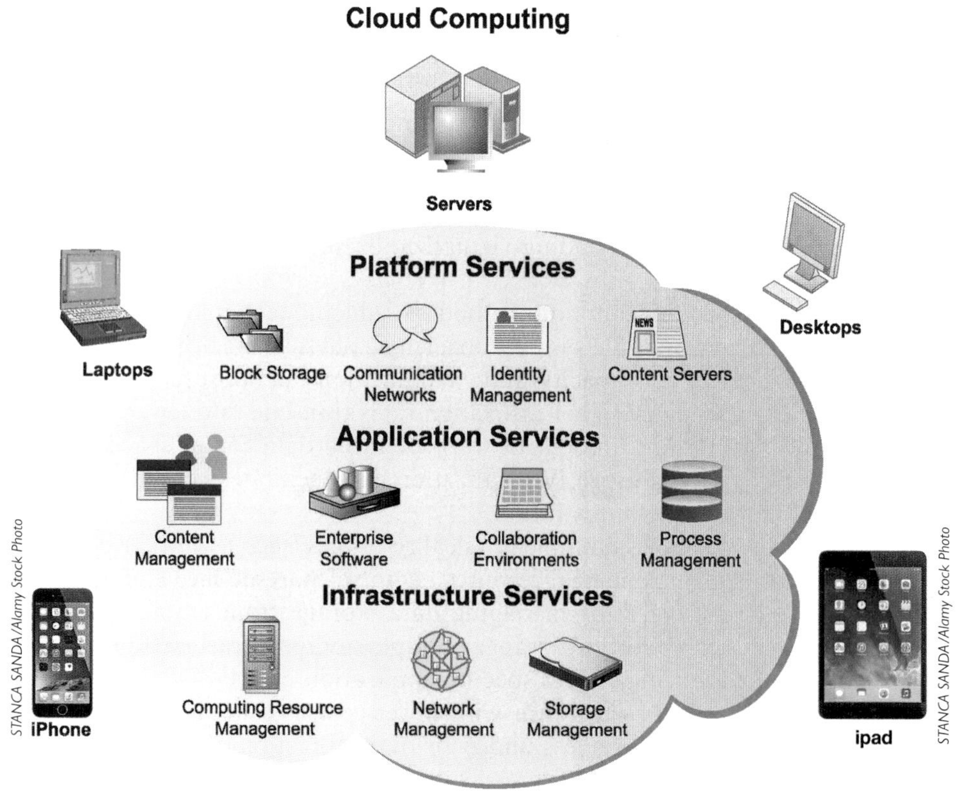

- **Rapid elasticity:** Computing resources can be rapidly provisioned, increased, or decreased to meet changing user demand.
- **Measured service:** Charges for cloud resources are based on number of resources actually used.

Cloud computing consists of three types of services:

- **Infrastructure as a service (IaaS):** Customers use processing, storage, networking, and other computing resources from cloud service providers to run their information systems. For example, Amazon uses the spare capacity of its IT infrastructure to provide a broadly based cloud environment selling IT infrastructure services. These include its Simple Storage Service (S3) for storing customers' data and its Elastic Compute Cloud (EC2) service for running their applications. Users pay only for the amount of computing and storage capacity they actually use. (See the Interactive Session on Organizations.) Figure 5.5 shows some of the major services Amazon Web Services offers.
- **Software as a service (SaaS):** Customers use software hosted by the vendor on the vendor's cloud infrastructure and delivered as a service over a network. Leading **software as a service (SaaS)** examples are G Suite, which provides common business applications online, and Salesforce.com, which leases customer relationship management and related software services over the Internet. Both charge users an annual subscription fee, although Google also has a pared-down free version. Users access these applications from a web browser, and the data and software are maintained on the providers' remote servers.
- **Platform as a service (PaaS):** Customers use infrastructure and programming tools supported by the cloud service provider to develop their own applications. For example, IBM offers Bluemix for software development and testing on its cloud infrastructure. Another example is Salesforce.com's Force.com, which allows developers to build applications that are hosted on its servers as a service.

Chapter 2 discussed Google Docs, G Suite, and related software services for desktop productivity and collaboration. These are among the most popular software services for consumers, although they are increasingly used in business. Salesforce.com is a leading software service for business, providing customer relationship management (CRM) and other application software solutions as software services leased over the Internet. Its Sales Cloud and Service Cloud offer applications for improving

Figure 5.5
Major Amazon Web Services

Amazon Web Services (AWS) is a collection of web services that Amazon provides to users of its cloud platform. AWS now offers over 90 services and is the largest provider of public cloud-based services.

Computing Takes Off in the Cloud

Cloud computing is now the fastest-growing form of computing. The biggest players in the cloud computing marketplace include Amazon Web Services (AWS), Microsoft, and Google. These companies have made cloud computing an affordable and sensible option for companies ranging from tiny Internet start-ups to established companies like Netflix and FedEx.

For example, AWS provides subscribing companies with flexible computing power and data storage as well as data management, messaging, payment, and other services that can be used together or individually as the business requires. Anyone with an Internet connection and a little bit of money can harness the same computing systems that Amazon itself uses to run its retail business. If customers provide specifications on the amount of server space, bandwidth, storage, and any other services they require, AWS can automatically allocate those resources. You don't pay a monthly or yearly fee to use Amazon's computing resources—instead, you pay for exactly what you use. Economies of scale keep costs astonishingly low, and AWS has been able to keep reducing prices. To remain competitive, other cloud computing vendors have had to follow suit.

Cloud computing also appeals to many businesses because the cloud services provider will handle all of the maintenance and upkeep of their IT infrastructures, allowing these businesses to spend more time on higher-value work. Start-up companies and smaller companies are finding that they no longer need to build their own data center. With cloud infrastructures like Amazon's readily available, they have access to technical capability that was formerly available to only much larger businesses. Hi-Media is the Internet publisher of the Fotolog photo blogging website. Hi-Media rebuilt the site and moved it to AWS where it can easily scale computing capacity to meet the demands of Fotolog's 32 million global users who have collectively posted 1 billion photos and 10 billion comments.

Although cloud computing has been touted as a cheap and more flexible alternative to buying and owning information technology, this isn't always the case. For large companies, paying a public cloud provider a monthly service fee for 10,000 or more employees may actually be more expensive than having the company maintain its own IT infrastructure and staff. Companies also worry about unexpected "runaway costs" from using a pay-per-use model. Integrating cloud services with existing IT infrastructures, errors, mismanagement, or unusually high volumes of web traffic will run up the bill for cloud service users.

Gartner, Inc. technology consultants advise clients contemplating public cloud services to take into account the number of machines an organization will run, the number of hours per day or per week they'll run, and the amount of storage their data will require. Additional costs include licenses that need to be paid for on a recurring basis, the rate of change for the data, and how much new data the business is expected to generate. A very large company may find it cheaper to own and manage its own data center or private cloud. But as public clouds become more efficient and secure and the technology grows cheaper, large companies will start using more cloud resources.

A major barrier to widespread cloud adoption has been concerns about cloud reliability and security. Amazon's S3 cloud storage service experienced a four-hour outage February 28, 2017, shutting down thousands of websites across the Internet. There were also significant Amazon cloud outages in the preceding five years. As cloud computing continues to mature and the major cloud infrastructure providers gain more experience, cloud service and reliability have steadily improved. Experts recommend that companies for whom an outage would be a major risk consider using another computing service as a backup.

In February 2016 Netflix completed a decade-long project to shut down its own data centers and use Amazon's cloud exclusively to run its business. Management liked not having to guess months beforehand what the firm's hardware, storage, and networking needs would be. AWS would provide whatever Netflix needed at the moment.

Netflix had experienced a major hardware failure in 2008 at its own data center and began moving its computing to AWS the following year. The first thing Netflix shifted was its jobs page, followed by functions such as its video player, iPhone-related technology, discovery and search, and accounts pages. Netflix shifted its big data platform to AWS in 2013 and billing and payments in 2014. Netflix is now fully reliant on AWS, using a variety of web-based software tools such as human resources software from Workday Inc. for its business applications.

Netflix also maintains a content-delivery network through Internet service providers and other third parties to speed up the delivery of movies and web traffic between Netflix and its customers. Netflix competes with Amazon in the video-streaming business, and it wanted to retain control of its own content delivery network.

About 12 percent of companies run IT operations entirely in the cloud, and nearly all of these companies are small or medium-sized businesses, according to a recent survey by BetterCloud, which makes management and security products. BetterCloud predicts that by 2022, slightly more than 20 percent of large enterprise companies will operate entirely in the cloud.

Glenn O'Donnell, vice president and research director at Forrester Research, believes that a 100 percent cloud operation will be extremely rare for large established companies. Many large companies are moving more of their computing to the cloud but are unable to migrate completely. Legacy systems are the most difficult to switch over.

Most midsized and large companies will gravitate toward a hybrid approach. The top cloud providers themselves—Amazon, Google, Microsoft, and IBM—use their own public cloud services for some purposes, but they continue to keep certain functions on private servers. Worries about reliability, security, and risks of change have made it difficult for them to move critical computing tasks to the public cloud.

Giant Eagle, one of the largest U.S. privately held multiformat food, fuel, and pharmacy retailers, is adopting a hybrid cloud solution from IBM Cloud. The hybrid cloud will provide capabilities for consumption-based pricing, faster procurement, and customized deployment of applications along with integrated system management for greater visibility into enterprise data. Marriott is keeping its own data centers but is updating them to use the latest cloud technology. It also uses IBM's cloud to host apps that it doesn't want to host itself. The hybrid cloud environment offers faster digital services to web-savvy guests and helps Marriott use analytics to uncover insights about traveler preferences for its more than 4,000 properties across the globe.

Sources: Robert McMillan, "Amazon Grapples with Outage at AWS Cloud Service," *Wall Street Journal*, March 1, 2017; Brandon Butler, "Battle of the Clouds," *Network World*, February 22, 2017; "AWS Case Study: Hi-Media," www.aws.amazon.com, accessed May 14, 2017; Robert McMillan, "Cloud-Computing Kingpins Slow to Adapt to Own Movement," *Wall Street Journal*, August 4, 2015; Robert McMillan and Rachael King, "Netflix Is Ready to Pull Plug on Its Final Data Center," *Wall Street Journal*, August 14, 2015; Dan Berthiaume, "Giant Eagle Flies to the Cloud," *Chain Store Age*, December 4, 2015; Darryl K. Taft, "IBM Lands Cloud Deals with Marriott, Others," *eWeek*, February 2, 2015; and Kelly Bit, "The $10 Hedge Fund Supercomputer That's Sweeping Wall Street," *Bloomberg Business Week*, May 20, 2015.

CASE STUDY QUESTIONS

1. What business benefits do cloud computing services provide? What problems do they solve?

2. What are the disadvantages of cloud computing?

3. What kinds of businesses are most likely to benefit from using cloud computing? Why?

sales and customer service. A Marketing Cloud enables companies to engage in digital marketing interactions with customers through email, mobile, social, web, and connected products. Salesforce.com also provides a Community Cloud platform for online collaboration and engagement and an Analytics Cloud platform to deploy sales, service, marketing, and custom analytics apps.

Salesforce.com is also a leading example of PaaS. Its Force.com is an application development platform on which customers can develop their own applications for use within the broader Salesforce network. Force.com provides a set of development tools and IT services that enable users to customize their Salesforce.com CRM applications or build entirely new applications and run them in the cloud on Salesforce.com's data center infrastructure. Salesforce opened up Force.com to other independent software developers and listed their programs on its AppExchange, an online marketplace for third-party applications that run on the Force.com platform.

A cloud can be private or public. A **public cloud** is owned and maintained by a cloud service provider, such as Amazon Web Services, and made available to the general public or industry group. Public cloud services are often used for websites with public information and product descriptions, one-time large computing projects, new application development and testing, and consumer services such as online storage of data, music, and photos. Google Drive, Dropbox, and Apple iCloud are leading examples of these consumer cloud services.

A **private cloud** is operated solely for an organization. It might be managed by the organization or a third party and hosted either internally or externally. Like public clouds, private clouds can allocate storage, computing power, or other resources seamlessly to provide computing resources on an as-needed basis. Companies that want flexible IT resources and a cloud service model while retaining control over their own IT infrastructure are gravitating toward these private clouds. (Review the Interactive Session on Organizations.)

Because organizations using public clouds do not own the infrastructure, they do not have to make large investments in their own hardware and software. Instead, they purchase their computing services from remote providers and pay only for the amount of computing power they actually use (utility computing) or are billed on a monthly or annual subscription basis. The term **on-demand computing** has also been used to describe such services.

Cloud computing has some drawbacks. Unless users make provisions for storing their data locally, the responsibility for data storage and control is in the hands of the provider. Some companies worry about the security risks related to entrusting their critical data and systems to an outside vendor that also works with other companies. Companies expect their systems to be available 24/7 and do not want to suffer any loss of business capability if cloud infrastructures malfunction. Nevertheless, the trend is for companies to shift more of their computer processing and storage to some form of cloud infrastructure. Start-ups and small companies that do not have ample IT resources or budgets will find public cloud services especially helpful.

Large firms are most likely to adopt a **hybrid cloud** computing model, in which they use their own infrastructure for their most essential core activities and adopt public cloud computing for less-critical systems or for additional processing capacity during peak business periods. Table 5.2 compares the three cloud computing models.

TABLE 5.2

Cloud Computing Models Compared

Type of Cloud	Description	Managed By	Uses
Public cloud	Third-party service offering computing, storage, and software services to multiple customers and that is available to the public	Third-party service providers	Companies without major privacy concerns Companies seeking pay-as-you-go IT services Companies lacking IT resources and expertise
Private cloud	Cloud infrastructure operated solely for a single organization and hosted either internally or externally	In-house IT or private third-party host	Companies with stringent privacy and security requirements Companies that must have control over data sovereignty
Hybrid cloud	Combination of private and public cloud services that remain separate entities	In-house IT, private host, third-party providers	Companies requiring some in-house control of IT that are also willing to assign part of their IT infrastructures to a public cloud

Cloud computing will gradually shift firms from having a fixed infrastructure capacity toward a more flexible infrastructure, some of it owned by the firm, and some of it rented from giant computer centers owned by cloud vendors. You can find out more about cloud computing in the Learning Tracks for this chapter.

Green Computing

By curbing hardware proliferation and power consumption, virtualization has become one of the principal technologies for promoting green computing. **Green computing** or **green IT** refers to practices and technologies for designing, manufacturing, using, and disposing of computers, servers, and associated devices such as monitors, printers, storage devices, and networking and communications systems in order to minimize impact on the environment.

According to Green House Data, the world's data centers use as much energy as the output of 30 nuclear power plants, which is about 1.5 percent of all energy use in the world. Reducing computer power consumption has been a very high green priority. A corporate data center can easily consume more than 100 times more power than a standard office building. All this additional power consumption has a negative impact on the environment and corporate operating costs. Data centers are now being designed with energy efficiency in mind, using state-of-the-art air-cooling techniques, energy-efficient equipment, virtualization, and other energy-saving practices. Large companies such as Microsoft, Google, Facebook, and Apple are starting to reduce their carbon footprint with clean energy–powered data centers, including extensive use of wind and hydropower.

High-Performance and Power-Saving Processors

Another way to reduce power requirements and hardware sprawl is to use more efficient and power-saving processors. Contemporary microprocessors now feature multiple processor cores (which perform the reading and execution of computer instructions) on a single chip. A **multicore processor** is an integrated circuit to which two or more processor cores have been attached for enhanced performance, reduced power consumption, and more efficient simultaneous processing of multiple tasks. This technology enables two or more processing engines with reduced power requirements and heat dissipation to perform tasks faster than a resource-hungry chip with a single processing core. Today, you'll find PCs with dual-core, quad-core, six-core, and eight-core processors. Intel's Core i9 family of processors for high-end PCs has up to 18 cores.

Intel and other chip manufacturers are working on microprocessors that minimize power consumption, which is essential for prolonging battery life in small mobile digital devices. Highly power-efficient microprocessors, such as the A9 and A10 processors used in Apple's iPhone and iPad, and Intel's Atom processor, are used in lightweight smartphones and tablets, intelligent cars, and health care devices. The Apple processors have about one-fiftieth of the power consumption of a laptop dual-core processor.

5-3 What are the major types of computer software used in business and the major software trends?

To use computer hardware, you need software, which provides the detailed instructions that direct the computer's work. System software and application software are interrelated and can be thought of as a set of nested boxes, each of which must interact closely with the other boxes surrounding it. Figure 5.6 illustrates this relationship. The system software surrounds and controls access to the hardware. Application software must work through the system software to operate. End users work primarily with application software. Each type of software must be designed for a specific machine to ensure its compatibility.

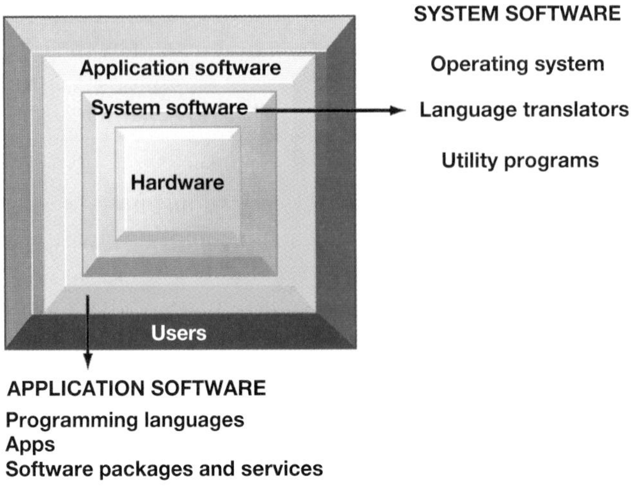

Figure 5.6
The Major Types of Software
The relationship between the system software, application software, and users can be illustrated by a series of nested boxes. System software—consisting of operating systems, language translators, and utility programs—controls access to the hardware. Application software, including programming languages and software packages, must work through the system software to operate. The user interacts primarily with the application software.

OPERATING SYSTEM SOFTWARE

The system software that manages and controls the computer's activities is called the **operating system**. Other system software consists of computer language translation programs that convert programming languages into machine language that can be understood by the computer and utility programs that perform common processing tasks, such as copying, sorting, or computing a square root.

The operating system is the computer system's chief manager, enabling the system to handle many tasks and users at the same time. The operating system allocates and assigns system resources, schedules the use of computer resources and computer jobs, and monitors computer system activities. The operating system provides locations in primary memory for data and programs and controls the input and output devices, such as printers, terminals, and telecommunication links. The operating system also coordinates the scheduling of work in various areas of the computer so that different parts of different jobs can be worked on simultaneously.

PC, Server, and Mobile Operating Systems

The operating system controls the way users interact with the computer. Contemporary PC operating systems and application software use a **graphical user interface**, often called a **GUI**, which makes extensive use of icons, buttons, bars, and boxes to perform tasks.

Conventional client operating system software was designed around the mouse and keyboard, but it is increasingly becoming more natural and intuitive by using **multitouch** technology. The multitouch interface on the iPhone and other smartphones and tablet computers as well as on newer PC models allows you to use one or more fingers to perform special gestures to manipulate lists or objects on a screen without using a mouse or a keyboard.

Table 5.3 compares leading PC and server operating systems. These include the Windows family of operating systems (Windows 10, Windows 8, Windows 7, and Windows Server), UNIX, Linux, and the operating system for the Macintosh computer.

The Microsoft Windows family of operating systems has both client and server versions and a streamlined GUI which now works with touch screens and mobile devices as well as with keyboards and traditional PCs. Windows systems can perform multiple programming tasks simultaneously and have powerful networking capabilities, including the ability to access information from the Internet. At the client level, most PCs use some form of the Microsoft Windows or Apple operating systems. The latest Windows client version is **Windows 10**.

Windows operating systems for servers provide network management functions, including support for virtualization and cloud computing. Windows Server has multiple versions for small, medium, and large businesses.

TABLE 5.3

Leading PC and Server Operating Systems

Operating System	Features
Windows 10	Most recent Windows client operating system, which supports multitouch and mobile devices as well as traditional PCs and includes voice search capabilities.
Windows Server	Windows operating system for servers.
UNIX	Used for PCs, workstations, and network servers. Supports multitasking, multiuser processing, and networking. Is portable to different models of computer hardware.
Linux	Open source, reliable alternative to UNIX and Windows operating systems that runs on many types of computer hardware and can be modified by software developers.
OS X and macOS	Operating system for the Macintosh computer that is highly visual and user-friendly, with support for multitouch. Most recent version is macOS Sierra.

Today there is a much greater variety of operating systems than in the past, with new operating systems for computing on handheld mobile digital devices or cloud-connected computers. Google's **Chrome OS** provides a lightweight operating system for cloud computing using a web-connected computer or mobile device. Programs are not stored on the user's computing device but are used over the Internet and accessed through the Chrome web browser. User data reside on servers across the Internet. **Android** is an open source operating system for mobile devices such as smartphones and tablet computers developed by the Open Handset Alliance led by Google. It has become the most popular smartphone platform worldwide, competing with **iOS**, Apple's mobile operating system for the iPhone, iPad, and iPod Touch.

UNIX is a multiuser, multitasking operating system developed by Bell Laboratories in 1969 to connect various machines and is highly supportive of communications and networking. UNIX is often used on workstations and servers and provides the reliability and scalability for running large systems on high-end servers. UNIX can run on many kinds of computers and can be easily customized. Application programs that run under UNIX can be ported from one computer to run on a different computer with little modification. Graphical user interfaces have been developed for UNIX. Vendors have developed different versions of UNIX that are incompatible, thereby limiting software portability.

Linux is a UNIX-like operating system that can be downloaded from the Internet free of charge or purchased for a small fee from companies that provide additional tools for the software. It is free, reliable, compactly designed, and capable of running on many hardware platforms, including servers, handheld computers, and consumer electronics.

Linux has become popular as a robust, low-cost alternative to UNIX and the Windows operating systems. For example, E*Trade Financial saves $13 million annually with improved computer performance by running Linux on a series of small inexpensive IBM servers instead of large expensive Oracle Sun servers running a proprietary version of UNIX.

Linux plays a major role in the back office, running web servers and local area networks in about 35 percent of the worldwide server market. IBM, HP, Dell, and Oracle have made Linux part of their offerings to corporations, and major software vendors offer versions of their products that can run on Linux.

APPLICATION SOFTWARE AND DESKTOP PRODUCTIVITY TOOLS

Today, businesses have access to an array of tools for developing their application software. These include traditional programming languages, application software packages, and desktop productivity tools; software for developing Internet applications; and software for enterprise integration. It is important to know which software tools and programming languages are appropriate for the work your business wants to accomplish.

Programming Languages for Business

Popular programming languages for business applications include C, C++, Visual Basic, and Java. **C** is a powerful and efficient language developed in the early 1970s that combines machine portability with tight control and efficient use of computer resources. It is used primarily by professional programmers to create operating systems and application software, especially for PCs. **C++** is a newer version of C that has all the capabilities of C plus additional features for working with software objects. Unlike traditional programs, which separate data from the actions to be taken on the data, a software **object** combines data and procedures. Chapter 12 describes object-oriented software development in more detail. **Visual Basic** is a widely used visual programming tool and environment for creating applications that run on Microsoft Windows operating systems. A **visual programming language** allows users to manipulate graphic or iconic elements to create programs. COBOL (COmmon Business Oriented Language), was developed in the early 1960s for business processing and can still be found in large legacy systems in banking, insurance, and retail.

Java is an operating system–independent, processor-independent, object-oriented programming language created by Sun Microsystems that has become the leading interactive programming environment for the web. The Java platform has migrated into mobile phones, smartphones, automobiles, music players, game machines, and finally, into set-top cable television systems serving interactive content and pay-per-view services. Java software is designed to run on any computer or computing device, regardless of the specific microprocessor or operating system the device uses. For each of the computing environments in which Java is used, a Java Virtual Machine interprets Java programming code for that machine. In this manner, the code is written once and can be used on any machine for which there exists a Java Virtual Machine.

Other popular programming tools for web applications include Ruby, Python, and PHP. Ruby is an object-oriented programming language known for speed and ease of use in building web applications, and Python (praised for its clarity) is being used for building cloud computing applications.

Software Packages and Desktop Productivity Tools

Much of the software used in businesses today is not custom programmed but consists of application software packages and desktop productivity tools. A **software package** is a prewritten, precoded, commercially available set of programs that eliminates the need for individuals or organizations to write their own software programs for certain functions. Software packages that run on mainframes and larger computers usually require professional programmers for their installation and support, but desktop productivity software packages for consumer users can easily be installed and run by the users themselves. Table 5.4 describes the major desktop productivity software tools.

Software Suites The major desktop productivity tools are bundled together as a software suite. Microsoft Office is an example. Core office tools include Word processing software, Excel **spreadsheet software** (see Figure 5.7), Access database software, PowerPoint presentation graphics software, and Outlook, a set of tools for email, scheduling, and contact management. Microsoft now offers a hosted cloud version of its productivity and collaboration tools as a subscription service called **Office 365**. Competing with Microsoft Office are low-cost office productivity suites such as the open source OpenOffice (downloadable free over the Internet) and cloud-based Google Docs and G Suite (see Chapter 2).

TABLE 5.4
Desktop Productivity Software.

Software Tool	Capabilities	Example
Word processing	Allows the user to make changes in a document electronically, with various formatting options.	Microsoft Word WordPerfect
Spreadsheet	Organizes data into a grid of columns and rows. When the user changes a value or values, all other related values on the spreadsheet are automatically recalculated. Used for modeling and what-if analysis (see Figure 5.7) and can also present numeric data graphically.	Microsoft Excel iWork Numbers
Data management	Creates files and databases in which users can store, manipulate, and retrieve related data. Suitable for building small information systems.	Microsoft Access
Presentation graphics	Creates professional-quality electronic graphics presentations and computerized slide shows; can include multimedia displays of sound, animation, photos, and video clips.	Microsoft PowerPoint iWork Keynote
Personal information management	Creates and maintains appointments, calendars, to-do lists, and business contact information; also used for email.	Microsoft Outlook
Desktop publishing	Creates professional-looking documents, brochures, or books.	Adobe InDesign

Web Browsers Easy-to-use software called **web browsers** are used for displaying web pages and for accessing the web and other Internet resources. Browsers can display or present graphics, audio, and video information as well as traditional text, and they allow you to click (or touch) on-screen buttons or highlighted words to link to related websites. Web browsers have become the primary interface for accessing the Internet or for using networked systems based on Internet technology. The leading web browsers today are Microsoft Internet Explorer, Mozilla Firefox, Apple Safari, and Google Chrome.

Total fixed cost	19,000.00
Variable cost per unit	3.00
Average sales price	17.00
Contribution margin	14.00
Break-even point	1,357

Custom Neckties Pro Forma Income Statement

Units sold	0.00	679	1,357	2,036	2,714
Revenue	0	11,536	23,071	34,607	46,143
Fixed cost	19,000	19,000	19,000	19,000	19,000
Variable cost	0	2,036	4,071	6,107	8,143
Total cost	19,000	21,036	23,071	25,107	27,143
Profit/Loss	(19,000)	(9,500)	0	9,500	19,000

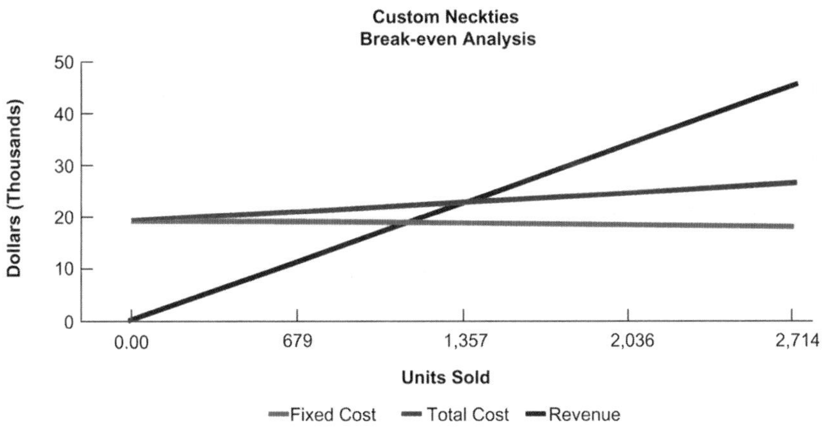

Figure 5.7
Spreadsheet Software
Spreadsheet software organizes data into columns and rows for analysis and manipulation. Contemporary spreadsheet software provides graphing abilities for a clear, visual representation of the data in the spreadsheets. This sample break-even analysis is represented as numbers in a spreadsheet as well as a line graph for easy interpretation.

TABLE 5.5

Examples of HTML

Plain English	HTML
Subcompact	<TITLE>Subcompact</TITLE>
4 passenger	<LI>4 passenger</LI>
$16,800	<LI>$16,800</LI>

HTML AND HTML5

Hypertext Markup Language (HTML) is a page description language for specifying how text, graphics, video, and sound are placed on a web page and for creating dynamic links to other web pages and objects. Using these links, a user need only point at a highlighted keyword or graphic, click it, and immediately be transported to another document. Table 5.5 illustrates some sample HTML statements.

HTML programs can be custom written, but they also can be created using the HTML authoring capabilities of web browsers or of popular word processing, spreadsheet, data management, and presentation graphics software packages. HTML editors, such as Adobe Dreamweaver, are more powerful HTML authoring programs for creating web pages.

HTML was originally designed to create and link static documents composed largely of text. Today, however, the web is much more social and interactive, and many web pages have multimedia elements—images, audio, and video. Third-party plug-in applications such as Flash, Silverlight, and Java have been required to integrate these rich media with web pages. However, these add-ons require additional programming and put strains on computer processing. The most recent version of HTML, called **HTML5**, solves this problem by making it possible to embed images, audio, video, and other elements directly into a document without processor-intensive add-ons. HTML5 also makes it easier for web pages to function across different display devices, including mobile devices as well as desktops. Web pages will execute more quickly, and web-based mobile apps will work like web pages.

WEB SERVICES

Web services refer to a set of loosely coupled software components that exchange information with each other using universal web communication standards and languages. They can exchange information between two systems regardless of the operating systems or programming languages on which the systems are based. They can be used to build open-standard, web-based applications linking systems of different organizations, and they can be used to create applications that link disparate systems within a single company. Different applications can use them to communicate with each other in a standard way without time-consuming custom coding.

The foundation technology for web services is **XML**, which stands for **Extensible Markup Language**. This language was developed in 1996 by the World Wide Web Consortium (W3C, the international body that oversees the development of the web) as a more powerful and flexible markup language than HTML for web pages. Whereas HTML is limited to describing how data should be presented in the form of web pages, XML can perform presentation, communication, and storage of data. In XML, a number is not simply a number; the XML tag specifies whether the number represents a price, a date, or a zip code. Table 5.6 illustrates some sample XML statements.

By tagging selected elements of the content of documents for their meanings, XML makes it possible for computers to manipulate and interpret their data automatically and perform operations on the data without human intervention. XML provides a standard format for data exchange, enabling web services to pass data from one process to another.

TABLE 5.6
Examples of XML

Plain English	XML
Subcompact	<AUTOMOBILETYPE="Subcompact">
4 passenger	<PASSENGERUNIT="PASS">4</PASSENGER>
$16,800	<PRICE CURRENCY="USD">$16,800</PRICE>

Web services communicate through XML messages over standard web protocols. Companies discover and locate web services through a directory much as they would locate services in the Yellow Pages of a telephone book. Using web protocols, a software application can connect freely to other applications without custom programming for each application with which it wants to communicate. Everyone shares the same standards.

The collection of web services that are used to build a firm's software systems constitutes what is known as a service-oriented architecture. A **service-oriented architecture (SOA)** is set of self-contained services that communicate with each other to create a working software application. Software developers reuse these services in other combinations to assemble other applications as needed.

Virtually all major software vendors, such as IBM, Microsoft, Oracle, and HP, provide tools and entire platforms for building and integrating software applications using web services. IBM includes web service tools in its WebSphere e-business software platform, and Microsoft has incorporated web services tools in its Microsoft.NET platform.

Dollar Rent-A-Car's systems use web services to link its online booking system with the Southwest Airlines website. Although both companies' systems are based on different technology platforms, a person booking a flight on Southwest.com can reserve a car from Dollar without leaving the airline's website. Instead of struggling to get Dollar's reservation system to share data with Southwest's information systems, Dollar used Microsoft.NET web services technology as an intermediary. Reservations from Southwest are translated into web services protocols, which are then translated into formats that Dollar's computers can understand.

Other car rental companies have linked their information systems to airline companies' websites before, but without web services, these connections had to be built one at a time. Web services provide a standard way for Dollar's computers to talk to other companies' information systems without having to build special links to each one. Dollar is expanding its use of web services to link directly to the systems of a small tour operator and a large travel reservation system as well as a wireless website for mobile phones. It does not have to write new software code for each new partner's information systems or each new wireless device (see Figure 5.8).

SOFTWARE TRENDS

Today there are many more sources for obtaining software and many more capabilities for users to create their own customized software applications. Expanding use of open source software and cloud-based software tools and services exemplify this trend.

Open Source Software

Open source software provides all computer users with free access to its program code, so they can modify the code to fix errors or to make improvements. Open source software is not owned by any company or individual. A global network of programmers and users manages and modifies the software, usually without being paid to do so. Popular open source software tools include the Linux operating system (described earlier in this chapter), Apache HTTP web server, the Mozilla Firefox web browser, and the Apache OpenOffice desktop productivity suite. Google's Android mobile

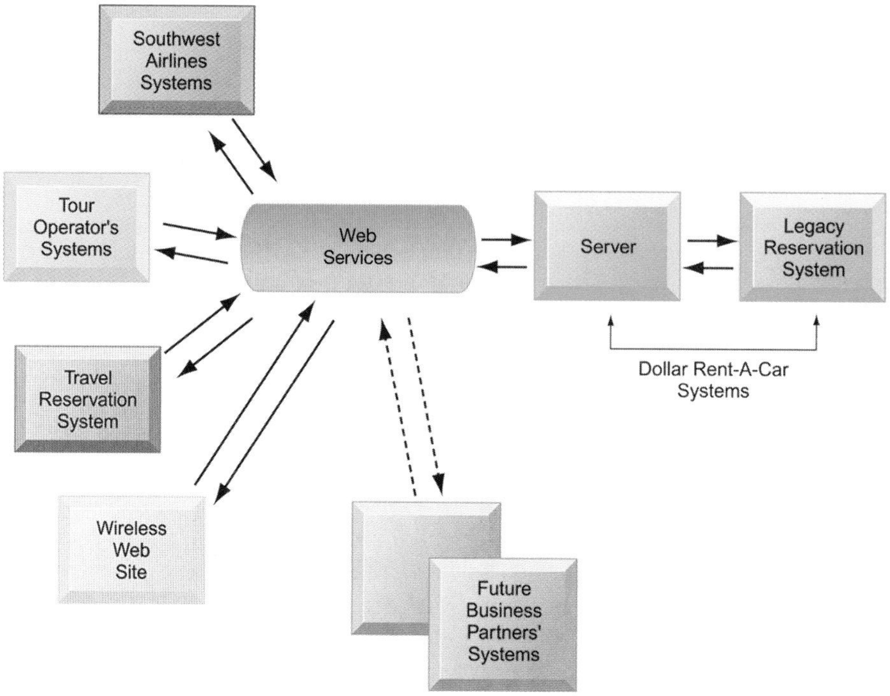

Figure 5.8
How Dollar Rent-A-Car Uses Web Services
Dollar Rent-A-Car uses web services to provide a standard intermediate layer of software to talk to other companies' information systems. Dollar Rent-A-Car can use this set of web services to link to other companies' information systems without having to build a separate link to each firm's systems.

operating system and Chrome web browser are based on open source code. Today you can find thousands of open source computer programs to accomplish everything from e-commerce shopping carts and funds clearance to sales force management.

Cloud-Based Software Services and Tools

In the past, software such as Microsoft Word or Adobe Illustrator came in a box and was designed to operate on a single machine. Today, you're more likely to download the software from the vendor's website or use the software as a cloud service delivered over the Internet. (Review our discussion of SaaS in Section 5-2.) In addition to free or low-cost tools for individuals and small businesses provided by Google and Yahoo, enterprise software and other software for running larger businesses are available as cloud services from the major commercial software vendors.

Mashups and Apps The software you use for both personal and business tasks may consist of large self-contained programs, or it may be composed of interchangeable components that integrate freely with other applications on the Internet. Individual users and entire companies mix and match these software components to create their own customized applications and to share information with others. The resulting software applications are called **mashups**. The idea is to produce from different sources a new work that is greater than the sum of its parts. You have performed a mashup if you've ever personalized your Facebook profile or your blog with a capability to display videos or slide shows.

Web mashups combine the capabilities of two or more online applications to create a kind of hybrid that provides more customer value than the original sources alone. For instance, ZipRealty uses Google Maps and data provided by online real estate database Zillow.com to display a complete list of multiple listing service (MLS) real estate listings for any zip code the user specifies.

Apps are small specialized software programs that run on the Internet, on your computer, or on your mobile phone or tablet and are generally delivered over the Internet. Google refers to its online services as apps, but when we talk about apps today, most of the attention goes to the apps that have been developed for the mobile digital platform. It is these apps that turn smartphones and other mobile handheld devices into general-purpose computing tools. There are now millions of apps for the iOS and Android operating systems.

Some downloaded apps do not access the web, but many do, providing faster access to web content than traditional web browsers. They feature a streamlined, nonbrowser pathway for users to experience the web and perform a number of tasks, ranging from reading the newspaper to shopping, searching, and buying. Because so many people are now accessing the Internet from their mobile devices, some say that apps are the new browsers. Apps are also starting to influence the design and function of traditional websites because consumers are attracted to the look and feel of apps and their speed of operation.

Many apps are free or purchased for a small charge, much less than conventional software, which further adds to their appeal. There are already over 2.2 million apps for the Apple iPhone and iPad platform and a similar number that run on devices using the Android operating system. The success of these mobile platforms depends in large part on the quantity and the quality of the apps they provide. Apps tie the customer to a specific hardware platform; as the user adds more and more apps to his or her mobile phone, the cost of switching to a competing mobile platform rises.

At the moment, the most commonly downloaded apps are games, news and weather, maps/navigation, social networking, music, and video/movies. But there are also serious apps for business users that make it possible to create and edit documents, connect to corporate systems, schedule and participate in meetings, track shipments, and dictate voice messages (see the Chapter 1 Interactive Session on People). There are also a huge number of e-commerce apps for researching and buying goods and services online.

5-4 What are the principal issues in managing hardware and software technology?

Selection and use of computer hardware and software technology have a profound impact on business performance. We now describe the most important issues you will face when managing hardware and software technology: capacity planning and scalability; determining the total cost of technology assets; determining whether to own and maintain your own hardware, software, and other infrastructure components or lease them from an external technology service provider; and managing mobile platforms and software localization.

CAPACITY PLANNING AND SCALABILITY

E-commerce and e-business need much larger processing and storage resources to handle the surging digital transactions flowing between different parts of the firm and between the firm and its customers and suppliers. Many people using a website simultaneously place strains on a computer system, as does hosting large numbers of interactive web pages with data-intensive graphics or video.

Managers and information systems specialists now need to pay more attention to hardware capacity planning and scalability than before. From an IT perspective, **capacity planning** is the process of predicting when a computer hardware system becomes saturated. It considers factors such as the maximum number of users that the system can accommodate at one time, the impact of existing and future software applications, and performance measures, such as minimum response time for processing business transactions. Capacity planning ensures that the firm has enough computing power for its current and future needs. For example, the NASDAQ stock market performs ongoing capacity planning to identify peaks in the volume of stock trading transactions and to ensure that it has enough computing capacity to handle large surges in volume when trading is very heavy.

Scalability refers to the ability of a computer, product, or system to expand to serve a large number of users without breaking down. Electronic commerce and electronic business both call for scalable IT infrastructures that have the capacity to grow with the business as the size of a website and number of visitors increase. Organizations must make sure they have sufficient computer processing, storage, and network resources to handle surging volumes of digital transactions and to make such data immediately available online.

TOTAL COST OF OWNERSHIP (TCO) OF TECHNOLOGY ASSETS

When you calculate how much your hardware and software cost, their purchase price is only the beginning. You must also consider ongoing administration costs for hardware and software upgrades, maintenance, technical support, training, and even utility and real estate costs for running and housing the technology. The **total cost of ownership (TCO)** model can be used to analyze these direct and indirect costs to help determine the actual cost of owning a specific technology. Table 5.7 describes the most important TCO components to consider in a TCO analysis.

When all these cost components are considered, the hidden costs for support staff, downtime, and additional network management can make distributed client/server architectures—especially those incorporating handheld computers and wireless devices—more expensive than centralized mainframe architectures.

Many large firms are saddled with redundant, incompatible hardware and software because of poor planning. These firms could reduce their TCO through greater centralization and standardization of their hardware and software resources. Companies could reduce the size of the information systems staff required to support their infrastructure if the firm minimized the number of computer models and pieces of software that employees are allowed to use.

USING TECHNOLOGY SERVICE PROVIDERS

Some of the most important questions facing managers are "How should we acquire and maintain our technology assets?" "Should we build software applications ourselves or outsource them to an external contractor?" "Should we purchase and run

TABLE 5.7
TCO Components

Hardware acquisition	Purchase price of computer hardware equipment, including computers, displays, storage, and printers
Software acquisition	Purchase or license of software for each user
Installation	Cost to install computers and software
Training	Cost to provide training to information systems specialists and end users
Support	Cost to provide ongoing technical support, help desks, and so forth
Maintenance	Cost to upgrade the hardware and software
Infrastructure	Cost to acquire, maintain, and support related infrastructure, such as networks and specialized equipment (including storage backup units)
Downtime	Lost productivity if hardware or software failures cause the system to be unavailable for processing and user tasks
Space and energy	Real estate and utility costs for housing and providing power for the technology

them ourselves or rent them from external service providers?" In the past, most companies ran their own computer facilities and developed their own software. Today, more and more companies are obtaining their hardware and software technology from external service vendors.

Outsourcing

A number of firms are **outsourcing** the maintenance of their IT infrastructures and the development of new systems to external vendors. They may contract with an external service provider to run their computer center and networks, to develop new software, or to manage all the components of their IT infrastructures. For example, FedEx outsourced 30 percent of its IT system operations and software development to external IT service providers.

Specialized web hosting services are available for companies that lack the financial or technical resources to operate their own websites. A **web hosting service** maintains a large web server, or a series of servers, and provides fee-paying subscribers with space to maintain their websites. The subscribing companies may create their own web pages or have the hosting service, or a web design firm, create them. Some services offer *co-location*, in which the firm actually purchases and owns the server computer housing its website but locates the server in the physical facility of the hosting service.

Firms often retain control over their hardware resources but outsource custom software development or maintenance to outside firms, frequently firms that operate offshore in low-wage areas of the world. When firms outsource software work outside their national borders, the practice is called **offshore software outsourcing**. Until recently, this type of software development involved lower-level maintenance, data entry, and call center operations, but with the growing sophistication and experience of offshore firms, particularly in India, more and more new program development is taking place offshore. Chapter 12 discusses offshore software outsourcing in more detail.

To manage their relationship with an outsourcer or technology service provider, firms will need a contract that includes a **service level agreement (SLA)**. The SLA is a formal contract between customers and their service providers that defines the specific responsibilities of the service provider and the level of service the customer expects. SLAs typically specify the nature and level of services provided, criteria for performance measurement, support options, provisions for security and disaster recovery, hardware and software ownership and upgrades, customer support, billing, and conditions for terminating the agreement. For example, PeroxyChem, described in the chapter-opening case, and IBM have a service-level agreement (SLA) for high input/output requirements and standardization.

Using Cloud Services

Firms now have the option of maintaining their own IT infrastructures or using cloud-based hardware and software services. Companies considering the cloud computing model need to assess the costs and benefits of external services carefully, weighing all management, organizational, and technology issues, including the level of service and performance that is acceptable for the business.

Cloud computing is more immediately appealing to small and medium-sized businesses that lack resources to purchase and own their own hardware and software. However, large corporations have huge investments in complex proprietary systems supporting unique business processes, some of which give them strategic advantages. Moreover, the cost savings from switching to cloud services are not always easy to determine for large companies that already have their own IT infrastructures in place.

Pricing for cloud services is usually based on a per-hour or other per-use charge. Even if a company can approximate the hardware and software costs to run a specific computing task on premises, it still needs to figure in how much of the firm's network management, storage management, system administration, electricity, and real estate costs should be allocated to a specific, individual, on-premises IT service. An information systems department might not have the right information to analyze those factors on a service-by-service basis.

MANAGING MOBILE PLATFORMS

Gains in productivity from equipping employees with mobile computing devices must be balanced against increased costs from integrating these devices into the firm's IT infrastructure and providing technical support. This is especially true when the organization allows employees to use their own personal devices for their jobs (BYOD).

In the past, companies tried to limit business smartphone use to a single platform. This made it easier to keep track of each mobile device and roll out software upgrades or fixes, because all employees were using the same devices or, at the very least, the same operating system. Today, employees want to be able to use a variety of personally owned mobile devices, including the iPad, iPhone, and Android handhelds, to access corporate systems such as email, databases, and applications.

For personal mobile devices to access company information, the company's networks must be configured to receive connections from that device. Firms need an efficient inventory management system that keeps track of which devices employees are using, where each device is, and what software is installed on it. They also need to know what pieces of corporate data are on those personal devices, and this is not always easy to determine. It is more difficult to protect the company's network and data when employees access them from their privately owned devices.

If a device is stolen or compromised, companies need to ensure that sensitive or confidential company information isn't exposed. Companies often use technologies that allow them to wipe data from devices remotely or encrypt data so that, if stolen, they cannot be used. You'll find a detailed discussion of mobile security issues in Chapter 8.

Many companies only allow employee mobile devices access to a limited set of applications and noncritical corporate data. For more critical business systems, more company control is required, and firms often turn to **mobile device management (MDM)** software, which monitors, manages, and secures mobile devices that are deployed across multiple mobile service providers and across multiple mobile operating systems used in the organization. MDM tools enable the IT department to monitor mobile usage, install or update mobile software, back up and restore mobile devices, and remove software and data from devices that are stolen or lost.

MANAGING SOFTWARE LOCALIZATION FOR GLOBAL BUSINESS

If you are operating a global company, all the management issues we have just described will be affected by the need to create systems that can be realistically used by multiple business units in different countries. Although English has become a kind of standard business language, this is truer at higher levels of companies and not throughout the middle and lower ranks. Software may have to be built with local language interfaces before a new information system can be successfully implemented worldwide.

These interfaces can be costly and messy to build. Menu bars, commands, error messages, reports, queries, online data entry forms, and system documentation may need to be translated into all the languages of the countries where the system will be used. To be truly useful for enhancing productivity of a global workforce, the software interfaces must be easily understood and mastered quickly. The entire process of converting software to operate in a second language is called *software localization*.

Global systems must also consider differences in local cultures and business processes. Cross-functional systems such as enterprise and supply chain management systems are not always compatible with differences in languages, cultural heritages, and business processes in other countries. In a global systems environment, all these factors add to the TCO and will influence decisions about whether to outsource or use technology service providers.

5-5 How will MIS help my career?

Here is how Chapter 5 and this book can help you find a job as an entry-level IT consultant.

THE COMPANY

A1 Tech IT Consulting, a national technology consulting firm headquartered in Atlanta, is looking for an entry-level IT consultant. The company partners with technology vendors to create and sell leading-edge technology solutions based on cloud, network, and managed IT services to small, medium-sized, and enterprise-size companies. The company has 65 employees and is noted for outstanding customer service.

POSITION DESCRIPTION

The entry-level IT consultant will work with the firm's account managers to maintain good relationships with existing clients and help its technology consultants to create solutions and proposals for prospective customers. The company will provide on-the-job training about the technology industry and its technology consulting process. Job responsibilities include:

- Providing research on potential and existing clients and the competitive landscape.
- Managing digital marketing campaigns.
- Assisting in identifying potential business opportunities.
- Preparing periodic reports on screening, tracking, and monitoring clients and prospects.

JOB REQUIREMENTS

- Bachelor's degree or equivalent
- Ability to communicate well with clients by phone, by email, and face-to-face
- Strong organizational, presentation, and writing skills
- Ability to work in a fast-paced environment and collaborate effectively as a team member
- Proficiency in Microsoft Office (Word, Excel, and PowerPoint)

INTERVIEW QUESTIONS

1. What do you know about cloud computing and managed IT services? Are you familiar with common operating system, security, and data management platforms? Have you ever used these services on the job? What did you do with them?
2. Have you had much face-to-face contact with customers? Can you describe what work you did with customers? Have you ever helped customers with a technology problem?
3. Do you have any digital marketing experience?
4. Can you give us an example of a sales-related problem or other business problem that you helped solve? Do you do any writing and analysis? Can you provide examples?
5. What is your level of proficiency with Microsoft Office? What work have you done with Excel spreadsheets?

AUTHOR TIPS

1. Review this chapter and also Chapters 6–8 of this text, paying special attention to cloud computing, networking technology, and managed technology services.
2. Use the web to research the company and how it works with other technology companies to provide its IT services. Learn what you can about these partner companies as well and the tools and services they offer.
3. Inquire exactly how you would be using Microsoft Office and if possible provide examples of how you used these tools to solve problems in the classroom or for a job assignment. Bring examples of your writing (including some from your Digital Portfolio described in MyLab MIS) demonstrating your analytical skills and project experience.
4. Indicate that you are very interested in learning more about the technology industry and technologies and services the company works with.
5. Review postings on the company's LinkedIn page and Facebook and Twitter channels to learn about strategic trends and important topics for the company.

Review Summary

5-1 **What are the components of IT infrastructure?** IT infrastructure consists of the shared technology resources that provide the platform for the firm's specific information system applications. Major IT infrastructure components include computer hardware, software, data management technology, networking and telecommunications technology, and technology services.

5-2 **What are the major computer hardware, data storage, input, and output technologies used in business and the major hardware trends?** Computers are categorized as mainframes, midrange computers, PCs, workstations, or supercomputers. Mainframes are the largest computers, midrange computers are primarily servers, PCs are desktop or laptop machines, workstations are desktop machines with powerful mathematical and graphic capabilities, and supercomputers are sophisticated, powerful computers that can perform massive and complex computations rapidly. Computing power can be further increased by creating a computational grid that combines the computing power of all the computers on a network. In the client/server model of computing, computer processing is split between clients and servers connected by a network. The exact division of tasks between client and server depends on the application.

Traditional secondary storage technologies include magnetic disk, optical disc, and magnetic tape. Optical CD-ROM and DVD discs can store vast amounts of data compactly, and some types are rewritable. Cloud-based storage services are increasingly being used for personal an corporate data. The principal input devices are keyboards, computer mice, touch screens (including those with multitouch), magnetic ink and optical character recognition devices, pen-based instruments, digital scanners, sensors, audio input devices, and radio-frequency identification devices. The principal output devices are display screens, printers, and audio output devices.

Major hardware trends include the mobile digital platform, nanotechnology, quantum computers, consumerization of IT, virtualization, cloud computing, green computing, and high-performance/power-saving processors. Cloud computing provides computer processing, storage, software, and other services as virtualized resources over a network, primarily the Internet, on an as-needed basis.

5-3 **What are the major types of computer software used in business and the major software trends?** The two major types of software are system software and application software. System software coordinates the various parts of the computer system and mediates between application software and computer hardware. Application software is used to develop specific business applications.

The system software that manages and controls the activities of the computer is called the operating system. Leading PC and server operating systems include Windows 10, Windows Server, UNIX, Linux, and the Macintosh operating system. Linux is a powerful, resilient, open source operating system that can run on multiple hardware platforms and is used widely to run web servers.

The principal programming languages used in business application software include Java, C, C++, and Visual Basic. PC and cloud-based productivity tools include word processing, spreadsheet, data management, presentation graphics, and web browser software. Java is an operating system-independent and hardware-independent programming language that is the leading interactive programming environment for the web. Ruby and Python are used in web and cloud computing applications. HTML is a page description language for creating web pages.

Web services are loosely coupled software components based on XML and open web standards that can work with any application software and operating system. They can be used as components of applications to link the systems of two organizations or to link disparate systems of a single company.

Software trends include the expanding use of open source software and cloud-based software tools and services (including SaaS, mashups, and apps).

5-4 **What are the principal issues in managing hardware and software technology?** Managers and information systems specialists need to pay special attention to hardware capacity planning and scalability to ensure that the firm has enough computing power for its current and future needs. Businesses also need to balance the costs and benefits of building and maintaining their own hardware and software versus outsourcing or using an on-demand computing model. The total cost of ownership (TCO) of the organization's technology assets includes not only the original cost of computer hardware and software but also costs for hardware and software upgrades, maintenance, technical support, and training, including the costs for managing and maintaining mobile devices. Companies with global operations need to manage software localization.

Key Terms

Android, 173
Application server, 160
Application software, 157
Apps, 178
BYOD, 164
C, 174
C++, 174
Capacity planning, 179
Centralized processing, 160
Chrome OS, 173
Client, 160
Client/server computing, 160
Cloud computing, 166
Consumerization of IT, 164
Data center, 156
Data management software, 158
Distributed processing, 160
Extensible Markup Language (XML), 176
Graphical user interface (GUI), 172
Green computing (green IT), 171
Grid computing, 159
HTML5, 176
Hybrid cloud, 170
Hypertext Markup Language (HTML), 176
Input devices, 161
iOS, 173
Java, 174
Legacy systems, 158
Linux, 173
Mainframe, 159
Mashups, 178
Mobile device management (MDM), 182
Multicore processor, 171
Multitouch, 172
Nanotechnology, 164
N-tier client/server architectures, 160
Object, 174
Office 365, 174
Offshore software outsourcing, 181
On-demand computing, 170
Open source software, 177
Operating system, 172
Output devices, 161
Outsourcing, 181
Personal computer (PC), 159
Private cloud, 170
Public cloud, 170
Quantum computing, 164
Scalability, 180
Server, 159
Service level agreement (SLA), 181
Service-oriented architecture (SOA), 177
Software as a service (SaaS), 167
Software package, 174
Software-defined storage (SDS), 165
Solid state drive (SSD), 161
Spreadsheet software, 174
Supercomputer, 159
System software, 157

MyLab MIS™

To complete the problems with **MyLab MIS**, go to EOC Discussion Questions in MyLab MIS

Review Questions

5-1 What are the components of IT infrastructure?

- Define information technology (IT) infrastructure and describe each of its components.

5-2 What are the major computer hardware, data storage, input, and output technologies used in business and the major hardware trends?

- List and describe the various type of computers available to businesses today.
- Define the client/server model of computing and describe the difference between two-tiered and n-tier client/server architecture.
- Define and describe the mobile digital platform, BYOD, nanotechnology, grid computing, cloud computing, virtualization, green computing, and multicore processing.

5-3 What are the major types of computer software used in business and the major software trends?

- Distinguish between application software and system software and explain the role the operating system of a computer plays.
- List and describe the major PC and server operating systems.
- Name and describe the major desktop productivity software tools.
- Explain how Java and HTML are used in building applications for the web.
- Define web services, describe the technologies they use, and explain how web services benefit businesses.
- Explain why open source software is so important today and its benefits for business.
- Define and describe cloud computing software services, mashups, and apps and explain how they benefit individuals and businesses.

5-4 What are the principal issues in managing hardware and software technology?

- Explain why managers need to pay attention to capacity planning and scalability of technology resources.
- Describe the cost components used to calculate the TCO of technology assets.
- Identify the benefits and challenges of using outsourcing, cloud computing services, and mobile platforms.
- Explain why software localization has become an important management issue for global companies.

Discussion Questions

5-5 MyLab MIS Why is selecting computer hardware and software for the organization an important business decision? What people, organization, and technology issues should be considered when selecting computer hardware and software?

5-6 MyLab MIS Should organizations use software service providers (including cloud services) for all their software needs? Why or why not? What people, organization, and technology factors should be considered when making this decision?

5-7 MyLab MIS What are the advantages and disadvantages of cloud computing?

Hands-On MIS Projects

The projects in this section give you hands-on experience in developing solutions for managing IT infrastructures and IT outsourcing, using spreadsheet software to evaluate alternative desktop systems, and using web research to budget for a sales conference. Visit **MyLab MIS** to access this chapter's Hands-On MIS Projects.

MANAGEMENT DECISION PROBLEMS

5-8 The University of Pittsburgh Medical Center (UPMC) relies on information systems to operate 19 hospitals, a network of other care sites, and international and commercial ventures. Demand for additional servers and storage technology was growing by 20 percent each year. UPMC was setting up a separate server for every application, and its servers and other computers were running a number of operating systems, including several versions of UNIX and Windows. UPMC had to manage technologies from many vendors, including Hewlett-Packard (HP), Oracle Sun, Microsoft, and IBM. Assess the impact of this situation on business performance. What factors and management decisions must be considered when developing a solution to this problem?

5-9 Qantas Airways, Australia's leading airline, faces cost pressures from high fuel prices and lower levels of global airline traffic. To remain competitive, the airline must find ways to keep costs low while providing a high level of customer service. Qantas had a 30-year-old data center. Management had to decide whether to replace its IT infrastructure with newer technology or outsource it. What factors should Qantas management consider when deciding whether to outsource? If Qantas decides to outsource, list and describe points that should be addressed in a service level agreement.

IMPROVING DECISION MAKING: USING A SPREADSHEET TO EVALUATE HARDWARE AND SOFTWARE OPTIONS

Software skills: Spreadsheet formulas
Business skills: Technology pricing

5-10 In this exercise, you will use spreadsheet software to calculate the cost of desktop systems, printers, and software.

Use the Internet to obtain pricing information on hardware and software for an office of 30 people. You will need to price 30 PC desktop systems (monitors, computers, and keyboards) manufactured by Lenovo, Dell, and HP. (For the purposes of this exercise, ignore the fact that desktop systems usually come with preloaded software packages.) Obtain pricing on 15 desktop printers manufactured by HP, Canon, and Dell. Each desktop system must satisfy the minimum specifications shown in tables that you can find in MyLab MIS™. Also, obtain pricing on 30 copies of the most recent versions of Microsoft Office and OpenOffice. Each desktop productivity package should contain programs for word processing, spreadsheets, database, and presentations. Prepare a spreadsheet showing your research results for the software and the desktop system, printer, and software combination offering the best performance and pricing per worker. Because every two workers share one printer (15 printers/30 systems), your calculations should assume only half a printer cost per worker.

IMPROVING DECISION MAKING: USING WEB RESEARCH TO BUDGET FOR A SALES CONFERENCE

Software skills: Internet-based software
Business skills: Researching transportation and lodging costs

5-11 In this exercise, you'll use software at various online travel sites to obtain pricing for total travel and lodging costs for a sales conference.

The Foremost Composite Materials Company is planning a two-day sales conference for October 19–20, starting with a reception on the evening of October 18. The conference consists of all-day meetings that the entire sales force, numbering 120 sales representatives and their 16 managers, must attend. Each sales representative requires his or her own room, and the company needs two common meeting rooms, one large enough to hold the entire sales force plus a few visitors (200 total) and the other able to hold half the force. Management has set a budget of $200,000 for the representatives' room rentals. The company would like to hold the conference in either Miami or Marco Island, Florida, at a Hilton- or Marriott-owned hotel.

Use the Hilton and Marriott websites to select a hotel in whichever of these cities would enable the company to hold its sales conference within its budget and meet its sales conference requirements. Then locate flights arriving the afternoon prior to the conference. Your attendees will be coming from Los Angeles (53), San Francisco (31), Seattle (21), Chicago (18), and Pittsburgh (13). Determine costs of each airline ticket from these cities. When you are finished, create a budget for the conference. The budget will include the cost of each airline ticket, the room cost, and $70 per attendee per day for food.

Collaboration and Teamwork Project

Evaluating Server and Mobile Operating Systems

5-12 Form a group with three or four of your classmates. Choose two server or mobile operating systems to evaluate. You might research and compare the capabilities and costs of Linux versus UNIX or the most recent version of the Windows operating system for servers. Alternatively, you could compare the capabilities of the Android mobile operating system with iOS for the iPhone. If possible, use Google Docs and Google Drive or Google Sites to brainstorm; organize and develop a presentation of your findings for the class.

BUSINESS PROBLEM-SOLVING CASE

Is BYOD Good for Business?

Just about everyone who has a smartphone wants to be able to bring it to work and use it on the job. And why not? Employees using their own smartphones would allow companies to enjoy all the same benefits of a mobile workforce without spending their own money to purchase these devices. Smaller companies are able to go mobile without making large investments in devices and mobile services. Gartner, Inc. consultants have predicted that by 2017, 50 percent of employers will require employees to supply their own mobile devices for the workplace. BYOD is becoming the "new normal."

Shouldn't businesses rejoice? Not necessarily. Half of all enterprises believe that BYOD represents a growing problem for their organizations, according to a number of studies. Although BYOD can improve employee job satisfaction and productivity, it also can cause a number of problems if not managed properly. Support for personally owned devices is more difficult than it is for company-supplied devices, the cost of managing mobile devices can increase, and protecting corporate data and networks becomes more difficult.

When employees bring their own devices to work, IT departments lose almost all control over the hardware. They can't control what apps or programs are installed, how the devices are secured, or what files are downloaded. In the past the firm was able to control who had what technology in order to prevent privacy breaches, hacking, and unauthorized access to corporate information. Inability to control the hardware means more vulnerabilities. That is the big tradeoff with BYOD: offering employees greater flexibility while potentially exposing the company to danger.

Certain industries, such as healthcare, have incredibly strict regulations about the use and distribution of personal information. Companies must comply with these policies, even if the data reside on an employee-owned device. A failure to comply can result in significant legal penalties, and allowing employees to load confidential data onto their personal devices greatly increases the risk of compliance failure.

BYOD advocates have argued that it increases employee productivity, but that is not always the case. When employees bring their own devices to work, they may be tempted to use them on the job for entertainment or catching up with friends. It's incredibly easy for employees to get sucked into an endless black hole of text messaging, YouTube videos, and checking Facebook updates. Productivity will suffer (see the Chapter 7 Interactive Session on People).

BYOD requires a significant portion of corporate IT resources dedicated to managing and maintaining a large number of devices within the organization. In the past, companies tried to limit business smartphone use to a single platform. This made it easier to keep track of each mobile device and to roll out software upgrades or fixes because all employees were using the same devices or, at the very least, the same operating system. Today, the mobile digital landscape is much more complicated, with a variety of devices and operating systems on the market that do not have well-developed tools for administration and security. Android has over 80 percent of the worldwide smartphone market, but it is more difficult to use for corporate work than Apple mobile devices using the iOS operating system. IOS is considered a closed system and runs only on a limited number of different Apple mobile devices. In contrast, Android's fragmentation makes it more difficult and costly for corporate IT to manage. There are about 25,000 different models of Android-based devices available around the world, according to a report by OpenSignal, which researches wireless networks and devices. Android's huge consumer market share attracts many hackers. Android is also vulnerable because it has an open source architecture and comes in multiple versions.

If employees are allowed to work with more than one type of mobile device and operating system, companies need an effective way to keep track of all the devices employees are using. To access company information, the company's networks must be configured to receive connections from that device. When employees make changes to their personal phone, such as switching cellular carriers, changing their phone number, or buying a new mobile device altogether, companies will need to quickly and flexibly ensure that their employees are still able to remain productive. Firms need a system that keeps track of which devices employees are using, where the device is located, whether it is being used, and what software it is equipped with. For unprepared companies, keeping track of who gets access to what data could be a nightmare.

With the large variety of mobile devices and operating systems available, providing adequate technical support for every employee could be difficult. When employees are not able to access critical data or encounter other problems with their mobile devices, they will need assistance from the information systems department. Companies that rely on desktop computers tend to have many of the same computers with the same specs and operating systems, making tech support that much easier. Mobility introduces a new layer of variety and complexity to tech support that companies need to be prepared to handle.

There are significant concerns with securing company information accessed with mobile devices. If a device is stolen or compromised, companies need ways to ensure that sensitive or confidential information isn't freely available to anyone. Mobility puts assets and data at greater risk than if they were only located within company walls and on company machines. Marble Security Labs analyzed 1.2 million Android and iOS apps and found that the consumer apps on mobile devices did not adequately protect business information. Companies often use technologies that allow them to wipe data from devices remotely or encrypt data so that if the device is stolen, it cannot be used. You'll find a detailed discussion of mobile security issues in Chapter 8.

Intel was a pioneer in the BYOD movement and has successfully implemented an enterprise-wide policy covering more than 30,000 employee mobile devices. Another major issue surrounding a corporate BYOD policy is the potential lack of trust between workers and management when management has access to personal data on employee devices. To deal with this issue, Intel has established clear-cut guidelines informing employees about exactly what information can and can't be seen when administrators manage personal devices. Intel will quickly respond to any questions employees might have regarding BYOD. The company also allows employees to choose among different levels of mobile access to corporate systems, with each tier accompanied by different levels of security.

SAP, a leading global vendor of enterprise software, is another tech company that has implemented BYOD successfully. The company developed a specialized mobile platform for various work-related applications, enabling employees to work from anywhere with their mobile devices. SAP has also created a security system for decommissioning a mobile device within a minute whenever a smartphone or tablet is lost or stolen. All SAP divisions across the globe have reported some form of success with BYOD. SAP Australia/New Zealand reports that the policy is key in attracting younger workers who are attached to their mobile devices and constantly use the apps.

Blackstone, a global investment and advisory firm, has implemented a BYOD policy, but it has placed limitations on the types of devices employees can use. Blackstone's BYOD policy only allows employees to use their own Apple products such as iPads. For that company, Apple devices were the easiest to support and required little maintenance compared to other mobile tools. Any other devices would add to the workload of Blackstone's IT department, thus eliminating the cost savings that often come with BYOD. Due to Apple's popularity, few employees have objected.

At Venafi, a cybersecurity company, employees have the option of bringing their own smartphones, tablets, and notebooks to work with them or using company-issued devices. The company has a well-developed BYOD policy. Venafi's IT department does not support employees' hardware devices because it would be too difficult to handle all the different mobile devices and software available to consumers. That means employees are responsible for troubleshooting and repairs of their personal equipment. However, Venafi does ensure that each device each device is securely connected to the corporate network.

According to Tammy Moskites, Venafi CISO and CIO, the biggest challenge in defining a BYOD policy that leaves everyone satisfied has been balancing risk with flexibility. Although Venafi has given employees the choice of using their own mobile devices, it has also written contracts with language describing the terms and conditions for bringing personal devices into work, including the ability to remove company data from the device if needed.

Many corporate BYOD policies restrict access to time-wasting sites like Facebook, YouTube, or Twitter. But Venafi management believes that instead of resorting to measures like blocking YouTube or Facebook and forbidding the use of mobile phones, companies should focus more on performance. As long as the employees are motivated and performing well, they shouldn't be subjected to unnecessary restrictions. Employees typically don't understand the implications of BYOD and the dangers of lax security. Venafi's IT department tries to educate employees about the realities of BYOD and gives them the power to use their devices responsibly.

Iftekhar Khan, IT director at Toronto's Chelsea Hotel, remains less sanguine. He believes BYOD might work for his company down the road but not in the immediate future. Khan notes that the hospitality industry and many others still want employees to use corporate-owned devices for any laptop, tablet, or smartphone requiring access to the corporate network. His business has sensitive information and needs that level of control. Although the hotel might possibly save money with BYOD, it's ultimately all about productivity.

Sources: *Lisa Phifer*, "The Challenges of a Bring Your Own Device (BYOD) Policy," *Simple MDM*, January 5, 2017; Sarah K. White, "How to Implement an Effective BYOD Policy," *CIO*, September 26, 2016; Ryan Patrick, "Is a BYOD Strategy Best for Business?" *IT World Canada*, March 22, 2016; "5 BYOD Management Case Studies," Sunviewsoftware.com, accessed May 5, 2016; Linda Gimmeson, "3 Companies Showing Success with BYOD," Toolbox.com, July 9, 2015; Aruba Networks, "Enterprise Security Threat Level Directly Linked to User Demographics, Industry and Geography," *Business Wire*, April 14, 2015; Alan F., "Open Signal: 24,093 Unique and Different Android-Powered Devices Are Available," Phonearena.com, August 5, 2015.

CASE STUDY QUESTIONS

5-13 What are the advantages and disadvantages of allowing employees to use their personal mobile devices for work?

5-14 What people, organization, and technology factors should be addressed when deciding whether to allow employees to use their personal mobile devices for work?

5-15 Evaluate how the companies described in this case study dealt with the challenges of BYOD.

5-16 Allowing employees to use their own smartphones for work will save the company money. Do you agree? Why or why not?

MyLab MIS

Go to the Assignments section of MyLab MIS to complete these writing exercises.

5-17 What are the distinguishing characteristics of cloud computing and what are the three types of cloud services?

5-18 What is the total cost of ownership of technology assets and what are its cost components?

Chapter 5 References

Amazon Web Services. "Overview of Amazon Web Services." (April 2017).

Andersson, Henrik, James Kaplan, and Brent Smolinski. "Capturing Value from IT Infrastructure Innovation." *McKinsey Quarterly* (October 2012).

Babcock, Charles. "Cloud's Thorniest Question: Does It Pay Off?" *Information Week* (June 4, 2012).

Benlian, Alexander, Marios Koufaris, and Thomas Hess. "Service Quality in Software-as-a-Service: Developing the SaaS-Qual Measure and Examining Its Role in Usage Continuance." *Journal of Management Information Systems* 28, No. 3 (Winter 2012).

Butler, Brandon. "Battle of the Clouds: Amazon Web Services vs. Microsoft Azure vs. Google Cloud Platform." Network World (February 22, 2017).

Castellanos, Sara. "Companies Look to Make a Quantum Leap with New Technology." *New York Times* (May 6, 2017).

Carr, Nicholas. *The Big Switch* (New York: Norton, 2008.)

Clark, Don. "Intel Unveils Tiny Quark Chips for Wearable Devices." *Wall Street Journal* (September 10, 2013).

Choi, Jae, Derek L. Nazareth, and Hemant K. Jain. "Implementing Service-Oriented Architecture in Organizations." *Journal of Management Information Systems* 26, No. 4 (Spring 2010).

Follow, Jaewon Kang. "IBM Bets on Next-Gen Technologies as It Tries to Stave Off Rivals." TheStreet.com (May 5, 2016).

Gartner, Inc. "Gartner Says by 2020 'Cloud Shift' Will Affect More Than $1 Trillion in IT Spending" (July 20, 2016).

Gartner, Inc. "Gartner Says Worldwide IT Spending Forecast to Grow 2.7 Percent in 2017." www.gartner.com (January 12, 2017).

Greengard, Samuel. "The Challenges and Rewards of Enterprise SaaS." *CIO Insight* (February 10, 2015).

Gómez, Jaime, Idana Salazar, and Pilar Vargas. "Firm Boundaries, Information Processing Capacity, and Performance in Manufacturing Firms." *Journal of Management Information Systems* 33 No. 3 (2016).

Hu, Paul Jen-Hwa, Han-Fen Hu, Chih-Ping Wei, and Pei-Fang Hsu. "Examining Firms' Green Information Technology Practices: A Hierarchical View of Key Drivers and Their Effects." *Journal of Management Information Systems* 33, No. 4 (2016).

"Hybrid IT Takes Center Stage." Harvard Business Review Analytic Services (2016).

International Data Corporation. "Strategies for Effectively Implementing a Mobile Device Management Solution" (July 2014).

Letschin, Michael. "Six Trends That Will Change How You Think About Data Storage." *Information Management* (February 8, 2016).

Li, Shengli, Hsing Kenneth Cheng, Yang Duan, and Yu-Chen Yang. "A Study of Enterprise Software Licensing Models." *Journal of Management Information Systems* 34 No. 1 (2017).

Mell, Peter, and Tim Grance. "The NIST Definition of Cloud Computing, Version 15." NIST (October 17, 2009).

Mueller, Benjamin, Goetz Viering, Christine Legner, and Gerold Riempp. "Understanding the Economic Potential of Service-Oriented Architecture." *Journal of Management Information Systems* 26, No. 4 (Spring 2010).

Osterman Research Inc. "The What, the Why, and the How of the Hybrid Cloud" (April 2016).

Schuff, David, and Robert St. Louis. "Centralization vs. Decentralization of Application Software." *Communications of the ACM* 44, No. 6 (June 2001).

Torode, Christine, Linda Tucci, and Karen Goulart. "Managing the Next-Generation Data Center." *Modern Infrastructure CIO Edition* (January 2013).

Walden, Stephanie. "The Pros and Cons of Public, Private, and Hybrid Clouds." *Mashable* (April 2, 2015).

CHAPTER

6

Foundations of Business Intelligence: Databases and Information Management

LEARNING OBJECTIVES

After reading this chapter, you will be able to answer the following questions:

6-1 What is a database, and how does a relational database organize data?

6-2 What are the principles of a database management system?

6-3 What are the principal tools and technologies for accessing information from databases to improve business performance and decision making?

6-4 Why are information policy, data administration, and data quality assurance essential for managing the firm's data resources?

6-5 How will MIS help my career?

CHAPTER CASES

- Data Management Helps the Charlotte Hornets Learn More About Their Fans
- Kraft Heinz Finds a New Recipe for Analyzing Its Data
- Keurig Green Mountain Improves Its Data Management
- How Reliable Is Big Data?

VIDEO CASES

- Dubuque Uses Cloud Computing and Sensors to Build a Smarter City
- Brooks Brothers Closes in on Omnichannel Retail
- Maruti Suzuki Business Intelligence and Enterprise Databases

MyLab MIS

- Discussion Questions: 6-5, 6-6, 6-7
- Hands-on MIS Projects: 6-8, 6-9, 6-10, 6-11;
- Writing Assignments: 6-17, 6-18;
- eText with Conceptual Animations

DATA MANAGEMENT HELPS THE CHARLOTTE HORNETS LEARN MORE ABOUT THEIR FANS

The NBA's Charlotte Hornets have millions of fans, but until recently they didn't know very much about them. The Charlotte, North Carolina-based basketball team had many millions of records of fan data—online ticket and team gear purchases, food and beverage purchases at games, and comments about the team on social media. Every time a fan performs one of these actions, more data about that fan are created. Three million records of food and beverage purchase transactions are generated during each Hornets game. There was too much unorganized customer data for decision makers to digest.

All of this accumulating data, which came from many different sources, started to overtax the team's Microsoft Dynamics customer relationship management system. There were 12 to 15 different sources of data on Hornets fan behavior, and they were maintained in separate data repositories that could not communicate with each other. It became increasingly harder for the Hornets to understand their fans and how they were interacting with the organization.

Five years ago, Hornets management decided to improve its approach to data management. The team needed technology that could easily maintain data from 12 to 15 different sources and 12 different vendors, and it needed to be able to combine and integrate what amounted to 12 different profiles on each fan into a single profile. This would enable the Hornets to understand each fan and that person's behavior in much greater detail and offer fans a more personalized experience.

Under the leadership of Chris Zeppenfield, the Hornets' senior director of business intelligence, the team implemented a data warehouse that would consolidate all of the Hornets' customer data from its various data sources in a single location where the data could be easily accessed and analyzed by business users. The warehouse was based on a SAP HANA database optimized to process very large quantities of data at ultra-high speed and included Phizzle FanTracker™ software to cleanse, streamline, and combine millions of fan records to create a single profile for each Hornets fan. Phizzle FanTracker™ is a fan engagement platform designed to consolidate, analyze, and act on multiple data sources. The platform's data aggregation capabilities, innovative data visualization tools, and

© Oleksii Sidorov/Shutterstock

social listening solutions provide sports properties and brands the ability to gather and analyze digital, social, and real-world fan engagements. FanTracker™ works with the SAP HANA database to consolidate customer profiles, analyze and act on real-time online behavior, and consolidate all existing data sources to uniquely identify fan records. The solution provides a unified overview and deeper understanding of each fan, allowing clubs to offer their fans a more personalized experience.

By using FanTracker™ and a unified data warehouse, the Hornets have compiled and synthesized 25 million fan and consumer interactions, saving over $1.5 million in consulting expenses. They now have a real-time data profile for every one of their 1.5 million fans, which includes up-to-the minute behavioral data on each fan from third-party applications as well as the Hornets' own sources. Each profile reveals detailed insights into a fan's behavior including sentiment, purchase history, interactions, and fan value across multiple points of contact. Zeppenfeld believes that better fan data management has helped the team rank among the top five NBA franchises for new full season ticket sales each year.

Sources: Jim O'Donnell, "Charlotte Hornets Use Phizzle Built on HANA to Analyze Fan Behavior," SearchSAPtechtarget.com, February 6, 2017; Mark J. Burns, "Why the Charlotte Hornets Are Using Phizzle to Streamline Their Data Warehouse," *Sport Techie*, September 2016; "NBA Team Charlotte Hornets/SAP Case Study," www.phizzle.com, accessed February 16, 2017; and "Phizzle and SAP Unveil Bundled Solution for Automated Fan Engagement," *Marketwired*, March 3, 2015.

The experience of the Charlotte Hornets illustrates the importance of data management. Business performance depends on what a firm can or cannot do with its data. The Charlotte Hornets NBA basketball team was a thriving business, but both operational efficiency and management decision making were hampered by fragmented data stored in multiple locations that were difficult to access and analyze. How businesses store, organize, and manage their data has an enormous impact on organizational effectiveness.

The chapter-opening diagram calls attention to important points raised by this case and this chapter. The Charlotte Hornets had accumulated very large quantities of fan data from many different sources. Marketing campaigns and personalized offers to fans were not as effective as they could be because it was so difficult to assemble and analyze the data required to obtain a detailed understanding of each customer. The solution was to combine the Hornets' customer data from all sources in a data warehouse that provided a single source of data for reporting and analysis and use FanTracker™ software to consolidate disparate pieces of customer data into a single profile for each customer. The Hornets had to reorganize their data into a standard companywide format; establish rules, responsibilities, and procedures for accessing and using the data; and provide tools for making the data accessible to users for querying and reporting.

The data warehouse integrated company data from all of its disparate sources into a single comprehensive database that could be queried directly. The data were reconciled to prevent multiple profiles on the same customer. The solution improved customer marketing, sales, and service while reducing costs. The Hornets increased their ability to quickly analyze very large quantities of data by using SAP HANA high-speed database technology.

The data warehouse boosted operational efficiency and decision making by making more comprehensive and accurate customer data available and by making it easier to access all the business's data on each customer. By helping the Hornets understand their own customers better, the solution increased opportunities for selling to customers as well as the effectiveness of marketing and sales campaigns.

Here are some questions to think about: What was the business impact of the Hornets' data management problems? How did better use of the Hornets' customer data improve operational efficiency and management decision making?

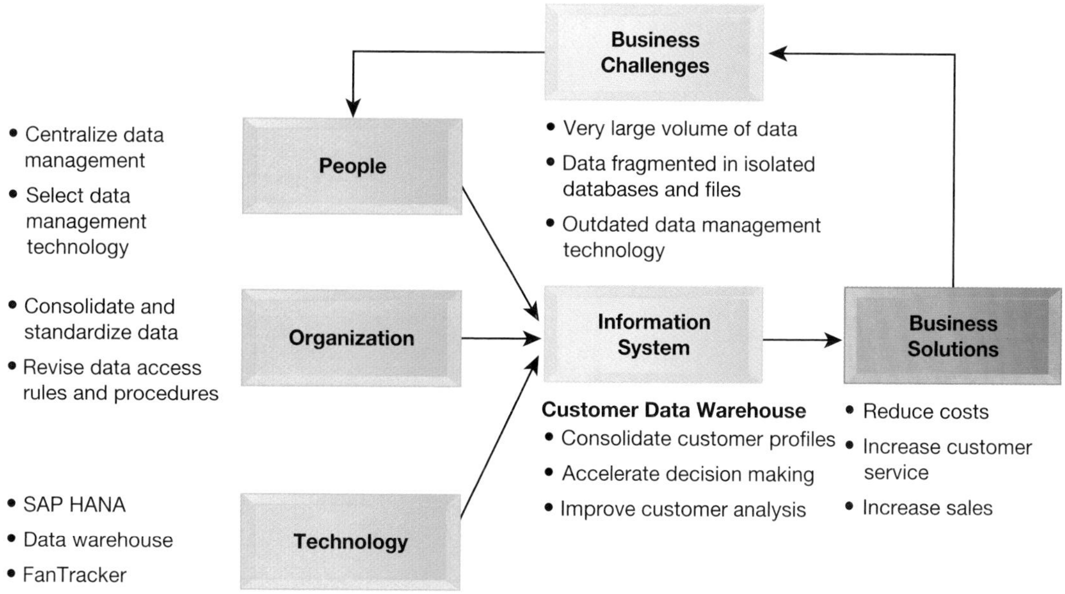

6-1 What is a database, and how does a relational database organize data?

A computer system organizes data in a hierarchy that starts with bits and bytes and progresses to fields, records, files, and databases (see Figure 6.1). A **bit** represents the smallest unit of data a computer can handle. A group of bits, called a **byte**, represents a single character, which can be a letter, a number, or another symbol. A grouping of characters into a word, a group of words, or a complete number (such as a person's name or age) is called a **field**. A group of related fields, such as a student's identification number (ID), the course taken, the date, and the grade, comprises a **record**; a group of records of the same type is called a **file**. For example, the records in Figure 6.1 could constitute a student course file. A group of related files makes up a **database**. The student course file illustrated in Figure 6.1 could be grouped with files on students' personal histories and financial backgrounds to create a student database. Databases are at the heart of all information systems because they keep track of the people, places, and things that a business must deal with on a continuing, often instant basis.

ENTITIES AND ATTRIBUTES

To run a business, you most likely will be using data about categories of information such as customers, suppliers, employees, orders, products, shippers, and perhaps parts. Each of these generalized categories representing a person, place, or thing on which we store information is called an **entity**. Each entity has specific characteristics called **attributes**. For example, in Figure 6.1, COURSE would be an entity, and Student_ID, Course, Date, and Grade would be its attributes. If you were a business keeping track of parts you used and their suppliers, the entity SUPPLIER would have attributes such as the supplier's name and address, which would most likely include the street, city, state, and zip code. The entity PART would typically have attributes such as part description, price of each part (unit price), and the supplier who produced the part.

ORGANIZING DATA IN A RELATIONAL DATABASE

If you stored this information in paper files, you would probably have a file on each entity and its attributes. In an information system, a database organizes the data much the same way, grouping related pieces of data. The **relational database**

Figure 6.1
The Data Hierarchy
A computer system organizes data in a hierarchy that starts with the bit, which represents either a 0 or a 1. Bits can be grouped to form a byte to represent one character, number, or symbol. Bytes can be grouped to form a field, and related fields can be grouped to form a record. Related records can be collected to form a file, and related files can be organized into a database.

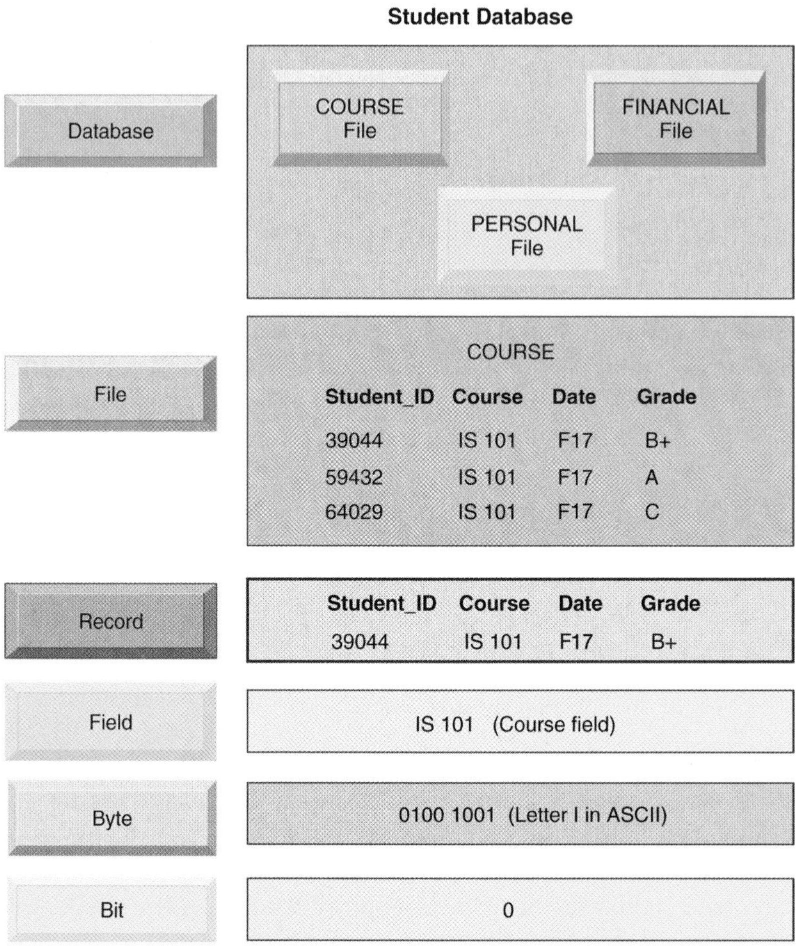

is the most common type of database today. Relational databases organize data into two-dimensional tables (called *relations*) with columns and rows. Each table contains data about an entity and its attributes. For the most part, there is one table for each business entity, so, at the most basic level, you will have one table for customers and a table each for suppliers, parts in inventory, employees, and sales transactions.

Let's look at how a relational database would organize data about suppliers and parts. Look at the SUPPLIER table illustrated in Figure 6.2. It consists of a grid of columns and rows of data. Each element of data about a supplier, such as the supplier name, street, city, state, and zip code, is stored as a separate field within the SUPPLIER table. Each field represents an attribute for the entity SUPPLIER. Fields in a relational database are also called *columns*.

The actual information about a single supplier that resides in a table is called a *row*. Rows are commonly referred to as records, or, in very technical terms, as **tuples**.

Note that there is a field for Supplier_Number in this table. This field uniquely identifies each record so that the record can be retrieved, updated, or sorted, and it is called a **key field**. Each table in a relational database has one field designated as its **primary key**. This key field is the unique identifier for all the information in any row of the table, and this primary key cannot be duplicated.

We could use the supplier's name as a key field. However, if two suppliers had the same name (which does happen from time to time), supplier name would not uniquely identify each, so it is necessary to assign a special identifier field for this purpose. For example, if you had two suppliers, both named "CBM," but one was based in Dayton and the other in St. Louis, it would be easy to confuse them. However, if each has a unique supplier number, such confusion is prevented.

SUPPLIER

Columns (Attributes, Fields)

Supplier_Number	Supplier_Name	Supplier_Street	Supplier_City	Supplier_State	Supplier_Zip
8259	CBM Inc.	74 5th Avenue	Dayton	OH	45220
8261	B. R. Molds	1277 Gandolly Street	Cleveland	OH	49345
8263	Jackson Composites	8233 Micklin Street	Lexington	KY	56723
8444	Bryant Corporation	4315 Mill Drive	Rochester	NY	11344

Rows (Records, Tuples)

Key Field (Primary Key)

Figure 6.2
A Relational Database Table
A relational database organizes data in the form of two-dimensional tables. Illustrated here is a table for the entity SUPPLIER showing how it represents the entity and its attributes. Supplier_Number is the key field.

We also see that the address information has been separated into four fields: Supplier_Street, Supplier_City, Supplier_State, and Supplier_Zip. Data are separated into the smallest elements that one would want to access separately to make it easy to select only the rows in the table that match the contents of one field, such as all the suppliers in Ohio (OH). The rows of data can also be sorted by the contents of the Supplier_State field to get a list of suppliers by state regardless of their cities.

So far, the SUPPLIER table does not have any information about the parts that a particular supplier provides for your company. PART is a separate entity from SUPPLIER, and fields with information about parts should be stored in a separate PART table (see Figure 6.3).

Why not keep information on parts in the same table as suppliers? If we did that, each row of the table would contain the attributes of both PART and SUPPLIER. Because one supplier could supply more than one part, the table would need many extra rows for a single supplier to show all the parts that supplier provided. We would be maintaining a great deal of redundant data about suppliers, and it would be difficult to search for the information on any individual part because you would not know whether this part is the first or fiftieth part in this supplier's record. A separate table, PART, should be created to store these three fields and solve this problem.

PART

Part_Number	Part_Name	Unit_Price	Supplier_Number
137	Door latch	22.00	8259
145	Side mirror	12.00	8444
150	Door molding	6.00	8263
152	Door lock	31.00	8259
155	Compressor	54.00	8261
178	Door handle	10.00	8259

Primary Key

Foreign Key

Figure 6.3
The PART Table
Data for the entity PART have their own separate table. Part_Number is the primary key and Supplier_Number is the foreign key, enabling users to find related information from the SUPPLIER table about the supplier for each part.

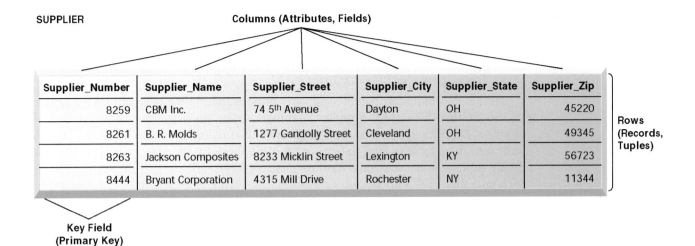

The PART table would also have to contain another field, Supplier_Number, so that you would know the supplier for each part. It would not be necessary to keep repeating all the information about a supplier in each PART record because having a Supplier_ Number field in the PART table allows you to look up the data in the fields of the SUPPLIER table.

Notice that Supplier_Number appears in both the SUPPLIER and PART tables. In the SUPPLIER table, Supplier_Number is the primary key. When the field Supplier_Number appears in the PART table, it is called a **foreign key** and is essentially a look-up field to find data about the supplier of a specific part. Note that the PART table would itself have its own primary key field, Part_Number, to identify each part uniquely. This key is not used to link PART with SUPPLIER but could be used to link PART with a different entity.

As we organize data into tables, it is important to make sure that all the attributes for a particular entity apply only to that entity. If you were to keep the supplier's address with the PART record, that information would not really relate only to PART; it would relate to both PART and SUPPLIER. If the supplier's address were to change, it would be necessary to alter the data in every PART record rather than only once in the SUPPLIER record.

ESTABLISHING RELATIONSHIPS

Now that we've broken down our data into a SUPPLIER table and a PART table, we must make sure we understand the relationship between them. A schematic called an **entity-relationship diagram** clarifies table relationships in a relational database. The most important piece of information an entity-relationship diagram provides is the manner in which two tables are related to each other. Tables in a relational database may have one-to-one, one-to-many, and many-to-many relationships.

An example of a one-to-one relationship is a human resources system that stores confidential data about employees. The system stores data, such as the employee name, date of birth, address, and job position, in one table and confidential data about that employee, such as salary or pension benefits, in another table. These two tables pertaining to a single employee would have a one-to-one relationship because each record in the EMPLOYEE table with basic employee data has only one related record in the table storing confidential data.

The relationship between the SUPPLIER and PART entities in our database is a one-to-many relationship. Each supplier can supply more than one part, but each part has only one supplier. For every record in the SUPPLIER table, many related records might be in the PART table.

Figure 6.4 illustrates how an entity-relationship diagram would depict this one-to-many relationship. The boxes represent entities. The lines connecting the boxes represent relationships. A line connecting two entities that ends in two short marks designates a one-to-one relationship. A line connecting two entities that ends with a crow's foot preceded by a short mark indicates a one-to-many relationship. Figure 6.4 shows that each part has only one supplier, but the same supplier can provide many parts.

We would also see a one-to-many relationship if we wanted to add a table about orders to our database because one supplier services many orders. The ORDER table would contain only the Order_Number and Order_Date fields. Figure 6.5 illustrates a report showing an order of parts from a supplier. If you look at the report, you can see that the information on the top-right portion of the report comes from the ORDER table. The actual line items ordered are listed in the lower portion of the report.

Figure 6.4
A Simple Entity-Relationship Diagram
This diagram shows the relationship between the entities SUPPLIER and PART.

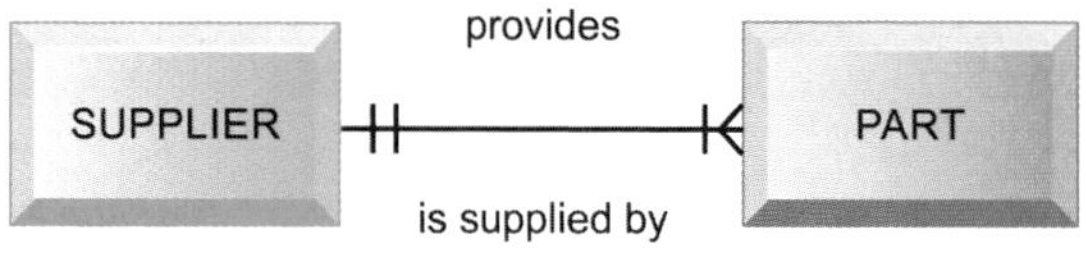

Order Number: 3502
Order Date: 1/15/2018

Supplier Number: 8259
Supplier Name: CBM Inc.
Supplier Address: 74 5th Avenue, Dayton, OH 45220

Order_Number	Part_Number	Part_Quantity	Part_Name	Unit_Price	Extended Price
3502	137	10	Door latch	22.00	$220.00
3502	152	20	Door lock	31.00	620.00
3502	178	5	Door handle	10.00	50.00
			Order Total:		$890.00

Figure 6.5
Sample Order Report
The shaded areas show which data came from the ORDER, SUPPLIER, and LINE_ITEM tables. The database does not maintain data on extended price or order total because they can be derived from other data in the tables.

Because one order can be for many parts from a supplier, and a single part can be ordered many times on different orders, this creates a many-to-many relationship between the PART and ORDER tables. Whenever a many-to-many relationship exists between two tables, it is necessary to link these two tables in a table that joins this information. Creating a separate table for a line item in the order would serve this purpose. This table is often called a *join table* or an *intersection relation*. This join table contains only three fields: Order_Number and Part_Number, which are used only to link the ORDER and PART tables, and Part_Quantity. If you look at the bottom-left part of the report, this is the information coming from the LINE_ITEM table.

We would thus wind up with a total of four tables in our database. Figure 6.6 illustrates the final set of tables, and Figure 6.7 shows what the entity-relationship diagram for this set of tables would look like. Note that the ORDER table does not contain data on the extended price because that value can be calculated by multiplying Unit_Price by Part_Quantity. This data element can be derived when needed, using information that already exists in the PART and LINE_ITEM tables. Order_Total is another derived field, calculated by totaling the extended prices for items ordered.

The process of streamlining complex groups of data to minimize redundant data elements and awkward many-to-many relationships and increase stability and flexibility is called **normalization**. A properly designed and normalized database is easy to maintain and minimizes duplicate data. The Learning Tracks for this chapter direct you to more-detailed discussions of database design, normalization, and entity-relationship diagramming.

Relational database systems enforce **referential integrity** rules to ensure that relationships between coupled tables remain consistent. When one table has a foreign key that points to another table, you may not add a record to the table with the foreign key unless there is a corresponding record in the linked table. In the database we have just created, the foreign key Supplier_Number links the PART table to the SUPPLIER table. We may not add a new record to the PART table for a part with supplier number 8266 unless there is a corresponding record in the SUPPLIER table for supplier number 8266. We must also delete the corresponding record in the PART table if we delete the record in the SUPPLIER table for supplier number 8266. In other words, we shouldn't have parts from nonexistent suppliers!

The example provided here for parts, orders, and suppliers is a simple one. Even in a very small business, you will have tables for other important entities such as customers, shippers, and employees. A very large corporation typically has databases with thousands of entities (tables) to maintain. What is important for any business, large or small, is to have a good data model that includes all its entities and the relationships among them, one that is organized to minimize redundancy, maximize accuracy, and make data easily accessible for reporting and analysis.

PART

Part_Number	Part_Name	Unit_Price	Supplier_Number
137	Door latch	22.00	8259
145	Side mirror	12.00	8444
150	Door molding	6.00	8263
152	Door lock	31.00	8259
155	Compressor	54.00	8261
178	Door handle	10.00	8259

LINE_ITEM

Order_Number	Part_Number	Part_Quantity
3502	137	10
3502	152	20
3502	178	5

ORDER

Order_Number	Order_Date
3502	1/15/2018
3503	1/16/2018
3504	1/17/2018

SUPPLIER

Supplier_Number	Supplier_Name	Supplier_Street	Supplier_City	Supplier_State	Supplier_Zip
8259	CBM Inc.	74 5th Avenue	Dayton	OH	45220
8261	B. R. Molds	1277 Gandolly Street	Cleveland	OH	49345
8263	Jackson Components	8233 Micklin Street	Lexington	KY	56723
8444	Bryant Corporation	4315 Mill Drive	Rochester	NY	11344

Figure 6.6
The Final Database Design with Sample Records
The final design of the database for suppliers, parts, and orders has four tables. The LINE_ITEM table is a join table that eliminates the many-to-many relationship between ORDER and PART.

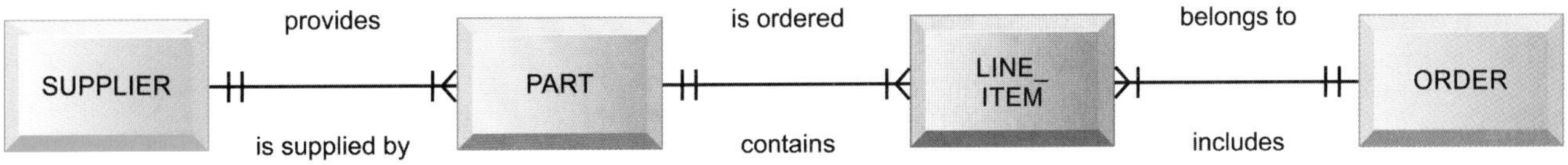

Figure 6.7
Entity-Relationship Diagram for the Database with Four Tables
This diagram shows the relationship between the SUPPLIER, PART, LINE_ITEM, and ORDER entities.

It cannot be emphasized enough: If the business does not get its data model right, the system will not be able to serve the business properly. The company's systems will not be as effective as they could be because they will have to work with data that may be inaccurate, incomplete, or difficult to retrieve. Understanding the organization's data and how they should be represented in a database is perhaps the most important lesson you can learn from this course.

For example, Famous Footwear, a shoe store chain with more than 1,100 locations in 49 states, could not achieve its goal of having the right style of shoe in the right store for sale at the right price because its database was not properly designed for a rapidly adjusting store inventory. The company had a database that was designed primarily for producing standard reports for management rather than for reacting to marketplace changes. Management could not obtain precise data on specific items in inventory in each of its stores. The company had to work around this problem by building a new database that organized the sales and inventory data better for analysis and inventory management.

6-2 What are the principles of a database management system?

Now that you have started creating the files and identifying the data your business requires, you will need a database management system to help you manage and use the data. A **database management system (DBMS)** is a specific type of software for creating, storing, organizing, and accessing data from a database. Microsoft Access is a DBMS for desktop systems, whereas DB2, Oracle Database, and Microsoft SQL Server are DBMS for large mainframes and midrange computers. MySQL is a popular open-source DBMS. All these products are relational DBMS that support a relational database.

The DBMS relieves the end user or programmer from the task of understanding where and how the data are actually stored by separating the logical and physical views of the data. The *logical view* presents data as end users or business specialists would perceive them, whereas the *physical view* shows how data are actually organized and structured on physical storage media, such as a hard disk.

The database management software makes the physical database available for different logical views required by users. For example, for the human resources database illustrated in Figure 6.8, a benefits specialist typically will require a view consisting of the employee's name, social security number, and health insurance coverage. A payroll department member will need data such as the employee's name, social security number, gross pay, and net pay. The data for all of these views is stored in a single database, where the organization can managed it more easily.

OPERATIONS OF A RELATIONAL DBMS

In a relational database, tables can be easily combined to deliver data that users require, provided that any two tables share a common data element. Let's return to the database we set up earlier with PART and SUPPLIER tables illustrated in Figures 6.2 and 6.3.

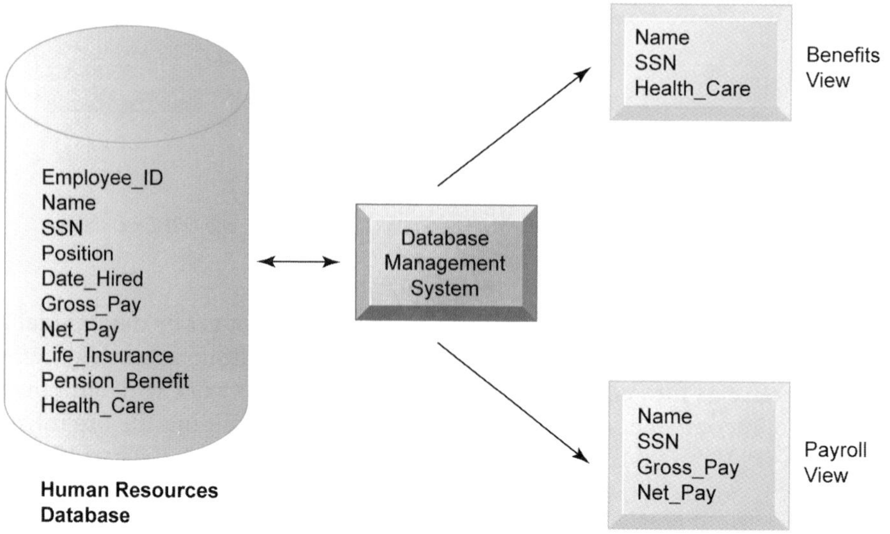

Figure 6.8
Human Resources Database with Multiple Views
A single human resources database provides many views of data, depending on the information requirements of the user. Illustrated here are two possible views, one of interest to a benefits specialist and one of interest to a member of the company's payroll department.

Suppose we wanted to find in this database the names of suppliers who could provide us with part number 137 or part number 150. We would need information from two tables: the SUPPLIER table and the PART table. Note that these two tables have a shared data element: Supplier_Number.

In a relational database, three basic operations, as shown in Figure 6.9, are used to develop useful sets of data: select, project, and join. The *select* operation creates a subset consisting of all records in the file that meet stated criteria. Select creates, in other words, a subset of rows that meet certain criteria. In our example, we want to select records (rows) from the PART table where the Part_Number equals 137 or 150. The *join* operation combines relational tables to provide the user with more information than is available in individual tables. In our example, we want to join the now-shortened PART table (only parts 137 or 150 are presented) and the SUPPLIER table into a single new table.

The *project* operation creates a subset consisting of columns in a table, permitting the user to create new tables that contain only the information required. In our example, we want to extract from the new table only the following columns: Part_Number, Part_Name, Supplier_Number, and Supplier_Name (see Figure 6.9).

CAPABILITIES OF DATABASE MANAGEMENT SYSTEMS

A DBMS includes capabilities and tools for organizing, managing, and accessing the data in the database. The most important are its data definition capability, data dictionary, and data manipulation language.

DBMS have a **data definition** capability to specify the structure of the content of the database. It would be used to create database tables and to define the characteristics of the fields in each table. This information about the database would be documented in a **data dictionary**. A data dictionary is an automated or manual file that stores definitions of data elements and their characteristics. Microsoft Access has a rudimentary data dictionary capability that displays information about the name, description, size, type, format, and other properties of each field in a table (see Figure 6.10). Data dictionaries for large corporate databases may capture additional information, such as usage, ownership (who in the organization is responsible for maintaining the data), authorization, security, and the individuals, business functions, programs, and reports that use each data element.

Querying and Reporting

DBMS include tools for accessing and manipulating information in databases. Most DBMS have a specialized language called a **data manipulation language** that is used to add, change, delete, and retrieve the data in the database. This language

PART

Part_Number	Part_Name	Unit_Price	Supplier_Number
137	Door latch	22.00	8259
145	Side mirror	12.00	8444
150	Door molding	6.00	8263
152	Door lock	31.00	8259
155	Compressor	54.00	8261
178	Door handle	10.00	8259

Select Part_Number = 137 or 150

SUPPLIER

Supplier_Number	Supplier_Name	Supplier_Street	Supplier_City	Supplier_State	Supplier_Zip
8259	CBM Inc.	74 5th Avenue	Dayton	OH	45220
8261	B. R. Molds	1277 Gandolly Street	Cleveland	OH	49345
8263	Jackson Components	8233 Micklin Street	Lexington	KY	56723
8444	Bryant Corporation	4315 Mill Drive	Rochester	NY	11344

Join by Supplier_Number

Part_Number	Part_Name	Supplier_Number	Supplier_Name
137	Door latch	8259	CBM Inc.
150	Door molding	8263	Jackson Components

Project selected columns

Figure 6.9
The Three Basic Operations of a Relational DBMS
The select, join, and project operations enable data from two tables to be combined and only selected attributes to be displayed.

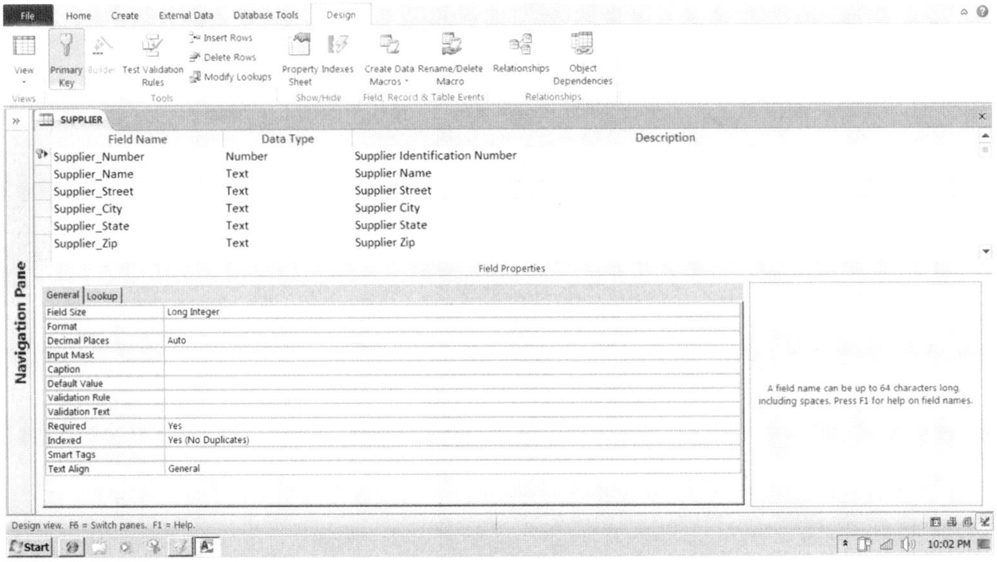

Figure 6.10
Access Data Dictionary Features
Microsoft Access has a rudimentary data dictionary capability that displays information about the size, format, and other characteristics of each field in a database. Displayed here is the information maintained in the SUPPLIER table. The small key icon to the left of Supplier_Number indicates that it is a key field.

Source: Courtesy of Microsoft Corporation

contains commands that permit end users and programming specialists to extract data from the database to satisfy information requests and develop applications. The most prominent data manipulation language today is **Structured Query Language**, or **SQL**. Figure 6.11 illustrates the SQL **query** that would produce the new resultant table in Figure 6.9. A query is a request for data from a database. You can find out more about how to perform SQL queries in our Learning Tracks for this chapter.

Users of DBMS for large and midrange computers, such as DB2, Oracle, or SQL Server, would employ SQL to retrieve information they needed from the database. Microsoft Access also uses SQL, but it provides its own set of user-friendly tools for querying databases and for organizing data from databases into more polished reports.

Microsoft Access has capabilities to help users create queries by identifying the tables and fields they want and the results and then selecting the rows from the database that meet particular criteria. These actions in turn are translated into SQL commands. Figure 6.12 illustrates how the SQL query to select parts and suppliers in Figure 6.11 would be constructed using Microsoft Access.

DBMS typically include capabilities for report generation so that the data of interest can be displayed in a more structured and polished format than would be possible just by querying. Crystal Reports is a popular **report generator** for large corporate DBMS, although it can also be used with Microsoft Access.

Microsoft Access also has capabilities for developing desktop system applications. These include tools for creating data entry screens and reports and developing the logic for processing transactions. Information systems specialists primarily use these capabilities.

```
SELECT PART.Part_Number, PART.Part_Name, SUPPLIER.Supplier_Number,
SUPPLIER.Supplier_Name
FROM PART, SUPPLIER
WHERE PART.Supplier_Number = SUPPLIER.Supplier_Number AND
Part_Number = 137 OR Part_Number = 150;
```

Figure 6.11
Example of a SQL Query
Illustrated here are the SQL statements for a query to select suppliers for parts 137 or 150. They produce a list with the same results as Figure 6.9.

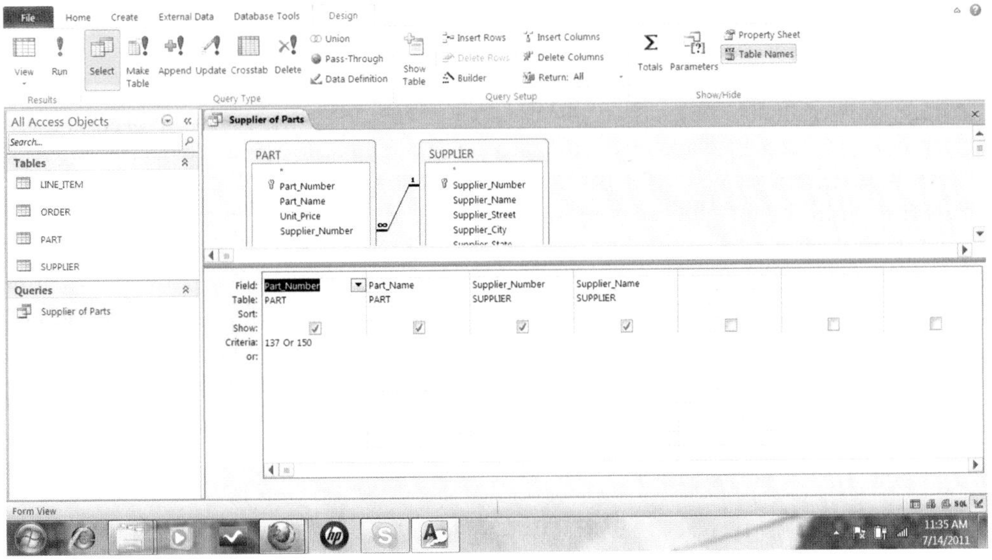

Figure 6.12
An Access Query
Illustrated here is how the query in Figure 6.11 would be constructed using Microsoft Access query-building tools. It shows the tables, fields, and selection criteria used for the query.

Source: Courtesy of Microsoft Corporation

NON-RELATIONAL DATABASES AND DATABASES IN THE CLOUD

For more than three decades, relational database technology has been the gold standard. Cloud computing, unprecedented data volumes, massive workloads for web services, and the need to store new types of data require database alternatives to the traditional relational model of organizing data in the form of tables, columns, and rows. Companies are turning to *NoSQL* non-relational-database technologies for this purpose. **Non-relational database management systems** use a more flexible data model and are designed for managing large data sets across many distributed machines and for easily scaling up or down. They are useful for accelerating simple queries against large volumes of structured and unstructured data, including web, social media, graphics, and other forms of data that are difficult to analyze with traditional SQL-based tools.

There are several kinds of NoSQL databases, each with its own technical features and behavior. Oracle NoSQL Database is one example, as is Amazon's SimpleDB, one of the Amazon Web Services that run in the cloud. SimpleDB provides a simple web services interface to create and store multiple data sets, query data easily, and return the results. There is no need to predefine a formal database structure or change that definition if new data sets are added later.

MetLife's MongoDB open source NoSQL database brings together data from more than 70 administrative systems, claims systems, and other data sources, including semi-structured and unstructured data, such as images of health records and death certificates. The NoSQL database can handle structured, semi-structured, and unstructured information without requiring tedious, expensive, and time-consuming database-mapping to normalize all data to a rigid schema, as required by relational databases.

Cloud Databases and Distributed Databases

Among the services Amazon and other cloud computing vendors provide are relational database engines. Amazon Relational Database Service (Amazon RDS) offers MySQL, Microsoft SQL Server, Oracle Database, PostgreSQL, or Amazon Aurora as database engines. Pricing is based on usage. Oracle has its own Database Cloud Services using its relational Oracle Database, and Microsoft Windows Azure SQL Database is a cloud-based relational database service based on the Microsoft SQL Server DBMS. Cloud-based data management services have special appeal for web-focused start-ups or small to medium-sized businesses seeking database capabilities at a lower price than in-house database products.

Google now offers its Spanner distributed database technology as a cloud service. A **distributed database** is one that is stored in multiple physical locations. Parts or copies of the database are physically stored in one location and other parts or copies are maintained in other locations. Spanner makes it possible to store information across millions of machines in hundreds of data centers around the globe, with special time-keeping tools to synchronize the data precisely in all of its locations and ensure the data are always consistent. Google uses Spanner to support its various cloud services, including Google Photos, AdWords (Google's online ad system), and Gmail, and is now making the technology available to other companies that might need such capabilities to run a global business.

6-3 What are the principal tools and technologies for accessing information from databases to improve business performance and decision making?

Businesses use their databases to keep track of basic transactions, such as paying suppliers, processing orders, serving customers, and paying employees, but they also need databases to provide information that will help the company run the business more efficiently and help managers and employees make better decisions. If a company wants to know which product is the most popular or who is its most profitable customer, the answer lies in the data.

THE CHALLENGE OF BIG DATA

Most of the data that organizations collected was transaction data that could easily fit into rows and columns of relational database management systems. There has been an explosion of data from many different sources, including web traffic, email messages, and social media content (tweets, status messages) as well as machine-generated data from sensors. These data may be unstructured or semi-structured and thus not suitable for relational database products that organize data in the form of columns and rows. We now use the term **big data** to describe these data sets with volumes so huge that they are beyond the ability of typical DBMS to capture, store, and analyze.

Big data is often characterized by the "3Vs": the extreme *volume* of data, the wide *variety* of data types and sources, and the *velocity* at which the data must be processed. Big data doesn't designate any specific quantity but usually refers to data in the petabyte and exabyte range—in other words, billions to trillions of records, respectively, from different sources. Big data are produced in much larger quantities and much more rapidly than traditional data. For example, a single jet engine is capable of generating 10 terabytes of data in just 30 minutes, and there are more than 25,000 airline flights each day. Even though tweets are limited to 140 characters each, Twitter generates more than 8 terabytes of data daily. Digital information is growing exponentially, from 1.8 zettabytes in 2011 to an expected 35 zettabytes in 2020. According to a Cisco Systems report, if an 11-ounce cup of coffee represented one gigabyte, then one zettabyte would have the same volume as the Great Wall of China.

Businesses are interested in big data because they contain more patterns and interesting relationships than smaller data sets, with the potential to provide new insights into customer behavior, weather patterns, financial market activity, or other phenomena. For example, Shutterstock, the global online image marketplace, stores 24 million images and adds 10,000 more each day. To find ways to optimize the Shutterstock experience, it analyzes its big data to find out where its website visitors place their cursors and how long they hover over an image before making a purchase. Big data is also finding many uses in the public sector (see the chapter-ending case study).

However, to derive business value from these data, organizations need new technologies and tools capable of managing and analyzing nontraditional data along with their traditional enterprise data. They also need to know what questions to ask of the data and the limitations of big data. Capturing, storing, and analyzing big data can be expensive, and information from big data may not necessarily help decision makers. It's important to have a clear understanding of the problems big data will solve for the business. The chapter-ending case explores these issues.

BUSINESS INTELLIGENCE TECHNOLOGY INFRASTRUCTURE

Suppose you wanted concise, reliable information about current operations, trends, and changes across the entire company. If you worked in a large company, the data you need might have to be pieced together from separate systems, such as sales, manufacturing, and accounting, and even from external sources, such as demographic or competitor data. Increasingly, you might need to use big data. A technology infrastructure for business intelligence has an array of tools for obtaining useful information from all the different types of data used by businesses today, including semi-structured and unstructured big data in vast quantities. These capabilities include data warehouses and data marts, Hadoop, in-memory computing, and analytical platforms. Some of these capabilities are available as cloud services.

Data Warehouses and Data Marts

The traditional tool for analyzing corporate data for the past two decades has been the data warehouse. A **data warehouse** is a database that stores current and historical data of potential interest to decision makers throughout the company. The data originate in many core operational transaction systems, such as systems for sales, customer accounts, and manufacturing, and may include data from website transactions. The data warehouse extracts current and historical data from multiple operational systems inside the organization. These data are combined with data from external sources and transformed by correcting inaccurate and incomplete data and structuring the data in a common repository for management reporting and analysis. The Charlotte Hornets data warehouse described in the chapter-opening case is an example.

The data warehouse makes the data available for anyone to access as needed, but it cannot be altered. A data warehouse system also provides a range of ad hoc and standardized query tools, analytical tools, and graphical reporting facilities. A data warehouse can be deployed on premises, in the cloud, or in a hybrid cloud environment (review Chapter 5).

Companies often build enterprise-wide data warehouses, where a central data warehouse serves the entire organization, or they create smaller, decentralized warehouses called data marts. A **data mart** is a subset of a data warehouse in which a summarized or highly focused portion of the organization's data is placed in a separate database for a specific population of users. For example, a company might develop marketing and sales data marts to deal with customer information. Dell maintains a data mart for its sales team that consolidates and streamlines information from a variety of data sources, legacy systems, and reporting systems.

Hadoop

Relational DBMS and data warehouse products are not well suited for organizing and analyzing big data or data that do not easily fit into columns and rows used in their data models. For handling unstructured and semi-structured data in vast quantities, as well as structured data, organizations are using **Hadoop**. Hadoop is an open source software framework managed by the Apache Software Foundation that enables distributed parallel processing of huge amounts of data across inexpensive computers. It breaks a big data problem down into sub-problems, distributes them among up to thousands of inexpensive computer processing nodes, and then combines the result into a smaller data set that is easier to analyze. You've probably used Hadoop to find the best airfare on the Internet, get directions to a restaurant, do a search on Google, or connect with a friend on Facebook.

Hadoop consists of several key services: the Hadoop Distributed File System (HDFS) for data storage and MapReduce for high-performance parallel data processing. HDFS links together the file systems on the numerous nodes in a Hadoop cluster to turn them into one big file system. Hadoop's MapReduce was inspired by Google's MapReduce system for breaking down processing of huge data sets and assigning work to the various nodes in a cluster. HBase, Hadoop's non-relational database, provides rapid access to the data stored on HDFS and a transactional platform for running high-scale real-time applications.

Hadoop can process large quantities of any kind of data, including structured transactional data, loosely structured data such as Facebook and Twitter feeds, complex data such as web server log files, and unstructured audio and video data. Hadoop runs on a cluster of inexpensive servers, and processors can be added or removed as needed. Companies use Hadoop for analyzing very large volumes of data as well as for a staging area for unstructured and semi-structured data before they are loaded into a data warehouse. Yahoo uses Hadoop to track user behavior so it can modify its home page to fit their interests. Life sciences research firm NextBio uses Hadoop and HBase to process data for pharmaceutical companies conducting genomic research. Top database vendors such as IBM, Hewlett-Packard, Oracle, and Microsoft have their own Hadoop software distributions. Other vendors offer tools for moving data into and out of Hadoop or for analyzing data within Hadoop.

In-Memory Computing

Another way of facilitating big data analysis is to use **in-memory computing**, which relies primarily on a computer's main memory (RAM) for data storage. (Conventional DBMS use disk storage systems.) Users access data stored in system's primary memory, thereby eliminating bottlenecks from retrieving and reading data in a traditional, disk-based database and dramatically shortening query response times. In-memory processing makes it possible for very large sets of data, amounting to the size of a data mart or small data warehouse, to reside entirely in memory. Complex business calculations that used to take hours or days are able to be completed within seconds, and this can even be accomplished on handheld devices.

The previous chapter describes some of the advances in contemporary computer hardware technology that make in-memory processing possible, such as powerful high-speed processors, multicore processing, and falling computer memory prices. These technologies help companies optimize the use of memory and accelerate processing performance while lowering costs.

Leading in-memory database products include SAP HANA, Oracle Database In-Memory, Microsoft SQL Server 2016, and Teradata Intelligent Memory. The chapter-opening case on the Charlotte Hornets and the Interactive Session on the Kraft Heinz Company show how organizations are benefiting from in-memory technology.

Analytic Platforms

Commercial database vendors have developed specialized high-speed **analytic platforms** using both relational and non-relational technology that are optimized for analyzing large data sets. Analytic platforms such as IBM PureData System for Analytics feature preconfigured hardware-software systems that are specifically designed for query processing and analytics. For example, IBM PureData System for Analytics features tightly integrated database, server, and storage components that handle complex analytic queries 10 to 100 times faster than traditional systems. Analytic platforms also include in-memory systems and NoSQL non-relational database management systems. Analytic platforms are now available as cloud services.

Kraft Heinz Finds a New Recipe for Analyzing Its Data

When the Kraft Foods Group and Heinz finalized their merger in July 2015 it was the marriage of two giants. The new Kraft Heinz Company became the fifth-largest consumer-packaged food and beverage organization in the world, with more than 200 global brands, $27.4 billion in revenue, and over 40,000 employees. Eight of the brands each have annual revenue exceeding $1 billion: Heinz, Maxwell House, Kraft, Lunchables, Planters, Velveeta, Philadelphia, and Oscar Mayer. Running these companies required huge amounts of data from all of these brands. This is clearly the world of big data.

To remain profitable, enterprises in the fast-moving consumer goods industry require very lean operations. The uncertain global economy has dampened consumer spending, so companies such as Kraft Heinz must constantly identify opportunities for improving operational efficiencies to protect their profit margins. Kraft Heinz decided to deal with this challenge by focusing on optimizing its supply chain—manufacturing optimal quantities of each of its products and delivering them to retailers at the best time and least cost to capitalize on consumer demand.

Managing a supply chain as large as that of Kraft Heinz requires timely and accurate data on sales forecasts, manufacturing plans, and logistics, often from multiple sources. To ensure that Kraft Heinz would be able to use all of its enterprise business data effectively, management decided to split the data among two large SAP enterprise resource planning (ERP) systems, one for North America business and the other for all other global business. The combined company also had to rethink its data warehouse.

Before the merger, the North America business had maintained nearly 18 terabytes of data in a SAP Business Warehouse and was using SAP Business Warehouse Accelerator to facilitate operational reporting. SAP Business Warehouse is SAP's data warehouse software for consolidating organizational data and supporting data analytics and reporting. The SAP Business Warehouse (BW) Accelerator is used to speed up database queries. Kraft Heinz management wanted decision makers to obtain more fine-grained views of the data that would reveal new opportunities for improving efficiency, self-service reporting, and real-time analytics.

SAP BW Accelerator was not suitable for these tasks. It could optimize query runtime (the period of time when a query program is running) only for a specific subset of data in the warehouse and was limited to reporting on selected views of the data. It could not deal with data load and calculation performance and required replication of Business Warehouse data in a separate accelerator. With mushrooming data on the merged company's sales, logistics, and manufacturing, the warehouse was too overtaxed to generate timely reports for decision makers. Moreover, Kraft Heinz's complex data model made building new reports very time-consuming—as long as six months to complete. Kraft Heinz needed a solution that would deliver more detailed reports more quickly without affecting the performance of underlying operational systems.

Kraft Heinz business users had been building some of their own reports using SAP Business Objects Analysis edition for Microsoft Office, which integrates with Microsoft Excel and PowerPoint. This tool allows ad hoc multidimensional analysis of online analytical processing (OLAP). What these users needed was to be able to build self-service reports from a single source of data and find an efficient way to collate data from multiple sources to obtain an enterprise-wide view of what was going on.

Kraft Heinz decided to migrate its data warehouse from its legacy database to SAP BW powered by SAP HANA, SAP's in-memory database platform, which dramatically improves the efficiency at which data can be loaded and processed, calculations can be computed, and queries and reports can be run. The new data warehouse would be able to integrate with existing SAP ERP applications driving day-to-day business operations. The company worked with IBM Global Services consultants to cleanse and streamline its existing databases. It archived and purged unwanted or unused data, with the IT department working closely with business professionals to jointly determine what was essential, what was still being used, and what data thought to be unused had been moved to a different functional area of the company. Cleansing and streamlining data reduced the database size almost 50 percent, to 9 TB.

According to Sundar Dittakavi, Kraft Heinz Group Leader of Global Business Intelligence, in addition to providing better insights, the new data warehouse environment has achieved a 98 percent improvement in the production of standard reports.

This is due to the 83 percent reduction in load time to execution time to make the data available and reduction in execution time to complete the analysis. Global key performance indicators for the Kraft side of the business are built into SAP HANA.

Kraft Heinz can now accommodate exploding volumes of data and database queries easily while maintaining enough processing power to handle unexpected issues. The company is also able to build new reports much faster, and the flexibility of SAP HANA makes it much easier to change the company's data model. Now Kraft Heinz can produce new reports for business users in weeks instead of months and give decision makers the insights they need to boost efficiency and lower operating costs.

Sources: Ken Murphy, "The Kraft-Heinz Company Unlocks Recipe for Strategic Business Insight," *SAP Insider Profiles*, January 25, 2017; "The Kraft Heinz Company Migrates SAP Business Warehouse to the Lightning-Fast SAP HANA Database," IBM Corp. and SAP SE, 2016; and www.kraftheinzcompany.com, accessed February 15, 2017.

CASE STUDY QUESTIONS

1. Identify the problem in this case study. To what extent was it a technology problem? Were any people and organizational factors involved?
2. How was information technology affecting business performance at Kraft Heinz?
3. How did new technology provide a solution to the problem? How effective was the solution?
4. Identify the people, organization, and technology factors that had to be addressed in selecting and implementing Kraft Heinz's new data warehouse solution.

Figure 6.13 illustrates a contemporary business intelligence technology infrastructure using the technologies we have just described. Current and historical data are extracted from multiple operational systems along with web data, social media data, Internet of Things (IoT) machine-generated data, unstructured audio/visual data, and other data from external sources. Some companies are starting to pour all of these types of data into a data lake. A **data lake** is a repository for raw unstructured data or structured data that for the most part have not yet been analyzed, and the data can be accessed in many ways. The data lake stores these data in their native format until they are needed. The Hadoop Distributed File System (HDFS) is often used to store the data lake contents across a set of clustered computer nodes, and Hadoop clusters may be used to pre-process some of these data for use in the data warehouse, data marts, or an analytic platform or for direct querying by power users. Outputs include reports and dashboards as well as query results. Chapter 12 discusses the various types of BI users and BI reporting in greater detail.

ANALYTICAL TOOLS: RELATIONSHIPS, PATTERNS, TRENDS

When data have been captured and organized using the business intelligence technologies we have just described, they are available for further analysis by using software for database querying and reporting, multidimensional data analysis (OLAP), and data mining. This section will introduce you to these tools, with more detail about business intelligence analytics and applications in Chapter 11.

Online Analytical Processing (OLAP)

Suppose your company sells four products—nuts, bolts, washers, and screws—in the East, West, and Central regions. If you wanted to ask a straightforward question, such as how many washers sold during the past quarter, you could easily find the answer by querying your sales database. However, what if you wanted to know how many washers sold in each of your sales regions and compare actual results with projected sales?

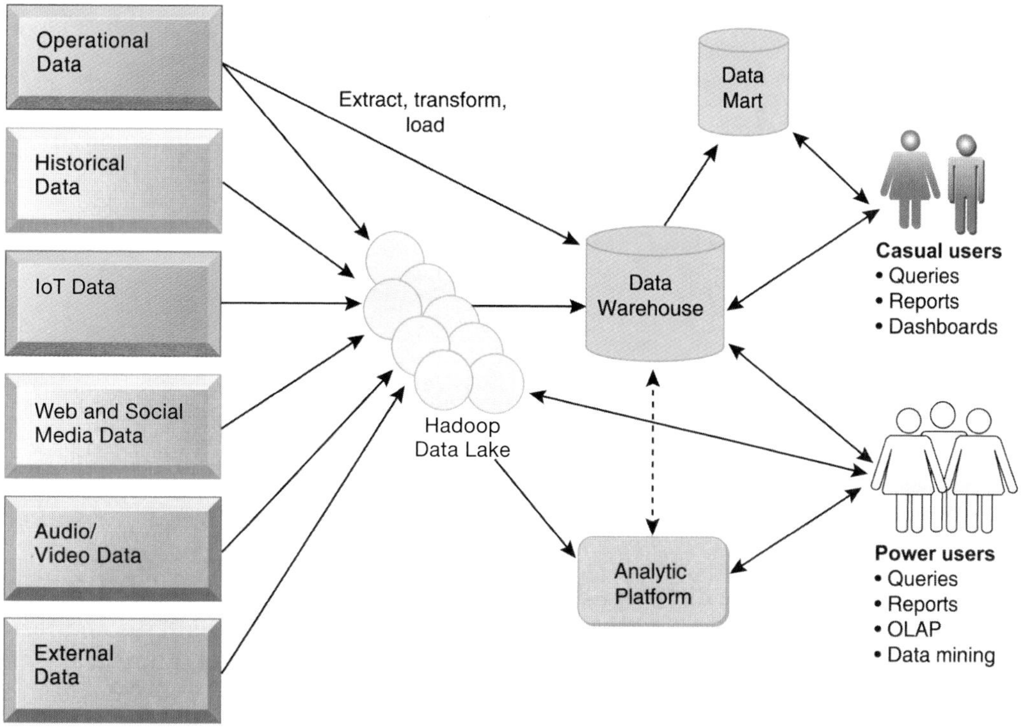

Figure 6.13
Business Intelligence Technology Infrastructure
A contemporary business intelligence technology infrastructure features capabilities and tools to manage and analyze large quantities and different types of data from multiple sources. Easy-to-use query and reporting tools for casual business users and more sophisticated analytical toolsets for power users are included.

To obtain the answer, you would need **online analytical processing (OLAP)**. OLAP supports multidimensional data analysis, enabling users to view the same data in different ways using multiple dimensions. Each aspect of information—product, pricing, cost, region, or time period—represents a different dimension. A product manager could use a multidimensional data analysis tool to learn how many washers were sold in the East in June, how that compares with the previous month and the previous June, and how it compares with the sales forecast. OLAP enables users to obtain online answers to ad hoc questions such as these in rapid time, even when the data are stored in very large databases, such as sales figures for multiple years.

Figure 6.14 shows a multidimensional model that could be created to represent products, regions, actual sales, and projected sales. A matrix of actual sales can be stacked on top of a matrix of projected sales to form a cube with six faces. If you rotate the cube 90 degrees one way, the face showing will be product versus actual and projected sales. If you rotate the cube 90 degrees again, you will see region versus actual and projected sales. If you rotate 180 degrees from the original view, you will see projected sales and product versus region. Cubes can be nested within cubes to build complex views of data. A company would use either a specialized multidimensional database or a tool that creates multidimensional views of data in relational databases.

Data Mining

Traditional database queries answer such questions as "How many units of product number 403 were shipped in February 2017?" OLAP, or multidimensional analysis, supports much more complex requests for information, such as, "Compare sales of product 403 relative to plan by quarter and sales region for the past two years." With OLAP and query-oriented data analysis, users need to have a good idea about the information for which they are looking.

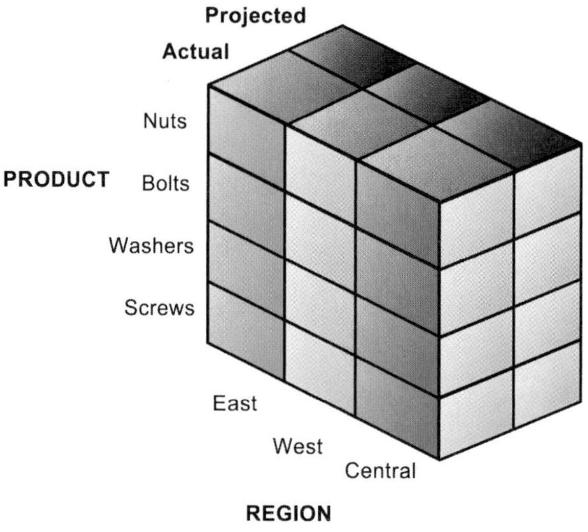

Figure 6.14
Multidimensional Data Model
This view shows product versus region. If you rotate the cube 90 degrees, the face that will show is product versus actual and projected sales. If you rotate the cube 90 degrees again, you will see region versus actual and projected sales. Other views are possible.

Data mining is more discovery-driven. Data mining provides insights into corporate data that cannot be obtained with OLAP by finding hidden patterns and relationships in large databases and inferring rules from them to predict future behavior. The patterns and rules are used to guide decision making and forecast the effect of those decisions. The types of information obtainable from data mining include associations, sequences, classifications, clusters, and forecasts.

- *Associations* are occurrences linked to a single event. For instance, a study of supermarket purchasing patterns might reveal that, when corn chips are purchased, a cola drink is purchased 65 percent of the time, but when there is a promotion, cola is purchased 85 percent of the time. This information helps managers make better decisions because they have learned the profitability of a promotion.
- In *sequences*, events are linked over time. We might find, for example, that if a house is purchased, a new refrigerator will be purchased within two weeks 65 percent of the time, and an oven will be bought within one month of the home purchase 45 percent of the time.
- *Classification* recognizes patterns that describe the group to which an item belongs by examining existing items that have been classified and by inferring a set of rules. For example, businesses such as credit card or telephone companies worry about the loss of steady customers. Classification helps discover the characteristics of customers who are likely to leave and can provide a model to help managers predict who those customers are so that the managers can devise special campaigns to retain such customers.
- *Clustering* works in a manner similar to classification when no groups have yet been defined. A data-mining tool can discover different groupings within data, such as finding affinity groups for bank cards or partitioning a database into groups of customers based on demographics and types of personal investments.
- Although these applications involve predictions, *forecasting* uses predictions in a different way. It uses a series of existing values to forecast what other values will be. For example, forecasting might find patterns in data to help managers estimate the future value of continuous variables, such as sales figures.

These systems perform high-level analyses of patterns or trends, but they can also drill down to provide more detail when needed. There are data-mining applications for all the functional areas of business and for government and scientific work. One popular use for data mining is to provide detailed analyses of patterns in customer data for one-to-one marketing campaigns or for identifying profitable customers.

Caesars Entertainment, formerly known as Harrah's Entertainment, is the largest gaming company in the world. It continually analyzes data about its customers gathered when people play its slot machines or use its casinos and hotels. The corporate marketing department uses this information to build a detailed gambling profile, based on a particular customer's ongoing value to the company. For instance, data mining tells Caesars the favorite gaming experience of a regular customer at one of its riverboat casinos, along with that person's preferences for room accommodations, restaurants, and entertainment. This information guides management decisions about how to cultivate the most profitable customers, encourage those customers to spend more, and attract more customers with high revenue-generating potential. Business intelligence improved Caesar's profits so much that it became the centerpiece of the firm's business strategy, and customer data are Caesar's most valuable asset (O'Keefe, 2015).

Text Mining and Web Mining

Unstructured data, most in the form of text files, is believed to account for more than 80 percent of useful organizational information and is one of the major sources of big data that firms want to analyze. Email, memos, call center transcripts, survey responses, legal cases, patent descriptions, and service reports are all valuable for finding patterns and trends that will help employees make better business decisions. **Text mining** tools are now available to help businesses analyze these data. These tools can extract key elements from unstructured big data sets, discover patterns and relationships, and summarize the information.

Businesses might turn to text mining to analyze transcripts of calls to customer service centers to identify major service and repair issues or to measure customer sentiment about their company. **Sentiment analysis** software can mine text comments in an email message, blog, social media conversation, or survey form to detect favorable and unfavorable opinions about specific subjects. For example, Kraft Foods uses a Community Intelligence Portal and sentiment analysis to tune into consumer conversations about its products across numerous social networks, blogs, and other websites. Kraft tries to make sense of relevant comments rather than just track brand mentions and can identify customers'emotions and feelings when they talk about how they barbecue and what sauces and spices they use.

The web is another rich source of unstructured big data for revealing patterns, trends, and insights into customer behavior. The discovery and analysis of useful patterns and information from the World Wide Web is called **web mining**. Businesses might turn to web mining to help them understand customer behavior, evaluate the effectiveness of a particular website, or quantify the success of a marketing campaign. For instance, marketers use Google Trends, which tracks the popularity of various words and phrases used in Google search queries to learn what people are interested in and what they are interested in buying.

Web mining looks for patterns in data through content mining, structure mining, and usage mining. Web content mining is the process of extracting knowledge from the content of web pages, which may include text, image, audio, and video data. Web structure mining examines data related to the structure of a particular website. For example, links pointing to a document indicate the popularity of the document; links coming out of a document indicate the richness or perhaps the variety of topics covered in the document. Web usage mining examines user interaction data a web server records whenever requests for a website's resources are received. The usage data records the user's behavior when the user browses or makes transactions on the website and collects the data in a server log. Analyzing such data can help companies determine the value of particular customers, cross-marketing strategies across products, and the effectiveness of promotional campaigns.

DATABASES AND THE WEB

Many companies are using the web to make some of the information in their internal databases available to customers and business partners. Prospective customers might use a company's website to view the company's product catalog or to place an order.

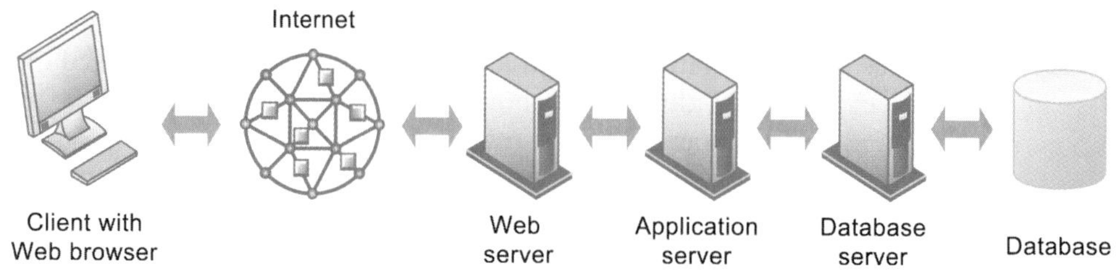

Figure 6.15 Linking Internal Databases to the Web
Users access an organization's internal database through the web, using their desktop PCs or mobile devices and web browser software.

The company in turn might use the web to check inventory availability for that product from its supplier.

These actions involve accessing and (in the case of ordering) updating corporate databases through the web. Suppose, for example, a customer with a web browser wants to search an online retailer's database for pricing information. Figure 6.15 illustrates how that customer might access the retailer's internal database over the web. The user would access the retailer's website over the Internet using web browser software on his or her client PC or mobile device. The user's web browser software would request data from the organization's database, using HTML commands to communicate with the web server.

Because many back-end databases cannot interpret commands written in HTML, the web server would pass these requests for data to software that translates HTML commands into SQL so the DBMS working with the database can process them. In a client/server environment, the DBMS often resides on a dedicated computer called a **database server**. The DBMS receives the SQL requests and provides the required data. The information is transferred from the organization's internal database back to the web server for delivery in the form of a web page to the user.

Figure 6.15 shows that the software working between the web server and the DBMS could be on an application server running on its own dedicated computer (see Chapter 5). The application server takes requests from the web server, runs the business logic to process transactions based on those requests, and provides connectivity to the organization's back-end systems or databases. Alternatively, the software for handling these operations could be a custom program or a CGI script. A CGI script is a compact program using the *Common Gateway Interface* (*CGI*) specification for processing data on a web server.

There are a number of advantages to using the web to access an organization's internal databases. First, everyone knows how to use web browser software, and employees require much less training than if they used proprietary query tools. Second, the web interface requires few or no changes to the internal database. Companies leverage their investments in older systems because it costs much less to add a web interface in front of a legacy system than to redesign and rebuild the system to improve user access.

Accessing corporate databases through the web is creating new efficiencies and opportunities, and, in some cases, it is even changing the way business is being done. ThomasNet.com provides an up-to-date directory of information from more than 700,000 suppliers of industrial products such as chemicals, metals, plastics, rubber, and automotive equipment. Formerly called Thomas Register, the company used to send out huge paper catalogs with this information. Now, it provides this information to users on its website and has become a smaller, leaner company.

Other companies have created entirely new businesses based on access to large databases through the web. One is the social networking service Facebook, which helps users stay connected with each other and meet new people. Facebook features profiles with information about more than 1.9 billion active users with information about themselves, including interests, friends, photos, and groups with which they are affiliated. Facebook maintains a massive database to house and manage all this content.

6-4 Why are information policy, data administration, and data quality assurance essential for managing the firm's data resources?

Setting up a database is only a start. To make sure that the data for your business remain accurate, reliable, and readily available to those who need it, your business will need special policies and procedures for data management.

ESTABLISHING AN INFORMATION POLICY

Every business, large and small, needs an information policy. Your firm's data are an important resource, and you don't want people doing whatever they want with them. You need to have rules on how the data are to be organized and maintained and who is allowed to view the data or change them.

An **information policy** specifies the organization's rules for sharing, disseminating, acquiring, standardizing, classifying, and inventorying information. Information policies identify which users and organizational units can share information, where information can be distributed, and who is responsible for updating and maintaining the information. For example, a typical information policy would specify that only selected members of the payroll and human resources department would have the right to change or view sensitive employee data, such as an employee's salary or social security number, and that these departments are responsible for making sure that such employee data are accurate.

If you were in a small business, the owners or managers would establish and implement the information policy. In a large organization, managing and planning for information as a corporate resource often requires a formal data administration function. **Data administration** is responsible for the specific policies and procedures through which data can be managed as an organizational resource. These responsibilities include developing information policy, planning for data, overseeing logical database design and data dictionary development, and monitoring how information system's specialists and end-user groups use data.

A large organization will also have a database design and management group within the corporate information systems division that is responsible for defining and organizing the structure and content of the database and maintaining it. In close cooperation with users, the design group establishes the physical database, the logical relations among elements, and the access rules and security procedures. The functions it performs are called **database administration**.

ENSURING DATA QUALITY

What would happen if a customer's telephone number or account balance were incorrect? What would be the impact if the database had the wrong price for the product you sold? Data that are inaccurate, untimely, or inconsistent with other sources of information create serious operational and financial problems for businesses, even with a well-designed database and information policy. When faulty data go unnoticed, they often lead to incorrect decisions, product recalls, and even financial losses.

Gartner Inc. reported that more than 25 percent of the critical data in large *Fortune* 1000 companies' databases is inaccurate or incomplete, including bad product codes and product descriptions, faulty inventory descriptions, erroneous financial data, incorrect supplier information, and incorrect employee data.

Some of these data quality problems are caused by redundant and inconsistent data produced by multiple systems. For example, the sales ordering system and the inventory management system might both maintain data on the organization's products. However, the sales ordering system might use the term *Item Number*, and the inventory system might call the same attribute *Product Number*. The sales, inventory, or manufacturing systems of a clothing retailer might use different codes to represent values for an attribute. One system might represent clothing size as extra large, whereas the other system might use the code XL for the same purpose. During the design process for a database, data describing entities, such as a customer, product, or order, should be named and defined consistently for all business areas using the database.

If a database is properly designed and enterprise-wide data standards established, duplicate or inconsistent data elements should be minimal. Most data quality problems, however, such as misspelled names, transposed numbers, or incorrect or missing codes, stem from errors during data input. The incidence of such errors is rising as companies move their businesses to the web and allow customers and suppliers to enter data into their websites that directly update internal systems.

Think of all the times you have received several pieces of the same direct mail advertising on the same day. This is very likely the result of your name being maintained multiple times in a database. Your name may have been misspelled or you used your middle initial on one occasion and not on another or the information was initially entered on a paper form and not scanned properly into the system. Because of these inconsistencies, the database would treat you as different people! We often receive redundant mail addressed to Laudon, Lavdon, Lauden, or Landon.

Before a new database is in place, organizations need to identify and correct their faulty data and establish better routines for editing data once their database is in operation. Analysis of data quality often begins with a **data quality audit**, which is a structured survey of the accuracy and level of completeness of the data in an information system. Data quality audits can be performed by surveying entire data files, surveying samples from data files, or surveying end users for their perceptions of data quality.

Data cleansing, also known as *data scrubbing*, consists of activities for detecting and correcting data in a database that are incorrect, incomplete, improperly formatted, or redundant. Data cleansing not only corrects data but also enforces consistency among different sets of data that originated in separate information systems. Specialized data-cleansing software is available to survey data files automatically, correct errors in the data, and integrate the data in a consistent, companywide format.

The Interactive Session on Organizations describes Keurig Green Mountain's experience managing data as a resource. As you read this case, try to identify the policies, procedures, and technologies that were required to improve data management at this company.

6-5 How will MIS help my career?

Here is how Chapter 6 and this book can help you find a job as an entry-level data analyst.

THE COMPANY

Mega Midwest Power, a large diversified energy company headquartered in Cleveland, Ohio, has an open position for an entry-level data analyst. The company is involved in the distribution, transmission, and generation of electricity as well as energy management and other energy-related services for 5 million customers in the Midwest and mid-Atlantic regions.

POSITION DESCRIPTION

Job responsibilities include:

- Maintaining the integrity of substation equipment and related data in multiple databases, including SAP.

Keurig Green Mountain Improves Its Data Management

More than 25 percent of all coffee consumed in the United States today comes from Keurig Green Mountain single-serve K-Cups. Keurig Green Mountain, headquartered in Waterbury, Vermont, has expanded so rapidly over the past decade that it has over 75 brands and over 530 product varieties of hot and cold coffees (including Green Mountain), teas, cocoas, dairy-based beverages, cider, and fruit-based drinks. It also partners with other vendors such as Dunkin Donuts, Newman's Own, and Starbucks to package and sell their products in K-Cup pods. The company has 5,700 employees globally and generated $4.2 billion in revenue in 2016. A business this large and complex must maintain a very large amount of data.

Keurig Green Mountain's meteoric growth called for a better approach to managing that data. The company had relied on what it called a "hero culture" for that purpose. Different groups in charge of providing data would set up the data they were responsible for, such as customer records, vendor records, or material master data. The department receiving the data would correct any inaccuracies to make sure that the right products were produced, orders were placed, and items were shipped. The data providers were called "heroes" because their work was of such high value to the company. This way of working sufficed before Keurig's growth spurt took off. However, because the data corrections that were made downstream were not always conveyed to the data providers, the process was not repeatable and corrections might have to be made again the next time the data were used. This added to the time and cost to conduct business. Additionally, having different groups of "heroes" fix the data only for their specific business processes meant that managing data from a companywide standpoint was limited.

By 2013 Keurig Green Mountain had outgrown its legacy ERP system and switched to SAP ERP. This gave the entire company the opportunity to review how it was managing data and to take the necessary steps toward master data management, well-defined processes, standards for the maintenance of data across the organization, and comprehensive data cleansing. Master data management (MDM) is the organizational effort to create one single master reference source for all critical business data, leading to fewer errors and less redundancy in business processes. By providing one point of reference for critical information, MDM eliminates costly redundancies that occur when organizations rely upon multiple conflicting sources of data.

Keurig Green Mountain enlisted DATUM LLC to help it establish a strong enterprise data management framework. This was necessary to ensure that as the company's volume of data increased, it wouldn't return to disparate data management practices that would negate the efficiencies and benefits of the SAP ERP software. DATUM LLC is an information management solutions company based in Annapolis, Maryland, that provides software and consulting services. Its Information Value Management® SaaS (software as a service) translates business objectives into functional designs that improve quality and processing speed.

DATUM supplies expertise on defining data-centric processes, information value, and accountability. By incorporating best practices, Information Value Management® provides a framework of data standards, governance rules, business metrics, and business processes that is useful for analytics, business intelligence, process improvement, performance management, ERP implementation, and managing big data.

Information Value Management® (IVM) can be integrated with SAP® Information Steward software, which provides a single environment to discover, assess, define, monitor, and improve the quality of enterprise data assets. Information Steward's functionality includes modules for discovering data characteristics and relationships, creating and running data validation rules, identifying bad data and improving data quality, cataloging data, defining business terms for data, and organizing the terms into categories, as well as data cleansing tools. Information Steward helps ensure companywide reporting consistency so that the company's data stewards can easily monitor hanging data and make sure these changes are reflected in the organization's master data management. IVM can also be used with other SAP solutions for enterprise information management (EIM), including data quality assurance, master data management, content management, and information lifecycle management.

Keurig Green Mountain has used Information Steward to implement data quality reports. As data are collected, the tool alerts users to missing required fields. This capability lessens the need for a "hero culture," repeated errors, and repeated fixes to data downstream. Better data quality leads to more informed business decisions, and users of company data will have more trust in the data behind their business processes. Keurig believes the entire company will be aligned to an enterprise-wide data strategy and standards won't be completed by 2020.

Sources: "Keurig Green Mountain Brews Up Data Governance," www.datumstrategy.com, accessed February 19, 2017; Ken Murphy, "Keurig Green Mountain Brews Up Data Governance," *SAP Insider Profiles*, January 2016; www.sap.com, accessed March 5, 2016; and www.keurig-greenmountain.com, accessed February 19, 2017.

CASE STUDY QUESTIONS

1. Identify the problem described in this case.

2. What people, organization, and technology issues had to be addressed in order to come up with a solution?

3. What were the business benefits of improving enterprise-wide data management for Keurig Green Mountain?

4. How did better data management improve operations and management decision making?

- Querying databases in multiple systems.
- Modifying systems for proper data management and procedural controls.
- Recommending and implementing process changes based on data problems that are identified.
- Conducting business-specific research, gathering data, and compiling reports and summaries
- Expanding knowledge of policies, practices, and procedures.

JOB REQUIREMENTS

- BA/BS degree in business, finance, accounting, economics, engineering, or related discipline
- 1–2 years professional work experience desirable
- Knowledge of Microsoft Office tools (Excel, PowerPoint, Access, and Word)
- Strong analytical capabilities, including attention to detail, problem solving, and decision making
- Strong oral and written communication and teamwork skills
- Familiarity with transmission substation equipment desirable

INTERVIEW QUESTIONS

1. What do you know about substation equipment? Have you ever worked with SAP for Utilities?
2. What do you know about data management and databases? Have you ever worked with data management software? If so, what exactly have you done with it?
3. Tell us what you can do with Access and Excel. What kinds of problems have you used these tools to solve? Did you take courses in Access or Excel?
4. What experience do you have analyzing problems, and developing specific or programmatic solutions? Can you give an example of a problem you helped solve?

AUTHOR TIPS

1. Do some research on the electric utility industry equipment maintenance and software for electric utility asset management and predictive maintenance. Read available blogs from IBM, Deloitte, and Intel about predictive maintenance and watch YouTube videos from GE and IBM on this subject.

2. Review Chapter 6 of this text on data management and databases along with the Chapter 11 discussion of operational intelligence and ending case study on GE and predictive maintenance. Inquire what you would be expected to do with databases in this job position.
3. Do some research on the capabilities of SAP for Utilities and ask exactly how you would be using this software and what skills would be required. Watch SAP's YouTube video on SAP for Utilities.
4. Inquire about how you would be using Microsoft Office tools for the job and what Excel and Access skills you would be expected to demonstrate. Show that you would be eager to learn what you don't know about these tools to fulfill your job assignments.

Review Summary

6-1 **What is a database, and how does a relational database organize data?** A database is a group of related files that keeps track of people, places, and things (entities) about which organizations maintain information. The relational database is the primary method for organizing and maintaining data today in information systems. It organizes data in two-dimensional tables with rows and columns called relations. Each table contains data about an entity and its attributes. Each row represents a record and each column represents an attribute or field. Each table also contains a key field to identify each record uniquely for retrieval or manipulation. An entity-relationship diagram graphically depicts the relationship between entities (tables) in a relational database. The process of breaking down complex groupings of data and streamlining them to minimize redundancy and awkward many-to-many relationships is called normalization.

6-2 **What are the principles of a database management system?** A DBMS consists of software that permits centralization of data and data management so that businesses have a single consistent source for all their data needs. A single database services multiple applications. The DBMS separates the logical and physical views of data so that the user does not have to be concerned with the data's physical location. The principal capabilities of a DBMS include a data definition capability, a data dictionary capability, and a data manipulation language. Non-relational databases are becoming popular for managing types of data that can't be handled easily by the relational data model.

6-3 **What are the principal tools and technologies for accessing information from databases to improve business performance and decision making?** Contemporary data management technology has an array of tools for obtaining useful information from all the types of data businesses use today, including semi-structured and unstructured big data in very large quantities from many different sources. These capabilities include data warehouses and data marts, Hadoop, in-memory computing, and analytical platforms. OLAP represents relationships among data as a multidimensional structure, which can be visualized as cubes of data and cubes within cubes of data. Data mining analyzes large pools of data, including the contents of data warehouses, to find patterns and rules that can be used to predict future behavior and guide decision making. Text mining tools help businesses analyze large unstructured data sets consisting of text. Web mining tools focus on analyzing useful patterns and information from the World Wide Web, examining the structure of websites, activities of website users, and the contents of web pages. Conventional databases can be linked to the web or a web interface to facilitate user access to an organization's internal data.

6-4 Why are information policy, data administration, and data quality assurance essential for managing the firm's data resources? Developing a database environment requires policies and procedures for managing organizational data as well as a good data model and database technology. A formal information policy governs the maintenance, distribution, and use of information in the organization. In large corporations, a formal data administration function is responsible for information policy as well as for data planning, data dictionary development, and monitoring data usage in the firm. Data that are inaccurate, incomplete, or inconsistent create serious operational and financial problems for businesses if they lead to bad decisions about the actions the firm should take. Assuring data quality involves using enterprise-wide data standards, databases designed to minimize inconsistent and redundant data, data quality audits, and data cleansing software.

Key Terms

Analytic platform, 210
Attributes, 197
Big data, 208
Bit, 197
Byte, 197
Data administration, 217
Data cleansing, 217
Data definition, 204
Data dictionary, 204
Data lake, 212
Data manipulation language, 204
Data mart, 209
Data mining, 214
Data quality audit, 218
Data warehouse, 209
Database, 197
Database administration, 217
Database management system (DBMS), 203
Database server, 216
Distributed database, 208
Entity, 197
Entity-relationship diagram, 200
Field, 197
File, 197
Foreign key, 200
Hadoop, 209
Information policy, 217
In-memory computing, 210
Key field, 198
Non-relational database management systems, 207
Normalization, 201
Online analytical processing (OLAP), 213
Primary key, 198
Query, 206
Record, 197
Referential integrity, 201
Relational database, 197
Report generator, 206
Sentiment analysis, 215
Structured Query Language (SQL), 206
Text mining, 215
Tuples, 198
Web mining, 215

MyLab MIS™

To complete the problems with **MyLab MIS**, go to EOC Discussion Questions in MyLab MIS.

Review Questions

6-1 What is a database, and how does a relational database organize data?

- Define a database.
- Define and explain the significance of entities, attributes, and key fields.
- Define a relational database and explain how it organizes and stores information.
- Explain the role of entity-relationship diagrams and normalization in database design.

6-2 What are the principles of a database management system?

- Define a database management system (DBMS), describe how it works, and explain how it benefits organizations.
- Define and compare the logical and physical views of data.
- Define and describe the three operations of a relational database management system.
- Name and describe the three major capabilities of a DBMS.

- Define a non-relational database management system and explain how it differs from a relational DBMS.

6-3 What are the principal tools and technologies for accessing information from databases to improve business performance and decision making?

- Define big data and describe the technologies for managing and analyzing big data.
- List and describe the components of a contemporary business intelligence infrastructure.
- Describe the capabilities of online analytical processing (OLAP).
- Define data mining, describe what types of information can be obtained from it, and explain how it differs from OLAP.
- Explain how text mining and web mining differ from conventional data mining.
- Explain how users can access information from a company's internal databases through the web.

6-4 Why are information policy, data administration, and data quality assurance essential for managing the firm's data resources?

- Define information policy and data administration and explain how they help organizations manage their data.
- List and describe the most common data quality problems.
- List and describe the most important tools and techniques for assuring data quality.

Discussion Questions

6-5 MyLab MIS It has been said that you do not need database management software to create a database environment. Discuss.

6-6 MyLab MIS To what extent should end users be involved in the selection of a database management system and database design?

6-7 MyLab MIS What are the consequences of an organization not having an information policy?

Hands-On MIS Projects

MANAGEMENT DECISION PROBLEMS

The projects in this section give you hands-on experience in analyzing data quality problems, establishing companywide data standards, creating a database for inventory management, and using the web to search online databases for overseas business resources. Visit **MyLab MIS** to access this chapter's Hands-On MIS Projects.

6-8 Emerson Process Management, a global supplier of measurement, analytical, and monitoring instruments and services based in Austin, Texas, had a new data warehouse designed for analyzing customer activity to improve service and marketing. However, the data warehouse was full of inaccurate and redundant data. The data in the warehouse came from numerous transaction processing systems in Europe, Asia, and other locations around the world. The team that designed the warehouse had assumed that sales groups in all these areas would enter customer names and addresses the same way. In fact, companies in different countries were using multiple ways of entering quote, billing, shipping, and other data. Assess the potential business impact of these data quality problems. What decisions have to be made and steps taken to reach a solution?

6-9 Your industrial supply company wants to create a data warehouse from which management can obtain a single corporate-wide view of critical sales information to identify bestselling products, key customers, and sales trends. Your sales and product information are stored in several systems: a divisional sales system running on a UNIX server and a corporate sales system running on an IBM mainframe. You would like to create a single standard format that consolidates these data from both systems. In MyLab MIS, you can review the proposed format along with sample files from the two systems that would supply the data for the data warehouse. Then answer the following questions:

- What business problems are created by not having these data in a single standard format?
- How easy would it be to create a database with a single standard format that could store the data from both systems? Identify the problems that would have to be addressed.
- Should the problems be solved by database specialists or general business managers? Explain.
- Who should have the authority to finalize a single companywide format for this information in the data warehouse?

ACHIEVING OPERATIONAL EXCELLENCE: BUILDING A RELATIONAL DATABASE FOR INVENTORY MANAGEMENT

Software skills: Database design, querying, and reporting
Business skills: Inventory management

6-10 In this exercise, you will use database software to design a database for managing inventory for a small business. Sylvester's Bike Shop, located in San Francisco, California, sells road, mountain, hybrid, leisure, and children's bicycles. Currently, Sylvester's purchases bikes from three suppliers but plans to add new suppliers in the near future. Using the information found in the tables in MyLab MIS, build a simple relational database to manage information about Sylvester's suppliers and products. MyLab MIS contains more details about the specifications for the database.

After you have built the database, perform the following activities.

- Prepare a report that identifies the five most expensive bicycles. The report should list the bicycles in descending order from most expensive to least expensive, the quantity on hand for each, and the markup percentage for each.
- Prepare a report that lists each supplier, its products, the quantities on hand, and associated reorder levels. The report should be sorted alphabetically by supplier. Within each supplier category, the products should be sorted alphabetically.
- Prepare a report listing only the bicycles that are low in stock and need to be reordered. The report should provide supplier information for the identified items.
- Write a brief description of how the database could be enhanced to improve management of the business further. What tables or fields should be added? What additional reports would be useful?

IMPROVING DECISION MAKING: SEARCHING ONLINE DATABASES FOR OVERSEAS BUSINESS RESOURCES

Software skills: Online databases
Business skills: Researching services for overseas operations

6-11 This project develops skills in searching online web-enabled databases with-information about products and services in faraway locations.

Your company is located in Greensboro, North Carolina, and manufactures office furniture of various types. You are considering opening a facility to manufacture and sell your products in Australia. You would like to contact organizations that offer many services necessary for you to open your Australian office and manufacturing facility, including attorneys, accountants, import-export experts, and telecommunications equipment and support firms. Access the following online databases to locate companies that you would like to meet with during your upcoming trip: Australian Business Register and the Nationwide Business Directory of Australia. If necessary, use search engines such as Yahoo and Google.

- List the companies you would contact on your trip to determine whether they can help you with these and any other functions you think are vital to establishing your office.
- Rate the databases you used for accuracy of name, completeness, ease of use, and general helpfulness.

Collaboration and Teamwork Project

Identifying Entities and Attributes in an Online Database

6-12 With your team of three or four students, select an online database to explore, such as AOL Music, iGo.com, or the Internet Movie Database. Explore one of these websites to see what information it provides. List the entities and attributes that the company running the website must keep track of in its databases. Diagram the relationships between the entities you have identified. If possible, use Google Docs and Google Drive or Google Sites to brainstorm, organize, and develop a presentation of your findings for the class.

BUSINESS PROBLEM-SOLVING CASE

How Reliable Is Big Data?

Today's companies are dealing with an avalanche of data from social media, search, and sensors as well as from traditional sources. According to one estimate, 2.5 quintillion bytes of data per day are generated around the world. Making sense of "big data" to improve decision making and business performance has become one of the primary opportunities for organizations of all shapes and sizes, but it also represents big challenges.

Big data helps streaming music service Spotify create a service that feels personal to each of its 75 million global users. Spotify uses the big data it collects on user listening habits (over 600 gigabytes daily) to design highly individualized products that captivate its users around a particular mood or moment in time rather than offering the same tired genres. Users can constantly enhance their listening experience with data-driven features such as Discovery tool for new music, a Running tool that curates music timed to the beat of their workout, and Taste Rewind—which tells what they would have listened to in the past by analyzing what they listen to now.

A number of services have emerged to analyze big data to help consumers. There are now online services to enable consumers to find the lowest price on autos, computers, mobile phone plans, clothing, airfare, hotel rooms, and many other types of goods and services. Big data is also providing benefits in sports (see the chapter-opening case), education, science, healthcare, and law enforcement.

For example, New York city analyzes all the crime-related data it collects to lower the crime rate. Its CompStat crime-mapping program uses a comprehensive citywide database of all reported crimes or complaints, arrests, and summonses in each of the city's 76 precincts to report weekly on crime complaint and arrest activity at the precinct, patrol borough, and citywide levels. CompStat data can be displayed on maps showing crime and arrest locations, crime hot spots, and other relevant information to help precinct commanders quickly identify patterns and trends and deploy policemen where they are most needed. Big data on criminal activity also powers New York city's Crime Strategies Unit, which targets the worst offenders for aggressive prosecution. Healthcare companies are currently analyzing big data to determine the most effective and economical treatments for chronic illnesses and common diseases and provide personalized care recommendations to patients.

There are limits to using big data. A number of companies have rushed to start big data projects without first establishing a business goal for this new information. Swimming in numbers doesn't necessarily mean that the right information is being collected or that people will make smarter decisions. Experts in big data analysis believe too many companies, seduced by the promise of big data, jump into big data projects with nothing to show for their efforts. They start amassing mountains of data with no clear objective or understanding of exactly how analyzing big data will achieve their goal or what questions they are trying to answer.

Just because something can be measured doesn't mean it should be measured. Suppose, for instance, that a large company wants to measure its website traffic in relation to the number of mentions on Twitter. It builds a digital dashboard to display the results continuously. In the past, the company had generated most of its sales leads and eventual sales from trade shows and conferences. Switching to Twitter mentions as the key metric to measure changes the sales department's focus. The department pours its energy and resources into monitoring website clicks and social media traffic, which produce many unqualified leads that never lead to sales.

Although big data is very good at detecting correlations, especially subtle correlations that an analysis of smaller data sets might miss, big data analysis doesn't necessarily show causation or which correlations are meaningful. For example, examining big data might show that from 2006 to 2011 the United States murder rate was highly correlated with the market share of Internet Explorer, since both declined sharply. But that doesn't necessarily mean there is any meaningful connection between the two phenomena. Data analysts need some business knowledge of the problem they are trying to solve with big data.

Big data predictive models don't necessarily give you a better idea of what will happen in the future. Meridian Energy Ltd., an electricity generator and distributor operating in New Zealand and Australia, moved away from using an aging predictive equipment maintenance system. The software was supposed to predict the maintenance needs of all the large equipment the company owns and operates, including generators, wind turbines, transformers, circuit breakers and industrial batteries. However, the system used outdated modeling techniques and could not actually predict equipment failures. It ran simulations of different scenarios and predicted when assets would fail the simulated tests. The recommendations of the software were useless because they did not accurately predict which pieces of equipment actually failed in the real world. Meridian eventually replaced the old system with IBM's Predictive Maintenance and Quality software, which bases predictions on more real-time data from equipment.

All data sets and data-driven forecasting models are a reflection of the biases of the people selecting the data and performing the analysis. Several years ago, Google developed what it thought was a leading-edge algorithm using data it collected from web searches to determine exactly how many people had influenza and how the disease was spreading. It tried to calculate the number of people with flu in the United States by relating people's location to flu-related search queries on Google. The service has consistently overestimated flu rates, when compared to conventional data collected afterward by the U.S. Centers for Disease Control (CDC). According to Google Flu Trends, nearly 11 percent of the U.S. population was supposed to have had influenza at the flu season's peak in mid-January 2013. However, an article in the science journal *Nature* stated that Google's results were twice the actual amount estimated by the CDC, which had 6 percent of the population coming down with the disease.

Why did this happen? Several scientists suggested that Google was "tricked" by widespread media coverage of this year's severe flu season in the United States, which was further amplified by social media coverage. The model developed for forecasting flu trends was based on a flawed assumption—that the incidence of flu-related searches on Googles was a precise indicator of the number of people who actually came down with the flu. Google's algorithm only looked at numbers, not the context of the search results.

Insufficient attention to context and flawed assumptions also played a role in the failure of most political experts to predict Donald Trump's victory over Hillary Clinton in the 2016 U.S. presidential election, perhaps the biggest upset in modern American politics. Trump's victory ran counter to almost every major forecast, which had put Clinton's chances of winning between 70 to 99 percent.

Tons of data had been analyzed by political experts and the candidates' campaign teams. Clinton ran an overwhelmingly data-driven campaign, and big data had played a large role in Barack Obama's victories in 2008 and 2012. Clinton's team added to the database the Obama campaigns had built, which connected personal data from traditional sources, such as reports from pollsters and field workers, with other data from social media posts and other online behavior as well as data used to predict consumer behavior. The Clinton team assumed that the same voters who supported Obama would turn out for their candidate and focused on identifying voters in areas with a likelihood of high voter turnout. However, turnout for Clinton among the key groups who had supported Obama—women, minorities, college graduates, and blue-collar workers—fell short of expectations. (Trump had turned to big data as well but put more emphasis on tailoring campaign messages to targeted voter groups.)

Political experts were misled into thinking Clinton's victory was assured because some predictive models lacked context in explaining potentially wide margins of error. There were shortcomings in polling, analysis, and interpretation, and analysts did not spend enough time examining how the data used in the predictive models were created. Many polls used in election forecasts underestimated the strength of Trump's support. State polls were off, perhaps failing to capture Republicans who initially refused to vote for Trump and then changed their minds at the last moment. Polls from Wisconsin shortly before the election had put Clinton well ahead of Trump. Polls are important for election predictions, but they are only one of many sources of data that should be consulted. Predictive models were unable to fully determine who would actually turn out to vote as opposed to how people think they will vote. Analysts overlooked signs that Trump was forging ahead in the battleground states and Florida. Britain had a similar surprise when polls mistakenly predicted the nation would vote in June 2016 to stay in the European Union.

And let's not forget that big data poses some challenges to information security and privacy. As Chapter 4 pointed out, companies are now aggressively collecting and mining massive data sets on people's shopping habits, incomes, hobbies, residences, and (via mobile devices) movements from place to place. They are using such big data to discover new facts about people, to classify them based on subtle patterns, to flag them as "risks" (for example, loan default risks or health risks), to predict their behavior, and to manipulate them for maximum profit.

When you combine someone's personal information with pieces of data from many different sources, you can infer new facts about that person (such as the fact that they are showing early signs of Parkinson's disease, or are unconsciously drawn toward products that are colored blue or green). If asked, most people might not want to disclose such information, but they might not even know such information about them exists. Privacy experts worry that people will be tagged and suffer adverse consequences without due process, the ability to fight back, or even knowledge that they have been discriminated against.

Sources: Ed Burns, "When Predictive Models Are Less Than Presidential," *Business Information*, February 2017; Craig Stedman, "Don't Let a Data-Driven Approach Ax Judgment from Analytics Equation" SearchBusinessAnalytics.com, January 12, 2017; Aaron Timms, "Is Donald Trump's Surprise Win a Failure of Big Data? Not Really," *Fortune*, November 14, 2016; Steve Lohr and Natasha Singer, "The Data Said Clinton Would Win. Why You Shouldn't Have Believed It," *New York Times*, November 10, 2016; "Big Data Helped Donald Trump Even After He Scorned It," *Agence France-Presse*, December 4, 2016; Nicole Laskowski and Niel Nikolaisen, "Seven Big Data Problems and How to Avoid Them," TechTarget Inc., 2016; "The Most Innovative Companies of 2016: Top Companies by Sector," www.fastcompany.com, accessed March 4. 2016; Ed Burns, "Big Data Analytics Not Just a Grab and Go Process," *Business Information*, February 2015; Joseph Stromberg, "Why Google Flu Trends Can't Track the Flu (Yet)," smithsonianmag.com, March 13, 2014; and Gary Marcus and Ernest Davis, "Eight (No, Nine!) Problems with Big Data," *New York Times*, April 6, 2014.

CASE STUDY QUESTIONS

6-13 What business benefits did the organizations described in this case achieve by analyzing and using big data?

6-14 Identify two decisions at the organizations described in this case that were improved by using big data and two decisions using big data that were not improved.

6-15 List and describe the limitations to using big data.

6-16 Should all organizations try to analyze big data? Why or why not? What people, organization, and technology issues should be addressed before a company decides to work with big data?

MyLab MIS

Go to the Assignments section of MyLab MIS to complete these writing exercises.

6-17 Define web mining and describe the three ways that web mining looks for patterns in data.

6-18 Discuss how the following facilitate the management of big data: Hadoop, in-memory computing, analytic platforms.

Chapter 6 References

Aiken, Peter, Mark Gillenson, Xihui Zhang, and David Rafner. "Data Management and Data Administration. Assessing 25 Years of Practice." *Journal of Database Management* (July–September 2011).

Barton, Dominic, and David Court. "Making Advanced Analytics Work for You." *Harvard Business Review* (October 2012).

Beath, Cynthia, Irma Becerra-Fernandez, Jeanne Ross, and James Short. "Finding Value in the Information Explosion." *MIT Sloan Management Review* 53, No. 4 (Summer 2012).

Bughin, Jacques, John Livingston, and Sam Marwaha. "Seizing the Potential for Big Data." *McKinsey Quarterly* (October 2011).

Byerly, Jonathan. "Dell and the Agile Data Mart." *SAP Insider Profiles* (December 15, 2016).

Caserta, Joe, and Elliott Cordo. "Data Warehousing in the Era of Big Data." *Big Data Quarterly* (January 19, 2016).

Chai, Sen and Willy Shih. "Why Big Data Isn't Enough." *MIT Sloan Management Review* (Winter 2017).

Clifford, James, Albert Croker, and Alex Tuzhilin. "On Data Representation and Use in a Temporal Relational DBMS." *Information Systems Research* 7, No. 3 (September 1996).

DalleMule, Leandro, and Thomas H. Davenport. "What's Your Data Strategy?" *Harvard Business Review* (May–June 2017).

DataInformed. "The Database Decision: Key Considerations to Keep in Mind." Wellesley Information Services (2015).

Davenport, Thomas H. *Big Data at Work: Dispelling the Myths, Uncovering the Opportunities.* (Boston, MA: Harvard Business School, 2014.)

Duncan, Alan D., Mei Yang Selvage, and Saul Judah. "How a Chief Data Officer Should Drive a Data Quality Program." Gartner Inc. (October 14, 2016).

Eckerson, Wayne W. "Analytics in the Era of Big Data: Exploring a Vast New Ecosystem." TechTarget (2012).

Experian Data Quality. "Connecting Data Quality Initiatives with Business Drivers." Experian Data Solutions (2016).

______ "Using Quality Data for Competitive Advantage." Experian Data Solutions (2016).

Experian Information Solutions. "The 2016 Global Data Management Benchmark Report." (2016).

Henschen, Doug. "MetLife Uses NoSQL for Customer Service Breakthrough." *Information Week* (May 13, 2013).

Hoffer, Jeffrey A., Ramesh Venkataraman, and Heikki Toppi. *Modern Database Management*, 12th ed. (Upper Saddle River, NJ: Prentice-Hall, 2016).

Horst, Peter and Robert Dubroff. "Don't Let Big Data Bury Your Brand." *Harvard Business Review* (November 2015).

Jordan, John. "The Risks of Big Data for Companies." *Wall Street Journal* (October 20, 2013).

Kroenke, David M., and David Auer. *Database Processing: Fundamentals, Design, and Implementation*, 14th ed. (Upper Saddle River, NJ: Prentice-Hall, 2016).

Lee, Yang W., and Diane M. Strong. "Knowing-Why About Data Processes and Data Quality." *Journal of Management Information Systems* 20, No. 3 (Winter 2004).

Loveman, Gary. "Diamonds in the Datamine." *Harvard Business Review* (May 2003).

Marcus, Gary, and Ernest Davis. "Eight (No, Nine!) Problems with Big Data." *New York Times* (April 6, 2014).

Martens, David, and Foster Provost. "Explaining Data-Driven Document Classifications." *MIS Quarterly* 38, No. 1 (March 2014).

McAfee, Andrew, and Erik Brynjolfsson. "Big Data: The Management Revolution." *Harvard Business Review* (October 2012).

McKinsey Global Institute. "Big Data: The Next Frontier for Innovation, Competition, and Productivity." McKinsey & Company (2011).

Morrow, Rich. "Apache Hadoop: The Swiss Army Knife of IT." Global Knowledge (2013).

Mulani, Narendra. "In-Memory Technology: Keeping Pace with Your Data." *Information Management* (February 27, 2013).

O'Keefe, Kate. "Real Prize in Caesars Fight: Data on Players." *Wall Street Journal* (March 19, 2015).

Redman, Thomas. *Data Driven: Profiting from Your Most Important Business Asset*. (Boston, MA: Harvard Business Press, 2008).

Redman, Thomas C. "Data's Credibility Problem" *Harvard Business Review* (December 2013).

Ross, Jeanne W., Cynthia M. Beath, and Anne Quaadgras. "You May Not Need Big Data After All." *Harvard Business Review* (December 2013).

SAP. "Data Warehousing and the Future." (February 2017).

TechTarget Inc. "Identifying and Meeting the Challenges of Big Data." (2016).

Wallace, David J. "How Caesar's Entertainment Sustains a Data-Driven Culture." *DataInformed* (December 14, 2012).

Zoumpoulis, Spyros, Duncan Simester, and Theos Evgeniou, "Run Field Experiments to Make Sense of Your Big Data." *Harvard Business Review* (November 12, 2015).

CHAPTER

7 Telecommunications, the Internet, and Wireless Technology

LEARNING OBJECTIVES

After reading this chapter, you will be able to answer the following questions:

7-1 What are the principal components of telecommunications networks and key networking technologies?

7-2 What are the different types of networks?

7-3 How do the Internet and Internet technology work, and how do they support communication and e-business?

7-4 What are the principal technologies and standards for wireless networking, communication, and Internet access?

7-5 How will MIS help my career?

CHAPTER CASES

- RFID Helps Macy's Pursue an Omnichannel Strategy
- Net Neutrality: The Battle Continues
- Monitoring Employees on Networks: Unethical or Good Business?
- Google, Apple, and Facebook Battle for Your Internet Experience

VIDEO CASES

- Telepresence Moves out of the Boardroom and into the Field
- Virtual Collaboration with IBM Sametime

MyLab MIS

- Discussion Questions: 7-5, 7-6, 7-7;
- Hands-on MIS Projects: 7-8, 7-9, 7-10, 7-11;
- Writing Assignments: 7-18, 7-19
- eText with Conceptual Animations

RFID HELPS MACY'S PURSUE AN OMNICHANNEL STRATEGY

Macy's is a major retail chain with 850 department stores (including Bloomingdale's) throughout the United States, Puerto Rico, Guam, and Dubai as well as e-commerce websites for online sales. The Macy's chain is known for its diversity of popular clothing, shoe, furniture, and houseware brands.

To remain competitive, Macy's has adopted an omnichannel retail strategy, which seeks to provide the customer with a seamless shopping experience, whether the customer is purchasing online from a desktop or mobile device, by telephone, or in a brick-and-mortar store. Macy's wants its customers to be able to shop anywhere, anytime, and any way they choose. Macy's sales staff are allowed to sell an item that may be out of stock locally by selecting merchandise from other store locations or from its online fulfillment centers. That means that Macy's brick-and-mortar retail stores are serving as potential fulfillment centers for orders coming in from all sources. If the customer sees online that a pair of boy's shorts is on the selling floor at the Southlake Mall Macy's in Indiana, those shorts need to be in stock at that location.

This is not so easy. Retailers don't typically list the last remaining item of a specific product as being available for online purchasing because they don't have enough confidence in their inventory accuracy to ensure that the item is actually in stock. These last remaining units are usually marked down or not sold, and they account for 15 to 20 percent of inventory, significantly raising costs and lowering profits.

To solve this problem, Macy's implemented an item-level radio frequency identification (RFID) system called Pick to the Last Unit (P2LU) based on Tyco's TrueVUE RFID Inventory Visibility Platform. P2LU attempts to ensure that the last unit of an item in any store is able to be easily located and made available for sale. Macy's suppliers attach ultrahigh-frequency RFID tags to each item in frequently replenished products, such as men's dress, shirts, underwear, and women's shoes, throughout all of its U.S. stores. Macy's sales staff use Zebra Technologies MC3190-Z handheld RFID readers to activate each RFID tag to broadcast data about the item to which it is attached. The RFID reader in turn transmits the RFID data to Macy's corporate inventory system. With an RFID reader Macy's staff can scan each pair of Levi's jeans stacked on shelves and determine what is in the backroom that should be

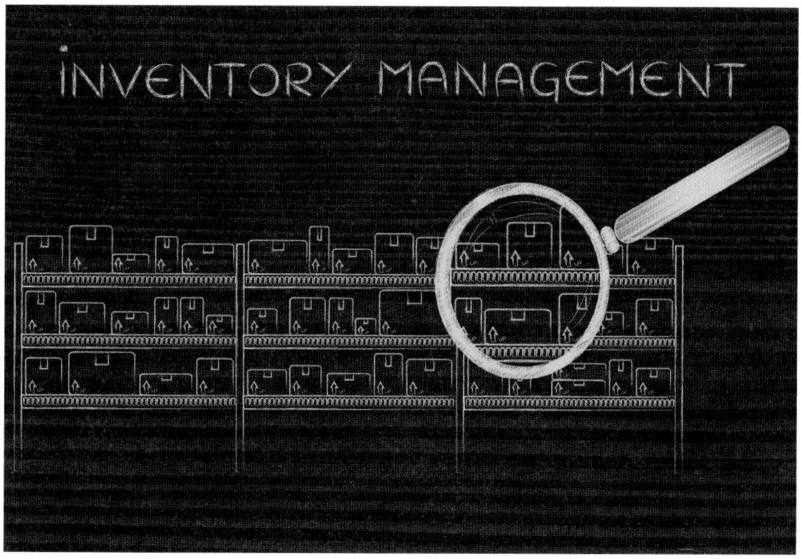

© Faithie/Shutterstock

on the sales floor. Data from the scan automatically update Macy's inventory system and are used to generate replenishment orders.

Before Macy's implemented this system, inventory was degrading at a rate of 2 to 3 percent per month due to theft or items checked out improperly at the register. By the beginning of retailers' peak selling season in November, inventory count at the floor levels was only 60 to 70 percent accurate. So much inaccuracy about inventory led to very large numbers of lost sales.

Macy's now has enough confidence in its inventory accuracy so that even if only one of an item is left in stock, it can leverage every unit in every store to fulfill orders. Deploying RFID has reduced costs by lowering interim inventory requirements by a third, eliminating $1 billion of inventory from Macy's stores. And, of course, having more items actually available when customers need them boosts sales.

Sources: Claire Swedberg, "Platt Retail Institute Finds RFID-Based Inventory Accuracy, Sales, and Satisfaction," *RFID Journal*, January 20, 2017, and "Macy's Launches Pick to the Last Unit Program for Omnichannel Sales," *RFID Journal*, January 26, 2016; Tyco Retail Solutions, "Macy's Leverages the Power of RFID to Fuel Successful Omni-Channel Fulfillment Strategy," January 18, 2016, and "The Magic of Macy's: Leveraging RFID for 'Pick to the Last Unit' Omni-Channel Fulfillment," 2016; and www.sensormatic.com, accessed May 5, 2017.

The experience of Macy's illustrates some of the powerful capabilities and opportunities provided by contemporary networking technology. The Macy's chain uses wireless networking and radio frequency identification (RFID) technology to track inventory more precisely.

The chapter-opening diagram calls attention to important points raised by this case and this chapter. Macy's has many competitors and feels it has to adopt an omnichannel strategy to remain competitive. It also wants to take advantage of new mobile networking technologies.

Improving inventory accuracy is absolutely critical for omnichannel fulfillment and a "buy anywhere, fulfill anywhere" model. Instead of tracking cases of goods or pallets, Macy's P2LU uses RFID to track individual items on store shelves. Thanks to its RFID inventory tracking system, Macy's has a complete view of inventory in stores, online, and across the supply chain.

Now, Macy's is able to maximize revenue. Macy's is able to sell every single unit in inventory. There is no longer wasted inventory, and Macy's maximizes revenue from omnichannel programs and improves the overall customer experience.

Here are some questions to think about: Why has wireless technology played such a key role at Macy's? Describe how the RFID system changed the sales and ordering processes at Macy's.

7-1 What are the principal components of telecommunications networks and key networking technologies?

If you run or work in a business, you can't do without networks. You need to communicate rapidly with your customers, suppliers, and employees. Until about 1990, businesses used the postal system or telephone system with voice or fax for communication. Today, however, you and your employees use computers, email, text messaging, the Internet, mobile phones, and mobile computers connected to wireless networks for this purpose. Networking and the Internet are now nearly synonymous with doing business.

NETWORKING AND COMMUNICATION TRENDS

Firms in the past used two fundamentally different types of networks: telephone networks and computer networks. Telephone networks historically handled voice communication, and computer networks handled data traffic. Telephone companies built

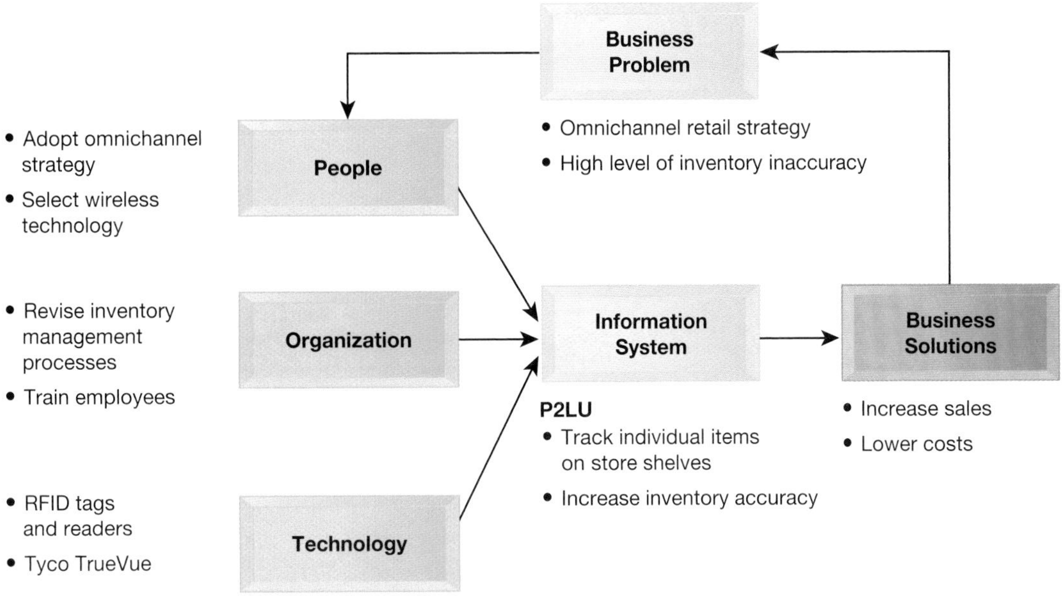

telephone networks throughout the twentieth century by using voice transmission technologies (hardware and software), and these companies almost always operated as regulated monopolies throughout the world. Computer companies originally built computer networks to transmit data between computers in different locations.

Thanks to continuing telecommunications deregulation and information technology innovation, telephone and computer networks are converging into a single digital network using shared Internet-based standards and technology. Telecommunications providers today, such as AT&T and Verizon, offer data transmission, Internet access, mobile phone service, and television programming as well as voice service. Cable companies, such as Cablevision and Comcast, offer voice service and Internet access. Computer networks have expanded to include Internet telephone and video services.

Both voice and data communication networks have also become more powerful (faster), more portable (smaller and mobile), and less expensive. For instance, the typical Internet connection speed in 2000 was 56 kilobits per second, but today the majority of U.S. households have high-speed **broadband** connections provided by telephone and cable TV companies running at 1 to 15 million bits per second. The cost for this service has fallen exponentially, from 25 cents per kilobit in 2000 to a tiny fraction of a cent today.

Increasingly, voice and data communication, as well as Internet access, are taking place over broadband wireless platforms such as mobile phones, mobile handheld devices, and PCs in wireless networks. More than half the Internet users in the United States use smartphones and tablets to access the Internet.

WHAT IS A COMPUTER NETWORK?

If you had to connect the computers for two or more employees in the same office, you would need a computer network. In its simplest form, a network consists of two or more connected computers. Figure 7.1 illustrates the major hardware, software, and transmission components in a simple network: a client computer and a dedicated server computer, network interfaces, a connection medium, network operating system software, and either a hub or a switch.

Each computer on the network contains a network interface device to link the computer to the network. The connection medium for linking network components can be a telephone wire, coaxial cable, or radio signal in the case of cell phone and wireless local area networks (Wi-Fi networks).

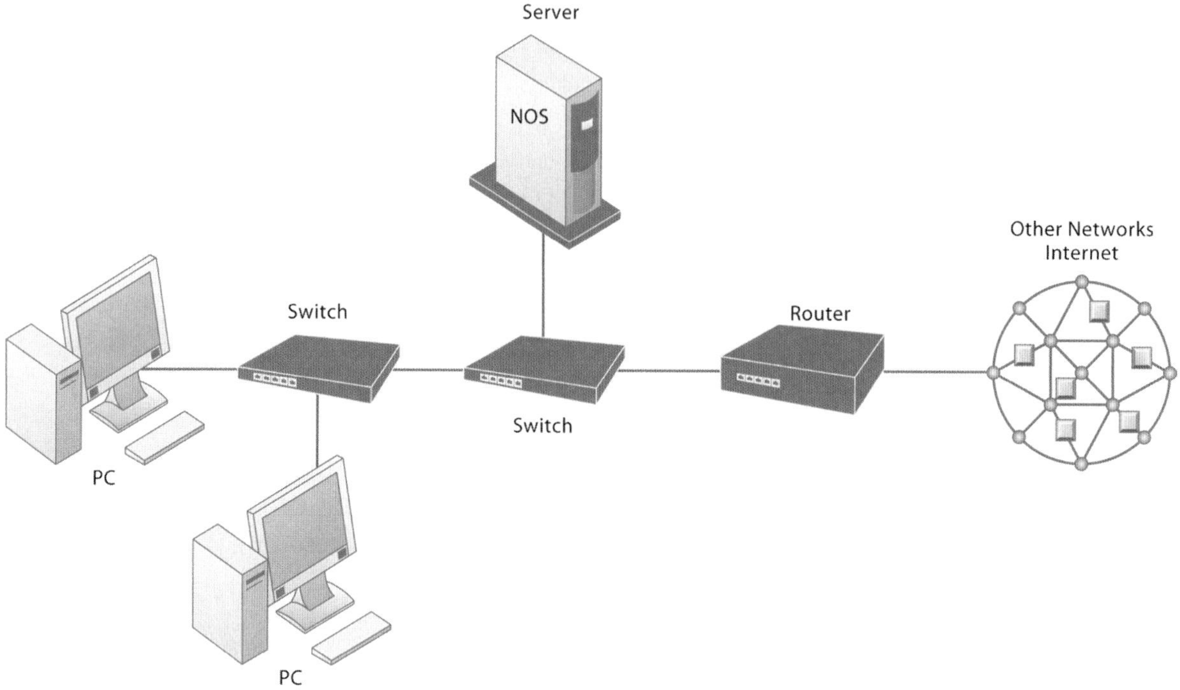

Figure 7.1
Components of a Simple Computer Network
Illustrated here is a simple computer network consisting of computers, a network operating system (NOS) residing on a dedicated server computer, cable (wiring) connecting the devices, switches, and a router.

The **network operating system (NOS)** routes and manages communications on the network and coordinates network resources. It can reside on every computer in the network or primarily on a dedicated server computer for all the applications on the network. A server is a computer on a network that performs important network functions for client computers, such as displaying web pages, storing data, and storing the network operating system (hence controlling the network). Microsoft Windows Server, Linux, and Novell Open Enterprise Server are the most widely used network operating systems.

Most networks also contain a switch or a hub acting as a connection point between the computers. **Hubs** are simple devices that connect network components, sending a packet of data to all other connected devices. A **switch** has more intelligence than a hub and can filter and forward data to a specified destination on the network.

What if you want to communicate with another network, such as the Internet? You would need a router. A **router** is a communications processor that routes packets of data through different networks, ensuring that the data sent get to the correct address.

Network switches and routers have proprietary software built into their hardware for directing the movement of data on the network. This can create network bottlenecks and makes the process of configuring a network more complicated and time-consuming. **Software-defined networking (SDN)** is a new networking approach in which many of these control functions are managed by one central program, which can run on inexpensive commodity servers that are separate from the network devices themselves. This is especially helpful in a cloud computing environment with many pieces of hardware because it allows a network administrator to manage traffic loads in a flexible and more efficient manner.

Networks in Large Companies

The network we've just described might be suitable for a small business, but what about large companies with many locations and thousands of employees? As a firm grows, its small networks can be tied together into a corporate-wide networking

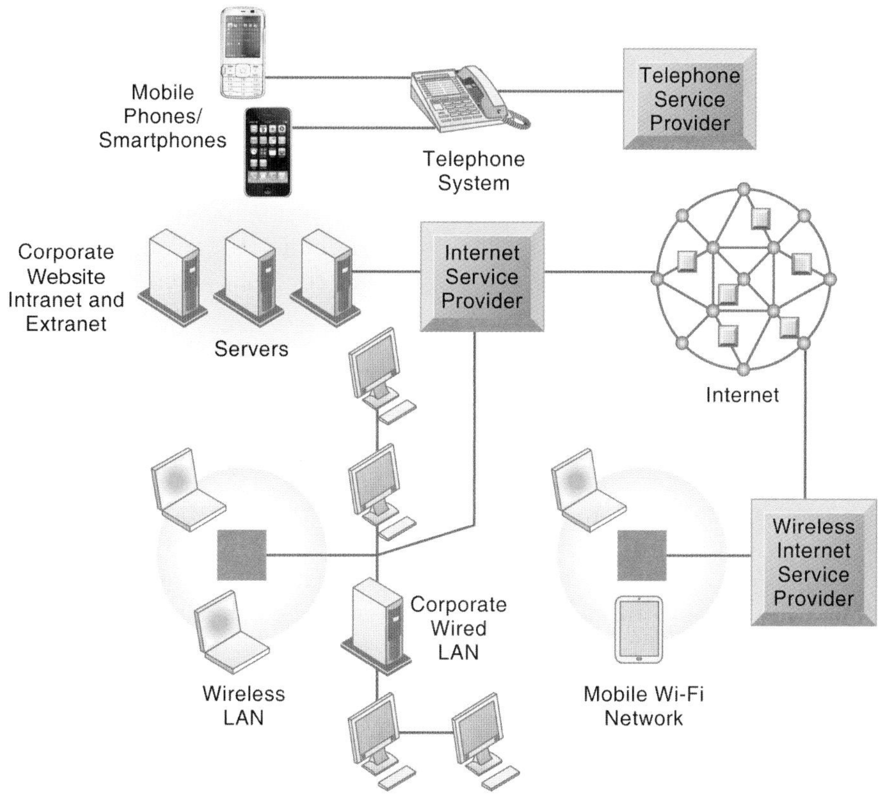

Figure 7.2
Corporate Network Infrastructure
Today's corporate network infrastructure is a collection of many networks from the public switched telephone network to the Internet to corporate local area networks linking workgroups, departments, or office floors.

infrastructure. The network infrastructure for a large corporation consists of a large number of these small local area networks linked to other local area networks and to firmwide corporate networks. A number of powerful servers support a corporate website, a corporate intranet, and perhaps an extranet. Some of these servers link to other large computers supporting back-end systems.

Figure 7.2 provides an illustration of these more complex, larger scale corporate-wide networks. Here the corporate network infrastructure supports a mobile sales force using mobile phones and smartphones, mobile employees linking to the company website, and internal company networks using mobile wireless local area networks (Wi-Fi networks). In addition to these computer networks, the firm's infrastructure may include a separate telephone network that handles most voice data. Many firms are dispensing with their traditional telephone networks and using Internet telephones that run on their existing data networks (described later).

As you can see from this figure, a large corporate network infrastructure uses a wide variety of technologies—everything from ordinary telephone service and corporate data networks to Internet service, wireless Internet, and mobile phones. One of the major problems facing corporations today is how to integrate all the different communication networks and channels into a coherent system that enables information to flow from one part of the corporation to another and from one system to another.

KEY DIGITAL NETWORKING TECHNOLOGIES

Contemporary digital networks and the Internet are based on three key technologies: client/server computing, the use of packet switching, and the development of widely used communications standards (the most important of which is Transmission Control Protocol/Internet Protocol, or TCP/IP) for linking disparate networks and computers.

Client/Server Computing

Client/server computing, introduced in Chapter 5, is a distributed computing model in which some of the processing power is located within small, inexpensive client computers and resides literally on desktops or laptops or in handheld devices. These powerful clients are linked to one another through a network that is controlled by a network server computer. The server sets the rules of communication for the network and provides every client with an address so others can find it on the network.

Client/server computing has largely replaced centralized mainframe computing in which nearly all the processing takes place on a central large mainframe computer. Client/server computing has extended computing to departments, workgroups, factory floors, and other parts of the business that could not be served by a centralized architecture. It also makes it possible for personal computing devices such as PCs, laptops, and mobile phones to be connected to networks such as the Internet. The Internet is the largest implementation of client/server computing.

Packet Switching

Packet switching is a method of slicing digital messages into parcels called packets, sending the packets along different communication paths as they become available and then reassembling the packets once they arrive at their destinations (see Figure 7.3). Prior to the development of packet switching, computer networks used leased, dedicated telephone circuits to communicate with other computers in remote locations. In circuit-switched networks, such as the telephone system, a complete point-to-point circuit is assembled, and then communication can proceed. These dedicated circuit-switching techniques were expensive and wasted available communications capacity—the circuit was maintained regardless of whether any data were being sent.

Packet switching is more efficient. Messages are first broken down into small fixed bundles of data called packets. The packets include information for directing the packet to the right address and for checking transmission errors along with the data. The packets are transmitted over various communications channels by using routers, each packet traveling independently. Packets of data originating at one source will be routed through many paths and networks before being reassembled into the original message when they reach their destinations.

TCP/IP and Connectivity

In a typical telecommunications network, diverse hardware and software components need to work together to transmit information. Different components in a network communicate with each other by adhering to a common set of rules called protocols. A **protocol** is a set of rules and procedures governing transmission of information between two points in a network.

Figure 7.3
Packet-Switched Networks and Packet Communications
Data are grouped into small packets, which are transmitted independently over various communications channels and reassembled at their final destination.

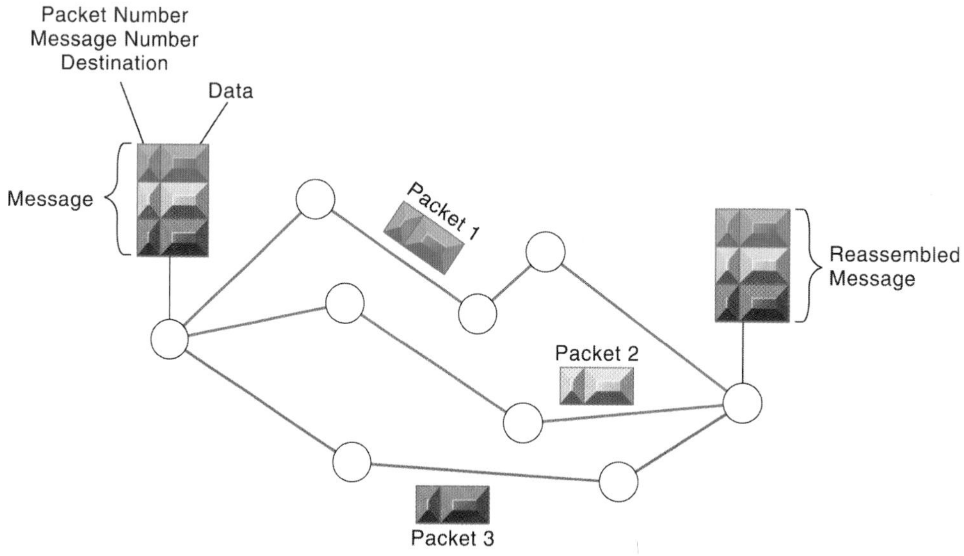

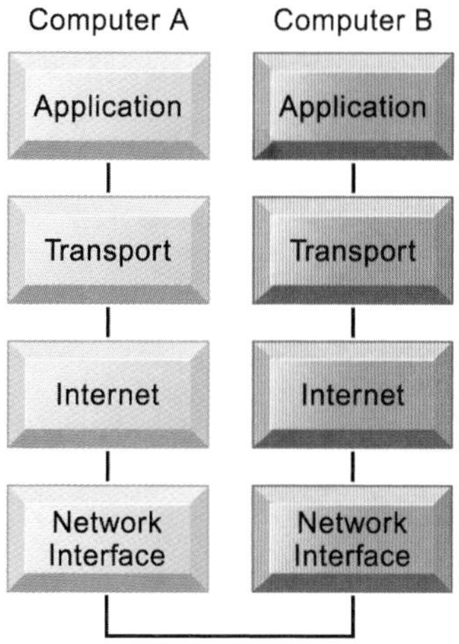

Figure 7.4
The Transmission Control Protocol/Internet Protocol (TCP/IP) Reference Model
This figure illustrates the four layers of the TCP/IP reference model for communications.

In the past, diverse proprietary and incompatible protocols often forced business firms to purchase computing and communications equipment from a single vendor. However, today, corporate networks are increasingly using a single, common, worldwide standard called **Transmission Control Protocol/Internet Protocol (TCP/IP)**. TCP/IP was developed during the early 1970s to support U.S. Department of Defense Advanced Research Projects Agency (DARPA) efforts to help scientists transmit data among different types of computers over long distances.

TCP/IP uses a suite of protocols, the main ones being TCP and IP. TCP refers to the Transmission Control Protocol, which handles the movement of data between computers. TCP establishes a connection between the computers, sequences the transfer of packets, and acknowledges the packets sent. IP refers to the Internet Protocol (IP), which is responsible for the delivery of packets and includes the disassembling and reassembling of packets during transmission. Figure 7.4 illustrates the four-layered Department of Defense reference model for TCP/IP, and the layers are described as follows:

1. Application layer. The Application layer enables client application programs to access the other layers and defines the protocols that applications use to exchange data. One of these application protocols is the Hypertext Transfer Protocol (HTTP), which is used to transfer web page files.
2. Transport layer. The Transport layer is responsible for providing the Application layer with communication and packet services. This layer includes TCP and other protocols.
3. Internet layer. The Internet layer is responsible for addressing, routing, and packaging data packets called IP datagrams. The Internet Protocol is one of the protocols used in this layer.
4. Network Interface layer. At the bottom of the reference model, the Network Interface layer is responsible for placing packets on and receiving them from the network medium, which could be any networking technology.

Two computers using TCP/IP can communicate even if they are based on different hardware and software platforms. Data sent from one computer to the other passes downward through all four layers, starting with the sending computer's Application layer and passing through the Network Interface layer. After the data reach the recipient host computer, they travel up the layers and are reassembled into a format the receiving computer can use. If the receiving computer finds a damaged packet, it asks the sending computer to retransmit it. This process is reversed when the receiving computer responds.

7-2 What are the different types of networks?

Let's look more closely at alternative networking technologies available to businesses.

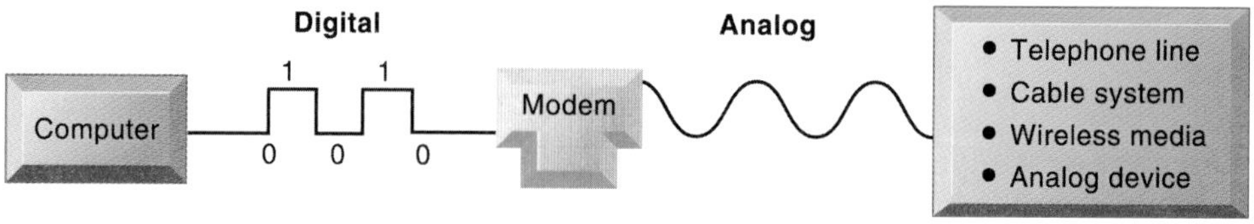

Figure 7.5
Functions of the Modem
A modem is a device that translates digital signals into analog form (and vice versa) so that computers can transmit data over analog networks such as telephone and cable networks.

SIGNALS: DIGITAL VERSUS ANALOG

There are two ways to communicate a message in a network: an analog signal or a digital signal. An *analog signal* is represented by a continuous waveform that passes through a communications medium and has been used for voice communication. The most common analog devices are the telephone handset, the speaker on your computer, or your iPod earphone, all of which create analog waveforms that your ear can hear.

A *digital signal* is a discrete, binary waveform rather than a continuous waveform. Digital signals communicate information as strings of two discrete states: one bits and zero bits, which are represented as on-off electrical pulses. Computers use digital signals and require a modem to convert these digital signals into analog signals that can be sent over (or received from) telephone lines, cable lines, or wireless media that use analog signals (see Figure 7.5). **Modem** stands for modulator-demodulator. Cable modems connect your computer to the Internet by using a cable network. DSL modems connect your computer to the Internet using a telephone company's landline network. Wireless modems perform the same function as traditional modems, connecting your computer to a wireless network that could be a cell phone network or a Wi-Fi network.

TYPES OF NETWORKS

There are many kinds of networks and ways of classifying them. One way of looking at networks is in terms of their geographic scope (see Table 7.1).

Local Area Networks

If you work in a business that uses networking, you are probably connecting to other employees and groups via a local area network. A **local area network (LAN)** is designed to connect personal computers and other digital devices within a half-mile or 500-meter radius. LANs typically connect a few computers in a small office, all the computers in one building, or all the computers in several buildings in close proximity. LANs also are used to link to long-distance wide area networks (WANs, described later in this section) and other networks around the world, using the Internet.

Review Figure 7.1, which could serve as a model for a small LAN that might be used in an office. One computer is a dedicated network server, providing users with access to shared computing resources in the network, including software programs and data files.

The server determines who gets access to what and in which sequence. The router connects the LAN to other networks, which could be the Internet, or another corporate network, so that the LAN can exchange information with networks external to it. The most common LAN operating systems are Windows and Linux.

TABLE 7.1
Types of Networks

Type	Area
Local area network (LAN)	Up to 500 meters (half a mile); an office or floor of a building
Campus area network (CAN)	Up to 1,000 meters (a mile); a college campus or corporate facility
Metropolitan area network (MAN)	A city or metropolitan area
Wide area network (WAN)	A regional, transcontinental, or global area

Ethernet is the dominant LAN standard at the physical network level, specifying the physical medium to carry signals between computers, access control rules, and a standardized set of bits that carry data over the system. Originally, Ethernet supported a data transfer rate of 10 megabits per second (Mbps). Newer versions, such as Gigabit Ethernet, support a data transfer rate of 1 gigabit per second (Gbps).

The LAN illustrated in Figure 7.1 uses a client/server architecture by which the network operating system resides primarily on a single server, and the server provides much of the control and resources for the network. Alternatively, LANs may use a **peer-to-peer** architecture. A peer-to-peer network treats all processors equally and is used primarily in small networks with 10 or fewer users. The various computers on the network can exchange data by direct access and can share peripheral devices without going through a separate server.

Larger LANs have many clients and multiple servers, with separate servers for specific services such as storing and managing files and databases (file servers or database servers), managing printers (print servers), storing and managing email (mail servers), or storing and managing web pages (web servers).

Metropolitan and Wide Area Networks

Wide area networks (WANs) span broad geographical distances—entire regions, states, continents, or the entire globe. The most universal and powerful WAN is the Internet. Computers connect to a WAN through public networks, such as the telephone system or private cable systems, or through leased lines or satellites. A **metropolitan area network (MAN)** is a network that spans a metropolitan area, usually a city and its major suburbs. Its geographic scope falls between a WAN and a LAN.

TRANSMISSION MEDIA AND TRANSMISSION SPEED

Networks use different kinds of physical transmission media, including twisted pair wire, coaxial cable, fiber-optic cable, and media for wireless transmission. Each has advantages and limitations. A wide range of speeds is possible for any given medium, depending on the software and hardware configuration. Table 7.2 compares these media.

TABLE 7.2

Physical Transmission Media

Transmission Medium	Description	Speed
Twisted pair wire (CAT 5)	Strands of copper wire twisted in pairs for voice and data communications. CAT 5 is the most common 10 Mbps LAN cable. Maximum recommended run of 100 meters.	10–100+ Mbps
Coaxial cable	Thickly insulated copper wire, which is capable of high-speed data transmission and less subject to interference than twisted wire. Currently used for cable TV and for networks with longer runs (more than 100 meters).	Up to 1 Gbps
Fiber-optic cable	Strands of clear glass fiber, transmitting data as pulses of light generated by lasers. Useful for high-speed transmission of large quantities of data. More expensive than other physical transmission media and harder to install; often used for network backbone.	15 Mbps to 6+ Tbps
Wireless transmission media	Based on radio signals of various frequencies and includes both terrestrial and satellite microwave systems and cellular networks. Used for long-distance, wireless communication and Internet access.	Up to 600+ Mbps

Bandwidth: Transmission Speed

The total amount of digital information that can be transmitted through any telecommunications medium is measured in bits per second (bps). One signal change, or cycle, is required to transmit one or several bits; therefore, the transmission capacity of each type of telecommunications medium is a function of its frequency. The number of cycles per second that can be sent through that medium is measured in **hertz**—one hertz is equal to one cycle of the medium.

The range of frequencies that can be accommodated on a particular telecommunications channel is called its **bandwidth**. The bandwidth is the difference between the highest and lowest frequencies that can be accommodated on a single channel. The greater the range of frequencies, the greater the bandwidth and the greater the channel's transmission capacity.

7-3 How do the Internet and Internet technology work, and how do they support communication and e-business?

The Internet has become an indispensable personal and business tool—but what exactly is the Internet? How does it work, and what does Internet technology have to offer for business? Let's look at the most important Internet features.

WHAT IS THE INTERNET?

The Internet is the world's most extensive public communication system. It's also the world's largest implementation of client/server computing and internetworking, linking millions of individual networks all over the world. This global network of networks began in the early 1970s as a U.S. Department of Defense network to link scientists and university professors around the world.

Most homes and small businesses connect to the Internet by subscribing to an Internet service provider. An **Internet service provider (ISP)** is a commercial organization with a permanent connection to the Internet that sells temporary connections to retail subscribers. EarthLink, NetZero, and AT&T are ISPs. Individuals also connect to the Internet through their business firms, universities, or research centers that have designated Internet domains.

There is a variety of services for ISP Internet connections. Connecting via a traditional telephone line and modem, at a speed of 56.6 kilobits per second (Kbps), used to be the most common form of connection worldwide, but high-speed broadband connections have largely replaced it. Digital subscriber line, cable, satellite Internet connections, and T lines provide these broadband services.

Digital subscriber line (DSL) technologies operate over existing telephone lines to carry voice, data, and video at transmission rates ranging from 385 Kbps all the way up to 40 Mbps, depending on usage patterns and distance. **Cable Internet connections** provided by cable television vendors use digital cable coaxial lines to deliver high-speed Internet access to homes and businesses. They can provide high-speed access to the Internet of up to 50 Mbps, although most providers offer service ranging from 1 Mbps to 6 Mbps. Where DSL and cable services are unavailable, it is possible to access the Internet via satellite, although some satellite Internet connections have slower upload speeds than other broadband services.

T1 and T3 are international telephone standards for digital communication. They are leased, dedicated lines suitable for businesses or government agencies requiring high-speed guaranteed service levels. **T1 lines** offer guaranteed delivery at 1.54 Mbps, and T3 lines offer delivery at 45 Mbps. The Internet does not provide similar guaranteed service levels but, simply, best effort.

INTERNET ADDRESSING AND ARCHITECTURE

The Internet is based on the TCP/IP networking protocol suite described earlier in this chapter. Every computer on the Internet is assigned a unique **Internet Protocol (IP) address**, which currently is a 32-bit number represented by four strings of numbers ranging from 0 to 255 separated by periods. For instance, the IP address of www.microsoft.com is 207.46.250.119.

When a user sends a message to another user on the Internet, the message is first decomposed into packets using the TCP protocol. Each packet contains its destination address. The packets are then sent from the client to the network server and from there on to as many other servers as necessary to arrive at a specific computer with a known address. At the destination address, the packets are reassembled into the original message.

The Domain Name System

Because it would be incredibly difficult for Internet users to remember strings of 12 numbers, the **Domain Name System (DNS)** converts domain names to IP addresses. The **domain name** is the English-like name that corresponds to the unique numeric IP address for each computer connected to the Internet. DNS servers maintain a database containing IP addresses mapped to their corresponding domain names. To access a computer on the Internet, users need only specify its domain name.

DNS has a hierarchical structure (see Figure 7.6). At the top of the DNS hierarchy is the root domain. The child domain of the root is called a top-level domain, and the child domain of a top-level domain is called a second-level domain. Top-level domains are two- and three-character names you are familiar with from surfing the web, for example, .com, .edu, .gov, and the various country codes such as .ca for Canada or .it for Italy. Second-level domains have two parts, designating a top-level name and a second-level name—such as buy.com, nyu.edu, or amazon.ca. A host name at the bottom of the hierarchy designates a specific computer on either the Internet or a private network.

The following list shows the most common domain extensions currently available and officially approved. Countries also have domain names such as .uk, .au, and .fr (United Kingdom, Australia, and France, respectively), and there is a new class of

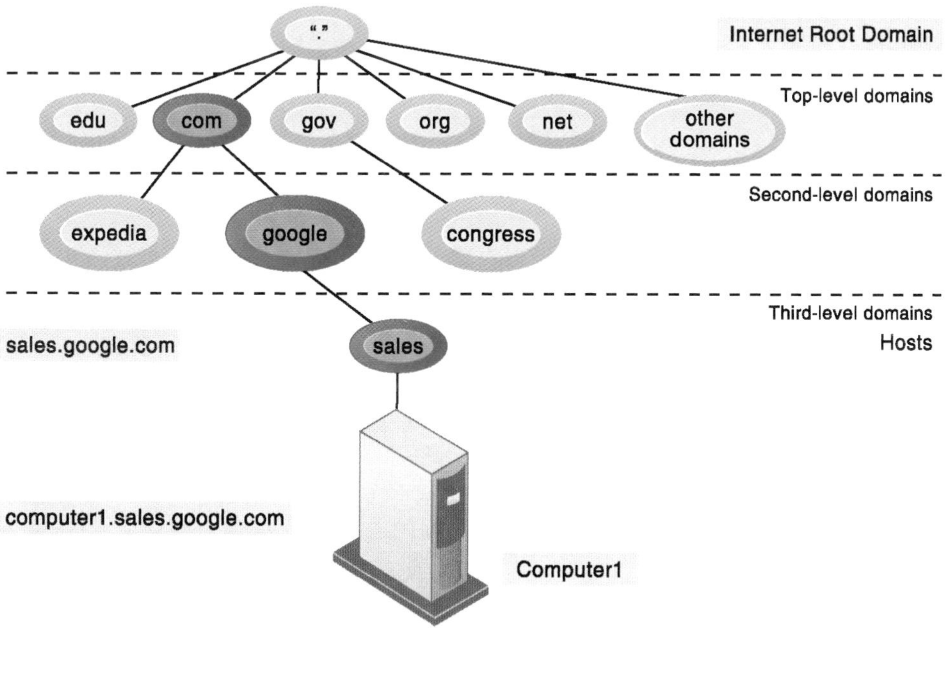

Figure 7.6
The Domain Name System
The Domain Name System is a hierarchical system with a root domain, top-level domains, second-level domains, and host computers at the third level.

internationalized top-level domains that use non-English characters. In the future, this list will expand to include many more types of organizations and industries as follows:

.com	Commercial organizations/businesses
.edu	Educational institutions
.gov	U.S. government agencies
.mil	U.S. military
.net	Network computers
.org	Any type of organization
.biz	Business firms
.info	Information providers

Internet Architecture and Governance

Internet data traffic is carried over transcontinental high-speed backbone networks that generally operate in the range of 155 Mbps to 2.5 Gbps (see Figure 7.7). These trunk lines are typically owned by long-distance telephone companies (called *network service providers*) or by national governments. Local connection lines are owned by regional telephone and cable television companies in the United States and in other countries that connect retail users in homes and businesses to the Internet. The regional networks lease access to ISPs, private companies, and government institutions.

Each organization pays for its own networks and its own local Internet connection services, a part of which is paid to the long-distance trunk line owners. Individual Internet users pay ISPs for using their service, and they generally pay a flat subscription fee, no matter how much or how little they use the Internet. A debate is now raging on whether this arrangement should continue or whether heavy Internet users who download large video and music files should pay more for the bandwidth they consume. The Interactive Session on Organizations explores this topic by examining the pros and cons of net neutrality.

No one owns the Internet, and it has no formal management. However, worldwide Internet policies are established by a number of professional organizations and government bodies, including the Internet Architecture Board (IAB), which helps define

Figure 7.7
Internet Network Architecture
The Internet backbone connects to regional networks, which in turn provide access to Internet service providers, large firms, and government institutions. Network access points (NAPs) and metropolitan area exchanges (MAEs) are hubs where the backbone intersects regional and local networks and where backbone owners connect with one another.

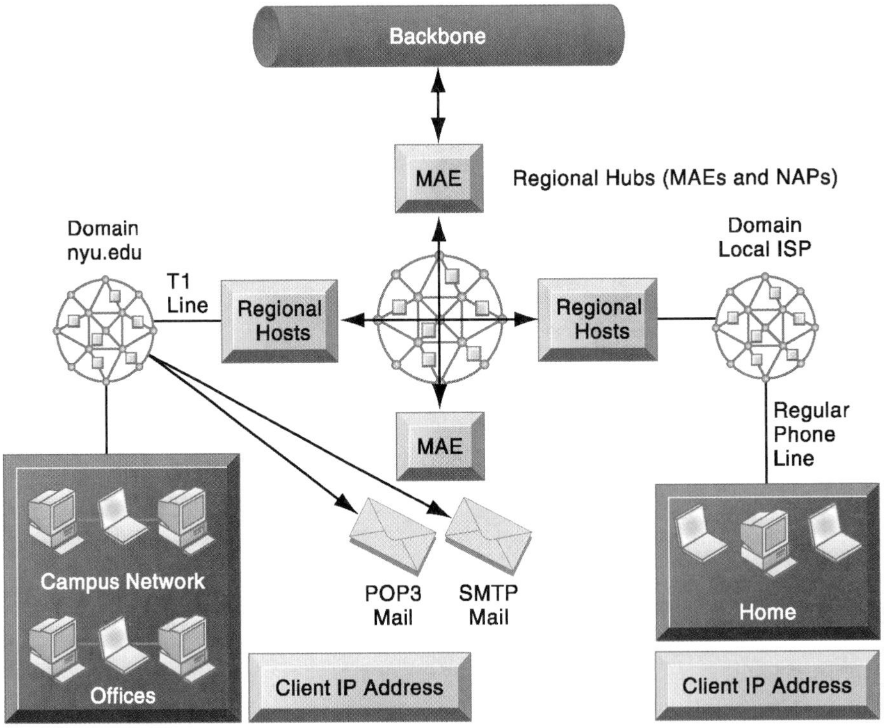

INTERACTIVE SESSION: ORGANIZATIONS Net Neutrality: The Battle Continues

What kind of Internet user are you? Do you primarily use the Net to do a little email and online banking? Or are you online all day, watching YouTube videos, downloading music files, or playing online games? Do you use your iPhone to stream TV shows and movies on a regular basis? If you're a power Internet or smartphone user, you are consuming a great deal of bandwidth. Could hundreds of millions of people like you start to slow the Internet down?

Video streaming on Netflix has accounted for 32 percent of all bandwidth use in the United States and Google's YouTube for 19 percent of web traffic at peak hours. If user demand overwhelms network capacity, the Internet might not come to a screeching halt, but users could face sluggish download speeds and video transmission.

Internet service providers (ISPs) assert that network congestion is a serious problem and that expanding their networks would require passing on burdensome costs to consumers. These companies believe differential pricing methods, which include data caps and metered use—charging based on the amount of bandwidth consumed—are the fairest way to finance necessary investments in their network infrastructures. However, metering Internet use is not universally accepted because of an ongoing debate about net neutrality.

Net neutrality is the idea that Internet service providers must allow customers equal access to content and applications, regardless of the source or nature of the content. The Internet has been neutral, with all Internet traffic treated equally on a first-come, first-served basis by Internet backbone owners. However, this arrangement prevents telecommunications and cable companies from charging differentiated prices based on the amount of bandwidth consumed by the content being delivered over the Internet.

Net neutrality advocates include the Electronic Frontier Foundation; data-intensive web businesses such as Netflix, Amazon, and Google; major consumer groups; and a host of bloggers and small businesses. They argue that differentiated pricing would impose heavy costs on heavy bandwidth users such as YouTube, Skype, and other innovative services, preventing high-bandwidth start-up companies from gaining traction. Net neutrality supporters also argue that without net neutrality, ISPs that are also cable companies, such as Comcast, might block online streaming video from Netflix or Hulu to force customers to use the cable company's on-demand movie rental services.

Network owners believe regulation to enforce net neutrality will impede U.S. competitiveness by discouraging capital expenditure for new networks and curbing their networks' ability to cope with the exploding demand for Internet and wireless traffic. U.S. Internet service lags behind many other nations in overall speed, cost, and quality of service, adding credibility to this argument.

On January 14, 2014, the U.S. Court of Appeals for the District of Columbia struck down the Federal Communication Commission (FCC) Open Internet rules that required equal treatment of Internet traffic and prevented broadband providers from blocking traffic favoring certain sites or charging special fees to companies that account for the most traffic. The court said the FCC saddled broadband providers with the same sorts of obligations as traditional common carrier telecommunications services, such as landline phone systems, even though the commission had explicitly decided not to classify broadband as a telecommunications service.

The Obama administration favored net neutrality and an open Internet and urged the FCC to implement the strongest possible rules to protect it. On February 26, 2015, the FCC decided to reclassify high-speed Internet as a telecommunications service in which outright blocking of content, slowing of transmissions, and the creation of so-called fast lanes would be prohibited. The new rules applied to mobile data service for smartphones and tablets in addition to wired lines. The order also included provisions to protect consumer privacy and ensure that Internet service would be available to people with disabilities and in remote areas. These rules were upheld by a June 14, 2016, decision by the U.S. Court of Appeals for the District of Columbia Circuit.

That has not stopped legal challenges to the government's net neutrality rules from being filed by a number of organizations, including the United States Telecom Association, AT&T, the National Cable & Telecommunications Association, and CTIA, which represents wireless carriers The Trump administration has unleashed efforts to roll back net neutrality rules as part of its push for government-wide deregulation. The battle over net neutrality is not yet over.

Sources: John J. McKinnon and Drew FitzGerald, "Regulator Outlines Net Neutrality Rollback," *Wall Street Journal*, April 26, 2017; Cecelia Kang, "FCC Chairman Poses Sweeping Changes to Net Neutrality Laws," *New York Times*, April 26, 2017; John D. McKinnon and Brett Kendall, "FCC's Net-Neutrality Rules Upheld by Appeals Court," *Wall Street Journal*, June 14, 2016; Darren Orf, "The Next Battle for Net Neutrality Is Getting Bloody," *Gizmodo*, May 25, 2016;Rebecca Ruiz, "FCC Sets Net Neutrality Rules," *New York Times*, March 12, 2015; Rebecca Ruiz and Steve Lohr, "F.C.C. Approves Net Neutrality Rules, Classifying Broadband Internet Service as a Utility," *New York Times*, February 26, 2015.

CASE STUDY QUESTIONS

1. What is net neutrality? Why has the Internet operated under net neutrality up to this point?
2. Who's in favor of net neutrality? Who's opposed? Why?
3. What would be the impact on individual users, businesses, and government if Internet providers switched to a tiered service model for transmission over landlines as well as wireless?
4. It has been said that net neutrality is the most important issue facing the Internet since the advent of the Internet. Discuss the implications of this statement.
5. Are you in favor of legislation enforcing network neutrality? Why or why not?

the overall structure of the Internet; the Internet Corporation for Assigned Names and Numbers (ICANN), which manages the domain name system; and the World Wide Web Consortium (W3C), which sets Hypertext Markup Language and other programming standards for the web.

These organizations influence government agencies, network owners, ISPs, and software developers with the goal of keeping the Internet operating as efficiently as possible. The Internet must also conform to the laws of the sovereign nation-states in which it operates as well as to the technical infrastructures that exist within the nation-states. Although in the early years of the Internet and the web there was very little legislative or executive interference, this situation is changing as the Internet plays a growing role in the distribution of information and knowledge, including content that some find objectionable.

The Future Internet: IPv6 and Internet2

The Internet was not originally designed to handle the transmission of massive quantities of data and billions of users. Because of sheer Internet population growth, the world is about to run out of available IP addresses using the old addressing convention. The old addressing system is being replaced by a new version of the IP addressing schema called **IPv6** (Internet Protocol version 6), which contains 128-bit addresses (2 to the power of 128), or more than a quadrillion possible unique addresses. IPv6 is compatible with most modems and routers sold today, and IPv6 will fall back to the old addressing system if IPv6 is not available on local networks. The transition to IPv6 will take several years as systems replace older equipment.

Internet2 is an advanced networking consortium representing more than 500 U.S. universities, private businesses, and government agencies working with 66,000 institutions across the United States and international networking partners from more than 100 countries. To connect these communities, Internet2 developed a high-capacity, 100 Gbps network that serves as a test bed for leading-edge technologies that may eventually migrate to the public Internet, including large-scale network performance measurement and management tools, secure identity and access management tools, and capabilities such as scheduling high-bandwidth, high-performance circuits.

TABLE 7.3
Major Internet Services

Capability	Functions Supported
Email	Person-to-person messaging; document sharing
Chatting and instant messaging	Interactive conversations
Newsgroups	Discussion groups on electronic bulletin boards
Telnet	Logging on to one computer system and doing work on another
File Transfer Protocol (FTP)	Transferring files from computer to computer
World Wide Web	Retrieving, formatting, and displaying information (including text, audio, graphics, and video) by using hypertext links

INTERNET SERVICES AND COMMUNICATION TOOLS

The Internet is based on client/server technology. Individuals using the Internet control what they do through client applications on their computers, such as web browser software. The data, including email messages and web pages, are stored on servers. A client uses the Internet to request information from a particular web server on a distant computer, and the server sends the requested information back to the client over the Internet. Client platforms today include not only PCs and other computers but also smartphones and tablets.

Internet Services

A client computer connecting to the Internet has access to a variety of services. These services include email, chatting and instant messaging, electronic discussion groups, **Telnet**, **File Transfer Protocol (FTP)**, and the web. Table 7.3 provides a brief description of these services.

Each Internet service is implemented by one or more software programs. All the services may run on a single server computer, or different services may be allocated to different machines. Figure 7.8 illustrates one way these services can be arranged in a multitiered client/server architecture.

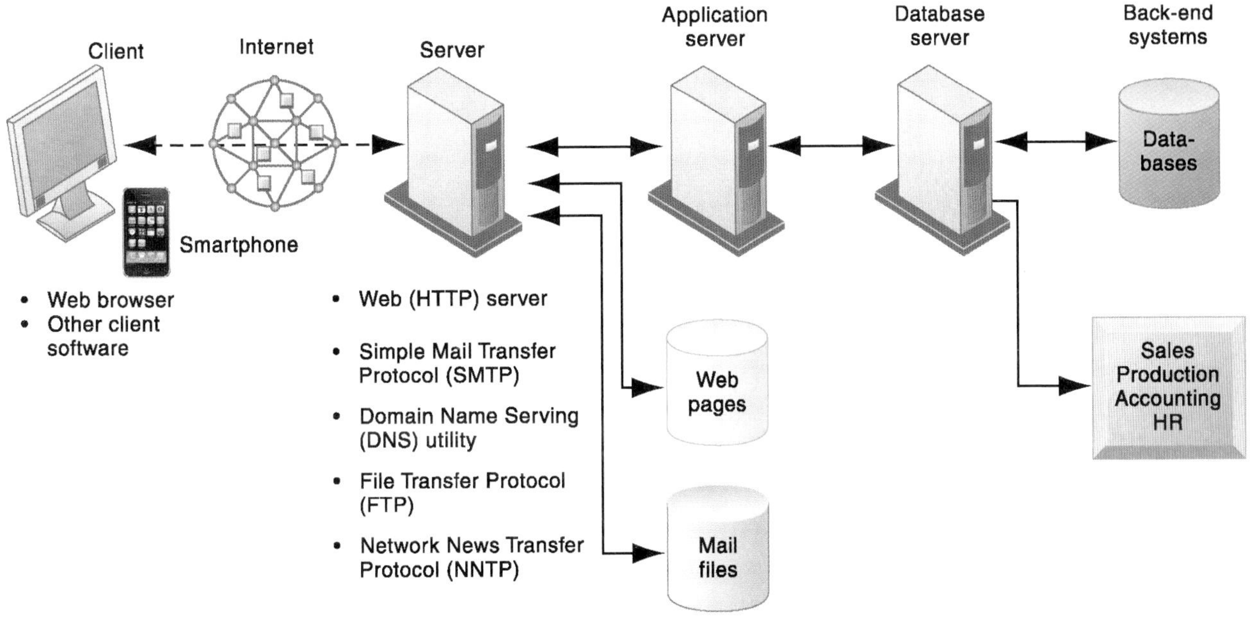

Figure 7.8
Client/Server Computing on the Internet
Client computers running web browsers and other software can access an array of services on servers over the Internet. These services may all run on a single server or on multiple specialized servers.

Email enables messages to be exchanged from computer to computer, with capabilities for routing messages to multiple recipients, forwarding messages, and attaching text documents or multimedia files to messages. Most email today is sent through the Internet. The cost of email is far lower than equivalent voice, postal, or overnight delivery costs, and email messages arrive anywhere in the world in a matter of seconds.

Chatting enables two or more people who are simultaneously connected to the Internet to hold live, interactive conversations. **Chat** systems now support voice and video chat as well as written conversations. Many online retail businesses offer chat services on their websites to attract visitors, to encourage repeat purchases, and to improve customer service.

Instant messaging is a type of chat service that enables participants to create their own private chat channels. The instant messaging system alerts the user whenever someone on his or her private list is online so that the user can initiate a chat session with other individuals. Instant messaging systems for consumers include Yahoo! Messenger, Google Hangouts, AOL Instant Messenger, and Facebook Chat. Companies concerned with security use proprietary communications and messaging systems such as IBM Sametime.

Newsgroups are worldwide discussion groups posted on Internet electronic bulletin boards on which people share information and ideas on a defined topic such as radiology or rock bands. Anyone can post messages on these bulletin boards for others to read.

Employee use of email, instant messaging, and the Internet is supposed to increase worker productivity, but the accompanying Interactive Session on People shows that this may not always be the case. Many company managers now believe they need to monitor and even regulate their employees' online activity, but is this ethical? Although there are some strong business reasons companies may need to monitor their employees' email and web activities, what does this mean for employee privacy?

Voice over IP

The Internet has also become a popular platform for voice transmission and corporate networking. **Voice over IP (VoIP)** technology delivers voice information in digital form using packet switching, avoiding the tolls charged by local and long-distance telephone networks (see Figure 7.9). Calls that would ordinarily be transmitted over public telephone networks travel over the corporate network based on the Internet protocol, or the public Internet. Voice calls can be made and received with a computer equipped with a microphone and speakers or with a VoIP-enabled telephone.

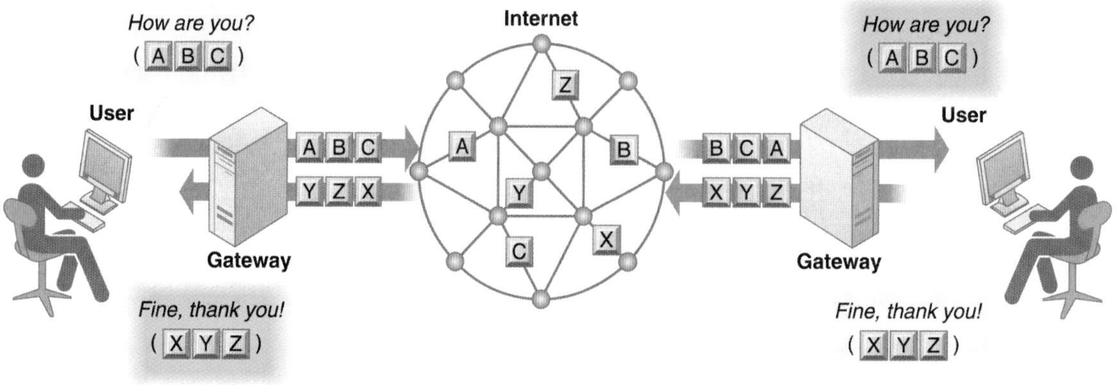

Figure 7.9
How Voice Over IP Works
A VoIP phone call digitizes and breaks up a voice message into data packets that may travel along different routes before being reassembled at the final destination. A processor nearest the call's destination, called a gateway, arranges the packets in the proper order and directs them to the telephone number of the receiver or the IP address of the receiving computer.

Cable firms such as Time Warner and Cablevision provide VoIP service bundled with their high-speed Internet and cable offerings. Skype offers free VoIP worldwide using a peer-to-peer network, and Google has its own free VoIP service.

Although up-front investments are required for an IP phone system, VoIP can reduce communication and network management costs by 20 to 30 percent. For example, VoIP saves Virgin Entertainment Group $700,000 per year in long-distance bills. In addition to lowering long-distance costs and eliminating monthly fees for private lines, an IP network provides a single voice-data infrastructure for both telecommunications and computing services. Companies no longer have to maintain separate networks or provide support services and personnel for each type of network.

Unified Communications

In the past, each of the firm's networks for wired and wireless data, voice communications, and videoconferencing operated independently of each other and had to be managed separately by the information systems department. Now, however, firms can merge disparate communications modes into a single universally accessible service using unified communications technology. **Unified communications** integrates disparate channels for voice communications, data communications, instant messaging, email, and electronic conferencing into a single experience by which users can seamlessly switch back and forth between different communication modes. Presence technology shows whether a person is available to receive a call.

CenterPoint Properties, a major Chicago area industrial real estate company, used unified communications technology to create collaborative websites for each of its real estate deals. Each website provides a single point for accessing structured and unstructured data. Integrated presence technology lets team members email, instant message, call, or videoconference with one click.

Virtual Private Networks

What if you had a marketing group charged with developing new products and services for your firm with members spread across the United States? You would want them to be able to email each other and communicate with the home office without any chance that outsiders could intercept the communications. Large private networking firms offer secure, private, dedicated networks to customers, but this is expensive. A lower-cost solution is to create a virtual private network within the public Internet.

A **virtual private network (VPN)** is a secure, encrypted, private network that has been configured within a public network to take advantage of the economies of scale and management facilities of large networks, such as the Internet (see Figure 7.10). A VPN provides your firm with secure, encrypted communications at a much lower cost than the same capabilities offered by traditional non-Internet providers that use their private networks to secure communications. VPNs also provide a network infrastructure for combining voice and data networks.

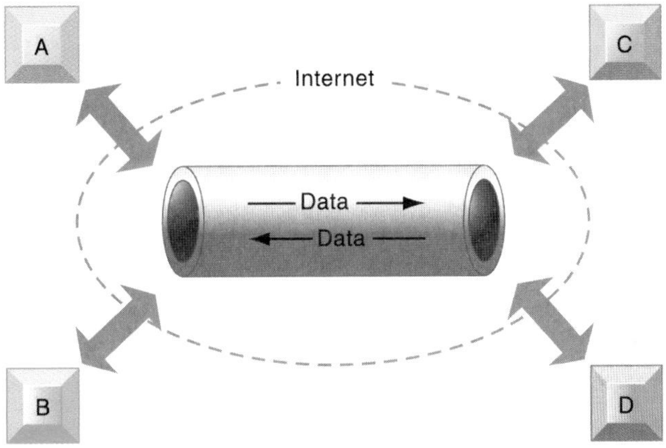

Figure 7.10
A Virtual Private Network Using the Internet
This VPN is a private network of computers linked using a secure tunnel connection over the Internet. It protects data transmitted over the public Internet by encoding the data and wrapping them within the Internet protocol. By adding a wrapper around a network message to hide its content, organizations can create a private connection that travels through the public Internet.

INTERACTIVE SESSION: PEOPLE

Monitoring Employees on Networks: Unethical or Good Business?

The Internet has become an extremely valuable business tool, but it's also a huge distraction for workers on the job. Employees are wasting valuable company time by surfing inappropriate websites (Facebook, shopping, sports, etc.), sending and receiving personal email, texting to friends, and downloading videos and music. According to a survey by International Data Corp (IDC), 30 to 40 percent of Internet access is spent on non-work-related browsing, and a staggering 60 percent of all online purchases are made during working hours. A series of studies have found that employees spend between one and three hours per day at work surfing the web on personal business. A company with 1,000 workers using the Internet could lose up to $35 million in productivity annually from just an hour of daily web surfing by workers.

Many companies have begun monitoring employee use of email and the Internet, sometimes without their knowledge. Many tools are now available for this purpose, including Spector CNE Investigator, OsMonitor, IMonitor, Work Examiner, Mobistealth, and Spytech. These products enable companies to record online searches, monitor file downloads and uploads, record keystrokes, keep tabs on emails, create transcripts of chats, or take certain screenshots of images displayed on computer screens. Instant messaging, text messaging, and social media monitoring are also increasing. Although U.S. companies have the legal right to monitor employee Internet and email activity while they are at work, is such monitoring unethical, or is it simply good business?

Managers worry about the loss of time and employee productivity when employees are focusing on personal rather than company business. Too much time on personal business translates into lost revenue. Some employees may even be billing time they spend pursuing personal interests online to clients, thus overcharging them.

If personal traffic on company networks is too high, it can also clog the company's network so that legitimate business work cannot be performed. GMI Insurance Services, which serves the U.S. transportation industry, found that employees were downloading a great deal of music and streaming video and storing them on company servers. GMI's server backup space was being eaten up.

When employees use email or the web (including social networks) at employer facilities or with employer equipment, anything they do, including anything illegal, carries the company's name. Therefore, the employer can be traced and held liable. Management in many firms fear that racist, sexually explicit, or other potentially offensive material accessed or traded by their employees could result in adverse publicity and even lawsuits for the firm. Even if the company is found not to be liable, responding to lawsuits could run up huge legal bills. Companies also fear leakage of confidential information and trade secrets through email or social networks. Another survey conducted by the American Management Association and the ePolicy Institute found that 14 percent of the employees polled admitted they had sent confidential or potentially embarrassing company emails to outsiders.

U.S. companies have the legal right to monitor what employees are doing with company equipment during business hours. The question is whether electronic surveillance is an appropriate tool for maintaining an efficient and positive workplace. Some companies try to ban all personal activities on corporate networks—zero tolerance. Others block employee access to specific websites or social sites, closely monitor email messages, or limit personal time on the web.

GMI Insurance implemented Veriato Investigator and Veriato 360 software to record and analyze the Internet and computer activities of each GMI employee. The Veriato software is able to identify which websites employees visit frequently, how much time employees spend at these sites, whether employees are printing out or copying confidential documents to take home on a portable USB storage device, and whether there are any inappropriate communication conversations taking place. GMI and its sister company, CCS, had an acceptable use policy (AUP) in place prior to monitoring, providing rules about what employees are allowed and not allowed to do with the organization's computing resources. However, GMI's AUP was nearly impossible to enforce until implementation of the Veriato employee monitoring software. To deal with music and video downloads, GMI additionally developed a "software download policy," which must be reviewed and signed by employees. Management at both GMI and CCS believe employee productivity increased by 15 to 20 percent as a result of using the Veriato monitoring software.

A number of firms have fired employees who have stepped out of bounds. A Proofpoint survey found that one in five large U.S. companies had fired an employee for violating email policies. Among managers who fired employees for Internet misuse, the majority did so because the employees' email contained sensitive, confidential, or embarrassing information.

No solution is problem-free, but many consultants believe companies should write corporate policies on employee email, social media, and Internet use. The policies should include explicit ground rules that state, by position or level, under what circumstances employees can use company facilities for email, blogging, or web surfing. The policies should also inform employees whether these activities are monitored and explain why.

The rules should be tailored to specific business needs and organizational cultures. For example, investment firms will need to allow many of their employees access to other investment sites. A company dependent on widespread information sharing, innovation, and independence could very well find that monitoring creates more problems than it solves.

Sources: "Office Slacker Stats," www.staffmonitoring.com, accessed May 3, 2017; "How Do Employers Monitor Internet Usage at Work?" wisegeek.org, accessed April 15, 2017; Susan M. Heathfield, "Surfing the Web at Work," About.com, May 27, 2016; Veriato, "Veriato 'Golden' for GMI Insurance Services," 2016; Marcell Gogan, "How Do Companies Monitor Employee Internet Usage?" *TGDaily*, November 24, 2016; and Dune Lawrence, "Companies Are Tracking Employees to Nab Traitors," *Bloomberg*, March 23, 2015.

CASE STUDY QUESTIONS

1. Should managers monitor employee email and Internet usage? Why or why not?

2. Describe an effective email and web use policy for a company.

3. Should managers inform employees that their web behavior is being monitored? Or should managers monitor secretly? Why or why not?

Several competing protocols are used to protect data transmitted over the public Internet, including Point-to-Point Tunneling Protocol (PPTP). In a process called *tunneling*, packets of data are encrypted and wrapped inside IP packets. By adding this wrapper around a network message to hide its content, business firms create a private connection that travels through the public Internet.

THE WEB

The web is the most popular Internet service. It's a system with universally accepted standards for storing, retrieving, formatting, and displaying information by using a client/server architecture. Web pages are formatted using hypertext with embedded links that connect documents to one another and that also link pages to other objects, such as sound, video, or animation files. When you click a graphic and a video clip plays, you have clicked a hyperlink. A typical **website** is a collection of web pages linked to a home page.

Hypertext

Web pages are based on a standard Hypertext Markup Language (HTML), which formats documents and incorporates dynamic links to other documents and other objects stored in the same or remote computers (see Chapter 5). Web pages are accessible through the Internet because web browser software operating your computer can request web pages stored on an Internet host server by using the **Hypertext Transfer Protocol (HTTP)**. HTTP is the communications standard that transfers pages on the web. For example, when you type a web address in your browser, such as http://www.sec.gov, your browser sends an HTTP request to the sec.gov server requesting the home page of sec.gov.

HTTP is the first set of letters at the start of every web address, followed by the domain name, which specifies the organization's server computer that is storing the web page. Most companies have a domain name that is the same as or closely related to their official corporate name. The directory path and web page name are two more pieces of information within the web address that help the browser track down the requested page. Together, the address is called a **uniform resource locator (URL)**. When typed into a browser, a URL tells the browser software exactly where to look for the information. For example, in the URL http://www.megacorp.com/content/features/082610.html, *http* names the protocol that displays web pages, www.megacorp.com is the domain name, content/features is the directory path that identifies where on the domain web server the page is stored, and 082610.html is the web page name and the name of the format it is in. (It is an HTML page.)

Web Servers

A web server is software for locating and managing stored web pages. It locates the web pages a user requests on the computer where they are stored and delivers the web pages to the user's computer. Server applications usually run on dedicated computers, although they can all reside on a single computer in small organizations.

The leading web servers in use today are Microsoft Internet Information Services (IIS) and Apache HTTP Server. Apache is an open source product that is free of charge and can be downloaded from the web.

Searching for Information on the Web

No one knows for sure how many web pages there really are. The surface web is the part of the web that search engines visit and about which information is recorded. For instance, Google indexed an estimated 60 trillion pages in 2016, and this reflects a large portion of the publicly accessible web page population. But there is a deep web that contains an estimated 1 trillion additional pages, many of them proprietary (such as the pages of *Wall Street Journal Online*, which cannot be visited without a subscription or access code) or that are stored in protected corporate databases. Searching for information on Facebook is another matter. With more than 1.9 billion members, each with pages of text, photos, and media, the population of web pages is larger than many estimates. However, Facebook is a closed web, and its pages are not completely searchable by Google or other search engines.

Search Engines Obviously, with so many web pages, finding specific ones that can help you or your business, nearly instantly, is an important problem. The question is, how can you find the one or two pages you really want and need out of billions of indexed web pages? **Search engines** attempt to solve the problem of finding useful information on the web nearly instantly and, arguably, they are the killer app of the Internet era. Today's search engines can sift through HTML files; files of Microsoft Office applications; PDF files; and audio, video, and image files. There are hundreds of search engines in the world, but the vast majority of search results come from Google, Baidu, Yahoo, and Microsoft's Bing (see Figure 7.11). While we typically think of Amazon as an online store, it is also a powerful product search engine.

Web search engines started out in the early 1990s as relatively simple software programs that roamed the nascent web, visiting pages and gathering information about the content of each page. The first search engines were simple keyword indexes of all the pages they visited, leaving users with lists of pages that may not have been truly relevant to their search.

In 1994, Stanford University computer science students David Filo and Jerry Yang created a hand-selected list of their favorite web pages and called it "Yet Another Hierarchical Officious Oracle," or Yahoo. Yahoo was not initially a search engine but rather an edited selection of websites organized by categories the editors found useful. Currently, Yahoo relies on Microsoft's Bing for search results.

In 1998, Larry Page and Sergey Brin, two other Stanford computer science students, released their first version of Google. This search engine was different. Not only did it

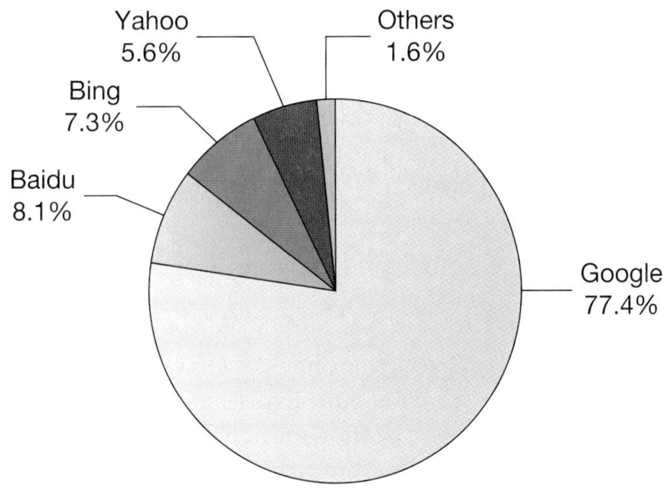

Figure 7.11
Top Web Search Engines Worldwide
Google is the world's most popular search engine.
Source: Based on data from Net Market Share, April 2017.

index each web page's words but it also ranked search results based on the relevance of each page. Page patented the idea of a page ranking system (called *PageRank System*), which essentially measures the popularity of a web page by calculating the number of sites that link to that page as well as the number of pages to which it links. The premise is that popular web pages are more relevant to users. Brin contributed a unique web crawler program that indexed not only keywords on a page but also combinations of words (such as authors and the titles of their articles). These two ideas became the foundation for the Google search engine. Figure 7.12 illustrates how Google works.

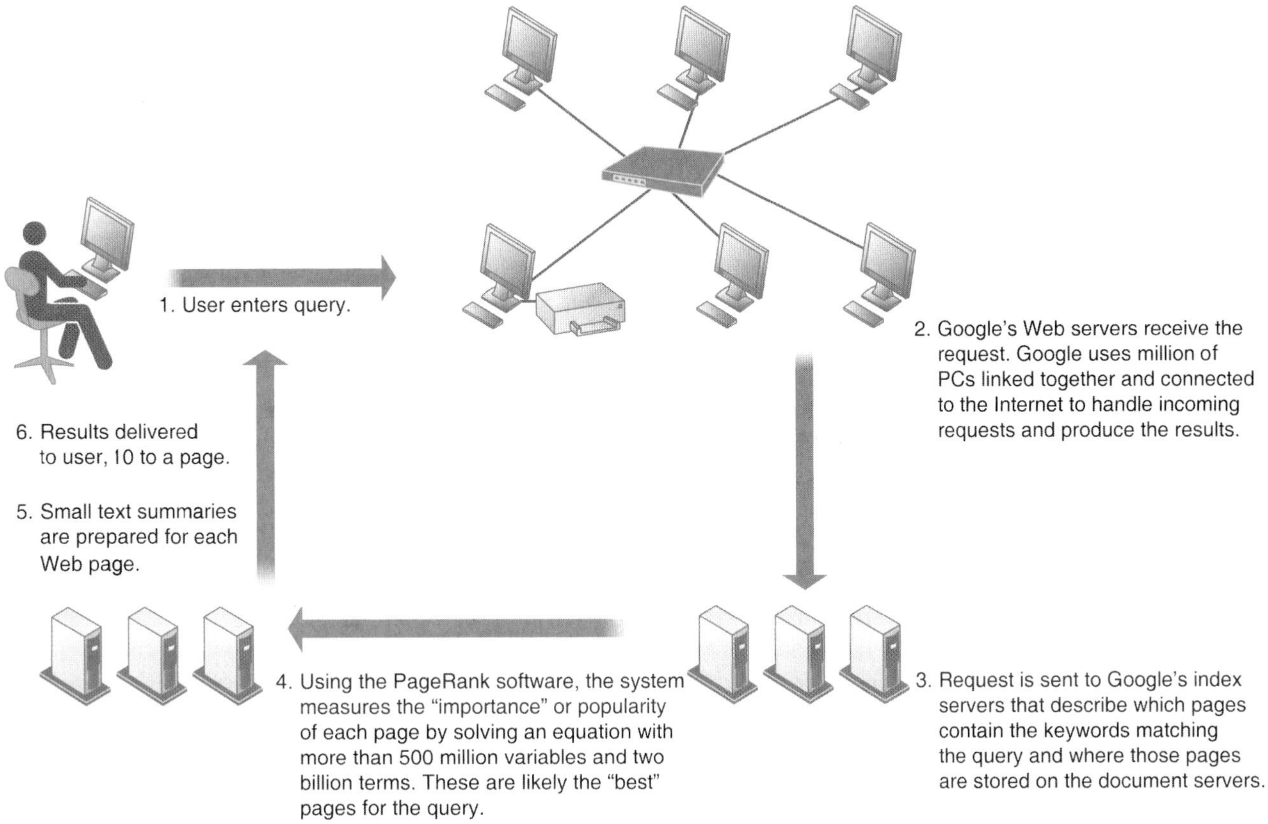

1. User enters query.
2. Google's Web servers receive the request. Google uses million of PCs linked together and connected to the Internet to handle incoming requests and produce the results.
3. Request is sent to Google's index servers that describe which pages contain the keywords matching the query and where those pages are stored on the document servers.
4. Using the PageRank software, the system measures the "importance" or popularity of each page by solving an equation with more than 500 million variables and two billion terms. These are likely the "best" pages for the query.
5. Small text summaries are prepared for each Web page.
6. Results delivered to user, 10 to a page.

Figure 7.12
How Google Works
The Google search engine is continuously crawling the web, indexing the content of each page, calculating its popularity, and storing the pages so that it can respond quickly to user requests to see a page. The entire process takes about half a second.

Mobile Search Mobile search from smartphones and tablets makes up more than 50 percent of all searches and will expand rapidly in the next few years. Google, Amazon, and Yahoo have developed new search interfaces to make searching and shopping from smartphones more convenient. Google revised its search algorithm to favor sites that look good on smartphone screens. Although smartphones are widely used to shop, actual purchases typically take place on laptops or desktops, followed by tablets.

Semantic Search Another way for search engines to become more discriminating and helpful is to make search engines capable of understanding what we are really looking for. Called **semantic search**, the goal is to build a search engine that could really understand human language and behavior. Google and other search engine firms are attempting to refine search engine algorithms to capture more of what the user intended and the meaning of a search. In September 2013, Google introduced its Hummingbird search algorithm. Rather than evaluate each word separately in a search, Google's semantically informed Hummingbird tries to evaluate an entire sentence, focusing on the meaning behind the words. For instance, if your search is a long sentence like "Google annual report selected financial data 2016," Hummingbird should be able to figure out that you really want Google's SEC Form 10K report filed with the Securities and Exchange Commission on March 31, 2017.

Google searches also take advantage of Knowledge Graph, an effort of the search algorithm to anticipate what you might want to know more about as you search on a topic. Results of the knowledge graph appear on the right of the screen and contain more information about the topic or person you are searching on. For example, if you search "Lake Tahoe," the search engine will return basic facts about Tahoe (altitude, average temperature, and local fish), a map, and hotel accommodations. Google has made **predictive search** part of most search results. This part of the search algorithm guesses what you are looking for and suggests search terms as you type your search words.

Social Search One problem with Google and mechanical search engines is that they are so thorough. Enter a search for "ultra computers" and, in 0.2 seconds, you will receive over 300 million responses! **Social search** is an effort to provide fewer, more relevant, and trustworthy search results based on a person's network of social contacts. In contrast to the top search engines that use a mathematical algorithm to find pages that satisfy your query, social search would highlight content that was created or touched by members of your social network.

Facebook Search is a social network search engine that responds to user search queries with information from the user's social network of friends and connections. Facebook Search relies on the huge amount of data on Facebook that is, or can be, linked to individuals and organizations. You might use Facebook Search to search for Boston restaurants that your friends like or pictures of your friends before 2014. Google has developed Google +1 as a social layer on top of its existing search engine. Users can place a +1 next to the websites they found helpful, and their friends will be informed.

Visual Search and the Visual Web Although search engines were originally designed to search text documents, the explosion of photos and videos on the Internet created a demand for searching and classifying these visual objects. Facial recognition software can create a digital version of a human face. Facebook has a tag suggest function to assist users in tagging their friends in photos. You can also search for people on Facebook by using their digital image to find and identify them. Facebook is now using artificial intelligence technology to make its facial recognition capabilities more accurate.

Searching photos, images, and video has become increasingly important as the web becomes more visual. The **visual web** refers to websites such as Pinterest, where pictures replace text documents, where users search pictures, and where pictures of products replace display ads for products. Pinterest is a social networking site that provides users (as well as brands) with an online board to which they can pin interesting pictures. Pinterest had 150 million active monthly users worldwide in 2017. Instagram is another example of the visual web. Instagram is a photo and video sharing site that allows users to take pictures, enhance them, and share them with friends on other social sites such as Facebook and Twitter. In 2017, Instagram had 700 million monthly active users.

Intelligent Agent Shopping Bots Chapter 11 describes the capabilities of software agents with built-in intelligence that can gather or filter information and perform other tasks to assist users. **Shopping bots** use intelligent agent software for searching the Internet for shopping information. Shopping bots such as MySimon or PriceGrabber can help people interested in making a purchase filter and retrieve information about products of interest, evaluate competing products according to criteria the users have established, and in some cases negotiate with vendors for price and delivery terms. Many of these shopping agents search the web for pricing and availability of products specified by the user and return a list of sites that sell the item along with pricing information and a purchase link.

Search Engine Marketing Search engines have become major advertising platforms and shopping tools by offering what is now called **search engine marketing**. Searching for information is one of the web's most popular activities; it is estimated that 236.4 million people in the United States will use search engines by 2019 and 216 million will use mobile search by that time. With this huge audience, search engines are the foundation for the most lucrative form of online marketing and advertising: search engine marketing. When users enter a search term on Google, Bing, Yahoo, or any of the other sites serviced by these search engines, they receive two types of listings: sponsored links, for which advertisers have paid to be listed (usually at the top of the search results page), and unsponsored, organic search results. In addition, advertisers can purchase small text boxes on the side of search results pages. The paid, sponsored advertisements are the fastest growing form of Internet advertising and are powerful new marketing tools that precisely match consumer interests with advertising messages at the right moment. Search engine marketing monetizes the value of the search process. In 2017, search engine marketing is expected to generate $36.69 billion, or 44.2 percent of digital ad spending, nearly half of all online advertising ($83 billion) (eMarketer, 2017). About 90 percent of Google's revenue of $90 billion in 2016 came from online advertising, and 90 percent of that ad revenue came from search engine marketing (Alphabet, 2017).

Because search engine marketing is so effective (it has the highest click-through rate and the highest return on ad investment), companies seek to optimize their websites for search engine recognition. The better optimized the page is, the higher a ranking it will achieve in search engine result listings. **Search engine optimization (SEO)** is the process of improving the quality and volume of web traffic to a website by employing a series of techniques that help a website achieve a higher ranking with the major search engines when certain keywords and phrases are put into the search field. One technique is to make sure that the keywords used in the website description match the keywords likely to be used as search terms by prospective customers. For example, your website is more likely to be among the first ranked by search engines if it uses the keyword *lighting* rather than *lamps* if most prospective customers are searching for *lighting*. It is also advantageous to link your website to as many other websites as possible because search engines evaluate such links to determine the popularity of a web page and how it is linked to other content on the web.

Search engines can be gamed by scammers who create thousands of phony website pages and link them or link them to a single retailer's site in an attempt to fool Google's search engine. Firms can also pay so-called link farms to link to their site. Google changed its search algorithm in 2012 to deal with this problem by examining the quality of links more carefully with the intent of down-ranking sites that have a suspicious pattern of sites linking to them.

In general, search engines have been very helpful to small businesses that cannot afford large marketing campaigns. Because shoppers are looking for a specific product or service when they use search engines, they are what marketers call hot prospects—people who are looking for information and often intending to buy. Moreover, search engines charge only for click-throughs to a site. Merchants do not have to pay for ads that don't work, only for ads that receive a click. Consumers benefit from search engine marketing because ads for merchants appear only when consumers are looking for a specific product. Thus, search engine marketing saves consumers cognitive energy and reduces search costs (including the cost of transportation needed to search for products physically). One study estimated the global value of search to both merchants and consumers to be more than $800 billion, with about 65 percent of the benefit going to consumers in the form of lower search costs and lower prices (McKinsey & Company, 2011).

Web 2.0

Today's websites don't just contain static content—they enable people to collaborate, share information, and create new services and content online. These second-generation interactive Internet-based services are referred to as **Web 2.0**. If you have pinned a photo on Pinterest, posted a video to YouTube, created a blog, or added an app to your Facebook page, you've used some of these Web 2.0 services.

Web 2.0 has four defining features: interactivity, real-time user control, social participation (sharing), and user-generated content. The technologies and services behind these features include cloud computing, software mashups and apps, blogs, RSS, wikis, and social networks. We have already described cloud computing, mashups, and apps in Chapter 5 and introduced social networks in Chapter 2.

A **blog**, the popular term for a weblog, is a personal website that typically contains a series of chronological entries (newest to oldest) by its author and links to related web pages. The blog may include a *blogroll* (a collection of links to other blogs) and *trackbacks* (a list of entries in other blogs that refer to a post on the first blog). Most blogs allow readers to post comments on the blog entries as well. The act of creating a blog is often referred to as blogging. Blogs can be hosted by a third-party service such as Blogger.com or TypePad.com, and blogging features have been incorporated into social networks such as Facebook and collaboration platforms such as IBM Notes. WordPress is a leading open source blogging tool and content management system. **Microblogging**, used in Twitter, is a type of blogging that features very short posts of 140 characters or fewer.

Blog pages are usually based on templates provided by the blogging service or software. Therefore, millions of people without HTML skills of any kind can post their own web pages and share content with others. The totality of blog-related websites is often referred to as the **blogosphere**. Although blogs have become popular personal publishing tools, they also have business uses (see Chapters 2 and 10).

If you're an avid blog reader, you might use RSS to keep up with your favorite blogs without constantly checking them for updates. **RSS**, which stands for Really Simple Syndication or Rich Site Summary, pulls specified content from websites and feeds it automatically to users' computers. RSS reader software gathers material from the websites or blogs that you tell it to scan and brings new information from those sites to you. RSS readers are available through websites such as Google and Yahoo, and they have been incorporated into the major web browsers and email programs.

Blogs allow visitors to add comments to the original content, but they do not allow visitors to change the original posted material. **Wikis**, in contrast, are collaborative websites on which visitors can add, delete, or modify content, including the work of previous authors. *Wiki* comes from the Hawaiian word for "quick."

Wiki software typically provides a template that defines layout and elements common to all pages, displays user-editable software program code, and then renders the content into an HTML-based page for display in a web browser. Some wiki software allows only basic text formatting, whereas other tools allow the use of tables, images, or even interactive elements, such as polls or games. Most wikis provide capabilities for monitoring the work of other users and correcting mistakes.

Because wikis make information sharing so easy, they have many business uses. The U.S. Department of Homeland Security's National Cyber Security Center (NCSC) deployed a wiki to facilitate information sharing with other federal agencies on threats, attacks, and responses and as a repository for technical and standards information. Pixar Wiki is a collaborative community wiki for publicizing the work of Pixar Animation Studios. The wiki format allows anyone to create or edit an article about a Pixar film.

Social networking sites enable users to build communities of friends and professional colleagues. Members typically create a profile—a web page for posting photos, videos, audio files, and text—and then share these profiles with others on the service identified as their friends or contacts. Social networking sites are highly interactive, offer real-time user control, rely on user-generated content, and are broadly based on social participation and sharing of content and opinions. Leading social networking sites include Facebook, Twitter (with more than 1.9 billion and 328 million monthly active users, respectively, in 2017), and LinkedIn (for professional contacts).

For many, social networking sites are the defining Web 2.0 application and one that has radically changed how people spend their time online; how people communicate and with whom; how business people stay in touch with customers, suppliers, and employees; how providers of goods and services learn about their customers; and how advertisers reach potential customers. The large social networking sites are also application development platforms where members can create and sell software applications to other members of the community. Facebook alone has more than 7 million apps and websites integrated with it, including applications for gaming, video sharing, and communicating with friends and family. We talk more about business applications of social networking in Chapters 2 and 10, and you can find social networking discussions in many other chapters of this book. You can also find a more detailed discussion of Web 2.0 in our Learning Tracks.

Web 3.0 and the Future Web

The future of the Internet, so-called Web 3.0, is becoming visible. The key features of **Web 3.0** are more tools for individuals to make sense out of the trillions of pages on the Internet, or the millions of apps available for smartphones and a visual, even three-dimensional (3D) Web where you can walk through pages in a 3D environment. (Review the discussion of semantic search and visual search earlier in this chapter.)

Even closer in time is a pervasive web that controls everything from a city's traffic lights and water usage, to the lights in your living room, to your car's rear view mirror, not to mention managing your calendar and appointments. This is referred to as the **Internet of Things (IoT)** and is based on billions of Internet-connected sensors throughout our physical world. Objects, animals, or people are provided with unique identifiers and the ability to transfer data over a network without requiring human-to-human or human-to-computer interaction. Firms such as General Electric, IBM, HP, and Oracle, and hundreds of smaller start-ups, are exploring how to build smart machines, factories, and cities through extensive use of remote sensors and fast cloud computing. We provide more detail on this topic in the following section.

The App Internet is another element in the future web. The growth of apps within the mobile platform is astounding. More than 80 percent of mobile minutes in the

United States are generated through apps, as opposed to browsers. Apps give users direct access to content and are much faster than loading a browser and searching for content.

Other complementary trends leading toward a future Web 3.0 include more widespread use of cloud computing and software as a service (SaaS) business models, ubiquitous connectivity among mobile platforms and Internet access devices, and the transformation of the web from a network of separate siloed applications and content into a more seamless and interoperable whole.

7-4 What are the principal technologies and standards for wireless networking, communication, and Internet access?

Welcome to the wireless revolution! Cell phones, smartphones, tablets, and wireless-enabled personal computers have morphed into portable media and computing platforms that let you perform many of the computing tasks you used to do at your desk, and a whole lot more. We introduced smartphones in our discussions of the mobile digital platform in Chapters 1 and 5. **Smartphones** such as the iPhone, Android phones, and BlackBerry combine the functionality of a cell phone with that of a mobile laptop computer with Wi-Fi capability. This makes it possible to combine music, video, Internet access, and telephone service in one device. A large part of the Internet is becoming a mobile, access-anywhere, broadband service for the delivery of video, music, and web search.

CELLULAR SYSTEMS

Today 95 percent of U.S. adults own mobile phones, and 77 percent own smartphones (Pew Research Center, 2017). Mobile is now the leading digital platform, with total activity on smartphones and tablets accounting for two-thirds of digital media time spent, and smartphone apps alone capturing more than half of digital media time (Comscore, 2016).

Digital cellular service uses several competing standards. In Europe and much of the rest of the world outside the United Sates, the standard is Global System for Mobile Communications (GSM). GSM's strength is its international roaming capability. There are GSM cell phone systems in the United States, including T-Mobile and AT&T.

A competing standard in the United States is Code Division Multiple Access (CDMA), which is the system Verizon and Sprint use. CDMA was developed by the military during World War II. It transmits over several frequencies, occupies the entire spectrum, and randomly assigns users to a range of frequencies over time, making it more efficient than GSM.

Earlier generations of cellular systems were designed primarily for voice and limited data transmission in the form of short text messages. Today wireless carriers offer 3G and 4G networks. **3G networks**, with transmission speeds ranging from 144 Kbps for mobile users in, say, a car, to more than 2 Mbps for stationary users, offer transmission speeds appropriate for email and web browsing, but are too slow for videos. **4G networks** have much higher speeds, up to 100 megabits/second download and 50 megabits upload, with more than enough capacity for watching high-definition video on your smartphone. Long Term Evolution (LTE) and mobile Worldwide Interoperability for Microwave Access (WiMax—see the following section) are the current 4G standards. The next generation of wireless technology called *5G* is still under development but is expected to transmit huge amounts of data in the gigabit range over short distances, with fewer transmission delays and the ability to connect many more devices than existing cellular systems.

WIRELESS COMPUTER NETWORKS AND INTERNET ACCESS

An array of technologies provides high-speed wireless access to the Internet for PCs and mobile devices. These new high-speed services have extended Internet access to numerous locations that could not be covered by traditional wired Internet services and have made ubiquitous computing, anywhere, anytime, a reality.

Bluetooth

Bluetooth is the popular name for the 802.15 wireless networking standard, which is useful for creating small **personal area networks (PANs)**. It links up to eight devices within a 10-meter area using low-power, radio-based communication and can transmit up to 722 Kbps in the 2.4-GHz band.

Wireless phones, pagers, computers, printers, and computing devices using Bluetooth communicate with each other and even operate each other without direct user intervention (see Figure 7.13). For example, a person could direct a notebook computer to send a document file wirelessly to a printer. Bluetooth connects wireless keyboards and mice to PCs or cell phones to earpieces without wires. Bluetooth has low power requirements, making it appropriate for battery-powered handheld computers or cell phones.

Although Bluetooth lends itself to personal networking, it has uses in large corporations. For example, FedEx drivers use Bluetooth to transmit the delivery data captured by their handheld computers to cellular transmitters, which forward the data to corporate computers. Drivers no longer need to spend time docking their handheld units physically in the transmitters, and Bluetooth has saved FedEx $20 million per year.

Wi-Fi and Wireless Internet Access

The 802.11 set of standards for wireless LANs and wireless Internet access is also known as **Wi-Fi**. The first of these standards to be widely adopted was 802.11b, which can transmit up to 11 Mbps in the unlicensed 2.4-GHz band and has an effective distance of 30 to 50 meters. The 802.11g standard can transmit up to 54 Mbps in the 2.4-GHz range. 802.11n is capable of transmitting over 100 Mbps. Today's PCs and tablets have built-in support for Wi-Fi, as do the iPhone, iPad, and other smartphones.

In most Wi-Fi communication, wireless devices communicate with a wired LAN using access points. An access point is a box consisting of a radio receiver/transmitter and antennas that links to a wired network, router, or hub.

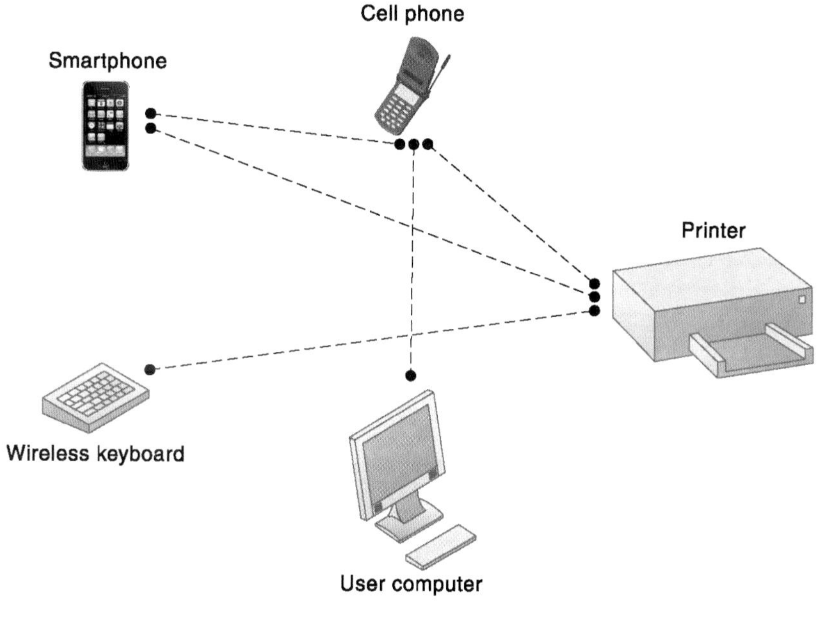

Figure 7.13
A Bluetooth Network (PAN)
Bluetooth enables a variety of devices, including cell phones, smartphones, wireless keyboards and mice, PCs, and printers, to interact wirelessly with each other within a small, 30-foot (10-meter) area. In addition to the links shown, Bluetooth can be used to network similar devices to send data from one PC to another, for example.

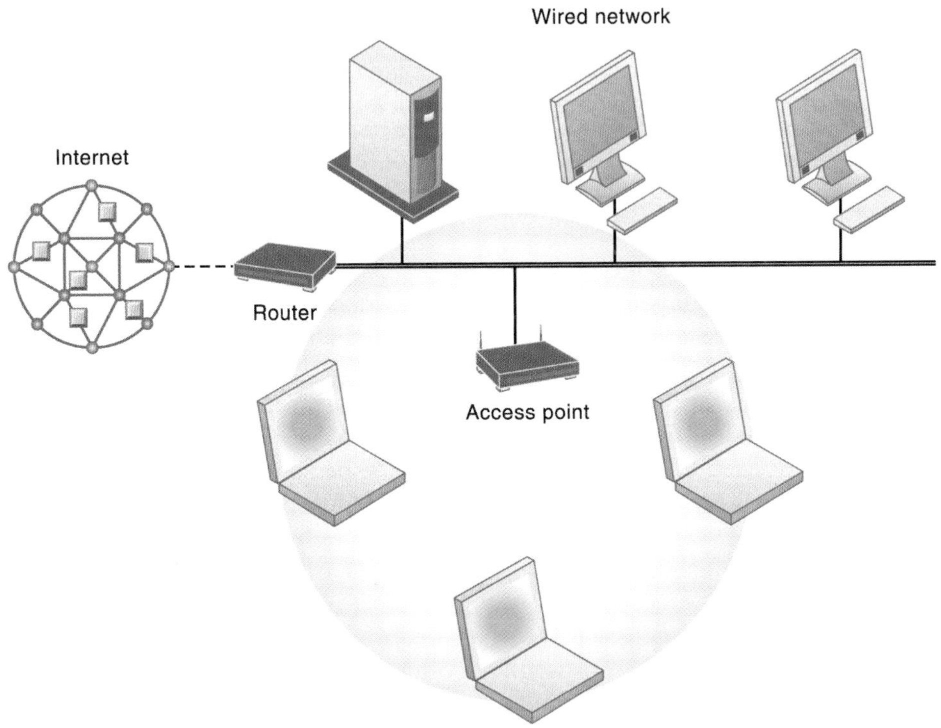

Figure 7.14
An 802.11 Wireless LAN
Mobile laptop computers equipped with network interface cards link to the wired LAN by communicating with the access point. The access point uses radio waves to transmit network signals from the wired network to the client adapters, which convert them to data that the mobile device can understand. The client adapter then transmits the data from the mobile device back to the access point, which forwards the data to the wired network.

Figure 7.14 illustrates an 802.11 wireless LAN that connects a small number of mobile devices to a larger wired LAN and to the Internet. Most wireless devices are client machines. The servers that the mobile client stations need to use are on the wired LAN. The access point controls the wireless stations and acts as a bridge between the main wired LAN and the wireless LAN. The access point also controls the wireless stations.

The most popular use for Wi-Fi today is for high-speed wireless Internet service. In this instance, the access point plugs into an Internet connection, which could come from a cable service or DSL telephone service. Computers within range of the access point use it to link wirelessly to the Internet.

Hotspots are locations with one or more access points providing wireless Internet access and are often in public places. Some hotspots are free or do not require any additional software to use; others may require activation and the establishment of a user account by providing a credit card number over the web.

Businesses of all sizes are using Wi-Fi networks to provide low-cost wireless LANs and Internet access. Wi-Fi hotspots can be found in hotels, airport lounges, libraries, cafes, and college campuses to provide mobile access to the Internet. Dartmouth College is one of many campuses where students now use Wi-Fi for research, course work, and entertainment.

Wi-Fi technology poses several challenges, however. One is Wi-Fi's security features, which make these wireless networks vulnerable to intruders. We provide more detail about Wi-Fi security issues in Chapter 8.

Another drawback of Wi-Fi networks is susceptibility to interference from nearby systems operating in the same spectrum, such as wireless phones, microwave ovens, or other wireless LANs. However, wireless networks based on the 802.11n standard solve this problem by using multiple wireless antennas in tandem to transmit and receive data and technology called MIMO (multiple input multiple output) to coordinate multiple simultaneous radio signals.

WiMax

A surprisingly large number of areas in the United States and throughout the world do not have access to Wi-Fi or fixed broadband connectivity. The range of Wi-Fi systems is no more than 300 feet from the base station, making it difficult for rural groups that don't have cable or DSL service to find wireless access to the Internet.

The Institute of Electrical and Electronics Engineers (IEEE) developed a family of standards known as WiMax to deal with these problems. **WiMax**, which stands for Worldwide Interoperability for Microwave Access, is the popular term for IEEE Standard 802.16. It has a wireless access range of up to 31 miles and transmission speed of up to 75 Mbps.

WiMax antennas are powerful enough to beam high-speed Internet connections to rooftop antennas of homes and businesses that are miles away. Cellular handsets and laptops with WiMax capabilities are appearing in the marketplace. Mobile WiMax is one of the 4G network technologies we discussed earlier in this chapter.

RFID AND WIRELESS SENSOR NETWORKS

Mobile technologies are creating new efficiencies and ways of working throughout the enterprise. In addition to the wireless systems we have just described, radio frequency identification systems and wireless sensor networks are having a major impact.

Radio Frequency Identification (RFID) and Near Field Communication (NFC)

Radio frequency identification (RFID) systems provide a powerful technology for tracking the movement of goods throughout the supply chain. RFID systems use tiny tags with embedded microchips containing data about an item and its location to transmit radio signals over a short distance to RFID readers. The RFID readers then pass the data over a network to a computer for processing. Unlike bar codes, RFID tags do not need line-of-sight contact to be read.

The RFID tag is electronically programmed with information that can uniquely identify an item plus other information about the item such as its location, where and when it was made, or its status during production. The reader emits radio waves in ranges anywhere from 1 inch to 100 feet. When an RFID tag comes within the range of the reader, the tag is activated and starts sending data. The reader captures these data, decodes them, and sends them back over a wired or wireless network to a host computer for further processing (see Figure 7.15). Both RFID tags and antennas come in a variety of shapes and sizes.

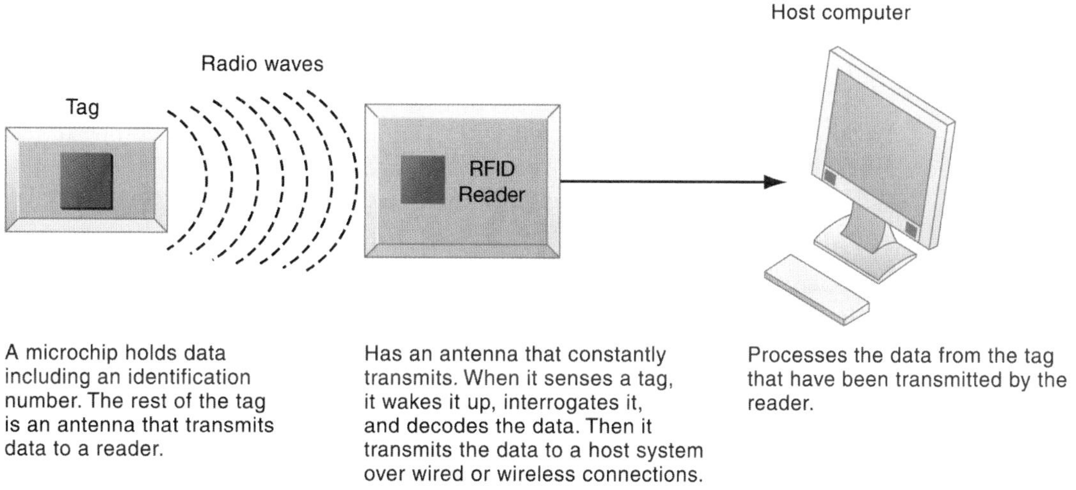

Host computer
Radio waves
Tag
RFID
Reader
A microchip holds data including an identification number. The rest of the tag is an antenna that transmits data to a reader.
Has an antenna that constantly transmits. When it senses a tag, it wakes it up, interrogates it, and decodes the data. Then it transmits the data to a host system over wired or wireless connections.
Processes the data from the tag that have been transmitted by the reader.

Figure 7.15
How RFID Works
RFID uses low-powered radio transmitters to read data stored in a tag at distances ranging from 1 inch to 100 feet. The reader captures the data from the tag and sends them over a network to a host computer for processing.

In inventory control and supply chain management, RFID systems capture and manage more detailed information about items in warehouses or in production than bar coding systems. If a large number of items are shipped together, RFID systems track each pallet, lot, or even unit item in the shipment. This technology may help companies such as Walmart improve receiving and storage operations by improving their ability to see exactly what stock is stored in warehouses or on retail store shelves. Macy's, described in the chapter-opening case, uses RFID technology to track individual items for sale on store shelves.

Walmart has installed RFID readers at store receiving docks to record the arrival of pallets and cases of goods shipped with RFID tags. The RFID reader reads the tags a second time just as the cases are brought onto the sales floor from backroom storage areas. Software combines sales data from Walmart's point-of-sale systems and the RFID data regarding the number of cases brought out to the sales floor. The program determines which items will soon be depleted and automatically generates a list of items to pick in the warehouse to replenish store shelves before they run out. This information helps Walmart reduce out-of-stock items, increase sales, and further shrink its costs.

The cost of RFID tags used to be too high for widespread use, but now it starts at around 7 cents per tag in the United States. As the price decreases, RFID is starting to become cost-effective for many applications.

In addition to installing RFID readers and tagging systems, companies may need to upgrade their hardware and software to process the massive amounts of data produced by RFID systems—transactions that could add up to tens or hundreds of terabytes.

Software is used to filter, aggregate, and prevent RFID data from overloading business networks and system applications. Applications often need to be redesigned to accept large volumes of frequently generated RFID data and to share those data with other applications. Major enterprise software vendors now offer RFID-ready versions of their supply chain management applications.

Tap-and-go services like Apple Pay or Google Wallet use an RFID-related technology called **near field communication (NFC)**. NFC is a short-range wireless connectivity standard that uses electromagnetic radio fields to enable two compatible devices to exchange data when brought within a few centimeters of each other. A smartphone or other NFC-compatible device sends out radio frequency signals that interact with an NFC tag found in compatible card readers or smart posters. The signals create a current that flows through the NFC tag, allowing the device and the tag to communicate with one another. In most cases the tag is passive and only sends out information while the other device (such as a smartphone) is active and can both send and receive information. (There are NFC systems where both components are active.)

NFC is used in wireless payment services, to retrieve information, and even to exchange videos or information with friends on the go. You could share a website link by passing your phone over a friend's phone, while waving the phone in front of a poster or display containing an NFC tag could show information about what you're viewing at a museum or exhibit.

Wireless Sensor Networks

If your company wanted state-of-the art technology to monitor building security or detect hazardous substances in the air, it might deploy a wireless sensor network. **Wireless sensor networks (WSNs)** are networks of interconnected wireless devices that are embedded in the physical environment to provide measurements of many points over large spaces. These devices have built-in processing, storage, and radio frequency sensors and antennas. They are linked into an interconnected network that routes the data they capture to a computer for analysis. These networks range from hundreds to thousands of nodes. Figure 7.16 illustrates one type of wireless sensor network, with data from individual nodes flowing across the network to a server

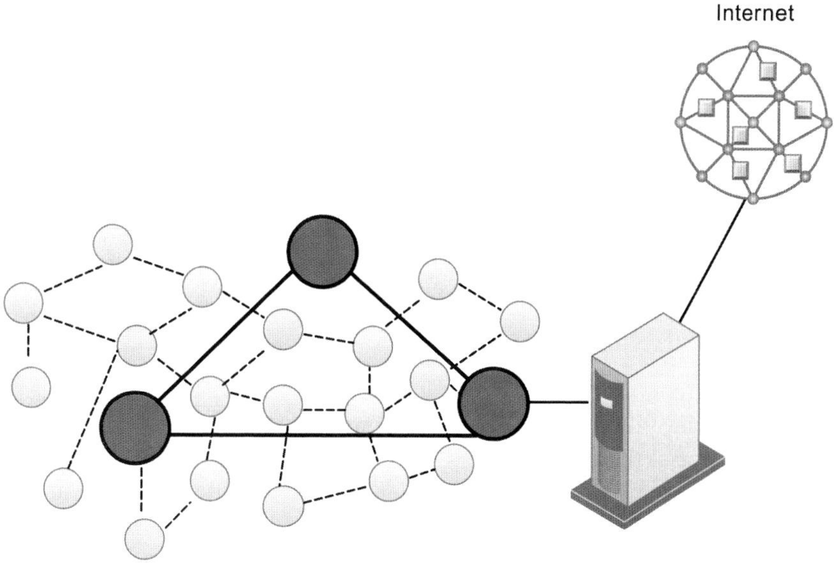

Figure 7.16
A Wireless Sensor Network
The small circles represent lower-level nodes, and the larger circles represent high-end nodes. Lower-level nodes forward data to each other or to higher-level nodes, which transmit data more rapidly and speed up network performance.

with greater processing power. The server acts as a gateway to a network based on Internet technology.

Wireless sensor networks are valuable for uses such as monitoring environmental changes; monitoring traffic or military activity; protecting property; efficiently operating and managing machinery and vehicles; establishing security perimeters; monitoring supply chain management; or detecting chemical, biological, or radiological material.

Output from RFID systems and wireless networks is fueling the Internet of Things (IoT), introduced earlier in this chapter, in which machines such as jet engines, power plant turbines, or agricultural sensors constantly gather data and send the data over the Internet for analysis. The data might signal the need to take action such as replacing a part that's close to wearing out, restocking a product on a store shelf, starting the watering system for a soybean field, or slowing down a turbine. Over time, more and more everyday physical objects will be connected to the Internet and will be able to identify themselves to other devices, creating networks that can sense and respond as data changes. Macy's Pick to the Last Unit system, described in the chapter-opening case, is an example of an IoT application. You'll find more examples of the Internet of Things in Chapters 2 and 12.

7-5 How will MIS help my career?

Here is how Chapter 7 and this book can help you find a job as an automotive digital advisor.

THE COMPANY

A1 Western Car Dealers, a large and fast-growing southern California automobile dealership, is looking for an automotive digital advisor to run its digital marketing program. The company has more than 500 vehicles for sale, 170 employees, and three locations for selling and servicing new and used vehicles.

POSITION DESCRIPTION

The automotive digital assistant will be part of a team assisting the dealership group with online marketing, including search engine optimization (SEO) and search engine marketing (SEM), social media and reputation management, and website management. Job responsibilities include coordinating efforts for the dealership owner, dealerships managers, and marketing manager in the following areas:

- Online advertising, SEO, and SEM
- Social media management, including managing the dealership's overall social media and content calendar and developing new content
- Online reputation management
- Website management
- Maintaining the dealership's blog

JOB REQUIREMENTS

- College graduate in marketing
- Knowledge of digital marketing and social media
- Microsoft Office skills
- Knowledge of automotive sales and content management systems desirable

INTERVIEW QUESTIONS

1. Have you ever taken any digital marketing courses?
2. Have you any experience running a digital marketing campaign? Did you use SEO and SEM? How did you measure the effectiveness of your social media campaign and audience growth?
3. Do you have any experience with social media management software?
4. Do you have any experience with online reputation management or online inventory management?
5. Have you ever maintained a blog?
6. What is your level of proficiency with Microsoft Office software?

AUTHOR TIPS

1. Review the discussions of search, search engine marketing, and blogs in this chapter and also the discussions of e-commerce marketing and building an e-commerce presence in Chapter 10.
2. Use the web to learn more about SEO, SEM, social media management, and online reputation management and software tools used for this work. Look into how to generate metrics reports using standardized tools and how to put together analyses and recommendations based on the social media data.
3. Look at how major auto dealers in large metropolitan areas are using social media channels. Are they creating content on YouTube, Instagram, Facebook and Twitter? Which channels are generating higher levels of audience engagement?
4. Inquire about exactly what you would have to do for website management and required software skills.
5. Inquire about the Microsoft Office skills you would need for this job. Bring examples of the work you have done with this software.

Review Summary

7-1 **What are the principal components of telecommunications networks and key networking technologies?** A simple network consists of two or more connected computers. Basic network components include computers, network interfaces, a connection medium, network operating system software, and either a hub or a switch. The networking infrastructure for a large company includes the traditional telephone system, mobile cellular communication, wireless local area networks, videoconferencing systems, a corporate website, intranets, extranets, and an array of local and wide area networks, including the Internet.

Contemporary networks have been shaped by the rise of client/server computing, the use of packet switching, and the adoption of Transmission Control Protocol/ Internet Protocol (TCP/IP) as a universal communications standard for linking disparate networks and computers, including the Internet. Protocols provide a common set of rules that enable communication among diverse components in a telecommunications network.

7-2 **What are the different types of networks?** The principal physical transmission media are twisted copper telephone wire, coaxial copper cable, fiber-optic cable, and wireless transmission.

Local area networks (LANs) connect PCs and other digital devices within a 500-meter radius and are used today for many corporate computing tasks. Wide area networks (WANs) span broad geographical distances, ranging from several miles to continents and are often private networks that are independently managed. Metropolitan area networks (MANs) span a single urban area.

Digital subscriber line (DSL) technologies, cable Internet connections, and T1 lines are often used for high-capacity Internet connections.

7-3 **How do the Internet and Internet technology work, and how do they support communication and e-business?** The Internet is a worldwide network of networks that uses the client/server model of computing and the TCP/IP network reference model. Every computer on the Internet is assigned a unique numeric IP address. The Domain Name System (DNS) converts IP addresses to more user-friendly domain names. Worldwide Internet policies are established by organizations and government bodies such as the Internet Architecture Board (IAB) and the World Wide Web Consortium (W3C).

Major Internet services include email, newsgroups, chatting, instant messaging, Telnet, FTP, and the web. Web pages are based on Hypertext Markup Language (HTML) and can display text, graphics, video, and audio. Website directories, search engines, and RSS technology help users locate the information they need on the web. RSS, blogs, social networking, and wikis are features of Web 2.0. The future Web 3.0 will feature more semantic search, visual search, prevalence of apps, and interconnectedness of many different devices (Internet of Things).

Firms are also starting to realize economies by using VoIP technology for voice transmission and virtual private networks (VPNs) as low-cost alternatives to private WANs.

7-4 **What are the principal technologies and standards for wireless networking, communication, and Internet access?** Cellular networks are evolving toward high-speed, high-bandwidth, digital packet-switched transmission. Broadband 3G networks are capable of transmitting data at speeds ranging from 144 Kbps to more than 2 Mbps. 4G networks capable of transmission speeds of 100 Mbps are starting to be rolled out.

Major cellular standards include Code Division Multiple Access (CDMA), which is used primarily in the United States, and Global System for Mobile Communications (GSM), which is the standard in Europe and much of the rest of the world.

Standards for wireless computer networks include Bluetooth (802.15) for small personal area networks (PANs), Wi-Fi (802.11) for local area networks (LANs), and WiMax (802.16) for metropolitan area networks (MANs).

Radio frequency identification (RFID) systems provide a powerful technology for tracking the movement of goods by using tiny tags with embedded data about an item and its location. RFID readers read the radio signals transmitted by these tags and pass the data over a network to a computer for processing. Wireless sensor networks (WSNs) are networks of interconnected wireless sensing and transmitting devices that are embedded in the physical environment to provide measurements of many points over large spaces.

Key Terms

3G networks, 256
4G networks, 256
Bandwidth, 240
Blog, 254
Blogosphere, 254
Bluetooth, 257
Broadband, 233
Cable Internet connections, 240
Chat, 246
Digital subscriber line (DSL), 240
Domain name, 241
Domain Name System (DNS), 241
Email, 246
File Transfer Protocol (FTP), 245
Hertz, 240
Hotspots, 258
Hubs, 234
Hypertext Transfer Protocol (HTTP), 249
Instant messaging, 246
Internet of Things (IoT), 255
Internet Protocol (IP) address, 241
Internet service provider (ISP), 240
Internet2, 244
IPv6, 244
Local area network (LAN), 238
Metropolitan area network (MAN), 239
Microblogging, 254
Modem, 238
Near field communication (NFC), 260
Network operating system (NOS), 234
Packet switching, 236
Peer-to-peer, 239
Personal area networks (PANs), 257
Predictive search, 252
Protocol, 236
Radio frequency identification (RFID), 259
Router, 234
RSS, 254
Search engine marketing, 253
Search engine optimization (SEO), 253
Search engines, 250
Semantic search, 252
Shopping bots, 253
Smartphones, 256
Social networking, 255
Social search, 252
Software-defined networking (SDN), 234
Switch, 234
T1 lines, 240
Telnet, 245
Transmission Control Protocol/Internet Protocol (TCP/IP), 237
Unified communications, 247
Uniform resource locator (URL), 250
Virtual private network (VPN), 247
Visual web, 252
Voice over IP (VoIP), 246
Web 2.0, 254
Web 3.0, 255
Website, 249
Wide area networks (WANs), 239
Wi-Fi, 257
Wiki, 254
WiMax, 259
Wireless sensor networks (WSNs), 260

MyLab MIS

To complete the problems with **MyLab MIS**, go to the EOC Discussion Questions in MyLab MIS.

Review Questions

7-1 What are the principal components of telecommunications networks and key networking technologies?

- Describe the features of a simple network and the network infrastructure for a large company.
- Name and describe the principal technologies and trends that have shaped contemporary telecommunications systems.

7-2 What are the different types of networks?

- Define an analog and a digital signal.
- Distinguish between a LAN, MAN, and WAN.

7-3 How do the Internet and Internet technology work, and how do they support communication and e-business?

- Define the Internet, describe how it works, and explain how it provides business value.
- Explain how the Domain Name System (DNS) and IP addressing system work.
- List and describe the principal Internet services.
- Define and describe VoIP and virtual private networks and explain how they provide value to businesses.

- List and describe alternative ways of locating information on the web.
- Describe how online search technologies are used for marketing.

7-4 What are the principal technologies and standards for wireless networking, communications, and Internet access?
- Define Bluetooth, Wi-Fi, WiMax, and 3G and 4G networks.
- Describe the capabilities of each and for which types of applications each is best suited.
- Define RFID, explain how it works, and describe how it provides value to businesses.
- Define WSNs, explain how they work, and describe the kinds of applications that use them.

Discussion Questions

7-5 MyLab MIS It has been said that within the next few years, smartphones will become the single-most important digital device we own. Discuss the implications of this statement.

7-6 MyLab MIS Should all major retailing and manufacturing companies switch to RFID? Why or why not?

7-7 MyLab MIS What are some of the issues to consider in determining whether the Internet would provide your business with a competitive advantage?

Hands-On MIS Projects

The projects in this section give you hands-on experience evaluating and selecting communications technology, using spreadsheet software to improve selection of telecommunications services, and using web search engines for business research. Visit **MyLab MIS** to access this chapter's Hands-On MIS Projects.

MANAGEMENT DECISION PROBLEMS

7-8 Your company supplies ceramic floor tiles to Home Depot, Lowe's, and other home improvement stores. You have been asked to start using radio frequency identification tags on each case of tiles you ship to help your customers improve the management of your products and those of other suppliers in their warehouses. Use the web to identify the cost of hardware, software, and networking components for an RFID system for your company. What factors should be considered? What are the key decisions that have to be made in determining whether your firm should adopt this technology?

7-9 BestMed Medical Supplies Corporation sells medical and surgical products and equipment from more than 700 manufacturers to hospitals, health clinics, and medical offices. The company employs 500 people at seven locations in western and midwestern states, including account managers, customer service and support representatives, and warehouse staff. Employees communicate by traditional telephone voice services, email, instant messaging, and cell phones. Management is inquiring about whether the company should adopt a system for unified communications. What factors should be considered? What are the key decisions that must be made in determining whether to adopt this technology? Use the web, if necessary, to find out more about unified communications and its costs.

IMPROVING DECISION MAKING: USING SPREADSHEET SOFTWARE TO EVALUATE WIRELESS SERVICES

Software skills: Spreadsheet formulas, formatting
Business skills: Analyzing telecommunications services and costs

7-10 In this project, you'll use the web to research alternative wireless services and use spreadsheet software to calculate wireless service costs for a sales force.

You would like to equip your sales force of 35, based in St. Louis, Missouri, with mobile phones that have capabilities for voice transmission, text messaging, Internet access, and taking and sending photos. Use the web to select two wireless providers that offer nationwide voice and data service as well as good service in your home area. Examine the features of the mobile handsets and wireless plans offered by each of these vendors. Assume that each of the 35 salespeople will need to spend three hours per weekday between 8 a.m. and 6 p.m. on mobile voice communication, send 30 text messages per weekday, use 1 gigabyte of data per month, and send five photos per week. Use your spreadsheet software to determine the wireless service and handset that will offer the best pricing per user over a two-year period. For the purposes of this exercise, you do not need to consider corporate discounts.

ACHIEVING OPERATIONAL EXCELLENCE: USING WEB SEARCH ENGINES FOR BUSINESS RESEARCH

Software skills: Web search tools
Business skills: Researching new technologies

7-11 This project will help develop your Internet skills in using web search engines for business research.

Use Google and Bing to obtain information about ethanol as an alternative fuel for motor vehicles. If you wish, try some other search engines as well. Compare the volume and quality of information you find with each search tool. Which tool is the easiest to use? Which produced the best results for your research? Why?

Collaboration and Teamwork Project

Evaluating Smartphones

7-12 Form a group with three or four of your classmates. Compare the capabilities of Apple's iPhone with a smartphone from another vendor with similar features. Your analysis should consider the purchase cost of each device, the wireless networks where each device can operate, plan and handset costs, and the services available for each device. You should also consider other capabilities of each device, including available software, security features, and the ability to integrate with existing corporate or PC applications. Which device would you select? On what criteria would you base your selection? If possible, use Google Docs and Google Drive or Google Sites to brainstorm, organize, and develop a presentation of your findings for the class.

BUSINESS PROBLEM SOLVING CASE

Google, Apple, and Facebook Battle for Your Internet Experience

Three Internet titans—Google, Apple, and Facebook—are in an epic struggle to dominate your Internet experience, and caught in the crossfire are search, music, video, and other media along with the devices you use for all of these things. Mobile devices with advanced functionality and ubiquitous Internet access are rapidly overtaking traditional desktop machines as the most popular form of computing. Today, people spend more than half their time online using mobile devices that take advantage of a growing cloud of computing capacity. It's no surprise, then, that today's tech titans are aggressively battling for control of this brave new online world.

Apple, which started as a personal computer company, quickly expanded into software and consumer electronics. Since upending the music industry with its MP3 player, the iPod, and the iTunes digital music service, Apple took mobile computing by storm with the iPhone, iPod Touch, and iPad. Now Apple wants to be the computing platform of choice for the Internet.

Apple's competitive strength is based not on its hardware platform alone but on its superior user interface and mobile software applications, in which it is a leader. Apple's App Store offers more than 2 million apps for mobile and tablet devices. Applications greatly enrich the experience of using a mobile device, and whoever creates the most appealing set of devices and applications will derive a significant competitive advantage over rival companies. Apps are the new equivalent of the traditional browser.

Apple thrives on its legacy of innovation. In 2011, it unveiled the potentially market-disrupting Siri (Speech Interpretation and Recognition Interface), a combination search/navigation tool and personal assistant. Siri promises personalized recommendations that improve as it gains user familiarity—all from a verbal command. Google countered by quickly releasing its own AI tool, Google Now.

Apple faces strong competition for its phones and tablets both in the United States and in developing markets like China from inexpensive Chinese smartphones and from Samsung Android phones that have larger screens and lower prices. iPhone sales have started to slow, but Apple is not counting on hardware devices alone for future growth. Services have always played a large part in the Apple ecosystem, and they have emerged as a major revenue source. Apple has more than 1 billion active devices in circulation, creating a huge installed base of users willing to purchase services and a source of new revenue streams. Apple's services business, which includes the App Store, Apple Music, and Apple Pay, has been growing at a double-digit rate and delivered $7.04 billion in revenue in the first quarter of 2017 alone. According to CEO Tim Cook, Apple has become one of the largest service businesses in the world. This service-driven strategy is not without worry because both Google and Facebook offer stiff competition in the services area. Google continues to be the world's leading search engine, accounting for over three-quarters of the world's web searches. About 90 percent of Google's revenue comes from ads, most of that on its search engine. Google dominates online advertising. However, Google is slipping in its position as the gateway to the Internet. New search start-ups focus on actions and apps instead of the web. Apple has also become a mobile search competitor. Its iOS mobile operating system software gives iPhone and iPad users the ability use Apple's own search engine for searches of music, apps and local services, bypassing Google.

In 2005, Google had purchased the Android open source mobile operating system to compete in mobile computing. Google provides Android at no cost to smartphone manufacturers, generating revenue indirectly through app purchases and advertising. Many different manufacturers have adopted Android as a standard. In contrast, Apple allows only its own devices to use its proprietary operating system, and all the apps it sells can run only on Apple products. Android is deployed on over 80 percent of smartphones worldwide, is the most common operating system for tablets, and runs on watches, car dashboards, and TVs—more than 4,000 distinct devices. Google wants to extend Android to as many devices as possible.

Google's Android could gain even more market share in the coming years, which could be problematic for Apple as it tries to maintain customer loyalty and keep software developers focused on the iOS platform. Whoever has the dominant smartphone operating system will have control over the apps where smartphone users spend most of their time and built-in channels for serving ads to mobile devices.

In 2017 Google accounted for 94 percent of the mobile search market in the United States. Although Google search technology can't easily navigate the mobile apps where users are spending most of their time, Google is starting to index the content inside mobile apps and provide links pointing to that content featured in Google's search results on smartphones. Since more than half of global search queries come from mobile devices, the company revised its search algorithms to add "mobile friendliness" to the 200 or so factors it uses to rank websites on its search engine. This favors sites that look good on smartphone screens. The cost-per-click paid for mobile ads has trailed desktop ads, but the gap between computer and mobile ads fees is narrowing. Google instituted a design change to merge PC ads and mobile ads and present a cleaner mobile search page.

Seven Google products and services, including Search, YouTube and Maps, have more than a billion users each. The Android operating system software is installed on more than two billion devices. Google's ultimate goal is to knit its services and devices together so that Google users will interact with the company seamlessly all day long and everyone will want to use Google. Much of Google's efforts to make its search and related services more powerful and user-friendly in the years ahead are based on the company's investments in artificial intelligence and machine learning. These technologies already have been implemented in applications such as voice search, Google Translate, and spam filtering. The goal is to evolve search into more of a smart assistance capability, where computers can understand what people are saying and respond conversationally with the right information at the right moment. Allo is a smart messaging app for iOS and Android that can learn your texting patterns over time to make conversations more expressive and productive. It suggests automatic replies to incoming messages, and you can get suggestions and even book a restaurant reservation without leaving the chat. Google Assistant is meant to provide a continuing, conversational dialogue between users and the search engine.

Facebook is the world's largest social networking service, with 1.9 billion monthly users. People use Facebook to stay connected with their friends and family and to express what matters most to them. Facebook Platform enables developers to build applications and websites that integrate with Facebook to reach its global network of users and to build personalized and social products.

Facebook has persistently worked on ways to convert its popularity and trove of user data into advertising dollars, with the expectation that these dollars will increasingly come from mobile smartphones and tablets. As of mid-2017 Facebook had 1.74 billion mobile active users. Facebook ads allow companies to target its users based on their real identities and expressed interests rather than educated guesses derived from web-browsing habits and other online behavior.

At the end of the first quarter of 2017, 98 percent of Facebook's revenue came from advertising, and 84 percent of that ad revenue was from mobile advertising. Many of those ads are highly targeted by age, gender, and other demographics. Facebook is now a serious competitor to Google in the mobile ad market and is even trying to compete with emerging mobile platforms, having purchased Oculus VR Inc., a maker of virtual reality goggles, for $2 billion. Together, Facebook and Google dominate the digital ad industry and have been responsible for almost all of its growth.

In March 2013, Facebook overhauled its home page to increase the size of both photos and links and allow users to create topical streams. This move gives advertisers more opportunities and more information with which to target markets. A "personalized newspaper" with, for example, an op-ed feed featuring followed commentary pages, a sports section tailored to preferred events and teams, and a hometown news feed will enrich Facebook's user database. Facebook has its own personalized search tool to challenge Google's dominance of search.

Facebook CEO Mark Zuckerberg is convinced that social networking is the ideal way to use the web and to consume all of the other content people might desire, including news and video. That makes it an ideal marketing platform for companies. But he also knows that Facebook can't achieve long-term growth and prosperity based on social networking alone. During the past few years Facebook has moved into virtual reality, messaging, video, and more. Facebook is challenging YouTube as the premier destination for personal videos, developing its own TV programming, and making its messages "smarter" by deploying chatbots. Chatbots are stripped-down software agents that understand what you type or say and respond by answering questions or executing tasks, and they run in the background of Facebook's Messenger service. Within Facebook Messenger, you can order a ride from Uber, get news updates, or check your flight status. A new standalone app will allow users to stream videos in their news feed through set-top boxes such as Apple Inc.'s Apple TV and Amazon.com Inc.'s Fire TV as well as Samsung Internet-connected TVs. Zuckerberg has said that he intends to help bring the next billion people online by attracting users in developing countries with affordable web connectivity. Facebook has launched several services in emerging markets, such as the Free Basics service designed to get people online so they can explore web applications including its social network. Facebook wants to beam the Internet to underserved areas through the use of drones and satellites along with other technologies. Zuckerberg thinks that Facebook could eventually be an Internet service provider to underserved areas. If Facebook can match Google on this front and succeed in making itself synonymous with mobile access, the company could very well compete for global advertising dominance.

Sources: David Streitfeld, "Google Wants to Be Everywhere with Everyone," New York Times, May 17, 2017; Tim Bajarin, "Learning This 1 Thing Helped Me Understand Apple's Strategy," *Time*, April 3, 2017; Mathew Ingram, "How Google and Facebook Have Taken Over the Digital Ad Industry," *Fortune*, January 4, 2017; Deepa Seetharaman, "Facebook Announces Launch of Television App," *Wall Street Journal*, February 14, 2017; Tripp Mickle, "Apple Continues Its Comeback Campaign, but iPhone Worries Persist," *Wall Street Journal*, May 2, 2017; David Ingraham, "Facebook Nears Ad-Only Business Model as Game Revenue Falls," Reuters, May 5, 2017; Don Reisinger, "How Mark Zuckerberg Is Shaping the Future of Facebook, Social Media," *eWeek*, May 16, 2016; Robert McMillan, "Facebook Hopes Chatbots Can Solve App Overload," *Wall Street Journal*, April 17, 2016; Eric Emin Wood, "Is a Shift to Being a Service Provider in Apple's Future?" IT World Canada, May 5, 2016; Yoni Heisler, "Apple's Growth Strategy Is Hiding in Plain Sight," BGR.com, January 28, 2016; Alistair Barr, "Mobile Devices Upend Google Search," *Wall Street Journal*, February 25, 2016, and " How Google Aims to Delve Deeper into Users' Lives," *Wall Street Journal*, May 28, 2015.

CASE STUDY QUESTIONS

7-13 Compare the business models and core competencies of Google, Apple, and Facebook.

7-14 Why is mobile computing so important to these three firms? Evaluate the mobile strategies of each firm.

7-15 What is the significance of search to the success or failure of mobile computing? How have Apple and Facebook attempted to compete with Google? Will their strategies succeed?

7-16 Which company and business model do you think is most likely to dominate the Internet, and why?

7-17 What difference would it make to a business or to an individual consumer if Apple, Google, or Facebook dominated the Internet experience? Explain your answer.

MyLab MIS

Go to the Assignments section of MyLab MIS to complete these writing exercises.

7-18 Compare Web 2.0 and Web 3.0.

7-19 How do social search, semantic search, and mobile search differ from searching for information on the web by using conventional search engines?

Chapter 7 References

Allen, Robert. "Search Engine Statistics 2017." *Smart Insights* (April 13, 2017).

Alphabet, Inc. "Form 10K for the Fiscal Year Ending December 31, 2016." Securities and Exchange Commission, filed February 2, 2017.

Barr, Alistair. "Mobile Devices Upend Google Search." *Wall Street Journal* (February 25, 2016).

Chiang, I. Robert, and Jhih-Hua Jhang-Li. "Delivery Consolidation and Service Competition Among Internet Service Providers." *Journal of Management Information Systems* 34, No. 3 (Winter 2014).

Comscore. "The 2016 Mobile App Report." (2016).

Deichmann, Johannes, Matthias Roggendorf, and Dominik Wee. "Preparing IT Systems and Organizations for the Internet of Things." McKinsey & Company (2015).

Eliason, Andy. "23 Search Engine Facts and Stats You Oughta Know." SEO.com, accessed May 8, 2017.

eMarketer. "US Ad Spending: The eMarketer Forecast for 2017." (2017).

IBM Global Technology Services. "Software-Defined Networking in the New Business Frontier." (July 2015).

Iyer, Bala. "To Project the Trajectory of the Internet of Things, Look to the Software Industry." *Harvard Business Review* (February 25, 2016).

Manyika, James, Michael Chui, Peter Bisson, Jonathan Woetzel, Richard Dobbs, Jacques Bughin, and Dan Aharon. "Unlocking the Potential of the Internet of Things." McKinsey Global Institute (2015).

McKinsey & Company. "The Impact of Internet Technologies: Search." (July 2011).

National Telecommunications and Information Agency. "NTIA Announces Intent to Transition Key Internet Domain Name Functions." (March 14, 2014).

Panko, Raymond R., and Julia Panko. *Business Data Networks and Security* , 10th ed. (Upper Saddle River, NJ: Prentice-Hall, 2015).

Pew Research Center. "Mobile Fact Sheet." (January 12, 2017).

Reisinger, Don. "How Mark Zuckerberg Is Shaping the Future of Facebook, Social Media." *eWeek* (May 16, 2016).

Segan, Sascha. "What Is 5G?" *PC Magazine* (May 1, 2017).

Varian, Hal. "Executive Assistants for Everyone." *MIT Sloan Management Review* (Fall 2016).

Vincent, James. "99.6 Percent of New Smartphones Run Android or iOS." *The Verge* (February 16, 2017).

Wang, Weiquan, and Izak Benbasat. "Empirical Assessment of Alternative Designs for Enhancing Different Types of Trusting Beliefs in Online Recommendation Agents." *Journal of Management Information Systems* 33, No. 3 (2016).

CHAPTER

8 Securing Information Systems

LEARNING OBJECTIVES

After reading this chapter, you will be able to answer the following questions:

8-1 Why are information systems vulnerable to destruction, error, and abuse?

8-2 What is the business value of security and control?

8-3 What are the components of an organizational framework for security and control?

8-4 What are the most important tools and technologies for safeguarding information resources?

8-5 How will MIS help my career?

CHAPTER CASES

- Hackers Target the U.S. Presidential Election: What Happened?
- WannaCry and the SWIFT System Hacking Attacks: Theft on a Worldwide Scale
- How Secure Is BYOD?
- U.S. Office of Personnel Management Data Breach: No Routine Hack

VIDEO CASES

- Stuxnet and Cyberwarfare
- Cyberespionage: The Chinese Threat

Instructional Videos:

- Sony PlayStation Hacked; Data Stolen from 77 Million Users
- Meet the Hackers: Anonymous Statement on Hacking Sony

MyLab MIS

- Discussion Questions: 8-5, 8-6, 8-7;
- Hands-on MIS Projects: 8-8, 8-9, 8-10, 8-11;
- Writing Assignments: 8-17, 8-18;
- eText with Conceptual Animations

HACKERS TARGET THE U.S. PRESIDENTIAL ELECTION: WHAT HAPPENED?

In September 2015 Special Agent Adrian Hawkins of the U.S. Federal Bureau of Investigation (FBI) phoned the Democratic National Committee (DNC) with troubling news about its computer network: At least one DNC computer system had been penetrated by hackers linked to the Russian government. Yared Tamene, the DNC tech-support contractor who fielded the calls, conducted a cursory search of the DNC computer system logs to look for signs of hacking. He stated that he did not look too hard, even after Special Agent Hawkins called back and left messages repeatedly over the next several weeks, because he thought the call might be a prank call from an imposter.

The DNC hack was the first sign of a Russian-led cyberwarfare campaign to disrupt the 2016 presidential election. DNC chairwoman Debbie Wasserman Schultz was forced to resign, and a torrent of confidential documents from the DNC and the Clinton campaign were released by WikiLeaks to the press during the campaign. In a stunning upset, Donald Trump won the presidential election, and his victory may have been facilitated by revelations in the leaked documents.

Several Russian hacker groups associated with Russian intelligence were identified as the source of the cyberattacks. The Russian hackers had moved freely through the DNC network for nearly 7 months before top DNC officials were alerted to the attack and hired cybersecurity firm CrowdStrike to beef up their system protection. The DNC computer system was replaced, and all laptops were turned in and their hard drives wiped clean to get rid of infected information.

In the meantime, the hackers gained access to systems of the Clinton campaign. The hackers did not have to use any sophisticated tools to gain access and were able

to deploy phishing emails to trick legitimate system users into revealing passwords for accessing the system. Clinton campaign aide Charles Delavan clicked on an email sent to the personal account of campaign chairman John Podesta thinking it was legitimate and opened another door for the Russians. Whenever someone clicked on a phishing message, the Russians would enter the network, "exfiltrate" documents of interest, and stockpile them for intelligence purposes. By the summer of 2016, Democrats' private emails and confidential documents were posted on WikiLeaks and other websites day after day and reported by the media,

The DNC thought it was well protected against cyberattacks but only had a fraction of the security budget that a corporation its size would have. It had a standard email spam-filtering service for blocking phishing attacks and malware created to resemble legitimate email, but it did not have the most advanced systems in place to track suspicious traffic.

Hacking during the 2016 presidential election went beyond the DNC and the Clinton campaign. Russian hackers tried to infiltrate voter databases and software systems in 39 states, targeting software used by poll workers on Election Day, accessing a campaign finance database in at least one state, and trying to delete or alter voter data in Illinois. (Officials don't believe the attackers changed any result.)

It looks like Russian hacking is not going to stop. Two days before the French presidential election on May 7, 2017, hackers leaked 14.5 gigabytes of email, personal, and business documents from candidate Emmanuel Macron's campaign onto the web. Experts believe hackers will be targeting the September 2017 German federal election campaigns—and future U.S. elections—as well.

Sources: Harold Stark, "How Russia 'Hacked' Us in 2016 [And What We did Wrong]," Forbes, January 24, 2017; Sue Marquette Poremba, "Data Security Lessons from the DNC Hack," ITBusinessEdge, March 7, 2017; Mark Moore, "Russian Hackers Infiltrated Voter Databases in Dozens of States," New York Post, June 13, 2017; and Eric Lipton, David E. Sanger, and Scott Shane,"The Perfect Weapon: How Russian Cyberpower Invaded the U.S.," New York Times, December 13, 2016.

Efforts to disrupt the 2016 U.S presidential election and other recent elections illustrate some of the reasons why organizations need to pay special attention to information systems security IT security breaches that enabled Russian hackers to penetrate information systems used by the Democratic Party have the potential to change the course of elections—and possibly the fate of nations. Weak IT security has been responsible for many billions of dollars of corporate and consumer financial losses as well.

The chapter-opening diagram calls attention to important points raised by this case and this chapter. The DNC and the Clinton campaign lacked IT security awareness, tools, and expertise to prevent employees from naively responding to hackers' phishing attacks. Also at work were human ignorance, error, and carelessness, evidenced by the DNC's unwillingness to respond quickly to the FBI's hacker attack warning and DNC and Clinton campaign members' inability to identify bogus phishing emails. Although the DNC and the Clinton campaign thought they had sufficient security tools to fend off unwanted intruders, they were not enough to protect them and the presidential campaign from Russian influence. Eventually the Democrats hired outside security experts to beef up system protection.

We will probably never really know exactly how much revelations from the emails exposed by the hackers affected the 2016 election outcome. But we do know that what happened was very serious and most likely a preview of future electoral trouble around the world. Equally disturbing, the security vulnerabilities that facilitated the DNC and Clinton campaign hacks are commonplace in businesses and other organizations as well.

Here are some questions to think about: What security vulnerabilities were exploited by the hackers? What people, organizational, and technological factors contributed to these security weaknesses? What was the business impact of these problems? Could the election hacking have been prevented?

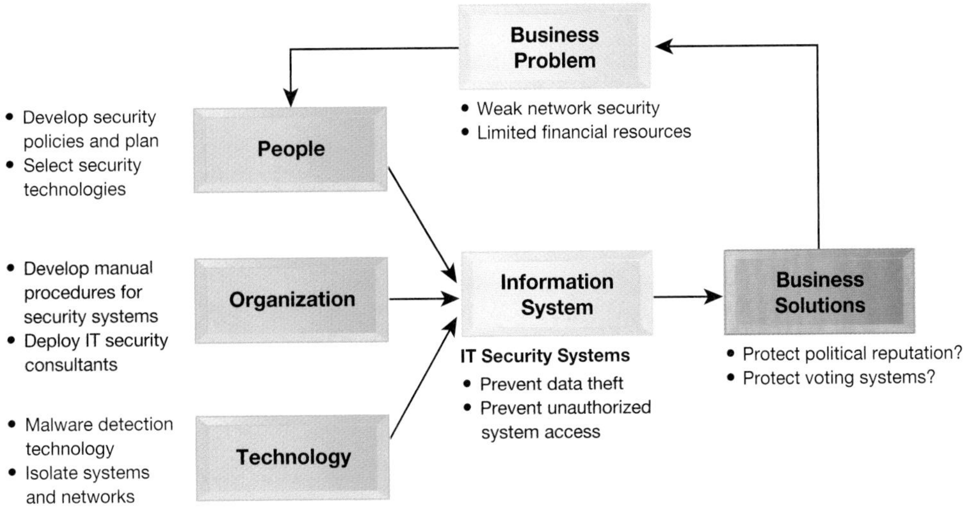

8-1 Why are information systems vulnerable to destruction, error, and abuse?

Can you imagine what would happen if you tried to link to the Internet without a firewall or antivirus software? Your computer would be disabled within a few seconds, and it might take you many days to recover. If you used the computer to run your business, you might not be able to sell to your customers or place orders with your suppliers while it was down. And you might find that your computer system had been penetrated by outsiders, who perhaps stole or destroyed valuable data, including confidential payment data from your customers. If too much data was destroyed or divulged, your business might never be able to recover!

In short, if you operate a business today, you need to make security and control a top priority. **Security** refers to the policies, procedures, and technical measures used to prevent unauthorized access, alteration, theft, or physical damage to information systems. **Controls** are methods, policies, and organizational procedures that ensure the safety of the organization's assets, the accuracy and reliability of its records, and operational adherence to management standards.

WHY SYSTEMS ARE VULNERABLE

When large amounts of data are stored in electronic form, they are vulnerable to many kinds of threats. Through communications networks, information systems in different locations are interconnected. The potential for unauthorized access or damage is not limited to a single location but can occur at many access points in the network. Figure 8.1 illustrates the most common threats against contemporary information systems. They can stem from technical, organizational, and environmental factors compounded by poor management decisions. In the multitier client/server computing environment illustrated here, vulnerabilities exist at each layer and in the communications between the layers. Users at the client layer can cause harm by introducing errors or by accessing systems without authorization. It is possible to access data flowing over networks, steal valuable data during transmission, or alter data without authorization. Radiation may disrupt a network at various points as well. Intruders can launch denial-of-service attacks or malicious software to disrupt the operation of websites. Those capable of penetrating corporate systems can steal, destroy, or alter corporate data stored in databases or files.

Systems malfunction if computer hardware breaks down, is not configured properly, or is damaged by improper use or criminal acts. Errors in programming, improper

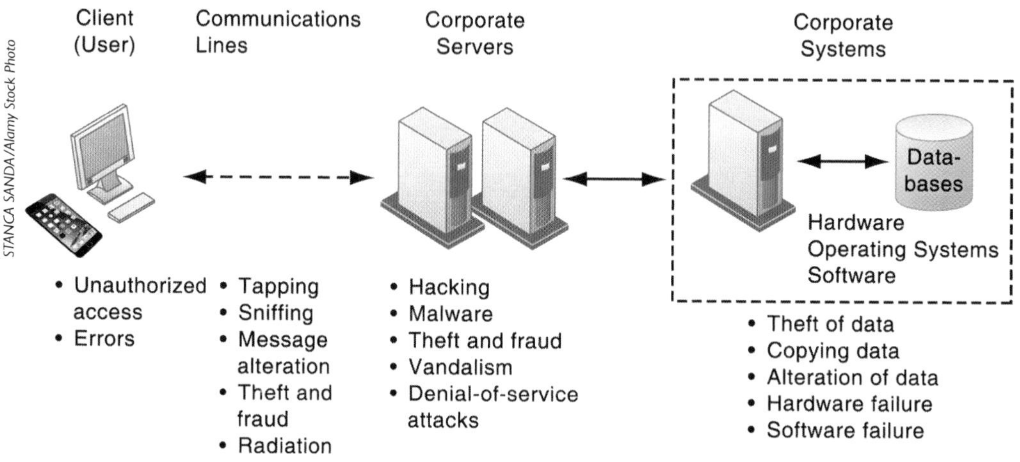

Figure 8.1 Contemporary Security Challenges and Vulnerabilities
The architecture of a web-based application typically includes a web client, a server, and corporate information systems linked to databases. Each of these components presents security challenges and vulnerabilities. Floods, fires, power failures, and other electrical problems can cause disruptions at any point in the network.

installation, or unauthorized changes cause computer software to fail. Power failures, floods, fires, or other natural disasters can also disrupt computer systems.

Domestic or offshore partnering with another company contributes to system vulnerability if valuable information resides on networks and computers outside the organization's control. Without strong safeguards, valuable data could be lost, be destroyed, or fall into the wrong hands, revealing important trade secrets or information that violates personal privacy.

The popularity of handheld mobile devices for business computing adds to these woes. Portability makes cell phones, smartphones, and tablet computers easy to lose or steal. Smartphones share the same security weaknesses as other Internet devices and are vulnerable to malicious software and penetration from outsiders. Smartphones that corporate employees use often contain sensitive data such as sales figures, customer names, phone numbers, and email addresses. Intruders may also be able to access internal corporate systems through these devices

Internet Vulnerabilities

Large public networks, such as the Internet, are more vulnerable than internal networks because they are virtually open to anyone. The Internet is so huge that when abuses do occur, they can have an enormously widespread impact. When the Internet becomes part of the corporate network, the organization's information systems are even more vulnerable to actions from outsiders.

Vulnerability has also increased from widespread use of email, instant messaging (IM), and peer-to-peer (P2P) file-sharing programs. Email may contain attachments that serve as springboards for malicious software or unauthorized access to internal corporate systems. Employees may use email messages to transmit valuable trade secrets, financial data, or confidential customer information to unauthorized recipients. Popular IM applications for consumers do not use a secure layer for text messages, so they can be intercepted and read by outsiders during transmission over the Internet. Instant messaging activity over the Internet can in some cases be used as a back door to an otherwise secure network. Sharing files over P2P networks, such as those for illegal music sharing, may also transmit malicious software or expose information on either individual or corporate computers to outsiders.

Wireless Security Challenges

Both Bluetooth and Wi-Fi networks are susceptible to hacking by eavesdroppers. Local area networks (LANs) using the 802.11 standard can be easily penetrated by outsiders armed with laptops, wireless cards, external antennae, and hacking software. Hackers use these tools to detect unprotected networks, monitor network traffic, and, in some cases, gain access to the Internet or to corporate networks.

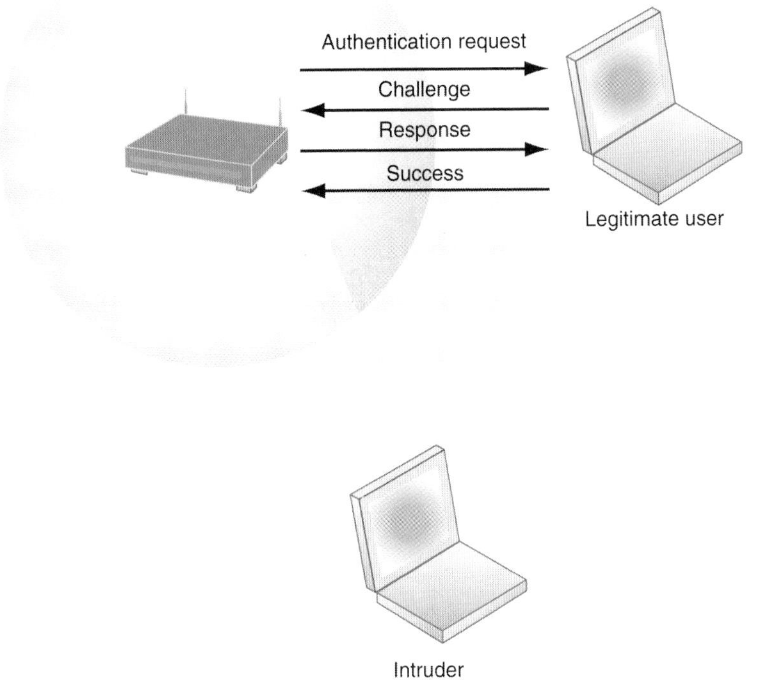

Figure 8.2
Wi-Fi Security Challenges
Many Wi-Fi networks can be penetrated easily by intruders using sniffer programs to obtain an address to access the resources of a network without authorization.

Wi-Fi transmission technology was designed to make it easy for stations to find and hear one another. The service set identifiers (SSIDs) that identify the access points in a Wi-Fi network are broadcast multiple times and can be picked up fairly easily by intruders' sniffer programs (see Figure 8.2). Wireless networks in many locations do not have basic protections against **war driving**, in which eavesdroppers drive by buildings or park outside and try to intercept wireless network traffic.

An intruder who has associated with an access point by using the correct SSID is capable of accessing other resources on the network. For example, the intruder could use the Windows operating system to determine which other users are connected to the network, access their computer hard drives, and open or copy their files.

Intruders also use the information they have gleaned to set up rogue access points on a different radio channel in physical locations close to users to force a user's radio network interface controller (NIC) to associate with the rogue access point. Once this association occurs, hackers using the rogue access point can capture the names and passwords of unsuspecting users.

MALICIOUS SOFTWARE: VIRUSES, WORMS, TROJAN HORSES, AND SPYWARE

Malicious software programs are referred to as **malware** and include a variety of threats such as computer viruses, worms, and Trojan horses. (See Table 8.1.) A **computer virus** is a rogue software program that attaches itself to other software programs or data files to be executed, usually without user knowledge or permission. Most computer viruses deliver a payload. The payload may be relatively benign, such as instructions to display a message or image, or it may be highly destructive—destroying programs or data, clogging computer memory, reformatting a computer's hard drive, or causing programs to run improperly. Viruses typically spread from computer to computer when humans take an action, such as sending an email attachment or copying an infected file.

TABLE 8.1

Examples of Malicious Code

Name	Type	Description
Cryp-tolocker	Ransomware/ Trojan	Hijacks users' photos, videos, and text documents; encrypts them with virtually unbreakable asymmetric encryption; and demands ransom payment for them.
Conficker	Worm	First detected in November 2008 and still a problem. Uses flaws in Windows software to take over machines and link them into a virtual computer that can be commanded remotely. Had more than 5 million computers worldwide under its control. Difficult to eradicate.
Sasser.ftp	Worm	First appeared in May 2004. Spread over the Internet by attacking random IP addresses. Causes computers to continually crash and reboot and infected computers to search for more victims. Affected millions of computers worldwide and caused an estimated $14.8 billion to $18.6 billion in damages.
ILOVEYOU	Virus	First detected on May 3, 2000. Script virus written in Visual Basic script and transmitted as an attachment to email with the subject line ILOVEYOU. Overwrites music, image, and other files with a copy of itself and did an estimated $10 billion to $15 billion in damage.

Most recent attacks have come from **worms**, which are independent computer programs that copy themselves from one computer to other computers over a network. Unlike viruses, worms can operate on their own without attaching to other computer program files and rely less on human behavior to spread from computer to computer. This explains why computer worms spread much more rapidly than computer viruses. Worms destroy data and programs as well as disrupt or even halt the operation of computer networks.

Worms and viruses are often spread over the Internet from files of downloaded software; from files attached to email transmissions; or from compromised email messages, online ads, or instant messaging. Viruses have also invaded computerized information systems from infected external storage devices or infected machines. Especially prevalent today are **drive-by downloads**, consisting of malware that comes with a downloaded file that a user intentionally or unintentionally requests.

Hackers can do to a smartphone just about anything they can do to any Internet-connected device: request malicious files without user intervention, delete files, transmit files, install programs running in the background to monitor user actions, and potentially convert the smartphone to a robot in a botnet to send email and text messages to anyone. According to IT security experts, mobile devices now pose the greatest security risks, outpacing those from larger computers. Kaspersky Lab reported that it had detected 8.5 million mobile malicious installation packages in 2016 (Kaspersky Lab, 2017),

Android, which is the world's leading mobile operating system, is the platform targeted by most hackers. Mobile device viruses pose serious threats to enterprise computing because so many wireless devices are now linked to corporate information systems (see the Interactive Session on Organizations in Section 8-4).

Blogs, wikis, and social networking sites such as Facebook, Twitter, and LinkedIn have emerged as new conduits for malware. Members are more likely to trust messages they receive from friends, even if this communication is not legitimate. For example, malware infected thousands of Facebook users worldwide in June 2016 by sending them a notification in the messenger app and/or in their email about a friend tagging in a comment. Upon clicking the link, the malware was downloaded on their device. The malware took control of users' Facebook accounts and sent malicious notifications to all of their Facebook friends (Amir, 2016).

The Internet of Things (IoT) introduces additional security challenges from the Internet-linked devices themselves, their platforms and operating systems, their communications, and even the systems to which they're connected. New security tools will be required to protect IoT devices and platforms from both information attacks and physical tampering, to encrypt their communications, and to address new challenges such as attacks that drain batteries. Many IoT devices such as sensors have simple processors and operating systems that may not support sophisticated security approaches.

Panda Security reported that it had identified and neutralized more than 20 million new malware samples in the fourth quarter of 2016 alone and that it had detected 200,000 new malware samples each day (Panda Security, 2016).

Many malware infections are Trojan horses. A **Trojan horse** is a software program that appears to be benign but then does something other than expected. The Trojan horse is not itself a virus because it does not replicate, but it is often a way for viruses or other malicious code to be introduced into a computer system. The term *Trojan horse* is based on the huge wooden horse the Greeks used to trick the Trojans into opening the gates to their fortified city during the Trojan War. Once inside the city walls, Greek soldiers hidden in the horse revealed themselves and captured the city.

An example of a modern-day Trojan horse is the Zeus Trojan. It is often used to steal login credentials for banking by surreptitiously capturing people's keystrokes as they use their computers. Zeus is spread mainly through drive-by downloads and phishing, and recent variants are hard for anti-malware tools to detect.

SQL injection attacks have become a major malware threat. SQL injection attacks take advantage of vulnerabilities in poorly coded web application software to introduce malicious program code into a company's systems and networks. These vulnerabilities occur when a web application fails to validate properly or filter data a user enters on a web page, which might occur when ordering something online. An attacker uses this input validation error to send a rogue SQL query to the underlying database to access the database, plant malicious code, or access other systems on the network. Large web applications have hundreds of places for inputting user data, each of which creates an opportunity for an SQL injection attack.

Malware known as **ransomware** is proliferating on both desktop and mobile devices. Ransomware tries to extort money from users by taking control of their computers, blocking access to files, or displaying annoying pop-up messages. The Interactive Session on Technology describes WannaCry, which encrypts an infected computer's files, forcing users to pay hundreds of dollars to regain access. You can get ransomware from downloading an infected attachment, clicking a link inside an email, or visiting the wrong website.

Some types of **spyware** also act as malicious software. These small programs install themselves surreptitiously on computers to monitor user web-surfing activity and serve up advertising. Thousands of forms of spyware have been documented.

Many users find such spyware annoying, and some critics worry about its infringement on computer users' privacy. Some forms of spyware are especially nefarious. **Keyloggers** record every keystroke made on a computer to steal serial numbers for software, to launch Internet attacks, to gain access to email accounts, to obtain passwords to protected computer systems, or to pick up personal information such as credit card or bank account numbers. The Zeus Trojan described earlier uses keylogging. Other spyware programs reset web browser home pages, redirect search requests, or slow performance by taking up too much computer resources.

HACKERS AND COMPUTER CRIME

A **hacker** is an individual who intends to gain unauthorized access to a computer system. Within the hacking community, the term *cracker* is typically used to denote a hacker with criminal intent, although in the public press, the terms *hacker* and

INTERACTIVE SESSION: TECHNOLOGY

WannaCry and the SWIFT System Hacking Attacks: Theft on a Worldwide Scale

On Friday, May 12, 2017, the world experienced its largest ransomware attack, known as WannaCry. Within a day, WannaCry had infected more than 230,000 computers in more than 150 countries. Parts of Britain's National Health Service (NHS), Spain's Telefónica, FedEx, and Deutsche Bahn (Germany's main rail system) were hit, along with many other organizations. The attack caused Britain's NHS to cancel surgeries, crippled a wide array of Russian and Chinese private and public institutions, and sent shock waves throughout the rest of the world.

The attack was the work of the WannaCry ransomware cryptoworm, which targeted computers running the Microsoft Windows operating system by encrypting data and demanding ransom payments in the Bitcoin cryptocurrency (described later in this chapter) to decrypt. The ransom amounted to 1781 bitcoins or about US$300. WannaCry used a Windows flaw to replicate itself and spread around a computer network. Global financial and economic losses from the ransomware attack could reach billions of dollars, much of that due to reduced productivity and efforts to mitigate the damage.

The U.S. National Security Agency (NSA) already knew about this Windows vulnerability, but instead of reporting it to Microsoft, it used this knowledge for its own purposes. Microsoft did not learn about the malware until it was revealed by the Shadow Brokers hacker group. On March 14, 2017, Microsoft issued a critical security patch to remove the underlying vulnerability on supported versions of Windows. However, at the time the WannaCry attacks began, many organizations had still not yet applied the patch. Those running Windows 7 and older, unsupported versions of Microsoft Windows, such as Windows XP and Windows Server 2003, were especially at risk. Microsoft subsequently released an emergency security patch for these platforms as well. Within four days of the initial outbreak, most organizations had applied updates, and new infections had slowed to a trickle. However, WannaCry is still active and capable of infecting organizations that have not made the necessary security upgrades.

Prominent cybersecurity companies Symantec and Kaspersky Lab both observed that the WannaCry code has some similarities with that previously used by the Lazarus Group linked to North Korea, which was believed to have carried out the cyberattack on Sony Pictures in 2014 and attacks on the SWIFT global banking network. North Korea itself denies being responsible for either cyberattack.

SWIFT, which stands for "Society for Worldwide Interbank Financial Telecommunication," is a system used by more than 11,000 financial institutions worldwide to authorize payments from one account to another. SWIFT's secure messaging system sends about 25 million messages on a typical day, including orders and confirmations for payments, securities settlements, and currency exchanges. Obviously, this is a very important system for global finance.

SWIFT has been a highly secure system, but not secure enough. In early 2016 there were multiple attempts to use SWIFT messaging to rob financial institutions. Bangladesh's central bank disclosed that in February 2016 it had lost $81 million to hackers who breached its security, accessed SWIFT, and tricked the Federal Reserve Bank of New York into sending funds it held for the bank to hacker-controlled accounts in the Philippines.

Hackers somehow managed to steal the Bangladesh bank's credentials to transmit the messages and used malware targeting a PDF reader for checking statements. SWIFT's core messaging system was not compromised. Security breaches occurred in the computers of individual institutions that interact with the system, and these computers remain the responsibility of individual SWIFT members. The hackers had access only to the compromised banks' funds but not to the funds of the thousands of other institutions that use SWIFT. However, investigators have identified breaches at 12 other banks, including Vietnam's Tien Phong Commercial Joint Stock Bank and Ecuador's Banco del Austro.

SWIFT is overseen by the National Bank of Belgium and representatives from the U.S. Federal Reserve, the Bank of England, the European Central Bank, the Bank of Japan, and other major banks. The system is based on flexibility and trust. A bank can choose to let employees access SWIFT's main interface right from their desktop browser. That same feature that makes SWIFT easy to use also makes the system susceptible to hacking. Hackers apparently were able to obtain the banks' SWIFT access codes, send authenticated but fraudulent requests to transfer funds, and cover their tracks with malware surreptitiously placed onto bank computer systems. These attacks showed a deep and sophisticated knowledge of specific controls at the targeted banks, which may have been acquired from insiders, cyberattacks, or both.

Most banks in the United States take special precautions with their SWIFT-linked computers, including multiple firewalls to isolate SWIFT from the bank's other networks and even operating the machines in separate locked rooms. Unfortunately some banks in other countries take fewer precautions. The Bangladesh bank may have been especially vulnerable, according to experts.

SWIFT plans to toughen system user authentication requirements, monitor compliance more rigorously, and provide more information about fraud detection. Ultimately, however, SWIFT can only do so much. The real solution must come from the participating banks themselves. Fully armoring the network's defenses is likely to take years.

Sources: Stu Woo and Robert McMillan, "Cybersecurity Experts Try to Understand How Ransomware Invaded Networks," *Wall Street Journal*, May 15, 2017; Russell Goldman, "What We Know and Don't Know About the International Cyberattack," *New York Times*, May 13, 2017; Nicole Perlroth and David E. Sanger, "In Computer Attacks, Clues Point to Frequent Culprit: North Korea," *New York Times*, May 15, 2017; Michael Corkery, "Hackers' $81 Million Sneak Attack on World Banking," *New York Times*, April 30, 2016; Katy Burne, Robin Sidel, and Syed Zain Al-Mahmood, "Swift Banking Network Struggles with Wave of Cyberattacks," *Wall Street Journal*, May 20, 2016; "What a Bank Heist Reveals About Global Security," *Bloomberg View*, May 31, 2016; John Detrixhe, Gavin Finch, and John Follain, "Swift CEO Expects More Hacking Surprises as Fix Is Years Away," *Bloomberg Business Week*, June 2, 2016.

CASE STUDY QUESTIONS

1. Compare the WannaCry and SWIFT system hacking attacks. What security vulnerabilities were exploited in each of these attacks?
2. What people, organization, and technology factors contributed to these security weaknesses?
3. How could these attacks have been prevented?
4. What was the business and social impact of these attacks?

cracker are used interchangeably. Hackers gain unauthorized access by finding weaknesses in the security protections websites and computer systems employ. Hacker activities have broadened beyond mere system intrusion to include theft of goods and information as well as system damage and **cybervandalism**, the intentional disruption, defacement, or even destruction of a website or corporate information system.

Spoofing and Sniffing

Hackers attempting to hide their true identities often spoof, or misrepresent, themselves by using fake email addresses or masquerading as someone else. **Spoofing** may also involve redirecting a web link to an address different from the intended one, with the site masquerading as the intended destination. For example, if hackers redirect customers to a fake website that looks almost exactly like the true site, they can then collect and process orders, effectively stealing business as well as sensitive customer information from the true site. We will provide more detail about other forms of spoofing in our discussion of computer crime.

A **sniffer** is a type of eavesdropping program that monitors information traveling over a network. When used legitimately, sniffers help identify potential network trouble spots or criminal activity on networks, but when used for criminal purposes, they can be damaging and very difficult to detect. Sniffers enable hackers to steal proprietary information from anywhere on a network, including email messages, company files, and confidential reports.

Denial-of-Service Attacks

In a **denial-of-service (DoS) attack**, hackers flood a network server or web server with many thousands of false communications or requests for services to crash the network. The network receives so many queries that it cannot keep up with them and is thus unavailable to service legitimate requests. A **distributed denial-of-service (DDoS)** attack uses numerous computers to inundate and overwhelm the network from numerous launch points.

Although DoS attacks do not destroy information or access restricted areas of a company's information systems, they often cause a website to shut down, making it impossible for legitimate users to access the site For busy e-commerce sites, these attacks are costly; while the site is shut down, customers cannot make purchases. Especially vulnerable are small and midsize businesses whose networks tend to be less protected than those of large corporations.

Perpetrators of DDoS attacks often use thousands of zombie PCs infected with malicious software without their owners' knowledge and organized into a **botnet**. Hackers create these botnets by infecting other people's computers with bot malware that opens a back door through which an attacker can give instructions. The infected computer then becomes a slave, or zombie, serving a master computer belonging to someone else. When hackers infect enough computers, they can use the amassed resources of the botnet to launch DDoS attacks, phishing campaigns, or unsolicited spam email.

Ninety percent of the world's spam and 80 percent of the world's malware are delivered by botnets. A recent example is the Mirai botnet, which infected numerous IoT devices (such as Internet-connected surveillance cameras) in October 2016 and then used them to launch a DDoS attack against Dyn, whose servers monitor and reroute Internet traffic. The Mirai botnet overwhelmed the Dyn servers, taking down Etsy, GitHub, Netflix, Shopify, SoundCloud, Spotify, Twitter, and a number of other major websites. The botnet took advantage of devices running out-of-date versions of Linux and relied on the fact that most users do not change default passwords on their devices.

Computer Crime

Most hacker activities are criminal offenses, and the vulnerabilities of systems we have just described make them targets for other types of **computer crime** as well. Computer crime is defined by the U.S. Department of Justice as "any violations of criminal law that involve a knowledge of computer technology for their perpetration, investigation, or prosecution." Table 8.2 provides examples of the computer as both a target and an instrument of crime. The Interactive Session on Technology describes one of the largest financial computer crime cases reported to date.

No one knows the magnitude of the computer crime problem—how many systems are invaded, how many people engage in the practice, or the total economic damage. According to the Ponemon Institute's 2016 Annual Cost of Cyber Crime Study, the average annualized cost of cybercrime for benchmarked companies in six different countries was $9 million (Ponemon Institute, 2016a). Many companies are reluctant to report computer crimes because the crimes may involve employees or the company fears that publicizing its vulnerability will hurt its reputation. The most economically damaging kinds of computer crime are DoS attacks, activities of malicious insiders, and web-based attacks.

Identity Theft

With the growth of the Internet and electronic commerce, identity theft has become especially troubling. **Identity theft** is a crime in which an imposter obtains key pieces of personal information, such as social security numbers, driver's license numbers, or credit card numbers, to impersonate someone else. The information may be used to obtain credit, merchandise, or services in the name of the victim or to provide the thief with false credentials. Identity theft has flourished on the Internet, with credit card files a major target of website hackers. According to the 2017 Identity Fraud Study by Javelin Strategy & Research, identity fraud affected 6.15 percent of U.S. consumers in 2016, and they lost $16 billion to identity fraud that year (Javelin, 2017).

TABLE 8.2

Examples of Computer Crime

Computers as Targets of Crime
Breaching the confidentiality of protected computerized data
Accessing a computer system without authority
Knowingly accessing a protected computer to commit fraud
Intentionally accessing a protected computer and causing damage negligently or deliberately
Knowingly transmitting a program, program code, or command that intentionally causes damage to a protected computer
Threatening to cause damage to a protected computer
Computers as Instruments of Crime
Theft of trade secrets
Unauthorized copying of software or copyrighted intellectual property, such as articles, books, music, and video
Schemes to defraud
Using email or messaging for threats or harassment
Intentionally attempting to intercept electronic communication
Illegally accessing stored electronic communications, including email and voice mail
Transmitting or possessing child pornography by using a computer

One increasingly popular tactic is a form of spoofing called **phishing**. Phishing involves setting up fake websites or sending email messages that look like those of legitimate businesses to ask users for confidential personal data. The email message instructs recipients to update or confirm records by providing social security numbers, bank and credit card information, and other confidential data either by responding to the email message, by entering the information at a bogus website, or by calling a telephone number. eBay, PayPal, Amazon.com, Walmart, and a variety of banks have been among the top spoofed companies. In a more targeted form of phishing called *spear phishing*, messages appear to come from a trusted source, such as an individual within the recipient's own company or a friend.

Phishing techniques called evil twins and pharming are harder to detect. **Evil twins** are wireless networks that pretend to offer trustworthy Wi-Fi connections to the Internet, such as those in airport lounges, hotels, or coffee shops. The bogus network looks identical to a legitimate public network. Fraudsters try to capture passwords or credit card numbers of unwitting users who log on to the network.

Pharming redirects users to a bogus web page, even when the individual types the correct web page address into his or her browser. This is possible if pharming perpetrators gain access to the Internet address information Internet service providers (ISPs) store to speed up web browsing and the ISP companies have flawed software on their servers that allows the fraudsters to hack in and change those addresses.

According to the Ponemon Institute's 2016 Cost of a Data Breach Study, the average cost of a data breach to the 383 companies it surveyed was $4 million (Ponemon, 2016b). Moreover, brand damage can be significant although hard to quantify. In addition to the data breaches described in case studies for this chapter, Table 8.3 describes other major data breaches.

The U.S. Congress addressed the threat of computer crime in 1986 with the Computer Fraud and Abuse Act, which makes it illegal to access a computer system without authorization. Most states have similar laws, and nations in Europe have

TABLE 8.3

Major Data Breaches

Data Breach	Description
Yahoo	In September and December 2016 Yahoo disclosed that it had been the target of two of the biggest data breaches ever, with sensitive information stolen involving more than 1 billion user accounts in 2013 and 500 million in 2014. State-sponsored hackers found a way to forge credentials to log into some users' accounts without a password. These data breaches forced Yahoo to lower its selling price by $300 million when it was acquired by Verizon in June 2017.
Anthem Health Insurance	In February 2015 hackers stole the personal information on more than 80 million customers of the giant health insurer, including names, birthdays, medical IDs, social security numbers, and income data. No medical or credit information was stolen. This was the largest healthcare breach ever recorded.
Sony	In November 2014 hackers stole more than 100 terabytes of corporate data, including trade secrets, email, personnel records, and copies of films for future release. Malware erased data from Sony's corporate systems, leading to hundreds of millions of dollars in losses as well as a tarnished brand image. Sony was hacked earlier in April 2011 when intruders obtained personal information, including credit, debit, and bank account numbers, from more than 100 million PlayStation Network users and Sony Online Entertainment users.
Home Depot	Hacked in 2014 with a malicious software program that plundered store registers while disguising itself as antivirus software. Fifty-six million credit card accounts were compromised, and 53 million customer email addresses were stolen.
eBay	Cyberattack on eBay servers during February and March 2014 compromised database containing customer names, encrypted passwords, email addresses, physical addresses, phone numbers, and birthdates; 145 million people were affected.

comparable legislation. Congress passed the National Information Infrastructure Protection Act in 1996 to make malware distribution and hacker attacks to disable websites federal crimes.

U.S. legislation, such as the Wiretap Act, Wire Fraud Act, Economic Espionage Act, Electronic Communications Privacy Act, CAN-SPAM Act, and Protect Act of 2003 (prohibiting child pornography), covers computer crimes involving intercepting electronic communication, using electronic communication to defraud, stealing trade secrets, illegally accessing stored electronic communications, using email for threats or harassment, and transmitting or possessing child pornography. A proposed federal Data Security and Breach Notification Act would mandate organizations that possess personal information to put in place "reasonable" security procedures to keep the data secure and notify anyone affected by a data breach, but it has not been enacted.

Click Fraud

When you click an ad displayed by a search engine, the advertiser typically pays a fee for each click, which is supposed to direct potential buyers to its products. **Click fraud** occurs when an individual or computer program fraudulently clicks an online ad without any intention of learning more about the advertiser or making a purchase. Click fraud has become a serious problem at Google and other websites that feature pay-per-click online advertising.

Some companies hire third parties (typically from low-wage countries) to click a competitor's ads fraudulently to weaken them by driving up their marketing costs. Click fraud can also be perpetrated with software programs doing the clicking, and botnets are often used for this purpose. Search engines such as Google attempt to monitor click fraud and have made some changes to curb it.

Global Threats: Cyberterrorism and Cyberwarfare

The cyber criminal activities we have described—launching malware, DoS attacks, and phishing probes—are borderless. Attack servers for malware are now hosted in more than 200 countries and territories. The leading sources of malware attacks include the United States, Netherlands, Germany, Russia, France, and China. The global nature of the Internet makes it possible for cybercriminals to operate—and to do harm—anywhere in the world.

Internet vulnerabilities have also turned individuals and even entire nation-states into easy targets for politically motivated hacking to conduct sabotage and espionage. **Cyberwarfare** is a state-sponsored activity designed to cripple and defeat another state or nation by penetrating its computers or networks to cause damage and disruption. One example is the efforts of Russian hackers to disrupt the U.S. 2016 presidential election described in the chapter-opening case. Cyberwarfare also includes defending against these types of attacks.

Cyberwarfare is more complex than conventional warfare. Although many potential targets are military, a country's power grids, financial systems, communications networks, and even voting systems can also be crippled. Non-state actors such as terrorists or criminal groups can mount attacks, and it is often difficult to tell who is responsible. Nations must constantly be on the alert for new malware and other technologies that could be used against them, and some of these technologies developed by skilled hacker groups are openly for sale to interested governments.

Preparations for cyberwarfare attacks have become much more widespread, sophisticated, and potentially devastating. Between 2011 and 2015, foreign hackers stole source code and blueprints to the oil and water pipelines and power grid of the United States and infiltrated the Department of Energy's networks 150 times (Perlroth, 2015). Over the years, hackers have stolen plans for missile tracking systems, satellite navigation devices, surveillance drones, and leading-edge jet fighters.

A 2015 report documented 29 countries with formal military and intelligence units dedicated to offensive cyberwarfare. Their cyberarsenals include collections of malware for penetrating industrial, military, and critical civilian infrastructure controllers, email lists and text for phishing attacks on important targets, and algorithms for DoS attacks. U.S. cyberwarfare efforts are concentrated in the United States Cyber Command, which coordinates and directs the operations and defense of Department of Defense information networks and prepares for military cyberspace operations. Cyberwarfare poses a serious threat to the infrastructure of modern societies, since their major financial, health, government, and industrial institutions rely on the Internet for daily operations.

INTERNAL THREATS: EMPLOYEES

We tend to think the security threats to a business originate outside the organization. In fact, company insiders pose serious security problems. Employees have access to privileged information, and in the presence of sloppy internal security procedures, they are often able to roam throughout an organization's systems without leaving a trace.

Studies have found that user lack of knowledge is the single greatest cause of network security breaches. Many employees forget their passwords to access computer systems or allow coworkers to use them, which compromises the system. Malicious intruders seeking system access sometimes trick employees into revealing their passwords by pretending to be legitimate members of the company in need of information. This practice is called **social engineering**, and the chapter-opening case shows how it was used to gain access to the Clinton campaign system.

Both end users and information systems specialists are also a major source of errors introduced into information systems. End users introduce errors by entering faulty data or by not following the proper instructions for processing data and using computer equipment. Information systems specialists may create software errors as they design and develop new software or maintain existing programs.

SOFTWARE VULNERABILITY

Software errors pose a constant threat to information systems, causing untold losses in productivity and sometimes endangering people who use or depend on systems. Growing complexity and size of software programs, coupled with demands for timely delivery to markets, have contributed to an increase in software flaws or vulnerabilities. For example, in February 2017 Cloudflare, a service provider that helps optimize website performance and security, reported that it had just fixed a software defect that had leaked sensitive data for months. The data included user passwords, cookies, and other authentication data. Although the amount of data leaked appeared to be small, the bug could have affected any of Cloudflare's 5.5 million customers (McMillan, 2017).

A major problem with software is the presence of hidden **bugs** or program code defects. Studies have shown that it is virtually impossible to eliminate all bugs from large programs. The main source of bugs is the complexity of decision-making code. A relatively small program of several hundred lines will contain tens of decisions leading to hundreds or even thousands of paths. Important programs within most corporations are usually much larger, containing tens of thousands or even millions of lines of code, each with many times the choices and paths of the smaller programs.

Zero defects cannot be achieved in larger programs. Complete testing simply is not possible. Fully testing programs that contain thousands of choices and millions of paths would require thousands of years. Even with rigorous testing, you would not know for sure that a piece of software was dependable until the product proved itself after much operational use.

Flaws in commercial software not only impede performance but also create security vulnerabilities that open networks to intruders. Each year security firms identify thousands of software vulnerabilities in Internet and PC software. A recent example is the Heartbleed bug, which is a flaw in OpenSSL, an open-source encryption technology that an estimated two-thirds of web servers use. Hackers could exploit the bug to access visitors' personal data as well as a site's encryption keys, which can be used to collect even more protected data.

Especially troublesome are **zero-day vulnerabilities**, which are holes in the software unknown to its creator. Hackers then exploit this security hole before the vendor becomes aware of the problem and hurries to fix it. This type of vulnerability is called *zero-day* because the author of the software has zero days after learning about it to patch the code before it can be exploited in an attack. Sometimes security researchers spot the software holes, but more often, they remain undetected until an attack has occurred.

To correct software flaws once they are identified, the software vendor creates small pieces of software called **patches** to repair the flaws without disturbing the proper operation of the software. It is up to users of the software to track these vulnerabilities, test, and apply all patches. This process is called *patch management*.

Because a company's IT infrastructure is typically laden with multiple business applications, operating system installations, and other system services, maintaining patches on all devices and services a company uses is often time-consuming and costly. Malware is being created so rapidly that companies have very little time to respond between the time a vulnerability and a patch are announced and the time malicious software appears to exploit the vulnerability.

8-2 What is the business value of security and control?

Companies have very valuable information assets to protect. Systems often house confidential information about individuals' taxes, financial assets, medical records, and job performance reviews. They also can contain information on corporate operations, including trade secrets, new product development plans, and marketing strategies. Government systems may store information on weapons systems, intelligence operations, and military targets. These information assets have tremendous value, and the repercussions can be devastating if they are lost, destroyed, or placed in the wrong hands. Systems that are unable to function because of security breaches, disasters, or malfunctioning technology can have permanent impacts on a company's financial health. Some experts believe that 40 percent of all businesses will not recover from application or data losses that are not repaired within three days.

Inadequate security and control may result in serious legal liability. Businesses must protect not only their own information assets but also those of customers, employees, and business partners. Failure to do so may open the firm to costly litigation for data exposure or theft. An organization can be held liable for needless risk and harm created if the organization fails to take appropriate protective action to prevent loss of confidential information, data corruption, or breach of privacy. For example, Target had to pay $39 million to several U.S. banks servicing Mastercard that were forced to reimburse Target customers millions of dollars when those customers lost money due to a massive 2013 hack of Target's payment systems affecting 40 million people. Target also paid $67 million to Visa for the data hack and $10 million to settle a class-action lawsuit brought by Target customers. A sound security and control framework that protects business information assets can thus produce a high return on investment. Strong security and control also increase employee productivity and lower operational costs.

LEGAL AND REGULATORY REQUIREMENTS FOR ELECTRONIC RECORDS MANAGEMENT

U.S. government regulations are forcing companies to take security and control more seriously by mandating the protection of data from abuse, exposure, and unauthorized access. Firms face new legal obligations for the retention and storage of electronic records as well as for privacy protection.

If you work in the healthcare industry, your firm will need to comply with the Health Insurance Portability and Accountability Act (HIPAA) of 1996. **HIPAA** outlines medical security and privacy rules and procedures for simplifying the administration of healthcare billing and automating the transfer of healthcare data between healthcare providers, payers, and plans. It requires members of the healthcare industry to retain patient information for six years and ensure the confidentiality of those records. It specifies privacy, security, and electronic transaction standards for healthcare providers handling patient information, providing penalties for breaches of medical privacy, disclosure of patient records by email, or unauthorized network access.

If you work in a firm providing financial services, your firm will need to comply with the Financial Services Modernization Act of 1999, better known as the **Gramm-Leach-Bliley Act** after its congressional sponsors. This act requires financial institutions to ensure the security and confidentiality of customer data. Data must be stored on a secure medium, and special security measures must be enforced to protect such data on storage media and during transmittal.

If you work in a publicly traded company, your company will need to comply with the Public Company Accounting Reform and Investor Protection Act of 2002, better known as the **Sarbanes-Oxley Act** after its sponsors Senator Paul Sarbanes of Maryland and Representative Michael Oxley of Ohio. This act was designed to protect investors after the financial scandals at Enron, WorldCom, and other public companies. It imposes responsibility on companies and their management to safeguard the accuracy and integrity of financial information that is used internally and released externally. One of the Learning Tracks for this chapter discusses Sarbanes-Oxley in detail.

Sarbanes-Oxley is fundamentally about ensuring that internal controls are in place to govern the creation and documentation of information in financial statements. Because information systems are used to generate, store, and transport such data, the legislation requires firms to consider information systems security and other controls required to ensure the integrity, confidentiality, and accuracy of their data. Each system application that deals with critical financial reporting data requires controls to make sure the data are accurate. Controls to secure the corporate network, prevent unauthorized access to systems and data, and ensure data integrity and availability in the event of disaster or other disruption of service are essential as well.

ELECTRONIC EVIDENCE AND COMPUTER FORENSICS

Security, control, and electronic records management have become essential for responding to legal actions. Much of the evidence today for stock fraud, embezzlement, theft of company trade secrets, computer crime, and many civil cases is in digital form. In addition to information from printed or typewritten pages, legal cases today increasingly rely on evidence represented as digital data stored on portable storage devices, CDs, and computer hard disk drives as well as in email, instant messages, and e-commerce transactions over the Internet.

In a legal action, a firm is obligated to respond to a discovery request for access to information that may be used as evidence, and the company is required by law to produce those data. The cost of responding to a discovery request can be enormous if the company has trouble assembling the required data or the data have been corrupted or destroyed. Courts now impose severe financial and even criminal penalties for improper destruction of electronic documents.

An effective electronic document retention policy ensures that electronic documents, email, and other records are well organized, accessible, and neither retained too long nor discarded too soon. It also reflects an awareness of how to preserve potential evidence for computer forensics. **Computer forensics** is the scientific collection, examination, authentication, preservation, and analysis of data held on or retrieved from computer storage media in such a way that the information can be used as evidence in a court of law. It deals with the following problems.

- Recovering data from computers while preserving evidential integrity
- Securely storing and handling recovered electronic data
- Finding significant information in a large volume of electronic data
- Presenting the information to a court of law

Electronic evidence may reside on computer storage media in the form of computer files and as *ambient data*, which are not visible to the average user. An example might be a file that has been deleted on a PC hard drive. Data that a computer user may have deleted on computer storage media can often be recovered through various techniques. Computer forensics experts try to recover such hidden data for presentation as evidence.

An awareness of computer forensics should be incorporated into a firm's contingency planning process. The CIO, security specialists, information systems staff, and corporate legal counsel should all work together to have a plan in place that can be executed if a legal need arises. You can find out more about computer forensics in the Learning Tracks for this chapter.

8-3 What are the components of an organizational framework for security and control?

Even with the best security tools, your information systems won't be reliable and secure unless you know how and where to deploy them. You'll need to know where your company is at risk and what controls you must have in place to protect your

TABLE 8.4 General Controls

Type of General Control	Description
Software controls	Monitor the use of system software and prevent unauthorized access and use of software programs, system software, and computer programs.
Hardware controls	Ensure that computer hardware is physically secure and check for equipment malfunction. Organizations that are critically dependent on their computers also must make provisions for backup or continued operation to maintain constant service.
Computer operations controls	Oversee the work of the computer department to ensure that programmed procedures are consistently and correctly applied to the storage and processing of data. They include controls over the setup of computer processing jobs and backup and recovery procedures for processing that ends abnormally.
Data security controls	Ensure that valuable business data files maintained internally or by an external hosting service are not subject to unauthorized access, change, or destruction while they are in use or in storage.
Implementation controls	Audit the systems development process at various points to ensure that the process is properly controlled and managed.
Administrative controls	Formalize standards, rules, procedures, and control disciplines to ensure that the organization's general and application controls are properly executed and enforced.

information systems. You'll also need to develop a security policy and plans for keeping your business running if your information systems aren't operational.

INFORMATION SYSTEMS CONTROLS

Information systems controls are both manual and automated and consist of general and application controls. **General controls** govern the design, security, and use of computer programs and the security of data files in general throughout the organization's information technology infrastructure. On the whole, general controls apply to all computerized applications and consist of a combination of hardware, software, and manual procedures that create an overall control environment.

General controls include software controls, physical hardware controls, computer operations controls, data security controls, controls over the systems development process, and administrative controls. Table 8.4 describes the functions of each of these controls.

Application controls are specific controls unique to each computerized application, such as payroll or order processing. They include both automated and manual procedures that ensure that only authorized data are completely and accurately processed by that application. Application controls can be classified as (1) input controls, (2) processing controls, and (3) output controls.

Input controls check data for accuracy and completeness when they enter the system. There are specific input controls for input authorization, data conversion, data editing, and error handling. *Processing controls* establish that data are complete and accurate during updating. *Output controls ensure* that the results of computer processing are accurate, complete, and properly distributed. You can find more detail about application and general controls in our Learning Tracks.

Information systems controls should not be an afterthought. They need to be incorporated into the design of a system and should consider not only how the system will perform under all possible conditions but also the behavior of organizations and people using the system

TABLE 8.5

Online Order Processing Risk Assessment

Exposure	Probability of Occurrence (%)	Loss Range/ Average ($)	Expected Annual Loss ($)
Power failure	30%	$5000–$200,000 ($102,500)	$30,750
Embezzlement	5%	$1000–$50,000 ($25,500)	$1275
User error	98%	$200–$40,000 ($20,100)	$19,698

RISK ASSESSMENT

Before your company commits resources to security and information systems controls, it must know which assets require protection and the extent to which these assets are vulnerable. A risk assessment helps answer these questions and determine the most cost-effective set of controls for protecting assets.

A **risk assessment** determines the level of risk to the firm if a specific activity or process is not properly controlled. Not all risks can be anticipated and measured, but most businesses will be able to acquire some understanding of the risks they face. Business managers working with information systems specialists should try to determine the value of information assets, points of vulnerability, the likely frequency of a problem, and the potential for damage. For example, if an event is likely to occur no more than once a year, with a maximum of a $1000 loss to the organization, it is not wise to spend $20,000 on the design and maintenance of a control to protect against that event. However, if that same event could occur at least once a day, with a potential loss of more than $300,000 a year, $100,000 spent on a control might be entirely appropriate.

Table 8.5 illustrates sample results of a risk assessment for an online order processing system that processes 30,000 orders per day. The likelihood of each exposure occurring over a one-year period is expressed as a percentage. The next column shows the highest and lowest possible loss that could be expected each time the exposure occurred and an average loss calculated by adding the highest and lowest figures and dividing by two. The expected annual loss for each exposure can be determined by multiplying the average loss by its probability of occurrence.

This risk assessment shows that the probability of a power failure occurring in a one-year period is 30 percent. Loss of order transactions while power is down could range from $5000 to $200,000 (averaging $102,500) for each occurrence, depending on how long processing is halted. The probability of embezzlement occurring over a yearly period is about 5 percent, with potential losses ranging from $1000 to $50,000 (and averaging $25,500) for each occurrence. User errors have a 98 percent chance of occurring over a yearly period, with losses ranging from $200 to $40,000 (and averaging $20,100) for each occurrence.

After the risks have been assessed, system builders will concentrate on the control points with the greatest vulnerability and potential for loss. In this case, controls should focus on ways to minimize the risk of power failures and user errors because anticipated annual losses are highest for these areas.

SECURITY POLICY

After you've identified the main risks to your systems, your company will need to develop a security policy for protecting the company's assets. A **security policy** consists of statements ranking information risks, identifying acceptable security goals, and identifying the mechanisms for achieving these goals. What are the firm's most important information assets? Who generates and controls this information in the firm? What existing security policies are in place to protect the information? What level of risk is management willing to accept for each of these assets? Is it willing, for instance,

SECURITY PROFILE 1

User: Personnel Dept. Clerk

Location: Division 1

Employee Identification Codes with This Profile:	00753, 27834, 37665, 44116
Data Field Restrictions	**Type of Access**
All employee data for Division 1 only	Read and Update
• Medical history data	None
• Salary	None
• Pensionable earnings	None

SECURITY PROFILE 2

User: Divisional Personnel Manager

Location: Division 1

Employee Identification Codes with This Profile:	27321
Data Field Restrictions	**Type of Access**
All employee data for Division 1 only	Read Only

Figure 8.3
Access Rules for a Personnel System

These two examples represent two security profiles or data security patterns that might be found in a personnel system. Depending on the security profile, a user would have certain restrictions on access to various systems, locations, or data in an organization.

to lose customer credit data once every 10 years? Or will it build a security system for credit card data that can withstand the once-in-a-hundred-years disaster? Management must estimate how much it will cost to achieve this level of acceptable risk.

The security policy drives other policies determining acceptable use of the firm's information resources and which members of the company have access to its information assets. An **acceptable use policy (AUP)** defines acceptable uses of the firm's information resources and computing equipment, including desktop and laptop computers, mobile devices, telephones, and the Internet. A good AUP defines unacceptable and acceptable actions for every user and specifies consequences for noncompliance.

Figure 8.3 is one example of how an identity management system might capture the access rules for different levels of users in the human resources function. It specifies what portions of a human resource database each user is permitted to access, based on the information required to perform that person's job. The database contains sensitive personal information such as employees' salaries, benefits, and medical histories.

The access rules illustrated here are for two sets of users. One set of users consists of all employees who perform clerical functions, such as inputting employee data into the system. All individuals with this type of profile can update the system but can neither read nor update sensitive fields, such as salary, medical history, or earnings data. Another profile applies to a divisional manager, who cannot update the system but who can read all employee data fields for his or her division, including medical history and salary. We provide more detail about the technologies for user authentication later on in this chapter.

DISASTER RECOVERY PLANNING AND BUSINESS CONTINUITY PLANNING

If you run a business, you need to plan for events, such as power outages, floods, earthquakes, or terrorist attacks, that will prevent your information systems and your business from operating. **Disaster recovery planning** devises plans for the restoration of disrupted computing and communications services. Disaster recovery plans focus primarily on the technical issues involved in keeping systems up and running, such as which files to back up and the maintenance of backup computer systems or disaster recovery services.

For example, MasterCard maintains a duplicate computer center in Kansas City, Missouri, to serve as an emergency backup to its primary computer center in St. Louis. Rather than build their own backup facilities, many firms contract with cloud-based disaster recovery services or firms such as SunGard Availability Services and Acronis providing sites with spare computers around the country where subscribing firms can run their critical applications in an emergency.

Business continuity planning focuses on how the company can restore business operations after a disaster strikes. The business continuity plan identifies critical business processes and determines action plans for handling mission-critical functions if systems go down. For example, Healthways, a well-being improvement company headquartered in Franklin, Tennessee, implemented a business continuity plan that identified the business processes of nearly 70 departments across the enterprise and the impact of system downtime on those processes. Healthways pinpointed its most critical processes and worked with each department to devise an action plan.

Business managers and information technology specialists need to work together on both types of plans to determine which systems and business processes are most critical to the company. They must conduct a business impact analysis to identify the firm's most critical systems and the impact a systems outage would have on the business. Management must determine the maximum amount of time the business can survive with its systems down and which parts of the business must be restored first.

THE ROLE OF AUDITING

How does management know that information systems security and controls are effective? To answer this question, organizations must conduct comprehensive and systematic audits. An **information systems audit** examines the firm's overall security environment as well as controls governing individual information systems. The auditor should trace the flow of sample transactions through the system and perform tests, using, if appropriate, automated audit software. The information systems audit may also examine data quality.

Security audits review technologies, procedures, documentation, training, and personnel. A thorough audit will even simulate an attack or disaster to test the response of the technology, information systems staff, and business employees.

The audit lists and ranks all control weaknesses and estimates the probability of their occurrence. It then assesses the financial and organizational impact of each threat. Figure 8.4 is a sample auditor's listing of control weaknesses for a loan system. It includes a section for notifying management of such weaknesses and for management's response. Management is expected to devise a plan for countering significant weaknesses in controls.

8-4 What are the most important tools and technologies for safeguarding information resources?

Businesses have an array of technologies for protecting their information resources. They include tools for managing user identities, preventing unauthorized access to systems and data, ensuring system availability, and ensuring software quality.

IDENTITY MANAGEMENT AND AUTHENTICATION

Midsize and large companies have complex IT infrastructures and many systems, each with its own set of users. **Identity management** software automates the process of keeping track of all these users and their system privileges, assigning each user a

Function: Loans Location: Peoria, IL	Prepared by: J. Ericson Date: June 16, 2017		Received by: T. Benson Review date: June 28, 2017	
Nature of Weakness and Impact	Chance for Error/Abuse		Notification to Management	
	Yes/No	Justification	Report date	Management response
User accounts with missing passwords	Yes	Leaves system open to unauthorized outsiders or attackers	5/10/17	Eliminate accounts without passwords
Network configured to allow some sharing of system files	Yes	Exposes critical system files to hostile parties connected to the network	5/10/17	Ensure only required directories are shared and that they are protected with strong passwords
Software patches can update production programs without final approval from Standards and Controls group	No	All production programs require management approval; Standards and Controls group assigns such cases to a temporary production status		

Figure 8.4
Sample Auditor's List of Control Weaknesses
This chart is a sample page from a list of control weaknesses that an auditor might find in a loan system in a local commercial bank. This form helps auditors record and evaluate control weaknesses and shows the results of discussing those weaknesses with management as well as any corrective actions management takes.

unique digital identity for accessing each system. It also includes tools for authenticating users, protecting user identities, and controlling access to system resources.

To gain access to a system, a user must be authorized and authenticated. **Authentication** refers to the ability to know that a person is who he or she claims to be. Authentication is often established by using **passwords** known only to authorized users. An end user uses a password to log on to a computer system and may also use passwords for accessing specific systems and files. However, users often forget passwords, share them, or choose poor passwords that are easy to guess, which compromises security. Password systems that are too rigorous hinder employee productivity. When employees must change complex passwords frequently, they often take shortcuts, such as choosing passwords that are easy to guess or keeping their passwords at their workstations in plain view. Passwords can also be sniffed if transmitted over a network or stolen through social engineering.

New authentication technologies, such as tokens, smart cards, and biometric authentication, overcome some of these problems. A **token** is a physical device, similar to an identification card, that is designed to prove the identity of a single user. Tokens are small gadgets that typically fit on key rings and display passcodes that change frequently. A **smart card** is a device about the size of a credit card that contains a chip formatted with access permission and other data. (Smart cards are also used in electronic payment systems.) A reader device interprets the data on the smart card and allows or denies access.

Biometric authentication uses systems that read and interpret individual human traits, such as fingerprints, irises, and voices to grant or deny access. Biometric authentication is based on the measurement of a physical or behavioral trait that makes each individual unique. It compares a person's unique characteristics, such as the fingerprints, face, or retinal image, against a stored profile of these characteristics to determine any differences between these characteristics and the stored profile. If the two profiles match, access is granted. Fingerprint and facial recognition technologies are just beginning to be used for security applications, with many PC laptops (and some smartphones) equipped with fingerprint identification devices and several models with built-in webcams and face recognition software.

The steady stream of incidents in which hackers have been able to access traditional passwords highlights the need for more secure means of authentication.

This smartphone has a biometric fingerprint reader for fast yet secure access to files and networks. New models of PCs and smartphones are starting to use biometric identification to authenticate users.

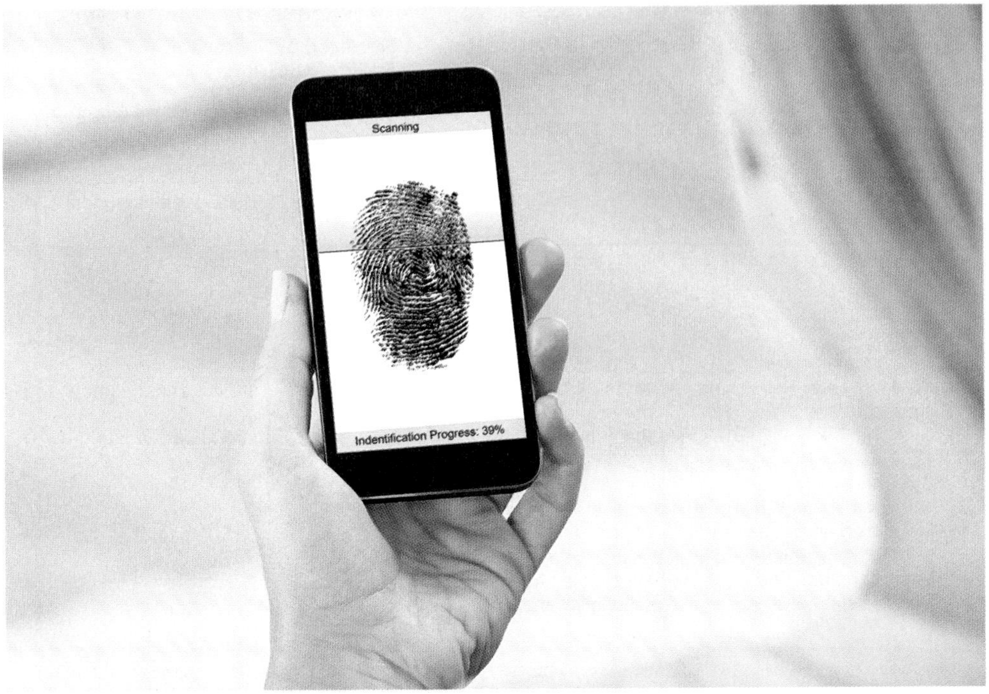

Two-factor authentication increases security by validating users through a multistep process. To be authenticated, a user must provide two means of identification, one of which is typically a physical token, such as a smartcard or chip-enabled bank card, and the other of which is typically data, such as a password or personal identification number (PIN). Biometric data, such as fingerprints, iris prints, or voice prints, can also be used as one of the authenticating mechanisms. A common example of two-factor authentication is a bank card; the card itself is the physical item, and the PIN is the data that go with it.

FIREWALLS, INTRUSION DETECTION SYSTEMS, AND ANTIVIRUS SOFTWARE

Without protection against malware and intruders, connecting to the Internet would be very dangerous. Firewalls, intrusion detection systems, and antivirus software have become essential business tools.

Firewalls

Firewalls prevent unauthorized users from accessing private networks. A firewall is a combination of hardware and software that controls the flow of incoming and outgoing network traffic. It is generally placed between the organization's private internal networks and distrusted external networks, such as the Internet, although firewalls can also be used to protect one part of a company's network from the rest of the network (see Figure 8.5).

The firewall acts like a gatekeeper that examines each user's credentials before it grants access to a network. The firewall identifies names, IP addresses, applications, and other characteristics of incoming traffic. It checks this information against the access rules that the network administrator has programmed into the system. The firewall prevents unauthorized communication into and out of the network.

In large organizations, the firewall often resides on a specially designated computer separate from the rest of the network, so no incoming request directly accesses private network resources. There are a number of firewall screening technologies, including static packet filtering, stateful inspection, Network Address Translation,

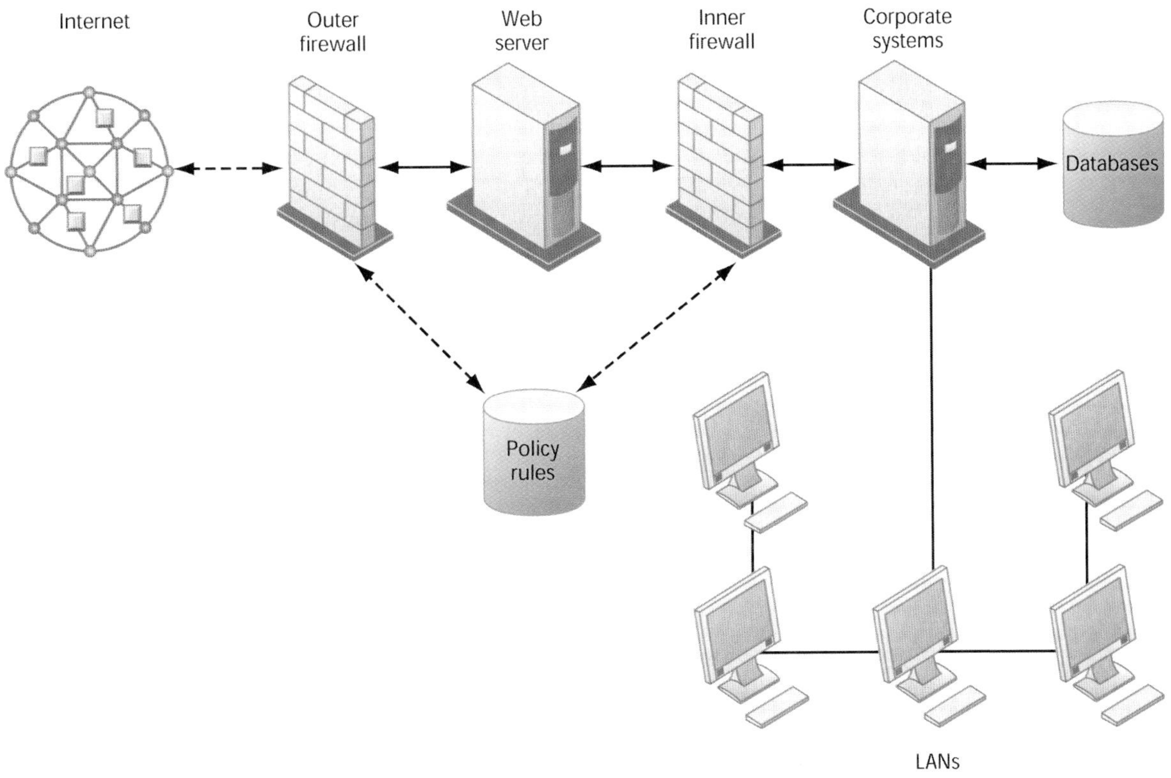

Figure 8.5
A Corporate Firewall
The firewall is placed between the firm's private network and the public Internet or another distrusted network to protect against unauthorized traffic.

and application proxy filtering. They are frequently used in combination to provide firewall protection.

Packet filtering examines selected fields in the headers of data packets flowing back and forth between the trusted network and the Internet, examining individual packets in isolation. This filtering technology can miss many types of attacks.

Stateful inspection provides additional security by determining whether packets are part of an ongoing dialogue between a sender and a receiver. It sets up state tables to track information over multiple packets. Packets are accepted or rejected based on whether they are part of an approved conversation or attempting to establish a legitimate connection.

Network Address Translation (NAT) can provide another layer of protection when static packet filtering and stateful inspection are employed. NAT conceals the IP addresses of the organization's internal host computer(s) to prevent sniffer programs outside the firewall from ascertaining them and using that information to penetrate internal systems.

Application proxy filtering examines the application content of packets. A proxy server stops data packets originating outside the organization, inspects them, and passes a proxy to the other side of the firewall. If a user outside the company wants to communicate with a user inside the organization, the outside user first communicates with the proxy application, and the proxy application communicates with the firm's internal computer. Likewise, a computer user inside the organization goes through the proxy to talk with computers on the outside.

To create a good firewall, an administrator must maintain detailed internal rules identifying the people, applications, or addresses that are allowed or rejected. Firewalls can deter, but not completely prevent, network penetration by outsiders and should be viewed as one element in an overall security plan.

Intrusion Detection Systems

In addition to firewalls, commercial security vendors now provide intrusion detection tools and services to protect against suspicious network traffic and attempts to access files and databases. **Intrusion detection systems** feature full-time monitoring tools placed at the most vulnerable points or hot spots of corporate networks to detect and deter intruders continually. The system generates an alarm if it finds a suspicious or anomalous event. Scanning software looks for patterns indicative of known methods of computer attacks such as bad passwords, checks to see whether important files have been removed or modified, and sends warnings of vandalism or system administration errors. The intrusion detection tool can also be customized to shut down a particularly sensitive part of a network if it receives unauthorized traffic.

Antivirus and Antispyware Software

Defensive technology plans for both individuals and businesses must include antimalware protection for every computer. **Antivirus software** prevents, detects, and removes malware, including computer viruses, computer worms, Trojan horses, spyware, and adware. However, most antivirus software is effective only against malware already known when the software was written. To remain effective, the antivirus software must be continually updated. Even then it is not always effective because some malware can evade antivirus detection. Organizations need to use additional malware detection tools for better protection.

Unified Threat Management Systems

To help businesses reduce costs and improve manageability, security vendors have combined into a single appliance various security tools, including firewalls, virtual private networks, intrusion detection systems, and web content filtering and antispam software. These comprehensive security management products are called **unified threat management (UTM)** systems. UTM products are available for all sizes of networks. Leading UTM vendors include Fortinent, Sophos, and Check Point, and networking vendors such as Cisco Systems and Juniper Networks provide some UTM capabilities in their products.

SECURING WIRELESS NETWORKS

The initial security standard developed for Wi-Fi, called Wired Equivalent Privacy (WEP), is not very effective because its encryption keys are relatively easy to crack. WEP provides some margin of security, however, if users remember to enable it. Corporations can further improve Wi-Fi security by using it in conjunction with virtual private network (VPN) technology when accessing internal corporate data.

In June 2004, the Wi-Fi Alliance industry trade group finalized the 802.11i specification (also referred to as Wi-Fi Protected Access 2 or WPA2) that replaces WEP with stronger security standards. Instead of the static encryption keys used in WEP, the new standard uses much longer keys that continually change, making them harder to crack.

ENCRYPTION AND PUBLIC KEY INFRASTRUCTURE

Many businesses use encryption to protect digital information that they store, physically transfer, or send over the Internet. **Encryption** is the process of transforming plain text or data into cipher text that cannot be read by anyone other than the sender and the intended receiver. Data are encrypted by using a secret numerical code, called an encryption key, that transforms plain data into cipher text. The message must be decrypted by the receiver.

Two methods for encrypting network traffic on the web are SSL and S-HTTP. **Secure Sockets Layer (SSL)** and its successor, Transport Layer Security (TLS), enable

Figure 8.6
Public Key Encryption
A public key encryption system can be viewed as a series of public and private keys that lock data when they are transmitted and unlock the data when they are received. The sender locates the recipient's public key in a directory and uses it to encrypt a message. The message is sent in encrypted form over the Internet or a private network. When the encrypted message arrives, the recipient uses his or her private key to decrypt the data and read the message.

client and server computers to manage encryption and decryption activities as they communicate with each other during a secure web session. **Secure Hypertext Transfer Protocol (S-HTTP)** is another protocol used for encrypting data flowing over the Internet, but it is limited to individual messages, whereas SSL and TLS are designed to establish a secure connection between two computers.

The capability to generate secure sessions is built into Internet client browser software and servers. The client and the server negotiate what key and what level of security to use. Once a secure session is established between the client and the server, all messages in that session are encrypted.

Two methods of encryption are symmetric key encryption and public key encryption. In symmetric key encryption, the sender and receiver establish a secure Internet session by creating a single encryption key and sending it to the receiver so both the sender and receiver share the same key. The strength of the encryption key is measured by its bit length. Today, a typical key will be 56 to 256 bits long (a string of from 56 to 256 binary digits) depending on the level of security desired. The longer the key, the more difficult it is to break the key. The downside is that the longer the key, the more computing power it takes for legitimate users to process the information.

The problem with all symmetric encryption schemes is that the key itself must be shared somehow among the senders and receivers, which exposes the key to outsiders who might just be able to intercept and decrypt the key. A more secure form of encryption called **public key encryption** uses two keys: one shared (or public) and one totally private as shown in Figure 8.6. The keys are mathematically related so that data encrypted with one key can be decrypted using only the other key. To send and receive messages, communicators first create separate pairs of private and public keys. The public key is kept in a directory, and the private key must be kept secret. The sender encrypts a message with the recipient's public key. On receiving the message, the recipient uses his or her private key to decrypt it.

Digital certificates are data files used to establish the identity of users and electronic assets for protection of online transactions (see Figure 8.7). A digital certificate system uses a trusted third party, known as a certificate authority (CA), to validate a user's identity. There are many CAs in the United States and around the world, including Symantec, GoDaddy, and Comodo.

The CA verifies a digital certificate user's identity offline. This information is put into a CA server, which generates an encrypted digital certificate containing owner identification information and a copy of the owner's public key. The certificate authenticates that the public key belongs to the designated owner. The CA makes its own public key available either in print or perhaps on the Internet. The recipient of an encrypted message uses the CA's public key to decode the digital certificate attached to the message, verifies it was issued by the CA, and then obtains the sender's public key and identification information contained in the certificate. By using

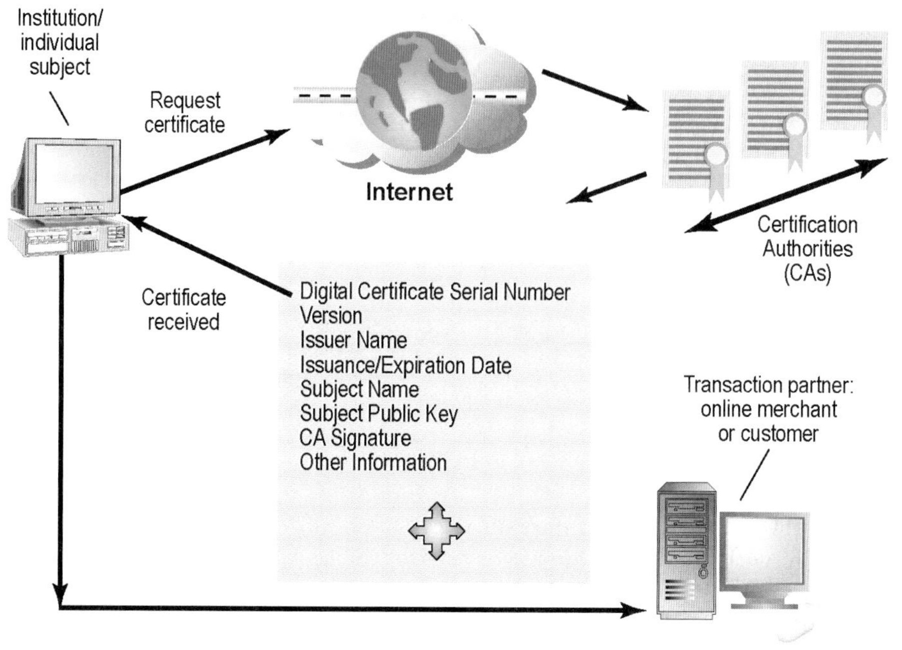

Figure 8.7
Digital Certificates
Digital certificates help establish the identity of people or electronic assets. They protect online transactions by providing secure, encrypted, online communication.

this information, the recipient can send an encrypted reply. The digital certificate system would enable, for example, a credit card user and a merchant to validate that their digital certificates were issued by an authorized and trusted third party before they exchange data. **Public key infrastructure (PKI)**, the use of public key cryptography working with a CA, is now widely used in e-commerce.

SECURING TRANSACTIONS WITH BLOCKCHAIN

Blockchain is gaining attention as a technology for enabling companies to create and verify transactions on a network instantaneously without a central authority. A blockchain is a type of distributed ledger that stores a permanent and tamper-proof record of transactions and shares them among a distributed network of computers. Unlike traditional databases, distributed ledgers are managed through a peer-to-peer (P2P) architecture and do not have a centralized data store.

The blockchain maintains a continuously growing list of records called blocks. Each block contains a timestamp and link to a previous block. Once a block of data is recorded on the blockchain ledger, it cannot be altered retroactively. When someone wants to add a transaction, participants in the network (all of whom have copies of the existing blockchain) run algorithms to evaluate and verify the proposed transaction. Legitimate changes to the ledger are recorded across the blockchain in a matter of seconds or minutes and records are protected through cryptography.

The simplicity and security that blockchain offers has made it attractive for storing and securing financial transactions, medical records, and other types of data. Blockchain is a foundational technology for Bitcoin, Ethereum, and other cryptocurrencies.

ENSURING SYSTEM AVAILABILITY

As companies increasingly rely on digital networks for revenue and operations, they need to take additional steps to ensure that their systems and applications are always available. Firms such as those in the airline and financial services industries with critical applications requiring online transaction processing have traditionally used fault-tolerant computer systems for many years to ensure 100 percent availability. In **online transaction processing**, transactions entered online are immediately processed by the computer. Multitudinous changes to databases, reporting, and requests for information occur each instant.

Fault-tolerant computer systems contain redundant hardware, software, and power supply components that create an environment that provides continuous, uninterrupted service. Fault-tolerant computers use special software routines or self-checking logic built into their circuitry to detect hardware failures and automatically switch to a backup device. Parts from these computers can be removed and repaired without disruption to the computer or downtime. **Downtime** refers to periods of time in which a system is not operational.

Controlling Network Traffic: Deep Packet Inspection

Have you ever tried to use your campus network and found that it was very slow? It may be because your fellow students are using the network to download music or watch YouTube. Bandwidth-consuming applications such as file-sharing programs, Internet phone service, and online video can clog and slow down corporate networks, degrading performance. For example, Ball State University in Muncie, Indiana, found its network had slowed because a small minority of students were using P2P file-sharing programs to download movies and music.

A technology called **deep packet inspection (DPI)** helps solve this problem. DPI examines data files and sorts out low-priority online material while assigning higher priority to business-critical files. Based on the priorities established by a network's operators, it decides whether a specific data packet can continue to its destination or should be blocked or delayed while more important traffic proceeds. Using a DPI system from Allot Communications, Ball State was able to cap the amount of file-sharing traffic and assign it a much lower priority. Ball State's preferred network traffic sped up.

Security Outsourcing

Many companies, especially small businesses, lack the resources or expertise to provide a secure high-availability computing environment on their own. They can outsource many security functions to **managed security service providers (MSSPs)** that monitor network activity and perform vulnerability testing and intrusion detection. SecureWorks, AT&T, Verizon, IBM, Perimeter eSecurity, and Symantec are leading providers of MSSP services.

SECURITY ISSUES FOR CLOUD COMPUTING AND THE MOBILE DIGITAL PLATFORM

Although cloud computing and the emerging mobile digital platform have the potential to deliver powerful benefits, they pose new challenges to system security and reliability. We now describe some of these challenges and how they should be addressed.

Security in the Cloud

When processing takes place in the cloud, accountability and responsibility for protection of sensitive data still reside with the company owning that data. Understanding how the cloud computing provider organizes its services and manages the data is critical.

Cloud computing is highly distributed. Cloud applications reside in large remote data centers and server farms that supply business services and data management for multiple corporate clients. To save money and keep costs low, cloud computing providers often distribute work to data centers around the globe where work can be accomplished most efficiently. When you use the cloud, you may not know precisely where your data are being hosted.

The dispersed nature of cloud computing makes it difficult to track unauthorized activity. Virtually all cloud providers use encryption to secure the data they handle while the data are being transmitted. However, if the data are stored on devices that also store other companies' data, it's important to ensure that these stored data are encrypted as well. DDoS attacks are especially harmful because they render cloud services unavailable to legitimate customers.

Companies expect their systems to be running 24/7. Cloud providers still experience occasional outages, but their reliability has increased to the point where a number of large companies are using cloud services for part of their IT infrastructures. Most keep their critical systems in-house.

Cloud users need to confirm that regardless of where their data are stored, they are protected at a level that meets their corporate requirements. They should stipulate that the cloud provider store and process data in specific jurisdictions according to the privacy rules of those jurisdictions. Cloud clients should find how the cloud provider segregates their corporate data from those of other companies and ask for proof that encryption mechanisms are sound. It's also important to know how the cloud provider will respond if a disaster strikes, whether the provider will be able to restore your data completely, and how long this should take. Cloud users should also ask whether cloud providers will submit to external audits and security certifications. These kinds of controls can be written into the service level agreement (SLA) before signing with a cloud provider. The Cloud Security Alliance (CSA) has created industrywide standards for cloud security, specifying best practices to secure cloud computing.

Securing Mobile Platforms

If mobile devices are performing many of the functions of computers, they need to be secured like desktops and laptops against malware, theft, accidental loss, unauthorized access, and hacking attempts. The Interactive Session on Organizations describes these mobile vulnerabilities in greater detail and their implications for both individuals and businesses.

Mobile devices accessing corporate systems and data require special protection. Companies should make sure that their corporate security policy includes mobile devices, with additional details on how mobile devices should be supported, protected, and used. They will need mobile device management tools to authorize all devices in use; to maintain accurate inventory records on all mobile devices, users, and applications; to control updates to applications; and to lock down or erase lost or stolen devices so they can't be compromised. Data loss prevention technology can identify where critical data are saved, who is accessing the data, how data are leaving the company, and where the data are going. Firms should develop guidelines stipulating approved mobile platforms and software applications as well as the required software and procedures for remote access of corporate systems. The organization's mobile security policy should forbid employees from using unsecured, consumer-based applications for transferring and storing corporate documents and files or sending such documents and files to oneself by email without encryption. Companies should encrypt communication whenever possible. All mobile device users should be required to use the password feature found in every smartphone.

ENSURING SOFTWARE QUALITY

In addition to implementing effective security and controls, organizations can improve system quality and reliability by employing software metrics and rigorous software testing. Software metrics are objective assessments of the system in the form of quantified measurements. Ongoing use of metrics allows the information systems department and end users to measure the performance of the system jointly and identify problems as they occur. Examples of software metrics include the number of transactions that can be processed in a specified unit of time, online response time, the number of payroll checks printed per hour, and the number of known bugs per

How Secure Is BYOD?

Attention all businesses: Every employee is carrying around a 5-ounce potential wireless network intrusion device: their smartphone. Thanks to BYOD, smartphones and other mobile devices pose one of the most serious security threats for organizations today.

Mobile devices are opening up new avenues for accessing corporate data that need to be closely monitored and protected. Sensitive data on mobile devices travel, both physically and electronically, from the office to home and possibly other off-site locations. According to a February 2016 Ponemon Institute study of 588 U.S. IT and security professionals, 67 percent of those surveyed reported that it was certain or likely that an employee's mobile access to confidential corporate data had resulted in a data breach. Unfortunately, only 41 percent of respondents said their companies had policies for accessing corporate data from mobile devices.

More than half of security breaches occur when devices are lost or stolen. That puts all of the personal and corporate data stored on the device, as well as access to corporate data on remote servers, at risk. Physical access to mobile devices may be a greater threat than hacking into a network because less effort is required to gain entry. Experienced attackers can easily circumvent passwords or locks on mobile devices or access encrypted data. Moreover, many smartphone users leave their phones totally unprotected to begin with or fail to keep the security features of their devices up-to-date. In the Websense and the Ponemon Institute's Global Study on Mobility Risks, 59 percent of respondents reported that employees circumvented or disabled security features such as passwords and key locks.

Another worry today is large-scale data leakage caused by use of cloud computing services. Employees are increasingly using public cloud services such as Google Drive or Dropbox for file sharing and collaboration and may be storing and exchanging files without their employers' approval. In early 2015 Dropbox had to patch a security flaw that allowed cyberattackers to steal new information uploaded to accounts through compromised third-party apps for Android devices. There's very little a company can do to prevent employees who are allowed to use their smartphones from downloading corporate data so they can work on those data remotely. Application downloads are risky as well. Employees downloading the latest gaming app can provide a direct path to confidential company data through malware or open hacker access.

Hacker attacks on mobile devices are escalating. Android is now the world's most popular operating system for mobile devices with 81 percent of the global market, and most mobile malware is targeted at the Android platform. Few smartphones are sold with anti-malware tools or firewalls.

Apple uses a closed "walled garden" model for managing its apps and reviews each one before releasing it on its App Store. A few vulnerabilities have been detected, Android application security is considered weaker, but it is improving. Android application security uses sandboxing, which confines apps, minimizing their ability to affect one another or manipulate device features without user permission. Google removes any apps that break its rules against malicious activity from Google Play, the official app store for the Android operating system. Google also vets the backgrounds of developers. Recent Android security enhancements include assigning varying levels of trust to each app, dictating what kind of data an app can access inside its confined domain, and providing a more robust way to store cryptographic credentials used to access sensitive information and resources.

Google Play now provides security scanning of all applications before they are available to download, ongoing security checks for as long as the application is available, and a Verify Apps service for mobile device protection for apps installed outside of Google Play. However, these Android improvements are largely only for people who use a phone or tablet running a newer version of Android and restrict their app downloads to Google's own Play store.

Companies need to develop mobile security strategies that strike the right balance between improving worker productivity and effective information security. Aetna's Chief Security Officer (CSO) Jim Routh says there is a certain minimum level of mobile security he requires regardless of whether a device is company- or personally owned. Aetna has about 6,000 users equipped with mobile devices that are either personally owned or issued by the company. Each device has mandatory protection that provides an encrypted channel to use in unsecured Wi-Fi networks and alerts the user and the company if a malicious app is about to be installed on the device.

Colin Minihan, director of security and best practices at VMWare AirWatch, believes that understanding users and their needs helps a mobile security strategy progress further. VmAirWatch categorizes similar groups of users and devises a specific plan of action for each group, choosing the right tools for the job.

According to Patrick Hevesi, Nordstrom's former director of security, if users need access to critical corporate data that must be protected, the firm should probably allow only fully managed, fully controlled, approved types of devices. Users who only want mobile tools for email and contacts can more easily bring their own devices. The key questions to ask are called the "three Ws": Who needs access? What do they need to access? What is the security posture of the device?

Sources: Howard Solomon, "Mobile Malware Trends: Trojans, Botnets, and More," *Canadian CIO*, April 2017; Michael Heller, "Mobile Security Strategy Matures with BYOD," and Kathleen Richards, "CISOs Battle to Control Mobile Risk in the Workplace," *Information Security Magazine*, June 1, 2016; Conner Forrest, "The State of Mobile Device Security," *ZDNet*, July 11, 2016; Nathan Olivarez-Giles, "Android's Security Improves—for the Few," *Wall Street Journal*, April 21, 2016; Ponemon Institute, "The Economic Risk of Confidential Data on Mobile Devices in the Workplace," February, 2016; and "Dropbox Patches Android Security Flaw," *Zero Day*, March 11, 2015.

CASE STUDY QUESTIONS

1. It has been said that a smartphone is a computer in your hand. Discuss the security implications of this statement.
2. What kinds of security problems do mobile computing devices pose?
3. What people, organizational, and technology issues must be addressed by smartphone security?
4. What steps can individuals and businesses take to make their smartphones more secure?

hundred lines of program code. For metrics to be successful, they must be carefully designed, formal, objective, and used consistently.

Early, regular, and thorough testing will contribute significantly to system quality. Many view testing as a way to prove the correctness of work they have done. In fact, we know that all sizable software is riddled with errors, and we must test to uncover these errors.

Good testing begins before a software program is even written, by using a *walkthrough*—a review of a specification or design document by a small group of people carefully selected based on the skills needed for the particular objectives being tested. When developers start writing software programs, coding walkthroughs can also be used to review program code. However, code must be tested by computer runs. When errors are discovered, the source is found and eliminated through a process called *debugging*. You can find out more about the various stages of testing required to put an information system into operation in Chapter 12. Our Learning Tracks also contain descriptions of methodologies for developing software programs that contribute to software quality.

8-5 How will MIS help my career?

Here is how Chapter 8 and this book can help you find an entry-level job as an identity access and management support specialist.

THE COMPANY

No. 1 Value Supermarkets, a major supermarket grocery store chain headquartered in Plano, Texas, is looking to fill an entry-level position for an identity access and management support specialist. The company has 59 retail locations in 23 Texas cities, more than 8,000 workers, and nearly a million weekly shoppers.

POSITION DESCRIPTION

The identity access and management support specialist will be responsible for monitoring the company's identity management system to ensure that the company is meeting its audit and compliance controls. This position reports to the company's security operations manager. Job responsibilities include:

- Performing data integrity testing of identity management system integrations with business applications.
- Integrating Windows Active Directory files with the identity management system.
- Maintaining information on system user roles and privileges.

JOB REQUIREMENTS

- Bachelor's degree
- Proficiency with computers
- Ability to multitask and work independently
- Attention to detail
- Strong time management skills
- Ability to communicate with both technical and non-technical staff

INTERVIEW QUESTIONS

1. What do know about authentication and identity management? Have you ever worked with identity management or other IT security systems? What did you do with this software?
2. Have you ever worked with Windows Active Directory? What exactly did you do with this software?
3. What knowledge and experience do you have with ensuring data integrity?
4. Can you give an example of a situation where you had to multitask and manage your time and how you handled it?
5. Can you tell us about the computer experience you've had? What software tools have you worked with?

AUTHOR TIPS

1. Review the last two sections of this chapter, especially the discussions of identity management and authentication. Also review the Chapter 6 discussions of data integrity and data quality.
2. Use the web to find out more about identity management, data integrity testing, leading identity management software tools, and Windows Active Directory.
3. Use the web to find out more about the company, the kinds of systems it uses, and who might be using those systems.

Review Summary

8-1 **Why are information systems vulnerable to destruction, error, and abuse?** Digital data are vulnerable to destruction, misuse, error, fraud, and hardware or software failures. The Internet is designed to be an open system and makes internal corporate systems more vulnerable to actions from outsiders. Hackers can unleash denial-of-service (DoS) attacks or penetrate corporate networks, causing serious system disruptions. Wi-Fi networks can easily be penetrated by intruders using sniffer programs to obtain an address to access the resources of the network. Computer viruses and worms can disable systems and websites. The dispersed nature of cloud computing makes it difficult to track unauthorized activity or to apply controls from afar. Software presents problems because software bugs may be impossible to eliminate and because software vulnerabilities can be exploited by hackers and malicious software. End users often introduce errors.

8-2 What is the business value of security and control? Lack of sound security and control can cause firms relying on computer systems for their core business functions to lose sales and productivity. Information assets, such as confidential employee records, trade secrets, or business plans, lose much of their value if they are revealed to outsiders or if they expose the firm to legal liability. Laws, such as HIPAA, the Sarbanes-Oxley Act, and the Gramm-Leach-Bliley Act, require companies to practice stringent electronic records management and adhere to strict standards for security, privacy, and control. Legal actions requiring electronic evidence and computer forensics also require firms to pay more attention to security and electronic records management.

8-3 What are the components of an organizational framework for security and control? Firms need to establish a good set of both general and application controls for their information systems. A risk assessment evaluates information assets, identifies control points and control weaknesses, and determines the most cost-effective set of controls. Firms must also develop a coherent corporate security policy and plans for continuing business operations in the event of disaster or disruption. The security policy includes policies for acceptable use and identity management. Comprehensive and systematic information systems auditing helps organizations determine the effectiveness of security and controls for their information systems.

8-4 What are the most important tools and technologies for safeguarding information resources? Firewalls prevent unauthorized users from accessing a private network when it is linked to the Internet. Intrusion detection systems monitor private networks for suspicious network traffic and attempts to access corporate systems. Passwords, tokens, smart cards, and biometric authentication are used to authenticate system users. Antivirus software checks computer systems for infections by viruses and worms and often eliminates the malicious software; antispyware software combats intrusive and harmful spyware programs. Encryption, the coding and scrambling of messages, is a widely used technology for securing electronic transmissions over unprotected networks. Blockchain technology enables companies to create and verify tamper-roof transactions on a network without a central authority. Digital certificates combined with public key encryption provide further protection of electronic transactions by authenticating a user's identity. Companies can use fault-tolerant computer systems to make sure that their information systems are always available. Use of software metrics and rigorous software testing help improve software quality and reliability.

Key Terms

Acceptable use policy (AUP), 291
Antivirus software, 296
Application controls, 289
Authentication, 293
Biometric authentication, 293
Blockchain, 298
Botnet, 282
Bugs, 286
Business continuity planning, 292
Click fraud, 284
Computer crime, 282
Computer forensics, 288
Computer virus, 277
Controls, 275
Cybervandalism, 281
Cyberwarfare, 285
Deep packet inspection (DPI), 299
Denial-of-service (DoS) attack, 281
Digital certificates, 297
Disaster recovery planning, 291
Distributed denial-of-service (DDoS) attack, 282
Downtime, 299
Drive-by download, 278
Encryption, 296
Evil twin, 283
Fault-tolerant computer systems, 299
Firewall, 294
General controls, 289

MyLab MIS

To complete the problems with **MyLab MIS**, go to the EOC Discussion Questions in MyLab MIS.

Review Questions

8-1 Why are information systems vulnerable to destruction, error, and abuse?

- List and describe the most common threats against contemporary information systems.
- Define malware and distinguish among a virus, a worm, and a Trojan horse.
- Define a hacker and explain how hackers create security problems and damage systems.
- Define computer crime. Provide two examples of crime in which computers are targets and two examples in which computers are used as instruments of crime.
- Define identity theft and phishing and explain why identity theft is such a big problem today.
- Describe the security and system reliability problems employees create.
- Explain how software defects affect system reliability and security.

8-2 What is the business value of security and control?

- Explain how security and control provide value for businesses.
- Describe the relationship between security and control and recent U.S. government regulatory requirements and computer forensics.

8-3 What are the components of an organizational framework for security and control?

- Define general controls and describe each type of general control.
- Define application controls and describe each type of application control.
- Describe the function of risk assessment and explain how it is conducted for information systems.
- Define and describe the following: security policy, acceptable use policy, and identity management.
- Explain how information systems auditing promotes security and control.

8-4 What are the most important tools and technologies for safeguarding information resources?

- Name and describe three authentication methods.
- Describe the roles of firewalls, intrusion detection systems, and antivirus software in promoting security.
- Explain how encryption protects information.

- Describe the role of encryption and digital certificates in a public key infrastructure.
- Distinguish between disaster recovery planning and business continuity planning.
- Identify and describe the security problems cloud computing poses.
- Describe measures for improving software quality and reliability.

Discussion Questions

8-5 MyLab MIS Security isn't simply a technology issue, it's a business issue. Discuss.

8-6 MyLab MIS If you were developing a business continuity plan for your company, where would you start? What aspects of the business would the plan address?

8-7 MyLab MIS Suppose your business had an e-commerce website where it sold goods and accepted credit card payments. Discuss the major security threats to this website and their potential impact. What can be done to minimize these threats?

Hands-On MIS Projects

The projects in this section give you hands-on experience analyzing security vulnerabilities, using spreadsheet software for risk analysis, and using web tools to research security outsourcing services. Visit **MyLab MIS** to access this chapter's Hands-On MIS Projects.

MANAGEMENT DECISION PROBLEMS

8-8 Reloaded Games is an online games platform that powers leading massively multiplayer online games. The Reloaded platform serves more than 30 million users. The games can accommodate millions of players at once and are played simultaneously by people all over the world. Prepare a security analysis for this Internet-based business. What kinds of threats should it anticipate? What would be their impact on the business? What steps can it take to prevent damage to its websites and continuing operations?

8-9 A survey of your firm's IT infrastructure has identified a number of security vulnerabilities. Review the data about these vulnerabilities, which can be found in a table in MyLab MIS. Use the table to answer the following questions:

- Calculate the total number of vulnerabilities for each platform. What is the potential impact of the security problems for each computing platform on the organization?
- If you only have one information systems specialist in charge of security, which platforms should you address first in trying to eliminate these vulnerabilities? Second? Third? Last? Why?
- Identify the types of control problems these vulnerabilities illustrate and explain the measures that should be taken to solve them.
- What does your firm risk by ignoring the security vulnerabilities identified?

IMPROVING DECISION MAKING: USING SPREADSHEET SOFTWARE TO PERFORM A SECURITY RISK ASSESSMENT

Software skills: Spreadsheet formulas and charts
Business skills: Risk assessment

8-10 This project uses spreadsheet software to calculate anticipated annual losses from various security threats identified for a small company.

Mercer Paints is a paint manufacturing company located in Alabama that uses a network to link its business operations. A security risk assessment that management requested identified a number of potential exposures. These exposures, their associated probabilities, and average losses are summarized in a table, which can be found in MyLab MIS. Use the table to answer the following questions:

- In addition to the potential exposures listed, identify at least three other potential threats to Mercer Paints, assign probabilities, and estimate a loss range.
- Use spreadsheet software and the risk assessment data to calculate the expected annual loss for each exposure.
- Present your findings in the form of a chart. Which control points have the greatest vulnerability? What recommendations would you make to Mercer Paints? Prepare a written report that summarizes your findings and recommendations.

IMPROVING DECISION MAKING: EVALUATING SECURITY OUTSOURCING SERVICES

Software skills: Web browser and presentation software
Business skills: Evaluating business outsourcing services

8-11 This project will help develop your Internet skills in using the web to research and evaluate security outsourcing services.

You have been asked to help your company's management decide whether to outsource security or keep the security function within the firm. Search the web to find information to help you decide whether to outsource security and to locate security outsourcing services.

- Present a brief summary of the arguments for and against outsourcing computer security for your company.
- Select two firms that offer computer security outsourcing services and compare them and their services.
- Prepare an electronic presentation for management, summarizing your findings. Your presentation should make the case of whether your company should outsource computer security. If you believe your company should outsource, the presentation should identify which security outsourcing service you selected and justify your decision.

Collaboration and Teamwork Project

Evaluating Security Software Tools

8-12 With a group of three or four students, use the web to research and evaluate security products from two competing vendors, such as for antivirus software, firewalls, or antispyware software. For each product, describe its capabilities, for what types of businesses it is best suited, and its cost to purchase and install. Which is the best product? Why? If possible, use Google Docs and Google Drive or Google Sites to brainstorm, organize, and develop a presentation of your findings for the class.

CASE STUDY

U.S. Office of Personnel Management Data Breach: No Routine Hack

The U.S. Office of Personnel Management (OPM) is responsible for recruiting and retaining a world-class workforce to serve the American people and is also responsible for background investigations on prospective employees and security clearances. In June 2015, the OPM announced that it had been the target of a data breach targeting the records of as many as 4 million people. In the following months, the number of stolen records was upped to 21.5 million. This was no routine hack. It is the greatest theft of sensitive personnel data in history.

Information targeted in the breach included personally identifiable information such as social security numbers as well as names, dates and places of birth, and addresses. Also stolen was detailed security clearance–related background information. This included records of people who had undergone background checks but who were not necessarily current or former government employees.

The data breach is believed to have begun in March 2014 and perhaps earlier, but it was not noticed by the OPM until April 2015, and it is unclear how it was actually discovered. The intrusion occurred before OPM had finished implementing new security procedures that restricted remote access for network administrators and reviewed all Internet connections to the outside world.

U.S. government officials suspect that the breach was the work of Chinese hackers, although there is no proof that it was actually sponsored by the Chinese government. Chinese officials have denied involvement. The attackers had stolen user credentials from contractor KeyPoint Government Solutions to access OPM networks, most likely through social engineering. The hackers then planted malware, which installed itself within OPM's network and established a backdoor for plundering data. From there, attackers escalated their privileges to gain access to a wide range of OPM systems.

The hackers' biggest prize was probably more than 20 years of background check data on the highly sensitive 127-page Standard Forms SF-86 Questionnaire for National Security Positions. SF-86 forms contain information about family members, college roommates, foreign contacts, and psychological information. OPM information related to the background investigations of current, former, and prospective federal government employees, including U.S. military personnel, and those for whom a federal background investigation was conducted, may have been extracted. Government officials say that the exposure of security clearance information could pose a problem for years.

The Central Intelligence Agency (CIA) does not use the OPM system, and its records were protected during the breach. However, intelligence and congressional officials worried that the hackers or Chinese intelligence operatives could still use the detailed OPM information they did obtain to identify U.S. spies by process of elimination. If they combined the stolen data with other information gathered over time, they could use big data analytics to identify operatives.

The potential exposure of U.S. intelligence officers could prevent many of them from ever being posted abroad again. Adm. Michael S. Rogers, director of the National Security Agency, suggested that the personnel data could also be used to develop "spear phishing" attacks on government officials. In such attacks, victims are duped into clicking on what appear to be emails from people they know, allowing malware into their computer networks.

The stolen data also included 5.6 million sets of fingerprints. According to biometrics expert Ramesh Kesanupalli, this could compromise secret agents because they could be identified by their fingerprints even if their names had been changed.

The OPM had been warned multiple times of security vulnerabilities and failings. A March 2015 OPM Office of the Inspector General semiannual report to Congress mentioned persistent deficiencies in OPM's information system security program, including incomplete security authorization packages, weaknesses in testing information security controls, and inaccurate plans of action and milestones.

Security experts have stated that the biggest problem with the breach was not OPM's failure to prevent remote break-ins but the absence of mechanisms to detect outside intrusion and inadequate encryption of sensitive data. Assistant Secretary for Cybersecurity and Communications Andy Ozment pointed out that if someone has the credentials of a user on the network, then he or she can access data even if they are encrypted, so encryption in this instance would not have protected the OPM data.

OPM was saddled with outdated technology and weak management. A DHS Federal Information Security Management Act (FISMA) Audit for fiscal year 2014 and audit of the Office of the Inspector General found serious flaws in OPM's network and the way it was managed. OPM did not maintain an inventory of systems and baseline configurations, with 11 servers operating without valid authorization. The auditors could not independently verify OPM's monthly automated vulnerability scanning program for all servers. There was no senior information security specialist or chief information security officer (CISO) responsible for network security. OPM lacked an effective multifactor authentication strategy and had poor management of user rights, inadequate monitoring of multiple systems, many unpatched computers, and a decentralized and ineffective cybersecurity function. Sensitive data were unencrypted and stored in old database systems that were vulnerable. What's more, OPM used contractors in China to manage some of its databases. These deficiencies had been pointed out to OPM over and over again since a FISMA audit in 2007. OPM had the vulnerabilities, no security-oriented leadership, and a skillful and motivated adversary.

Some security experts see OPM's vulnerabilities as a sign of the times, a reflection of large volumes of data, contemporary network complexity, weak organizational and cultural practices, and a legacy of outdated and poorly written software. As Thomas Bayer, CIO at Standard & Poor's Ratings, explained, until you have a serious data breach like the OPM hack, everyone invests in other things. It's only when a massive data breach occurs that organizations focus on their infrastructure. The expertise and technology for halting or slowing down cyberattacks such as that on OPM are not a mystery, and many companies and some government organizations are effectively defending themselves against most of the risks they face.

OPM lacked leadership and accountability. The prevailing mentality was for everyone to sit and bide their time. The CEO, CIO, and CISO in a private organization would be held accountable by the board of directors.

OPM is a top-heavy organization, with a large management layer of senior advisers to the director. For example, CIO Donna Seymour has 28 staff members under her and four direct reporting organizations, none of which is security-focused. There is no listed CISO function. OPM's director has 62 senior leaders in four groups. Many OPM managers are politically appointed and lack the expertise to make informed decisions about cybersecurity. It's only when managers in an organization understand and appreciate information security risks that they will authorize their IT department to develop an effective set of controls.

Most directors in the U.S. government do not have people in their organizations with the expertise and power to make changes, and many staff members are just not right for the job. OPM director Katherine Archuleta had formerly been the National Political Director for Barak Obama's 2012 presidential reelection campaign. CIO Donna Seymour, who was supposed to advise Archuleta on how to manage risk in IT systems, was a career government employee for more than 34 years. She had some IT and management roles at the Department of Defense and other agencies and has a degree in computer science but no specific expertise in cybersecurity. It is also difficult to bring in experienced managers from the business world because federal government pay scales are so low. A chief information officer (CIO) or chief information security officer (CISO) in the federal government would probably be paid about $168,000 annually, whereas an equivalent position in the private sector would probably have annual compensation of $400,000.

Since the OPM break-in, there has been a massive effort to rectify years of poor IT management. OPM is moving toward more centralized management of security. Information system security officers (ISSOs) report directly to a CISO. These positions are filled by individuals with professional security backgrounds. OPM hired a cybersecurity advisor, Clifton Triplett, and increased its IT modernization budget from $31 million to $87 million, with another $21 million scheduled for 2016.

OPM told current and former federal employees they could have free credit monitoring for 18 months to make sure their identities had not been stolen, but it has been slapped with numerous lawsuits from victims. Seymour faces a lawsuit for her role in failing to protect millions of personal employee data files, and Archuleta had to resign.

The FBI and Department of Homeland Security released a "cyber alert" memo describing lessons learned from the OPM hack. The memo lists generally recommended security practices for OPM to adopt, including encrypting data, activating a personal firewall at agency workstations, monitoring users' online habits, and blocking potentially malicious sites. The Obama administration ordered a 30-day Cybersecurity Sprint across all agencies to try to fix the big problems. Without a strong foundation, this investment could prove futile in the long run. OPM and the federal government as a whole need to invest more in managers with IT security expertise and give those individuals real authority to act.

What about other federal agencies storing sensitive information? The news is not good. An audit issued before the Chinese attacks pointed to lax security at the Internal Revenue Service, the Nuclear Regulatory Commission, the Energy Department, the Securities and Exchange Commission, and even the Department of Homeland Security, which is responsible for securing the nation's critical networks and infrastructure. Computer security failure remains across agencies even though the U.S. government has spent at least $65 billion on security since 2006.

Sources: Sean Lyngaas, "What DHS and the FBI Learned from the OPM Breach," *FCW*, January 11, 2016; Brendan L. Koerner, "Inside the Cyberattack that Shocked the U.S. Government," *Wired*, October 23, 2016; Michael Adams, "Why the OPM Hack Is Worse Than You Imagined," *Lawfare*, March 11, 2016; Adam Rice, "Warnings, Neglect and a Massive OPM Breach," SearchSecurity.com, accessed June 15, 2016; Steve Rosenbush, "The Morning Download: Outdated Tech Infrastructure Led to Massive OPM Breach," *Wall Street Journal*, July 10, 2015; Mark Mazzette and David E. Sanger, "U.S. Fears Data Stolen by Chinese Hacker Could Identify Spies," *New York Times*, July 24, 2015; Damian Paletta and Danny Yadron, "OPM Ratches Up Estimate of Hack's Scope" *Wall Street Journal*, July 9, 2015; and David E. Sanger, Nicole Perlroth, and Michael D. Shear, "Attack Gave Chinese Hackers Privileged Access to U.S. Systems," *New York Times*, June 20, 2015.

CASE STUDY QUESTIONS

8-13 List and describe the security and control weaknesses at OPM that are discussed in this case.

8-14 What people, organization, and technology factors contributed to these problems? How much was management responsible?

8-15 What was the impact of the OPM hack?

8-16 Is there a solution to this problem? Explain your answer.

MyLab MIS

Go to the Assignments section of MyLab MIS to complete these writing exercises.

8-17 Describe three spoofing tactics employed in identity theft by using information systems.

8-18 Describe four reasons mobile devices used in business are difficult to secure.

Chapter 8 References

Amir, Waqas. "Facebook 'Comment Tagging Malware' Spreading via Google Chrome." *HackRead* (June 27, 2016).

Anderson, Bonnie Brinton, Anthony Vance, C. Brock Kirwan, Jeffrey L, Jenkins, and David Eargle. "From Warning to Wallpaper: Why the Brain Habituates to Security Warnings and What Can Be Done About It." *Journal of Management Information Systems* 33, No. 3 (2016).

Bauer, Harald, Ondrej Burkacky, and Christian Knochenhauer. "Security in the Internet of Things." McKinsey and Company (May 2017).

Boss, Scott R., Dennis F. Galletta, Paul Benjamin Lowry, Gregory D. Moody, and Peter Polak. "What Do Systems Users Have to Fear? Using Fear Appeals to Engender Threats and Fear that Motivate Protective Security Behaviors." *MIS Quarterly* 39, No. 4 (December 2015).

Boyle, Randall J., and Raymond R. Panko. *Corporate Computer Security*, 4th ed. (Upper Saddle River, NJ: Prentice-Hall, 2015.)

Chen, Yan, and Fatemeh Mariam Zahedi. "Individuals' Internet Security Perceptions and Behaviors: Polycontextual Contrasts Between the United States and China." *MIS Quarterly* 40, No. 1 (March 2016).

Chen, Yan, K. Ram Ramamurthy, and Kuang-Wei Wen. "Organizations' Information Security Policy Compliance: Stick or Carrot Approach?" *Journal of Management Information Systems* 29, No. 3 (Winter 2013).

CSA Top Threats Working Group. "The Treacherous Twelve: CSA's Cloud Computing Top Threats in 2016." Cloud Security Alliance (February 2016).

Esteves, Jose, Elisabete Ramalho, and Guillermo de Haro. "To Improve Cybersecurity, Think Like a Hacker." *MIT Sloan Management Review* (Spring 2017).

FireEye. "Out of Pocket: A Comprehensive Mobile Threat Assessment of 7 Million iOS and Android Apps." (February 2015).

Focus Research. "Devastating Downtime: The Surprising Cost of Human Error and Unforeseen Events." (October 2010).

Galbreth, Michael R., and Mikhael Shor. "The Impact of Malicious Agents on the Enterprise Software Industry." *MIS Quarterly* 34, No. 3 (September 2010).

Hui, Kai-Lun, Seung Hyun Kim, and Qiu-Hong Wang. "Cybercrime Deterrence and International Legislation: Evidence from Distributed Denial of Service Attacks." *MIS Quarterly* 41, No. 2 (June 2017).

Hui, Kai Lung, Wendy Hui, and Wei T. Yue. "Information Security Outsourcing with System Interdependency and Mandatory Security Requirement." *Journal of Management Information Systems* 29, No. 3 (Winter 2013).

Iansiti, Marco, and Karim R. Lakhani. "The Truth About Blockchain." *Harvard Business Review* (January–February 2017).

Javelin Strategy & Research. "2017 Identity Fraud Study." (February 1, 2017).

Kaminski, Piotr, Chris Rezek, Wolf Richter, and Marc Sorel. "Protecting Your Digital Assets." McKinsey & Company (January 2017).

Kaplan, James, Chris Rezek, and Kara Sprague. "Protecting Information in the Cloud." *McKinsey Quarterly* (January 2013).

Karlovsky, Brian. "FireEye Names Malware's Favorite Targets, Sources." *Australian Reseller News* (March 2, 2014).

Kaspersky Lab. "Mobile Malware Evolution 2016." (2017).

Kirk, Jeremy. "Pushdo Spamming Botnet Gains Strength Again." IDG News Service (April 20, 2015).

McMillan, Robert. "Software Bug at Internet Service Provider Sparks Privacy Concerns." *Wall Street Journal* (February 24, 2017).

Osterman Research. "The Risks of Social Media and What Can Be Done to Manage Them." Commvault (June 2011).

Paletta, Damian, Danny Yadron, and Jennifer Valentino-Devries. "Cyberwar Ignites a New Arms Race." *Wall Street Journal* (October 11, 2015).

Panda Security. "Cybersecurity Predictions 2017." (2016).

Panko, Raymond R., and Julie L. Panko. *Business Data Networks and Security*. (Upper Saddle River, NJ: Pearson, 2015.)

Perlroth, Nicole. "Online Attacks on Infrastructure Are Increasing at a Worrying Pace." *New York Times* (October 1, 2015).

Ponemon Institute. "2016 Cost of Cybercrime Study and The Risk of Business Innovation." (October (2016a).

__________. "2016 Cost of Data Breach Study: Global Analysis." (2016b).

__________. "The Cost of Malware Containment." (January 2015).

Poremba, Sue Marquette. "Hackers Targeting the Cloud at Higher Rates Than Ever." *IT Business Edge* (October 15, 2015).

Posey, Clay, Tom L. Roberts, and Paul Benjamin Lowry. "The Impact of Organizational Commitment on Insiders' Motivation to Protect Organizational Information Assets." *Journal of Management Information Systems* 32, No. 4 (2015).

Reisinger, Don. "Android Security Remains a Glaring Problem: 10 Reasons Why." *eWeek* (March 2, 2014).

Ribeiro, John. "Hacker Group Targets Skype Social Media Accounts." *Computer World* (January 2, 2014).

Sadeh, Norman M. "Phish Isn't Spam." *Information Week* (June 25, 2012).

Samuel, Alexandra. "Online Security as Herd Immunity." *Harvard Business Review* (March 13, 2014).

Scharr, Jill. "Fake Instagram 'Image Viewers' Are Latest Malware Fad." *Tom's Guide* (May 8, 2014).

Schwartz, Matthew J. "Android Trojan Looks, Acts Like Windows Malware." *Information Week* (June 7, 2013).

Sen, Ravi, and Sharad Borle. "Estimating the Contextual Risk of Data Breach: An Empirical Approach." *Journal of Management Information Systems* 32, No. 2 (2015).

Sengupta, Somini. "Machines That Know You Without Using a Password." *New York Times* (September 10, 2013).

Snell, Bruce. "Mobile Threat Report." McAfee Inc. (2016).

Solutionary. "Solutionary Security Engineering Research Team Unveils Annual Global Threat Intelligence Report." (March 12, 2013).

Spears, Janine L., and Henri Barki. "User Participation in Information Systems Security Risk Management." *MIS Quarterly* 34, No. 3 (September 2010).

Tapscott, Don, and Alex Tapscott. "How Blockchain Will Change Organizations." *MIT Sloan Management Review* (Winter 2017).

Temizkan, Orcun, Ram L. Kumar, Sungjune Park, and Chandrasekar Subramaniam. "Patch Release Behaviors of Software Vendors in Response to Vulnerabilities: An Empirical Analysis." *Journal of Management Information Systems* 28, No. 4 (Spring 2012).

Thompson, Jadiann. "Scam Alert: Two Clicks on Facebook Could Leak All Your Personal Info to an International Scammer." Kshb.com (April 30, 2015).

Vance, Anthony, Paul Benjamin Lowry, and Dennis Eggett. "Using Accountability to Reduce Access Policy Violations in Information Systems." *Journal of Management Information Systems* 29, No. 4 (Spring 2013).

Verizon. "2017 Data Breach Investigations Report." (2017).

Wakida, Clayton. "Anonymous Accused of Hacking TMT Web Site." KMTV.com (April 27, 2015).

Wang, Jingguo, Manish Gupta, and H. Raghav Rao. "Insider Threats in a Financial Institution: Analysis of Attack-Proneness of Information Systems Applications." *MIS Quarterly* 39, No. 1 (March 2015).

Young, Carl S. "The Enemies of Data Security: Convenience and Collaboration." *Harvard Business Review* (February 11, 2015).

Zhao, Xia, Ling Xue, and Andrew B. Whinston. "Managing Interdependent Information Security Risks: Cyberinsurance, Managed Security Services, and Risk Pooling Arrangements." *Journal of Management Information Systems* 30, No. 1 (Summer 2013).

PART III

Key System Applications for the Digital Age

Part III examines the core information system applications businesses are using today to improve operational excellence and decision making. These applications include enterprise systems; systems for supply chain management, customer relationship management, and knowledge management; e-commerce applications; and business intelligence systems to enhance decision making. This part answers questions such as these: How can enterprise applications improve business performance? How do firms use e-commerce to extend the reach of their businesses? How can systems improve decision making and help companies make better use of their knowledge assets?

CHAPTER

9

Achieving Operational Excellence and Customer Intimacy: Enterprise Applications

LEARNING OBJECTIVES

After reading this chapter, you will be able to answer the following questions:

9-1 How do enterprise systems help businesses achieve operational excellence?

9-2 How do supply chain management systems coordinate planning, production, and logistics with suppliers?

9-3 How do customer relationship management systems help firms achieve customer intimacy?

9-4 What are the challenges that enterprise applications pose, and how are enterprise applications taking advantage of new technologies?

9-5 How will MIS help my career?

CHAPTER CASES

- Skullcandy Rocks with ERP in the Cloud
- Logistics and Transportation Management at LG Electronics
- Kenya Airways Flies High with Customer Relationship Management
- How Supply Chain Management Problems Killed Target Canada

VIDEO CASES

- Life Time Fitness Gets in Shape with Salesforce CRM
- Evolution Homecare Manages Patients with Microsoft Dynamics CRM

Instructional Video:

- GSMS Protects Patients by Serializing Every Bottle of Drugs

MyLab MIS

- Discussion Questions: 9-5, 9-6, 9-7;
- Hands-on MIS Projects: 9-8, 9-9, 9-10, 9-11;
- Writing Assignments: 9-18, 9-19;
- eText with Conceptual Animations

SKULLCANDY ROCKS WITH ERP IN THE CLOUD

Those colorful edgy earbuds for your mobile phone might very well come from Skullcandy, a leading maker of audio and gaming headphones, earbuds, speakers, and other accessories. Skullcandy was born in 2003 on a chairlift, when founder Rick Alden came up with the idea for a device that could control both a mobile phone and a MP3 music player with a hassle-free one-touch button built into a set of earbuds. Skullcandy's bold colors and designs as well as products that could be integrated directly into helmets and backpacks made the brand a favorite of skiers, surfers, skaters, and other action sports enthusiasts. Skullcandy became wildly popular worldwide, growing 200 percent each year, and has 330 employees and annual revenue exceeding $266 million.

With such explosive growth, the company quickly outgrew its distribution model, which consisted of Alden delivering products personally from his basement to ski and skate shops in the Park City, Utah, area (the site of Skullcandy corporate headquarters). Skullcandy's business processes were primarily manual, with individual spreadsheets serving as the system of record for its business transactions. In order to grow to a company that could ship a million items each year, Skullcandy needed to automate its processes and use a new set of information systems to support them.

In 2008, the company started to replace its spreadsheets and manual processes with the SAP Business ByDesign cloud-based enterprise resource planning (ERP) system. Business ByDesign software supports end-to-end business processes for financial management, project management, supply chain management, supplier relationship management, human resources management, customer relationship management, executive management support, and compliance management. The applications are integrated, and the system is the backbone for tracking all the transactions of the company. As Skullcandy continued to grow, it implemented additional Business ByDesign capabilities for managing third-party logistics (3PL) providers, omnichannel sales, and additional financial processes. (Omnichannel sales seek to provide the customer with a seamless shopping experience whether the customer is shopping online from a desktop or mobile device, by telephone, or in a brick-and-mortar store.) Skullcandy uses the Business ByDesign software running in SAP cloud computing centers. It doesn't need a computer center of its own to run these systems or more than a few people in its IT department.

How have the new ERP applications worked out? Very well, according to Skullcandy's management. The new system functionality has been credited with helping the business pursue a strategic acquisition, expand internationally, and significantly increase its customer base. In 2011, Skullcandy acquired Astro Gaming, a premium gaming headset company based in San Francisco. The Business ByDesign system was able to absorb this acquisition and run its transactions as a new and separate legal entity. The system also supports Sarbanes-Oxley (SOX) compliance, which is one of the requirements for filing as a public company, smoothing the way for Skullcandy to issue an IPO (initial public offering).

Shortly after going public, Skullcandy set up operations in Zurich, Switzerland, which became its European headquarters. The company also has locations in Canada, Mexico, Japan, and China. Business ByDesign already incorporated the regulations and laws of each country where Skullcandy operated. Skullcandy did not have to implement another system to transact in euros or deal with value-added taxes. This functionality was already included in the Business ByDesign software, so Skullcandy could easily set up operations in other countries with their own laws, regulations, languages, and currencies.

Skullcandy's distribution channels continued to expand. Best Buy, Target, and Walmart began selling its products. Today nearly 80 percent of Skullcandy's transactions are fully automated from point-of-sale through delivery. From the time a customer clicks "buy," it takes less than half an hour for the transaction to move through Skullcandy's systems with a credit check, a check for fraud, a check for product availability, and warehouse fulfillment. Accuracy of shipments to customers exceeds 99 percent. Skullcandy can better manage its inventory, accounts, and information as it grows.

Sources: Ken Murphy, "Skullcandy Rocks the Cloud," *SAP Insider Profiles* 7, No. 1 (January 2016); "SAP Business by Design Case Study: Skullcandy Inc." and "Inspiring People to Live at Full Volume," www.sap.com, accessed April 10, 2017; and www.skullcandy.com, accessed April 10, 2017.

Skullcandy's problems with its legacy systems and its need to find integrated systems to support its new distribution model and global growth strategy illustrate why companies need enterprise applications. Enterprise resource planning (ERP) systems as well as those for supply chain management and customer relationship management can dramatically improve operational effectiveness and decision making by integrating different business functions and providing consistent information throughout the company.

The chapter-opening case calls attention to important points raised by this case and this chapter. Skullcandy's business performance and ability to expand to new markets domestically and overseas suffered because it was saddled with outdated systems designed primarily for its old distribution model as a small company selling to local ski and skate shops. Its spreadsheet-based systems and manual processes made it difficult for different parts of the company to work together and respond to new market opportunities. They left the company operating too inefficiently and unable to pursue its new business goals. By implementing SAP's Business ByDesign enterprise applications, Skullcandy was able to transition to more efficient business processes for its new business model, including forecasting, planning, profitability analysis, and new-product development, and it could support its strategic growth plan based on new acquisitions.

Skullcandy's new systems made it possible to run its business more efficiently and effectively and also had the functionality to support global expansion. However, in order to obtain these benefits from the enterprise software, Skullcandy had change some of its outdated business processes as well as its old legacy systems.

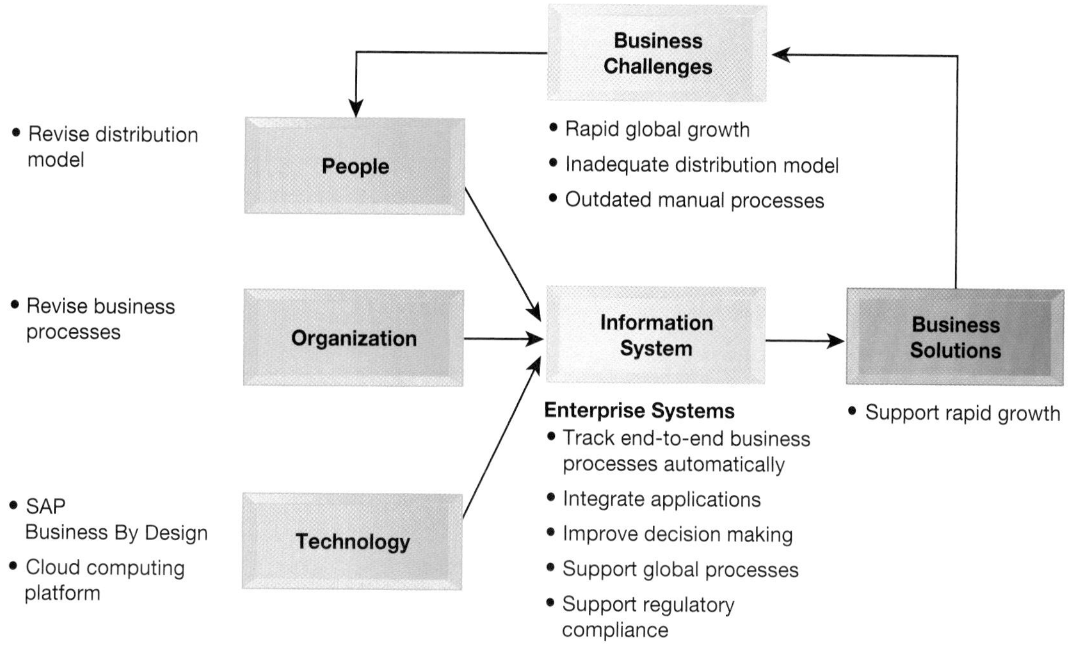

Here are some questions to think about: What problems did Skullcandy solve by implementing Business ByDesign? How did the new system change the way Skullcandy ran its business? What were the benefits of using cloud-based software for Skullcandy's solution?

9-1 How do enterprise systems help businesses achieve operational excellence?

Around the globe, companies are increasingly becoming more connected, both internally and with other companies. If you run a business, you'll want to be able to react instantaneously when a customer places a large order or when a shipment from a supplier is delayed. You may also want to know the impact of these events on every part of the business and how the business is performing at any point in time, especially if you're running a large company. Enterprise systems provide the integration to make this possible. Let's look at how they work and what they can do for the firm.

WHAT ARE ENTERPRISE SYSTEMS?

Imagine that you had to run a business based on information from tens or even hundreds of databases and systems, none of which could speak to one another. Imagine your company had 10 major product lines, each produced in separate factories and each with separate and incompatible sets of systems controlling production, warehousing, and distribution.

At the very least, your decision making would often be based on manual hard-copy reports, often out of date, and it would be difficult to understand what is happening in the business as a whole. Sales personnel might not be able to tell at the time they place an order whether the ordered items are in inventory, and manufacturing could not easily use sales data to plan for new production. You now have a good idea of why firms need a special enterprise system to integrate information.

Chapter 2 introduced enterprise systems, also known as enterprise resource planning (ERP) systems, which are based on a suite of integrated software modules

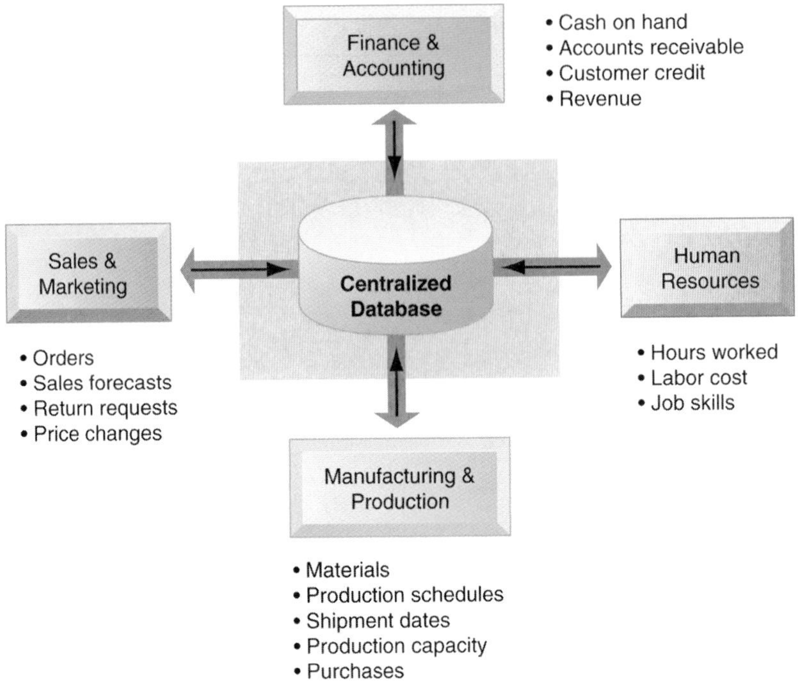

Figure 9.1
How Enterprise Systems Work
Enterprise systems feature a set of integrated software modules and a central database by which business processes and functional areas throughout the enterprise can share data.

and a common central database. The database collects data from many divisions and departments in a firm and from a large number of key business processes in manufacturing and production, finance and accounting, sales and marketing, and human resources, making the data available for applications that support nearly all an organization's internal business activities. When new information is entered by one process, the information is made immediately available to other business processes (see Figure 9.1).

If a sales representative places an order for tire rims, for example, the system verifies the customer's credit limit, schedules the shipment, identifies the best shipping route, and reserves the necessary items from inventory. If inventory stock is insufficient to fill the order, the system schedules the manufacture of more rims, ordering the needed materials and components from suppliers. Sales and production forecasts are immediately updated. General ledger and corporate cash levels are automatically updated with the revenue and cost information from the order. Users can tap into the system and find out where that particular order is at any minute. Management can obtain information at any point in time about how the business was operating. The system can also generate enterprise-wide data for management analyses of product cost and profitability.

ENTERPRISE SOFTWARE

Enterprise software is built around thousands of predefined business processes that reflect best practices. Table 9.1 describes some of the major business processes that enterprise software supports.

Companies implementing this software first have to select the functions of the system they wish to use and then map their business processes to the predefined business processes in the software. (One of our Learning Tracks shows how SAP enterprise software handles the procurement process for a new piece of equipment.) Configuration tables provided by the software manufacturer enable the firm to tailor a particular aspect of the system to the way it does business. For example, the firm could use these tables to select whether it wants to track revenue by product line, geographical unit, or distribution channel.

TABLE 9.1

Business Processes Supported by Enterprise Systems

Financial and accounting processes, including general ledger, accounts payable, accounts receivable, fixed assets, cash management and forecasting, product-cost accounting, cost-center accounting, asset accounting, tax accounting, credit management, and financial reporting

Human resources processes, including personnel administration, time accounting, payroll, personnel planning and development, benefits accounting, applicant tracking, time management, compensation, workforce planning, performance management, and travel expense reporting

Manufacturing and production processes, including procurement, inventory management, purchasing, shipping, production planning, production scheduling, material requirements planning, quality control, distribution, transportation execution, and plant and equipment maintenance

Sales and marketing processes, including order processing, quotations, contracts, product configuration, pricing, billing, credit checking, incentive and commission management, and sales planning

If the enterprise software does not support the way the organization does business, companies can rewrite some of the software to support the way their business processes work. However, enterprise software is unusually complex, and extensive customization may degrade system performance, compromising the information and process integration that are the main benefits of the system. If companies want to reap the maximum benefits from enterprise software, they must change the way they work to conform to the business processes defined by the software.

To implement a new enterprise system, Tasty Baking Company identified its existing business processes and then translated them into the business processes built into the SAP ERP software it had selected. To ensure that it obtained the maximum benefits from the enterprise software, Tasty Baking Company deliberately planned for customizing less than 5 percent of the system and made very few changes to the SAP software itself. It used as many tools and features that were already built into the SAP software as it could. SAP has more than 3,000 configuration tables for its enterprise software.

Leading enterprise software vendors include SAP, Oracle, IBM, Infor Global Solutions, and Microsoft. Versions of enterprise software packages are designed for small and medium-sized businesses and on-demand software services running in the cloud (see the chapter-opening case and Section 9-4).

BUSINESS VALUE OF ENTERPRISE SYSTEMS

Enterprise systems provide value by both increasing operational efficiency and providing firmwide information to help managers make better decisions. Large companies with many operating units in different locations have used enterprise systems to enforce standard practices and data so that everyone does business the same way worldwide.

Coca-Cola, for instance, implemented a SAP enterprise system to standardize and coordinate important business processes in 200 countries. Lack of standard, companywide business processes prevented the company from using its worldwide buying power to obtain lower prices for raw materials and from reacting rapidly to market changes.

Enterprise systems help firms respond rapidly to customer requests for information or products. Because the system integrates order, manufacturing, and delivery data, manufacturing is better informed about producing only what customers have ordered, procuring exactly the right number of components or raw materials to fill actual orders, staging production, and minimizing the time that components or finished products are in inventory.

Alcoa, the world's leading producer of aluminum and aluminum products with operations spanning 31 countries and more than 200 locations, had initially been organized around lines of business, each of which had its own set of information systems. Many of these systems were redundant and inefficient. Alcoa's costs for executing requisition-to-pay and financial processes were much higher, and its cycle times were longer than those of other companies in its industry. (Cycle time refers to the total elapsed time from the beginning to the end of a process.) The company could not operate as a single worldwide entity.

After implementing enterprise software from Oracle, Alcoa eliminated many redundant processes and systems. The enterprise system helped Alcoa reduce requisition-to-pay cycle time by verifying receipt of goods and automatically generating receipts for payment. Alcoa's accounts payable transaction processing dropped 89 percent. Alcoa was able to centralize financial and procurement activities, which helped the company reduce nearly 20 percent of its worldwide costs.

Enterprise systems provide much valuable information for improving management decision making. Corporate headquarters has access to up-to-the-minute data on sales, inventory, and production and uses this information to create more accurate sales and production forecasts. Enterprise software includes analytical tools to use data the system captures to evaluate overall organizational performance. Enterprise system data have common standardized definitions and formats that are accepted by the entire organization. Performance figures mean the same thing across the company. Enterprise systems allow senior management to find out easily at any moment how a particular organizational unit is performing, determine which products are most or least profitable, and calculate costs for the company as a whole.

For example, Alcoa's enterprise system includes functionality for global human resources management that shows correlations between investment in employee training and quality, measures the companywide costs of delivering services to employees, and measures the effectiveness of employee recruitment, compensation, and training.

9-2 How do supply chain management systems coordinate planning, production, and logistics with suppliers?

If you manage a small firm that makes a few products or sells a few services, chances are you will have a small number of suppliers. You could coordinate your supplier orders and deliveries by using just a telephone and fax machine. But if you manage a firm that produces more complex products and services, you will have hundreds of suppliers, and each of your suppliers will have its own set of suppliers. Suddenly, you will need to coordinate the activities of hundreds or even thousands of other firms to produce your products and services. Supply chain management (SCM) systems, which we introduced in Chapter 2, are an answer to the problems of supply chain complexity and scale.

THE SUPPLY CHAIN

A firm's **supply chain** is a network of organizations and business processes for procuring raw materials, transforming these materials into intermediate and finished products, and distributing the finished products to customers. It links suppliers, manufacturing plants, distribution centers, retail outlets, and customers to supply goods and services from source through consumption. Materials, information, and payments flow through the supply chain in both directions.

Goods start out as raw materials and, as they move through the supply chain, are transformed into intermediate products (also referred to as components or parts) and, finally, into finished products. The finished products are shipped to distribution centers and from there to retailers and customers. Returned items flow in the reverse direction from the buyer back to the seller.

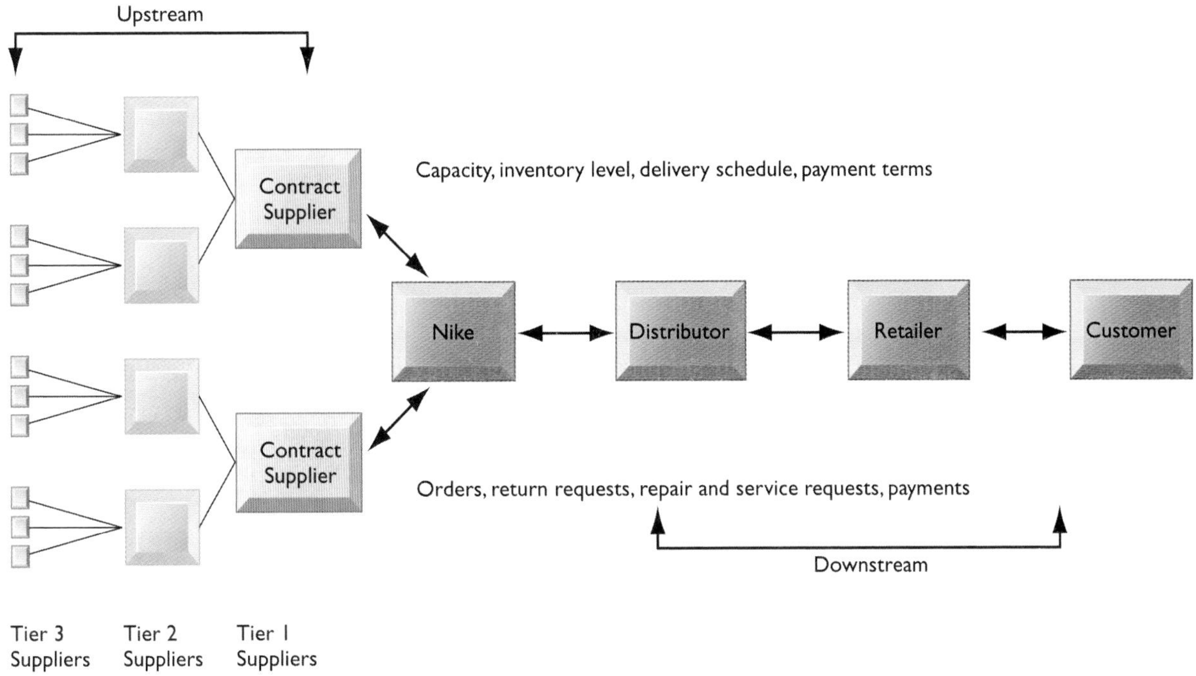

Figure 9.2
Nike's Supply Chain
This figure illustrates the major entities in Nike's supply chain and the flow of information upstream and downstream to coordinate the activities involved in buying, making, and moving a product. Shown here is a simplified supply chain, with the upstream portion focusing only on the suppliers for sneakers and sneaker soles.

Let's look at the supply chain for Nike sneakers as an example. Nike designs, markets, and sells sneakers, socks, athletic clothing, and accessories throughout the world. Its primary suppliers are contract manufacturers with factories in China, Thailand, Indonesia, Brazil, and other countries. These companies fashion Nike's finished products.

Nike's contract suppliers do not manufacture sneakers from scratch. They obtain components for the sneakers—the laces, eyelets, uppers, and soles—from other suppliers and then assemble them into finished sneakers. These suppliers in turn have their own suppliers. For example, the suppliers of soles have suppliers for synthetic rubber, suppliers for chemicals used to melt the rubber for molding, and suppliers for the molds into which to pour the rubber. Suppliers of laces have suppliers for their thread, for dyes, and for the plastic lace tips.

Figure 9.2 provides a simplified illustration of Nike's supply chain for sneakers; it shows the flow of information and materials among suppliers, Nike, Nike's distributors, retailers, and customers. Nike's contract manufacturers are its primary suppliers. The suppliers of soles, eyelets, uppers, and laces are the secondary (Tier 2) suppliers. Suppliers to these suppliers are the tertiary (Tier 3) suppliers.

The *upstream* portion of the supply chain includes the company's suppliers, the suppliers' suppliers, and the processes for managing relationships with them. The *downstream* portion consists of the organizations and processes for distributing and delivering products to the final customers. Companies that manufacture, such as Nike's contract suppliers of sneakers, also manage their own *internal supply chain processes* for transforming materials, components, and services their suppliers furnish into finished products or intermediate products (components or parts) for their customers and for managing materials and inventory.

The supply chain illustrated in Figure 9.2 has been simplified. It only shows two contract manufacturers for sneakers and only the upstream supply chain for sneaker soles. Nike has hundreds of contract manufacturers turning out finished sneakers, socks, and athletic clothing, each with its own set of suppliers. The upstream portion of Nike's supply chain actually comprises thousands of entities. Nike also has numerous distributors and many thousands of retail stores where its shoes are sold, so the downstream portion of its supply chain is also large and complex.

INFORMATION SYSTEMS AND SUPPLY CHAIN MANAGEMENT

Inefficiencies in the supply chain, such as parts shortages, underused plant capacity, excessive finished goods inventory, or high transportation costs, are caused by inaccurate or untimely information. For example, manufacturers may keep too many parts in inventory because they do not know exactly when they will receive their next shipments from their suppliers. Suppliers may order too few raw materials because they do not have precise information on demand. These supply chain inefficiencies waste as much as 25 percent of a company's operating costs.

If a manufacturer had perfect information about exactly how many units of product customers wanted, when they wanted them, and when they could be produced, it would be possible to implement a highly efficient **just-in-time strategy**. Components would arrive exactly at the moment they were needed, and finished goods would be shipped as they left the assembly line.

In a supply chain, however, uncertainties arise because many events cannot be foreseen—uncertain product demand, late shipments from suppliers, defective parts or raw materials, or production process breakdowns. To satisfy customers, manufacturers often deal with such uncertainties and unforeseen events by keeping more material or products in inventory than they think they may actually need. The *safety stock* acts as a buffer for the lack of flexibility in the supply chain. Although excess inventory is expensive, low fill rates are also costly because business may be lost from canceled orders.

One recurring problem in supply chain management is the **bullwhip effect**, in which information about the demand for a product gets distorted as it passes from one entity to the next across the supply chain. A slight rise in demand for an item might cause different members in the supply chain—distributors, manufacturers, suppliers, secondary suppliers (suppliers' suppliers), and tertiary suppliers (suppliers' suppliers' suppliers)—to stockpile inventory so each has enough just in case. These changes ripple throughout the supply chain, magnifying what started out as a small change from planned orders and creating excess inventory, production, warehousing, and shipping costs (see Figure 9.3).

For example, Procter & Gamble (P&G) found it had excessively high inventories of its Pampers disposable diapers at various points along its supply chain because of such distorted information. Although customer purchases in stores were fairly stable, orders from distributors spiked when P&G offered aggressive price promotions. Pampers and Pampers' components accumulated in warehouses along the supply chain to meet demand that did not actually exist. To eliminate this problem, P&G revised its marketing, sales, and supply chain processes and used more accurate demand forecasting.

The bullwhip effect is tamed by reducing uncertainties about demand and supply when all members of the supply chain have accurate and up-to-date information. If all supply chain members share dynamic information about inventory levels, schedules, forecasts, and shipments, they have more precise knowledge about how to adjust their sourcing, manufacturing, and distribution plans. Supply chain management systems provide the kind of information that helps members of the supply chain make better purchasing and scheduling decisions.

SUPPLY CHAIN MANAGEMENT SOFTWARE

Supply chain software is classified as either software to help businesses plan their supply chains (supply chain planning) or software to help them execute the supply chain steps (supply chain execution). **Supply chain planning systems** enable the firm to

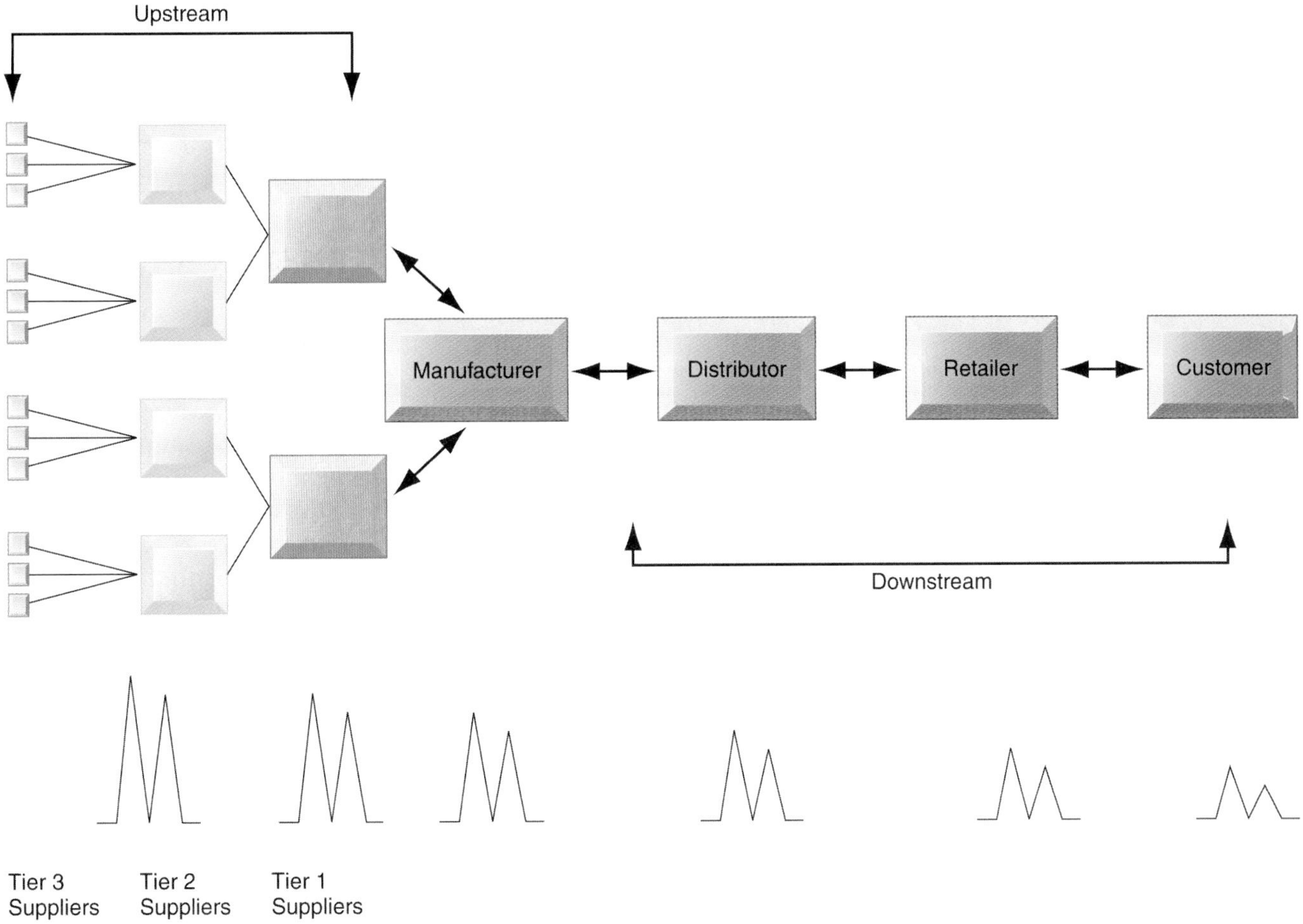

Figure 9.3
The Bullwhip Effect
Inaccurate information can cause minor fluctuations in demand for a product to be amplified as one moves further back in the supply chain. Minor fluctuations in retail sales for a product can create excess inventory for distributors, manufacturers, and suppliers.

model its existing supply chain, generate demand forecasts for products, and develop optimal sourcing and manufacturing plans. Such systems help companies make better decisions such as determining how much of a specific product to manufacture in a given time period; establishing inventory levels for raw materials, intermediate products, and finished goods; determining where to store finished goods; and identifying the transportation mode to use for product delivery.

For example, if a large customer places a larger order than usual or changes that order on short notice, it can have a widespread impact throughout the supply chain. Additional raw materials or a different mix of raw materials may need to be ordered from suppliers. Manufacturing may have to change job scheduling. A transportation carrier may have to reschedule deliveries. Supply chain planning software makes the necessary adjustments to production and distribution plans. Information about changes is shared among the relevant supply chain members so that their work can be coordinated. One of the most important—and complex—supply chain planning functions is **demand planning**, which determines how much product a business needs to make to satisfy all its customers' demands. JDA Software, SAP, and Oracle all offer supply chain management solutions.

Supply chain execution systems manage the flow of products through distribution centers and warehouses to ensure that products are delivered to the right locations in the most efficient manner. They track the physical status of goods, the management of materials, warehouse and transportation operations, and financial information involving all parties. An example is the Warehouse Management System (WMS) that Haworth Incorporated uses. Haworth is a world-leading manufacturer and designer of office furniture, with distribution centers in four states. The WMS tracks and controls the flow of finished goods from Haworth's distribution centers to its customers. Acting on shipping plans for customer orders, the WMS directs the movement of goods based on immediate conditions for space, equipment, inventory, and personnel.

GLOBAL SUPPLY CHAINS AND THE INTERNET

Before the Internet, supply chain coordination was hampered by the difficulties of making information flow smoothly among disparate internal supply chain systems for purchasing, materials management, manufacturing, and distribution. It was also difficult to share information with external supply chain partners because the systems of suppliers, distributors, or logistics providers were based on incompatible technology platforms and standards. Enterprise and supply chain management systems enhanced with Internet technology supply some of this integration.

A manager uses a web interface to tap into suppliers' systems to determine whether inventory and production capabilities match demand for the firm's products. Business partners use web-based supply chain management tools to collaborate online on forecasts. Sales representatives access suppliers' production schedules and logistics information to monitor customers' order status.

Global Supply Chain Issues

More and more companies are entering international markets, outsourcing manufacturing operations, and obtaining supplies from other countries as well as selling abroad. Their supply chains extend across multiple countries and regions. There are additional complexities and challenges to managing a global supply chain.

Global supply chains typically span greater geographic distances and time differences than domestic supply chains and have participants from a number of countries. Performance standards may vary from region to region or from nation to nation. Supply chain management may need to reflect foreign government regulations and cultural differences.

The Internet helps companies manage many aspects of their global supply chains, including sourcing, transportation, communications, and international finance. Today's apparel industry, for example, relies heavily on outsourcing to contract manufacturers in China and other low-wage countries. Apparel companies are starting to use the web to manage their global supply chain and production issues. (Review the discussion of Li & Fung in Chapter 3.)

In addition to contract manufacturing, globalization has encouraged outsourcing warehouse management, transportation management, and related operations to third-party logistics providers, such as UPS Supply Chain Solutions and Schneider National. These logistics services offer web-based software to give their customers a better view of their global supply chains. Customers can check a secure website to monitor inventory and shipments, helping them run their global supply chains more efficiently.

Demand-Driven Supply Chains: From Push to Pull Manufacturing and Efficient Customer Response

In addition to reducing costs, supply chain management systems facilitate efficient customer response, enabling the workings of the business to be driven more by customer demand. (We introduced efficient customer response systems in Chapter 3.)

Earlier supply chain management systems were driven by a push-based model (also known as build-to-stock). In a **push-based model**, production master schedules are based on forecasts or best guesses of demand for products, and products are pushed to customers. With new flows of information made possible by web-based

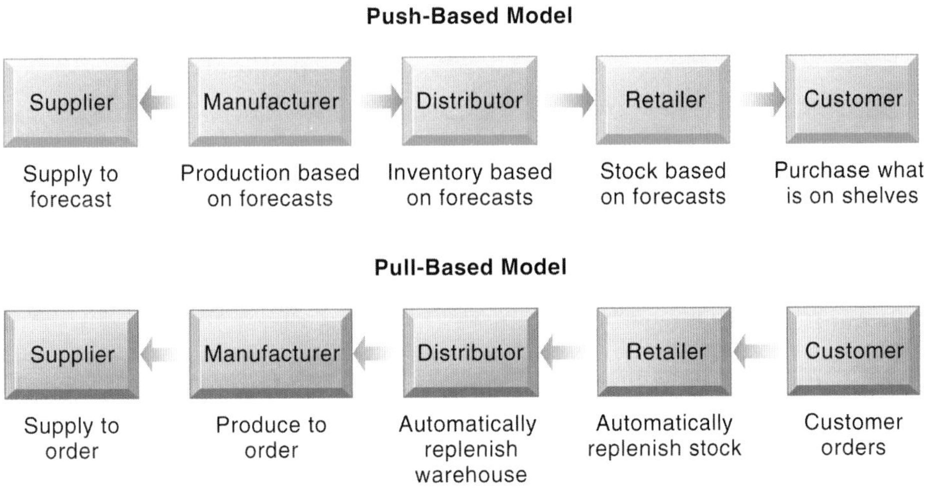

Figure 9.4
Push- Versus Pull-Based Supply Chain Models
The difference between push- and pull-based models is summarized by the slogan "Make what we sell, not sell what we make."

tools, supply chain management more easily follows a pull-based model. In a **pull-based model**, also known as a demand-driven or build-to-order model, actual customer orders or purchases trigger events in the supply chain. Transactions to produce and deliver only what customers have ordered move up the supply chain from retailers to distributors to manufacturers and eventually to suppliers. Only products to fulfill these orders move back down the supply chain to the retailer. Manufacturers use only actual order demand information to drive their production schedules and the procurement of components or raw materials, as illustrated in Figure 9.4. Walmart's continuous replenishment system described in Chapter 3 is an example of the pull-based model.

The Internet and Internet technology make it possible to move from sequential supply chains, where information and materials flow sequentially from company to company, to concurrent supply chains, where information flows in many directions simultaneously among members of a supply chain network. Complex supply networks of manufacturers, logistics suppliers, outsourced manufacturers, retailers, and distributors can adjust immediately to changes in schedules or orders. Ultimately, the Internet will enable a digital logistics nervous system for supply chains (see Figure 9.5).

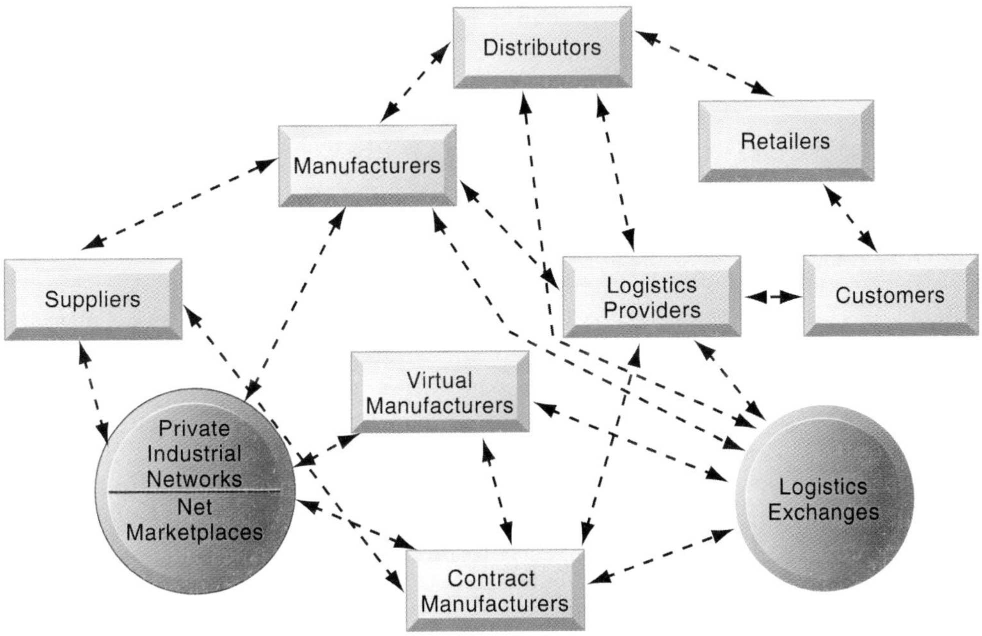

Figure 9.5
The Emerging Internet-Driven Supply Chain
The emerging Internet-driven supply chain operates like a digital logistics nervous system. It provides multidirectional communication among firms, networks of firms, and e-marketplaces so that entire networks of supply chain partners can immediately adjust inventories, orders, and capacities.

INTERACTIVE SESSION: TECHNOLOGY

Logistics and Transportation Management at LG Electronics

From its origins as the progenitor of South Korea's electronics industry and then its first global exporter, LG Electronics has evolved to a respected global brand with manufacturing facilities in China, India, Mexico, Brazil, Poland, and Russia and a presence in 49 countries. Headquartered in Seoul, South Korea, the company employs 75,000 people working in 118 locations around the world and had 2016 global sales of $47.9 billion. Perhaps best known today for its quality mobile phones, LG Electronics is also one of the world's top manufacturers of flat-screen televisions, air conditioners, washing machines, and refrigerators.

Led primarily by exploding demand for flat-screen televisions and mobile phones in the past 15 years, LG Electronics' European operations grew exponentially. By 2015, its logistics network was inadequate and severely overtaxed. Most of its transportation needs were outsourced to third-party logistics (3PL) providers. Internal knowledge and expertise were nonexistent. Management was clamoring for increased logistics visibility so that it could preempt bottlenecks rather than fashioning reflexive, and often imprudent, remedies. Dependent on their 3PL providers, managers had little to no control over transportation planning. Fixed routing in outsourced systems hamstrung management's ability to optimize carriers, loads, and overall capacity. In order to control performance and costs, LG Electronics Europe knew it had to take control of its logistics system and adopt robust performance evaluation tools so that it could continually adapt and revise transportation decisions.

LG Electronics Europe chose to implement JDA Software's Intelligent Fulfillment solutions: Transportation Modeler, Transportation Manager, and Transportation Planner. The ease of use and exceptional data-sharing capabilities of this unified supply chain planning, optimization, and business analytics platform immediately drew favorable reviews.

Once all managers could log in to a single source where all logistics data were shared, they could collaborate to find the most efficient and cost-effective transportation options. Transportation strategies could now be flexible and easily adapted to respond to fluctuations in product demand, shipping rates, fuel costs, and other factors.

LG used JDA Transportation Modeler to model an ideal logistics system that consolidated orders, established transportation hubs, and selected carriers in a flexible manner based on costs and service levels. With Transportation Modeler, LG Electronics Europe can assess the abilities of alternative transportation hubs and associated carriers to optimize order consolidation. What-if scenarios examine various requirements and objectives to design possible networks and outline the best way to run them.

Once a logistics system model has been settled upon, it is run through Transportation Manager to generate a new network. Transportation orders can then be dynamically managed. What's more, cross-company workflows now connect LG Electronics Europe to its supplier network. Freight audits reveal comprehensive statistical insight into logistics spending. Truck-loading efficiency ratios are used to optimize the vehicle-miles needed to transport like tonnages of freight. Consolidation ratios show how to combine two or more shipments to yield maximum cost savings.

Transportation Planner then weighs product availability, customer delivery commitments, and facility, inventory, and transportation network constraints to create benchmarks. By focusing managerial attention only on activities that fall outside of these accepted norms, labor productivity is maximized. This built-in exception-based management functionality minimizes the need for human intervention and review.

Three-dimensional load building automatically uses order line data to optimally configure pallets, taking into account weights, dimensions, stacking protocols, and other factors. A web-enabled interface displays this customizable 3-D view, and a Gantt bar chart illustrates the project schedule for dock and vehicle utilization. All transportation plans are archived so that they can be used in historical analysis and future what-if scenario construction, and previous asset allocations and carrier assignments are considered as new transportation plans are created. Multiple users can access and edit any active plan.

As LG Electronics Europe's users became comfortable with the system, they progressed beyond basic tasks such as loading trucks and scheduling deliveries to more complex issues including managing tariffs and checking for invoice duplication.

Workload efficiency was bolstered by the ability to access real-time information, the exception-based management tools, and the ability to tailor logistics to local environments. JDA Services—Consulting, Education, Performance Engineering, and Support Services—provided valuable support with system implementation. Change was introduced systematically with a comprehensive training regimen, JDA experts walked users through equipment use, interface details, tool usage minutiae, and other miscellaneous issues. In addition, LG participated in a JDA Special Interest Group (SIG), which organized and supervised group meetings with other JDA customers to share experiences and offer peer-to-peer support.

LG's new supply chain transportation knowledge base and increased visibility into its transportation network quickly produced significant cost savings,. Dedicated performance analysis using the built-in business intelligence (BI) tools resulted in improvements in all transportation metrics. Managers can now see a load plan's optimized cost compared with its implemented cost or how shipment costs are calculated from loads along with 60 other key metrics by selecting a report or dashboard directly within their current transportation workflow. Improved service (in-stock) levels, faster order cycle times, reduced time to implementation, and improvements in the freight audit process have all been achieved.

LG Electronics Europe can now also assess the performance of its carriers and allocate loads accordingly. Improved service levels have yielded increased customer satisfaction. Consolidation ratios in all implementations saw a 10 percent improvement, and optimized load configurations improved truck-loading efficiency ratios. In partnership with its 3PL providers, LG Electronics Europe is poised for continuing improvement in its service levels.

Sources: www.jda.com, accessed May 1, 2017; "LG Life's Good: Taking Control: LG Electronics Optimizes Its European Logistics with JDA Transportation Solutions," JDA Software Group Inc., July 8. 2015; and www.lg.com, accessed March 4, 2017.

CASE STUDY QUESTIONS

1. Identify the supply chain management problems LG Electronics faced. What was the business impact of its inability to manage its supply chain well?
2. What people, organization, and technology factors contributed to LG's supply chain problems?
3. How did implementing JDA Software solutions change the way LG ran its business?
4. How did LG's new logistics and transportation management system improve management decision making? Describe two decisions that the new system solution improved.

BUSINESS VALUE OF SUPPLY CHAIN MANAGEMENT SYSTEMS

You have just seen how supply chain management systems enable firms to streamline both their internal and external supply chain processes and provide management with more accurate information about what to produce, store, and move. By implementing a networked and integrated supply chain management system, companies match supply to demand, reduce inventory levels, improve delivery service, speed product time to market, and use assets more effectively (see the Interactive Session on Technology).

Total supply chain costs represent the majority of operating expenses for many businesses and in some industries approach 75 percent of the total operating budget. Reducing supply chain costs has a major impact on firm profitability.

In addition to reducing costs, supply chain management systems help increase sales. If a product is not available when a customer wants it, customers often try to purchase it from someone else. More precise control of the supply chain enhances the firm's ability to have the right product available for customer purchases at the right time.

9-3 How do customer relationship management systems help firms achieve customer intimacy?

You've probably heard phrases such as "the customer is always right" or "the customer comes first." Today these words ring truer than ever. Because competitive advantage based on an innovative new product or service is often very short lived, companies are realizing that their most enduring competitive strength may be their relationships with their customers. Some say that the basis of competition has switched from who sells the most products and services to who "owns" the customer and that customer relationships represent a firm's most valuable asset.

WHAT IS CUSTOMER RELATIONSHIP MANAGEMENT?

What kinds of information would you need to build and nurture strong, long-lasting relationships with customers? You'd want to know exactly who your customers are, how to contact them, whether they are costly to service and sell to, what kinds of products and services they are interested in, and how much money they spend on your company. If you could, you'd want to make sure you knew each of your customers well, as if you were running a small-town store. And you'd want to make your good customers feel special.

In a small business operating in a neighborhood, it is possible for business owners and managers to know their customers well on a personal, face-to-face basis, but in a large business operating on a metropolitan, regional, national, or even global basis, it is impossible to know your customer in this intimate way. In these kinds of businesses, there are too many customers and too many ways that customers interact with the firm (over the web, the phone, email, blogs, and in person). It becomes especially difficult to integrate information from all these sources and deal with the large number of customers.

A large business's processes for sales, service, and marketing tend to be highly compartmentalized, and these departments do not share much essential customer information. Some information on a specific customer might be stored and organized in terms of that person's account with the company. Other pieces of information about the same customer might be organized by products that were purchased. In this traditional business environment, there is no convenient way to consolidate all this information to provide a unified view of a customer across the company.

This is where customer relationship management systems help. Customer relationship management (CRM) systems, which we introduced in Chapter 2, capture and integrate customer data from all over the organization, consolidate the data, analyze the data, and then distribute the results to various systems and customer touch points across the enterprise. A **touch point** (also known as a contact point) is a method of interaction with the customer, such as telephone, email, customer service desk, conventional mail, Facebook, Twitter, website, wireless device, or retail store. Well-designed CRM systems provide a single enterprise view of customers that is useful for improving both sales and customer service (see Figure 9.6.)

Good CRM systems provide data and analytical tools for answering questions such as these: What is the value of a particular customer to the firm over his or her lifetime? Who are our most loyal customers? Who are our most profitable customers? What do these profitable customers want to buy? Firms use the answers to these questions to acquire new customers, provide better service and support to existing customers, customize their offerings more precisely to customer preferences, and provide ongoing value to retain profitable customers.

CUSTOMER RELATIONSHIP MANAGEMENT SOFTWARE

Commercial CRM software packages range from niche tools that perform limited functions, such as personalizing websites for specific customers, to large-scale enterprise applications that capture myriad interactions with customers, analyze them

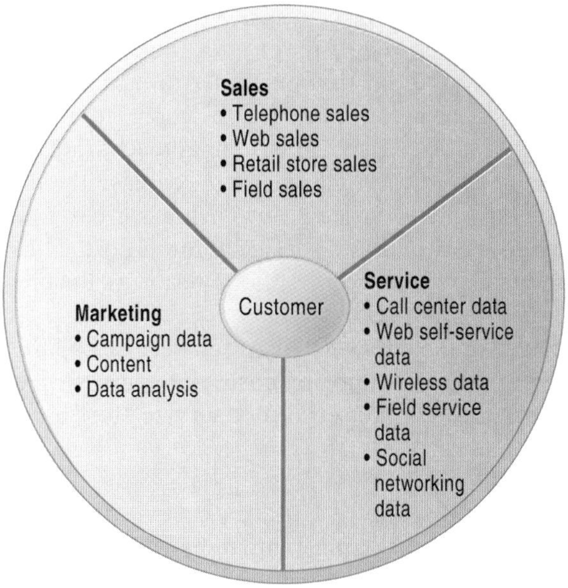

Figure 9.6
Customer Relationship Management (CRM)
CRM systems examine customers from a multifaceted perspective. These systems use a set of integrated applications to address all aspects of the customer relationship, including customer service, sales, and marketing.

with sophisticated reporting tools, and link to other major enterprise applications, such as supply chain management and enterprise systems. The more comprehensive CRM packages contain modules for **partner relationship management (PRM)** and **employee relationship management (ERM)**.

PRM uses many of the same data, tools, and systems as customer relationship management to enhance collaboration between a company and its selling partners. If a company does not sell directly to customers but rather works through distributors or retailers, PRM helps these channels sell to customers directly. It provides a company and its selling partners with the ability to trade information and distribute leads and data about customers, integrating lead generation, pricing, promotions, order configurations, and availability. It also provides a firm with tools to assess its partners' performances so it can make sure its best partners receive the support they need to close more business.

ERM software deals with employee issues that are closely related to CRM, such as setting objectives, employee performance management, performance-based compensation, and employee training. Major CRM application software vendors include Oracle, SAP, Salesforce.com, and Microsoft Dynamics CRM.

Customer relationship management systems typically provide software and online tools for sales, customer service, and marketing. We briefly describe some of these capabilities.

Sales Force Automation

Sales force automation (SFA) modules in CRM systems help sales staff increase productivity by focusing sales efforts on the most profitable customers, those who are good candidates for sales and services. SFA modules provide sales prospect and contact information, product information, product configuration capabilities, and sales quote generation capabilities. Such software can assemble information about a particular customer's past purchases to help the salesperson make personalized recommendations. SFA modules enable sales, marketing, and shipping departments to share customer and prospect information easily. SFA increases each salesperson's efficiency by reducing the cost per sale as well as the cost of acquiring new customers and retaining old ones. SFA modules also provide capabilities for sales forecasting, territory management, and team selling.

Customer Service

Customer service modules in CRM systems provide information and tools to increase the efficiency of call centers, help desks, and customer support staff. They have capabilities for assigning and managing customer service requests.

One such capability is an appointment or advice telephone line. When a customer calls a standard phone number, the system routes the call to the correct service person, who inputs information about that customer into the system only once. When the customer's data are in the system, any service representative can handle the customer relationship. Improved access to consistent and accurate customer information helps call centers handle more calls per day and decrease the duration of each call. Thus, call centers and customer service groups achieve greater productivity, reduced transaction time, and higher quality of service at lower cost. The customer is happier because he or she spends less time on the phone restating his or her problem to customer service representatives.

CRM systems may also include web-based self-service capabilities: The company website can be set up to provide inquiring customers personalized support information as well as the option to contact customer service staff by phone for additional assistance.

Marketing

CRM systems support direct-marketing campaigns by providing capabilities for capturing prospect and customer data, for providing product and service information, for qualifying leads for targeted marketing, and for scheduling and tracking direct-marketing mailings or email (see Figure 9.7). Marketing modules also include tools for analyzing marketing and customer data, identifying profitable and unprofitable customers, designing products and services to satisfy specific customer needs and interests, and identifying opportunities for cross-selling.

Cross-selling is the marketing of complementary products to customers. (For example, in financial services, a customer with a checking account might be sold a money market account or a home improvement loan.) CRM tools also help firms manage and execute marketing campaigns at all stages, from planning to determining the rate of success for each campaign.

Figure 9.8 illustrates the most important capabilities for sales, service, and marketing processes found in major CRM software products. Like enterprise software, this software is business-process driven, incorporating hundreds of business processes thought to represent best practices in each of these areas. To achieve maximum benefit, companies need to revise and model their business processes to conform to the best-practice business processes in the CRM software.

Figure 9.9 illustrates how a best practice for increasing customer loyalty through customer service might be modeled by CRM software. Directly servicing customers

Figure 9.7
How CRM Systems Support Marketing
Customer relationship management software provides a single point for users to manage and evaluate marketing campaigns across multiple channels, including email, direct mail, telephone, the web, and social media.

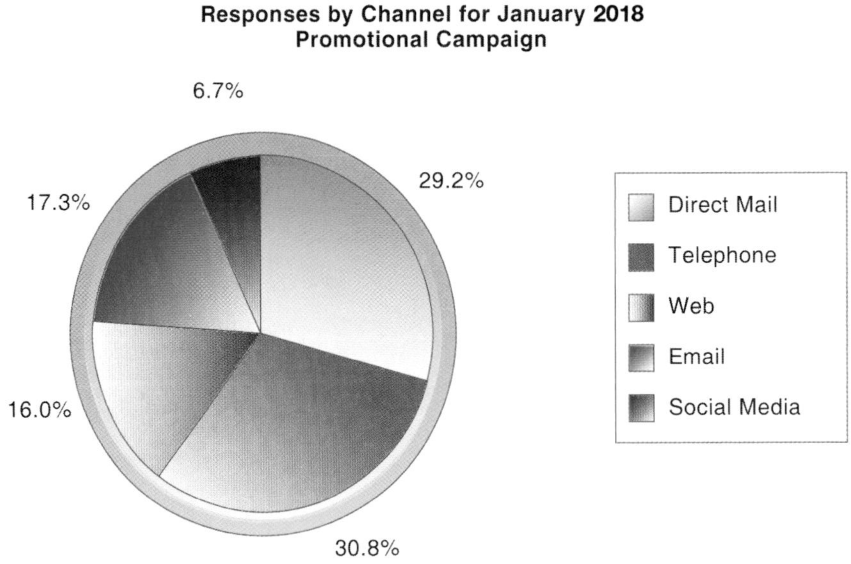

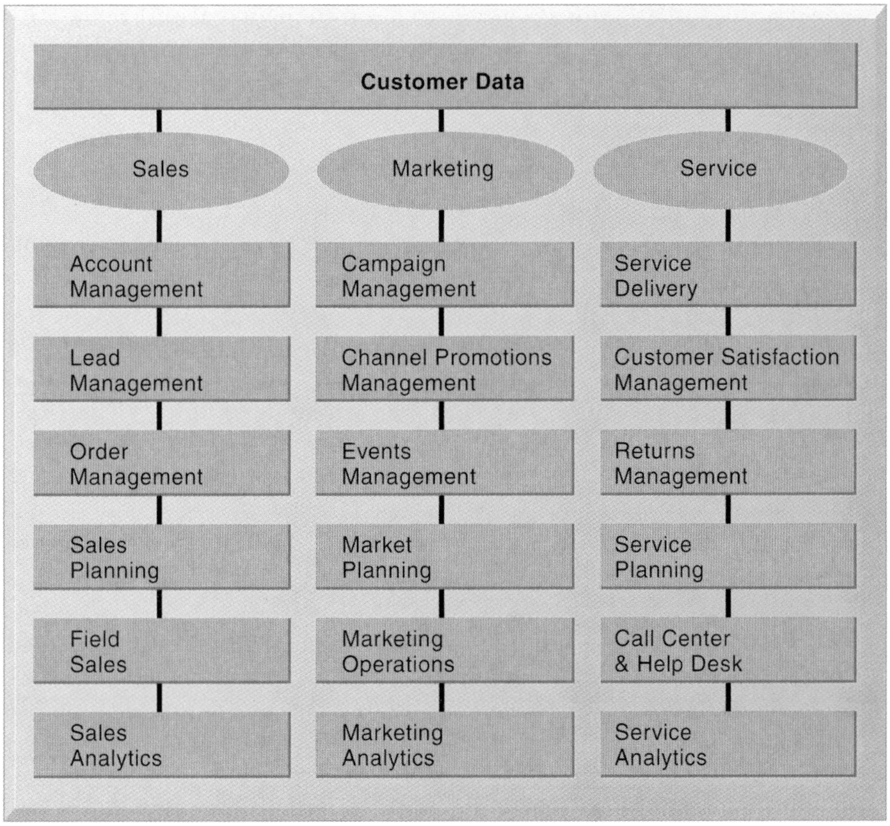

Figure 9.8
CRM Software Capabilities
The major CRM software products support business processes in sales, service, and marketing, integrating customer information from many sources. Included is support for both the operational and analytical aspects of CRM.

provides firms with opportunities to increase customer retention by singling out profitable long-term customers for preferential treatment. CRM software can assign each customer a score based on that person's value and loyalty to the company and provide that information to help call centers route each customer's service request to agents who can best handle that customer's needs. The system would automatically provide the service agent with a detailed profile of that customer that includes his or her score for value and loyalty. The service agent would use this information to

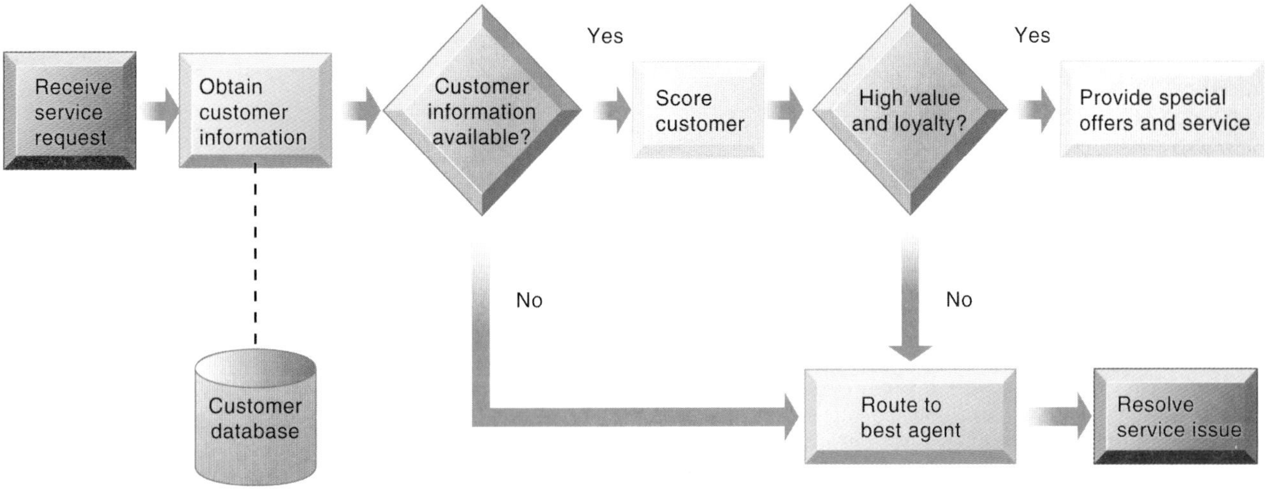

Figure 9.9
Customer Loyalty Management Process Map
This process map shows how a best practice for promoting customer loyalty through customer service would be modeled by customer relationship management software. The CRM software helps firms identify high-value customers for preferential treatment.

present special offers or additional service to the customer to encourage the customer to keep transacting business with the company. You will find more information on other best-practice business processes in CRM systems in our Learning Tracks.

OPERATIONAL AND ANALYTICAL CRM

All of the applications we have just described support either the operational or analytical aspects of customer relationship management. **Operational CRM** includes customer-facing applications, such as tools for sales force automation, call center and customer service support, and marketing automation. **Analytical CRM** includes applications that analyze customer data generated by operational CRM applications to provide information for improving business performance.

Analytical CRM applications are based on data from operational CRM systems, customer touch points, and other sources that have been organized in data warehouses or analytic platforms for use in online analytical processing (OLAP), data mining, and other data analysis techniques (see Chapter 6). Customer data collected by the organization might be combined with data from other sources, such as customer lists for direct-marketing campaigns purchased from other companies or demographic data. Such data are analyzed to identify buying patterns, to create segments for targeted marketing, and to pinpoint profitable and unprofitable customers (see Figure 9.10).

Another important output of analytical CRM is the customer's lifetime value to the firm. **Customer lifetime value (CLTV)** is based on the relationship between the revenue produced by a specific customer, the expenses incurred in acquiring and servicing that customer, and the expected life of the relationship between the customer and the company.

BUSINESS VALUE OF CUSTOMER RELATIONSHIP MANAGEMENT SYSTEMS

Companies with effective customer relationship management systems realize many benefits, including increased customer satisfaction, reduced direct-marketing costs, more effective marketing, and lower costs for customer acquisition and retention. Information from CRM systems increases sales revenue by identifying the most profitable customers and segments for focused marketing and cross-selling (see the Interactive Session on Organizations).

Figure 9.10
Analytical CRM
Analytical CRM uses a customer data warehouse or analytic platform and tools to analyze customer data collected from the firm's customer touch points and from other sources.

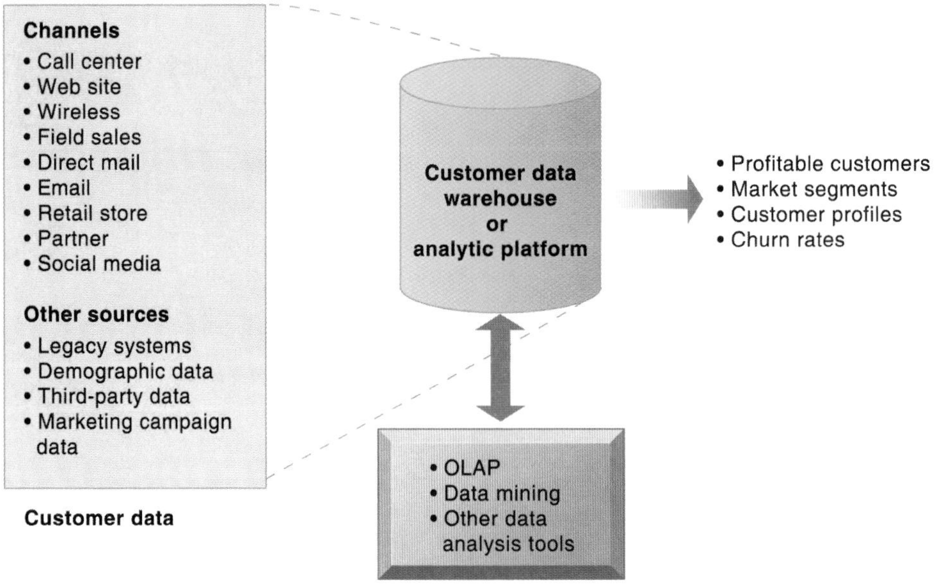

INTERACTIVE SESSION: ORGANIZATIONS

Kenya Airways Flies High with Customer Relationship Management

Kenya Airways is the flag carrier of Kenya and ranks fourth among the top ten African airlines in terms of seat capacity, with a fleet of 47 aircraft covering 62 destinations domestically and abroad. It is the only African airline in the SkyTeam alliance, whose 20 members include Delta Airlines, Air France, Alitalia, Aeromexico, China Airlines, and Korean Air, and is expected to live up to a very high global standard.

One area of the business that needed improvement was the airline's relationship to its customers. Africa's current population of 1 billion is expected to reach 1.5 billion within a decade, with a rapidly growing middle class in many countries. Until recently Kenya Airways was unable to fully capitalize on this market opportunity because it didn't know enough about its customers. Although the airline had added more planes, passenger numbers had been decreasing, partly due to the fear of Ebola virus outbreaks, regional terrorism, and increased competition from Persian Gulf carriers. Profitability suffered.

The airline didn't know who clicked on its email campaigns. It was advertising mostly on billboards, in newspapers, and on flyers, with no way to measure the effectiveness of those campaigns. There was no way to tell what its sales representatives in different offices were doing. Data on customers were located in many different repositories, such as spreadsheets and files in company and partner travel agent offices, reservation systems, and airport check-ins, and the data were not integrated. Without a single repository for customer data, Kenya Airways was unable to identify the preferences, special needs, or other personal characteristics of its "guests," who included commercial traders, business executives, government officials, students, missionaries, and medical tourists. Marketing, sales, and customer service activities were operating in the dark. For example, each May the airline would send every customer in its scattered data repositories a Mother's Day greeting, although many of the recipients were not mothers.

In 2014 Kenya Airways initiated a multiyear program to automate and integrate all of its customer data so that it could engage in effective customer relationship management using Oracle's Marketing, Sales, Data, and Service Clouds. Oracle Marketing Cloud provides a cloud-based platform to connect firms' marketing data, centrally orchestrate cross-channel customer interactions, engage the right audience, and analyze performance. It includes tools for managing marketing automation campaigns, providing cross-channel customer experiences, creating and managing engaging content, "listening" to customer conversations about a product, brand or service, and engaging with messaging (social marketing).

A few weeks after implementing Oracle Marketing Cloud, the airline ran its first automated marketing campaign, which directed emails, SMS texts, and social media posts about special holiday season fares to Kenyan emigrants in Dubai. Kenya Airways then created campaigns to promote new and expanded routes to Hanoi and Zanzibar. As time went on, the airline's marketing team became more skillful at tracking revenue flows generated by those campaigns and identifying new sources of data to target the campaigns more effectively. Kenya Airways marketing automation lead Harriet Luyai reported in early 2015 that "reachable contacts" rose from 40 percent to 89 percent, open rates on marketing emails rose from 40 percent to 65 percent, and the airline's "acquisition rate"—the percentage of respondents who opt in to its campaigns—was up to 20 percent. The airline can measure the impact of marketing campaigns on ticket sales. Campaigns that previously took three days to execute using an agency now take 30 minutes and are much less expensive.

After implementing Oracle Marketing Cloud, Kenya Airways started using Oracle Sales Cloud to automate its sales activities and Oracle RightNow Cloud Service for its customer service activities, linking all three clouds in one central data repository. Marketing, sales, and service could now integrate their customer data and coordinate business processes. The airline pulled together information on age, income, education level, job function, job level, revenue generated for the airline, geography, status, preferences, interest areas, service calls, email activity, form submissions, and purchase history to help it create very detailed customer profiles for personalizing offerings.

To help the Kenya Airways marketing team drive additional revenue by converting leads to ticket sales, increasing website traffic, and increasing social followers the airline implemented Oracle

Social Cloud. This tool helps the Kenya Airways customer service team follow social media posts and discussions about the airline's services and respond to questions and problems within 30 minutes. It also helps agents prioritize their follow-up posts and manage workflows for the appropriate approvals and for troubleshooting.

Although Kenya Airways had a customer loyalty program, it had previously been unable to identify high-value customers. Now Kenya Airways can track all its high-value customers and show how much revenue each customer generates. It can also segment customers across the customer life cycle, making it possible to distinguish a new customer from a longtime high-value customer. Kenya Airways now has a 360-degree view of each of its customers.

It took much more time to implement the Oracle Cloud suite than Kenya Airways had originally estimated—more than a year instead of six months. The required data, which resided in many different applications, needed to be cleansed to make sure they were all in the right format before they could be transferred to the new data repository. Much of this work was manual. Airline staff had to be trained in new ways of working with digital CRM tools because so much of its work had previously been manual. Kenya Airways management feels the airline has been richly rewarded for this effort.

Sources: Rob Preston, "First-Class Flight," *Profit Magazine*, August 2016; www.kenya-airways.com/us, accessed February 21, 2017; www.reuters.com, accessed February 21, 2017; "Kenya Airways Turns to McKinsey for Turnaround Strategy," Consultancy.uk, February 8, 2016; and Tilde Herrera, "Kenya Airways Fuels with Data to Lift Marketing," Ad Exchanger, October 29, 2015.

CASE STUDY QUESTIONS

1. What was the problem at Kenya Airways described in this case? What people, organization, and technology factors contributed to this problem?
2. What was the relationship of customer relationship management to Kenya Airways's business performance and business strategy?
3. Describe Kenya Airway's solution to its problem. What people, organization, and technology issues had to be addressed by the solution?
4. How effective was this solution? How did it affect the way Kenya Airways ran its business and its business performance?

Customer churn is reduced as sales, service, and marketing respond better to customer needs. The **churn rate** measures the number of customers who stop using or purchasing products or services from a company. It is an important indicator of the growth or decline of a firm's customer base.

9-4 What are the challenges that enterprise applications pose, and how are enterprise applications taking advantage of new technologies?

Many firms have implemented enterprise systems and systems for supply chain and customer relationship management because they are such powerful instruments for achieving operational excellence and enhancing decision making. But precisely because they are so powerful in changing the way the organization works, they are challenging to implement. Let's briefly examine some of these challenges as well as new ways of obtaining value from these systems.

ENTERPRISE APPLICATION CHALLENGES

Promises of dramatic reductions in inventory costs, order-to-delivery time, more efficient customer response, and higher product and customer profitability make enterprise systems and systems for SCM and CRM very alluring. But to obtain this value, you must clearly understand how your business has to change to use these systems effectively.

Enterprise applications involve complex pieces of software that are very expensive to purchase and implement. It might take a large *Fortune* 500 company several years to complete a large-scale implementation of an enterprise system or a system for SCM or CRM. According to a 2016 survey of 215 ERP users conducted by Panorama Consulting Solutions, the average cost of an ERP project was $3.8 million. Projects took an average of 21.1 months to complete, and 46 percent of the projects delivered 50 percent or less of the expected benefits. Approximately 57 percent of these projects experienced cost overruns and schedule overruns (Panorama Consulting Solutions, 2016). Changes in project scope and additional customization work add to implementation delays and costs.

Enterprise applications require not only deep-seated technological changes but also fundamental changes in the way the business operates. Companies must make sweeping changes to their business processes to work with the software. Employees must accept new job functions and responsibilities. They must learn how to perform a new set of work activities and understand how the information they enter into the system can affect other parts of the company. This requires new organizational learning and should also be factored into ERP implementation costs.

SCM systems require multiple organizations to share information and business processes. Each participant in the system may have to change some of its processes and the way it uses information to create a system that best serves the supply chain as a whole.

Some firms experienced enormous operating problems and losses when they first implemented enterprise applications because they didn't understand how much organizational change was required. For example, Kmart had trouble getting products to store shelves when it first implemented i2 Technologies (now JDA Software) SCM software. The i2 software did not work well with Kmart's promotion-driven business model, which created sharp spikes in demand for products. Overstock.com's order tracking system went down for a full week when the company replaced a homegrown system with an Oracle enterprise system. The company rushed to implement the software and did not properly synchronize the Oracle software's process for recording customer refunds with its accounts receivable system. The chapter-ending case shows how rushed implementation of enterprise applications contributed to Target Canada's business failure.

Enterprise applications also introduce switching costs. When you adopt an enterprise application from a single vendor, such as SAP, Oracle, or others, it is very costly to switch vendors, and your firm becomes dependent on the vendor to upgrade its product and maintain your installation.

Enterprise applications are based on organization-wide definitions of data. You'll need to understand exactly how your business uses its data and how the data would be organized in a CRM, SCM, or ERP system. CRM systems typically require some data cleansing work.

Enterprise software vendors are addressing these problems by offering pared-down versions of their software and fast-start programs for small and medium-sized businesses and best-practice guidelines for larger companies. Companies are also achieving more flexibility by using cloud applications for functions not addressed by the basic enterprise software so that they are not constrained by a single do-it-all type of system.

Companies adopting enterprise applications can also save time and money by keeping customizations to a minimum. For example, Kennametal, a $2 billion metal-cutting tools company in Pennsylvania, had spent $10 million over 13 years maintaining an ERP system with more than 6,400 customizations. The company replaced it with a plain-vanilla, uncustomized version of SAP enterprise software and changed its business processes to conform to the software.

NEXT-GENERATION ENTERPRISE APPLICATIONS

Today, enterprise application vendors are delivering more value by becoming more flexible, user-friendly, web-enabled, mobile, and capable of integration with other systems. Stand-alone enterprise systems, customer relationship management systems, and SCM systems are becoming a thing of the past. The major enterprise software vendors have created what they call *enterprise solutions*, *enterprise suites*, or e-business suites to make their CRM, SCM, and ERP systems work closely with each other and link to systems of customers and suppliers. SAP Business Suite, Oracle E-Business Suite, and Microsoft Dynamics Suite (aimed at midsized companies) are examples, and they now use web services and service-oriented architecture (SOA) (see Chapter 5).

Next-generation enterprise applications also include open source and cloud solutions as well as more functionality available on mobile platforms. Open source products such as Compiere, Apache Open for Business (OFBiz) and Openbravo do not offer as many capabilities as large commercial enterprise software but are attractive to companies such as small manufacturers because of their low cost.

Large enterprise software vendors such as SAP, Oracle, Microsoft, and Epicor now feature cloud versions of their flagship ERP systems and also cloud-based products for small and medium-sized businesses. SAP, for example, offers the SAP HANA Cloud Platform and cloud-first SAP Business ByDesign enterprise software for small and medium-sized businesses. Microsoft recently released a cloud-first upgrade of its Dynamics AX ERP, which is deployed on the Microsoft Azure cloud platform. Cloud-based enterprise systems are also offered by smaller vendors such as NetSuite and Plex Systems.

The undisputed global market leader in cloud-based CRM systems is Salesforce.com, which we described in Chapter 5. Salesforce.com delivers its service through Internet-connected computers or mobile devices, and it is widely used by small, medium-sized, and large enterprises. As cloud-based products mature, more companies, including very large *Fortune* 500 firms, will be choosing to run all or part of their enterprise applications in the cloud.

Social CRM

CRM software vendors are enhancing their products to take advantage of social networking technologies. These social enhancements help firms identify new ideas more rapidly, improve team productivity, and deepen interactions with customers (see Chapter 10). Using **social CRM** tools, businesses can better engage with their customers by, for example, analyzing their sentiments about their products and services.

Social CRM tools enable a business to connect customer conversations and relationships from social networking sites to CRM processes. The leading CRM vendors now offer such tools to link data from social networks to their CRM software. SAP, Salesforce.com, and Oracle CRM products now feature technology to monitor, track, and analyze social media activity on Facebook, LinkedIn, Twitter, YouTube, and other sites. Business intelligence and analytics software vendors such as SAS also have capabilities for social media analytics (with several measures of customer engagement across a variety of social networks) along with campaign management tools for testing and optimizing both social and traditional web-based campaigns.

Salesforce.com connected its system for tracking leads in the sales process with social-listening and social-media marketing tools, enabling users to tailor their social-marketing dollars to core customers and observe the resulting comments. If an ad agency wants to run a targeted Facebook or Twitter ad, these capabilities make it possible to aim the ad specifically at people in the client's lead pipeline who are already being tracked in the CRM system. Users will be able to view tweets as they take place in real time and perhaps uncover new leads. They can also manage multiple campaigns and compare them all to figure out which ones generate the highest click-through rates and cost per click.

Business Intelligence in Enterprise Applications

Enterprise application vendors have added business intelligence features to help managers obtain more meaningful information from the massive amounts of data these systems generate. SAP now makes it possible for its enterprise applications to use HANA in-memory computing technology so that they are capable of much more rapid and complex data analysis. Included are tools for flexible reporting, ad hoc analysis, interactive dashboards, what-if scenario analysis, and data visualization. Rather than requiring users to leave an application and launch separate reporting and analytics tools, the vendors are starting to embed analytics within the context of the application itself. They are also offering complementary analytics products such as SAP BusinessObjects and Oracle Business Intelligence Enterprise Edition.

The major enterprise application vendors offer portions of their products that work on mobile handhelds. You can find out more about this topic in our Learning Track on Wireless Applications for Customer Relationship Management, Supply Chain Management, and Healthcare.

9-5 How will MIS help my career?

Here is how this Chapter 9 and this book can help you find a job as a manufacturing management trainee.

THE COMPANY

XYZ Global Industrial Components is a large Michigan-headquartered company with 40 global manufacturing facilities and more than 4,000 employees worldwide, and it has an open position for a new college graduate in its Manufacturing Management Program. The company produces fastener, engineered, and linkage and suspension components for automotive, heavy duty trucks, aerospace, electric utility, telecommunications, and other industries worldwide.

POSITION DESCRIPTION

The Manufacturing Management Program is a rotational, two-year program designed to nurture and train future managers by enabling recent college graduates to acquire critical skills and industry experience in plant, technical, and corporate environments. Job responsibilities include:

- Working with business units and project teams on systems implementation, including implementation of ERP and JDA manufacturing systems.
- Understanding business processes and data requirements for each business unit.
- Proficiency in supporting and conducting business requirement analysis sessions.
- Tracking and documenting changes to functional and business specifications.
- Writing user documentation, instructions, and procedures.
- Monitoring and documenting post-implementation problems and revision requests.

JOB REQUIREMENTS

- Bachelor's degree in IT, MIS, engineering, or related field or equivalent, with a GPA higher than 3.0
- Demonstrated skills in Microsoft Office Suite
- Strong written and verbal communication skills
- Proven track record of accomplishments both inside and outside the educational setting
- Experience in a leadership role in a team

INTERVIEW QUESTIONS

1. Describe the projects you have worked on in a team. Did you play a leadership role? Exactly what did you do to help your team achieve its goal? Were any of these projects IT projects?

2. What do you know about ERP or JDA manufacturing systems? Have you ever worked with them? What exactly did you do with these systems?
3. Tell us what you can do with Microsoft Office software. Which tools have you used? Do you have any Access and Excel skills? What kinds of problems have you used these tools to solve? Did you take courses in Access or Excel?

AUTHOR TIPS

1. Do some research on the company, its industry, and the kinds of challenges it faces. Look through the company's LinkedIn page and read their posts over the past twelve months. Are there any key trends in the LinkedIn posts for this company?
2. Review this text's Chapter 9 on enterprise applications and Chapter 12 on developing systems and IT project management and implementation.
3. View YouTube videos created by major IT consulting firms that discuss the latest trends in manufacturing technology and enterprise systems.
4. Inquire about how you would be using Microsoft Office tools for the job and what Excel and Access skills you would be expected to demonstrate. Bring examples of the work you have done with this software. Show that you would be eager to learn what you don't know about these tools to fulfill your job assignments.
5. Bring examples of your writing (including some from your Digital Portfolio described in MyLab MIS) demonstrating your analytical skills and project experience.

Review Summary

9-1 **How do enterprise systems help businesses achieve operational excellence?** Enterprise software is based on a suite of integrated software modules and a common central database. The database collects data from and feeds the data into numerous applications that can support nearly all of an organization's internal business activities. When one process enters new information, the information is made available immediately to other business processes.

Enterprise systems support organizational centralization by enforcing uniform data standards and business processes throughout the company and a single unified technology platform. The firmwide data that enterprise systems generate help managers evaluate organizational performance.

9-2 **How do supply chain management systems coordinate planning, production, and logistics with suppliers?** Supply chain management (SCM) systems automate the flow of information among members of the supply chain so they can use it to make better decisions about when and how much to purchase, produce, or ship. More accurate information from supply chain management systems reduces uncertainty and the impact of the bullwhip effect.

Supply chain management software includes software for supply chain planning and for supply chain execution. Internet technology facilitates the management of global supply chains by providing the connectivity for organizations in different countries to share supply chain information. Improved communication among supply chain members also facilitates efficient customer response and movement toward a demand-driven model.

9-3 **How do customer relationship management systems help firms achieve customer intimacy?** Customer relationship management (CRM) systems integrate and automate customer-facing processes in sales, marketing, and customer service, providing an enterprise-wide view of customers. Companies can use this customer knowledge when they interact with customers to provide them with better service or sell new products and services. These systems also identify profitable or unprofitable customers or opportunities to reduce the churn rate.

The major customer relationship management software packages provide capabilities for both operational CRM and analytical CRM. They often include modules for managing relationships with selling partners (partner relationship management) and for employee relationship management.

9-4 **What are the challenges that enterprise applications pose, and how are enterprise applications taking advantage of new technologies?** Enterprise applications are difficult to implement. They require extensive organizational change, large new software investments, and careful assessment of how these systems will enhance organizational performance. Enterprise applications cannot provide value if they are implemented atop flawed processes or if firms do not know how to use these systems to measure performance improvements. Employees require training to prepare for new procedures and roles. Attention to data management is essential.

Enterprise applications are now more flexible, web-enabled, and capable of integration with other systems, using web services and service-oriented architecture (SOA). They also have open source and on-demand versions and can run in cloud infrastructures or on mobile platforms. CRM software has added social networking capabilities to enhance internal collaboration, deepen interactions with customers, and use data from social networking sites. Open source, mobile, and cloud versions of some of these products are becoming available.

Key Terms

Analytical CRM, 332
Bullwhip effect, 322
Churn rate, 334
Cross-selling, 330
Customer lifetime value (CLTV), 332
Demand planning, 323
Employee relationship management (ERM), 329
Enterprise software, 318
Just-in-time strategy, 322
Operational CRM, 332
Partner relationship management (PRM), 329
Pull-based model, 325
Push-based model, 324
Sales force automation (SFA), 329
Social CRM, 336
Supply chain, 320
Supply chain execution systems, 323
Supply chain planning systems, 322
Touch point, 328

MyLab MIS

To complete the problems with **MyLab MIS**, go to the EOC Discussion Questions in MyLab MIS.

Review Questions

9-1 How do enterprise systems help businesses achieve operational excellence?
- Define an enterprise system and explain how enterprise software works.
- Describe how enterprise systems provide value for a business.

9-2 How do supply chain management systems coordinate planning, production, and logistics with suppliers?
- Define a supply chain and identify each of its components.
- Explain how supply chain management systems help reduce the bullwhip effect and how they provide value for a business.
- Define and compare supply chain planning systems and supply chain execution systems.
- Describe the challenges of global supply chains and how Internet technology can help companies manage them better.
- Distinguish between a push-based and a pull-based model of supply chain management and explain how contemporary supply chain management systems facilitate a pull-based model.

9-3 How do customer relationship management systems help firms achieve customer intimacy?

- Define customer relationship management and explain why customer relationships are so important today.
- Describe how partner relationship management (PRM) and employee relationship management (ERM) are related to customer relationship management (CRM).
- Describe the tools and capabilities of customer relationship management software for sales, marketing, and customer service.
- Distinguish between operational and analytical CRM.

9-4 What are the challenges that enterprise applications pose, and how are enterprise applications taking advantage of new technologies?

- List and describe the challenges enterprise applications pose.
- Explain how these challenges can be addressed.
- Describe how enterprise applications are taking advantage of SOA, cloud computing, and open source software.
- Define social CRM and explain how customer relationship management systems are using social networking.

Discussion Questions

9-5 MyLab MIS Supply chain management is less about managing the physical movement of goods and more about managing information. Discuss the implications of this statement.

9-6 MyLab MIS If a company wants to implement an enterprise application, it had better do its homework. Discuss the implications of this statement.

9-7 MyLab MIS Which enterprise application should a business install first: ERP, SCM, or CRM? Explain your answer.

Hands-On MIS Projects

The projects in this section give you hands-on experience analyzing business process integration, suggesting supply chain management and customer relationship management applications, using database software to manage customer service requests, and evaluating supply chain management business services. Visit **MyLab MIS** to access this chapter's Hands-On MIS Projects,

MANAGEMENT DECISION PROBLEMS

9-8 Toronto-based Mercedes-Benz Canada, with a network of 55 dealers, did not know enough about its customers. Dealers provided customer data to the company on an ad hoc basis. Mercedes did not force dealers to report this information. There was no real incentive for dealers to share information with the company. How could CRM and PRM systems help solve this problem?

9-9 Office Depot sells a wide range of office supply products and services in the United States and internationally. The company tries to offer a wider range of office supplies at lower cost than other retailers by using just-in-time replenishment and tight inventory control systems. It uses information from a demand forecasting system and point-of-sale data to replenish its inventory in its 1,600 retail stores. Explain how these systems help Office Depot minimize costs and any other benefits they provide. Identify and describe other supply chain management applications that would be especially helpful to Office Depot.

IMPROVING DECISION MAKING: USING DATABASE SOFTWARE TO MANAGE CUSTOMER SERVICE REQUESTS

Software skills: Database design; querying and reporting
Business skills: Customer service analysis

9-10 In this exercise, you'll use database software to develop an application that tracks customer service requests and analyzes customer data to identify customers meriting priority treatment.

Prime Service is a large service company that provides maintenance and repair services for close to 1,200 commercial businesses in New York, New Jersey, and Connecticut. Its customers include businesses of all sizes. Customers with service needs call into its customer service department with requests for repairing heating ducts, broken windows, leaky roofs, broken water pipes, and other problems. The company assigns each request a number and writes down the service request number, the identification number of the customer account, the date of the request, the type of equipment requiring repair, and a brief description of the problem. The service requests are handled on a first-come-first-served basis. After the service work has been completed, Prime calculates the cost of the work, enters the price on the service request form, and bills the client. This arrangement treats the most important and profitable clients—those with accounts of more than $70,000—no differently from its clients with small accounts. Management would like to find a way to provide its best customers with better service. It would also like to know which types of service problems occur most frequently so that it can make sure it has adequate resources to address them.

Prime Service has a small database with client account information, which can be found in MyLab MIS. Use database software to design a solution that would enable Prime's customer service representatives to identify the most important customers so that they could receive priority service. Your solution will require more than one table. Populate your database with at least 10 service requests. Create several reports that would be of interest to management, such as a list of the highest—and lowest—priority accounts and a report showing the most frequently occurring service problems. Create a report listing service calls that customer service representatives should respond to first on a specific date.

ACHIEVING OPERATIONAL EXCELLENCE: EVALUATING SUPPLY CHAIN MANAGEMENT SERVICES

Software skills: Web browser and presentation software
Business skills: Evaluating supply chain management services

9-11 In addition to carrying goods from one place to another, some trucking companies provide supply chain management services and help their customers manage their information. In this project, you'll use the web to research and evaluate two of these business services. Investigate the websites of two companies, UPS Logistics and Schneider Logistics, to see how these companies' services can be used for supply chain management. Then respond to the following questions:

- What supply chain processes can each of these companies support for its clients?
- How can customers use the websites of each company to help them with supply chain management?
- Compare the supply chain management services these companies provide. Which company would you select to help your firm manage its supply chain? Why?

Collaboration and Teamwork Project

Analyzing Enterprise Application Vendors

9-12 With a group of three or four other students, use the web to research and evaluate the products of two vendors of enterprise application software. You could compare, for example, the SAP and Oracle enterprise systems, the supply chain management systems from JDA Software and SAP, or the customer relationship management systems of Oracle and Salesforce.com. Use what you have learned from these companies' websites to compare the software products you have selected in terms of business functions supported, technology platforms, cost, and ease of use. Which vendor would you select? Why? Would you select the same vendor for a small business (50–300 employees) as well as for a large one? If possible, use Google Docs and Google Drive or Google Sites to brainstorm, organize, and develop a presentation of your findings for the class.

BUSINESS PROBLEM SOLVING CASE

How Supply Chain Management Problems Killed Target Canada

Target is one of the world's most successful general merchandise retailers, with 1,795 retail store locations and a powerful brand image as a fashion-forward discounter. It is not as big or far-flung as Walmart, with $70 billion in annual revenue compared with $485 billion for Walmart, and all of its stores are located in the United States. (Walmart has 11,695 stores all over the world.) Target is very good at what it does and, ideally, would to like to grow like Walmart. In 2011 it decided to make its first foray into global expansion by opening up retail stores in Canada. That year Target acquired the leaseholds of 189 locations operated by Hudson's Bay Company's Zellers discount chain for $1.8 billion, hoping to open Target stores in 124 of these sites by the end of 2013. This was a very ambitious—and possibly unrealistic—timetable.

Target opened its first Canadian stores in March 2013. Target's expansion into Canada was highly anticipated by consumers and feared by rivals, but it failed miserably. On January 15, 2015, Target Canada filed for bankruptcy protection, announcing that it would close all of its 133 Canadian stores, and began liquidating their inventory. All Target Canada stores were closed by April 12, 2015. Some experts consider Target Canada a case study in what retailers should not do when they enter a new market.

Target quickly moved to build three new gigantic distribution centers in Canada. (A distribution center is where all the products from thousands of vendors are sorted and prepared for shipment to individual stores.) Unfortunately, Target Canada was unable to keep track of its products or make sure that the right amounts of products were being ordered, stored, and shipped. At first too few products were arriving at the distribution centers, leaving store shelves bare and Canadian customers empty-handed. Later the distribution centers became overwhelmed with too much product. Target's information systems could not properly compute shelving locations. Target had the stock, but it was stuck in the distribution centers and store shelves still remained empty. Making matters worse, the retail store checkout system was unreliable and didn't process transactions properly. And Target Canada also had higher product prices and less product selection than U.S. Target stores. Canadian sales never took off, and Target had to end its business in Canada.

How could this have happened? First, Target's business was geared to operating domestically in the United States. To operate in Canada, its information systems would have to be able to calculate prices in Canadian currency, which is worth about 75 percent of a U.S. dollar, with the conversion rate constantly fluctuating. Canada also uses the metric system, so the system would have to convert inches and feet into centimeters and meters as well. Knowing the size of an item and the size of packaging is essential for stocking shelves and inventory management. Target's supply chain management and pricing software would have to be modified to handle multiple measurement systems and currencies. Adding to the complexity, products for Target's Canadian market might have different dimensions from those for the United States. A box of shower curtain hooks for the U.S. market might be 12 inches long but only 11 ½ inches for Canada, expressed in centimeters. In other words, internationalizing systems takes a great deal of work and planning.

Target's U.S. operations used custom-built systems for ordering products from vendors, moving goods through warehouses, and stocking store shelves. These systems worked very well, and Target's IT staff and business end users were highly experienced in using them. Target's management had to decide whether to customize these domestic systems so they could work abroad or move to completely new systems for Canada. Because it would require considerable time and effort to internationalize these systems, Target's management opted for a new ready-made software package solution, thinking that it could be implemented faster, even if the company had little experience actually using the new system.

SAP was selected because of its functionality in enterprise resource planning (ERP) and supply chain management as well as capabilities for supporting different languages and currencies. Data on the products in Target's Canadian stores would be fed from the SAP system to other systems to forecast demand for products, manage its distribution centers, and replenish stock in the stores. Target hoped that eventually it could replace its custom homegrown systems with SAP so that the entire company would have the same set of systems worldwide. However, SAP implementations in large companies typically take a long time—often three to five years—and many millions of dollars. Target wanted to go live with SAP in only two years. This was exceedingly, if not unrealistically, ambitious, but management thought using consultants from

Accenture who were highly experienced in SAP implementations would speed things up.

In 2012, once Target began ordering items for its pending Canadian launch, items sourced overseas with long lead times were stalled. Products weren't fitting into shipping containers as expected, and tariff codes were missing or incomplete. Other items weren't able to fit properly onto store shelves. The data used by Target's supply chain software was full of flaws, and the system required correct data to function properly and ensure products moved as anticipated Product dimensions were in inches, not centimeters, or entered in the wrong order. Sometimes the wrong currency was used. Important information was missing, and there were numerous typos.

Target's rush to launch pressured suppliers to enter data quickly into SAP for roughly 75,000 different products. The data had to either be imported from other systems or entered from scratch. A record for a single item might have dozens of fields to fill out, such as fields for the manufacturer, the model, the dimensions, the weight, and how many units can fit into a shipping case. Much of the data were entered incorrectly. Widths were entered instead of lengths, and prices and item descriptions were entered incorrectly as well. Young merchandising assistants in charge of obtaining the details from suppliers were often not experienced enough to challenge vendors on the accuracy of the product information they provided. Information in Target's system was estimated to be only 30 percent accurate, compared with an accuracy rate of 98 to 99 percent for similar data in U.S. firms.

It also turned out that Manhattan, the company's software for running its warehouses, did not communicate well with SAP. For example, an employee at headquarters might have ordered 1,000 toothbrushes but mistakenly entered into SAP data that the shipment would be packaged as 10 boxes of 100 toothbrushes each. But the shipment might actually be configured differently as four large packages containing 250 toothbrushes each. Target's distribution system would treat this shipment as if it didn't exist and couldn't process the information. It would identify the shipment as a "problem area." These kinds of problems crop up at any warehouse, but at Target Canada, they occurred way too often.

Target had purchased a sophisticated and highly regarded system from JDA Software for supply chain forecasting and replenishment. However, this software typically requires years of historical data before it can provide accurate sales forecasts. Lacking such data to feed the system, Target's buying team instead used wildly optimistic projections, which assumed Canadian store sales from the start would be as high as operational stores in the United States even though Target Canada was not yet that well established.

Adding to Target Canada's system woes, the point-of-sale (POS) system was not working properly. Terminals for cash payments took too long to boot up and sometimes froze, items wouldn't scan, the self-checkout stations gave incorrect change, or the POS system would not provide the correct price. Target Canada had purchased POS software from an Israeli company called Retalix. Unlike SAP, Retalix is not an industry standard. It is believed that Target chose this software package because of touted capabilities for processing payments on mobile devices. Target Canada didn't have time to replace this software and kept going with all these bugs.

By fall of 2013, Target's three distribution centers were overflowing with goods. Target had to rent additional storage facilities to accommodate the inventory overflow, making it even more difficult to track down items. Target stores might end up with too much of some products and too little of others. The auto-replenishment system, which kept track of what a store had in stock, wasn't functioning properly, either. Target Canada's system required data about the exact dimensions of every product and every shelf in order to calculate whether employees needed to fill an empty rack. Much of the data were still incorrect, so the system couldn't make accurate calculations. The auto-replenishment system performed so badly that Target shut off the system at its three test stores and had employees replenish shelves manually. Auto-replenishment wasn't reinstated until months later.

There was another reason for the discrepancies between what items appeared to be in stock at headquarters and were actually missing from stores. Target Canada's replenishment system had a feature to notify distribution centers to ship more product when a store ran out. Some of the business analysts responsible for this function, however, were purposely turning it off. These business analysts were judged based on the percentage of their products that were in stock at any given time. When the auto-replenishment switch was turned off, the system wouldn't report an item as out of stock, so the analyst's numbers would look good on paper. To prevent further gaming the system, Target's IT team built a tool that reported when the system was turned on or off and determined whether there was a legitimate reason for it to be turned off (for example, if an item was seasonal.) The analysts were denied access to these controls.

In 2014 Target's IT staff was finally able to install an automatic verification tool to catch bad data before they could enter SAP. The system wouldn't allow a purchase order to proceed until an employee entered product code data that were correct. The problem was that the verification tool was deployed too late. On January 15, 2015, Target Canada announced it was filing for bankruptcy protection. The company had already spent $7 billion on expanding into Canada and was not projected to show a profit until 2021 at the earliest. All of Target Canada's 133 stores were closed, and 17,600 employees lost their jobs.

Sources: David Gewirtz, "Billion Dollar Mistake: How Inferior IT Killed Target Canada," *ZDNet*, February 11, 2016; Joe Castaldo, "The Last Days of Target," www.canadianbusiness.com, accessed April 10, 2017; www.target.com, accessed March 1, 2017; and Marc Wulfraat, "The Aftermath of Target Canada's Collapse," Canadian Grocer, March 10, 2015.

CASE STUDY QUESTIONS

9-13 How important was supply chain management for Target Canada? How did it relate to its business model? Explain your answer.

9-14 Identify all the problems Target Canada encountered that prevented it from becoming a successful retailer. What were the people, organization, and technology factors that contributed to these problems?

9-15 How much of Target Canada's problems were technology based? Explain your answer.

9-16 How responsible was management for Target Canada's problems? Explain your answer.

9-17 What things should Target Canada have done differently to be successful?

MyLab MIS

Go to the Assignments section of MyLab MIS to complete these writing exercises.

9-18 What are three reasons a company would want to implement an enterprise resource planning (ERP) system and two reasons it might not want to do so?

9-19 What are the sources of data for analytical CRM systems? Provide three examples of outputs from analytical CRM systems.

Chapter 9 References

Bozarth, Cecil, and Robert B. Handfield. *Introduction to Operations and Supply Chain Management*, 4th ed. (Upper Saddle River, NJ: Prentice-Hall, 2016.)

D'Avanzo, Robert, Hans von Lewinski, and Luk N. van Wassenhove. "The Link Between Supply Chain and Financial Performance." *Supply Chain Management Review* (November 1, 2003).

Davenport, Thomas H. *Mission Critical: Realizing the Promise of Enterprise Systems.* (Boston: Harvard Business School Press, 2000.)

Davenport, Thomas H., Leandro Dalle Mule, and John Lucke. "Know What Your Customers Want Before They Do." *Harvard Business Review* (December 2011).

Hitt, Lorin, D. J. Wu, and Xiaoge Zhou. "Investment in Enterprise Resource Planning: Business Impact and Productivity Measures." *Journal of Management Information Systems* 19, No. 1 (Summer 2002).

Hu, Michael, and Sean T. Monahan. "Sharing Supply Chain Data in the Digital Era." *MIT Sloan Management Review* (Fall 2015).

Kanaracus, Chris. "ERP Software Project Woes Continue to Mount, Survey Says." *IT World* (February 20, 2013).

Kimberling, Eric. "5 Lessons from Successful CRM Implementations." Panorama-consulting.com (January 28, 2015).

Klein, Richard, and Arun Rai. "Interfirm Strategic Information Flows in Logistics Supply Chain Relationships." *MIS Quarterly* 33, No. 4 (December 2009).

Laudon, Kenneth C. "The Promise and Potential of Enterprise Systems and Industrial Networks." Working paper, The Concours Group. Copyright Kenneth C. Laudon (1999).

Lee, Hau L., V. Padmanabhan, and Seugin Whang. "The Bullwhip Effect in Supply Chains." *Sloan Management Review* (Spring 1997).

Liang, Huigang, Nilesh Sharaf, Quing Hu, and Yajiong Xue. "Assimilation of Enterprise Systems: The Effect of Institutional Pressures and the Mediating Role of Top Management." *MIS Quarterly* 31, No. 1 (March 2007).

Liang, Huigang, Zeyu Peng, Yajiong Xue, Xitong Guo, and Nengmin Wang. "Employees' Exploration of Complex Systems: An Integrative View." *Journal of Management Information Systems* 32, No. 1 (2015).

Maklan, Stan, Simon Knox, and Joe Peppard. "When CRM Fails." *MIT Sloan Management Review* 52, No. 4 (Summer 2011).

Malik, Yogesh, Alex Niemeyer, and Brian Ruwadi. "Building the Supply Chain of the Future." *McKinsey Quarterly* (January 2011).

Oracle Corporation. "Alcoa Implements Oracle Solution 20% Below Projected Cost, Eliminates 43 Legacy Systems." www.oracle.com, accessed August 21, 2005.

Panorama Consulting Solutions. "2016 Report on ERP Systems and Enterprise Software." (2016).

Rai, Arun, Paul A. Pavlou, Ghiyoung Im, and Steve Du. "Interfirm IT Capability Profiles and Communications for Cocreating Relational Value: Evidence from the Logistics Industry." *MIS Quarterly* 36, No. 1 (March 2012).

Rai, Arun, Ravi Patnayakuni, and Nainika Seth. "Firm Performance Impacts of Digitally Enabled Supply Chain Integration Capabilities." *MIS Quarterly* 30, No. 2 (June 2006).

Ranganathan, C., and Carol V. Brown. "ERP Investments and the Market Value of Firms: Toward an Understanding of Influential ERP Project Variables." *Information Systems Research* 17, No. 2 (June 2006).

Sarker, Supreteek, Saonee Sarker, Arvin Sahaym, and Bjørn-Andersen. "Exploring Value Cocreation in Relationships Between an ERP Vendor and its Partners: A Revelatory Case Study." *MIS Quarterly* 36, No. 1 (March 2012).

SAS. "Data Elevates the Customer Experience." *Forbes Insights* (April 2016).

Seldon, Peter B., Cheryl Calvert, and Song Yang. "A Multi-Project Model of Key Factors Affecting Organizational Benefits from Enterprise Systems." *MIS Quarterly* 34, No. 2 (June 2010).

Sodhi, ManMohan S., and Christopher S. Tang. "Supply Chains Built for Speed and Customization." *MIT Sloan Management Review* (Summer 2017).

Strong, Diane M., and Olga Volkoff. "Understanding Organization-Enterprise System Fit: A Path to Theorizing the Information Technology Artifact." *MIS Quarterly* 34, No. 4 (December 2010).

SupplyChainBrain. "Trends in Enterprise Resource Planning Cloud Technology." (February 25, 2015).

Sussin, Jenny. "Top Use Cases and Benefits of Social for CRM in 2015." Gartner, Inc. (February 12, 2015).

Sykes, Tracy Ann, Viswanath Venkatesh, and Jonathan L. Johnson. "Enterprise System Implementation and Employee Job Performance: Understanding the Role of Advice Networks." *MIS Quarterly* 38, No. 1 (March 2014).

Tate, Wendy L., Diane Mollenkopf, Theodore Stank, and Andrea Lago da Silva. "Integrating Supply and Demand." *MIT Sloan Management Review* (Summer 2015).

Tian, Feng, and Sean Xin Xu. "How Do Enterprise Resource Planning Systems Affect Firm Risk? Post-Implementation Impact." *MIS Quarterly* 39, No. 1 (March 2015).

"Top 5 Reasons ERP Implementations Fail and What You Can Do About It." Ziff Davis (2013).

"Trends in Enterprise Resource Planning Cloud Technology." *SupplyChainBrain* (February 25, 2015).

Van Caeneghem, Alexander, and Jean-Marie Becquevort. "Turning on ERP Systems Can Turn Off People." *CFO* (February 5, 2016).

Wong, Christina W.Y., Kee-Hung Lai, and T.C.E. Cheng. "Value of Information Integration to Supply Chain Management: Roles of Internal and External Contingencies." *Journal of Management Information Systems* 28, No. 3 (Winter 2012).

CHAPTER

10 E-commerce: Digital Markets, Digital Goods

LEARNING OBJECTIVES

After reading this chapter, you will be able to answer the following questions:

10-1 What are the unique features of e-commerce, digital markets, and digital goods?

10-2 What are the principal e-commerce business and revenue models?

10-3 How has e-commerce transformed marketing?

10-4 How has e-commerce affected business-to-business transactions?

10-5 What is the role of m-commerce in business, and what are the most important m-commerce applications?

10-6 What issues must be addressed when building an e-commerce presence?

10-7 How will MIS help my career?

CHAPTER CASES

- YouTube Transforms the Media Landscape
- Uber: Digital Disruptor
- "Socializing" with Customers
- A Nasty Ending for Nasty Gal

VIDEO CASES

- Walmart Takes On Amazon: A Battle of IT and Management Systems
- Groupon: Deals Galore
- Etsy: A Marketplace and Community

Instructional Videos:

- Walmart's E-commerce Fulfillment Center Network
- Behind the Scenes of an Amazon Warehouse

MyLab MIS

- Discussion Questions: 10-7; 10-8, 10-9;
- Hands-on MIS Projects: 10-10, 10-11; 10-12, 10-13;
- Writing Assignments: 10-18, 10-19;
- eText with Conceptual Animations

YOUTUBE TRANSFORMS THE MEDIA LANDSCAPE

The first video posted on YouTube was a 19-second clip from 2005 of one of the company's founders standing in front of the San Diego Zoo elephant cage. Who would have thought that the online video-sharing service would mushroom into the world's second most popular website, with more than 1 billion users—almost a third of all the people on the Internet? YouTube viewers worldwide now watch more than 1 billion hours of videos a day. Four hundred hours of video are uploaded to YouTube every minute, equivalent to 65 years of video daily.

YouTube allows users to view, rate, share, add to favorites, report, and comment on videos and subscribe to other users' video channels. Although hundreds of millions of people love to post YouTube videos of their growing children, dogs, and cats, YouTube offers much more: clips from major motion pictures and TV shows, music videos, sports videos, videos from companies promoting their brands, and numerous "how-to" videos about home repair, gardening, and computer troubleshooting. Most YouTube content has been uploaded by individuals, but media corporations such as CBS, the BBC, Vevo, and Hulu offer some of their material via YouTube as part of a partnership program.

YouTube maintains very large databases for video content and tracking the behavior of its users. It carefully mines data to give each user personalized video recommendations that will entice that person to watch longer. There are so many eyeballs affixed to YouTube—it's a gold mine for marketers, and YouTube content gets richer by the minute. About 2 billion unique users now watch a YouTube video every 90 days. More than half of YouTube views come from mobile devices.

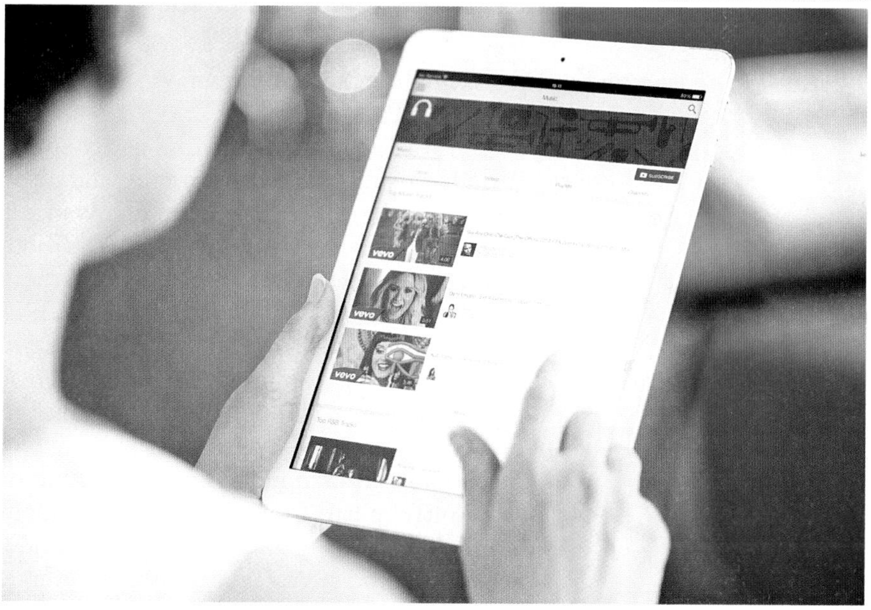

YouTube was purchased by Google in 2006 and benefits from Google's enormous reach, since Google handles nearly 80 percent of global Internet searches. YouTube revenue comes from ads accompanying videos that are targeted to site content and audiences. YouTube also offers subscription-based premium channels, film rentals, and a subscription service called YouTube Red that provides ad-free access to the website and some exclusive content. It is unclear if YouTube is actually profitable at this point.

Once known as a magnet for pirated video, YouTube has been embraced by Hollywood and the entertainment world. Almost every movie trailer or music video is released onto YouTube; all major sports leagues upload highlights there; and networks supplement traditional programming with videos that can be shared, like the talk show host James Corden's "Carpool Karaoke" series. YouTube has become a major destination entertainment site, and it is about to alter the media landscape even further.

YouTube has joined services targeting consumers who want to give up cable or satellite TV without losing access to live television. In early 2017, YouTube announced a subscription service called YouTube TV. For $35 per month, the service offers more than 40 channels, including the major networks, FX, ESPN, and the Disney Channel, as well as the ability to store an unlimited number of programs on a cloud-based digital video recorder for up to six accounts. YouTube TV subscribers will be able to watch content on any platform, including PCs, tablets, smartphones, and big-screen TVs.

After the cost of acquiring all this television content is considered, Google may not make much on YouTube TV subscription revenue. That's fine right now because Google is using YouTube TV is to break into the television advertising market, selling targeted advertising in ad slots that typically went to cable operators. Long term that could be significant: Roughly $70 billion is spent annually on TV ads.

Sources: Jack Nicas, "YouTube Tops 1 Billion Hours of Video a Day, on Pace to Eclipse TV," *Wall Street Journal*, February 27, 2017; Jack Nicas and Shalini Ramachandran, "Google's YouTube to Launch $35-a-Month Web-TV Service," *Wall Street Journal*, February 28, 2017; Daisuke Wakabayashi, "YouTube Unveils Subscription Television Service," *New York Times*, February 28, 2017; and "36 Mind Blowing YouTube Facts, Figures and Statistics—2017," *Fortunelords*, March 23, 2017.

YouTube exemplifies some of the major trends in e-commerce today. It does not sell a product, it sells an innovative service, as e-commerce businesses are increasingly trying to do. YouTube's service delivers streaming video content either for free (supported by advertising) or by subscription and also enables users to upload and store their own videos. YouTube makes use of advanced data mining and search technology to generate revenue from advertising. YouTube is "social," linking people to each other through their shared interests and fascination with video. And it is mobile: YouTube can be viewed on smartphones and tablets as well as conventional computers and TV screens, and more than half of YouTube views are on mobile devices.

The chapter-opening diagram calls attention to important points raised by this case and this chapter. YouTube's primary business challenge is how to take advantage of opportunities presented by the Internet and new developments in search and data mining technology to wring profits from the billions of videos it streams to viewers. Obviously YouTube had to make major investments in technology to support video uploads and downloads, gigantic databases of videos and users, tagging images, and social networking tools. YouTube generates revenue from ads targeted to video viewers and to subscriptions to its streaming content services, including its new lineup of major TV channels. It is unclear whether YouTube has achieved long-term profitability, but it is very valuable to Google as another outlet for its advertising.

Here are some questions to think about: How does YouTube provide value? Why is YouTube an expensive business to operate? Is it a viable business model? Why or why not?

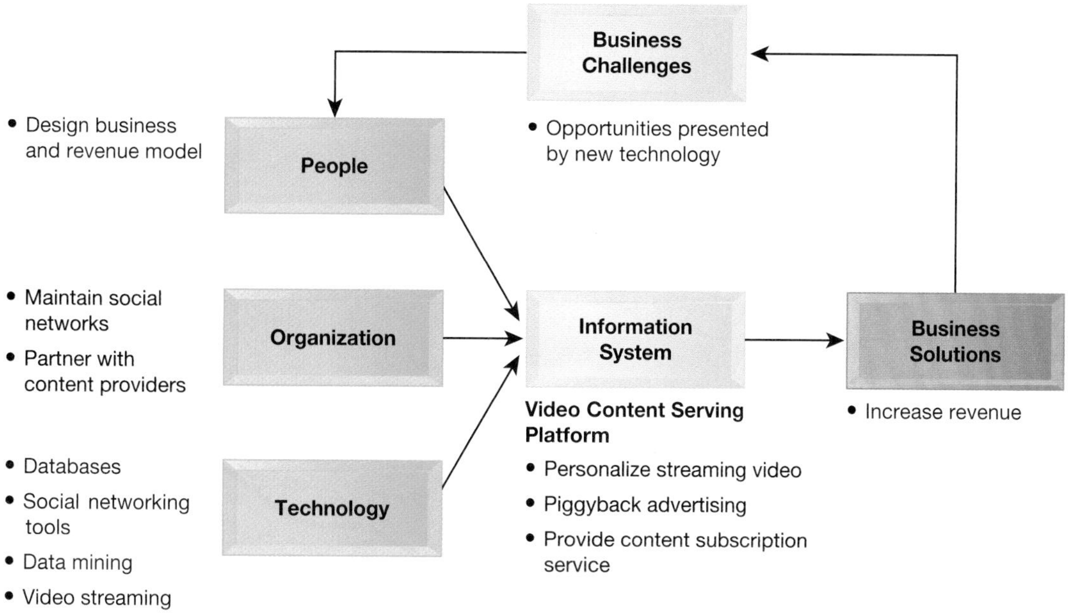

10-1 What are the unique features of e-commerce, digital markets, and digital goods?

In 2018, purchasing goods and services online by using smartphones, tablets, and desktop computers will be ubiquitous. In 2018, an estimated 219 million Americans will shop online, and 189 million will purchase something online, as did millions of others worldwide. Although most purchases still take place through traditional channels, e-commerce continues to grow rapidly and to transform the way many companies do business. In 2018, e-commerce consumer sales of goods, services, travel, and online content, about 10 percent of total retail sales of $5.17 trillion, are growing at 15 percent annually (compared with 3.3 percent for traditional retailers) (eMarketer, 2017a). E-commerce has expanded from the desktop and home computer to mobile devices, from an isolated activity to a new social commerce, and from a *Fortune* 1000 commerce with a national audience to local merchants and consumers whose location is known to mobile devices. At the top 100 e-commerce retail sites, more than half of online shoppers arrive from their smartphones, although most continue to purchase using a PC or tablet. The key words for understanding this new e-commerce in 2018 are "social, mobile, local."

E-COMMERCE TODAY

E-commerce refers to the use of the Internet and the web to transact business. More formally, e-commerce is about digitally enabled commercial transactions between and among organizations and individuals. For the most part, this refers to transactions that occur over the Internet and the web. Commercial transactions involve the exchange of value (e.g., money) across organizational or individual boundaries in return for products and services.

E-commerce began in 1995 when one of the first Internet portals, Netscape.com, accepted the first ads from major corporations and popularized the idea that the web could be used as a new medium for advertising and sales. No one envisioned at the time what would turn out to be an exponential growth curve for e-commerce retail sales, which doubled and tripled in the early years. E-commerce grew at double-digit rates until the recession of 2008–2009, when growth slowed to a crawl and revenues flattened (see Figure 10.1), not bad considering that traditional retail sales were

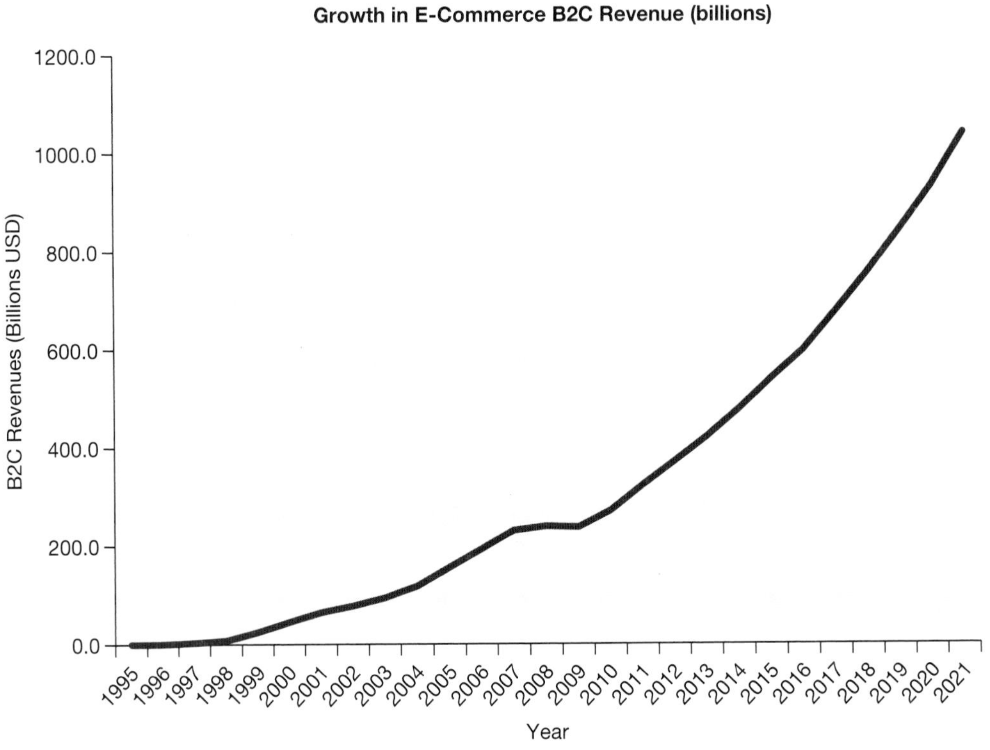

Figure 10.1
The Growth of E-commerce
Retail e-commerce revenues grew 15–25 percent per year until the recession of 2008–2009, when they slowed measurably. In 2017, e-commerce revenues grew at an estimated 16 percent annually.

Sources: Based on data from eMarketer, "US Retail Ecommerce Sales, 2015–2021," 2017a; eMarketer, "US Digital Travel Sales, 2014–2020," 2016; and eMarketer chart, "US Mobile Downloads and In-App Revenues, 2013–2016," 2016.

shrinking by 5 percent annually. Since then, offline retail sales have increased only a few percentage points a year, whereas online e-commerce has been a stellar success.

The very rapid growth in e-commerce in the early years created a market bubble in e-commerce stocks, which burst in March 2001. A large number of e-commerce companies failed during this process. Yet for many others, such as Amazon, eBay, Expedia, and Google, the results have been more positive: soaring revenues, fine-tuned business models that produce profits, and rising stock prices. By 2006, e-commerce revenues returned to solid growth and have continued to be the fastest-growing form of retail trade in the United States, Europe, and Asia.

- Online consumer sales will grow to an estimated $678 billion in 2018, an increase of more than 16 percent over 2017 (including travel services and digital downloads), with 189 million people purchasing online and an additional 219 million shopping and gathering information but not purchasing (eMarketer, 2017b). The Internet influences more than $2 trillion in retail commerce that takes places in physical stores, about 40 percent of all retail sales.
- The number of individuals of all ages online in the United States is expected to grow to 278 million in 2018, up from 147 million in 2004. In the world, more than 3.7 billion people are now connected to the Internet. Growth in the overall Internet population has spurred growth in e-commerce (Internet World Stats, 2017).
- Approximately 96 million U.S. households will have broadband access to the Internet in 2018, representing about 77 percent of all households.
- About 232 million Americans will access the Internet by using a smartphone. Mobile e-commerce has begun a rapid growth based on apps, ringtones, downloaded entertainment, and location-based services. Mobile e-commerce will account for about $207 billion in 2018, 30 percent of all e-commerce, and about 39 percent of all retail e-commerce. Mobile phones and tablets are becoming the most common Internet access device. Currently, more than 80 percent of all mobile phone users access the Internet by using their phones (eMarketer, 2017f).
- B2B e-commerce (use of the Internet for business-to-business commerce and collaboration among business partners) expanded to more than $7 trillion. Table 10.1 highlights these new e-commerce developments.

TABLE 10.1

The Growth of E-commerce

Business Transformation
E-commerce remains the fastest-growing form of commerce when compared to physical retail stores, services, and entertainment. Social, mobile, and local commerce have become the fastest-growing forms of e-commerce.
The breadth of e-commerce offerings grows, especially in the services economy of social networking, travel, entertainment, retail apparel, jewelry, appliances, and home furnishings.
The online demographics of shoppers broaden to match that of ordinary shoppers.
Pure e-commerce business models are refined further to achieve higher levels of profitability, and traditional retail firms, such as Walmart, JCPenney, L.L.Bean, and Macy's, are developing omnichannel business models to strengthen their dominant physical retail assets. Walmart, the world's largest retailer, has decided to take on Amazon with a more than $1 billion investment in its e-commerce efforts.
Small businesses and entrepreneurs continue to flood the e-commerce marketplace, often riding on the infrastructures created by industry giants, such as Amazon, Apple, and Google, and increasingly taking advantage of cloud-based computing resources.
Mobile e-commerce has taken off in the United States with location-based services and entertainment downloads, including e-books, movies, music, and television shows. Mobile e-commerce will generate more than $207 billion in 2018.
Technology Foundations
Wireless Internet connections (Wi-Fi, WiMax, and 4G smartphones) continue to expand.
Powerful smartphones and tablet computers provide access to music, web surfing, and entertainment as well as voice communication. Podcasting and streaming take off as platforms for distribution of video, radio, and user-generated content.
Mobile devices expand to include wearable computers such as Apple Watch and Fitbit trackers.
The Internet broadband foundation becomes stronger in households and businesses as transmission prices fall.
Social networking apps and sites such as Facebook, Twitter, LinkedIn, Instagram, and others seek to become a major new platform for e-commerce, marketing, and advertising. Facebook has 1.94 billion users worldwide and 201 million in the United States (Facebook, 2017). One hundred ninety-six million Americans use social networks in 2018, about 70 percent of the Internet user population.
Internet-based models of computing, such as smartphone apps, cloud computing, software as a service (SaaS), and database software, greatly reduce the cost of e-commerce websites.
New Business Models Emerge
More than 70 percent of the Internet population has joined an online social network, created blogs, and shared photos and music. Together, these sites create an online audience as large as that of television that is attractive to marketers. In 2018, social networking will account for an estimated 20 percent of online time. Social sites have become the primary gateway to the Internet in news, music, and, increasingly, products.
The traditional advertising industry is disrupted as online advertising grows twice as fast as TV and print advertising; Google, Yahoo, and Facebook display more than 1 trillion ads a year.
On-demand service e-commerce sites such as Uber and Airbnb extend the market creator business model (on-demand model) to new areas of the economy.
Newspapers and other traditional media adopt online, interactive models but are losing advertising revenues to the online players despite gaining online readers. The *New York Times* succeeds in capturing more than 1 million subscribers, growing at 15 percent annually and adding 500,000 new digital subscribers in 2016. Book publishing thrives because of the growth in e-books and the continuing appeal of traditional books.
Online entertainment business models offering television, movies, music, and games grow with cooperation among the major copyright owners in Hollywood and New York and with Internet distributors such as Apple, Amazon, Google, YouTube, and Facebook. Increasingly, the online distributors are moving into movie and TV production. Cable television is in modest decline.

THE NEW E-COMMERCE: SOCIAL, MOBILE, LOCAL

One of the biggest changes is the extent to which e-commerce has become more social, mobile, and local. Online marketing once consisted largely of creating a corporate website, buying display ads on Yahoo, purchasing ad words on Google, and sending email messages. The workhorse of online marketing was the display ad. It still is, but it's increasingly being replaced by video ads, which are far more effective. Display ads from the very beginning of the Internet were based on television ads, where brand messages were flashed before millions of users who were not expected to respond immediately, ask questions, or make observations. If the ads did not work, the solution was often to repeat the ad. The primary measure of success was how many eyeballs (unique visitors) a website produced and how many impressions a marketing campaign generated. (An impression was one ad shown to one person.) Both of these measures were carryovers from the world of television, which measures marketing in terms of audience size and ad views.

From Eyeballs to Conversations: Conversational Commerce

After 2007, all this changed with the rapid growth of Facebook and other social sites, the explosive growth of smartphones beginning with the Apple iPhone, and the growing interest in local marketing. What's different about the new world of social-mobile-local e-commerce is the dual and related concepts of conversations and engagement. In the popular literature, this is often referred to as conversational commerce. Marketing in this new period is based on firms engaging in multiple online conversations with their customers, potential customers, and even critics. Your brand is being talked about on the web and social media (that's the conversation part), and marketing your firm, building, and restoring your brands require you to locate, identify, and participate in these conversations. Social marketing means all things social: listening, discussing, interacting, empathizing, and engaging. The emphasis in online marketing has shifted from a focus on eyeballs to a focus on participating in customer-oriented conversations. In this sense, social marketing is not simply a new ad channel but a collection of technology-based tools for communicating with shoppers. The leading social commerce platforms are Facebook, Instagram, Twitter, and Pinterest.

In the past, firms could tightly control their brand messaging and lead consumers down a funnel of cues that ended in a purchase. That is not true of social marketing. Consumer purchase decisions are increasingly driven by the conversations, choices, tastes, and opinions of their social network. Social marketing is all about firms participating in and shaping this social process.

From the Desktop to the Smartphone

Traditional online marketing (browser-based, search, display ads, video ads, email, and games) still constitutes the majority (58 percent) of all online marketing ($93 billion), but it's growing much more slowly than social-mobile-local marketing. The marketing dollars are following customers and shoppers from the PC to mobile devices.

Social, mobile, and local e-commerce are connected. As mobile devices become more powerful, they are more useful for accessing Facebook and other social sites. As mobile devices become more widely adopted, customers can use them to find local merchants, and merchants can use them to alert customers in their neighborhood of special offers.

WHY E-COMMERCE IS DIFFERENT

Why has e-commerce grown so rapidly? The answer lies in the unique nature of the Internet and the web. Simply put, the Internet and e-commerce technologies are much richer and more powerful than previous technology revolutions such as radio, television, and the telephone. Table 10.2 describes the unique features of the Internet and web as a commercial medium. Let's explore each of these unique features in more detail.

TABLE 10.2

Eight Unique Features of E-commerce Technology

E-Commerce Technology Dimension	Business Significance
Ubiquity. Internet/web technology is available everywhere: at work, at home, and elsewhere by desktop and mobile devices. Mobile devices extend service to local areas and merchants.	The marketplace is extended beyond traditional boundaries and is removed from a temporal and geographic location. Marketspace is created; shopping can take place anytime, anywhere. Customer convenience is enhanced, and shopping costs are reduced.
Global Reach. The technology reaches across national boundaries, around the earth.	Commerce is enabled across cultural and national boundaries seamlessly and without modification. The marketspace includes, potentially, billions of consumers and millions of businesses worldwide.
Universal Standards. There is one set of technology standards, namely Internet standards.	With one set of technical standards across the globe, disparate computer systems can easily communicate with each other.
Richness. Video, audio, and text messages are possible.	Video, audio, and text marketing messages are integrated into a single marketing message and consumer experience.
Interactivity. The technology works through interaction with the user.	Consumers are engaged in a dialogue that dynamically adjusts the experience to the individual and makes the consumer a participant in the process of delivering goods to the market.
Information Density. The technology reduces information costs and raises quality.	Information processing, storage, and communication costs drop dramatically, whereas currency, accuracy, and timeliness improve greatly. Information becomes plentiful, cheap, and more accurate.
Personalization/Customization. The technology allows personalized messages to be delivered to individuals as well as to groups.	Personalization of marketing messages and customization of products and services are based on individual characteristics.
Social Technology. The technology supports content generation and social networking.	New Internet social and business models enable user content creation and distribution and support social networks.

Ubiquity

In traditional commerce, a marketplace is a physical place, such as a retail store, that you visit to transact business. E-commerce is ubiquitous, meaning that it is available just about everywhere all the time. It makes it possible to shop from your desktop, at home, at work, or even from your car, using smartphones. The result is called a **marketspace**—a marketplace extended beyond traditional boundaries and removed from a temporal and geographic location.

From a consumer point of view, ubiquity reduces **transaction costs**—the costs of participating in a market. To transact business, it is no longer necessary for you to spend time or money traveling to a market, and much less mental effort is required to make a purchase.

Global Reach

E-commerce technology permits commercial transactions to cross cultural and national boundaries far more conveniently and cost effectively than is true in traditional commerce. As a result, the potential market size for e-commerce merchants is roughly equal to the size of the world's online population (estimated to be more than 3 billion).

In contrast, most traditional commerce is local or regional—it involves local merchants or national merchants with local outlets. Television, radio stations, and newspapers, for instance, are primarily local and regional institutions with limited, but powerful, national networks that can attract a national audience but not easily cross national boundaries to a global audience.

Universal Standards

One strikingly unusual feature of e-commerce technologies is that the technical standards of the Internet and, therefore, the technical standards for conducting e-commerce are universal standards. All nations around the world share them and enable any computer to link with any other computer regardless of the technology platform each is using. In contrast, most traditional commerce technologies differ from one nation to the next. For instance, television and radio standards differ around the world, as does cellular telephone technology.

The universal technical standards of the Internet and e-commerce greatly lower **market entry costs**—the cost merchants must pay simply to bring their goods to market. At the same time, for consumers, universal standards reduce **search costs**—the effort required to find suitable products.

Richness

Information **richness** refers to the complexity and content of a message. Traditional markets, national sales forces, and small retail stores have great richness; they can provide personal, face-to-face service, using aural and visual cues when making a sale. The richness of traditional markets makes them powerful selling or commercial environments. Prior to the development of the web, there was a trade-off between richness and reach; the larger the audience reached, the less rich the message. The web makes it possible to deliver rich messages with text, audio, and video simultaneously to large numbers of people.

Interactivity

Unlike any of the commercial technologies of the twentieth century, with the possible exception of the telephone, e-commerce technologies are interactive, meaning they allow for two-way communication between merchant and consumer and peer-to-peer communication among friends. Television, for instance, cannot ask viewers any questions or enter conversations with them, and it cannot request customer information to be entered on a form. In contrast, all these activities are possible on an e-commerce website or mobile app. Interactivity allows an online merchant to engage a consumer in ways similar to a face-to-face experience but on a massive, global scale.

Information Density

The Internet and the web vastly increase **information density**—the total amount and quality of information available to all market participants, consumers, and merchants alike. E-commerce technologies reduce information collection, storage, processing, and communication costs while greatly increasing the currency, accuracy, and timeliness of information.

Information density in e-commerce markets make prices and costs more transparent. **Price transparency** refers to the ease with which consumers can find out the variety of prices in a market; **cost transparency** refers to the ability of consumers to discover the actual costs merchants pay for products.

There are advantages for merchants as well. Online merchants can discover much more about consumers than in the past. This allows merchants to segment the market into groups that are willing to pay different prices and permits the merchants to engage in **price discrimination**—selling the same goods, or nearly the same goods, to different targeted groups at different prices. For instance, an online merchant can discover a consumer's avid interest in expensive, exotic vacations and then pitch high-end vacation plans to that consumer at a premium price, knowing this person is willing to pay extra for such a vacation. At the same time, the online merchant can pitch the same vacation plan at a lower price to a more price-sensitive consumer. Information density also helps merchants differentiate their products in terms of cost, brand, and quality.

Personalization/Customization

E-commerce technologies permit **personalization**. Merchants can target their marketing messages to specific individuals by adjusting the message to a person's clickstream behavior, name, interests, and past purchases. The technology also permits **customization**—changing the delivered product or service based on a user's preferences or prior behavior. Given the interactive nature of e-commerce technology, much information about the consumer can be gathered in the marketplace at the moment of purchase. With the increase in information density, a great deal of information about the consumer's past purchases and behavior can be stored and used by online merchants.

The result is a level of personalization and customization unthinkable with traditional commerce technologies. For instance, you may be able to shape what you see on television by selecting a channel, but you cannot change the content of the channel you have chosen. In contrast, online news outlets such as the *Wall Street Journal Online* allow you to select the type of news stories you want to see first and give you the opportunity to be alerted when certain events happen.

Social Technology: User Content Generation and Social Networking

In contrast to previous technologies, the Internet and e-commerce technologies have evolved to be much more social by allowing users to create and share with their friends (and a larger worldwide community) content in the form of text, videos, music, or photos. By using these forms of communication, users can create new social networks and strengthen existing ones.

All previous mass media in modern history, including the printing press, use a broadcast model (one-to-many) in which content is created in a central location by experts (professional writers, editors, directors, and producers), and audiences are concentrated in huge numbers to consume a standardized product. The new Internet and e-commerce empower users to create and distribute content on a large scale and permit users to program their own content consumption. The Internet provides a unique many-to-many model of mass communications.

KEY CONCEPTS IN E-COMMERCE: DIGITAL MARKETS AND DIGITAL GOODS IN A GLOBAL MARKETPLACE

The location, timing, and revenue models of business are based in some part on the cost and distribution of information. The Internet has created a digital marketplace where millions of people all over the world can exchange massive amounts of information directly, instantly, and free. As a result, the Internet has changed the way companies conduct business and increased their global reach.

The Internet reduces information asymmetry. An **information asymmetry** exists when one party in a transaction has more information that is important for the transaction than the other party. That information helps determine their relative bargaining power. In digital markets, consumers and suppliers can see the prices being charged for goods, and in that sense, digital markets are said to be more transparent than traditional markets.

For example, before automobile retailing sites appeared on the web, there was significant information asymmetry between auto dealers and customers. Only the auto dealers knew the manufacturers' prices, and it was difficult for consumers to shop around for the best price. Auto dealers' profit margins depended on this asymmetry of information. Today's consumers have access to a legion of websites providing competitive pricing information, and three-fourths of U.S. auto buyers use the Internet to shop around for the best deal. Thus, the web has reduced the information asymmetry surrounding an auto purchase. The Internet has also helped businesses seeking to purchase from other businesses reduce information asymmetries and locate better prices and terms.

Digital markets are very flexible and efficient because they operate with reduced search and transaction costs, lower **menu costs** (merchants' costs of changing prices), greater price discrimination, and the ability to change prices dynamically based on market conditions. In **dynamic pricing**, the price of a product varies depending on the demand characteristics of the customer or the supply situation of the seller. For instance, online retailers from Amazon to Walmart change prices on many products based on time of day, demand for the product, and users' prior visits to their sites. Using big data analytics, some online firms can adjust prices at the individual level based on behavioral targeting parameters such as whether the consumer is a price haggler (who will receive a lower price offer) versus a person who accepts offered prices and does not search for lower prices. Prices can also vary by zip code, with higher prices set for poor sections of a community. Uber, along with other ride services, uses surge pricing to adjust prices of a ride based on demand (which always rises during storms and major conventions).

These new digital markets can either reduce or increase switching costs, depending on the nature of the product or service being sold, and they might cause some extra delay in gratification due to shipping times. Unlike a physical market, you can't immediately consume a product such as clothing purchased over the web (although immediate consumption is possible with digital music downloads and other digital products).

Digital markets provide many opportunities to sell directly to the consumer, bypassing intermediaries such as distributors or retail outlets. Eliminating intermediaries in the distribution channel can significantly lower purchase transaction costs. To pay for all the steps in a traditional distribution channel, a product may have to be priced as high as 135 percent of its original cost to manufacture.

Figure 10.2 illustrates how much savings result from eliminating each of these layers in the distribution process. By selling directly to consumers or reducing the number of intermediaries, companies can raise profits while charging lower prices. The removal of organizations or business process layers responsible for intermediary steps in a value chain is called **disintermediation**. E-commerce has also given rise to a completely new set of new intermediaries such as Amazon, eBay, PayPal, and Blue Nile. Therefore, disintermediation differs from one industry to another.

Disintermediation is affecting the market for services. Airlines and hotels operating their own reservation sites online earn more per ticket because they have eliminated travel agents as intermediaries. Table 10.3 summarizes the differences between digital markets and traditional markets.

Figure 10.2
The Benefits of Disintermediation to the Consumer
The typical distribution channel has several intermediary layers, each of which adds to the final cost of a product, such as a sweater. Removing layers lowers the final cost to the customer.

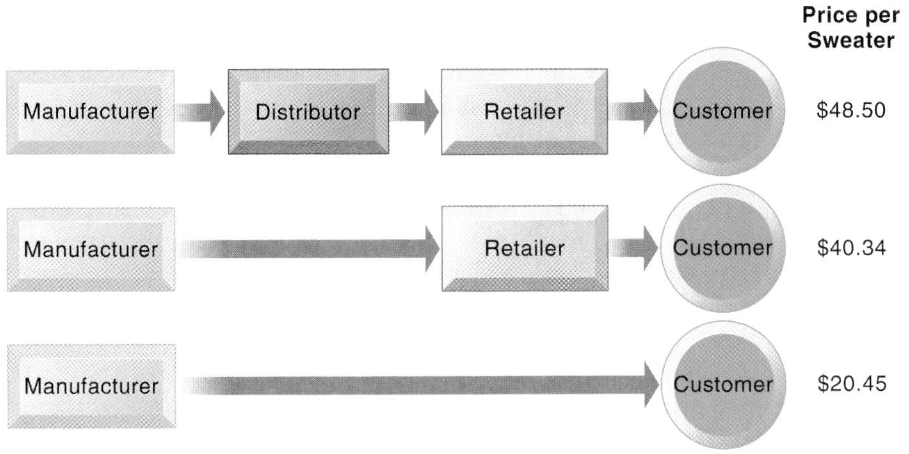

TABLE 10.3

Digital Markets Compared with Traditional Markets

	Digital Markets	Traditional Markets
Information asymmetry	Asymmetry reduced	Asymmetry high
Search costs	Low	High
Transaction costs	Low (sometimes virtually nothing)	High (time, travel)
Delayed gratification	High (or lower in the case of a digital good)	Lower: purchase now
Menu costs	Low	High
Dynamic pricing	Low cost, instant	High cost, delayed
Price discrimination	Low cost, instant	High cost, delayed
Market segmentation	Low cost, moderate precision	High cost, less precision
Switching costs	Higher/lower (depending on product characteristics)	High
Network effects	Strong	Weaker
Disintermediation	More possible/likely	Less possible/unlikely

Digital Goods

The Internet digital marketplace has greatly expanded sales of **digital goods**—goods that can be delivered over a digital network. Music tracks, video, Hollywood movies, software, newspapers, magazines, and books can all be expressed, stored, delivered, and sold as purely digital products. For the most part, digital goods are intellectual property, which is defined as "works of the mind." Intellectual property is protected from misappropriation by copyright, patent, trademark, and trade secret laws (see Chapter 4). Today, all these products are delivered as digital streams or downloads while their physical counterparts decline in sales.

In general, for digital goods, the marginal cost of producing another unit is about zero (it costs nothing to make a copy of a music file). However, the cost of producing the original first unit is relatively high—in fact, it is nearly the total cost of the product because there are few other costs of inventory and distribution. Costs of delivery over the Internet are very low, marketing costs often remain the same, and pricing can be highly variable. On the Internet, the merchant can change prices as often as desired because of low menu costs.

The impact of the Internet on the market for these kinds of digital goods is nothing short of revolutionary, and we see the results around us every day. Businesses dependent on physical products for sales—such as bookstores, music stores, book publishers, music labels, and film studios—face the possibility of declining sales and even destruction of their businesses. Newspapers and magazines subscriptions to hard copies are declining, while online readership and subscriptions are expanding.

Total record label industry revenues have fallen nearly 50 percent from $14 billion in 1999 to about $7.7 billion in 2016, due almost entirely to the rapid decline in CD album sales and the growth of digital music services (both legal and illegal music piracy). On the plus side, the Apple iTunes Store has sold more than 50 billion songs for 99 cents each since opening in 2003, providing the industry with a digital distribution model that has restored some of the revenues lost to digital music channels. Yet the download business is rapidly fading at Apple, down more than 25 percent in recent years, as streaming becomes the dominant consumer path to music. Since iTunes, illegal downloading has been cut in half, and legitimate online music sales (both downloads and streaming) amounted to $5.7 billion in 2016. As cloud streaming services expand, illegal downloading will decline further. Digital music sales, both digital download and streaming, account for more than 75 percent of all music revenues. The music labels make only about 32 cents from a single track download and only 0.5 cents for a streamed track. Although the record labels make revenue from ownership of the song (both words and music), the artists who perform the music make virtually nothing from streamed music. Artists' earnings on a streamed song on an ad-supported platform like Spotify are pennies per million streams.

Hollywood has not been severely disrupted by digital distribution platforms, in part because it is more difficult to download high-quality, pirated copies of full-length movies and because of the availability of low-cost, high-quality legal movies. Hollywood has also struck lucrative distribution deals with Netflix, Google, Hulu, Amazon, and Apple, making it convenient to download and pay for high-quality movies and television series. These arrangements are not enough to compensate entirely for the loss in DVD sales, which fell 60 percent from 2006 to 2016, more than 15 percent in 2016 alone. Digital format streaming and downloads grew by 31 percent in 2016. In 2017, for the first time, consumers viewed more downloaded movies than DVDs or related physical products. As with television series, the demand for feature-length Hollywood movies appears to be expanding in part because of the growth of smartphones, tablets, and smart TVs, making it easier to watch movies in more locations.

In 2018, about 135 million Internet users are expected to view movies, about one-half of the adult Internet audience. Although this rapid growth will not continue forever, there is little doubt that the Internet is becoming a major movie distribution and television channel that rivals cable television, and someday may replace cable television entirely. Table 10.4 describes digital goods and how they differ from traditional physical goods.

10-2 What are the principal e-commerce business and revenue models?

E-commerce is a fascinating combination of business models and new information technologies. Let's start with a basic understanding of the types of e-commerce and then describe e-commerce business and revenue models.

TYPES OF E-COMMERCE

There are many ways to classify electronic commerce transactions—one is by looking at the nature of the participants. The three major electronic commerce categories are

TABLE 10.4

How the Internet Changes the Markets for Digital Goods

	Digital Goods	Traditional Goods
Marginal cost/unit	Zero	Greater than zero, high
Cost of production	High (most of the cost)	Variable
Copying cost	Approximately zero	Greater than zero, high
Distributed delivery cost	Low	High
Inventory cost	Low	High
Marketing cost	Variable	Variable
Pricing	More variable (bundling, random pricing games)	Fixed, based on unit costs

business-to-consumer (B2C) e-commerce, business-to-business (B2B) e-commerce, and consumer-to-consumer (C2C) e-commerce.

- **Business-to-consumer (B2C)** electronic commerce involves retailing products and services to individual shoppers. Amazon, Walmart, and iTunes are examples of B2C commerce. BarnesandNoble.com, which sells books, software, and music to individual consumers, is an example of B2C e-commerce.
- **Business-to-business (B2B)** electronic commerce involves sales of goods and services among businesses. Elemica's website for buying and selling chemicals and energy is an example of B2B e-commerce.
- **Consumer-to-consumer (C2C)** electronic commerce involves consumers selling directly to consumers. For example, eBay, the giant web auction site, enables people to sell their goods to other consumers by auctioning their merchandise off to the highest bidder or for a fixed price. eBay acts as a middleman by creating a digital platform for peer-to-peer commerce. Craigslist is the most widely used platform consumers use to buy from and sell directly to others.

Another way of classifying electronic commerce transactions is in terms of the platforms participants use in a transaction. Until recently, most e-commerce transactions took place using a desktop PC connected to the Internet over a wired network. Several wireless mobile alternatives have emerged, such as smartphones and tablet computers. The use of handheld wireless devices for purchasing goods and services from any location is termed **mobile commerce** or **m-commerce**. All three types of e-commerce transactions can take place using m-commerce technology, which we discuss in detail in Section 10.3.

E-COMMERCE BUSINESS MODELS

Changes in the economics of information described earlier have created the conditions for entirely new business models to appear while destroying older business models. Table 10.5 describes some of the most important Internet business models that have emerged. All, in one way or another, use the Internet (including apps on mobile devices) to add extra value to existing products and services or to provide the foundation for new products and services.

Portal

Portals are gateways to the web and are often defined as those sites that users set as their home page. Some definitions of a portal include search engines such as Google and Bing even if few make these sites their home page. Portals such as Yahoo, Facebook, MSN, and AOL offer web search tools as well as an integrated package of content and services such as news, email, instant messaging, maps, calendars, shopping, music downloads, video streaming, and more all in one place. The portal business model now provides a destination site where users start their web searching and linger to read news, find entertainment, meet other people, and, of course, be exposed to advertising. Facebook is a very different kind of portal based on social networking, and in 2018 Americans will spend more than half their online time at Facebook, about two hours per day! Portals generate revenue primarily by attracting very large audiences, charging advertisers for display ad placement (similar to traditional newspapers), collecting referral fees for steering customers to other sites, and charging for premium services. In 2018, portals (not including Google or Bing) will generate an estimated $41 billion in display ad revenues. Although there are hundreds of portal/search engine sites, the top four portals (Yahoo, Facebook, MSN, and AOL) gather more than 95 percent of the Internet portal traffic because of their superior brand recognition.

E-tailer

Online retail stores, often called **e-tailers**, come in all sizes, from giant Amazon with 2016 retail sales revenues of more than $80 billion to tiny local stores that have

TABLE 10.5

Internet Business Models

Category	Description	Examples
E-tailer	Sells physical products directly to consumers or to individual businesses.	Amazon Blue Nile
Transaction broker	Saves users money and time by processing online sales transactions and generating a fee each time a transaction occurs.	ETrade.com Expedia
Market creator	Provides a digital environment where buyers and sellers can meet, search for products, display products, and establish prices for those products; can serve consumers or B2B e-commerce, generating revenue from transaction fees.	eBay Priceline.com Exostar Elemica
Content provider	Creates revenue by providing digital content, such as news, music, photos, or video, over the web. The customer may pay to access the content, or revenue may be generated by selling advertising space.	WSJ.com GettyImages.com iTunes.com MSN Games
Community provider	Provides an online meeting place where people with similar interests can communicate and find useful information.	Facebook Google+ Twitter
Portal	Provides initial point of entry to the web along with specialized content and other services.	Yahoo Bing Google
Service provider	Provides applications such as photo sharing, video sharing, and user-generated content as services; provides other services such as online data storage and backup.	Google Apps Photobucket.com Dropbox

websites. An e-tailer is similar to the typical brick-and-mortar storefront, except that customers only need to connect to the Internet to check their inventory and place an order. Altogether, online retail (the sale of physical goods online) will generate about $532 billion in revenues in 2018. The value proposition of e-tailers is to provide convenient, low-cost shopping 24/7; large selections; and consumer choice. Some e-tailers, such as Walmart.com or Staples.com, referred to as bricks-and-clicks, are subsidiaries or divisions of existing physical stores and carry the same products. Others, however, operate only in the virtual world, without any ties to physical locations. Ashford.com and eVitamins.com are examples of this type of e-tailer. Several other variations of e-tailers—such as online versions of direct-mail catalogs, online malls, and manufacturer-direct online sales—also exist.

Content Provider

E-commerce has increasingly become a global content channel. *Content* is defined broadly to include all forms of intellectual property. **Intellectual property** refers to tangible and intangible products of the mind for which the creator claims a property right. Content providers distribute information content—such as digital video, music, photos, text, and artwork—over the web. The value proposition of online content providers is that consumers can conveniently find a wide range of content online and purchase this content inexpensively to be played or viewed on multiple computer devices or smartphones.

Providers do not have to be the creators of the content (although sometimes they are, like Disney.com) and are more likely to be Internet-based distributors of content produced and created by others. For example, Apple sells music tracks at its iTunes Store, but it does not create or commission new music.

The phenomenal popularity of the iTunes Store and Apple's Internet-connected devices such as the iPhone, iPod, and iPad has enabled new forms of digital content delivery from podcasting to mobile streaming. **Podcasting** is a method of publishing audio or video broadcasts through the Internet, allowing subscribing users to download audio or video files onto their personal computers, smartphones, tablets, or portable music players. **Streaming** is a publishing method for music and video files that flows a continuous stream of content to a user's device without being stored locally on the device.

Estimates vary, but total online content will generate about around $28 billion in 2018, one of the fastest-growing e-commerce segments, growing at an estimated 18 percent annual rate.

Transaction Broker

Sites that process transactions for consumers normally handled in person, by phone, or by mail are transaction brokers. The largest industries using this model are financial services and travel services. The online transaction broker's primary value propositions are savings of money and time and providing an extraordinary inventory of financial products and travel packages in a single location. Online stockbrokers and travel booking services charge fees that are considerably less than traditional versions of these services. Fidelity Financial Services and Expedia are the largest online financial and travel service firms based on a transaction broker model.

Market Creator

Market creators build a digital environment in which buyers and sellers can meet, display products, search for products, and establish prices. The value proposition of online market creators is that they provide a platform where sellers can easily display their wares and purchasers can buy directly from sellers. Online auction markets such as eBay and Priceline are good examples of the market creator business model. Another example is Amazon's Merchants platform (and similar programs at eBay), where merchants are allowed to set up stores on Amazon's website and sell goods at fixed prices to consumers. The so-called on-demand economy (mistakenly referred to often as the sharing economy), exemplified by Uber (described in the Interactive Session on Organizations) and Airbnb, is based on the idea of a market creator building a digital platform where supply meets demand; for instance, spare auto or room rental capacity finds individuals who want transportation or lodging. Crowdsource funding markets such as Kickstarter.com bring together private equity investors and entrepreneurs in a funding marketplace.

Service Provider

Whereas e-tailers sell products online, service providers offer services online. Photo sharing and online sites for data backup and storage all use a service provider business model. Software is no longer a physical product with a CD in a box but, increasingly, software as a service (SaaS) that you subscribe to online rather than purchase from a retailer, such as Office 365. Google has led the way in developing online software service applications such as Google Apps, Google Sites, Gmail, and online data storage services. Salesforce.com is a major provider of cloud-based software for customer management (see Chapter 5).

Community Provider (Social Networks)

Community providers are sites that create a digital online environment where people with similar interests can transact (buy and sell goods); share interests, photos, videos; communicate with like-minded people; receive interest-related information; and even play out fantasies by adopting online personalities called *avatars*. Social networking sites Facebook, Google+, Tumblr, Instagram, LinkedIn, and Twitter and

INTERACTIVE SESSION: ORGANIZATIONS Uber: Digital Disruptor

You're in New York, Paris, Chicago, or another major city and need a ride. Instead of trying to hail a cab, you pull out your smartphone and tap the Uber app. A Google map pops up displaying your nearby surroundings. You select a spot on the screen designating an available driver, and the app secures the ride, showing how long it will take for the ride to arrive and how much it will cost. Once you reach your destination, the fare is automatically charged to your credit card. No fumbling for money.

Rates take into account the typical factors of time and distance but also demand. Uber's software predicts areas where rides are likely to be in high demand at different times of the day. This information appears on a driver's smartphone so that the driver knows where to linger and, ideally, pick up customers within minutes of a request for a ride. Uber also offers a higher-priced town car service for business executives and a ride-sharing service. Under certain conditions, if demand is high, Uber can be more expensive than taxis, but it still appeals to riders by offering a reliable, fast, convenient alternative to traditional taxi services.

Uber runs much leaner than a traditional taxi company does. Uber does not own taxis and has no maintenance and financing costs. It does not have employees, so it claims, but instead calls the drivers independent contractors, who receive a cut of each fare. Uber is not encumbered with employee costs such as workers' compensation, minimum wage requirements, background checks on drivers, driver training, health insurance, or commercial licensing costs. Uber has shifted the costs of running a taxi service entirely to the drivers and to the customers using their cell phones. Drivers pay for their own cars, fuel, and insurance. What Uber does is provide a smartphone-based platform that enables people who want a service—like a taxi—to find a provider who can meet that need.

Uber relies on user reviews of drivers and the ride experience to identify problematic drivers and driver reviews of customers to identify problematic passengers. It also sets standards for cleanliness. It uses the reviews to discipline drivers. Uber does not publicly report how many poorly rated drivers or passengers there are in its system. Uber also uses software that monitors sensors in drivers' smartphones to monitor their driving behavior.

Uber is headquartered in San Francisco and was founded in 2009 by Travis Kalanick and Garrett Camp. In 2016, it had more than 400,000 drivers working in 570 cities worldwide, generating revenue of $6.5 billion. After paying for drivers, marketing, and other operating expenses, Uber lost $2.8 billion that year. More than 40 million people use Uber each month. However, Uber's over-the-top success has created its own set of challenges.

By digitally disrupting a traditional and highly regulated industry, Uber has ignited a firestorm of opposition from existing taxi services in the United States and around the world. Who can compete with an upstart firm offering a 40 percent price reduction when demand for taxis is low? (When demand is high, Uber prices surge.) What city or state wants to give up regulatory control over passenger safety, protection from criminals, driver training, and a healthy revenue stream generated by charging taxi firms for a taxi license?

If Uber is the poster child for the new on-demand economy, it's also an iconic example of the social costs and conflict associated with this new kind of business model. Uber has been accused of denying its drivers the benefits of employee status by classifying them as contractors; violating public transportation laws and regulations throughout the United States and the world; abusing the personal information it has collected on ordinary people; and failing to protect public safety by refusing to perform criminal, medical, and financial background checks on its drivers. Uber's brand image has been further tarnished by negative publicity about its aggressive, unrestrained workplace culture and the behavior of CEO Kalanick.

Uber has taken some remediating steps. It enhanced its app to make it easier for drivers to take breaks while they are on the job. Drivers can now also be paid instantly for each ride they complete rather than weekly and see on the app's dashboard how much they have earned. Uber added an option to its app for passengers to tip its U.S. drivers, and Kalanick resigned as head of Uber in June 2017.

Critics fear that Uber and other on-demand firms have the potential for creating a society of part-time, low-paid, temp work, displacing traditionally full-time, secure jobs—the so-called Uberization of work. Uber responds to this fear by saying it is lowering the cost of transportation, expanding the demand for ride services, and expanding opportunities for car drivers, whose pay is about the same as other taxi drivers.

Does Uber have a sustainable business model? The company is still not profitable, although if Uber continues to triple revenue every year, the answer could be yes. But Uber has competitors, including Lyft in the United States and local firms in Asia and Europe. New, smaller competing firms offering app-based cab-hailing services are cropping up, such as Sidecar and Via. Established taxi firms in New York and other cities are launching their own hailing apps and trumpeting their fixed-rate prices. Uber is pressing on, with new services for same-day deliveries, business travel accounts, and experiments with self-driving cars, which management believes will be key to long-term profitability. It is still too early to tell whether Uber and other on-demand businesses will succeed.

Sources: Reuters, "Here's How Much Uber Made in 2016," *Fortune*, April 14, 2017; Rob Berger, "Uber Settlement Takes Customers for a Ride," *Forbes*, April 22, 2016; Mike Isaac and Noam Scheiber, "Uber Settles Cases with Concessions, but Drivers Stay Freelancers," *New York Times*, April 21, 2016; Brian Solomon, "Leaked: Uber's Financials Show Huge Growth, Even Bigger Losses," *Forbes*, January 12, 2016; Douglas MacMillan, "Uber's App Will Soon Begin Tracking Driving Behavior," *Wall Street Journal*, June 29, 2016; and Douglas MacMillan, "The $50 Billion Question: Can Uber Deliver?" *Wall Street Journal*, June 15, 2015.

CASE STUDY QUESTIONS

1. Analyze Uber using the competitive forces and value chain models. What is its competitive advantage?

2. What is the relationship between information technology and Uber's business model? Explain your answer.

3. How disruptive is Uber?

4. Is Uber a viable business? Explain your answer.

hundreds of other smaller, niche sites such as Sportsvite all offer users community-building tools and services. Social networking sites have been the fastest-growing websites in recent years, often doubling their audience size in a year.

E-COMMERCE REVENUE MODELS

A firm's **revenue model** describes how the firm will earn revenue, generate profits, and produce a superior return on investment. Although many e-commerce revenue models have been developed, most companies rely on one, or some combination, of the following six revenue models: advertising, sales, subscription, free/freemium, transaction fee, and affiliate.

Advertising Revenue Model

In the **advertising revenue model**, a website generates revenue by attracting a large audience of visitors who can then be exposed to advertisements. The advertising model is the most widely used revenue model in e-commerce, and arguably, without advertising revenues, the web would be a vastly different experience from what it is now because people would be asked to pay for access to content. Content on the web—everything from news to videos and opinions—is free to visitors because advertisers pay the production and distribution costs in return for the right to expose visitors to ads. Companies will spend an estimated $93 billion on online advertising in 2018 (in the form of a paid message on a website, paid search listing, video, app, game, or other online medium, such as instant messaging). About $70 billion of this will be for mobile ads. Mobile ads will account for 74 percent percent of all digital advertising. In the past five years, advertisers have increased online spending and cut outlays on traditional channels such as radio and newspapers. In 2018, online advertising will grow at 28 percent and constitute about 32 percent of all advertising in the United States (eMarketer, 2017e).

Websites with the largest viewership or that attract a highly specialized, differentiated viewership and are able to retain user attention (stickiness) can charge higher advertising rates. Yahoo, for instance, derives nearly all its revenue from display ads (banner ads), video ads, and, to less extent, search engine text ads. Ninety percent of Google's revenue derives from advertising, including selling keywords (AdWords), selling ad spaces (AdSense), and selling display ad spaces to advertisers (DoubleClick). Facebook displayed one-third of the trillion display ads shown on all sites in 2016.

Sales Revenue Model

In the **sales revenue model**, companies derive revenue by selling goods, information, or services to customers. Companies such as Amazon (which sells books, music, and other products), LLBean.com, and Gap.com all have sales revenue models. Content providers make money by charging for downloads of entire files such as music tracks (iTunes Store) or books or for downloading music and/or video streams (Hulu.com TV shows). Apple has pioneered and strengthened the acceptance of micropayments. **Micropayment systems** provide content providers with a cost-effective method for processing high volumes of very small monetary transactions (anywhere from 25 cents to $5.00 per transaction). The largest micropayment system on the web is Apple's iTunes Store, which has more than 1 billion customers worldwide who purchase individual music tracks for 99 cents and feature length movies for various prices.

Subscription Revenue Model

In the **subscription revenue model**, a website offering content or services charges a subscription fee for access to some or all of its offerings on an ongoing basis. Content providers often use this revenue model. For instance, the online version of *Consumer Reports* provides access to premium content, such as detailed ratings, reviews, and recommendations, only to subscribers, who have a choice of paying a $6.99 monthly subscription fee or a $35.00 annual fee. Netflix is one of the most successful subscriber sites with nearly 100 million customers worldwide in 2017. To be successful, the subscription model requires the content to be perceived as differentiated, having high added value, and not readily available elsewhere or easily replicated. Other companies offering content or services online on a subscription basis include Match.com and eHarmony (dating services), Ancestry.com (genealogy research), and Microsoft Xbox Live.

Free/Freemium Revenue Model

In the **free/freemium revenue model**, firms offer basic services or content for free and charge a premium for advanced or special features. For example, Google offers free applications but charges for premium services. Pandora, the subscription radio service, offers a free service with limited play time and advertising and a premium service with unlimited play. Spotify music service also uses a freemium business model. The idea is to attract very large audiences with free services and then convert some of this audience to pay a subscription for premium services. One problem with this model is converting people from being free loaders into paying customers. "Free" can be a powerful model for losing money. None of the freemium music streaming sites have earned a profit to date. Nevertheless, they are finding that free service with ad revenue is more profitable than the paid subscriber part of their business.

Transaction Fee Revenue Model

In the **transaction fee revenue model**, a company receives a fee for enabling or executing a transaction. For example, eBay provides an online auction marketplace and receives a small transaction fee from a seller if the seller is successful in selling an item. E*Trade, an online stockbroker, receives transaction fees each time it executes a stock transaction on behalf of a customer. The transaction revenue model enjoys wide acceptance in part because the true cost of using the platform is not immediately apparent to the user.

Online financial services, from banking to payment systems, rely on a transaction fee model. While online banking and services are dominated by large banks with millions of customers, start-up financial technology firms, also known as **FinTech** firms, have grown rapidly to compete with banks for peer-to-peer (P2P), bill payment, money transfer, lending, crowdsourcing, financial advice, and account aggregation services. The largest growth in FinTech has involved P2P payment services, such as Venmo and Square, two of hundreds of FinTech firms competing in this space with banks and online payment giants such as PayPal (PayPal purchased Venmo in 2013). FinTech firms are typically not profitable and are often bought out by larger financial service firms for their technology and customer base.

Affiliate Revenue Model

In the **affiliate revenue model**, websites (called *affiliate websites*) send visitors to other websites in return for a referral fee or percentage of the revenue from any resulting sales. Referral fees are also referred to as lead generation fees. For example, MyPoints makes money by connecting companies to potential customers by offering special deals to its members. When members take advantage of an offer and make a purchase, they earn points they can redeem for free products and services, and MyPoints receives a referral fee. Community feedback sites such as Epinions and Yelp receive much of their revenue from steering potential customers to websites where they make a purchase. Amazon uses affiliates that steer business to the Amazon website by placing the Amazon logo on their blogs. Personal blogs often contain display ads as part of affiliate programs. Some bloggers are paid directly by manufacturers, or receive free products, for speaking highly of products and providing links to sales channels.

10-3 How has e-commerce transformed marketing?

Although e-commerce and the Internet have changed entire industries and enabled new business models, no industry has been more affected than marketing and marketing communications.

The Internet provides marketers with new ways of identifying and communicating with millions of potential customers at costs far lower than traditional media, including search engine marketing, data mining, recommender systems, and targeted email. The Internet enables **long tail marketing**. Before the Internet, reaching a large audience was very expensive, and marketers had to focus on attracting the largest number of consumers with popular hit products, whether music, Hollywood movies, books, or cars. In contrast, the Internet allows marketers to find potential customers inexpensively for products where demand is very low. For instance, the Internet makes it possible to sell independent music profitably to very small audiences. There's always some demand for almost any product. Put a string of such long tail sales together and you have a profitable business.

The Internet also provides new ways—often instantaneous and spontaneous—to gather information from customers, adjust product offerings, and increase customer value. Table 10.6 describes the leading marketing and advertising formats used in e-commerce.

BEHAVIORAL TARGETING

Many e-commerce marketing firms use **behavioral targeting** techniques to increase the effectiveness of banners, rich media, and video ads. Behavioral targeting refers to tracking the clickstreams (history of clicking behavior) of individuals on thousands of websites to understand their interests and intentions and expose them to

TABLE 10.6

Online Display Ad Spending by Formats (Billions)

Marketing Format	2018 Revenue	Description
Search engine	$42.1	Text ads targeted at precisely what the customer is looking for at the moment of shopping and purchasing. Sales oriented.
Display ads	$46.1	Banner ads (pop-ups and leave-behinds) with interactive features; increasingly behaviorally targeted to individual web activity. Brand development and sales. Includes social media and blog display ads.
Video	$14.4	Fastest-growing format, engaging and entertaining; behaviorally targeted, interactive. Branding and sales.
Classified	$2.1	Job, real estate, and services ads; interactive, rich media, and personalized to user searches. Sales and branding.
Rich media	$11.7	Animations, games, and puzzles. Interactive, targeted, and entertaining. Branding orientation.
Lead generation	$2.0	Marketing firms that gather sales and marketing leads online and then sell them to online marketers for a variety of campaign types. Sales or branding orientation.
Sponsorships	$2.1	Online games, puzzles, contests, and coupon sites sponsored by firms to promote products. Sales orientation.
Email	$0.37	Effective, targeted marketing tool with interactive and rich media potential. Sales oriented.

advertisements that are uniquely suited to their online behavior. Marketers and most researchers believe this more precise understanding of the customer leads to more efficient marketing (the firm pays for ads only to those shoppers who are most interested in their products) and larger sales and revenues. Unfortunately, behavioral targeting of millions of web users also leads to the invasion of personal privacy without user consent. When consumers lose trust in their web experience, they tend not to purchase anything. Backlash is growing against the aggressive uses of personal information as consumers seek out safer havens for purchasing and messaging. Snapchat offers disappearing messages, and even Facebook has retreated by making its default for new posts "for friends only."

Behavioral targeting takes place at two levels: at individual websites or from within apps and on various advertising networks that track users across thousands of websites. All websites collect data on visitor browser activity and store it in a database. They have tools to record the site that users visited prior to coming to the website, where these users go when they leave that site, the type of operating system they use, browser information, and even some location data. They also record the specific pages visited on the particular site, the time spent on each page of the site, the types of pages visited, and what the visitors purchased (see Figure 10.3). Firms analyze this information about customer interests and behavior to develop precise profiles of existing and potential customers. In addition, most major websites have hundreds of tracking programs on their home pages, which track your clickstream behavior across the web by following you from site to site and re-target ads to you by showing you the same ads on different sites. The leading online advertising network is Google's DoubleClick.

This information enables firms to understand how well their website is working, create unique personalized web pages that display content or ads for products or services of special interest to each user, improve the customer's experience, and create

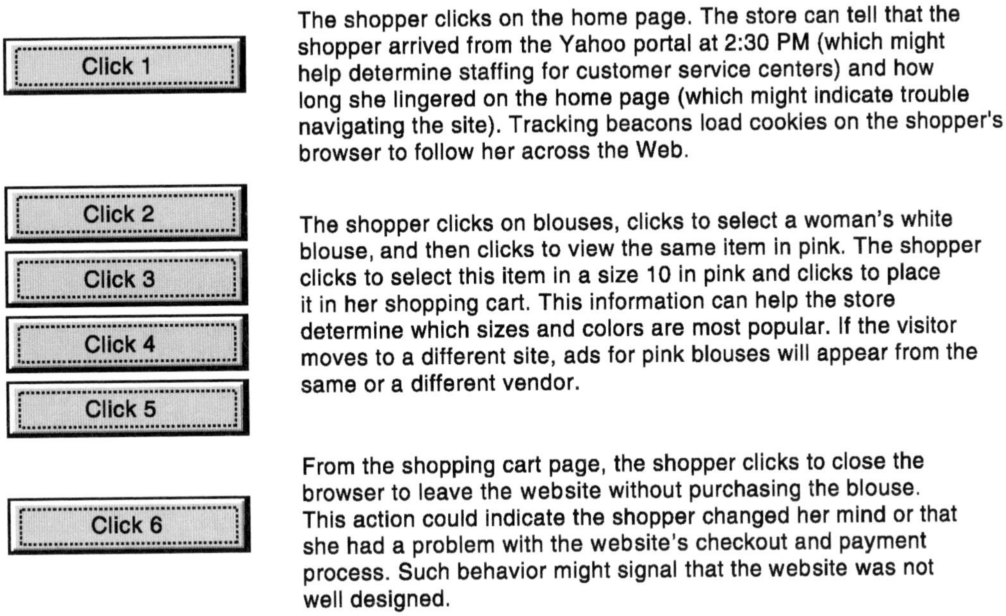

Click 1
The shopper clicks on the home page. The store can tell that the shopper arrived from the Yahoo portal at 2:30 PM (which might help determine staffing for customer service centers) and how long she lingered on the home page (which might indicate trouble navigating the site). Tracking beacons load cookies on the shopper's browser to follow her across the Web.
Click 2
Click 3
Click 4
Click 5
The shopper clicks on blouses, clicks to select a woman's white blouse, and then clicks to view the same item in pink. The shopper clicks to select this item in a size 10 in pink and clicks to place it in her shopping cart. This information can help the store determine which sizes and colors are most popular. If the visitor moves to a different site, ads for pink blouses will appear from the same or a different vendor.
Click 6
From the shopping cart page, the shopper clicks to close the browser to leave the website without purchasing the blouse. This action could indicate the shopper changed her mind or that she had a problem with the website's checkout and payment process. Such behavior might signal that the website was not well designed.

Figure 10.3
Website Visitor Tracking
E-commerce websites and advertising platforms like Google's DoubleClick have tools to track a shopper's every step through an online store and then across the web as shoppers move from site to site. Close examination of customer behavior at a website selling women's clothing shows what the store might learn at each step and what actions it could take to increase sales.

additional value through a better understanding of the shopper (see Figure 10.4). By using personalization technology to modify the web pages presented to each customer, marketers achieve some of the benefits of using individual salespeople at dramatically lower costs. For instance, General Motors will show a Chevrolet banner ad to women emphasizing safety and utility, whereas men will receive ads emphasizing power and ruggedness.

It's a short step from ad networks to programmatic ad buying. Ad networks create real-time bidding platforms (RTB) where marketers bid in an automated environment for highly targeted slots available from web publishers. Here, ad platforms can predict how many targeted individuals will view the ads, and ad buyers can estimate how much this exposure is worth to them.

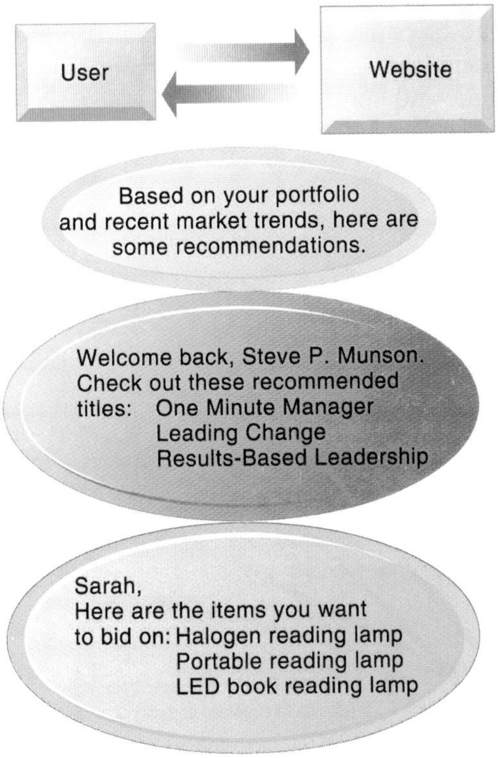

Figure 10.4
Website Personalization
Firms can create unique personalized web pages that display content or ads for products or services of special interest to individual users, improving the customer experience and creating additional value.

What if you are a large national advertising company with many clients trying to reach millions of consumers? What if you were a large global manufacturer trying to reach potential consumers for your products? With millions of websites, working with each one would be impractical. Advertising networks solve this problem by creating a network of several thousand of the most popular websites millions of people visit, tracking the behavior of these users across the entire network, building profiles of each user, and then selling these profiles to advertisers in a real-time bidding environment. Popular websites download dozens of web tracking cookies, bugs, and beacons, which report user online behavior to remote servers without the users' knowledge. Looking for young, single consumers with college degrees, living in the Northeast, in the 18–34 age range who are interested in purchasing a European car? Advertising networks can identify and deliver thousands of people who fit this profile and expose them to ads for European cars as they move from one website to another. Estimates vary, but behaviorally targeted ads are generally 10 times more likely to produce a consumer response than a randomly chosen banner or video ad (see Figure 10.5). So-called advertising exchanges use this same technology to auction access to people with very specific profiles to advertisers in a few milliseconds. In 2016, about 50 percent of online display ads were targeted ads developed by programmatic ad buys, and the rest depended on the context of the pages shoppers visited—the estimated demographics of visitors, or so-called blast-and-scatter advertising—which is placed randomly on any available page with minimal targeting, such as time of day or season.

It's another short step to **native advertising**. Native advertising involves placing ads in social network newsfeeds or within traditional editorial content, such as a newspaper article. This is also referred to as organic advertising, where content and advertising are in very close proximity or integrated together.

Two-thirds (68 percent) of Internet users disapprove of search engines and websites tracking their online behavior to aim targeted ads at them. Twenty-eight percent of those surveyed approve of behavioral targeting because they believe it produces more relevant ads and information. A majority of Americans want a Do Not Track option in browsers that will stop websites from collecting information about their online behavior. More than 50 percent are very concerned about the wealth of personal data online; 86 percent have taken steps to mask their online behavior; 25 percent of web users use ad-blocking software. Next to hackers, Americans try to avoid advertisers pursuing them while online, and 64 percent block cookies to make tracking more difficult (Rainie and Duggan, 2016).

Figure 10.5
How an Advertising Network Such as Doubleclick Works
Advertising networks and their use of tracking programs have become controversial among privacy advocates because of their ability to track individual consumers across the Internet.

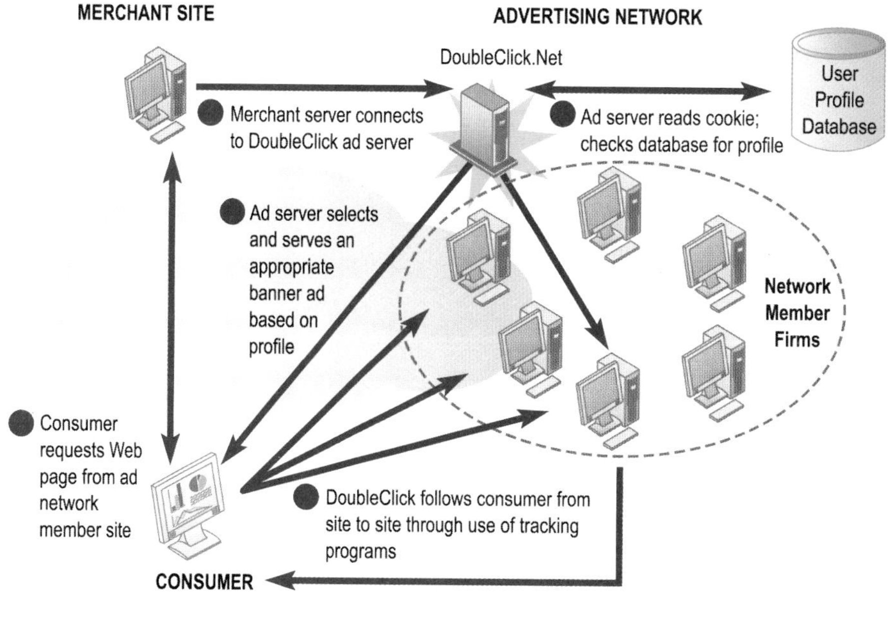

SOCIAL E-COMMERCE AND SOCIAL NETWORK MARKETING

Social e-commerce is commerce based on the idea of the digital **social graph**, a mapping of all significant online social relationships. The social graph is synonymous with the idea of a social network used to describe offline relationships. You can map your own social graph (network) by drawing lines from yourself to the 10 closest people you know. If they know one another, draw lines between these people. If you are ambitious, ask these 10 friends to list and draw in the names of the 10 people closest to them. What emerges from this exercise is a preliminary map of your social network. Now imagine if everyone on the Internet did the same and posted the results to a very large database with a website. Ultimately, you would end up with Facebook or a site like it.

According to small world theory, you are only six links away from any other person on earth. If you entered your personal address book, which has, say, 100 names in it, in a list and sent it to your friends, and they in turn entered 50 new names of their friends, and so on, five times, the social network created would encompass 31 billion people! The social graph is therefore a collection of millions of personal social graphs (and all the people in them). So, it's a small world indeed, and we are all more closely linked than we ever thought.

If you understand the interconnectedness of people, you will see just how important this concept is to e-commerce: The products and services you buy will influence the decisions of your friends, and their decisions will in turn influence you. If you are a marketer trying to build and strengthen a brand, the implication is clear: Take advantage of the fact that people are enmeshed in social networks, share interests and values, and communicate and influence one another. As a marketer, your target audience is not a million isolated people watching a TV show but the social network of people who watch the show and the viewers' personal networks. Table 10.7 describes the features of social commerce that are driving its growth.

In 2018, one of the fastest-growing media for branding and marketing is social media. Companies spent an estimated $21 billion in 2017 using social networks such

TABLE 10.7

Features of Social Commerce

Social Commerce Feature	Description
Newsfeed	A stream of notifications from friends and advertisers that social users find on their home pages.
Timelines	A stream of photos and events in the past that create a personal history for users, one that can be shared with friends.
Social sign-on	Websites allow users to sign into their sites through their social network pages on Facebook or another social site. This allows websites to receive valuable social profile information from Facebook and use it in their own marketing efforts.
Collaborative shopping	An environment where consumers can share their shopping experiences with one another by viewing products, chatting, or texting. Friends can chat online about brands, products, and services.
Network notification	An environment where consumers can share their approval (or disapproval) of products, services, or content or share their geolocation, perhaps a restaurant or club, with friends. Facebook's ubiquitous "like" button is an example, as are Twitter's tweets and followers.
Social search (recommendations)	An environment where consumers can ask their friends for advice on purchases of products, services, and content. Although Google can help you find things, social search can help you evaluate the quality of things by listening to the evaluations of your friends or their friends. For instance, Amazon's social recommender system can use your Facebook social profile to recommend products.

as Facebook to reach millions of consumers who spend hours a day on the Facebook site. Facebook accounts for 74 percent of all social marketing in the United States. Expenditures for social media marketing are much smaller than for television, magazines, and even newspapers, but this will change in the future. Social networks in the offline world are collections of people who voluntarily communicate with one another over an extended period of time. Online social networks, such as Facebook, LinkedIn YouTube, Twitter, Tumblr, and Google+, along with other sites with social components, are websites that enable users to communicate with one another, form group and individual relationships, and share interests, values, and ideas. Individuals establish online profiles with text and photos, creating an online profile of how they want others to see them, and then invite their friends to link to their profile. The network grows by word of mouth and through email links.

Facebook, with 203 million U.S. monthly visitors, receives most of the public attention given to social networking, but the other top four social sites are also growing, though at slower rates than in the past. Facebook user growth has slowed in the United States. LinkedIn growth slowed in 2017, and it had 102 million visitors a month in 2017. Twitter grew to reach 101 million active users, with stronger offshore growth than in the United States. Pinterest hit the top 50 websites with 90 million, a 30 percent increase from 2016. According to ComScore, nearly half of the total time spent online in the United States was spent on social network sites, and social networking is the most common online activity (ComScore, 2017). The fastest-growing smartphone applications are social network apps; nearly half of smartphone users visit social sites daily. More than 65 percent of all visits to Facebook in 2017 came from smartphones.

At **social shopping** sites such as Pinterest you can swap shopping ideas with friends. Facebook offers the "like" button and Google the +1 button to let your friends know you admire a product, service, or content and, in some cases, purchase something online. Facebook processes around 5 billion likes a day worldwide. Online communities are also ideal venues to employ viral marketing techniques. Online viral marketing is like traditional word-of-mouth marketing except that the word can spread across an online community at the speed of light and go much further geographically than a small network of friends.

The Wisdom of Crowds

Creating sites where thousands, even millions, of people can interact offers business firms new ways to market and advertise and to discover who likes (or hates) their products. In a phenomenon called the **wisdom of crowds**, some argue that large numbers of people can make better decisions about a wide range of topics or products than a single person or even a small committee of experts.

Obviously, this is not always the case, but it can happen in interesting ways. In marketing, the wisdom of crowds concept suggests that firms should consult with thousands of their customers first as a way of establishing a relationship with them and, second, to understand better how their products and services are used and appreciated (or rejected). Actively soliciting the comments of your customers builds trust and sends the message to your customers that you care what they are thinking and that you need their advice.

Beyond merely soliciting advice, firms can be actively helped in solving some business problems by using **crowdsourcing**. For instance, BMW launched a crowdsourcing project to enlist the aid of customers in designing an urban vehicle for 2025. Kickstarter.com is arguably one of the most famous e-commerce crowdfunding sites where visitors invest in start-up companies. Other examples include Caterpillar working with customers to design better machinery, IKEA for designing furniture, and Pepsico using Super Bowl viewers to build an online video.

Marketing through social media is still in its early stages, and companies are experimenting in hopes of finding a winning formula. Social interactions and customer sentiment are not always easy to manage, presenting new challenges for companies eager to protect their brands. The Interactive Session on People provides specific examples of companies' social marketing efforts using Facebook and Twitter.

INTERACTIVE SESSION: PEOPLE "Socializing" with Customers

More than 2 billion people worldwide use social media, making it an obvious platform for companies seeking to engage consumers, amplify product messages, discover trends and influencers, build brand awareness, and take action on customer requests and recommendations. More than 30 million businesses have active Facebook brand pages, enabling users to interact with the brand through blogs, comment pages, contests, and offerings on the brand page. The "like" button gives users a chance to share with their social network their feelings about content and other objects they are viewing and websites they are visiting. With like buttons on many millions of websites, Facebook can track user behavior on other sites and then sell this information to marketers. Facebook also sells display ads to firms that show up in the right column of users' home pages and most other pages in the Facebook interface such as photos and apps. Twitter features such as "promoted tweets" and "promoted trends" enable advertisers to have their tweets displayed more prominently when Twitter users search for certain keywords.

Lowe's has used Facebook mobile video and Snapchat image messaging to help first-time millennial home buyers learn home improvement skills. The home improvement retailer launched a new series of social videos in April 2016 to showcase spring cleaning and do-it-yourself projects. Lowe's believes this is a more immediate and interactive way to reach younger consumers who are increasingly spending time on visual-driven social media platforms.

Lowe's "FlipSide" videos are short, two-sided live action videos that show simultaneously what can happen if a homeowner doesn't clean the gutters and air filters or prune overgrown shrubs compared with the results of proper spring cleaning. These videos take advantage of the flip video application in Facebook's mobile feed that enables users to change the orientation of the video, and the videos link back to the Lowes.com website.

Lowe's "In-a-Snap" Snapchat series tries to inspire young homeowners and renters to undertake simple home improvement projects such as installing shelves to build a study nook. During the Lowe's Snapchat story, users can tap on the screen to put a nail in a wall or chisel off an old tile.

Lowe's social media activities have helped increase brand engagement. Although the company's social campaigns are designed to teach first-time homeowners or young renters about home improvement, the company is also hoping they will encourage consumers to think differently about the brand beyond its products and services. Management believes millennials who are becoming first-time homeowners want to know the deeper meaning of what a company is trying to stand for, not just the products and services it offers.

An estimated 90 percent of customers are influenced by online reviews, and nearly half of U.S. social media users actively seek customer service through social media. As a result, marketing is now placing much more emphasis on customer satisfaction and service. Social media monitoring helps marketers and business owners understand more about buyers' likes, dislikes, and complaints concerning products, additional products or product modifications customers want, and how people are talking about a brand (positive or negative sentiment).

General Motors (GM) has 26 full-time social media customer care advisors for North America alone, covering more than 150 company social channels from GM, Chevrolet, Buick, GMC, and Cadillac and approximately 85 sites such as automotive enthusiast forums. These advisors are available to assist customers seven days a week, 16 operational hours per day. GM believes that the processes for identifying and resolving quality concerns are very important.

GM recognized early on that there was a wealth of information in online vehicle owner forums that should be utilized in product development. GM social media advisors actively monitor vehicle owner forums and other social media platforms to identify potential issues and provide real-time customer feedback to the company's brand quality and engineering leaders. In some cases, GM social media advisors were able to identify issues much earlier than traditional surveying or dealer feedback.

For example, GM's social media team identified a faulty climate-control part when a customer posted the issue on a product-owner blog. The complaint received dozens of replies and thousands of views, prompting GM that it needed to investigate further. Once GM specialists determined the root cause of the issue, the company released a technical service bulletin to all dealerships to replace the affected HVAC control modules on vehicles already built. GM fixed the original customer's vehicle within 10 days and adjusted production to ensure no additional customers would be affected.

Other companies have used social media feedback to improve their products as well. Prompted by customer social media comments about meats other than roast beef, fast food sandwich restaurant chain Arby's launched a "Meat Mountain" campaign poster showing various meats other than roast beef. Arby's customers mistakenly thought the poster displayed a new sandwich and, through social media, indicated they were anxious to try it. Arby's then responded with a new $10 Meat Mountain sandwich.

Still, the results of a social presence can be unpredictable and not always beneficial, as a number of companies have learned. A few days before September 11, 2016, San Antonio–based Miracle Mattress provoked angry social media backlash when it posted a video to Facebook advertising a "Twin Towers Sale." The video encouraged customers to "remember 9/11" and "get any size mattress for a twin price." Miracle Mattress removed the video from its Facebook timeline, and owner Mike Bonanno posted an apology letter.

Sources: Farhad Manjoo "How Battling Brands Online Has Gained Urgency, and Impact," *New York Times*, June 21, 2017; Lindsay Friedman, "The 12 Worst Social-Media Fails of 2016," www.entrepreneur.com, accessed July 5, 2017; Rob Petersen, "12 Inspiring Social-Media Monitoring Case Studies," *Business 2 Community*, August 11, 2016; Claudia Kubowicz Malhotra and Arvind Malhotra, "How CEOs Can Leverage Twitter," *MIT Sloan Management Review*, Winter 2016; Daniel Matthews, "Social Customer Service Metrics: 3 Case Studies," Ducttapemarketing.com, accessed July 1, 2016; and Nathalie Tadena, "Lowe's Enlists Snapchat, Facebook Mobile Video in New Push to Reach Millennials," *Wall Street Journal*, April 25, 2016.

CASE STUDY QUESTIONS

1. Assess the people, organization, and technology issues for using social media technology to engage with customers.
2. What are the advantages and disadvantages of using social media for advertising, brand building, market research, and customer service?
3. Give an example of a business decision in this case study that was facilitated by using social media to interact with customers.
4. Should all companies use social media technology for customer service and marketing? Why or why not? What kinds of companies are best suited to use these platforms?

10-4 How has e-commerce affected business-to-business transactions?

The trade between business firms (business-to-business commerce, or B2B) represents a huge marketplace. The total amount of B2B trade in the United States in 2017 was estimated to be about $13.3 trillion, with B2B e-commerce (online B2B) contributing about $6.3 trillion of that amount (U.S. Bureau of the Census, 2017; authors' estimates). By 2020, B2B e-commerce is expected to grow to about $7.2 trillion in the United States. The process of conducting trade among business firms is complex and requires considerable human intervention; therefore, it consumes significant resources. Some firms estimate that each corporate purchase order for support products costs them, on average, at least $100 in administrative overhead. Administrative overhead includes processing paper, approving purchase decisions, spending time using the telephone and fax machines to search for products and arrange for purchases, arranging for shipping, and receiving the goods. Across the economy, this adds up to trillions of dollars annually spent for procurement processes that could be automated. If even just a portion of inter-firm trade were automated and parts of the entire procurement process were assisted by the Internet, literally trillions of dollars might be released for more productive uses, consumer prices potentially would fall, productivity would increase, and the economic wealth of the nation would expand. This is the promise of B2B e-commerce. The challenge of B2B e-commerce

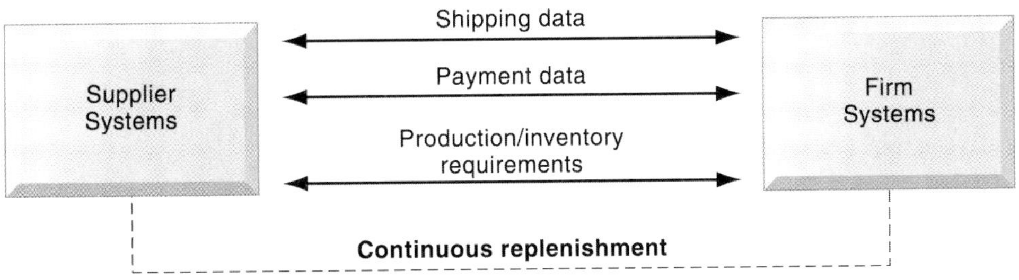

Figure 10.6
Electronic Data Interchange (EDI)
Companies use EDI to automate transactions for B2B e-commerce and continuous inventory replenishment. Suppliers can automatically send data about shipments to purchasing firms. The purchasing firms can use EDI to provide production and inventory requirements and payment data to suppliers.

is changing existing patterns and systems of procurement and designing and implementing new Internet-based B2B solutions.

ELECTRONIC DATA INTERCHANGE (EDI)

B2B e-commerce refers to the commercial transactions that occur among business firms. Increasingly, these transactions are flowing through a variety of Internet-enabled mechanisms. About 80 percent of online B2B e-commerce is still based on proprietary systems for **Electronic Data Interchange (EDI)**. EDI enables the computer-to-computer exchange between two organizations of standard transactions such as invoices, bills of lading, shipment schedules, or purchase orders. Transactions are automatically transmitted from one information system to another through a network, eliminating the printing and handling of paper at one end and the inputting of data at the other. Each major industry in the United States and much of the rest of the world has EDI standards that define the structure and information fields of electronic transactions for that industry.

EDI originally automated the exchange of documents such as purchase orders, invoices, and shipping notices. Although many companies still use EDI for document automation, firms engaged in just-in-time inventory replenishment and continuous production use EDI as a system for continuous replenishment. Suppliers have online access to selected parts of the purchasing firm's production and delivery schedules and automatically ship materials and goods to meet prespecified targets without intervention by firm purchasing agents (see Figure 10.6).

Although many organizations still use private networks for EDI, they are increasingly web-enabled because Internet technology provides a much more flexible and low-cost platform for linking to other firms. Businesses can extend digital technology to a wider range of activities and broaden their circle of trading partners.

Procurement, for example, involves not only purchasing goods and materials but also sourcing, negotiating with suppliers, paying for goods, and making delivery arrangements. Businesses can now use the Internet to locate the lowest-cost supplier, search online catalogs of supplier products, negotiate with suppliers, place orders, make payments, and arrange transportation. They are not limited to partners linked by traditional EDI networks.

NEW WAYS OF B2B BUYING AND SELLING

The Internet and web technology enable businesses to create electronic storefronts for selling to other businesses using the same techniques as used for B2C commerce. Alternatively, businesses can use Internet technology to create extranets or electronic marketplaces for linking to other businesses for purchase and sale transactions.

Private industrial networks typically consist of a large firm using a secure website to link to its suppliers and other key business partners (see Figure 10.7). The buyer owns the network, and it permits the firm and designated suppliers, distributors, and other business partners to share product design and development, marketing, production scheduling, inventory management, and unstructured communication,

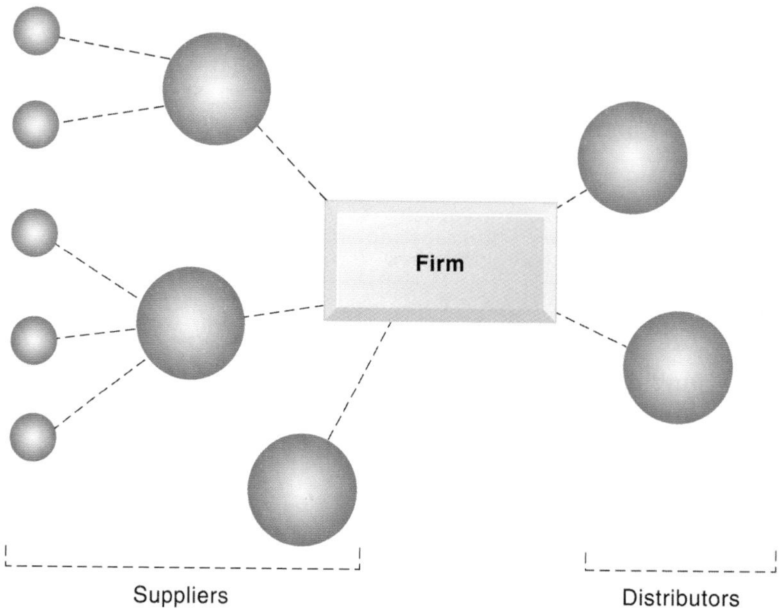

Figure 10.7
A Private Industrial Network
A private industrial network, also known as a private exchange, links a firm to its suppliers, distributors, and other key business partners for efficient supply chain management and other collaborative commerce activities.

including graphics and email. Another term for a private industrial network is a **private exchange**.

An example is VW Group Supply, which links the Volkswagen Group and its suppliers. VW Group Supply handles 90 percent of all global purchasing for Volkswagen, including all automotive and parts components.

Net marketplaces, which are sometimes called e-hubs, provide a single, digital marketplace based on Internet technology for many buyers and sellers (see Figure 10.8). They are industry-owned or operate as independent intermediaries between buyers and sellers. Net marketplaces generate revenue from purchase and sale transactions and other services provided to clients. Participants in Net marketplaces can establish prices through online negotiations, auctions, or requests for quotations, or they can use fixed prices.

There are many types of Net marketplaces and ways of classifying them. Some sell direct goods and some sell indirect goods. **Direct goods** are goods used in a production process, such as sheet steel for auto body production. **Indirect goods** are all

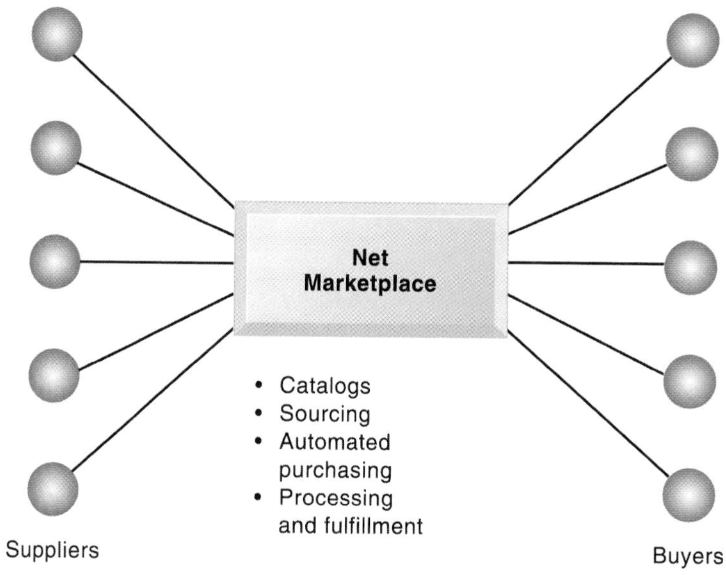

Figure 10.8
A Net Marketplace
Net marketplaces are online marketplaces where multiple buyers can purchase from multiple sellers.

other goods not directly involved in the production process, such as office supplies or products for maintenance and repair. Some Net marketplaces support contractual purchasing based on long-term relationships with designated suppliers, and others support short-term spot purchasing, where goods are purchased based on immediate needs, often from many suppliers.

Some Net marketplaces serve vertical markets for specific industries, such as automobiles, telecommunications, or machine tools, whereas others serve horizontal markets for goods and services that can be found in many industries, such as office equipment or transportation.

Exostar is an example of an industry-owned Net marketplace, focusing on long-term contract purchasing relationships and on providing common networks and computing platforms for reducing supply chain inefficiencies. This aerospace and defense industry-sponsored Net marketplace was founded jointly by BAE Systems, Boeing, Lockheed Martin, Raytheon, and Rolls-Royce plc to connect these companies to their suppliers and facilitate collaboration. More than 125,000 trading partners in the commercial, military, and government sectors use Exostar's sourcing, e-procurement, and collaboration tools for both direct and indirect goods.

Exchanges are independently owned third-party Net marketplaces that connect thousands of suppliers and buyers for spot purchasing. Many exchanges provide vertical markets for a single industry, such as food, electronics, or industrial equipment, and they primarily deal with direct inputs. For example, Go2Paper enables a spot market for paper, board, and craft among buyers and sellers in the paper industries from more than 75 countries.

Exchanges proliferated during the early years of e-commerce, but many have failed. Suppliers were reluctant to participate because the exchanges encouraged competitive bidding that drove prices down and did not offer any long-term relationships with buyers or services to make lowering prices worthwhile. Many essential direct purchases are not conducted on a spot basis because they require contracts and consideration of issues such as delivery timing, customization, and quality of products.

10-5 What is the role of m-commerce in business, and what are the most important m-commerce applications?

Walk down the street in any major metropolitan area and count how many people are pecking away at their iPhones, Samsungs, or BlackBerrys. Ride the trains or fly the planes, and you'll see fellow travelers reading an online newspaper, watching a video on their phone, or reading a novel on their Kindle. As the mobile audience has expanded in leaps and bounds, mobile advertising and m-commerce have taken off.

In 2017, retail m-commerce constituted about 35 percent of all e-commerce, with about $157 billion in annual revenues generated by retail goods and services, apps, advertising, music, videos, ring tones, movies, television, and location-based services such as local restaurant locators and traffic updates. However, m-commerce is the fastest-growing form of e-commerce, expanding at a rate of 20 percent or more per year, and is estimated to grow to $337 billion by 2020 (see Figure 10.9) (eMarketer, 2017f).

The main areas of growth in mobile e-commerce are mass market retailing such as Amazon ($70 billion) and Apple (about $12 billion); sales of digital content such as music, TV shows, movies, and e-books (about $12 billion); and in-app sales to mobile devices (about $7 billion) (eMarketer, 2016d). These estimates do not include mobile advertising or location-based services. On-demand firms such as Uber (described earlier in this chapter) and Airbnb are location-based services, but they are certainly examples of mobile commerce as well. Larger screens and more convenient payment procedures also play a role in the expansion of m-commerce.

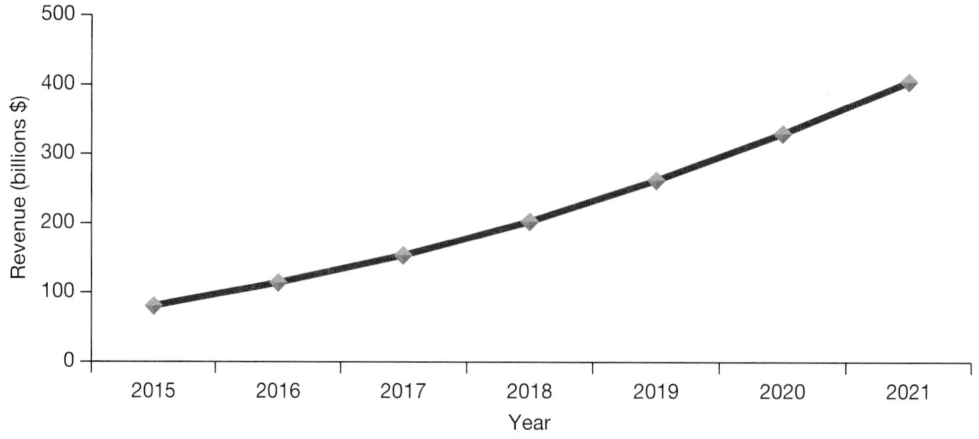

Figure 10.9
Mobile Retail Commerce Revenues
Mobile e-commerce is the fastest-growing type of B2C e-commerce and represented about 34 percent of all e-commerce in 2017.

Sources: Data from eMarketer chart "Retail Mcommerce Sales, US, (billions) 2015–2021," eMarketer, 2017

LOCATION-BASED SERVICES AND APPLICATIONS

Location-based services include geosocial, geoadvertising, and geoinformation services. Seventy-four percent of smartphone owners use location-based services. What ties these activities together and is the foundation for mobile commerce is the global positioning system (GPS)–enabled map services available on smartphones. A **geosocial service** can tell you where your friends are meeting. **Geoadvertising services** can tell you where to find the nearest Italian restaurant, and **geoinformation services** can tell you the price of a house you are looking at or about special exhibits at a museum you are passing. In 2018, the fastest-growing and most popular location-based services are on-demand economy firms such as Uber, Lyft, Airbnb, and hundreds more that provide services to users in local areas and are based on the user's location (or, in the case of Airbnb, the user's intended travel location).

Waze is an example of a popular, social geoinformation service. Waze is a GPS-based map and navigational app for smartphones, now owned by Google. Waze locates the user's car on a digital map using GPS and, like other navigation programs, collects information on the user's speed and direction continuously. What makes Waze different is that it collects traffic information from users who submit accident reports, speed traps, landmarks, street fairs, protests, and even addresses. Waze uses this information to come up with suggested alternative routes, travel times, and warnings and can even make recommendations for gas stations along the way. The Waze app is used extensively by Uber and Lyft drivers and more than 35 million other drivers in the United States.

Foursquare and new offerings by Facebook and Google are examples of geosocial services. Geosocial services help you find friends, or your friends to find you, by checking in to the service, announcing your presence in a restaurant or other place. Your friends are instantly notified. About 20 percent of smartphone owners use geosocial services.

Foursquare provides a location-based social networking service to 50 million registered individual users, who may connect with friends, update their location, and provide reviews and tips for enjoying a location. Points are awarded for checking in at designated venues. Users choose to post their check-ins on their accounts on Twitter, Facebook, or both. Users also earn badges by checking in at locations with certain tags, for check-in frequency, or for the time of check-in.

Connecting people to local merchants in the form of geoadvertising is the economic foundation for mobile commerce. Geoadvertising sends ads to users based on their GPS locations. Smartphones report their locations back to Google and Apple. Merchants buy access to these consumers when they come within range of a merchant. For instance, Kiehl Stores, a cosmetics retailer, sent special offers and announcements to customers who came within 100 yards of their store.

OTHER MOBILE COMMERCE SERVICES

Banks and credit card companies have developed services that let customers manage their accounts from their mobile devices. JPMorgan Chase and Bank of America customers can use their cell phones to check account balances, transfer funds, and pay bills. Apple Pay for the iPhone and Apple Watch, along with other Android and Windows smartphone models, allows users to charge items to their credit card accounts with a swipe of their phone. (See our Learning Track on mobile payment systems.)

The mobile advertising market is the fastest-growing online ad platform, racking up $70 billion in ad revenue in 2017 and growing at 25 percent annually. Ads eventually move to where the eyeballs are, and increasingly that means mobile phones and, to less extent, tablets. Google is the largest mobile advertising market, posting about $19 billion in mobile ads, with Facebook number two with $14.3 billion (nearly 90 percent of its total digital ad business). Google is displaying ads linked to cell phone searches by users of the mobile version of its search engine; Ads are embedded in games, videos, and other mobile applications.

Shopkick is a mobile application that enables retailers such as Best Buy, Sports Authority, and Macy's to offer coupons to people when they walk into their stores. The Shopkick app automatically recognizes when the user has entered a partner retail store and offers a new virtual currency called kickbucks, which can be redeemed for store gift cards.

Fifty-five percent of online retailers now have m-commerce websites—simplified versions of their websites that enable shoppers to use cell phones to shop and place orders. Sephora, Home Depot, Amazon, and Walmart are among those retailers with apps for m-commerce sales. In 2017, more than half of m-commerce sales occurred within apps rather than mobile web browsers.

10-6 What issues must be addressed when building an e-commerce presence?

Building a successful e-commerce presence requires a keen understanding of business, technology, and social issues as well as a systematic approach. Today, an e-commerce presence is not just a corporate website but also includes a social network site on Facebook, a Twitter feed, and smartphone apps where customers can access your services. Developing and coordinating all these customer venues can be difficult. A complete treatment of the topic is beyond the scope of this text, and students should consult books devoted to just this topic (Laudon and Traver, 2018). The two most important management challenges in building a successful e-commerce presence are (1) developing a clear understanding of your business objectives and (2) knowing how to choose the right technology to achieve those objectives.

DEVELOP AN E-COMMERCE PRESENCE MAP

E-commerce has moved from being a PC-centric activity on the web to a mobile and tablet-based activity. Currently, a majority of Internet users in the United States use smartphones and tablets to shop for goods and services, look up prices, enjoy entertainment, and access social sites, less so to make purchases. Your potential customers use these various devices at different times during the day and involve themselves in different conversations, depending what they are doing—touching base with friends, tweeting, or reading a blog. Each of these is a touch point where you can meet the customer, and you have to think about how you develop a presence in these different virtual places. Figure 10.10 provides a roadmap to the platforms and related activities you will need to think about when developing your e-commerce presence.

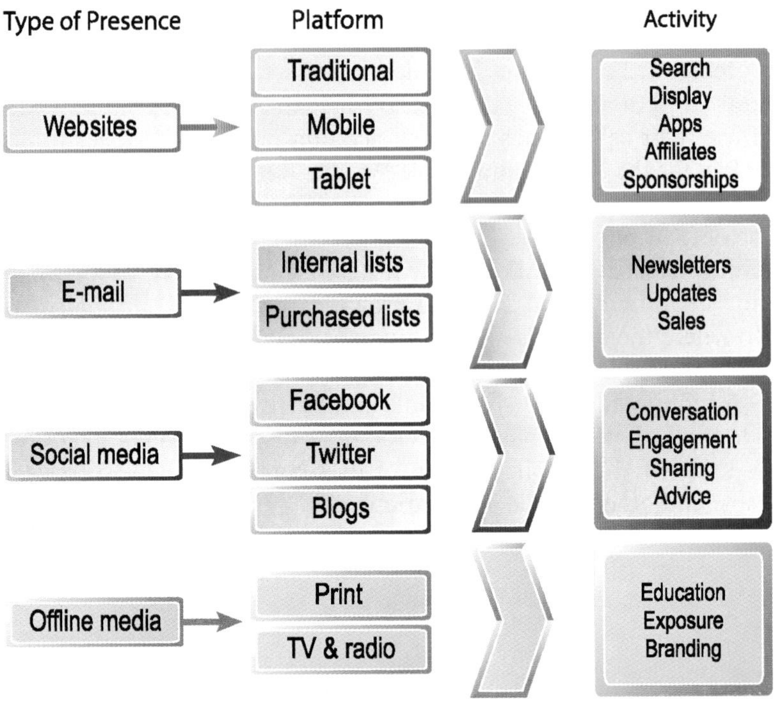

Figure 10.10
E-commerce Presence Map
An e-commerce presence requires firms to consider the four types of presence, with specific platforms and activities associated with each.

Figure 10.10 illustrates four kinds of e-commerce presence: websites, email, social media, and offline media. You must address different platforms for each of these types. For instance, in the case of website presence, there are three platforms: traditional desktop, tablets, and smartphones, each with different capabilities. Moreover, for each type of e-commerce presence, there are related activities you will need to consider. For instance, in the case of websites, you will want to engage in search engine marketing, display ads, affiliate programs, and sponsorships. Offline media, the fourth type of e-commerce presence, is included here because many firms use multiplatform or integrated marketing by which print ads refer customers to websites.

DEVELOP A TIMELINE: MILESTONES

Where would you like to be a year from now? It's very helpful for you to have a rough idea of the time frame for developing your e-commerce presence when you begin. You should break your project down into a small number of phases that could be completed within a specified time. Table 10.8 illustrates a one-year timeline for the

TABLE 10.8
E-commerce Presence Timeline

Phase	Activity	Milestone
Phase 1: Planning	Envision web presence; determine personnel.	Web mission statement
Phase 2: Website development	Acquire content; develop a site design; arrange for hosting the site.	Website plan
Phase 3: Web implementation	Develop keywords and metatags; focus on search engine optimization; identify potential sponsors.	A functional website
Phase 4: Social media plan	Identify appropriate social platforms and content for your products and services.	A social media plan
Phase 5: Social media implementation	Develop Facebook, Twitter, and Pinterest presence.	Functioning social media presence
Phase 6: Mobile plan	Develop a mobile plan; consider options for porting your website to smartphones.	A mobile media plan

development of an e-commerce presence for a start-up company devoted to fashions for teenagers. You can also find more detail about developing an e-commerce website in the Learning Tracks for this chapter.

10-7 How will MIS help my career?

Here is how Chapter 10 can help you find a job as a junior e-commerce data analyst.

THE COMPANY

SportsFantasy Empire, a technology company that creates digital sports competitions, is looking for a recent college graduate to fill a junior e-commerce data analyst position. SportsFantasy Empire offers players the opportunity to compete through web and mobile devices in fantasy sports contests for cash prizes. The company was founded in 2011 and is headquartered in Los Angeles, with additional offices in San Francisco and New York.

JOB DESCRIPTION

The junior e-commerce data analyst will work with SportsFantasy Empire's analytics team to analyze large volumes of data to derive business insights about the company's games and customers that will increase revenue. Job responsibilities include:

- Setting up contest sizing that defines the user experience and business efficiency.
- Optimizing acquisition spending and marketing strategies to drive growth.
- Identifying ways to improve customer game play through on-site changes.
- Measuring how new features or site changes are driving changes in customer behavior.
- Developing standard reporting for key business results, including reports on contest performance, player activity, segment performance, and key player performance.

JOB REQUIREMENTS

- Bachelor's degree in engineering, mathematics, business, or a related field
- E-commerce data analytics experience desirable
- Knowledge of statistics
- Demonstrated history of independently developing new insights from data
- Experience with model building, SQL, SAS, or other programming language desirable
- Strong communication and organizational skills
- Avid fantasy sports player a plus

INTERVIEW QUESTIONS

1. Do you play fantasy sports? How often? Have you ever worked with data about fantasy sports? Why do you think you would be a good fit for this job?
2. What is your background in statistics? What courses did you take? Have you any job experience where you had to use statistics?
3. Have you ever analyzed data about website performance or online customer behavior?
4. What is your know about the cost of acquiring a customer through social media channels (i.e. measuring the average customer acquisition cost on social networks; acquisition vs. retention costs)?

5. How would you propose working with our non-technical teams in telling a story about customer data insights so that they are able to drive customer engagement and loyalty and execute more effectively?
6. What is your proficiency level with SQL or SAS and site analytics tools? Have you ever used these tools on the job? What did you do with them?
7. Can you give an example of a problem you solved using data analytics? Did you do any writing and analysis? Can you provide examples?

AUTHOR TIPS

1. Review this chapter and also the discussion of search and search engine marketing in Chapter 7. To qualify for this job, you should also have taken course work in statistics. Course work or on-the-job training in SQL and SAS would also be helpful.
2. Use the web to do more research on the company. Try to find out more about its strategy, competitors, and business challenges. Additionally, look over the company's social media channels over the past 12 months. Are there any trends you can identify or certain themes the social media channels seem to focus on?
3. Be prepared to talk about SportsFantasy Empire's games as well as the games offered by competitors to show you are familiar with the industry. Inquire about some of the ways the company fine-tunes its online presence. Be prepared to give an example of how you think a fantasy game could improve its online presence.
4. Use the web to find examples of data analytics used by fantasy sports companies.

Review Summary

10-1 **What are the unique features of e-commerce, digital markets, and digital goods?** E-commerce involves digitally enabled commercial transactions between and among organizations and individuals. Unique features of e-commerce technology include ubiquity, global reach, universal technology standards, richness, interactivity, information density, capabilities for personalization and customization, and social technology. E-commerce is becoming increasingly social, mobile, and local.

Digital markets are said to be more transparent than traditional markets, with reduced information asymmetry, search costs, transaction costs, and menu costs along with the ability to change prices dynamically based on market conditions. Digital goods, such as music, video, software, and books, can be delivered over a digital network. Once a digital product has been produced, the cost of delivering that product digitally is extremely low.

10-2 **What are the principal e-commerce business and revenue models?** E-commerce business models are e-tailers, transaction brokers, market creators, content providers, community providers, service providers, and portals. The principal e-commerce revenue models are advertising, sales, subscription, free/freemium, transaction fee, and affiliate.

10-3 **How has e-commerce transformed marketing?** The Internet provides marketers with new ways of identifying and communicating with millions of potential customers at costs far lower than traditional media. Crowdsourcing using the wisdom of crowds helps companies learn from customers to improve product offerings and increase customer value. Behavioral targeting techniques increase the effectiveness of banner, rich media, and video ads. Social commerce uses social networks and social network sites to improve targeting of products and services.

10-4 How has e-commerce affected business-to-business transactions? B2B e-commerce generates efficiencies by enabling companies to locate suppliers, solicit bids, place orders, and track shipments in transit electronically. Net marketplaces provide a single, digital marketplace for many buyers and sellers. Private industrial networks link a firm with its suppliers and other strategic business partners to develop highly efficient and responsive supply chains.

10-5 What is the role of m-commerce in business, and what are the most important m-commerce applications? M-commerce is especially well suited for location-based applications such as finding local hotels and restaurants, monitoring local traffic and weather, and providing personalized location-based marketing. Mobile phones and handhelds are being used for mobile bill payment, banking, securities trading, transportation schedule updates, and downloads of digital content such as music, games, and video clips. M-commerce requires wireless portals and special digital payment systems that can handle micropayments. The GPS capabilities of smartphones make geoadvertising, geosocial, and geoinformation services possible.

10-6 What issues must be addressed when building an e-commerce presence? Building a successful e-commerce presence requires a clear understanding of the business objectives to be achieved and selection of the right platforms, activities, and timeline to achieve those objectives. An e-commerce presence includes not only a corporate website but also a presence on Facebook, Twitter, and other social networking sites and smartphone apps.

Key Terms

Advertising revenue model, 365
Affiliate revenue model, 367
Behavioral targeting, 367
Business-to-business (B2B), 361
Business-to-consumer (B2C), 361
Community providers, 363
Consumer-to-consumer (C2C), 361
Cost transparency, 356
Crowdsourcing, 372
Customization, 357
Digital goods, 359
Direct goods, 376
Disintermediation, 358
Dynamic pricing, 358
Electronic Data Interchange (EDI), 375
E-tailer, 361
Exchanges, 377
FinTech, 367
Free/freemium revenue model, 366
Geoadvertising services, 378
Geoinformation services, 378
Geosocial services, 378
Indirect goods, 376
Information asymmetry, 357
Information density, 356
Intellectual property, 362
Location-based services, 378
Long tail marketing, 367
Market creator, 363
Market entry costs, 356
Marketspace, 355
Menu costs, 358
Micropayment systems, 366
Mobile commerce (m-commerce), 361
Native advertising, 370
Net marketplaces, 376
Personalization, 357
Podcasting, 363
Price discrimination, 356
Price transparency, 356
Private exchange, 376
Private industrial networks, 375
Revenue model, 365
Richness, 356
Sales revenue model, 366
Search costs, 356
Social graph, 371
Social shopping, 372
Streaming, 363
Subscription revenue model, 366
Transaction costs, 355
Transaction fee revenue model, 366
Wisdom of crowds, 372

MyLab MIS

To complete the problems with **MyLab MIS**, go to the EOC Discussion Questions in MyLab MIS.

Review Questions

10-1 What are the unique features of e-commerce, digital markets, and digital goods?
- Name and describe four business trends and three technology trends shaping e-commerce today.
- List and describe the eight unique features of e-commerce.
- Define a digital market and digital goods and describe their distinguishing features.

10-2 What are the principal e-commerce business and revenue models?
- Name and describe the principal e-commerce business models.
- Name and describe the e-commerce revenue models.

10-3 How has e-commerce transformed marketing?
- Explain how social networking and the wisdom of crowds help companies improve their marketing.
- Define behavioral targeting and explain how it works at individual websites and on advertising networks.
- Define the social graph and explain how it is used in e-commerce marketing.

10-4 How has e-commerce affected business-to-business transactions?
- Explain how Internet technology supports business-to-business electronic commerce.
- Define and describe Net marketplaces and explain how they differ from private industrial networks (private exchanges).

10-5 What is the role of m-commerce in business, and what are the most important m-commerce applications?
- List and describe important types of m-commerce services and applications.

10-6 What issues must be addressed when building an e-commerce presence?
- List and describe the four types of e-commerce presence.

Discussion Questions

10-7 MyLab MIS How does the Internet change consumer and supplier relationships?

10-8 MyLab MIS The Internet may not make corporations obsolete, but the corporations will have to change their business models. Do you agree? Why or why not?

10-9 MyLab MIS How have social technologies changed e-commerce?

Hands-On MIS Projects

The projects in this section give you hands-on experience developing e-commerce strategies for businesses, using spreadsheet software to research the profitability of an e-commerce company, and using web tools to research and evaluate e-commerce hosting services. Visit **MyLab MIS** to access this chapter's Hands-On MIS Projects.

MANAGEMENT DECISION PROBLEMS

10-10 Columbiana is a small, independent island in the Caribbean that has many historical buildings, forts, and other sites along with rain forests and striking mountains. A few first-class hotels and several dozen less expensive accommodations lie along its beautiful white-sand beaches. The major airlines have regular flights to Columbiana, as do several small airlines. Columbiana's government wants to increase tourism and develop new markets for the country's tropical agricultural products. How can an e-commerce presence help? What Internet business model would be appropriate? What functions should the e-commerce presence perform?

10-11 Explore the websites of the following companies: Blue Nile, Swatch, Lowe's, and Priceline. Determine which of these websites would benefit most from adding a company-sponsored blog to the website. List the business benefits of the blog. Specify the intended audience for the blog. Decide who in the company should author the blog and select some topics for the blog.

IMPROVING DECISION MAKING: USING SPREADSHEET SOFTWARE TO ANALYZE A DOT-COM BUSINESS

Software skills: Spreadsheet downloading, formatting, and formulas
Business skills: Financial statement analysis

10-12 Pick one e-commerce company on the Internet—for example, Ashford, Yahoo, or Priceline. Study the web pages that describe the company and explain its purpose and structure. Use the web to find articles that comment on the company. Then visit the Securities and Exchange Commission's website at www.sec.gov to access the company's 10-K (annual report) form showing income statements and balance sheets. Select only the sections of the 10-K form containing the desired portions of financial statements that you need to examine and download them into your spreadsheet. (MyLab MIS provides more detailed instructions on how to download this 10-K data into a spreadsheet.) Create simplified spreadsheets of the company's balance sheets and income statements for the past three years.

- Is the company a dot-com success, borderline business, or failure? What information provides the basis of your decision? Why? When answering these questions, pay special attention to the company's three-year trends in revenues, costs of sales, gross margins, operating expenses, and net margins.
- Prepare an overhead presentation (with a minimum of five slides), including appropriate spreadsheets or charts, and present your work to your professor and classmates.

ACHIEVING OPERATIONAL EXCELLENCE: EVALUATING E-COMMERCE HOSTING SERVICES

Software skills: Web browser software
Business skills: Evaluating e-commerce hosting services

10-13 This project will help develop your Internet skills in evaluating commercial services for hosting an e-commerce site for a small start-up company.

You would like to set up a website to sell towels, linens, pottery, and tableware from Portugal and are examining services for hosting small business Internet storefronts. Your website should be able to take secure credit card payments and calculate shipping costs and taxes. Initially, you would like to display photos and descriptions of 40 products. Visit eHost.com, GoDaddy, and iPage and compare the range of e-commerce hosting services they offer to small businesses, their capabilities, and their costs. Examine the tools they provide for creating an e-commerce site. Compare these services and decide which you would use if you were actually establishing a web store. Write a brief report indicating your choice and explaining the strengths and weaknesses of each service.

Collaboration and Teamwork Project

Performing a Competitive Analysis of E-commerce Sites

10-14 Form a group with three or four of your classmates. Select two businesses that are competitors in the same industry and that use their websites for electronic commerce. Visit these websites. You might compare, for example, the websites for Pandora and Spotify, Amazon and BarnesandNoble.com, or E*Trade and Scottrade. Prepare an evaluation of each business's website in terms of its functions, user friendliness, and ability to support the company's business strategy. Which website does a better job? Why? Can you make some recommendations to improve these websites? If possible, use Google Docs and Google Drive or Google Sites to brainstorm, organize, and develop a presentation of your findings for the class.

BUSINESS PROBLEM-SOLVING CASE

A Nasty Ending for Nasty Gal

In 2006, Sophia Amoruso was a 22-year-old hitchhiking, dumpster-diving community college dropout with a lot of time on her hands. After reading a book called *Starting an eBay Business for Dummies*, she launched an eBay store called Nasty Gal Vintage, named after a song and 1975 album by the jazz singer Betty Davis, second wife of the legendary Miles Davis.

Nasty Gal's styling was edgy and fresh—a little bit rock and roll, a little bit disco, modern, but never hyper-trendy. Eight years after its founding, Nasty Gal had sold more than $100 million in new and vintage clothing and accessories, employed more than 350 people, had more than a million fans on Facebook and Instagram, and was a global brand. It looked like a genuine e-commerce success story. Or was it?

When Amoruso began her business, she did everything herself out of her tiny San Francisco apartment—merchandising, photographing, copywriting, and shipping. She got up at the crack of dawn to make 6 a.m. estate sales, haggled with thrift stores, spent hours photoshopping the images she styled and shot herself using models she recruited herself, and ensured that packaging was high quality.

She would inspect items to make sure they were in good enough shape to sell. She zipped zippers, buttoned buttons, connected hooks, folded each garment, and slid it into a clear plastic bag that was sealed with a sticker. Then she boxed the item and affixed a shipping label on it. She had to assume that her customers were as particular and as concerned with aesthetics as she was.

Amoruso had taken photography classes at a community college, where she learned to understand the importance of silhouette and composition. She bought vintage pieces with dramatic silhouettes—a coat with a big funnel collar, a '50s dress with a flared skirt, or a Victorian jacket with puffy sleeves. Exaggerating everything about the silhouette through the angle from which it was photographed helped Amoruso produce tiny thumbnails for eBay that attracted serious bidders. She was able to take an object, distill what was best about it, and then exaggerate those qualities so they were visible even in its tiniest representation. When the thumbnail was enlarged, it looked amazing.

Amoruso has been a heavy user of social tools to promote her business. When she first started out, she used MySpace, where she attracted a cult following of more than 60,000 fans. The company gained traction on social media with Nasty Gal's aesthetic that could be both high and low, edgy and glossy.

Amoruso took customer feedback very seriously and believed customers were at the center of everything Nasty Gal did. When she sold on eBay, she learned to respond to every customer comment to help her understand precisely who was buying her goods and what they wanted. Amoruso said that the content Nasty Gal customers created has always been a huge part of the Nasty Gal brand. It was very important to see how customers wore Nasty Gal's pieces and the types of photographs they took. They were inspiring.

Social media is built on sharing, and Nasty Gal gave its followers compelling images, words, and content to share and talk about each day. They could be a crazy vintage piece, a quote, or a behind-the-scenes photo. At most companies the person manning the Twitter and Facebook accounts is far removed from senior management. Amoruso did not always author every Nasty Gal tweet, but she still read every comment. If the customers were unhappy about something, she wanted to hear about it right away. At other businesses, it might take months for customer feedback to filter up to the CEO. When Nasty Gal first joined Snapchat, Amoruso tested the water with a few Snaps, and Nasty Gal followers responded in force.

In June 2008, Amoruso moved Nasty Gal Vintage off eBay and onto its own destination website, www.nastygal.com. In 2012, Nasty Gal began selling clothes under its own brand label and also invested $18 million in a 527,000-square-foot national distribution center in Shepherdsville, Kentucky, to handle its own shipping and logistics. Venture capitalists Index Ventures provided at least $40 million in funding. Nasty Gal opened a brick-and-mortar store in Los Angeles in 2014 and another in Santa Monica in 2015.

With growing direct-to-consumer demand and higher inventory replenishment requirements driven by new store openings, Nasty Gal invested in a new warehouse management system. The warehouse management system investment was designed to increase warehouse productivity and shorten order cycle times so that Nasty Gal's supply chain could better service its mushrooming sales. (Order cycle time refers to the time period between placing of one order and the next order.) The company selected HighJump's Warehouse Management System (WMS) with the goal of increasing visibility and overall productivity while keeping fill rates above 99 percent. (The fill rate is the percentage of orders satisfied from stock at hand.)

Key considerations were scalability and capabilities for handling retail replenishment in addition to direct-to-consumer orders. HighJump's implementation team customized the WMS software to optimize the business processes that worked best for an e-commerce retailer that ships most of its items straight to the customer, with a small subset going to retail stores. The WMS software was also configured to support processes that would scale with future growth. Picking efficiency and fill rates shot up, with fill rates above 99 percent, even though order volume climbed.

Nasty Gal experienced tremendous growth in its early years, being named *INC Magazine*'s fastest-growing retailer in 2012 and earning number one ranking in *Internet Retailer's* Top 500 Guide in 2016. By 2011, annual sales hit $24 million and then nearly $100 million in 2012. However, sales started dropping to $85 million in 2014 and then $77 million in 2015. Nasty Gal's rapid expansion had been fueled by heavy spending in advertising and marketing. This is a strategy used by many startups, but it only pays off in the long run if one-time buyers become loyal shoppers. Otherwise, too much money is spent on online marketing like banner ads and paying for influencers. If a company pays $70 on marketing to acquire a customer and that customer only buys once from it, the company won't make money. A company that spends $200 million to make $100 million in revenue is not a sustainable business. Nasty Gal had a "leaky bucket" situation: Once it burned through its fundraising capital and cut down on marketing, sales continued to drop.

Nasty Gal couldn't hold onto customers. Some were dissatisfied with product quality, but many were more attracted to fast-fashion retailers such as Zara and H&M, which both deliver a wider array of trendy clothes through online and brick-and-mortar stores at lower prices and are constantly changing their merchandise. The actual market for the Nasty Gal brand was quickly saturated. There was a limit to the number of women Nasty Gal appealed to: Nasty Gal had a California cool, young girl look, and it was unclear how much it was attractive in other parts of the United States and around the world.

Nasty Gal also wasted money on things that didn't warrant large expenditures. The company quintupled the size of its headquarters by moving into a 50,300-square-foot location in downtown Los Angeles in 2013—far more space than the company needed, according to industry experts. The company had also opened a 500,000-square-foot fulfillment center in Kentucky to handle its own distribution and logistics as well as two brick-and-mortar stores in Los Angeles and Santa Monica. Even in the hyper-trendy fashion business, companies have to closely monitor production, distribution, and expenses for operations to move products at a scale big enough to make a profit. Nasty Gal's mostly young staff focused too much on the creative side of the business.

While it was growing, Nasty Gal built its management team, hiring sizzling junior talent from retail outlets such as Urban Outfitters. But their traditional retail backgrounds clashed with the startup mentality. As Nasty Gal expanded, Amoruso's own fame also grew, and she was sidetracked by other projects. She wrote two books. The first, titled *#Girlboss*, described the founding of Nasty Gal and Amoruso's business philosophy and was adapted by Netflix into a show with Amoruso as executive producer. Employees complained about Amoruso's management style and lack of focus.

Amoruso resigned as chief executive in 2015 but remained on Nasty Gal's board of directors until the company filed for Chapter 11 bankruptcy on November 9, 2016. Between 2015 and 2016, Nasty Gal had raised an additional $24 million in equity and debt financing from venture-focused Stamos Capital Partners LP and Hercules Technology Growth Capital Inc. Even though the funding helped Nasty Gal stay afloat, the company still had trouble paying for new inventory, rent, and other operating expenses.

Within weeks of filing for Chapter 11 protection, Nasty Gal sold its brand name and other intellectual property on February 28, 2017, for $20 million to a rival online fashion site, the United Kingdom's Boohoo.com. Boohoo is operating Nasty Gal as a standalone website, but Nasty Gal's stores are closing. Boohoo believes Nasty Gal's arresting style and loyal customer base will complement Boohoo and expand global opportunities for growth.

Sources: Sarah Chaney, "How Nasty Gal Went from an $85 Million Company to Bankruptcy," *Wall Street Journal*, February 24, 2017; Shan Li, "Nasty Gal, Once a Fashion World Darling, Went Bankrupt: What Went Wrong?," *Los Angeles Times*, February 24, 2017; "Case Study Nasty Gal," *HighJump*, 2016; and Yelena Shuster, "NastyGal Founder Sophia Amoruso on How to Become a #GirlBoss," *Elle*, May 15, 2014.

CASE STUDY QUESTIONS

10-15 How was social media related to Nasty Gal's business model? To what extent was Nasty Gal a "social" business?

10-16 What people, organization, and technology problems were responsible for Nasty Gal's failure as a business?

10-17 Could Nasty Gal have avoided bankruptcy? Explain your answer.

MyLab MIS

Go to the Assignments section of MyLab MIS to complete these writing exercises.

10-18 Describe the six features of social commerce. Provide an example for each feature, describing how a business could use that feature for selling to consumers online.

10-19 List and describe the main activities involved in building an e-commerce presence.

Chapter 10 References

Bapna, Ravi, Alok Gupta, Sarah Rice, and Arun Sundararajan. "Trust and the Strength of Ties in Online Social Networks: An Exploratory Field Experiment." *MIS Quarterly* 41, No. 1 (March 2017).

Brynjolfsson, Erik, Yu Hu, and Michael D. Smith. "Consumer Surplus in the Digital Economy: Estimating the Value of Increased Product Variety at Online Booksellers." *Management Science* 49, No. 11 (November 2003).

Brynjolfsson, Erik, Yu Jeffrey Hu, and Mohammad S. Rahman. "Competing in the Age of Multichannel Retailing." *MIT Sloan Management Review* (May 2013).

Brynjolfsson, Erik, Tomer Geva, and Shachar Reichman. "Crowd-Squared: Amplifying the Predictive Power of Search Trend Data." *MIS Quarterly* 40, No. 4 (December 2016).

Cervellon, Marie-Cecile, and Pamela Lirio, "When Employees Don't 'Like' Their Employers on Social Media." *MIT Sloan Management Review* (Winter 2017).

ComScore. "The Top U.S. Media Publishers on Social Media." (June 2017).

"Do Search Ads Really Work?" *Harvard Business Review* (March–April 2017).

Doyle, Cathy. "US Mobile StatPack." eMarketer (March 2016).

eMarketer. "US Retail Ecommerce Sales, 2015–2021 (Billions, % Change, and % of Total Retail Sales)." eMarketer Chart (February 21, 2017a).

eMarketer. "Digital Buyers, United States, 2014–2020 (in Millions)." eMarketer Estimates (May 2017b).

eMarketer. "Retail Mcommerce Sales, US, (Billions) 2015–2021." eMarketer Chart (February 1, 2017c).

eMarketer. "US Ad Spending: The eMarketer Forecast for 2017." eMarketer Report (March 2017d).

eMarketer. "US Time Spent with Media." eMarketer Chart (April 2017e).

eMarketer. "Retail Mcommerce Sales, US, (Billions) 2015–2021." eMarketer Chart (February 1, 2017f).

Facebook. "Stats." www.newsroom.fb.com, accessed July 20, 2017.

Federal Trade Commission. "Big Data: A Tool for Inclusion or Exclusion? Understanding the Issues." Federal Trade Commission (January 2016a).

Federal Trade Commission. "Data Brokers: A Call for Transparency and Accountability." Federal Trade Commission (May 2016b).

Fisman, Ray and Michael Luca. "Fixing Discrimination in Online Marketplaces." *Harvard Business Review* (December 2016).

Forrester Data. "Web-Influenced Retail Sales Forecast, 2016 To 2021 (US)." *Forrester Research* (November 4, 2016).

Hinz, Oliver, Il-Horn Hann, and Martin Spann. "Price Discrimination in E-Commerce? An Examination of Dynamic Pricing in Name-Your-Own Price Markets." *MIS Quarterly* 35, No. 1 (March 2011).

Holt, Douglas. "Branding in the Age of Social Media." *Harvard Business Review* (March 2016).

Hu, Nan, Paul A. Pavlou, and Jie Zhang." On Self-Selection Biases in Online Product Reviews." *MIS Quarterly* 41, No. 2 (June 2017).

Im, Il, Jongkun Jun, Wonseok Oh, and Seok-Oh Jeong. "Deal-Seeking Versus Brand-Seeking: Search Behaviors and Purchase Propensities in Sponsored Search Platforms." *MIS Quarterly* 40, No. 1 (March 2016).

Internet World Stats. "Internet Users in the World." Internetworldstats.com (2017).

John, Leslie K., Daniel Mochon, Oliver Emrich, and Janet Schwartz. "What's the Value of a 'Like'?" *Harvard Business Review* (March–April 2017).

Laudon, Kenneth C., and Carol Guercio Traver. *E-commerce: Business, Technology, Society*, 14th ed. Upper Saddle River, NJ: Prentice-Hall (2018).

Lin Zhije, Khim-Yong Goh, and Cheng-Suang Heng. "The Demand Effects of Product Recommendation Networks: An Empirical Analysis of Network Diversity and Stability." *MIS Quarterly* 41, No. 2 (June 2017).

Liu, Qianqian Ben, and Elena Karahanna. "The Dark Side of Reviews: The Swaying Effects of Online Product Reviews on Attribute Preference Construction." *MIS Quarterly* 41, No. 2 (June 2017).

Luo, Xueming, Bin Gu, Jie Zhang, and Chee Wei Phang. "Expert Blogs and Consumer Perceptions of Competing Brands." *MIS Quarterly* 41, No. 2 (June 2017).

Oh, Hyelim, Animesh Animesh, and Alain Pinsonneault. "Free Versus For-a-Fee: The Impact of a Paywall on the Pattern and Effectiveness of Word-of-Mouth via Social Media." *MIS Quarterly* 40, No. 1 (March 2016).

Orlikowski, Wanda, and Susan V. Scott. "The Algorithm and the Crowd: Considering the Materiality of Service Innovation." *MIS Quarterly* 39, No.1 (March 2015).

Rainie, Lee, and Maeve Duggan. "Privacy and Information Sharing." Pew Research Center (January, 2016).

Richardson Gosline, Renee, Jeffrey Lee, and Glen Urban. "The Power of Customer Stories in Digital Marketing." *MIT Sloan Management Review* (Summer 2017).

Rigby, Darrell K. "Digital Physical Mashups." *Harvard Business Review* (September 2014).

Shuk, Ying Ho, and David Bodoff. "The Effects of Web Personalization on User Attitude and Behavior: An Integration of the Elaboration Likelihood Model and Consumer Search Theory." *MIS Quarterly* 38, No. 2 (June 2014).

Susarla, Anjana, Jeong-Ha Oh, and Young Tan. "Influentials, Imitables, or Susceptibles? Virality and Word-of-Mouth Conversations in Online Social Networks." *Journal of Management Information Systems* 33, No.1 (2016).

U.S. Bureau of the Census. "E-Stats." www.census.gov, accessed July 8, 2017.

Zhang, Zan, Guofang Nan, Minqiang Li, and Yong Tan. "Duopoly Pricing Strategy for Information Products with Premium Service: Free Product or Bundling?" *Journal of Management Information Systems* 33, No. 1 (2016).

Zhou, Wenqi, and Wenjing Duan. "Do Professional Reviews Affect Online User Choices Through User Reviews? An Empirical Study." *Journal of Management Information Systems* 33, No. 1 (2016).

CHAPTER

11

Improving Decision Making and Managing Knowledge

LEARNING OBJECTIVES

After reading this chapter, you will be able to answer the following questions.

11-1 What are the different types of decisions, and how does the decision-making process work?

11-2 How do business intelligence and business analytics support decision making?

11-3 What are the business benefits of using artificial intelligence techniques in decision making and knowledge management?

11-4 What types of systems are used for enterprise-wide knowledge management and knowledge work, and how do they provide value for businesses?

11-5 How will MIS help my career?

CHAPTER CASES

- Can Big Data Analytics Help People Find Love?
- Does IBM's Watson Have a Future in Business?
- Will Robots Replace People in Manufacturing?
- GE Bets on the Internet of Things and Big Data Analytics

VIDEO CASES

- How IBM's Watson Became a Jeopardy Champion
- Business Intelligence Helps the Cincinnati Zoo Work Smarter

Instructional Video:

- IBM Watson Demo Oncology Diagnosis and Treatment

MyLab MIS

- Discussion Questions: 11-5, 11-6, 11-7;
- Hands-on MIS Projects: 11-8, 11-9, 11-10, 11-11;
- Writing Assignments: 11-18, 11-19;
- eText with Conceptual Animations

CAN BIG DATA ANALYTICS HELP PEOPLE FIND LOVE?

Can computers help people find love? Online dating website eHarmony, with more than 20 million registered users, thinks so. eHarmony is the first online dating service to use a "scientific" approach to matching highly compatible singles. The company employs a 29 Dimensions® model to match couples based on features of compatibility found in thousands of successful relationships, processing more than 3.5 million matches daily using 30 gigabytes of data and the MongoDB non-relational database management system.

Users joining eHarmony are required to fill out a questionnaire containing 200 questions that cover everything from characteristics to values. The information is then run through an eHarmony-patented algorithm, where matches are found for users. This may not be the most romantic way to find a spouse, but according to a survey conducted by Harris Interactive, 438 people on average get married every day in the United States after meeting through the eHarmony website. That's nearly 4 percent of new U.S. marriages!

eHarmony also mines terabytes of data on its users, collected mainly from their activities on its website. This helps predict how users will behave. For example, people using eHarmony have different communication levels. From data such as how many times users log on to the website, how many photos they post, and the number of words they use to describe themselves on their eHarmony profiles, eHarmony can tell who is more introverted or who is likely to be an initiator. The data also helps eHarmony determine whether users would be more likely to communicate with their matches at certain times of the day. The matching process is highly automated, allowing eHarmony to generate matches for users in a matter of minutes most of the time.

eHarmony's couple-matching algorithm varies from country to country and is regularly refined based on user behavior and new relationship research from educational institutions. The algorithm has been adjusted to add some flexibility into the matchmaking process so that a person's likes or dislikes do not overshadow other attributes that might make a match desirable. Big data analysis is also helpful for marketing, indicating when is a good time for eHarmony to send out promotions to individual users.

Drawing on its success in matching couples, eHarmony tried to apply its expertise to matching people with the right job. On April 1, 2016, the company launched Elevated Careers, a new service to match job seekers with potential employers based on 24 value, culture, and personality factors. Sixteen of those factors dealt with culture and how well employee values match with the target company. The goal was to make employees happier while reducing churn and improving company business performance. However, 10 months after launching the Elevated Careers website, eHarmony put the site up for sale, citing lack of experience in the human resources technology market.

Sources: Sarah Knapton, "Secret of eHarmony Algorithm Is Revealed," *The Telegraph*, May 14, 2017; Alia D. Wright, "eHarmony Seeks Buyer for Job Matching Site Elevated Careers," Society for Human Resource Management, February 16, 2017; "eHarmony Inc.," www.ibm.com, accessed May 12, 2017; "Big Dating at eHarmony," www.mongodb.com, accessed May 20, 2017; and Conner Forrest, "eHarmony's Elevated Careers Uses Big Data to Match You with the Perfect Job," *Tech Republic*, April 1, 2016.

eHarmony is a powerful illustration of how information systems improve decision making. This is a relatively new company that uses big data and sophisticated models to analyze the data to carve out a new web-based service and business model. There are many other online dating sites that use personal data to help people find dating or marital prospects. However, eHarmony claims to have the competitive edge because it has powerful and unique analytic tools to analyze large quantities of detailed data, generate accurate predictions of couples that will be most compatible, and recommend potential partners to customers. Other online dating sites lack the range of data and analytic tools to predict compatibility that eHarmony has.

The chapter-opening diagram calls attention to important points raised by this case and this chapter. eHarmony is an Internet business with many competitors, it is an online matchmaking service, and its business strategy is based on skillful analysis of detailed data. eHarmony was able to take advantage of new opportunities offered by big data and business intelligence technology. eHarmony collects vast quantities of detailed personal and behavioral data about its customers and uses the data along with relationship research findings to analyze these data along 29 dimensions to predict a couple's potential compatibility. eHarmony also uses big data to fine-tune its marketing decisions, and it used its business intelligence expertise to launch a new business matching companies and job seekers. Big data and data analytics have made it possible for eHarmony to make more accurate and insightful decisions and to offer the results of those decisions as a service. Better decision making using business intelligence has clearly made eHarmony more profitable and competitive.

The chapter-opening case also shows that it takes more than just the data and powerful analytics tools to produce successful products and decisions. eHarmony lacked sufficient knowledge of human resources to create a successful data-driven matchmaking system for job hunters and employers. Knowledge of a specific business and its business processes is also essential.

Here are some questions to think about: What is the relationship between big data and big data analytics to eHarmony's business model and business strategy? How easily can eHarmony expand its business beyond online matchmaking?

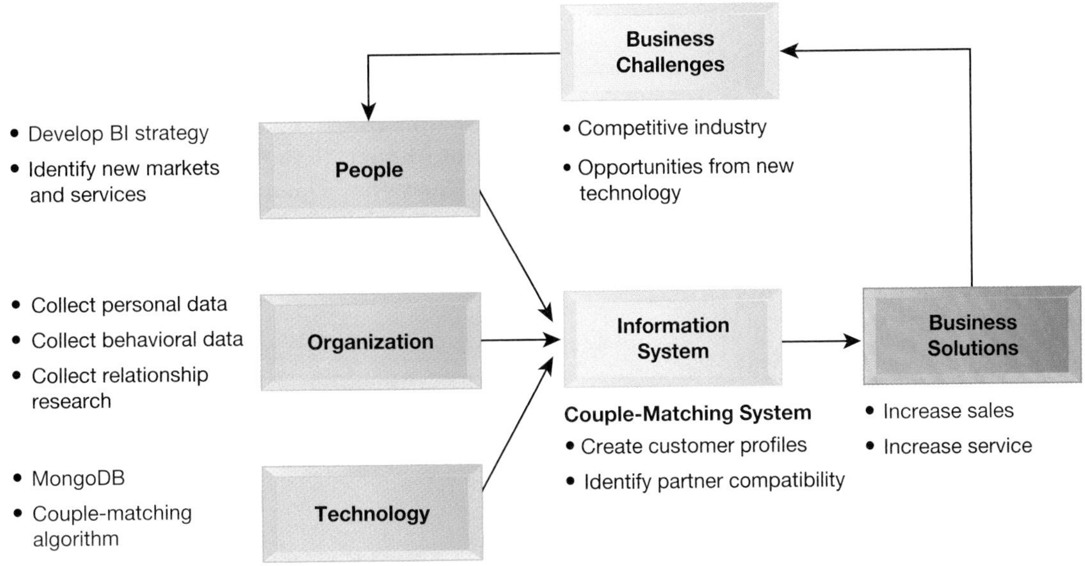

11-1 What are the different types of decisions, and how does the decision-making process work?

One of the main contributions of information systems has been to improve decision making for both individuals and groups. Decision making in businesses used to be limited to management. Today, lower-level employees are responsible for some of these decisions as information systems make information available to lower levels of the business. However, what do we mean by better decision making? How does decision making take place in businesses and other organizations? Let's take a closer look.

BUSINESS VALUE OF IMPROVED DECISION MAKING

What does it mean to the business to be able to make a better decision? What is the monetary value to the business of improved decision making? Table 11.1 measures the monetary value of improved decision making for a small U.S. manufacturing firm with $280 million in annual revenue and 140 employees. The firm has identified a number of key decisions where new system investments might improve the quality of decision making. The table provides selected estimates of annual value (in the form of cost savings or increased revenue) from improved decision making in selected areas of the business.

We can see from Table 11.1 that decisions are made at all levels of the firm and that some of these decisions are common, routine, and numerous. Although the value of improving any single decision may be small, improving hundreds of thousands of small decisions adds up to a large annual value for the business.

TYPES OF DECISIONS

Chapter 2 showed that there are different levels in an organization. Each of these levels has different information requirements for decision support and responsibility for different types of decisions (see Figure 11.1). Decisions are classified as structured, semi-structured, and unstructured.

Unstructured decisions are those in which the decision maker must provide judgment, evaluation, and insight to solve the problem. Each of these decisions is novel, important, and not routine, and there is no well-understood or agreed-on procedure for making them.

TABLE 11.1

Business Value of Enhanced Decision Making

Example Decision Value	Decision Maker	Number of Annual Decisions	Estimated Value to Firm of a Single Improved Decision	Annual
Allocate support to most valuable customers	Accounts manager	12	$100,000	$1,200,000
Predict call center daily demand	Call center management	4	$150,000	$600,000
Decide parts inventory levels daily	Inventory manager	365	$5,000	$1,825,000
Identify competitive bids from major suppliers	Senior management	1	$2,000,000	$2,000,000
Schedule production to fill orders	Manufacturing manager	150	$10,000	$1,500,000
Allocate labor to complete a job	Production floor manager	100	$4,000	$400,000

Structured decisions, by contrast, are repetitive and routine, and they involve a definite procedure for handling them so that they do not have to be treated each time as if they were new. Many decisions have elements of both types and are **semi-structured decisions**, when only part of the problem has a clear-cut answer provided by an accepted procedure. In general, structured decisions are more prevalent at lower organizational levels, whereas unstructured problems are more common at higher levels of the firm.

Senior executives face many unstructured decision situations, such as establishing the firm's 5-year or 10-year goals or deciding new markets to enter. Answering the question, "Should we enter a new market?" would require access to news, government reports, and industry views as well as high-level summaries of firm performance. However, the answer would also require senior managers to use their own best judgment and poll other managers for their opinions.

Middle management faces more structured decision scenarios, but their decisions may include unstructured components. A typical middle-level management decision might be "Why is the reported order fulfillment showing a decline over the past

Figure 11.1
Information Requirements of Key Decision-Making Groups in a Firm
Senior managers, middle managers, operational managers, and employees have different types of decisions and information requirements.

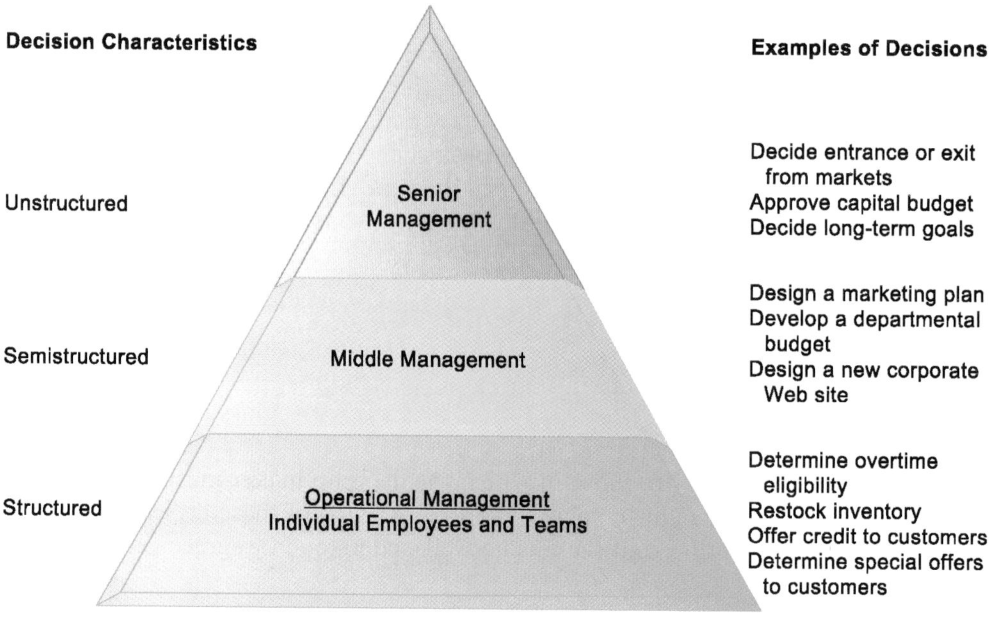

six months at a distribution center in Minneapolis?" This middle manager could obtain a report from the firm's enterprise system or distribution management system on order activity and operational efficiency at the Minneapolis distribution center. This is the structured part of the decision, but before arriving at an answer, this middle manager will have to interview employees and gather more unstructured information from external sources about local economic conditions or sales trends.

Operational management and rank-and-file employees tend to make more structured decisions. For example, a supervisor on an assembly line has to decide whether an hourly paid worker is entitled to overtime pay. If the employee worked more than eight hours on a particular day, the supervisor would routinely grant overtime pay for any time beyond eight hours that was clocked on that day.

A sales account representative often has to make decisions about extending credit to customers by consulting the firm's customer database that contains credit information. If the customer met the firm's specific criteria for granting credit, the account representative would grant that customer credit to make a purchase. In both instances, the decisions are highly structured and routinely made thousands of times each day in most large firms. The answer has been programmed into the firm's payroll and accounts receivable systems.

THE DECISION-MAKING PROCESS

Making a decision is a multistep process. Simon (1960) described four stages in decision making: intelligence, design, choice, and implementation (see Figure 11.2). These stages correspond to the four steps in problem solving used throughout this book.

Intelligence consists of discovering, identifying, and understanding the problems occurring in the organization—why the problem exists, where, and what effects it is

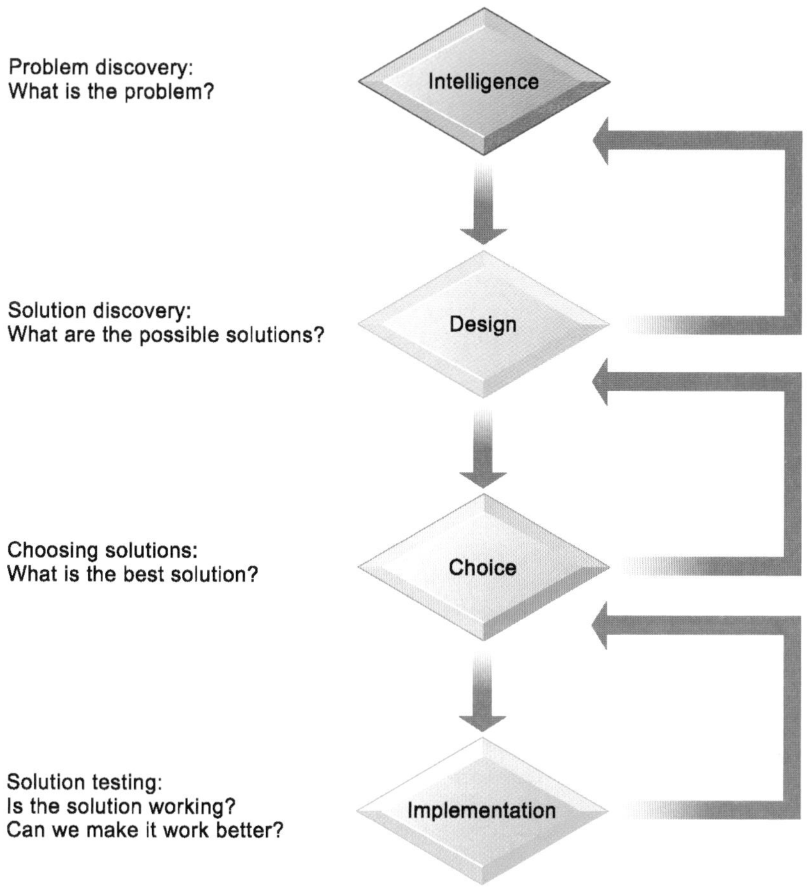
Problem discovery:
What is the problem?
Intelligence
Solution discovery:
What are the possible solutions?
Design
Choosing solutions:
What is the best solution?
Choice
Solution testing:
Is the solution working?
Can we make it work better?
Implementation

Figure 11.2
Stages in Decision Making
The decision-making process can be broken down into four stages.

having on the firm. **Design** involves identifying and exploring various solutions to the problem. **Choice** consists of choosing among solution alternatives. **Implementation** involves making the chosen alternative work and continuing to monitor how well the solution is working.

What happens if the solution you have chosen does not work? Figure 11.2 shows that you can return to an earlier stage in the decision-making process and repeat it if necessary. For instance, in the face of declining sales, a sales management team may decide to pay the sales force a higher commission for making more sales to spur on the sales effort. If this does not increase sales, managers would need to investigate whether the problem stems from poor product design, inadequate customer support, or a host of other causes that call for a different solution.

HIGH-VELOCITY AUTOMATED DECISION MAKING

Today, many decisions organizations make are not made by managers or any humans. For instance, when you enter a query in Google's search engine, Google's computer system has to decide which URLs to display in about half a second on average (500 milliseconds). High-frequency trading programs at electronic stock exchanges in the United States execute their trades within nanoseconds. Humans are eliminated from the decision chain because they are too slow.

In these high-speed automated decisions, the intelligence, design, choice, and implementation parts of the decision-making process are captured by computer algorithms that precisely define the steps to be followed to produce a decision. The people who wrote the software identified the problem, designed a method for finding a solution, defined a range of acceptable solutions, and implemented the solution. In these situations, organizations are making decisions faster than managers can monitor or control, and great care needs to be taken to ensure the proper operation of these systems to prevent significant harm.

QUALITY OF DECISIONS AND DECISION MAKING

How can you tell whether a decision has become better or the decision-making process improved? Accuracy is one important dimension of quality; in general, we think decisions are better if they accurately reflect the real-world data. Speed is another dimension; we tend to think that the decision-making process should be efficient, even speedy. For instance, when you apply for car insurance, you want the insurance firm to make a fast and accurate decision. However, there are many other dimensions of quality in decisions and the decision-making process to consider. Which is important for you will depend on the business firm where you work, the various parties involved in the decision, and your own personal values. Table 11.2 describes some quality dimensions

TABLE 11.2

Qualities of Decisions and the Decision-Making Process

Quality Dimension	Description
Accuracy	Decision reflects reality
Comprehensiveness	Decision reflects a full consideration of the facts and circumstances
Fairness	Decision faithfully reflects the concerns and interests of affected parties
Speed (efficiency)	Decision making is efficient with respect to time and other resources, including the time and resources of affected parties, such as customers
Coherence	Decision reflects a rational process that can be explained to others and made understandable
Due process	Decision is the result of a known process and can be appealed to a higher authority

for decision making. When we describe how systems "improve decisions and the decision-making process" in this chapter, we are referencing the dimensions in this table.

11-2 How do business intelligence and business analytics support decision making?

Chapter 2 introduced you to different kinds of systems for supporting the levels and types of decisions we have just described. The foundation for all of these systems is a business intelligence and business analytics infrastructure that supplies data and the analytic tools for supporting decision making.

WHAT IS BUSINESS INTELLIGENCE?

"Business intelligence" (BI) is a term hardware and software vendors and information technology consultants use to describe the infrastructure for warehousing, integrating, reporting, and analyzing data that come from the business environment. The foundation infrastructure collects, stores, cleans, and makes available relevant data to managers. Think databases, data warehouses, data marts, Hadoop, and analytic platforms, which we described in Chapter 6. "Business analytics" (BA) is also a vendor-defined term; it focuses more on tools and techniques for analyzing and understanding data. Think OLAP (online analytical processing), statistics, models, and data mining, which we also introduced in Chapter 6.

BI and analytics are essentially about integrating all the information streams a firm produces into a single, coherent enterprise-wide set of data and then using modeling, statistical analysis, and data mining tools to make sense out of all these data so managers can make better decisions and better plans. eHarmony, described in the chapter-opening case, is using BI and analytics to make some very fine-grained decisions about matching potential couples based on personality traits.

It is important to remember that BI and analytics are products defined by technology vendors and consulting firms. The largest five providers of these products are SAP, Oracle, IBM, SAS, and Microsoft. A number of BI and BA products now have cloud and mobile versions.

THE BUSINESS INTELLIGENCE ENVIRONMENT

Figure 11.3 gives an overview of a BI environment, highlighting the kinds of hardware, software, and management capabilities that the major vendors offer and that firms develop over time. There are six elements in this BI environment:

Data from the business environment: Businesses must deal with both structured and unstructured data from many sources, including big data. The data need to be integrated and organized so that they can be analyzed and used by human decision makers.

Business intelligence infrastructure: The underlying foundation of BI is a powerful database system that captures all the relevant data to operate the business. The data may be stored in transactional databases or combined and integrated into an enterprise data warehouse, series of interrelated data marts, or analytic platforms.

Business analytics toolset: A set of software tools is used to analyze data and produce reports, respond to questions managers pose, and track the progress of the business by using key indicators of performance.

Managerial users and methods: BI hardware and software are only as intelligent as the human beings who use them. Managers impose order on the analysis of data by using a variety of managerial methods that define strategic business goals and specify how progress will be measured. These include business performance management and balanced scorecard approaches that focus on key performance indicators, with special attention to competitors.

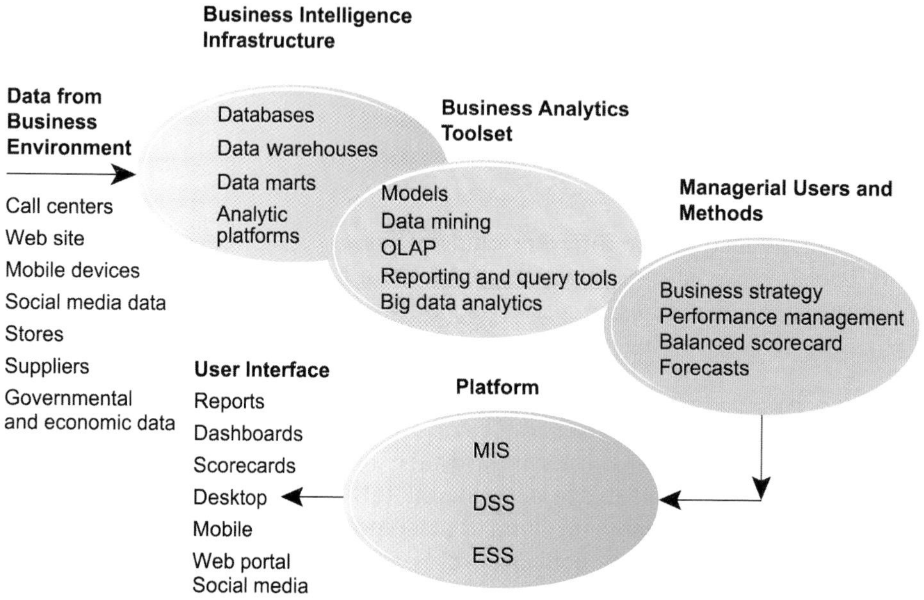

Figure 11.3
Business Intelligence and Analytics for Decision Support
Business intelligence and analytics require a strong database foundation, a set of analytic tools, and an involved management team that can ask intelligent questions and analyze data.

Delivery platform—MIS, DSS, ESS: The results from BI and analytics are delivered to managers and employees in a variety of ways, depending on what they need to know to perform their job. MIS, decision-support systems (DSS), and executive support systems (ESS), which we introduced in Chapter 2, deliver information and knowledge to different people and levels in the firm—operational employees, middle managers, and senior executives. In the past, these systems could not easily share data and operated as independent systems. Today, business intelligence and analytics tools can integrate all this information and bring it to managers' desktops or mobile platforms.

User interface: Business people often learn quicker from a visual representation of data than from a dry report with columns and rows of information. Today's business analytics software suites feature **data visualization** tools, such as rich graphs, charts, dashboards, and maps. They also can deliver reports on mobile phones and tablets as well as on the firm's web portal. An example are the interactive data visualization tools offered by Tableau Software. Tableau enables non-technical users to quickly and easily create and share customized interactive dashboards to provide business insights from a broad

Data visualization tools facilitate creation of graphs, charts, dashboards and maps to make it easier for users to obtain insights from data.

TABLE 11.3

Examples of Predefined Business Intelligence Production Reports

Business Functional Area	Production Reports
Sales	Sales forecasts, sales team performance, cross selling, sales cycle times
Service/Call Center	Customer satisfaction, service cost, resolution rates, churn rates
Marketing	Campaign effectiveness, loyalty and attrition, market basket analysis
Procurement and Support	Direct and indirect spending, off-contract purchases, supplier performance
Supply Chain	Backlog, fulfillment status, order cycle time, bill of materials analysis
Financials	General ledger, accounts receivable and payable, cash flow, profitability
Human Resources	Employee productivity, compensation, workforce demographics, retention

spectrum of data. Tableau works with many different sources of data including data from spreadsheets, corporate databases, and the web. BA software is adding capabilities to post information on Twitter, Facebook, or internal social media to support decision making in an online group setting rather than in a face-to-face meeting.

BUSINESS INTELLIGENCE AND ANALYTICS CAPABILITIES

BI and analytics promise to deliver correct, nearly real-time information to decision makers, and the analytic tools help them quickly understand the information and take action. There are five analytic functionalities that BI systems deliver to achieve these ends:

Production reports: These are predefined reports based on industry-specific requirements (see Table 11.3).

Parameterized reports: Users enter several parameters to filter data and isolate impacts of parameters. For instance, you might want to enter region and time of day to understand how sales of a product vary by region and time. If you were Starbucks, you might find that customers in the eastern United States buy most of their coffee in the morning, whereas in the northwest customers buy coffee throughout the day. This finding might lead to different marketing and ad campaigns in each region. (See the discussion of pivot tables later in this section.)

Dashboards/scorecards: These are visual tools for presenting performance data users define.

Ad hoc query/search/report creation: This allows users to create their own reports based on queries and searches.

Drill down: This is the ability to move from a high-level summary to a more detailed view.

Forecasts, scenarios, models: These include capabilities for linear forecasting, what-if scenario analysis, and data analysis, using standard statistical tools.

Predictive Analytics

An important capability of BI analytics is the ability to model future events and behaviors, such as the probability that a customer will respond to an offer to purchase a product. **Predictive analytics** use statistical analysis, data mining techniques, historical data, and assumptions about future conditions to predict future trends and behavior patterns. Variables that can be measured to predict future behavior are identified. For example, an insurance company might use variables such as age, gender, and driving record as predictors of driving safety when issuing auto insurance policies. A collection of such predictors is combined into a predictive model for forecasting future probabilities with an acceptable level of reliability. Georgia State and other colleges and universities are using predictive analytics to examine millions of student academic and personal records to spot students in danger of dropping out.

FedEx has been using predictive analytics to develop models that predict how customers will respond to price changes and new services, which customers are most at risk of switching to competitors, and how much revenue will be generated by new storefront or drop-box locations. The accuracy rate of FedEx's predictive analytics system ranges from 65 to 90 percent.

Predictive analytics are being incorporated into numerous BI applications for sales, marketing, finance, fraud detection, and healthcare. One of the best-known applications is credit scoring, which is used throughout the financial services industry. When you apply for a new credit card, scoring models process your credit history, loan application, and purchase data to determine your likelihood of making future credit payments on time. Healthcare insurers have been analyzing data for years to identify which patients are most likely to generate high costs.

Many companies employ predictive analytics to predict response to marketing campaigns and other efforts to cultivate them. By identifying customers more likely to respond, companies can lower their marketing and sales costs by focusing their resources on customers who have been identified as more promising. For instance, Slack Technologies, which provides cloud-based team collaboration tools and services for 6.8 million active users, uses predictive analytics to identify customers who are most likely to use its products very frequently and upgrade to its paid services (McDonough, 2017).

Big Data Analytics

Predictive analytics are starting to use big data from both private and public sectors, including data from social media, customer transactions, and output from sensors and machines. In e-commerce, many online retailers have capabilities for making personalized online product recommendations to their website visitors to help stimulate purchases and guide their decisions about what merchandise to stock. However, most of these product recommendations are based on the behaviors of similar groups of customers, such as those with incomes under $50,000 or whose ages are between 18 and 25. Now some firms are starting to analyze the tremendous quantities of online and in-store customer data they collect along with social media data to make these recommendations more individualized. These efforts are translating into higher customer spending and retention rates. Table 11.4 provides examples of companies using big data analytics.

In the public sector, big data analytics are driving the movement toward smart cities, which make intensive use of digital technology and public record data stores to make better decisions about running cities and serving their residents. Municipalities are capturing more data through sensors, location data from mobile phones, and targeted smartphone apps. Predictive modeling programs now inform public policy decisions on utility management, transportation operation, healthcare delivery, and public safety. For example, the city of Barcelona is using big data to improve operations and decisions. Sensors attached to trash cans alert workers when they need to be emptied. Drivers can use a smartphone application to find the nearest available parking spot on city streets. Irrigation systems built into Barcelona's parks monitor soil moisture and turn on sprinklers when water is needed. The city expects to reduce its water bill by 25 percent per year after installing sensors in local parks, producing estimated annual savings of almost $60 million.

Operational Intelligence and Analytics

Many decisions deal with how to run the business on a day-to-day basis. These are largely operational decisions, and this type of business activity monitoring is called **operational intelligence**. Another example of operational intelligence is the use of data

TABLE 11.4

What Big Data Analytics Can Do

Organization	Big Data Capabilities
Bank of America	Able to analyze all of its 50 million customers at once to understand each customer across all channels and interactions and present consistent, finely customized offers. Can determine which of its customers has a credit card or a mortgage loan that could benefit from refinancing at a competitor. When the customer visits BofA online, calls a call center, or visits a branch, that information is available for an online app or sales associate to present BofA's competing offer.
Vestas Wind Systems	Improves wind turbine placement for optimal energy output by using IBM Big-Insights software and an IBM Firestorm supercomputer to analyze 2.8 petabytes of structured and unstructured data such as weather reports, tidal phases, geospatial and sensor data, satellite images, deforestation maps, and weather modeling research. The analysis, which used to take weeks, can now be completed in less than one hour.
Hunch.com	Analyzes massive database with data from customer purchases, social networks, and signals from around the web to produce a taste graph that maps users with their predicted affinity to products, services, and websites. The taste graph includes predictions about 500 million people, 200 million objects (videos, gadgets, books), and 30 billion connections between people and objects. Helps eBay develop more finely customized recommendations on items to offer. Hunch was acquired by eBay where it is used to target marketing campaigns.
German World Cup Soccer Team	Analyzed very large amounts of video and numeric data about individual player and team performance on itself and competing teams and then used what it had learned to improve how it played and to capitalize on competitors' strengths and weaknesses. Superior use of big data analytics helped the team win the 2014 World Cup.

generated by sensors on trucks, trailers, and intermodal containers owned by Schneider National, one of North America's largest truckload, logistics, and intermodal services providers. The sensors monitor location, driving behaviors, fuel levels, and whether a trailer or container is loaded or empty. Data from fuel tank sensors help Schneider identify the optimal location at which a driver should stop for fuel based on how much is left in the tank, the truck's destination, and fuel prices en route. The chapter-ending case describes how General Electric Company (GE) is using operational intelligence and cloud-based software tools to monitor and analyze the performance of generators, jet engines, locomotives, and oil-refining gear.

The Internet of Things is creating huge streams of data from web activities, smartphones, sensors, gauges, and monitoring devices that can be used for operational intelligence about activities inside and outside the organization. Software for operational intelligence and analytics enables organizations to analyze these streams of big data as they are generated in real time. Companies can set trigger alerts on events or have them fed into live dashboards to help managers with their decisions. For example, Schneider's sensors capture hard braking in a moving truck and relay the data to corporate headquarters, where the data are tracked in dashboards monitoring safety metrics. The event initiates a conversation between the driver and that person's supervisor.

Location Analytics and Geographic Information Systems

Big data analytics include **location analytics**, the ability to gain business insight from the location (geographic) component of data, including location data from mobile phones, output from sensors or scanning devices, and data from maps. For example, location analytics might help a marketer determine which people to target with mobile ads about nearby restaurants and stores or quantify the impact of mobile ads

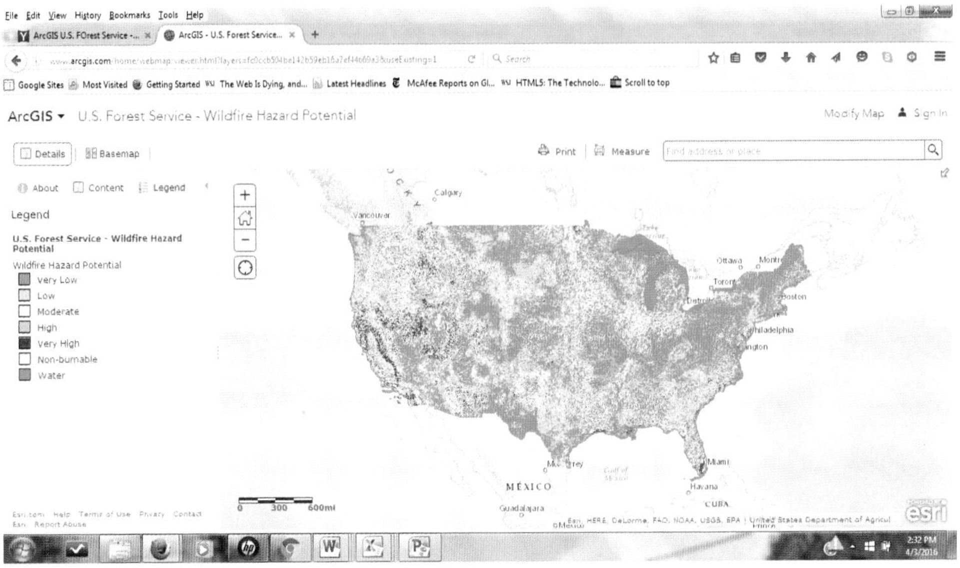

The U.S. Forest Service and Fire Modeling Institute created this map of Wildfire Hazard Potential (WHP) to assess wildfire risk and for prioritization of fuel management needs across large landscapes.

on in-store visits. Location analytics would help a utility company identify, view, and measure outages and their associated costs as related to customer location to help prioritize marketing, system upgrades, and customer service efforts. UPS's package tracking and delivery routing systems, described in Chapter 1, use location analytics, as does an application Starbucks uses to determine where to open new stores. (The system identifies geographic locations that will produce a high sales-to-investment ratio and per-store sales volume.)

The Starbucks and utility company applications are examples of **geographic information systems (GIS)**. GIS provide tools to help decision makers visualize problems that benefit from mapping. GIS software ties location data about the distribution of people or other resources to points, lines, and areas on a map. Some GIS have modeling capabilities for changing the data and automatically revising business scenarios. GIS might be used to help state and local governments calculate response times to natural disasters and other emergencies, to help banks identify the best locations for new branches or ATM terminals, or to help police forces pinpoint locations with the highest incidence of crime.

BUSINESS INTELLIGENCE USERS

Figure 11.4 shows that more than 80 percent of the audience for BI consists of casual users. Senior executives tend use BI to monitor firm activities by using visual interfaces such as dashboards and scorecards. Middle managers and analysts are much more likely to be immersed in the data and software, entering queries and slicing and dicing the data along different dimensions. Operational employees will, along with customers and suppliers, be looking mostly at prepackaged reports.

Support for Semi-structured Decisions

Many BI prepackaged production reports are MIS reports supporting structured decision making for operational and middle managers. We described operational and middle management, and the systems they use, in Chapter 2. However, some managers are super users and keen business analysts who want to create their own reports; they use more sophisticated analytics and models to find patterns in data, to model alternative business scenarios, or to test specific hypotheses. DSS are the BI delivery platform for this category of users, with the ability to support semi-structured decision making.

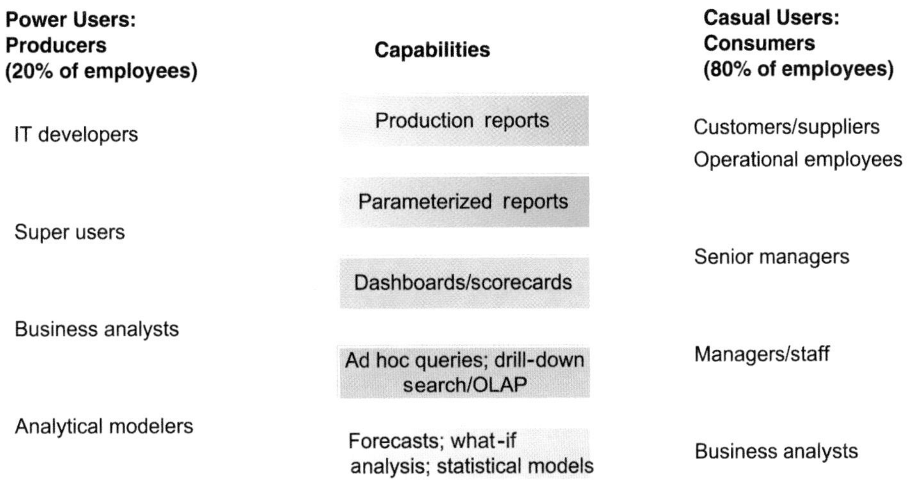

Figure 11.4
Business Intelligence Users
Casual users are consumers of BI output, whereas intense power users are the producers of reports, new analyses, models, and forecasts.

DSS rely more heavily on modeling than MIS, using mathematical or analytical models to perform what-if or other kinds of analysis. What-if analysis, working forward from known or assumed conditions, allows the user to vary certain values to test results to predict outcomes if changes occur in those values. What happens if we raise product prices by 5 percent or increase the advertising budget by $1 million? **Sensitivity analysis** models ask what-if questions repeatedly to predict a range of outcomes when one or more variables are changed multiple times (see Figure 11.5). Backward sensitivity analysis helps decision makers with goal seeking: If I want to sell 1 million product units next year, how much must I reduce the price of the product?

Chapter 6 described multidimensional data analysis and OLAP as one of the key business intelligence technologies. Spreadsheets have a similar feature for multidimensional analysis, called a **pivot table**, which super-user managers and analysts employ to identify and understand patterns in business information that may be useful for semi-structured decision making.

Figure 11.6 illustrates a Microsoft Excel pivot table that examines a large list of order transactions for a company selling online management training videos and books. It shows the relationship between two dimensions: the sales region and the source of contact (web banner ad or email) for each customer order. It answers the question of whether the source of the customer makes a difference in addition to region. The pivot table in this figure shows that most customers come from the West and that banner advertising produces most of the customers in all the regions.

Total fixed costs	**19000**					
Variable cost per unit	**3**					
Average sales price	**17**					
Contribution margin	**14**					
Break-even point	**1357**					
			Variable Cost per Unit			
Sales	**1357**	**2**	**3**	**4**	**5**	**6**
Price	**14**	1583	1727	1900	2111	2375
	15	1462	1583	1727	1900	2111
	16	1357	1462	1583	1727	1900
	17	1267	1357	1462	1583	1727
	18	1188	1267	1357	1462	1583

Figure 11.5
Sensitivity Analysis
This table displays the results of a sensitivity analysis of the effect of changing the sales price of a necktie and the cost per unit on the product's break-even point. It answers the question, "What happens to the break-even point if the sales price and the cost to make each unit increase or decrease?"

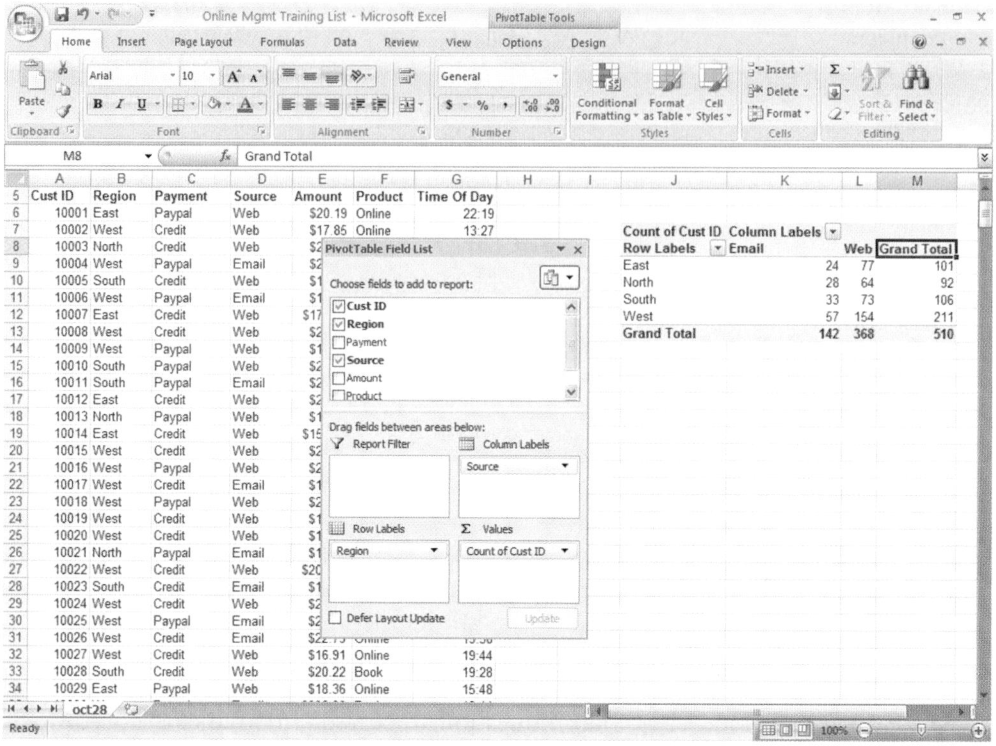

Figure 11.6
A Pivot Table That Examines Customer Regional Distribution and Advertising Source

In this pivot table, we can examine where an online training company's customers come from in terms of region and advertising source.

Source: Courtesy of Microsoft Corporation

One of the Hands-on MIS projects for this chapter asks you to use a pivot table to find answers to a number of other questions by using the same list of transactions for the online training company as we used in this discussion. The complete Excel file for these transactions is available in MyLab MIS. We have a Learning Track on creating pivot tables by using Excel.

In the past, much of this modeling was done with spreadsheets and small standalone databases. Today these capabilities are incorporated into large enterprise BI systems, and they can analyze data from large corporate databases. BI analytics include tools for intensive modeling. Such capabilities help Progressive Insurance identify the best customers for its products. Using widely available insurance industry data, Progressive defines small groups of customers, or cells, such as motorcycle riders aged 30 or older with college educations, credit scores over a certain level, and no accidents. For each cell, Progressive performs a regression analysis to identify factors most closely correlated with the insurance losses that are typical for this group. It then sets prices for each cell and uses simulation software to test whether this pricing arrangement will enable the company to make a profit. These analytic techniques make it possible for Progressive to insure customers profitably in traditionally high-risk categories that other insurers would have rejected.

Decision Support for Senior Management: The Balanced Scorecard and Enterprise Performance Management

BI delivered in the form of ESS helps senior executives focus on the most important performance information that affects the overall profitability and success of the firm. A leading methodology for understanding this important information a firm's executives need is called the **balanced scorecard method**. The balanced scorecard is a framework for operationalizing a firm's strategic plan by focusing on measurable outcomes of four dimensions of firm performance: financial, business process, customer, and learning and growth (see Figure 11.7).

Performance of each dimension is measured using **key performance indicators (KPIs)**, which are the measures proposed by senior management for understanding how well the firm is performing along any given dimension. For instance, one key

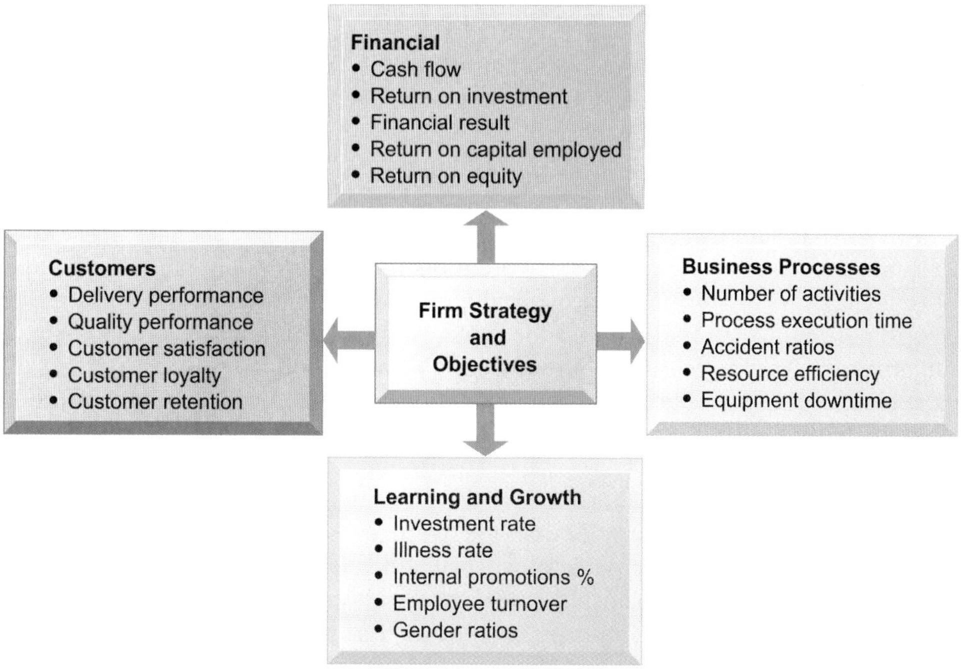

Figure 11.7
The Balanced Scorecard Framework
In the balanced scorecard framework, the firm's strategic objectives are operationalized along four dimensions: financial, business process, customer, and learning and growth. Each dimension is measured, using several KPIs.

indicator of how well an online retail firm is meeting its customer performance objectives is the average length of time required to deliver a package to a consumer. If your firm is a bank, one KPI of business process performance is the length of time required to perform a basic function such as creating a new customer account.

The balanced scorecard framework is thought to be balanced because it causes managers to focus on more than just financial performance. In this view, financial performance is past history—the result of past actions—and managers should focus on the things they can influence today, such as business process efficiency, customer satisfaction, and employee training. Once consultants and senior executives develop a scorecard, the next step is automating a flow of information to executives and other managers for each of the key performance indicators.

Another closely related management methodology is **business performance management (BPM)**. Originally defined by an industry group in 2004 (led by the same companies that sell enterprise and database systems, such as Oracle, SAP, and IBM), BPM attempts to translate a firm's strategies (e.g., differentiation, low-cost producer, market share growth, and scope of operation) systematically into operational targets. Once the strategies and targets are identified, a set of key performance indicators is developed to measure progress toward the targets. The firm's performance is then measured with information drawn from the firm's enterprise database systems.

Corporate data for contemporary ESS are supplied by the firm's existing enterprise applications (enterprise resource planning, supply chain management, and customer relationship management). ESS also provide access to news services, financial market databases, economic information, and whatever other external data senior executives require. ESS have significant **drill-down** capabilities if managers need more detailed views of data.

Well-designed ESS help senior executives monitor organizational performance, track activities of competitors, recognize changing market conditions, and identify problems and opportunities. Employees lower down in the corporate hierarchy also use these systems to monitor and measure business performance in their areas of responsibility. For these and other business intelligence systems to be truly useful, the information must be actionable—readily available and easy to use when making decisions. If users have difficulty identifying critical metrics within the reports they receive, employee productivity and business performance will suffer.

GROUP DECISION-SUPPORT SYSTEMS

The systems we have just described focus primarily on helping you make a decision acting alone. What if you are part of a team and need to make a decision as a group? **Group decision-support systems (GDSS)** are available for this purpose. The collaboration environments described in Chapter 2 can be used to help a set of decision makers working together as a group tin the same location or different locations to solve unstructured problems. Originally, GDSS required dedicated conference rooms with special hardware and software tools to facilitate group decision making. But today GDSS capabilities have evolved along with the power of desktop PCs, the explosion of mobile computing, and the rapid expansion of bandwidth on Wi-Fi and cellular networks. Dedicated rooms for collaboration can be replaced with much less expensive and flexible virtual collaboration rooms which can connect mobile employees with colleagues in the office sitting at desktops in a high quality video and audio environment.

For example, Cisco's Collaboration Meeting Rooms Hybrid (CMR) allows groups of employees to meet using any device, via WebEx video software, which does not require any special network connections, special displays, or complex software. The software to run CMR can be hosted on company servers or in the cloud. This allows even customers to participate in group meetings. The meetings can be scheduled by employees whenever needed. CMR can handle up to 500 video participants. Skype began deploying a cloud-based collaboration environment integrated with Microsoft Office called Skype for Business to support online meetings, sharing of documents, audio, and video.

11-3 What are the business benefits of using artificial intelligence techniques in decision making and knowledge management?

Decision making is also enhanced by "intelligent" techniques and knowledge management systems. The **"intelligent" techniques** most widely used in business are machine learning, neural networks, genetic algorithms, intelligent agents, natural language processing, computer vision systems, robotics, and expert systems. "Intelligent" techniques aid decision makers by capturing individual and collective knowledge, discovering patterns and behaviors in very large quantities of data, performing some human-like actions, and generating solutions to problems that are too large and complex for human beings to solve on their own.

These techniques are often described in popular writing as **artificial intelligence (AI)**, defined as computer-based systems (both hardware and software) that attempt to emulate human behavior and thought patterns, However, although AI technology can model certain limited aspects of human behavior, it does not yet exhibit the breadth, complexity, originality, and generality of human intelligence. Human intelligence is vastly more complex than the most sophisticated computer programs and covers a broader range of activities than is currently possible with "intelligent" systems and devices. AI technologies do what humans program or intend them to do. "Intelligent" techniques can extend the powers of humans but do not capture much of their intelligence. They do, nevertheless, have important business uses.

MACHINE LEARNING

Machine learning is the study of how computers can improve their performance without explicit commands programmed by humans by training algorithms to learn patterns from previous data and examples provided by humans. A machine that learns can recognize patterns in data based on its experience or prior learnings. For instance, researchers studying acute myelogenous leukemia (AML), a blood and bone

INTERACTIVE SESSION: TECHNOLOGY Does IBM's Watson Have a Future in Business?

IBM is betting much of its future on Watson, a supercomputing system that uses machine learning, statistical analysis, and natural language processing to extract meaning from images, videos, text, and speech. Watson can digest thousands of documents in minutes. To solve a typical problem, Watson tries many of the thousands of algorithms it has been programmed to use and is able to learn from its mistakes as well as its successes. Watson debuted in a televised 2011 *Jeopardy!* challenge where it beat the show's two greatest champions. Watson was able to register the intent of a question, search through millions of lines of text and data, pick up nuances of meaning and context, and rank potential responses for a user to select, all in less than three seconds. IBM terms Watson's ability to interpret speech and text, rapidly mine large volumes of data, answer questions, draw conclusions, and learn from its mistakes *cognitive computing.*

IBM sees its multi-billion-dollar investment in the Watson ecosystem as a stepping stone to broader commercial uses of its AI technology, including applications for healthcare, financial services, or any industry where sifting through large amounts of data (including unstructured data) to answer questions is important. In 2015 IBM created its Cognitive Business Solutions Unit, an internal consulting group, to develop cognitive technology applications for a wide range of industries and business needs. IBM has created about 100 commercial products based on this technology so far.

IBM has made Watson technology available via the Internet as a cloud service that could be used by many different industries, with parts of the system open to outside developers to create business and mobile applications based on cognitive computing. A Watson Developer Cloud provides tools and methodologies for developers to work with a Watson system, a content store supplying both free and fee-based data for new applications, and about 500 subject matter experts from IBM and third parties. IBM has also made Watson increasingly easier and less expensive to use.

Some of the earliest applications for Watson have been in healthcare, where medical information doubles every three years and in 2020 will be doubling every 73 days. IBM believes Watson can read and understand all this information in context, serve as an assistant to medical professionals, and potentially suggest therapies precisely tailored to individual patients.

In 2012, Memorial Sloan Kettering Cancer Center began work on a Watson for Oncology application to recommend personalized cancer treatments, using data from Sloan Kettering's clinical database of more than a million patients, 500 medical journals and textbooks, and 12 million pages of medical literature. Currently, the system offers recommendations for lung, breast, and colorectal cancers and is expanding to gastric-related cancers. Once Watson for Oncology has a patient's information, it can instantly search through medical literature from all over the world to identify the literature that is most relevant to that patient's specific cancer and prioritize potential treatment options based on the evidence and the patient's health record. Watson is able to present an analysis in about 15 minutes that would typically take humans months to develop.

Using Watson for Oncology turned out to be more complex than originally envisioned. For instance, Sloan Kettering oncologist Dr. Mark Kris displayed a screen from Watson that listed three potential treatments, but Watson was less than 32 percent confident that any of them were correct. But progress is genuine, and Watson for Oncology is now used at a number of hospitals worldwide, including the Cleveland Clinic, Jupiter Medical Center, Bumrungrad International Hospital in Bangkok, and Manipal Hospitals in seven cities in India as well as Memorial Sloan Kettering in New York. The University of Texas MD Anderson Cancer Center worked for five years on a Watson pilot system to digest Anderson's electronic medical records, academic literature, research data, and treatment options to recommend appropriate treatments for lung cancer. Although the pilot achieved a 90 percent accuracy rate in making the same treatment recommendations as MD Anderson physicians for selected cases, the project halted in late 2016 due to mismanagement.

IBM has aggressively been moving away from hardware and focusing on cloud-based analytic and artificially intelligent software. Although Watson is one key to IBM's future, analysts believe it's not growing fast enough to offset the weakness in its legacy computer and consulting businesses. Although many companies are experimenting with Watson, actual implementations of new Watson-based systems remain in their infancy.

In order to effectively commercialize the technology, IBM will need to expand Watson's knowledge domains, and this is its greatest challenge. Turning Watson into a useful business tool requires an enormous amount of work. Watson has to learn the terminology and master the domains of expertise in many different areas, including healthcare and scientific research, understand the context of how that language is used, and learn how to correlate questions with the correct answers. Watson can't come up yet with its own ideas.

It remains to be seen whether establishing a body of knowledge and training for one domain of knowledge, say, breast cancer diagnosis, can be used in other domains of knowledge and work and whether it creates opportunities for competitive advantage. All the major technology companies are investing aggressively in AI software, including Salesforce, SAP, Oracle, Google, Microsoft, and Amazon. Watson is very much a work in progress.

Sources: Daniela Hernandez, "Hospital Stumbles in Bid to Teach a Computer to Treat Cancer," *Wall Street Journal*, March 8, 2017; "Watson for Oncology," www.ibm.com, accessed May 22, 2017; Ed Burns, "Users Still Kicking the Tires on IBM's Cognitive Applications," TechTarget.com, October 27, 2016; Steve Lohr, "Artificial Intelligence: What Is Now, What's New and What's Next," *eMarketer*, May 2017; "IBM Is Counting on Its Bet on Watson, and Paying Big Money for It," *New York Times*, October 17, 2016; and Virginia Lau, "How Watson for Oncology Is Advancing Cancer Care," *Medical Marketing & Media*, April 19, 2016.

CASE STUDY QUESTIONS

1. How "intelligent" is Watson? What can it do? What can't it do?
2. What kinds of problems is Watson able to solve? How useful a tool is it for knowledge management and decision making?
3. Do you think Watson will be as useful in other industries and disciplines as IBM hopes? Will it be beneficial to everyone? Explain your answer.

marrow cancer, used bone marrow data, medical histories of affected patients, and blood data from healthy individuals to teach a standard 64-bit Windows workstation to accurately predict which AML patients diagnosed will go into remission following treatment and which ones will relapse. Google's ability to recognize the meaning and intent behind user queries rather than merely matching keywords is based on machine learning. The Interactive Session on Technology describes another leading example of machine learning, IBM's Watson, a question-answering computing system (both hardware and software) that can analyze very large quantities of data, answer questions using natural language, and learn from its mistakes and successes. Whatever machine learning programs do learn is domain specific and cannot be generalized to other topic areas without human intervention and training of the software.

NEURAL NETWORKS

Neural networks find patterns and relationships in very large amounts of data that would be too complicated and difficult for a human being to analyze by using machine learning algorithms and computational models that emulate the processing patterns of the biological human brain. Neural networks learn patterns from large quantities of data by sifting through data, searching for relationships, building models, and correcting over and over again the model's own mistakes.

A neural network has a large number of sensing and processing nodes that continuously interact with each other. Figure 11.8 represents one type of neural network comprising an input layer, a hidden processing layer, and an output layer. Humans train the network by feeding it a set of training data for which the inputs produce a known set of outputs or conclusions. This helps the computer learn the correct solution by example. As the computer is fed more data, each case is compared with the known outcome. If it differs, a correction is calculated and applied to the nodes in the hidden processing layer. These steps are repeated until a condition, such as corrections being less than a certain amount, is reached. The neural network in Figure 11.8

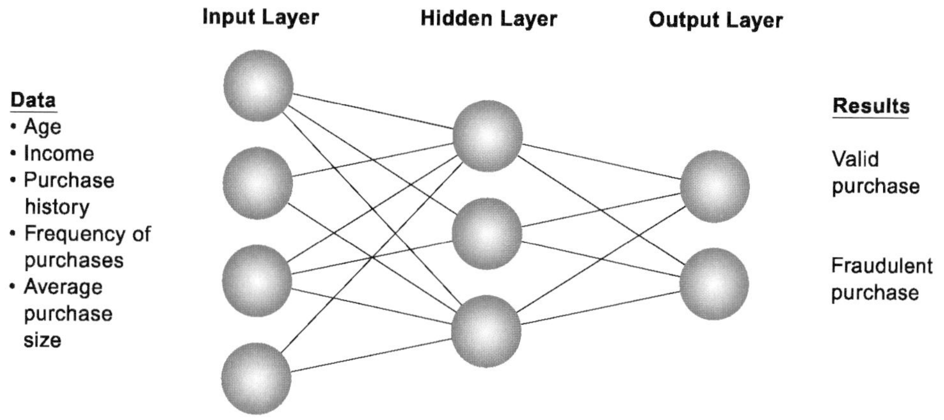

Figure 11.8
How a Neural Network Works
A neural network uses rules it learns from patterns in data to construct a hidden layer of logic. The hidden layer then processes inputs, classifying them based on the experience of the model. In this example, the neural network has been trained to distinguish between valid and fraudulent credit card purchases.

has learned how to identify a likely fraudulent credit card purchase. "Deep learning" neural networks are more complex, with many layers of transformation of the input data to produce a target output.

Neural network applications in medicine, science, and business address problems in pattern classification, prediction, and control and optimization. In medicine, neural network applications are used for screening patients for coronary artery disease, for diagnosing patients with epilepsy and Alzheimer's disease, and for performing pattern recognition of pathology images, including certain cancers. The financial industry uses neural networks to discern patterns in vast pools of data that might help investment firms predict the performance of equities, corporate bond ratings, or corporate bankruptcies. Visa International uses a neural network to help detect credit card fraud by monitoring all Visa transactions for sudden changes in the buying patterns of cardholders.

Neural networks cannot always explain why they arrived at a particular solution. They may not perform well if their training covers too little or too much data. In most current applications, neural networks are best used as aids to human decision makers instead of substitutes for them.

GENETIC ALGORITHMS

Genetic algorithms are useful for finding the optimal solution for a specific problem by examining a very large number of alternative solutions for that problem. They are based on machine learning techniques inspired by evolutionary biology such as inheritance, mutation, selection, and crossover (recombination).

A genetic algorithm works by searching a population of randomly generated strings of binary digits to identify the right string representing the best possible solution for the problem. As solutions alter and combine, the worst ones are discarded and the better ones survive to go on to produce even better solutions.

In Figure 11.9, each string corresponds to one of the variables in the problem. One applies a test for fitness, ranking the strings in the population according to their level of desirability as possible solutions. After the initial population is evaluated for fitness, the algorithm then produces the next generation of strings, consisting of strings that survived the fitness test plus offspring strings produced from mating pairs of strings, and tests their fitness. The process continues until a solution is reached.

Genetic algorithms are used to solve problems that are very dynamic and complex, involving hundreds or thousands of variables or formulas. The problem must be one whose range of possible solutions can be represented genetically and for which criteria can be established for evaluating fitness. Genetic algorithms expedite the

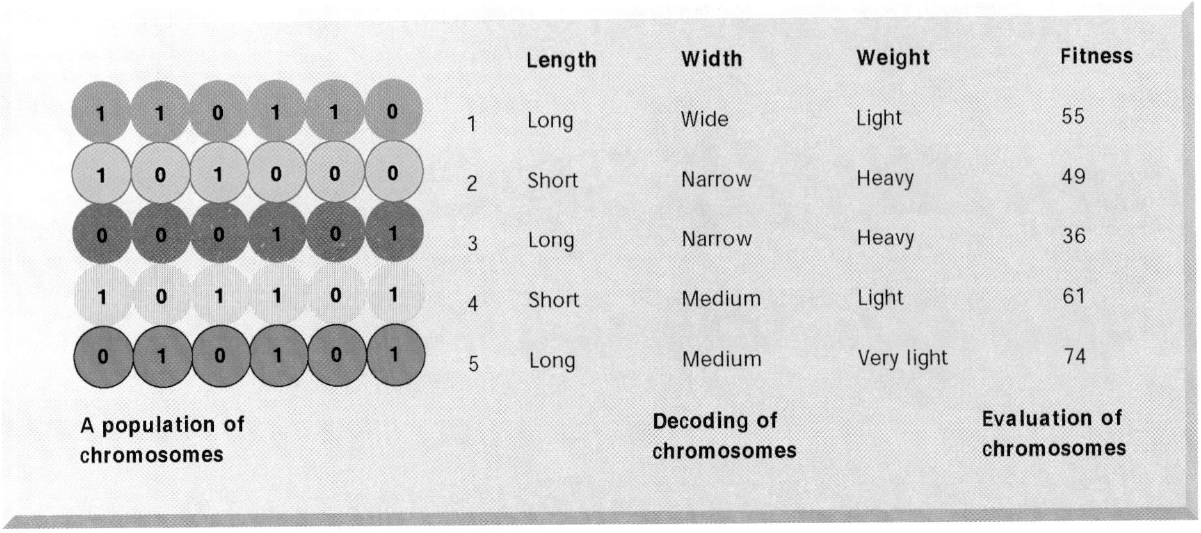

Figure 11.9
The Components of a Genetic Algorithm
This example illustrates an initial population of chromosomes, each representing a different solution. The genetic algorithm uses an iterative process to refine the initial solutions so that the better ones, those with the higher fitness, are more likely to emerge as the best solution.

solution because they can evaluate many solution alternatives quickly to find the best one. For example, General Electric engineers used genetic algorithms to help optimize the design for jet turbine aircraft engines, in which each design change required changes in up to 100 variables. The supply chain management software from JDA software uses genetic algorithms to optimize production-scheduling models, incorporating hundreds of thousands of details about customer orders, material and resource availability, manufacturing and distribution capability, and delivery dates.

INTELLIGENT AGENTS

Intelligent agent technology helps businesses and decision makers navigate through large amounts of data to locate and act on information they consider important. **Intelligent agents** are software programs that work in the background without direct human intervention to carry out specific, repetitive, and predictable tasks for an individual user, business process, or software application. The agent uses a limited built-in or learned knowledge base to accomplish tasks or make decisions on the user's behalf, such as deleting junk email, scheduling appointments, or finding the cheapest airfare to California.

There are many intelligent agent applications today in operating systems, application software, email systems, mobile computing software, and network tools. Of special interest to business are intelligent agents that search for information on the Internet. Chapter 7 describes how intelligent agent shopping bots help consumers find products they want and assist them in comparing prices and other features.

Although some intelligent agents are programmed to follow a simple set of rules, others are capable of learning from experience and adjusting their behavior. Siri, an application on Apple's iPhone and iPad, is an example. Siri uses voice recognition technology to answer questions, make recommendations, and perform actions. The software adapts to the user's individual preferences over time and personalizes results, performing tasks such as getting directions, scheduling appointments, and sending messages. Similar products include Google Now, Microsoft's Cortana, and Amazon's Alexa.

Chatbots (chatterbots) are software agents designed to simulate a conversation with one or more human users via textual or auditory methods. They try to

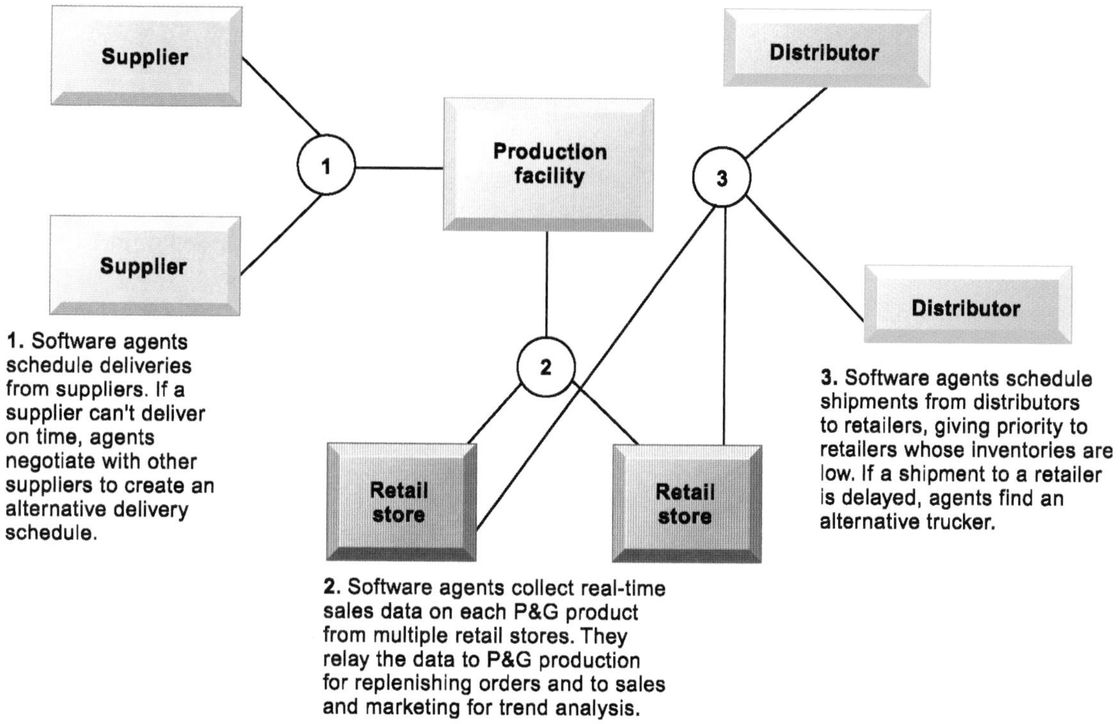

Figure 11.10
Intelligent Agents in P&G's Supply Chain Network
Intelligent agents are helping Procter & Gamble shorten the replenishment cycles for products such as a box of Tide.

understand what you type or say and respond by answering questions or executing tasks. They provide automated conversations that allow users to do things like check the weather, manage personal finances, and shop online. Facebook has integrated chatbots into its Messenger messaging app so that an outside company with a Facebook brand page can interact with Facebook users through the chat program. Today's chatbots perform very basic functions but will become more technologically advanced in the future.

Procter & Gamble (P&G) used intelligent agent technology to make its supply chain more efficient (see Figure 11.10). It modeled a complex supply chain as a group of semiautonomous agents representing individual supply chain components such as trucks, production facilities, distributors, and retail stores. The behavior of each agent is programmed to follow rules that mimic actual behavior, such as "order an item when it is out of stock." Simulations using the agents enable the company to perform what-if analyses on inventory levels, in-store stockouts, and transportation costs.

Using intelligent agent models, P&G discovered that trucks should often be dispatched before being fully loaded. Although transportation costs would be higher using partially loaded trucks, the simulation showed that retail store stockouts would occur less often, thus reducing the number of lost sales, which would more than make up for the higher distribution costs. Agent-based modeling has saved P&G $300 million annually on an investment of less than 1 percent of that amount.

NATURAL LANGUAGE PROCESSING, COMPUTER VISION SYSTEMS, AND ROBOTICS

Intelligent assistants such as Siri, Google Now, Cortana, and Alexa are able to respond to human voice commands with useful information in voice or written form. They employ **natural language processing**, a technology that makes it possible for a machine to understand spoken or written words expressed in human (natural) language and to

Will Robots Replace People in Manufacturing?

Robots have been muscling their way into almost every single occupation. Will they eventually replace people? Not likely, even in manufacturing, where they have made the greatest inroads so far. Industrial robots—with mechanical arms that can be programmed to weld, paint, and pick up and place objects with predictable regularity—have not taken over many tasks performed by humans on manufacturing assembly lines in Europe, Japan, the United States, and China. The biggest users of robotic technology have been automobile manufacturing plants, where robots do heavy lifting, welding, applying glue, and painting. People still do most of the final assembly of cars, especially when installing small parts or wiring that needs to be guided into place.

For most manufacturing work, it has been less expensive to use manual labor than it is to own, operate, and maintain a robotics system, given the tasks that robots can perform. But this is changing. Robots have become smaller, more mobile, more collaborative, and more adaptable, and their uses are widening. New robot models can work alongside humans without endangering them and help assemble all types of objects, as large as aircraft engines and as small and delicate as smartphones. They can also sense whether parts are being assembled correctly.

Robots are becoming easier to operate. Companies no longer need a software engineer to write program code to get a robot to perform a task. With some of today's robots, you can simply push a button, turn the robot's arm, and move it through the operation you want it to perform. The robot learns by doing.

A Renault SA plant in Cleon, France, now uses robots made by Universal Robots AS of Denmark to drive screws into engines, especially those that go into places people find hard to access. The robots have reach of more than 50 inches and six rotating joints to do the work. They also verify that parts are properly fastened and check to make sure the correct part is being used. The Renault robots weigh only about 64 pounds each, so they can easily be moved around to different locations as needed. They are also "collaborative," designed to work in proximity to people. Using sonar, cameras, or other technologies, these robots can sense where people are and slow down or stop to avoid hurting them.

These new-style robots are moving into other industries as well. ABB Ltd of Switzerland and others have recently introduced robots to help assemble consumer-electronics items. The robots were designed to work close to people and handle small parts. JCB Laboratories is using robots at its Wichita, Kansas, plant to pick up syringes, fill them with medications, and snap on caps. The robots work five to six times faster than people.

This new generation of robots will bring changes to the factory floor and perhaps the global competitive landscape. The Boston Consulting Group predicts that by 2025 the share of tasks performed by robots will rise from a global average of about 10 percent across all manufacturing industries to about 25 percent. In some industries, more than 40 percent of manufacturing tasks could be performed by robots. There will be dramatic productivity gains in many industries around the world (potentially boosting output per worker by 30 percent) and shifts in competitiveness among manufacturing countries.

Does this mean that robots will take over the production line? Not at this point. They still lack the flexibility, delicacy, and insight provided by humans. For example, today's collaborative robots often have to slow down or stop whenever people veer into their paths, disrupting production. Sales have been disappointing for Baxter, a two-armed collaborative robot from Rethink, which is used primarily for simple tasks such as moving materials, picking up parts, and packing or unpacking boxes. The robot's speed is restricted by safety considerations. For all their recent advances, robots still can't duplicate a human being's fine motor skills in manipulating materials and small parts. Robots still have trouble dealing with soft or floppy material, such as cloth or bundles of electrical wire.

Although robots are good at reliably and repeatedly performing defined tasks, they're not yet good at adapting. Mercedes-Benz had to cut back on its use of robots on the production line because the level of customization demanded by its customers requires a level of flexibility and dexterity that only humans can provide. Today's Mercedes customer wants to configure his or her own car, choosing among customization options such as carbon-fiber trim, four types of tire valve caps, and heated and cooled cup holders for 30 different models. Robots can't deal with the amount of variation in options that Mercedes cars have today.

Mercedes has found that if manufacturing focuses around a skilled crew of workers, it can shift a production line in a weekend. It would take weeks to reprogram robots and shift assembly patterns, and during that downtime, production would be at a standstill. Going forward, robots won't completely disappear from the Mercedes factory floor, but they'll be smaller and more flexible, operating alongside human workers.

As robots become more widespread, manufacturing tasks performed by humans will become higher-level and more complex. Workers will be expected to supervise and perhaps even program robots, and there will be fewer low-level manufacturing jobs. Workers will need more sophisticated skills to succeed in tomorrow's manufacturing plants.

Sources: Jack Hough, "Rise of the Robots," *Barrons,* March 4, 2017; Bloomberg, "Why Mercedes Is Halting Robots' Reign on the Production Line," *Industry Week*, February 25, 2016; Harold L. Sirkin, Michael Zinser, and Justin Rose, "The Robotics Revolution: The Next Great Leap in Manufacturing," *BCG Perspectives*, September 23, 2015; "Industries and Economies Leading the Robotics Revolution," *BCG Perspectives*, September 23, 2015; and James R. Hagerty, "Meet the New Generation of Robots for Manufacturing," *Wall Street Journal*, June 2, 2015.

CASE STUDY QUESTIONS

1. Why have robots caught on in manufacturing? What knowledge do they require?

2. Can robots replace human workers in manufacturing? Explain your answer.

3. If you were considering introducing robots in your manufacturing plant, what people, organization, and technology issues would you need to address?

process that information. You can also see natural language processing at work in the voice search feature of contemporary search engines such as Google or Yahoo, spam filtering systems, and text mining sentiment analysis (discussed in Chapter 6).

Computer vision systems deal with how computers can emulate the human visual system to view and extract information from real-world images. Such systems also incorporate image processing, pattern recognition, and image understanding. An example is Facebook's facial recognition tool called DeepFace, which is nearly as accurate as the human brain in recognizing a face. DeepFace will help Facebook improve the accuracy of Facebook's existing facial recognition capabilities to ensure that every photo of a Facebook user is connected to that person's Facebook account. Computer vision systems are also used in autonomous vehicles such as drones and self-driving cars, industrial machine vision systems (e.g. inspecting bottles), military applications, and robotic tools.

Robotics deals with the design, construction, operation, and use of movable machines that can substitute for humans along with computer systems for their control, sensory feedback, and information processing. Robots cannot substitute entirely for people but are programmed to perform a specific series of actions automatically. They are often are used in dangerous environments (such as bomb detection and deactivation), manufacturing processes, military operations (drones), and medical procedures (surgical robots). Of special interest today are robots used in manufacturing, which are increasingly taking over more production functions that used to be performed by humans. Many employees now worry whether robots will replace people entirely and take away their jobs. The Interactive Session on People explores this topic.

EXPERT SYSTEMS

What if employees in your firm had to make decisions that required some special knowledge, such as how to formulate a fast-drying sealing compound or how to diagnose and repair a malfunctioning diesel engine, but all the people with that expertise had left the firm? An **expert system** is an intelligent technique that captures human expertise in a limited domain of knowledge as a set of rules in a software system that

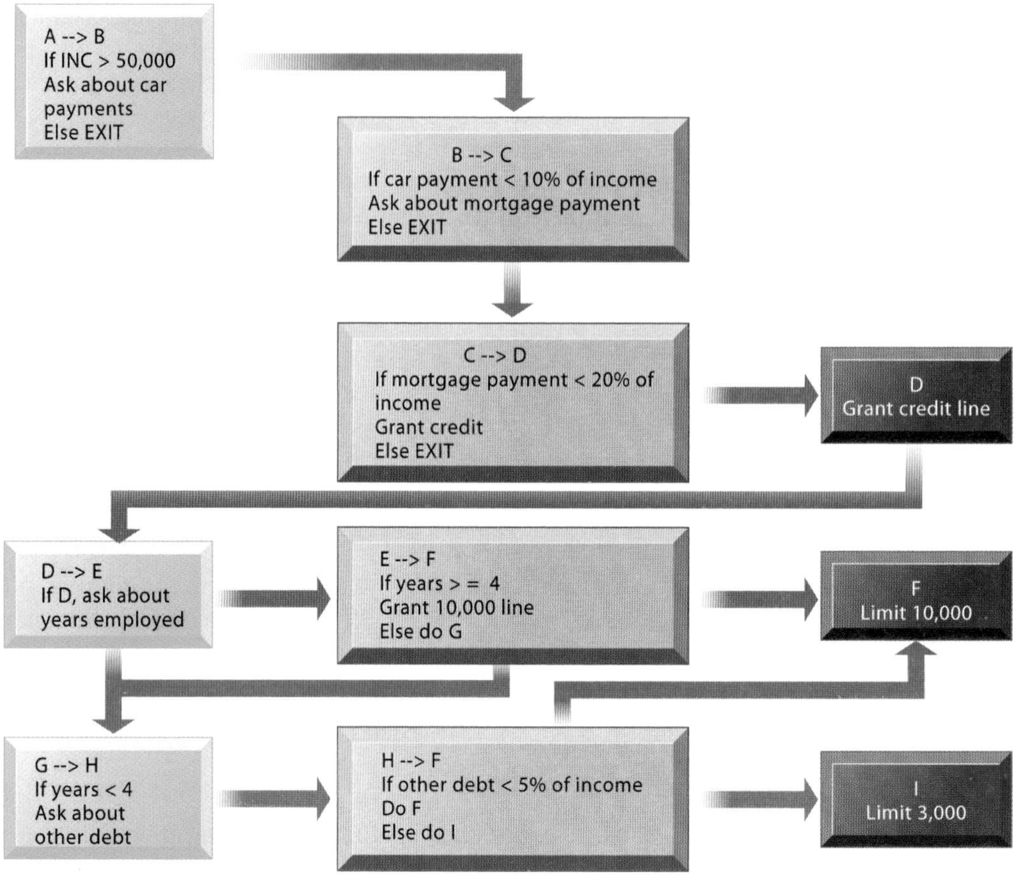

Figure 11.11
Rules in an Expert System
An expert system contains a set of rules to be followed when used. The rules are interconnected, the number of outcomes is known in advance and is limited, there are multiple paths to the same outcome, and the system can consider multiple rules at a single time. The rules illustrated are for a simple credit-granting expert system.

can be used by others in the organization. These systems typically perform a limited number of tasks that can be performed by professionals in a few minutes or hours, such as diagnosing a malfunctioning machine, determining whether to grant credit for a loan, or scanning legal documents for completeness. They are useful in decision-making situations when expertise is expensive or in short supply and needs to be captured by the firm in some systematic way.

How Expert Systems Work

Expert systems model human knowledge as a set of rules that collectively are called the **knowledge base**. Expert systems can have from 200 to as many as 10,000 or more of these rules, depending on the complexity of the decision-making problem (see Figure 11.11).

The strategy used to search through the collection of rules and formulate conclusions is called the **inference engine**. The inference engine works by searching through the rules and firing those rules that are triggered by facts the user gathers and enters.

Expert systems provide benefits such as improved decisions, reduced errors, reduced costs, reduced training time, and better quality and service. Thy have been used in applications for making decisions about granting credit and for diagnosing equipment problems. For example, Con-way Inc., now part of XPO Logistics, built an expert system called Line-haul to automate and optimize planning of overnight shipment routes for its nationwide freight-trucking business. The expert system captured thousands of business rules that dispatchers follow when assigning drivers, trucks, and trailers to transport 50,000 shipments of heavy freight each night across 25 U.S. states and Canada and when plotting their routes. This system was able to create optimum routing plans for 95 percent of daily freight shipments.

Only certain classes of problems can be solved using expert systems. Virtually all successful expert systems deal with problems of classification in which there are relatively few alternative outcomes and in which these possible outcomes are all known in advance. Expert systems are much less useful for dealing with unstructured problems that managers typically encounter.

Expert systems primarily capture the knowledge of individual experts. Collective knowledge that organizations have built up over the years can be captured and stored using case-based reasoning. You can find out more about case-based reasoning in our Learning Tracks. The Learning Tracks for this chapter also include a discussion of fuzzy logic systems, which are another way of representing knowledge more subjectively than crisp IF-THEN rules.

11-4 What types of systems are used for enterprise-wide knowledge management and knowledge work, and how do they provide value for businesses?

Systems for knowledge management improve the quality and usage of knowledge in the decision-making process. **Knowledge management** refers to the set of business processes developed in an organization to create, store, transfer, and apply knowledge. Knowledge management increases the ability of the organization to learn from its environment and to incorporate knowledge into its business processes and decision making.

Knowledge that is not shared and applied to the problems facing firms and managers does not add any value to the business. Knowing how to do things effectively and efficiently in ways that other organizations cannot duplicate is a major source of profit and competitive advantage. Businesses will operate less effectively and efficiently if this unique knowledge is not available for decision making and ongoing operations. There are two major types of knowledge management systems: enterprise-wide knowledge management systems and knowledge work systems.

ENTERPRISE-WIDE KNOWLEDGE MANAGEMENT SYSTEMS

Firms must deal with at least three kinds of knowledge. Some knowledge exists within the firm in the form of structured text documents (reports and presentations). Decision makers also need knowledge that is semi-structured, such as email, voice mail, chat room exchanges, videos, digital pictures, brochures, or bulletin board postings. In still other cases, there is no formal or digital information of any kind, and the knowledge resides in the heads of employees. Much of this knowledge is **tacit knowledge** and is rarely written down.

Enterprise-wide knowledge management systems deal with all three types of knowledge. Enterprise-wide knowledge management systems are general-purpose, firm-wide systems that collect, store, distribute, and apply digital content and knowledge. These systems include capabilities for searching for information, storing both structured and unstructured data, and locating employee expertise within the firm. They also include supporting technologies such as portals, search engines, collaboration and social business tools, and learning management systems.

Enterprise Content Management Systems

Businesses today need to organize and manage both structured and semi-structured knowledge assets. **Structured knowledge** is explicit knowledge that exists in formal documents as well as in formal rules that organizations derive by observing experts

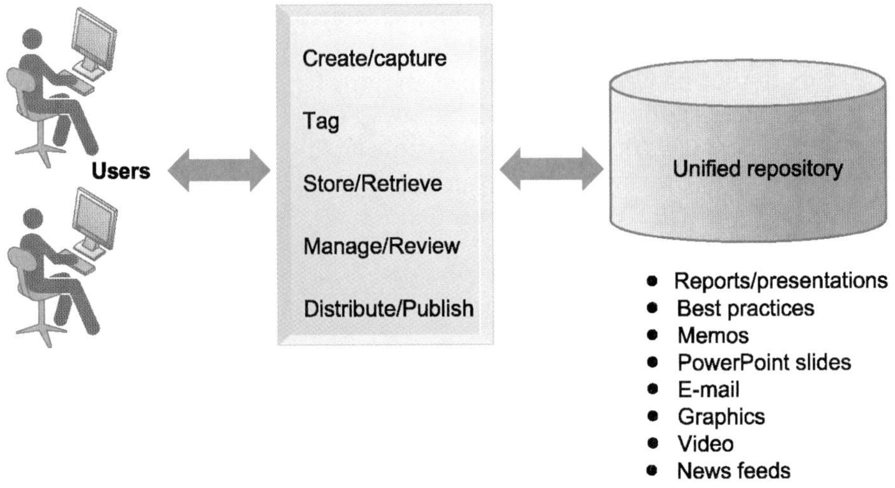

Figure 11.12
An Enterprise Content Management System
An enterprise content management system has capabilities for classifying, organizing, and managing structured and semi-structured knowledge and making it available throughout the enterprise.

and their decision-making behaviors. Nevertheless, according to experts, at least 80 percent of an organization's business content is semi-structured or unstructured—information in folders, messages, memos, proposals, emails, graphics, electronic slide presentations, and even videos created in different formats and stored in many locations.

Enterprise content management (ECM) systems help organizations manage both types of information. They have capabilities for knowledge capture, storage, retrieval, distribution, and preservation to help firms improve their business processes and decisions. Such systems include corporate repositories of documents, reports, presentations, and best practices as well as capabilities for collecting and organizing semi-structured knowledge such as email (see Figure 11.12). Major ECM systems also enable users to access external sources of information, such as news feeds and research, and to communicate by email, chat/instant messaging, discussion groups, and videoconferencing. They are starting to incorporate blogs, wikis, and other enterprise social networking tools.

A key problem in managing knowledge is the creation of an appropriate classification scheme to organize information into meaningful categories. Once the categories for classifying knowledge have been created, each knowledge object needs to be tagged, or classified, so that it can be easily retrieved. ECM systems have capabilities for tagging, interfacing with corporate databases where the documents are stored, and creating an enterprise portal environment for employees to use when searching for corporate knowledge. Open Text, EMC, IBM, and Oracle are leading vendors of enterprise content management software.

The New Zealand Department of Conservation, which is responsible for overseeing national parks and protecting wildlife and ecosystems, created a cloud-based enterprise content management system to facilitate storage, organization, and searching of 2.3 million documents related to its work. The ECM, called ContentWorX, enables participating government agencies to deploy web content, manage digital assets, and systemize documents and records, all on a common platform. Eighty percent of the documents are now accessible and searchable, and documents can be retrieved within seconds (Carr, 2016).

Firms in publishing, advertising, broadcasting, and entertainment have special needs for storing and managing unstructured digital data such as photographs, graphic images, video, and audio content. **Digital asset management systems** help them classify, store, and distribute these digital objects.

Locating and Sharing Expertise

Some of the knowledge businesses need is not in the form of a digital document but, instead, resides in the memory of individual experts in the firm. Contemporary enterprise content management systems, along with the systems for collaboration and social business introduced in Chapter 2, have capabilities for locating experts and tapping their knowledge. These include online directories of corporate experts and their profiles, with details about their job experience, projects, publications, and educational degrees, and repositories of expert-generated content. Specialized search tools make it easier for employees to find the appropriate expert in a company.

For knowledge resources outside the firm, social networking and social business tools enable users to bookmark web pages of interest, tag these bookmarks with keywords, and share the tags and web page links with other people. These bookmarks are often public on sites such as Delicious and Reddit, but some can be saved privately and shared only with specified people or groups.

Learning Management Systems

Companies need ways to keep track of and manage employee learning and to integrate it more fully into their knowledge management and other corporate systems. **Learning management systems (LMS)** provide tools for the management, delivery, tracking, and assessment of various types of employee learning and training.

Contemporary LMS support multiple modes of learning, including downloadable videos, web-based classes, live instruction in classes or online, and group learning in online forums and chat sessions. LMS consolidate mixed-media training, automate the selection and administration of courses, assemble and deliver learning content, and measure learning effectiveness.

CVM Solutions, LLC (CVM) uses Digitec's Knowledge Direct learning management system to provide training about how to manage suppliers for clients such as Procter & Gamble, Colgate-Palmolive, and Delta Airlines. Knowledge Direct provides a portal for accessing course content online along with hands-free administration features such as student registration and assessment tools, built-in Help and Contact Support, automatic email triggers to remind users of courses or deadlines, automatic email acknowledgement of course completions, and web-based reporting for accessed courses.

Businesses run their own learning management systems, but they are also turning to publicly available **massive open online courses (MOOCs)** to educate their employees. A MOOC is an online course made available via the web to very large numbers of participants Companies view MOOCs as a new way to design and deliver online learning where learners can collaborate with each other, watch short videos, and participate in threaded discussion groups. Firms such as Microsoft and AT&T have developed their own MOOCs, while others such as Bank of America and Qualcomm are using publicly available MOOCs aligned with their core competencies.

KNOWLEDGE WORK SYSTEMS

The enterprise-wide knowledge systems we have just described provide a wide range of capabilities that many, if not all, the workers and groups use in an organization. Firms also have specialized systems for knowledge workers to help them create new knowledge for improving the firm's business processes and decision making. **Knowledge work systems (KWS)** are specialized systems for engineers, scientists, and other knowledge workers that are designed to promote the creation of knowledge and ensure that new knowledge and technical expertise are properly integrated into the business.

Requirements of Knowledge Work Systems

Knowledge work systems give knowledge workers the specialized tools they need, such as powerful graphics, analytical tools, and communications and document management. These systems require great computing power to handle the sophisticated graphics or complex calculations necessary for such knowledge workers as scientific researchers, product designers, and financial analysts. Because knowledge workers are so focused on knowledge in the external world, these systems also must

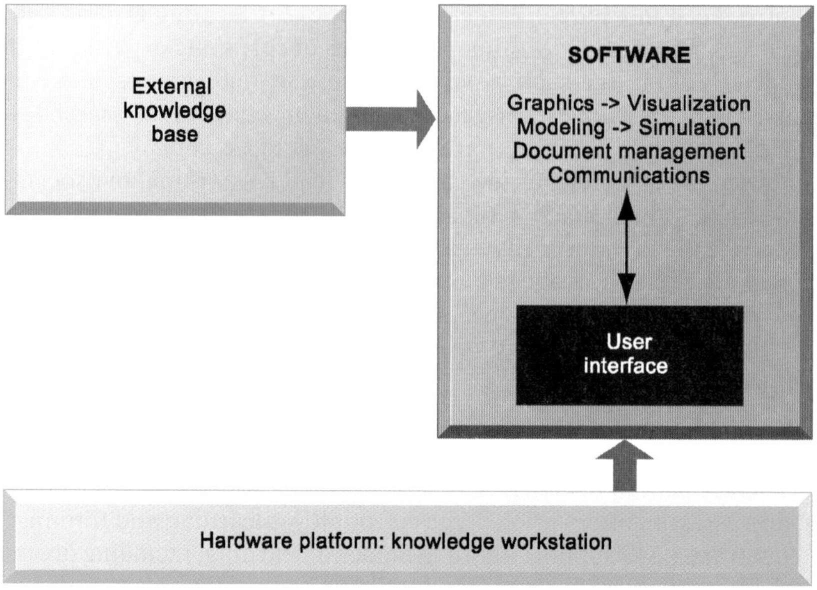

Figure 11.13
Requirements of Knowledge Work Systems
Knowledge work systems require strong links to external knowledge bases in addition to specialized hardware and software.

give the worker quick and easy access to external databases. They typically feature user-friendly interfaces that enable users to perform needed tasks without having to spend a lot of time learning how to use the computer. Figure 11.13 summarizes the requirements of knowledge work systems.

Knowledge workstations often are designed and optimized for the specific tasks to be performed. Design engineers need graphics with enough power to handle three-dimensional CAD systems. However, financial analysts are more interested in access to a myriad of external databases and technology for efficiently storing and accessing massive amounts of financial data.

Examples of Knowledge Work Systems

Major knowledge work applications include CAD systems (which we introduced in Chapter 3) and virtual reality systems for simulation and modeling.

Contemporary CAD systems are capable of generating realistic-looking three-dimensional graphic designs that can be rotated and viewed from all sides. The CAD software produces design specifications for manufacturing, reducing both errors and production time. **Virtual reality systems** use interactive graphics software to create computer-generated simulations that are so close to reality that users almost believe they are participating in a real-world situation. In many virtual reality systems, the user dons special clothing, headgear, and equipment, depending on the application. The clothing contains sensors that record the user's movements and immediately transmit that information back to the computer. For instance, to walk through a virtual reality simulation of a house, you would need garb that monitors the movement of your feet, hands, and head. You also would need goggles containing video screens and, sometimes, audio attachments and feeling gloves so that you are immersed in the computer feedback.

Audi has used virtual reality technology in its "dealership in a briefcase" program. By donning an Oculus Rift virtual reality headset, prospective buyers can feel as if they are sitting behind the wheel of a car or opening up the trunk. A camera tracks viewer's head movements and adjusts the image on the goggles accordingly. The VR headset displays in 3-D exactly what you'd see if you were looking over a real-life Audi. Bang & Olufsen headphones simulate the sounds of doors slamming shut and music from the stereo system of the cars being browsed. This VR experience is available for the entire Audi model range and customization options, including colors, upholstery, and infotainment systems. Facebook has been working on a virtual reality app for mobile phones, and both Facebook and Google have been experimenting with virtual reality headsets for immersive entertainment and other experiences.

Augmented reality (AR) is a related technology for enhancing visualization. AR provides a live direct or indirect view of a physical real-world environment whose elements are augmented by virtual computer-generated imagery. The user is grounded in the real physical world, and the virtual images are merged with the real view to create the augmented display. The digital technology provides additional information to enhance the perception of reality, making the surrounding real world of the user more interactive and meaningful. The yellow first-down markers shown on televised football games are examples of AR, as are medical procedures such as image-guided surgery, by which data acquired from computerized tomography (CT) and magnetic resonance imaging (MRI) scans or from ultrasound imaging are superimposed on the patient in the operating room. Facebook is planning to use smartphone cameras to overlay virtual items on the real world, enabling people to use their phones, for example, to play games virtually on coffee tables or overlay statistics on a video of their daily run.

Virtual reality applications developed for the web use a standard called **Virtual Reality Modeling Language (VRML)**. VRML is a set of specifications for interactive, three-dimensional modeling on the World Wide Web that organizes multiple media types, including animation, images, and audio, to put users in a simulated real-world environment. VRML is platform independent, operates over a desktop computer, and requires little bandwidth.

DuPont, the Wilmington, Delaware, chemical company, created a VRML application called HyperPlant, which enables users to access three-dimensional data over the Internet using web-browser software. Engineers can go through three-dimensional models as if they were physically walking through a plant, viewing objects at eye level. This level of detail reduces the number of mistakes they make during construction of oil rigs, oil plants, and other structures.

11-5 How will MIS help my career?

Here is how Chapter 11 can help you find a job as an entry-level data analyst.

THE COMPANY

Western Well Health, a major provider of healthcare services for the Denver Colorado metropolitan area is looking for an entry-level data analyst to perform data analysis and reporting for operational/clinical departments. The company's healthcare network includes 18 hospitals, six senior living communities, urgent care clinics, partner hospitals, and home care and hospice services in Colorado and Western Kansas.

POSITION DESCRIPTION

The data analyst will be responsible for coordinating a variety of quality and performance measurement initiatives, including satisfaction survey programs, benchmarking and tracking quality of care, clinical outcome performance, and asset utilization. Job responsibilities include:

- Performing data analysis based on SAS data sets, MS Access databases, external websites, and business intelligence platforms to produce reports for key stakeholder groups and decision makers.
- Eliciting data and reporting requirements using interviews, document analysis, requirements workshops, site visits, use cases, data analysis, and workflow analysis.
- Working with staff on the design, maintenance, and distribution of reports and incorporation of reports into the balanced scorecard.
- Analyzing, testing, and modifying databases and reports as needed to meet end user specifications and quality assurance procedures.
- Assisting in enhancing business intelligence reporting tools, dashboards, and mobile BI to improve usability, increase user adoption, and streamline support.

JOB REQUIREMENTS

- Bachelor's degree in Information Systems or Statistics
- Knowledge of Microsoft Access, SQL, and business intelligence tools such as Business Objects, SAS BI, or Tableau
- Data management, analytics, and information system experience preferred
- Some knowledge of the healthcare business and medical record systems desirable
- Project management skills and/or experience desirable

INTERVIEW QUESTIONS

1. Have you worked with any business intelligence software? Which tools? What is your level of proficiency? Can you give examples of the kinds of data analysis work and reports you used these tools for?
2. In your experience with data analysis and business intelligence, did you ever work with tools that were not as user-friendly as they could have been? What would you have recommended to improve the tool(s) for users?
3. Have you ever developed an analytics report for users from scratch? What BI tools or tools and data sets did you use? Can you talk more about how you worked with users to elicit the information requirements for the report?
4. What do you know about the healthcare industry and electronic medical records? Have you ever worked with medical record systems and software? What work did you do with them?
5. Have you ever worked on a project team? What were your responsibilities? Did you play a leadership role?

AUTHOR TIPS

1. Review the first two sections of this chapter on decision making and also Chapter 6 on data management and the first three sections of Chapter 12 on building systems and information requirements.
2. Use the web to do more research on the company. Try to find out more about its strategy, competitors, and business challenges. Additionally, look at the company's social media channels over the past 12 months. Are there any trends you can identify or certain themes the social media channels seem to focus on?
3. If you don't have experience with the BI software tools required for the job, use the web to learn more about these tools and how other healthcare companies are using them. Go to websites of major consulting companies such McKinsey & Co., Boston Consulting Group, Bain & Co., and Accenture to read their research articles on how technology is changing the healthcare service industry.
4. Be prepared to bring examples of the querying/reporting work you have done in your course work and your Microsoft Access proficiency.

Review Summary

11-1 What are the different types of decisions, and how does the decision-making process work? Decisions may be structured, semi-structured, or unstructured, with structured decisions clustering at the operational level of the organization and unstructured decisions at the strategic level. Decision making can be performed by individuals or groups and includes employees as well as operational, middle, and senior managers. There are four stages in decision making: intelligence, design, choice, and implementation.

11-2 How do business intelligence and business analytics support decision making? Business intelligence and analytics promise to deliver correct, nearly real-time information to decision makers, and the analytic tools help them quickly understand the information and take action. A business intelligence environment consists of data from the business environment, the BI infrastructure, a BA toolset, managerial users and methods, a BI delivery platform (MIS, DSS, or ESS), and the user interface. There are six analytic functionalities that BI systems deliver to achieve these ends: predefined production reports, parameterized reports, dashboards and scorecards, ad hoc queries and searches, the ability to drill down to detailed views of data, and the ability to model scenarios and create forecasts. BI analytics are starting to handle big data. Predictive analytics, location analytics, and operational intelligence are important analytic capabilities.

Management information systems (MIS) producing prepackaged production reports are typically used to support operational and middle management, whose decision making is fairly structured. For making unstructured decisions, analysts and super users employ decision-support systems (DSS) with powerful analytics and modeling tools, including spreadsheets and pivot tables. Senior executives making unstructured decisions use dashboards and visual interfaces displaying key performance information affecting the overall profitability, success, and strategy of the firm. The balanced scorecard and business performance management are two methodologies used in designing executive support systems (ESS).

Group decision-support systems (GDSS) help people meeting in a group arrive at decisions more efficiently. Contemporary GDSS use collaboration and videoconferencing platforms for soliciting ideas, gathering information, and documenting meeting sessions.

11-3 What are the business benefits of using artificial intelligence techniques in decision making and knowledge management? "Intelligent" techniques aid decision makers by capturing individual and collective knowledge, discovering patterns and behaviors in very large quantities of data, performing some human-like actions, and generating solutions to problems that are too large and complex for human beings to solve on their own. Machine learning is the study of how computers can improve their performance without explicit commands programmed by humans by training algorithms to learn from previous data and examples. Neural networks consist of hardware and software that attempt to mimic the thought processes of the human brain. Neural networks are able to learn without programming and to recognize patterns in massive amounts of data. Genetic algorithms develop solutions to particular problems using genetically based processes, such as fitness, crossover, and mutation. Intelligent agents are software programs with built-in or learned knowledge bases that carry out specific, repetitive, and predictable tasks for an individual user, business process, or software application. Chatbots are software agents designed to simulate a conversation with one or more human users via textual or auditory methods. Natural language processing technology makes it possible for a machine to understand spoken or written words expressed in human (natural) language and to process that information. Computer vision systems deal with how computers can emulate the human visual system to view and extract information from real-world images. Such systems incorporate image processing, pattern recognition, and image understanding. Robotics deals with the design, construction, operation, and use of movable machines that can substitute for some human actions. Expert systems capture tacit knowledge from a limited domain of human expertise and express that knowledge in the form of rules. The strategy to search through the knowledge base is called the inference engine.

11-4 What types of systems are used for enterprise-wide knowledge management and knowledge work, and how do they provide value for businesses? Enterprise content management systems feature databases and tools for organizing and storing structured documents and semi-structured knowledge such as email or rich media. Often these systems include group collaboration and social tools, portals to simplify information access, search tools, and tools for classifying information based on a taxonomy that is appropriate for the organization. Learning management systems provide tools for the management, delivery, tracking, and assessment of various types of employee learning and training.

Knowledge work systems (KWS) support the creation of new knowledge and its integration into the organization. KWS require easy access to an external knowledge base; powerful computer hardware that can support software with intensive graphics, analysis, document management, and communications capabilities; and a user-friendly interface.

Key Terms

Artificial intelligence (AI), 408
Augmented reality (AR), 421
Balanced scorecard method, 406
Business performance management (BPM), 407
Chatbot, 412
Choice, 398
Computer vision systems, 415
Data visualization, 400
Design, 398
Digital asset management systems, 418
Drill down, 407
Enterprise content management (ECM) systems, 418
Enterprise-wide knowledge management systems, 417
Expert system, 415
Genetic algorithms, 411
Geographic information systems (GIS), 404
Group decision-support systems (GDSS), 408
Implementation, 398
Inference engine, 416
Intelligence, 397
Intelligent agents, 412
"Intelligent" techniques, 408
Key performance indicators (KPIs), 406
Knowledge base, 416
Knowledge management, 417
Knowledge work systems (KWS), 419
Learning management system (LMS), 419
Location analytics, 403
Machine learning, 408
Massive open online course (MOOC), 419
Natural language processing, 413
Neural networks, 410
Operational intelligence, 402
Pivot table, 405
Predictive analytics, 401
Robotics, 415
Semi-structured decisions, 396
Sensitivity analysis, 405
Structured decisions, 396
Structured knowledge, 417
Tacit knowledge, 417
Unstructured decisions, 395
Virtual Reality Modeling Language (VRML), 421
Virtual reality systems, 420

MyLab MIS

To complete the problems with **MyLab MIS**, go to EOC Discussion Questions in MyLab MIS.

Review Questions

11-1 What are the different types of decisions, and how does the decision-making process work?
- List and describe the different decision-making levels and groups in organizations and their decision-making requirements.
- Distinguish among an unstructured, semi-structured, and structured decision.
- List and describe the stages in decision making.

11-2 How do business intelligence and business analytics support decision making?
- Define and describe business intelligence and business analytics.
- List and describe the elements of a BI environment.
- List and describe the analytic functionalities BI systems provide.
- Define predictive analytics and location analytics and give two examples of each.
- List each of the types of BI users and describe the kinds of systems that provide decision support for each type of user.
- Define and describe the balanced scorecard method and business performance management.

11-3 What are the business benefits of using artificial intelligence techniques in decision making and knowledge management?
- Define machine learning and explain how it benefits business.
- Define a neural network and describe how it works and how it benefits businesses.
- Define and describe genetic algorithms and intelligent agents. Explain how each technology works and the kinds of problems for which each is suited.
- Define and describe natural language processing, computer vision systems, and robotics and give examples of their business applications.
- Define an expert system, describe how it works, and explain its value to businesses.

11-4 What types of systems are used for enterprise-wide knowledge management and knowledge work, and how do they provide value for businesses?
- Define knowledge management and explain its value to businesses.
- Define and describe the various types of enterprise-wide knowledge systems and explain how they provide value for businesses.
- Define knowledge work systems and describe the generic requirements of these systems.
- Describe how the following systems support knowledge work: computer-aided design (CAD), virtual reality, and augmented reality.

Discussion Questions

11-5 MyLab MIS If businesses used DSS, GDSS, and ESS more widely, would they make better decisions? Why or why not?

11-6 MyLab MIS Describe various ways that knowledge management systems could help firms with sales and marketing or with manufacturing and production.

11-7 MyLab MIS How intelligent are "intelligent" techniques? Explain your answer.

Hands-On MIS Projects

The projects in this section give you hands-on experience designing a knowledge portal, identifying opportunities for business intelligence, using a spreadsheet pivot table to analyze sales data, and using intelligent agents to research products for sale on the web. Visit **MyLab MIS** to access this chapter's Hands-On MIS Projects.

MANAGEMENT DECISION PROBLEMS

11-8 U.S. Pharma Corporation is headquartered in New Jersey but has research sites in Germany, France, the United Kingdom, Switzerland, and Australia. Research and development of new pharmaceuticals is crucial to ongoing profits, and U.S. Pharma researches and tests thousands of possible drugs. The company's researchers need to share information with others within and outside the company, including the U.S. Food and Drug Administration, the World Health Organization, and the International Federation of Pharmaceutical Manufacturers & Associations. Also critical is access to health information sites, such as the U.S. National Library of Medicine and to industry conferences and professional journals. Design a knowledge portal for U.S. Pharma's researchers. Include in your design specifications relevant internal systems and databases, external sources of information, and internal and external communication and collaboration tools. Design a home page for your portal.

11-9 Applebee's is the largest casual dining chain in the world, with more than 1800 locations throughout the United States and 20 other countries. The menu features beef, chicken, and pork items as well as burgers, pasta, and seafood. Applebee's CEO wants to make the restaurant more profitable by developing menus that are tastier and contain more items that customers want and are willing to pay for despite rising costs for gasoline and agricultural products. How might business intelligence help management implement this strategy? What pieces of data would Applebee's need to collect? What kinds of reports would be useful to help management make decisions about how to improve menus and profitability?

IMPROVING DECISION MAKING: USING PIVOT TABLES TO ANALYZE SALES DATA

Software skills: Pivot tables
Business skills: Analyzing sales data

11-10 This project gives you an opportunity to learn how to use Excel's PivotTable functionality to analyze a database or data list. Use the data file for Online Management Training Inc. described earlier in the chapter. This is a list of the sales transactions at OMT for one day. You can find this spreadsheet file at MyLab MIS. Use Excel's PivotTable to help you answer the following questions:

- Where are the average purchases higher? The answer might tell managers where to focus marketing and sales resources or pitch different messages to different regions.
- What form of payment is the most common? The answer could be used to emphasize in advertising the most preferred means of payment.
- Are there any times of day when purchases are most common? Do people buy products while at work (likely during the day) or at home (likely in the evening)?
- What's the relationship among region, type of product purchased, and average sales price?

We provide instructions on how to use Excel PivotTables in our Learning Tracks.

IMPROVING DECISION MAKING: USING INTELLIGENT AGENTS FOR COMPARISON SHOPPING

Software skills: Web browser and shopping bot software
Business skills: Product evaluation and selection

11-11 This project will give you experience using shopping bots to search online for products, find product information, and find the best prices and vendors. Select a digital camera you might want to purchase, such as the Canon PowerShot SX420 or the Olympus Tough TG-4. Visit MySimon (www.mysimon.com), BizRate.com (www.bizrate.com), and Google Shopping to do price comparisons for you. Evaluate these shopping sites in terms of their ease of use, number of offerings, speed in obtaining information, thoroughness of information offered about the product and seller, and price selection. Which site or sites would you use and why? Which camera would you select and why? How helpful were these sites in making your decision?

Collaboration and Teamwork Project

Analyzing MOOCs for College Degree Programs

11-12 With three or four of your classmates, research the issue of whether MOOCs can and should be used by university students pursuing a college degree. Search the web for articles and findings about the appropriateness of MOOCs for college degree programs. Can students learn effectively with MOOCs? Should universities provide MOOC courses for college credit? What are the pros and cons? If possible, use Google Docs and Google Drive or Google Sites to brainstorm, organize, and develop a presentation of your findings for the class.

BUSINESS PROBLEM-SOLVING CASE

GE Bets on the Internet of Things and Big Data Analytics

General Electric (GE) wants to be known as the world's Digital Industrial Company. It is moving away from traditional manufacturing toward a much more technology-centric business strategy and business model that focuses on electric power generators, jet engines, locomotives, and oil-refining gear and software to connect these devices to the cloud. GE is putting its money on the technology that controls and monitors industrial machines as well as software-powered, cloud-based services for analyzing and deriving value from the data. GE hopes this strategy will turn it into a major software company.

GE is using sensor-generated data from industrial machines to help customers monitor equipment performance, prevent breakdowns, and assess the machines' overall health. GE has committed $1 billion to installing sensors on gas turbines, jet engines, and other machines; connecting them to the cloud; and analyzing the resulting data to identify ways to improve machine productivity and reliability. In other words, GE is betting its future on software and the Internet of Things (IoT).

In a number of industries, improving the productivity of existing assets by even a single percentage point can generate significant benefits. This is true of the oil and gas sector, where average recovery rate of an oil well is 35 percent. That means 65 percent of a well's potential is left in the earth because available technology makes it too expensive to extract. If technology can help oil extraction companies raise the recovery rate from 35 to 36 percent, the world's output would increase by 80 billion barrels—the equivalent of three years of global supply.

The oil and gas industry is also deeply affected by unplanned downtime, when equipment cannot operate because of a malfunction. A single unproductive day on a platform can cost a liquefied natural gas (LNG) facility as much as $25 million, and an average midsized LNG facility experiences about five down days a year. That's $125 to $150 million lost. Minimizing downtime is critical, especially considering declining revenues from lower energy prices. GE sees a $1 billion opportunity for its IoT software.

The foundation for all of GE's Industrial Internet (IoT) applications is Predix, a software platform launched in 2015 to collect data from industrial sensors and analyze the information in the cloud. Predix can run on any cloud infrastructure. The platform has open standards and protocols that allow customers to more easily and quickly connect their machines to the Industrial Internet. The platform can accommodate the size and scale of industrial data for every customer at current levels of use, but it also has been designed to scale up as demand grows. Predix can offer apps developed by other companies as well as GE, is available for on-premises or cloud-based deployment, and can be extended by customers with their own data sources, algorithms, and software code. Customers may develop their own custom applications for the Predix platform. GE is also building a developer community to create apps that can be hosted on Predix. Predix is not limited to industrial applications. It could be used for analyzing data in healthcare systems, for example. GE now has a Health Cloud running on Predix. Data security is embedded at all platform application layers, and this is essential for companies linking their operations to the Internet.

GE currently uses Predix to monitor and maintain its own industrial products, such as wind turbines, jet engines, and hydroelectric turbine systems. Predix is able to provide GE corporate customers' machine operators and maintenance engineers with real-time information to schedule maintenance checks, improve machine efficiency, and reduce downtime. Helping customers collect and use this operational data proactively would lower costs in GE service agreements. When GE agrees to provide service for a customer's machine, it often comes with a performance guarantee. Proactive identification of potential issues that also takes the cost out of shop visits helps the customer and helps GE.

In early 2013, GE began to use Predix to analyze data across its fleet of machines. A single engine's operating data will only tell you there's a problem with that engine. But by collecting massive amounts of data and analyzing the data across its entire fleet of machines, GE was able to cluster engine data by operating environment. The company found that the hot and harsh environments in the Middle East and China caused engines to clog, heat up, and lose efficiency, so they required more maintenance. GE found that engines had far fewer of these problems if they were washed more frequently. Fleet analytics helped GE increase engine lifetime and reduce engine maintenance. The company thinks it can save its customers an average of $7 million of jet airplane fuel annually because their engines will be more efficient. Predix's robust data and analytics platform made it possible for GE to use data across every GE engine all over the world and cluster fleet data.

Predix is starting to provide solutions for GE customers. For example, Invenergy LLC, North America's largest independent, privately held renewable energy provider is implementing GE Asset Performance Management reliability management software on 13 turbines at six gas-operated thermal plants in the United States. The software is based upon Predix and will perform predictive analytics on turbines that produce an operating capacity of 3,159 megawatts, enough to power a half-million homes. The software will help plant technicians more accurately predict and diagnose equipment failures before they occur in order to avoid unplanned outages. During preliminary testing, the system identified a turbine journal bearing experiencing early-stage vibration. A failure could have damaged the turbine and produced an unplanned outage, but Invenergy technicians were able to detect and repair the malfunction three months before it would have occurred. The GE system will also help Invenergy better manage its assets to achieve the optimal solution for reducing cost, managing risk and improving availability and reliability.

British oil and gas company BP plc had been using its own software to monitor conditions in its oil wells but decided to get out of the software business and became a GE customer. By the end of 2015, BP equipped 650 of its thousands of oil wells with GE sensors linked to Predix. Each well was outfitted with 20 to 30 sensors to measure pressure and temperature, transmitting 500,000 data points to the Predix cloud every 15 seconds. BP hopes to use the data to predict well flows and the useful life of each well and ultimately to obtain an enterprise-wide view of its oil fields' performance.

GE identified pipeline risk management as a major challenge for the oil and gas industry. There are 2 million miles of transmission pipe throughout the globe, moving liquid oil or gas from its point of extraction to refining, processing, or market. About 55 percent of transmission pipeline in the United States was installed before 1970. Pipeline spills are not frequent, but when they occur, they cause serious economic and environmental damage as well as bad publicity for pipeline operators and energy companies. Pipeline operators are always anxious to know where their next rupture will be, but they typically lacked the data to measure pipeline fitness. Operators had no way of integrating multiple sources of data into one place so they could see and understand the risk in their pipelines.

GE developed a pipeline-management software suite for accessing, managing, and integrating critical data for the safe management of pipelines, including a risk assessment tool to monitor aging infrastructure. GE's risk-assessment solution combines internal and external factors (such as flooding) to provide an accurate, up-to-the minute visual representation of where risk exists in a pipeline. This risk assessment tool enables pipeline operators to see how recent events affect their risk and make real-time decisions about where field service crews should be deployed along the pipeline. The risk assessment tool visualization and analytics capabilities run on Predix.

Weather has a sizable impact on risk for pipelines in areas prone to seismic activity, waterways, and washouts. Checking weather patterns along thousands of miles of pipe for rain or flood zones, and integrating those data with other complex pipeline data sets is very difficult to perform manually. But by bringing all relevant data together in one place, GE gives pipeline operators easier access to information to help them address areas with the greatest potential impact.

GE expects customers to benefit immediately from having all of their data integrated. But it wants them to be able to do more. In addition to being able to examine all current risk, pipeline operators would benefit from a "what-if" calculation tool to model hypothetical scenarios, such as assessing the impact of adjusting operating pressures or addressing particular areas of corrosive pipe. GE would give them the tools for a color-coded view of how those actions affect pipeline risk.

GE wants to go beyond helping customers manage the performance of their GE machines to managing the data on all of the machines in their entire operations. Many customers use GE equipment alongside of equipment from competitors. The customer cares about running the whole plant, not just GE turbines, for example, and 80 percent of the equipment in these facilities is not from GE. If, for example, if an oil and gas customer has a problem with a turbo compressor, a heat exchanger upstream from that compressor may be the source of the problem, so analyzing data from the turbo compressor will only tell part of the story. Customers therefore want GE to analyze non-GE equipment and help them keep their entire plant running.

If a customer purchases a piece of GE equipment such as a gas turbine or aircraft engine, GE often enters into a 10- to 15-year contractual services agreement that allows GE to connect to and monitor that machine, perform basic maintenance and diagnostics, and provide scheduled repairs. GE receives a bonus payment for keeping the equipment running at a specified threshold. GE may now be able to apply such outcome-based pricing to coverage of non-GE machines.

GE CEO Jeffrey Immelt wants GE to become a top 10 software company by 2020. In order to do this, GE needs to sell vast amounts of applications and Predix-based analytics. Although few businesses have the capital or infrastructure to operate a platform for integrating and analyzing their IoT data, GE faces competition from many sources. Amazon, Google, IBM, and Microsoft are all getting into Internet of Things platforms, and dozens of start-ups have similar ambitions. The biggest question is whether other large industrial companies will turn to GE or to another cloud platform to manage their information. And if you're a manufacturer of some size and sophistication, will you allow GE to "own" the data on your business, or will you manage and analyze the data yourself?

Sources: Paul Gillin, "Industrial IoT Revs Up at Big Renewable Energy Provider," *Silicon Angle,* May 17, 2017; *www.predix.io*, accessed May 20, 2017; Laura Winig, "GE's Big Bet on Data and Analytics," *MIT Sloan Management Review,* February 2016; www.ge.com, accessed May *20, 2017;* Devin Leonard and Rick Clough, "How GE Exorcised the Ghost of Jack Welch to Become a 124-Year-Old Startup," *Bloomberg Businessweek,* March 21, 2016; Holly Lugassy, "GE Leverages Pivotal Cloud Foundry to Build Predix, First Cloud for Industry," CloudFoundry.org, May 11, 2016; Cliff Saran, "GE Predictive Analytics Optimises Irish Power Electricity Production," *Computer Weekly,* July 13, 2015; Charles Babcock, "GE Predix Cloud: Industrial Support for Machine Data," *Information Week,* August 6, 2015; and "GE: IoT Makes Power Plants $50M More Valuable," *Information Week,* September 29, 2015.

CASE STUDY QUESTIONS

11-13 How is GE changing its business strategy and business model? What is the role of information technology in GE's business?

11-14 On what business functions and level of decision making is GE focusing?

11-15 Describe three kinds of decisions that can be supported using Predix. What is the value to the firm of each of those decisions? Explain.

11-16 To what extent is GE becoming a software company? Explain your answer.

11-17 Do you think GE will become one of the top 10 U.S. software companies? Why or why not?

MyLab MIS

Go to the Assignments section of MyLab MIS to complete these writing exercises.

11-18 Give three examples of data used in location analytics and explain how each can help businesses.

11-19 How do each of the following types of systems acquire and represent knowledge: expert system, neural network, genetic algorithm?

Chapter 11 References

Agrawal, Ajay, Joshua S. Gans, and Avi Goldfarb. "What to Expect from Artificial Intelligence." *MIT Sloan Management Review* (February 7, 2017).

Alavi, Maryam, and Dorothy Leidner. "Knowledge Management and Knowledge Management Systems: Conceptual Foundations and Research Issues." *MIS Quarterly* 25, No. 1 (March 2001).

Ask, Julie A., Michael Facemire, and Andrew Hogan. "The State of Chatbots." Forrester Research (October 20, 2016).

Breuker, Dominic, Martin Matzner, Patrick Delfmann, and Jörg Becker. "Comprehensible Predictive Models for Business Processes." *MIS Quarterly* 40, No. 4 (September 2016).

Erik Brynjolfsson, Tomer Geva, and Shachar Reichman. "Crowd-Squared: Amplifying the Predictive Power of Search Trend Data." *MIS Quarterly* 40, No. 4 (December 2016).

Lacity, Mary C., and Leslie P. Willcocks. "A New Approach to Automating Services." *MIT Sloan Management Review* (August 2016).

Burtka, Michael. "Genetic Algorithms." *The Stern Information Systems Review* 1, No. 1 (Spring 1993).

Carr, David F. "Collaboration in the Cloud." *Profit* (February 2016).

Davenport, Thomas H. "Big Data at Work: Dispelling the Myths, Uncovering the Opportunities." *Harvard Business Review* (2014).

Davenport, Thomas H., Jeanne Harris, and Robert Morison. *Analytics at Work: Smarter Decisions, Better Results*. (Boston: Harvard Business Press, 2010).

Davenport, Thomas H., and Julia Kirby. "Just How Smart Are Smart Machines?" *MIT Sloan Management Review* 57, No. 3 (Spring 2016).

Dhar, Vasant, and Roger Stein. *Intelligent Decision Support Methods: The Science of Knowledge Work*. (Upper Saddle River, NJ: Prentice-Hall, 1997).

eMarketer. "Artificial Intelligence: What's Now, What's New, and What's Next." (May 2017).

Ghiassi, Manoochehr, David Zimbra, and Sean Lee. "Targeted Twitter Sentiment Analysis for Brands Using Supervised Feature Engineering and the Dynamic Architecture for Artificial Neural Networks." *Journal of Management Information Systems* 33, No. 4 (2016).

Gelernter, David. "Machines That Will Think and Feel." *Wall Street Journal* (March 18, 2016).

Grau, Jeffrey. "How Retailers Are Leveraging 'Big Data' to Personalize Ecommerce." *eMarketer* (May 2012).

Hackathorn, Richard. "Business Value from the Analytics of Things." Bolder Technology Inc. (2016).

Holland, John H. "Genetic Algorithms." *Scientific American* (July 1992).

Ihrig, Martin, and Ian MacMillan. "Managing Your Mission-Critical Knowledge." *Harvard Business Review* (January–February 2015).

Iyengar, Kishen, Jeffrey R. Sweeney, and Ramiro Montealegre."Information Technology Use as a Learning Mechanism: The Impact of IT Use on Knowledge Transfer Effectiveness, Absorptive Capacity, and Franchisee Performance." MIS Quarterly 39 No. 3 (September 2015).

Kahneman, Daniel. *Thinking, Fast and Slow* (New York: Farrar, Straus and Giroux, 2011).

Kim, Seung Hyun, Tridas Mukhopadhyay, and Robert E. Kraut. "When Does Repository KMS Use Lift Performance? The Role of Alternative Knowledge Sources and Task Environments?" *MIS Quarterly* 40, No. 1 (March 2016).

Kyriakou, Harris, Jeffrey V. Nickerson, and Gaurav Sabnis. "Knowledge Reuse for Customization: Metamodels in an Open Design Community for 3D Printing." *MIS Quarterly* 41, No. 1 (2017).

Lash, Michael T., and Kang Zhao. "Early Predictions of Movie Success: The Who, What, and When of Profitability." *Journal of Management Information Systems* 33, No. 3 (2016).

Lewis-Kraus, Gideon. "The Great AI Awakening." *New York Times* (December 14, 2016).

Luca, Michael, Jon Kleinberg, and Sendhil Mullainathan. "Algorithms Need Managers, Too." *Harvard Business Review* (January–February 2016).

Malhotra, Arvind, Ann Majchrzak, Lâle Kesebi, and Sean Looram. "Developing Innovative Solutions Through Internal Crowdsourcing" *MIT Sloan Management Review* (Summer 2017).

Malone, Thomas. "Rethinking Knowledge Work: A Strategic Approach." *McKinsey Quarterly* (February 2011).

Marchand, Donald A., and Joe Peppard. "Why IT Fumbles Analytics." *Harvard Business Review* (January–February 2013).

Markoff, John. "Innovators of Intelligence Look to Past." *New York Times* (December 15, 2014).

Martens, David, Foster Provost, Jessica Clark, and Enric Junqué de Fortuny. "Mining Massive Fine-Grained Behavior Data to Improve Predictive Analytics." *MIS Quarterly* 40, No. 4 (December 2016).

McDonough, Brian. "How Slack Uses Big Data to Grow Its Business." *Information Management* (May 3, 2017).

McKinsey Global Institute. "The Age of Analytics: Competing in a Data-Driven World" (December 2016).

Nurmohamed, Zafrin, Nabeel Gillani, and Michael Lenox. "A New Use for MOOCs: Real-World Problem Solving." *Harvard Business Review* (July 14, 2013).

Pugh, Katrina, and Lawrence Prusak. "Designing Effective Knowledge Networks." *MIT Sloan Management Review* (Fall 2013).

Pyle, Dorian, and Cristina San Jose. "An Executive's Guide to Machine Learning." *McKinsey Quarterly* (June 2015).

Ransbotham, Sam, David Kiron, and Pamela Kirk Prentice. "Minding the Analytics Gap." *MIT Sloan Management Review* (Spring 2015).

Samuelson, Douglas A., and Charles M. Macal. "Agent-Based Simulation." *OR/MS Today* (August 2006).

Simon, H. A. *The New Science of Management Decision.* (New York: Harper & Row, 1960).

"Smarter, Smaller, Safer Robots." *Harvard Business Review* (November 2015).

Trantopoulos, Knstantinos, Georg von Krogh, Martin W. Wallin, and Martin Woerter. "External Knowledge and Information Technology: Implications for Process Innovation Performance." *MIS Quarterly* 41, No. 1 (March 2017).

Wang, Weiquan, and Izak Benbasat. "Empirical Assessment of Alternative Designs for Enhancing Different Types of Trusting Beliefs in Online Recommendation Agents." *Journal of Management Information Systems* 33, No. 3 (2016).

Wang, Yinglei, Darren B. Meister, and Peter H. Gray. "Social Influence and Knowledge Management Systems Use: Evidence from Panel Data." *MIS Quarterly* 37, No. 1 (March 2013).

Zahedi, Fatemeh Mariam, Nitin Walia, and Hemant Jain. "Augmented Virtual Doctor Office: Theory-Based Design and Assessment." *Journal of Management Information Systems* 33, No. 3 (2016).

PART IV

Chapter 12
Building Information Systems and Managing Projects

Building and Managing Systems

Part IV shows how to use the knowledge acquired in earlier chapters to analyze and design information system solutions to business problems. This part answers questions such as these: How can I develop a solution to an information system problem that provides genuine business benefits? How can the firm adjust to the changes introduced by the new system solution? What alternative approaches are available for building system solutions?

CHAPTER 12

Building Information Systems and Managing Projects

LEARNING OBJECTIVES

After reading this chapter, you will be able to answer the following questions:

12-1 What are the core problem-solving steps for developing new information systems?

12-2 What are the alternative methods for building information systems?

12-3 What are the principal methodologies for modeling and designing systems?

12-4 How should information systems projects be selected and managed?

12-5 How will MIS help my career?

CHAPTER CASES

- Girl Scout Cookie Sales Go Digital
- Developing Mobile Apps: What's Different
- Snohomish County Public Utility District Implements a New Human Resources System
- The Philly311 Project: The City of Brotherly Love Turns Problems into Opportunities

VIDEO CASES

- PSEG Leverages Big Data and Business Analytics Using GE's Predix Platform
- IBM: BPM in a SaaS Environment
- IBM Helps the City of Madrid with Real-Time BPM Software

Instructional Videos:

- What is PaaS?
- BPM: Business Process Management Customer Story

MyLab MIS

- Discussion Questions: 12-5, 12-6, 12-7;
- Hands-on MIS Projects: 12-8, 12-9, 12-10, 12-11;
- Writing Assignments: 12-18, 12-19;
- eText with Conceptual Animations

GIRL SCOUT COOKIE SALES GO DIGITAL

Thin Mints, Samoas, and Trefoils may be fun to eat, but selling Girl Scout cookies is a serious business. Girl Scout cookie sales bring in about $850 million annually. Cookie sales are a major source of funding for the Girl Scouts and an opportunity for the 1.9 million girls who do the selling to develop valuable sales and money management skills. However, collecting, counting, and organizing the annual avalanche of cookie orders has become a tremendous challenge.

The Girl Scouts' traditional cookie-ordering process has been heavily manual. During the peak sales period in January, each Girl Scout would enter her sales on an individual order card and turn the card in to the troop leader when she was finished. The troop leader would transfer the information to a five-part form and give this form to a community volunteer who tabulated the orders. From there, the order data passed to a regional council headquarters, where they would be batched into final orders for the manufacturer. (Little Brownie Bakers in Louisville, Kentucky, and ABC Bakers in Richmond, Virginia, are the two licensed suppliers for Girl Scout Cookies.) It might take weeks or months for customers to receive the cookies they ordered.

The paperwork was overwhelming. Order transactions changed hands too many times, creating many opportunities for error. All the added columns, multiple prices per box, and calculations had to be made by different people, all on a deadline.

The Girl Scouts are trying to use information technology to improve this process. For example, the Patriots' Trail Girl Scout Council, representing 65 communities and 18,000 Girl Scouts in the greater Boston area, used Intuit's hosted QuickBase for Corporate WorkGroups to document, manage, and organize cookie sales and deliveries, including online entry of cookie orders over the web and electronic transmission of orders to ABC Bakers. Other regional Girl Scout councils have also moved to a QuickBase system. ABC Bakers and Little Brownie Bakers have their own order management systems for Girl Scout cookies.

© Rob Hainer/Shutterstock

Girl Scouts of the USA decided that instead of relying on all these disparate systems, it should develop a single nationwide digital solution for Girl Scout cookie sales for all Girl Scouts to use if they chose. Working with Accenture consultants and Hybris e-commerce specialists, Girl Scouts of the USA developed the Digital

Cookie system. The system includes capabilities for individual Girl Scouts to create their own personalized websites for taking cookie orders and a mobile app for cookie sales that runs on iOS and Android smartphones and tablets. The Hybris Commerce Suite provides a single system for managing product content, commerce operations, and multiple sales channels (including the web and mobile devices) to create a unified and consistent cross-channel experience for customers.

A scout with a mobile device would contact a potential customer, meet the customer in person, and help him or her fill out an online order form on the mobile device. The customer would enter his or her credit card information. A scout using her own personal website would contact the customer in person or via phone or email. The customer would be provided with information on how to access that particular scout's personal website and use the website to enter order and payment information online. Customer credit card payment data can be entered directly online. Both options perform the required order calculations and eliminate the need for paper order forms. In 2016 Visa and Dell contributed $3 million to enhance the digital cookie platform with games, videos, quizzes, and music to teach the Scouts more about marketing, budgeting, resource allocation, and other critical business skills.

The Digital Cookie websites and apps are available only to Girl Scouts. Customers must purchase cookies through an individual Girl Scout or troop, but there is a mobile app for customers to locate where Girl Scout cookies are being sold nearby. Cookies can be shipped directly to customers' homes for an additional fee, sometimes as quickly as three to five business days. Alternatively, scouts can still deliver the cookies to your door. Digital Cookie is optional. If a Girl Scout or troop wants to use the traditional paper order forms, they can do so. The system has been designed so that the Girl Scouts themselves are still the ones making the cookie sales.

Clearly, Digital Cookie is helping the Girl Scouts dramatically reduce paperwork, errors, and order processing time as well as develop strong technology, business, and social skills for the twenty-first century workforce.

Sources: "Digital Cookie," www.girlscouts.org, accessed April 15,2017; Trent Gilles, "Girl Scouts Acting CEO Explains Why the Charity Is More than the Sum of Its Cookies," msn.com, accessed April 12, 2017; Elizabeth Olson, "Girl Scout Cookies Go Digital, with Help from Visa and Dell," *New York Times*, January 3, 2016; and Emanuella Grinberg, "What Girl Scouts Can Learn from Online Cookie Sales," *CNN*, January 18, 2015.

The experience of the Girl Scouts illustrates some of the steps required to design and build new information systems. It also illustrates some of the benefits of a new system solution. The Girl Scouts had an outdated manual, paper-based system for processing cookie orders that was excessively time-consuming and error ridden. The Girl Scouts tried several alternative solutions before opting for a new online and mobile ordering system. In this chapter, we will examine the Girl Scouts' search for a system solution as we describe each step of building a new information system by using the problem-solving process.

Here are some questions to think about: Compare the traditional Girl Scout cookie-ordering process with the Digital Cookie online ordering process using the web and the process using a mobile device. Diagram each of these processes.

12-1 What are the core problem-solving steps for developing new information systems?

We have already described the problem-solving process and how it helps us analyze and understand the role of information systems in business. This problem-solving process is especially valuable when we need to build new systems. A new information system is built as a solution to a problem or set of problems the organization perceives it is facing. The problem may be one in which managers and employees believe

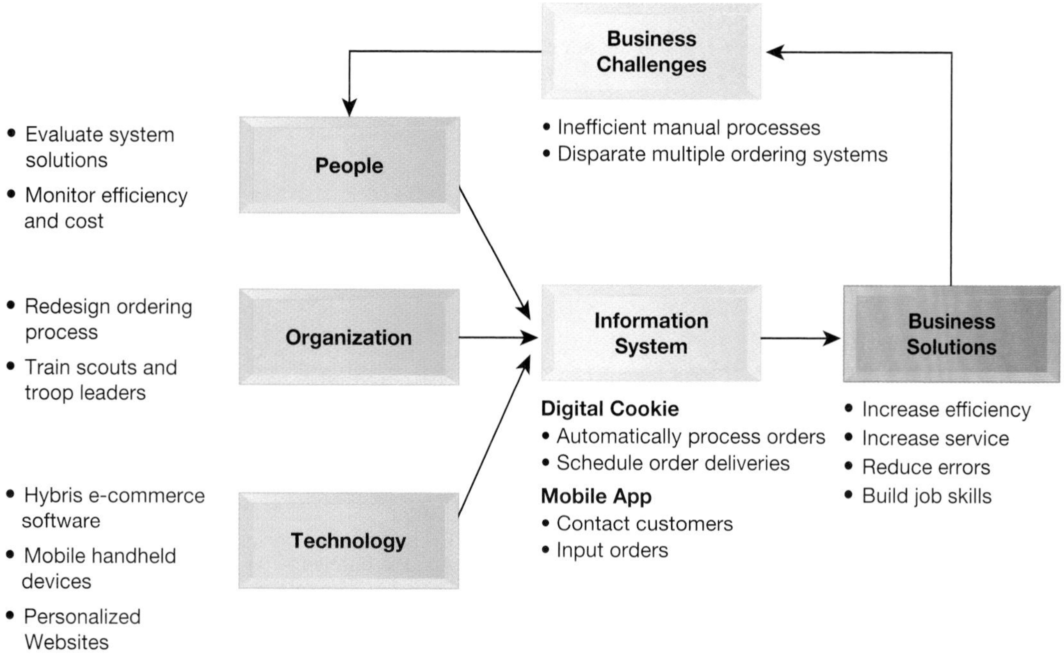

that the business is not performing as well as expected, or it may come from the realization that the organization should take advantage of new opportunities to perform more effectively.

Let's apply this problem-solving process to system building. Figure 12.1 illustrates the four steps we would need to take: (1) define and understand the problem, (2) develop alternative solutions, (3) choose the best solution, and (4) implement the solution.

Before a problem can be solved, first it must be properly defined. Members of the organization must agree that a problem actually exists and that it is serious. The problem must be investigated so that it can be better understood. Next comes a period of devising alternative solutions, then one of evaluating each alternative and selecting the best solution. The final stage is one of implementing the solution, in which a detailed design for the solution is specified, translated into a physical system, tested, introduced to the organization, and further refined as it is used over time.

In the information systems world, we have a special name for these activities. Figure 12.1 shows that the first three problem-solving steps, when we identify the problem, gather information, devise alternative solutions, and make a decision about the best solution, are called **systems analysis**.

DEFINING AND UNDERSTANDING THE PROBLEM

Defining the problem may take some work because various members of the company may have different ideas about the nature of the problem and its severity. What caused the problem? Why is it still around? Why wasn't it solved long ago? Systems analysts typically gather facts about existing systems and problems by examining documents, work papers, procedures, and system operations and by interviewing key users of the system.

Information systems problems in the business world typically result from a combination of people, organization, and technology factors. When identifying a key issue or problem, ask what kind of problem it is: Is it a people problem, an organizational problem, a technology problem, or a combination of these? What people, organizational, and technological factors contributed to the problem?

Once the problem has been defined and analyzed, it is possible to make some decisions about what should and can be done. What are the objectives of a solution

Figure 12.1
Developing an Information System Solution
Developing an information system solution is based on the problem-solving process.

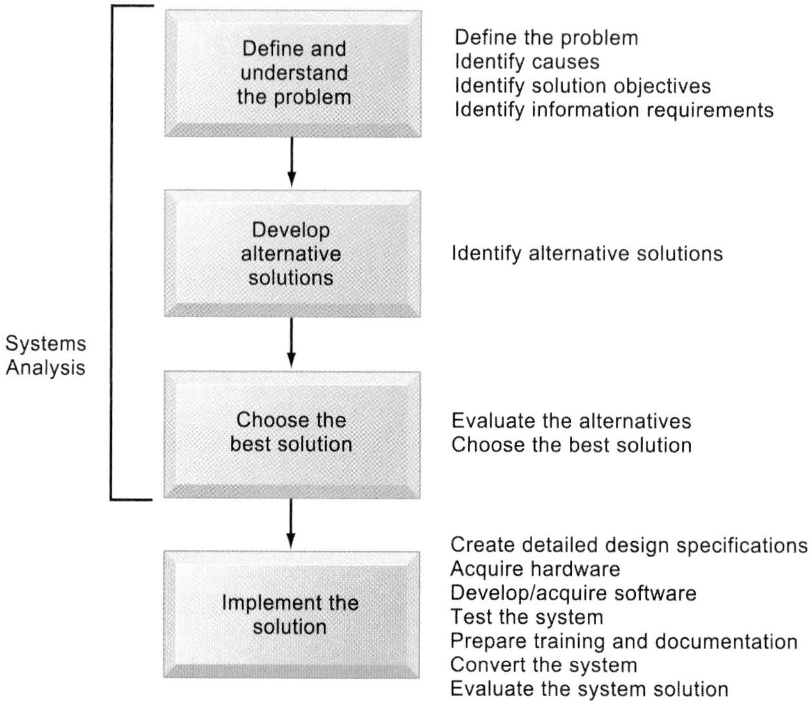

to the problem? Is the firm's objective to reduce costs, increase sales, or improve relationships with customers, suppliers, or employees? Do managers have sufficient information for decision making? What information is required to achieve these objectives?

At the most basic level, the **information requirements** of a new system identify who needs what information, where, when, and how. Requirements analysis carefully defines the objectives of the new or modified system and develops a detailed description of the functions that the new system must perform. A system designed around the wrong set of requirements will either have to be discarded because of poor performance or will need to undergo major modifications. Section 12-2 describes alternative approaches to eliciting requirements that help minimize this problem.

Let's return to our opening case about the Girl Scouts. The problem here is that the traditional ordering process for Girl Scout cookies has been heavily manual and time-consuming. Cookie ordering is extremely inefficient with high error rates and volunteers spending excessive time organizing orders and deliveries. Customers must pay in cash and wait weeks or months to receive their orders. This process is ripe for improvement with information technology. Tools for creating personalized e-commerce sales platforms on mobile devices and the web are readily available.

Organizationally, the Girl Scouts is a nationwide volunteer organization using cookie sales as the primary source of revenue. The Girl Scout cookie-ordering process requires many steps and coordination of multiple groups—individual Girl Scouts, volunteers, the council office, the cookie manufacturing factory, and delivery companies. The Girl Scout organization is also somewhat decentralized, with regional councils retaining the profits from cookie sales and deciding how to use them. Regional councils also have the power to decide whether to use automated tools.

The objectives of a solution for the Girl Scouts would be to reduce the amount of time, effort, and errors in the cookie-ordering process while providing an easier way to order cookies. Developing young women's leadership and business skills remains a high priority with the Girl Scouts, so the solution should ensure that scouts can still interact with customers and remain the primary sales channel for Girl Scout cookies.

Information requirements for the solution include the ability to take orders instantly and total and organize order transactions rapidly for transmittal to ABC Bakers or Little Brownie Bakers; the ability to track orders by type of cookie, troop, and individual Girl Scout; and the ability to schedule direct cookie deliveries to customers or bulk deliveries to individual Girl Scouts.

DEVELOPING ALTERNATIVE SOLUTIONS

What alternative solutions are possible for achieving these objectives and meeting these information requirements? The systems analysis lays out the most likely paths to follow given the nature of the problem. Some possible solutions do not require an information system solution but instead call for an adjustment in management, additional training, or refinement of existing organizational procedures. Some, however, do require modifications of the firm's existing information systems or an entirely new information system.

EVALUATING AND CHOOSING SOLUTIONS

The systems analysis includes a **feasibility study** to determine whether each proposed solution is feasible, or achievable, from financial, technical, and organizational standpoints. The feasibility study establishes whether each alternative solution is a good investment, whether the technology needed for the system is available and can be handled by the firm's information systems staff, and whether the organization is capable of accommodating the changes the system introduces.

A written systems proposal report describes the costs and benefits and advantages and disadvantages of each alternative solution. Which solution is best in a financial sense? Which works best for the organization? The systems analysis will detail the costs and benefits of each alternative and the changes that the organization will have to make to use the solution effectively. We provide a detailed discussion of how to determine the business value of systems and manage change in the following section. On the basis of this report, management will select what it believes is the best solution for the company.

The Girl Scouts had three alternative solutions. One was to maintain the status quo, a mixture of manual processes and multiple computerized order management systems that regional Girl Scout councils and licensed Girl Scout cookie baking companies used. The Girl Scouts of the USA did not favor this alternative because it was an uneven one. Some Girl Scout regional councils had their own automated ordering systems or access to the ABC and Little Brownies order management systems. Others were tied to the old manual processes. Girl Scout leadership worried that girls and their families versed in information technology would have an unfair advantage over those without such knowledge. The Girl Scouts wanted and needed a solution that was more uniform and capable of levelling the playing field.

A second alternative was to create a single standard digital system for ordering Girl Scout cookies online that would bypass individual Girl Scouts. Customers would be able to order Girl Scout cookies on their own online much as they would place a book order on Amazon.com. The Girl Scout leadership rejected this solution because it ran counter to the mission and goals of the organization, which were to develop members' leadership and interpersonal skills and to nurture the essential 5 Skills of goal setting, decision making, money management, people skills, and business ethics. Allowing customers to order cookies on their own would prevent the scouts from acquiring the valuable business and managerial skills that were among the main reasons for the organization's existence.

The third alternative was to develop a standard digital cookie ordering system for use nationwide that automates cookie ordering but still relies on individual Girl Scouts as the principal sales channel. Cookie customers would still have to place their orders with an individual Girl Scout or troop—they could not order online on their own. Nevertheless, they could take advantage of new online capabilities for locating cookie sellers, selecting cookies, paying by credit card, and arranging for cookie shipment directly to their homes. Use of the Digital Cookie system would be voluntary because some families and regional councils lacking access to computers or mobile devices would want to use the old manual order-taking system. This last alternative was the most feasible for the Girl Scouts.

IMPLEMENTING THE SOLUTION

The first step in implementing a system solution is to create detailed design specifications. **Systems design** shows how the chosen solution should be realized. The system design is the model or blueprint for an information system solution and consists of all the specifications that will deliver the functions identified during systems analysis. These specifications should address all the technical, organizational, and people components of the system solution.

Table 12.1 shows some of the design specifications for the Girl Scouts' new Digital Cookie system, which were based on information requirements for the solution that was selected. These design specifications apply to both the web and mobile app platforms.

TABLE 12.1

Design Specifications for the Digital Cookie System

Output	Online reports Hard-copy reports (web version) Online queries Order transactions for baking companies
Input	Order data entry screens Girl Scout data entry screen
Database	Database with cookie order file, Girl Scout file, troop file, regional council file, customer file
Processing	Calculate order totals by type of cookie and number of boxes Transmit orders to baking companies Track orders by customer Track orders by troop and individual Girl Scout Schedule deliveries or pickups Update Girl Scout and customer data for address changes
Manual procedures	Girl Scouts contact customers by phone, email, door-to-door, cookie sales booths Girl Scouts deliver cookies to customers requesting this option
Security and controls	Online passwords Only authorized Girl Scouts and troops can access Digital Cookie Parent must sign off on individual Girl Scout's site before it goes live Girl Scout's site can only list the scout's first name
Conversion	Input Girl Scout and troop data Input customer data Input bakery data Test system
Training and documentation	System guide for users Online practice demonstration Online training sessions and tutorials

Completing Implementation

In the final steps of implementing a system solution, the following activities would be performed:

- *Hardware selection and acquisition.* System builders select appropriate hardware for the application. They would either purchase the necessary computers and networking hardware or lease them from a technology provider.
- *Software development and programming.* Software is custom programmed in-house or purchased from an external source such as an outsourcing vendor, an application software package vendor, or an online software service provider. Individual Girl Scouts can use their own computers and mobile devices. The core ordering system and databases are maintained on remote servers accessed through the Internet. These servers are in private data centers, which may be hosted for the Girl Scouts or maintained by their own IT department. Consultants from Accenture and Hybris helped the Girl Scouts develop the software for the system and Web site, most likely using Hybris e-commerce software tools.
- *Testing.* The system is thoroughly tested to ensure that it produces the right results. The **testing process** requires detailed testing of individual computer programs, called **unit testing** as well as **system testing**, which tests the performance of the information system as a whole. **Acceptance testing** provides the final certification that the system is ready to be used in a production setting. Information systems tests are evaluated by users and reviewed by management. When all parties are satisfied that the new system meets their standards, the system is formally accepted for installation.

The systems development team works with users to devise a systematic test plan. The **test plan** includes all the preparations for the series of tests we have just described. Figure 12.2 shows a sample from a test plan that might have been used for the Girl Scout cookie system. The condition being tested is online access of the system by an authorized user.

Test Case Number: GS02-010

Prepared by: A. Patterson | **Date:** February 19, 2018

Objective: This subtest checks for an authorized user accessing the system.

Platform: Android

Procedure Description:
Select Sign In
Select Username
Enter Username
Select Password
Enter Password
Select Submit

Expected Result:
When user selects Sign In, the Sign In menu appears
When user selects User Name, the cursor moves to the User Name field
When user enters that person's system user name the user name appears on the screen
When user selects Password, the cursor moves to the Password field.
When user enters that person's password, the password appears on the screen as asterisks
When user selects Submit, the system verifies the entered data and allows the user to access the system
When user enters an incorrect (or unauthorized) username or password, the error message "Wrong User Name or Password" appears

Test Results:
All OK

Figure 12.2
A Sample Test Plan for the Girl Scout Digital Cookie System
When developing a test plan, it is imperative to include the various conditions to be tested, the requirements for each condition tested, and the expected results. Test plans require input from both end users and information systems specialists. Illustrated here is a test case for accessing the mobile Android app by an authorized Girl Scout user.

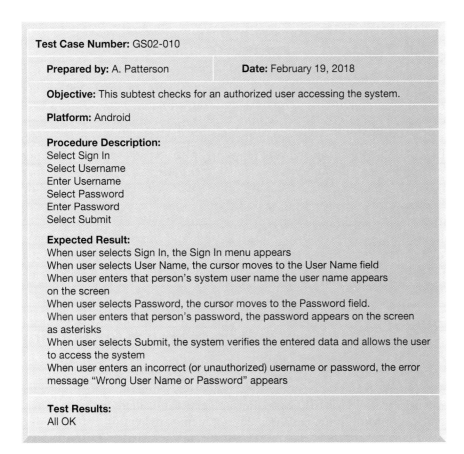

- *Training and documentation.* End users and information system specialists require training so that they will be able to use the new system. Detailed **documentation** showing how the system works from both a technical and end-user standpoint must be prepared.

The Digital Cookie System features hardcopy training manuals and online tutorials to help Girl Scouts and their leaders learn how to use the system.

- *Conversion* is the process of changing from the old to the new system. There are four main conversion strategies: the parallel strategy, the direct cutover strategy, the pilot study strategy, and the phased approach strategy.

In a **parallel strategy**, both the old system and its potential replacement are run together for a time until everyone is assured that the new one functions correctly. The old system remains available as a backup in case of problems. The **direct cutover strategy** replaces the old system entirely with the new system on an appointed day, carrying the risk that there is no system to fall back on if problems arise. The **pilot study** strategy introduces a new system to only a limited area of the organization, such as a single department or operating unit. Once this pilot version is working smoothly, it is installed throughout the rest of the organization. A **phased approach** introduces the system in stages (such as first introducing the modules for ordering Girl Scout cookies and then introducing the modules for transmitting orders and instructions to the cookie factory and shipper).

- *Production and maintenance.* After the new system is installed and conversion is complete, the system is said to be in **production**. During this stage, users and technical specialists review the solution to determine how well it has met its original objectives and to decide whether any revisions or modifications are in order. Changes in hardware, software, documentation, or procedures to a production system to correct errors, meet new requirements, or improve processing efficiency are termed **maintenance**.

The Girl Scouts continue to refine their Digital Cookie system. Future versions of Digital Cookie will see improvements in the user interface and user experience for both scouts and customers.

Managing the Change

Developing a new information systems solution is not merely a matter of installing hardware and software. The business must also deal with the organizational changes that the new solution will bring about—new information, new business processes, and perhaps new reporting relationships and decision-making power. A very well-designed solution may not work unless it is introduced to the organization very carefully. The process of planning change in an organization so that it is implemented in an orderly and effective manner is so critical to the success or failure of information system solutions that we devote Section 12-4 to a detailed discussion of this topic.

To manage the transition from the old system to the new Digital Cookie system, the Girl Scouts would have to inform troop leaders and volunteers about changes in cookie-ordering procedures, provide training, and provide resources for answering any questions that arose as scouts, parents, and administrators started using the system. They would need to work with ABC Bakers, Little Brownie Bakers, and their shippers on new procedures for transmitting and delivering orders.

12-2 What are the alternative methods for building information systems?

There are alternative methods for building systems by using the basic problem-solving model we have just described. These alternative methods include the traditional systems life cycle, prototyping, end-user development, application software packages, and outsourcing.

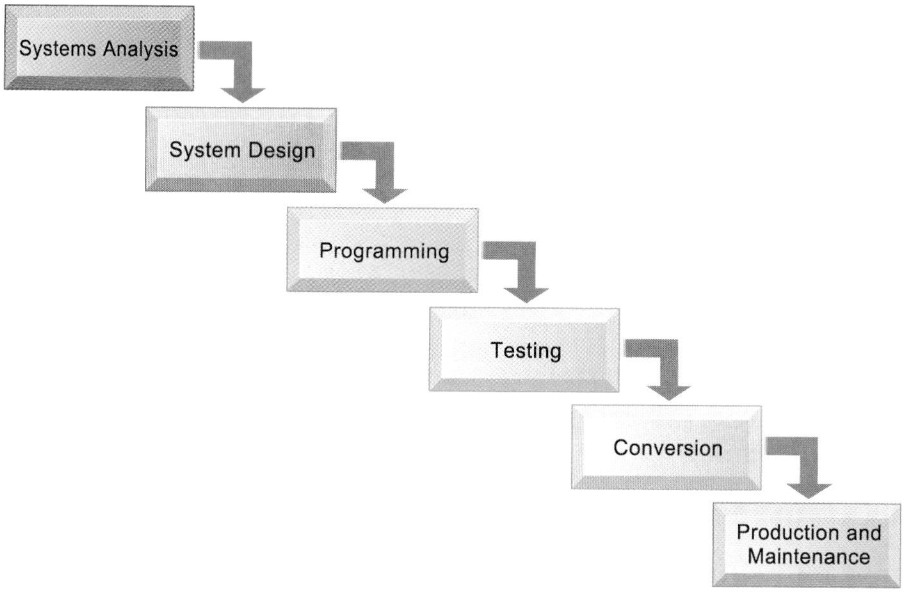

Figure 12.3
The Traditional Systems Development Life Cycle
The systems development life cycle partitions systems development into formal stages, with each stage requiring completion before the next stage can begin.

TRADITIONAL SYSTEMS DEVELOPMENT LIFE CYCLE

The **systems development life cycle (SDLC)** is the oldest method for building information systems. The life cycle methodology is a phased approach to building a system, dividing systems development into a series of formal stages, as illustrated in Figure 12.3. Although systems builders can go back and forth among stages in the life cycle, the systems life cycle is predominantly a waterfall approach in which tasks in one stage are completed before work for the next stage begins.

This approach maintains a very formal division of labor between end users and information systems specialists. Technical specialists, such as system analysts and programmers, are responsible for much of the systems analysis, design, and implementation work; end users are limited to providing information requirements and reviewing the technical staff's work. The life cycle also emphasizes formal specifications and paperwork, so many documents are generated during the course of a systems project.

The systems life cycle is still used for building large, complex systems that require rigorous and formal requirements analysis, predefined specifications, and tight controls over the systems-building process. However, this approach is also time-consuming and expensive to use. Tasks in one stage are supposed to be completed before work for the next stage begins. Activities can be repeated, but volumes of new documents must be generated and steps retraced if requirements and specifications need to be revised. This encourages freezing of specifications relatively early in the development process. The life cycle approach is also not suitable for many small desktop systems and apps, which tend to be less structured and more individualized.

PROTOTYPING

Prototyping consists of building an experimental system rapidly and inexpensively for end users to evaluate. The prototype is a working version of an information system or part of the system, but it is intended as only a preliminary model. Users interact with the prototype to get a better idea of their information requirements, refining the prototype multiple times. When the design is finalized, the prototype will be converted to a polished production system. Figure 12.4 shows a four-step model of the prototyping process.

Step 1: *Identify the user's basic requirements.* The system designer (usually an information systems specialist) works with the user only long enough to capture the user's basic information needs.

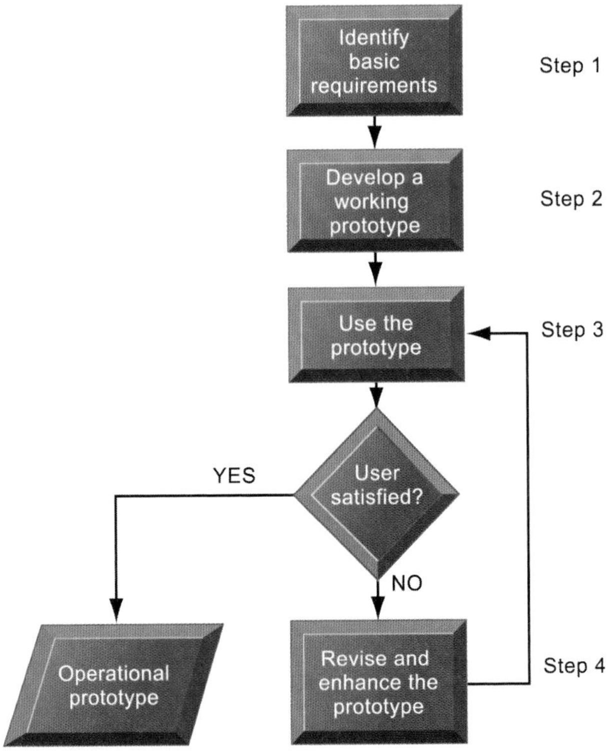

Figure 12.4
The Prototyping Process
The process of developing a prototype consists of four steps. Because a prototype can be developed quickly and inexpensively, systems builders can go through several iterations, repeating steps 3 and 4, to refine and enhance the prototype before arriving at the final operational one.

Step 2: *Develop an initial prototype.* The system designer creates a working prototype quickly, using tools for rapidly generating software.

Step 3: *Use the prototype.* The user is encouraged to work with the system to determine whether the prototype meets his or her needs and to suggest improvements for the prototype.

Step 4: *Revise and enhance the prototype.* The system builder notes all changes the user requests and refines the prototype accordingly. After the prototype has been revised, the cycle returns to step 3. Steps 3 and 4 are repeated until the user is satisfied.

Prototyping is especially useful in designing an information system's user interface. Because prototyping encourages intense end-user involvement throughout the systems development process, it is more likely to produce systems that fulfill user requirements.

However, rapid prototyping may gloss over essential steps in systems development, such as thorough testing and documentation. If the completed prototype works reasonably well, management may not see the need to build a polished production system. Some hastily constructed systems do not easily accommodate large quantities of data or a large number of users in a production environment.

END-USER DEVELOPMENT

End-user development allows end users, with little or no formal assistance from technical specialists, to create simple information systems, reducing the time and steps required to produce a finished application. Using user-friendly query, reporting, website development, graphics, and PC software tools, end users can access data, create reports, and develop simple applications on their own with little or no help from professional systems analysts or programmers. For example, Yellow Pages (YP), a digital media and marketing solutions company serving 260,000 small and medium-sized Canadian businesses, used Information Builders WebFOCUS to build a user-friendly analytics application that helps customers measure return on their advertising dollars and track the success of their campaigns. Users can customize the outputs they want (Information Builders, 2015).

On the whole, end-user-developed systems are completed more rapidly than those developed with conventional programming tools. Allowing users to specify their own business needs improves requirements gathering and often leads to a higher level of user involvement and satisfaction with the system. However, end-user development tools still cannot replace conventional tools for some business applications because they cannot easily handle the processing of large numbers of transactions or applications with extensive procedural logic and updating requirements.

End-user development also poses organizational risks because systems are created rapidly, without a formal development methodology, testing, and documentation. To help organizations maximize the benefits of end-user applications development, management should require cost justification of end-user information system projects and establish hardware, software, and quality standards for user-developed applications.

APPLICATION SOFTWARE PACKAGES, SOFTWARE SERVICES, AND OUTSOURCING

Chapter 5 points out that much of today's software underlying contemporary information systems is not developed in-house but is purchased from external sources. Firms can rent the software from an online software service provider, purchase a software package from a commercial vendor to run in-house, or have an in-house application developed by an external outsourcing firm. The Girl Scouts outsourced software development for the Digital Cookie System to Accenture and Hybris. Selection of the software or software service is often based on a **Request for Proposal (RFP)**, which is a detailed list of questions submitted to external vendors to see how well they meet the requirements for the proposed system.

Application Software Packages and Cloud Software Services

Systems are increasingly based on commercially available application software packages or cloud software as a service (SaaS). For example, companies can choose to implement Oracle enterprise resource planning, supply chain management, or human capital management software in-house or pay to use this software running on the Oracle Cloud platform. Microsoft Office desktop productivity software comes in both desktop and cloud (Office 365) versions.

If a cloud software service or software package can fulfill most of an organization's requirements, the company does not have to write its own software. The company saves time and money by using the prewritten, predesigned, pretested software programs from the package and SaaS vendors, who also provide ongoing maintenance and upgrades for the system. Many packages include capabilities for customization to meet unique requirements not addressed by the prewritten software. **Customization** features allow prewritten software to be modified to meet an organization's unique requirements without destroying the integrity of the software. However, if extensive customization is required, additional programming and customization work may become so expensive and time-consuming that it negates many of the advantages of software packages or services. If the software cannot be customized, the organization will have to adapt by changing its procedures.

Outsourcing

If a firm does not want to use its internal resources to build or operate information systems, it can outsource the work to an external organization that specializes in providing these services. The outsourcing vendor might be domestic or in another country. Domestic outsourcing is driven primarily by the fact that outsourcing firms possess skills, resources, and assets that their clients do not have. Installing a new supply chain management system in a very large company might require hiring an additional 30 to 50 people with specific expertise in supply chain management software. Rather than hire permanent new employees and then release them after the new system is built, it makes more sense, and is often less expensive, to outsource this work for a 12-month period.

In the case of offshore outsourcing, the decision tends to be driven by cost. A skilled programmer in India or Russia earns about U.S. $10,000 to $20,000 per year, compared to $60,000 or more per year for a comparable programmer in the United States. The Internet and low-cost communications technology have drastically reduced the expense and difficulty of coordinating the work of global teams in faraway locations. In addition to cost savings, many offshore outsourcing firms offer world-class technology assets and skills. For example, leading companies such as Hilton, NBC, Fox News, and Yahoo have outsourced website design and development work to India-based Profit By Outsourcing, which provides expertise in areas such as custom programmed content management, e-commerce solutions, mobile application development, and application development using Java and other tools that are not available internally in most companies. However, wage inflation outside the United States has eroded some of these advantages, and some jobs have moved back to the United States.

Your firm is most likely to benefit from outsourcing if it takes the time to evaluate all the risks and make sure outsourcing is appropriate for its particular needs. Any company that outsources its applications must thoroughly understand the project, including its requirements, method of implementation, source of expected benefits, cost components, and metrics for measuring performance.

Many firms underestimate costs for identifying and evaluating vendors of information technology services, for transitioning to a new vendor, for improving internal software development methods to match those of outsourcing vendors, and for monitoring vendors to make sure they are fulfilling their contractual obligations. Outsourcing offshore incurs additional costs for coping with cultural differences that drain productivity and dealing with human resources issues, such as terminating or relocating domestic employees. These hidden costs undercut some of the anticipated benefits from outsourcing. Firms should be especially cautious when using an outsourcer to develop or operate applications that give some type of competitive advantage.

Figure 12.5 shows best- and worst-case scenarios for the total cost of an offshore outsourcing project. It shows how much hidden costs affect the total project cost. The best case reflects the lowest estimates for additional costs, and the worst case reflects

Figure 12.5
Total Cost of Offshore Outsourcing
If a firm spends $10 million on offshore outsourcing contracts, that company will actually spend 15.2 percent in extra costs even in the best-case scenario. In the worst-case scenario, when there is a dramatic drop in productivity along with exceptionally high transition and layoff costs, a firm can expect to pay up to 57 percent in extra costs on top of the $10 million outlay for an offshore contract.

TOTAL COST OF OFFSHORE OUTSOURCING

Cost of outsourcing contract			**$10,000,000**	
Hidden Costs	Best Case	Additional Cost ($)	Worst Case	Additional Cost ($)
1. Vendor selection	0.2%	20,000	2%	200,000
2. Transition costs	2%	200,000	3%	300,000
3. Layoffs & retention	3%	300,000	5%	500,000
4. Lost productivity/cultural issues	3%	300,000	27%	2,700,000
5. Improving development processes	1%	100,000	10%	1,000,000
6. Managing the contract	6%	600,000	10%	1,000,000
Total additional costs		**1,520,000**		**5,700,000**
	Outstanding Contract ($)	Additional Cost ($)	Total Cost ($)	Additional Cost
Total cost of outsourcing (TCO) best case	10,000,000	1,520,000	11,520,000	15.2%
Total cost of outsourcing (TCO) worst case	10,000,000	5,700,000	15,700,000	57.0%

the highest estimates for these costs. As you can see, hidden costs increase the total cost of an offshore outsourcing project by an extra 15 to 57 percent. Even with these extra costs, many firms will benefit from offshore outsourcing if they manage the work well.

MOBILE APPLICATION DEVELOPMENT: DESIGNING FOR A MULTI-SCREEN WORLD

Today, employees and customers expect, and even demand, to be able to use a mobile device of their choice to obtain information or perform a transaction anywhere and at any time. To meet these needs, companies will need to develop mobile websites, mobile apps, and native apps as well as traditional information systems.

Once an organization decides to develop mobile apps, it has to make some important choices, including the technology it will use to implement these apps (whether to write software for a native app or mobile web app) and what to do about a mobile website. A **mobile website** is a version of a regular website that is scaled down in content and navigation for easy access and search on a small mobile screen. (Access Amazon's website from your computer and then from your smartphone to see the difference from a regular website.)

A **mobile web app** is an Internet-enabled app with specific functionality for mobile devices. Users access mobile web apps through their mobile device's web browser. The web app resides primarily on a server, is accessed through the Internet, and doesn't need to be installed on the device. The same application can be used by most devices that can surf the web, regardless of their brand.

A **native app** is a stand-alone application designed to run on a specific platform and device. The native app is installed directly on a mobile device. Native apps can connect to the Internet to download and upload data, and they can operate on these data even when not connected to the Internet. For example, an e-book reading app such as Kindle software can download a book from the Internet, disconnect from the Internet, and present the book for reading. Native mobile apps provide fast performance and a high degree of reliability. They can also take advantage of a mobile device's particular capabilities, such as its camera or touch features. However, native apps are expensive to develop because multiple versions of an app must be programmed for different mobile operating systems and hardware.

Developing applications for mobile platforms is quite different from development for PCs and their much larger screens. The reduced size of mobile devices makes using fingers and multi-touch gestures much easier than typing and using keyboards. Mobile apps need to be optimized for the specific tasks they are to perform. They should not try to carry out too many tasks, and they should be designed for usability. The user experience for mobile interaction is fundamentally different from using a desktop or laptop PC. Saving resources—bandwidth, screen space, memory, processing, data entry, and user gestures—is a top priority.

When a full website created for the desktop shrinks to the size of a smartphone screen, it is difficult for the user to navigate through the site. The user must continually zoom in and out and scroll to find relevant material. Therefore, companies need to design websites specifically for mobile interfaces and create multiple mobile sites to meet the needs of smartphones, tablets, and desktop browsers. This equates to at least three sites with separate content, maintenance, and costs. Currently, websites know what device you are using because your browser will send this information to the server when you log on. Based on this information, the server will deliver the appropriate screen.

One solution to the problem of having multiple websites is to use **responsive web design**. Responsive web design enables websites to change layouts automatically according to the visitor's screen resolution, whether on a desktop, laptop, tablet, or

Developing Mobile Apps: What's Different

Just about all businesses today want to deploy mobile apps. Studies show that mobile consumers look at their phones an average of 1,500 times each week and spend 177 minutes on their phone per day. With every swipe, tap, and zoom, customers are coming to expect the same experience in all their dealings with businesses, as are employees using mobile apps for internal corporate use. Businesses today know they must respond, and they want mobile apps developed in a very short time frame. That's not so easy.

Developing successful mobile apps poses some unique challenges. The user experience on a mobile device is fundamentally different from that on a PC. There are special features on mobile devices such as location-based services that give firms the potential to interact with customers in meaningful new ways. Firms need to be able to take advantage of those features while delivering an experience that is appropriate to a small screen. There are multiple mobile platforms to work with, including iOS, Android, and Windows 10, and a firm may need a different version of an application to run on each of these. System builders need to understand how, why, and where customers use mobile devices and how these mobile experiences change business interactions and behavior. You can't just port a website or desktop application to a smartphone or tablet. It's a different systems development process.

Let's look at mobile application development at Great-West Financial, the second-largest retirement services company in the United States with approximately 467,000 individual accounts and 8 million retirement plan participants under its administration. Company employees spend more time serving customers in the field than in the office and needed a connection to the company's ERP Financials system from wherever they were working to process accounts payable invoice approvals. Great-West decided to deploy the Dolphin Mobile Approvals app for this purpose.

Great-West selected Dolphin because it could handle all of its SAP workflows in a single app, so that employees did not have to go to one place to approve invoices and another to approve everything else. Great-West configured the app to make it look and feel as similar as possible to the application users accessed on their desktops. The user sees the same data fields on the invoice header and line item on a mobile device as on a desktop computer screen, and the steps in the invoice approval process are the same. However, given the difficulty of jumping back and forth between different screens on a mobile device, the mobile app incorporates the necessary invoice approval codes into its line-item detail rather than displaying these codes on a PDF attachment. On a desktop, users must sign into the SAP system in order to see an invoice and will receive notification that an invoice is available for approval via email. A pop-up notification on the mobile app eliminates the need for users to log into the app before knowing about an invoice

Before deploying the mobile app, Great-West had to set up an appropriate mobile infrastructure, considering factors such as security, sign-on, and back-end integration. Since this was the company's first mobile app interfacing to the SAP system, the company had to make sure the mobile app could incorporate the entire workflow from the SAP system and that all the data were encrypted and secure, Great-West purchased 1,000 licenses for the mobile approvals app (which is compatible with both iOS and Android devices) and issued company-owned devices to senior executives and the heaviest invoice users. Remaining users are allowed to use the app on their own devices as long as they conform to the firm's BYOD policy.

Mobile apps should not be built for the sake of going mobile but for genuinely helping the company become more successful. The mobile app must be connected in a meaningful way to the systems that power the business. Chicago-based TTX, which provides rail cars and freight rail management services to the railroad industry, found that the most critical aspect of its mobile application development project was having a firm idea of what it was trying to accomplish with the app. In 2014 the company developed a mobile app to improve billing accuracy and boost the productivity of its maintenance crews in its 50 maintenance shops that operate along the railroads. The app took about six months to design and build in-house.

The purpose of the app was to improve recordkeeping involved in TTX's maintenance work, which takes place in rough outdoor conditions where connectivity is spotty or nonexistent and is performed by employees who often wear gloves. Maintenance crews had used paper and pencil to record their notes on the rail car repairs. The mobile application was based on a

Windows platform for a plastic-encased PC with a touchscreen. TTX CIO and Vice President Bruce Schinelli and his systems development team recognized that what the app needed to do was replace pen and paper, and it had to work that well in the field. That early understanding of how the mobile app would provide value to the business drove the entire system design and implementation. Schinelli believes that if a company makes the wrong assumptions about the purpose of its mobile application, it will have to do a lot of rework. For TTX, the hard work was making sure its system builders knew exactly how the mobile app would work out in the field.

Sources: Mary K. Pratt and Linda Tucci, "Enterprise Mobile App Development: No Easy Answers," searchCIO.com, accessed April 14, 2017; Ken Murphy, "Great-West Financial Establishes Its Mobile Footprint," *SAP Insider Profiles*, October 31, 2016; David Smud, David Day, Paul Moceri, Shamou Maayr, and Sungkey Paik, "7 Principles for Appealing Mobile Apps," *Wall Street Journal*, April 11, 2017; and Brian Solis, "Mobile Is Eating the World," Sitecore Corporation, February 2016.

CASE STUDY QUESTIONS

1. What people, organization, and technology issues need to be addressed when building a mobile application?
2. How does user requirement definition for mobile applications differ from traditional systems analysis?
3. Describe how Great-West's invoice approval process changed after the mobile application was deployed.

smartphone. Responsive design uses tools such as flexible grid-based layouts, flexible images, and media queries to optimize the design for different viewing contexts. This eliminates the need for separate design and development work for each new device. HTML5, which we introduced in Chapter 5, is also used for mobile application development because it can support cross-platform mobile applications.

The Interactive Session on Technology describes how some companies have addressed the challenges of mobile development we have just identified.

RAPID APPLICATION DEVELOPMENT FOR E-BUSINESS

Technologies and business conditions are changing so rapidly that companies are adopting shorter, more informal development processes for many of their e-commerce and e-business applications. The term **rapid application development (RAD)** refers to the process of creating workable systems in a very short period of time. RAD includes the use of visual programming and other tools for building graphical user interfaces, iterative prototyping of key system elements, the automation of program code generation, and close teamwork among end users and information systems specialists. Simple systems often can be assembled from prebuilt components (see Section 12-3). The process does not have to be sequential, and key parts of development can occur simultaneously.

Sometimes a technique called **joint application design (JAD)** will be used to accelerate the generation of information requirements and to develop the initial systems design. JAD brings end users and information systems specialists together in an interactive session to discuss the system's design. Properly prepared and facilitated, JAD sessions can significantly speed up the design phase and involve users at an intense level.

Agile development focuses on rapid development and frequent delivery of working software, with continual user involvement. It breaks down a large project into a series of small subprojects that are completed in short periods of time using iteration and continuous feedback. Improvement or addition of new functionality takes place within the next iteration as developers clarify requirements.

DevOps is an organizational strategy to create a culture and environment that further promote rapid and agile development practices. *DevOps* stands for "development and operations" and emphasizes closer and more frequent communication and collaboration among the software developers who create applications and the IT operational staff who run and maintain the applications so teams can jointly build, test, release, and maintain new digital applications more frequently and more efficiently. With this type of organizational change along with agile techniques, standardized processes, and more powerful automated software creation and testing tools, it is possible to release more reliable applications more rapidly and more frequently. For example, DevOps helps developers at Netflix make hundreds of software changes each day.

12-3 What are the principal methodologies for modeling and designing systems?

We have just described alternative methods for building systems. There are also alternative methodologies for modeling and designing systems. The two most prominent are structured methodologies and object-oriented development.

STRUCTURED METHODOLOGIES

Structured methodologies have been used to document, analyze, and design information systems since the 1970s. **Structured** refers to the fact that the techniques are step by step, with each step building on the previous one. Structured methodologies are top-down, progressing from the highest, most abstract level to the lowest level of detail—from the general to the specific.

Structured development methods are process-oriented, focusing primarily on modeling the processes, or actions, that capture, store, manipulate, and distribute data as the data flow through a system. These methods separate data from processes. A separate programming procedure must be written every time someone wants to take an action on a particular piece of data. The procedures act on data that the program passes to them.

The primary tool for representing a system's component processes and the flow of data between them is the **data flow diagram (DFD)**. The DFD offers a logical graphic model of information flow, partitioning a system into modules that show manageable levels of detail. It rigorously specifies the processes or transformations that occur within each module and the interfaces that exist between them.

Figure 12.6 shows a simple data flow diagram for a mail-in university course registration system. The rounded boxes represent processes, which portray the transformation of data. The square box represents an external entity, which is an originator or

Figure 12.6
Data Flow Diagram for Mail-in University Registration System
The system has three processes: Verify availability (1.0), Enroll student (2.0), and Confirm registration (3.0). The name and content of each of the data flows appear adjacent to each arrow. There is one external entity in this system: the student. There are two data stores: the student master file and the course file.

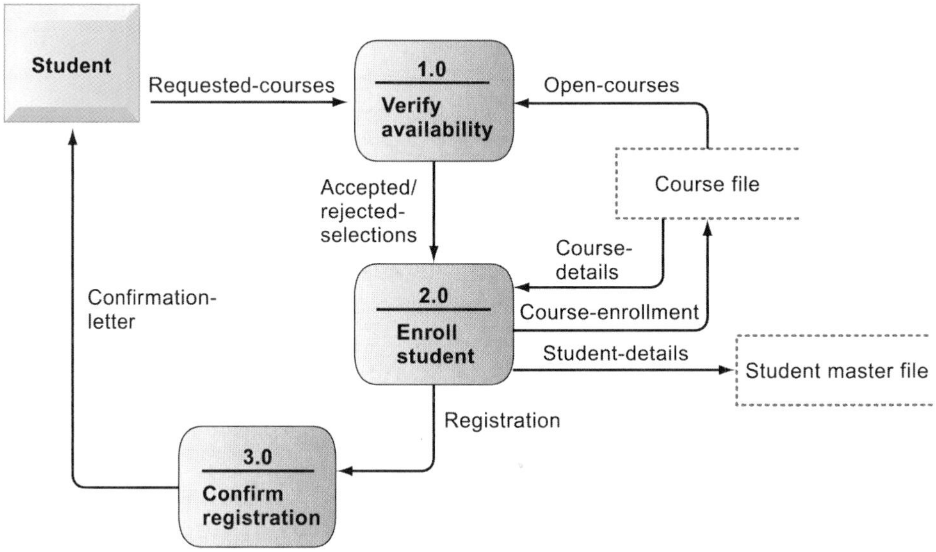

receiver of information located outside the boundaries of the system being modeled. The open rectangles represent data stores, which are either manual or automated inventories of data. The arrows represent data flows, which show the movement between processes, external entities, and data stores. They always contain packets of data with the name or content of each data flow listed beside the arrow.

This DFD shows that students submit registration forms with their names, identification numbers, and the numbers of the courses they wish to take. In Process 1.0, the system verifies that each course selected is still open by referencing the university's course file. The file distinguishes courses that are open from those that have been canceled or filled. Process 1.0 then determines which of the student's selections can be accepted or rejected. Process 2.0 enrolls the student in the courses for which he or she has been accepted. It updates the university's course file with the student's name and identification number and recalculates the class size. If maximum enrollment has been reached, the course number is flagged as closed. Process 2.0 also updates the university's student master file with information about new students or changes in address. Process 3.0 then sends each student applicant a confirmation-of-registration letter listing the courses for which he or she is registered and noting the course selections that could not be fulfilled.

Through leveled DFDs, a complex process can be broken down into successive levels of detail. An entire system can be divided into subsystems with a high-level data flow diagram. Each subsystem, in turn, can be divided into additional subsystems with lower-level DFDs, and the lower-level subsystems can be broken down again until the lowest level of detail has been reached. **Process specifications** describe the transformation occurring within the lowest level of the DFDs, showing the logic for each process.

In structured methodology, software design is modeled using hierarchical structure charts. The **structure chart** is a top-down chart, showing each level of design, its relationship to other levels, and its place in the overall design structure. The design first considers the main function of a program or system, then breaks this function into subfunctions, and decomposes each subfunction until the lowest level of detail has been reached. Figure 12.7 shows a high-level structure chart for a payroll system. If a design has too many levels to fit onto one structure chart, it can be broken down further on more detailed structure charts. A structure chart may document one program, one system (a set of programs), or part of one program.

OBJECT-ORIENTED DEVELOPMENT

Structured methods treat data and processes as logically separate entities, whereas in the real world such separation seems unnatural. **Object-oriented development** addresses these issues. Object-oriented development uses the object, which we introduced in Chapter 5, as the basic unit of systems analysis and design. An object

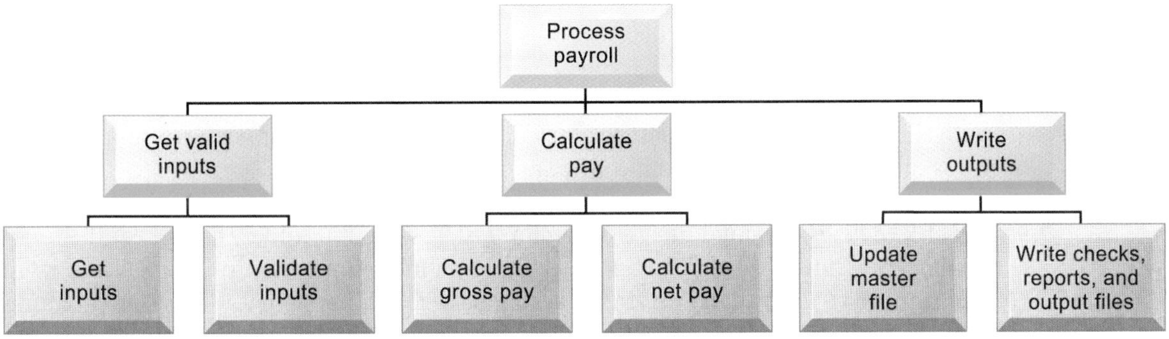

Figure 12.7
High-Level Structure Chart for a Payroll System
This structure chart shows the highest or most abstract level of design for a payroll system, providing an overview of the entire system.

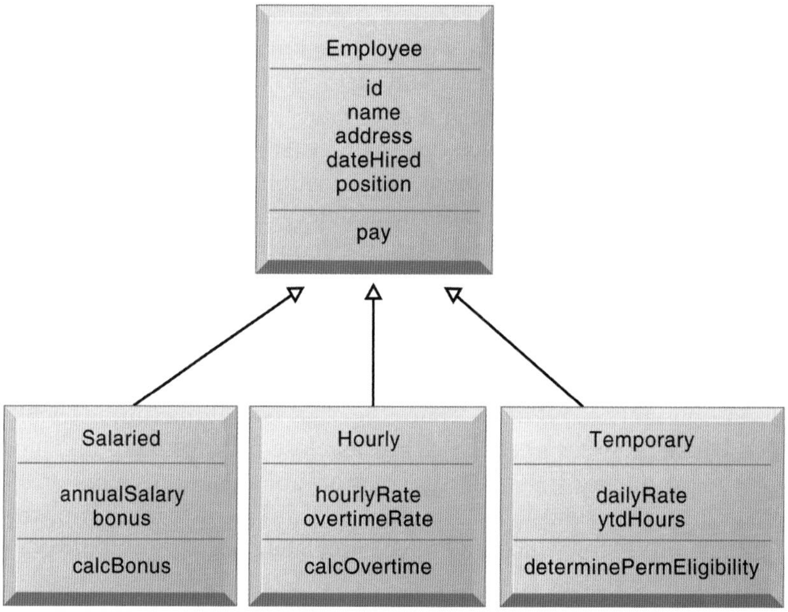

Figure 12.8
Class and Inheritance
This figure illustrates how classes inherit the common features of their superclass.

combines data and the specific processes that operate on those data. Data encapsulated in an object can be accessed and modified only by the operations, or methods, associated with that object. Instead of passing data to procedures, programs send a message for an object to perform an operation that is already embedded in it. The system is modeled as a collection of objects and the relationships among them. Because processing logic resides within objects rather than in separate software programs, objects must collaborate with each other to make the system work.

Object-oriented modeling is based on the concepts of *class* and *inheritance*. Objects belonging to a certain class, or general categories of similar objects, have the features of that class. Classes of objects in turn inherit all the structure and behaviors of a more general class and then add variables and behaviors unique to each object. New classes of objects are created by choosing an existing class and specifying how the new class differs from the existing class, instead of starting from scratch each time.

We can see how class and inheritance work in Figure 12.8, which illustrates the relationships among classes concerning employees and how they are paid. Employee is the common ancestor, or superclass, for the other three classes. Salaried, Hourly, and Temporary are subclasses of Employee. The class name is in the top compartment, the attributes for each class are in the middle portion of each box, and the list of operations is in the bottom portion of each box. The features that all employees share (ID, name, address, date hired, position, and pay) are stored in the Employee superclass, whereas each subclass stores features that are specific to that particular type of employee. Specific to Hourly employees, for example, are their hourly rates and overtime rates. A solid line from the subclass to the superclass is a generalization path showing that the subclasses Salaried, Hourly, and Temporary have common features that can be generalized into the superclass Employee.

Object-oriented development is more iterative and incremental than traditional structured development. During systems analysis, systems builders document the functional requirements of the system, specifying its most important properties and what the proposed system must do. Interactions between the system and its users are analyzed to identify objects, which include both data and processes. The object-oriented design phase describes how the objects will behave and how they will interact with one another. Similar objects are grouped to form a class, and classes are grouped into hierarchies in which a subclass inherits the attributes and methods from its superclass.

The information system is implemented by translating the design into program code, reusing classes that are already available in a library of reusable software objects and adding new ones created during the object-oriented design phase. Implementation may also involve the creation of an object-oriented database. The resulting system must be thoroughly tested and evaluated.

Because objects are reusable, object-oriented development could reduce the time and cost of writing software if organizations reuse software objects that have already been created as building blocks for other applications. New systems can be created by using some existing objects, changing others, and adding a few new objects.

Component-Based Development, Web Services, and Cloud-Based Development

To expedite software creation further, groups of objects have been assembled into software components for common functions, such as a graphical user interface or online ordering capability, and these components can be combined to create large-scale business applications. This approach to software development is called **component-based development**. Businesses are using component-based development to create their e-commerce applications by combining commercially available components for shopping carts, user authentication, search engines, and catalogs with pieces of software for their own unique business requirements.

Chapter 5 introduced web services as loosely coupled, reusable software components based on Extensible Markup Language (XML) and other open protocols and standards that enable one application to communicate with another with no custom programming required. In addition to supporting internal and external integration of systems, web services provide nonproprietary tools for building new information system applications or enhancing existing systems.

Platform as a service (PaaS), introduced in the Chapter 5 discussion of cloud computing, also holds considerable potential for helping system developers quickly write and test customer- or employee-facing applications. These online development environments come from a range of vendors, including Oracle, IBM, Salesforce.com (Force.com), and Microsoft (Azure). These platforms automate tasks such as setting up a newly composed application as a web service or linking to other applications and services. Some also offer a cloud infrastructure service, or links to cloud vendors such as Amazon, so that developers can launch what they build in a cloud infrastructure.

COMPUTER-AIDED SOFTWARE ENGINEERING (CASE)

Computer-aided software engineering (CASE)—sometimes called computer-aided systems engineering—provides software tools to automate the methodologies we have just described to reduce the amount of repetitive work in systems development. CASE tools provide automated graphics facilities for producing charts and diagrams, screen and report generators, data dictionaries, extensive reporting facilities, analysis and checking tools, code generators, and documentation generators. CASE tools also contain features for validating design diagrams and specifications.

CASE tools facilitate clear documentation and coordination of team development efforts. Team members can share their work by accessing each other's files to review or modify what has been done. Modest productivity benefits are achieved if the tools are used properly. Many CASE tools are PC based with powerful graphical capabilities.

12-4 How should information systems projects be selected and managed?

Your company might have developed what appears to be an excellent system solution. Yet when the system is in use, it does not work properly or it doesn't deliver the benefits that were promised. If this occurs, your firm is not alone. There is a very high failure rate among information systems projects because they have not been properly managed. A joint study by McKinsey and Oxford University found that large software projects on average run 66 percent over budget and 33 percent over schedule. Over 50 percent of businesses surveyed by cloud portfolio management provider Innotas in 2016 had experienced an IT project failure within the previous 12 months (Florentine, 2016). Firms may have incorrectly assessed the business value of the new system or were unable to manage the organizational change the new technology required. That's why it's essential to know how to manage information systems projects and the reasons they succeed or fail.

PROJECT MANAGEMENT OBJECTIVES

A **project** is a planned series of related activities for achieving a specific business objective. Information systems projects include the development of new information systems, enhancement of existing systems, or projects for replacing or upgrading the firm's information technology (IT) infrastructure.

Project management refers to the application of knowledge, skills, tools, and techniques to achieve specific targets within specified budget and time constraints. Project management activities include planning the work, assessing risk, estimating resources required to accomplish the work, organizing the work, acquiring human and material resources, assigning tasks, directing activities, controlling project execution, reporting progress, and analyzing the results. As in other areas of business, project management for information systems must deal with five major variables: scope, time, cost, quality, and risk.

Scope defines what work is or is not included in a project. For example, the scope of a project for a new order processing system might include new modules for inputting orders and transmitting them to production and accounting but not any changes to related accounts receivable, manufacturing, distribution, or inventory control systems. Project management defines all the work required to complete a project successfully and should ensure that the scope of a project does not expand beyond what was originally intended.

Time is the amount of time required to complete the project. Project management typically establishes the amount of time required to complete major components of a project. Each of these components is further broken down into activities and tasks. Project management tries to determine the time required to complete each task and establish a schedule for completing the work.

Cost is based on the time to complete a project multiplied by the daily cost of human resources required to complete the project. Information systems project costs also include the cost of hardware, software, and work space. Project management develops a budget for the project and monitors ongoing project expenses.

Quality is an indicator of how well the result of a project satisfies the objectives management specified. The quality of information systems projects usually boils down to improved organizational performance and decision making. Quality also considers the accuracy and timeliness of information the new system produces and ease of use.

Risk refers to potential problems that would threaten the success of a project. These potential problems might prevent a project from achieving its objectives by increasing time and cost, lowering the quality of project outputs, or preventing the project from being completed altogether. We discuss the most important risk factors for information systems projects later in this section.

SELECTING PROJECTS: MAKING THE BUSINESS CASE FOR A NEW SYSTEM

Companies typically are presented with many projects for solving problems and improving performance. There are far more ideas for systems projects than there are resources. You will need to select the projects that promise the greatest benefit to the business.

TABLE 12.2

Costs and Benefits of Information Systems

Implementation Costs
Hardware
Telecommunications
Software
Personnel costs

Operational Costs
Computer processing time
Maintenance
Operating staff
User time
Ongoing training costs
Facility costs

Tangible Benefits
Increased productivity
Lower operational costs
Reduced workforce
Lower computer expenses
Lower outside vendor costs
Lower clerical and professional costs
Reduced rate of growth in expenses
Reduced facility costs
Increased sales

Intangible Benefits
Improved asset usage
Improved resource control
Improved organizational planning
Increased organizational flexibility
More timely information
More information
Increased organizational learning
Legal requirements attained
Enhanced employee goodwill
Increased job satisfaction
Improved decision making
Improved operations
Higher client satisfaction
Better corporate image

Determining Project Costs and Benefits

As we pointed out earlier, the systems analysis includes an assessment of the economic feasibility of each alternative solution—whether each solution represents a good investment for the company. To identify the information systems projects that will deliver the most business value, you'll need to identify their costs and benefits and how they relate to the firm's information systems plan.

Table 12.2 lists some of the more common costs and benefits of systems. **Tangible benefits** can be quantified and assigned a monetary value. **Intangible benefits**, such as more efficient customer service or enhanced decision making, cannot be immediately quantified. Yet systems that produce mainly intangible benefits may still be good investments if they produce quantifiable gains in the long run.

To determine the benefits of a particular solution, you'll need to calculate all its costs and all its benefits. Obviously, a solution whose costs exceed benefits should be rejected, but even if the benefits outweigh the costs, some additional financial analysis is required to determine whether the investment represents a good return on the firm's invested capital. Capital budgeting methods, such as net present value, internal rate of return (IRR), or accounting rate of return on investment (ROI), would typically be employed to evaluate the proposed information system solution as an investment. You can find out more about how these capital budgeting methods are used to justify information system investments in our Learning Tracks.

Some of the tangible benefits the Girl Scouts obtained were increased productivity and lower operational costs resulting from streamlining the ordering process and reducing errors. Intangible benefits included customer satisfaction, more timely information, and improved operations.

The Information Systems Plan

An **information systems plan** shows how specific information systems fit into a company's overall business plan and business strategy. Table 12.3 lists the major components of such a plan. The plan contains a statement of corporate goals and specifies how information technology will help the business attain these goals. The report shows how general goals will be achieved by specific systems projects. It identifies specific

TABLE 12.3

Information Systems Plan

1. Purpose of the Plan
- Overview of plan contents
- Current business organization and future organization
- Key business processes
- Management strategy

2. Strategic Business Plan Rationale
- Current situation
- Current business organization
- Changing environments
- Major goals of the business plan
- Firm's strategic plan

3. Current Systems
- Major systems supporting business functions and processes
- Current infrastructure capabilities
  - Hardware
  - Software
  - Database
  - Telecommunications, mobile, and Internet
- Difficulties meeting business requirements
- Anticipated future demands

4. New Developments
- New system projects
  - Project descriptions
  - Business rationale
  - Applications' role in strategy
- New infrastructure capabilities required
  - Hardware
  - Software
  - Database
  - Telecommunications, mobile, and the Internet

5. Management Strategy
- Acquisition plans
- Milestones and timing
- Organizational realignment
- Internal reorganization
- Management controls
- Major training initiatives
- Personnel strategy

6. Implementation of the Plan
- Anticipated difficulties in implementation
- Progress reports

7. Budget Requirements
- Requirements
- Potential savings
- Financing
- Acquisition cycle

target dates and milestones that can be used later to evaluate the plan's progress in terms of how many objectives were actually attained in the time frame specified in the plan. The plan indicates the key management decisions concerning hardware acquisition; telecommunications; centralization/decentralization of authority, data, and hardware; and required organizational change.

The plan should describe organizational changes, including management and employee training requirements; changes in business processes; and changes in

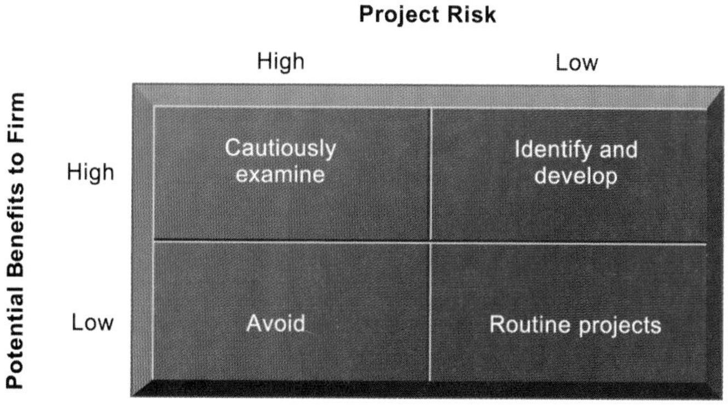

Figure 12.9
A System Portfolio
Companies should examine their portfolio of projects in terms of potential benefits and likely risks. Certain kinds of projects should be avoided altogether and others developed rapidly. There is no ideal mix. Companies in different industries have different information systems needs.

authority, structure, or management practice. When you are making the business case for a new information system project, you show how the proposed system fits into that plan.

Portfolio Analysis and Scoring Models

Once you have determined the overall direction of systems development, **portfolio analysis** will help you evaluate alternative system projects. Portfolio analysis inventories all of the firm's information systems projects and assets, including infrastructure, outsourcing contracts, and licenses. This portfolio of information systems investments can be described as having a certain profile of risk and benefit to the firm (see Figure 12.9), similar to a financial portfolio. Each information systems project carries its own set of risks and benefits. Firms try to improve the return on their information system portfolios by balancing the risk and return from their systems investments.

Obviously, you begin first by focusing on systems of high benefit and low risk. These promise early returns and low risks. Second, high-benefit, high-risk systems should be examined; low-benefit, high-risk systems should be totally avoided; and low-benefit, low-risk systems should be reexamined for the possibility of rebuilding and replacing them with more desirable systems having higher benefits. By using portfolio analysis, management can determine the optimal mix of investment risk and reward for their firms, balancing riskier, high-reward projects with safer, lower-reward ones.

Another method for evaluating alternative system solutions is a **scoring model**. Scoring models give alternative systems a single score based on the extent to which they meet selected objectives. Table 12.4 shows part of a simple scoring model that the Girl Scouts could have used in evaluating new system solutions (alternatives 2 and 3 described earlier). The first column lists the criteria that decision makers use to evaluate the systems. Table 12.4 shows that the Girl Scouts attach the most importance to capabilities for sales order processing, ease of use, ability to support individual Girl Scouts taking orders, and web access from multiple locations. The second column in Table 12.4 lists the weights that decision makers attached to the decision criteria. Columns 3 and 5 show the percentage of requirements for each function that each alternative system solution meets. Each alternative's score is calculated by multiplying the percentage of requirements met for each function by the weight attached to that function. Solution alternative 3 has the highest total score.

MANAGING PROJECT RISK AND SYSTEM-RELATED CHANGE

Some systems development projects are more likely to run into problems or to suffer delays because they carry a much higher level of risk than others. The level of project risk is influenced by project size, project structure, and the level of technical expertise

TABLE 12.4

Example of a Scoring Model for the Girl Scouts Cookie System

Criteria	Weight	Alternative 2 (%)	Alternative 2 Score	Alternative 3 (%)	Alternative 3 Score
1.1 Order processing					
1.2 Online order entry	5	67	335	83	415
1.3 Order tracking by customer	5	81	405	75	375
1.4 Order tracking by individual Girl Scout	5	30	150	80	400
Total order processing			890		1190
2.1 Ease of use					
2.2 Web access from multiple platforms	5	55	275	92	460
2.3 Short training time	4	79	316	85	340
2.4 User-friendly online screens and data entry	4	65	260	87	348
Total ease of use			851		1,148
3.1 Costs					
3.2 Software costs	3	51	153	65	195
3.3 Hardware (server) costs	4	57	228	90	360
3.4 Maintenance and support costs	4	42	168	89	356
Total costs			549		911
Grand Total			2290		3249

of the information systems staff and project team. The larger the project—as indicated by the dollars spent, project team size, and how many parts of the organization will be affected by the new system—the greater the risk. Very large-scale systems projects have a failure rate that is 50 to 75 percent higher than that for other projects because such projects are complex and difficult to control. Risks are also higher for systems where information requirements are not clear and straightforward or the project team must master new technology.

Implementation and Change Management

Dealing with these project risks requires an understanding of the implementation process and change management. A broader definition of **implementation** refers to all the organizational activities working toward the adoption and management of an innovation, such as a new information system. Successful implementation requires a high level of user involvement in a project and management support.

If users are heavily involved in the development of a system, they have more opportunities to mold the system according to their priorities and business requirements and to control the outcome. They also are more likely to react

TABLE 12.5

The User–Designer Communications Gap

User Concerns	Designer Concerns
Will the system deliver the information I need for my work?	What demands will this system put on our servers?
Can we access the data on our iPhones, tablets, and PCs?	What kind of programming demands will this place on our group?
What new procedures do we need to enter data into the system?	Where will the data be stored? What's the most efficient way to store them?
How will the operation of the system change employees' daily routines?	What technologies should we use to secure the data?

positively to the completed system because they have been active participants in the change process.

The relationship between end users and information systems specialists has traditionally been a problem area for information systems implementation efforts because of differing backgrounds, interests, and priorities. These differences create a **user–designer communications gap**. Information systems specialists often have a highly technical orientation to problem solving, focusing on technical solutions in which hardware and software efficiency is optimized at the expense of ease of use or organizational effectiveness. End users prefer systems that are oriented toward solving business problems or facilitating organizational tasks. Often the orientations of both groups are so at odds that they appear to speak in different tongues. These differences are illustrated in Table 12.5.

If an information systems project has the backing and commitment of management at various levels, it is more likely to receive higher priority from both users and the technical information systems staff. Management backing also ensures that a systems project receives sufficient funding and resources to be successful. Furthermore, to be enforced effectively, all the changes in work habits and procedures and any organizational realignments associated with a new system depend on management backing. According to the Project Management Institute, having executive sponsors who are actively engaged is the leading factor in project success (Project Management Institute, 2014).

Controlling Risk Factors

There are strategies you can follow to deal with project risk and increase the chances of a successful system solution. If the new system involves challenging and complex technology, you can recruit project leaders with strong technical and administrative experience. Outsourcing or using external consultants are options if your firm does not have staff with the required technical skills or expertise.

Large projects benefit from appropriate use of **formal planning and control tools** for documenting and monitoring project plans. The two most commonly used methods for documenting project plans are Gantt charts and PERT charts. A **Gantt chart** lists project activities and their corresponding start and completion dates. The Gantt chart visually represents the timing and duration of different tasks in a development project as well as their human resource requirements (see Figure 12.10). It shows each task as a horizontal bar whose length is proportional to the time required to complete it.

Although Gantt charts show when project activities begin and end, they don't depict task dependencies, how one task is affected if another is behind schedule or how tasks should be ordered. That is when **PERT charts** are useful. PERT stands for Program Evaluation and Review Technique, a methodology the U.S. Navy developed

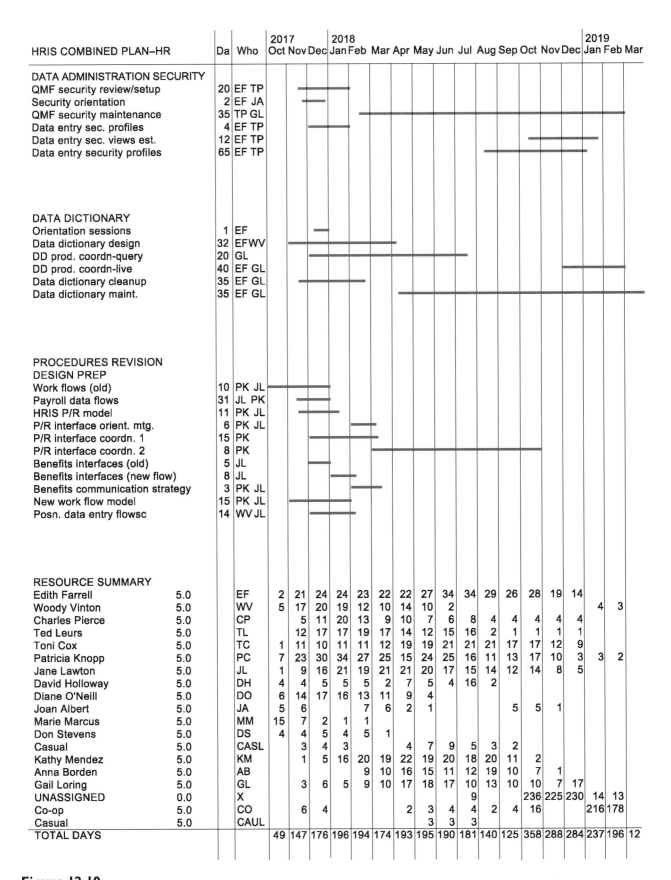

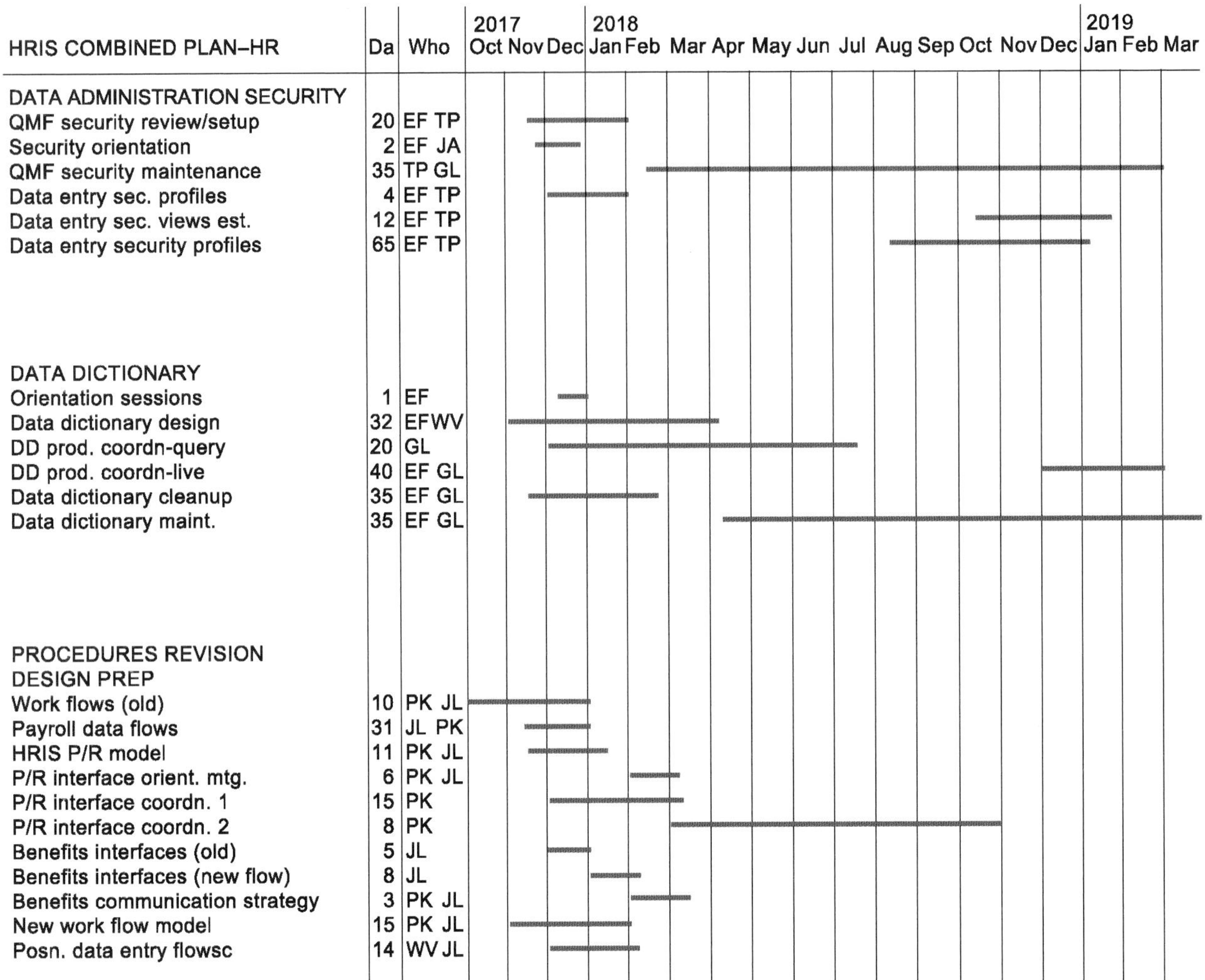

RESOURCE SUMMARY		Who	Oct 2017	Nov	Dec	Jan 2018	Feb	Mar	Apr	May	Jun	Jul	Aug	Sep	Oct	Nov	Dec	Jan 2019	Feb	Mar
Edith Farrell	5.0	EF	2	21	24	24	23	22	22	27	34	34	29	26	28	19	14			
Woody Vinton	5.0	WV	5	17	20	19	12	10	14	10	2							4	3	
Charles Pierce	5.0	CP		5	11	20	13	9	10	7	6	8	4	4	4	4	4			
Ted Leurs	5.0	TL		12	17	17	19	17	14	12	15	16	2	1	1	1	1			
Toni Cox	5.0	TC	1	11	10	11	11	12	19	19	21	21	21	17	17	12	9			
Patricia Knopp	5.0	PC	7	23	30	34	27	25	15	24	25	16	11	13	17	10	3	3	2	
Jane Lawton	5.0	JL	1	9	16	21	19	21	21	20	17	15	14	12	14	8	5			
David Holloway	5.0	DH	4	4	5	5	5	2	7	5	4	16	2							
Diane O'Neill	5.0	DO	6	14	17	16	13	11	9	4										
Joan Albert	5.0	JA	5	6			7	6	2	1				5	5	1				
Marie Marcus	5.0	MM	15	7	2	1	1													
Don Stevens	5.0	DS	4	4	5	4	5	1												
Casual	5.0	CASL		3	4	3			4	7	9	5	3	2						
Kathy Mendez	5.0	KM		1	5	16	20	19	22	19	20	18	20	11	2					
Anna Borden	5.0	AB					9	10	16	15	11	12	19	10	7	1				
Gail Loring	5.0	GL		3	6	5	9	10	17	18	17	10	13	10	10	7	17			
UNASSIGNED	0.0	X										9			236	225	230	14	13	
Co-op	5.0	CO		6	4				2	3	4	4	2	4	16			216	178	
Casual	5.0	CAUL								3	3	3								
TOTAL DAYS			49	147	176	196	194	174	193	195	190	181	140	125	358	288	284	237	196	12

Figure 12.10
A Gantt Chart
The Gantt chart in this figure shows the task, person-days, and initials of each responsible person as well as the start and finish dates for each task. The resource summary provides a good manager with the total person-days for each month and for each person working on the project to manage the project successfully. The project described here is a data administration project.

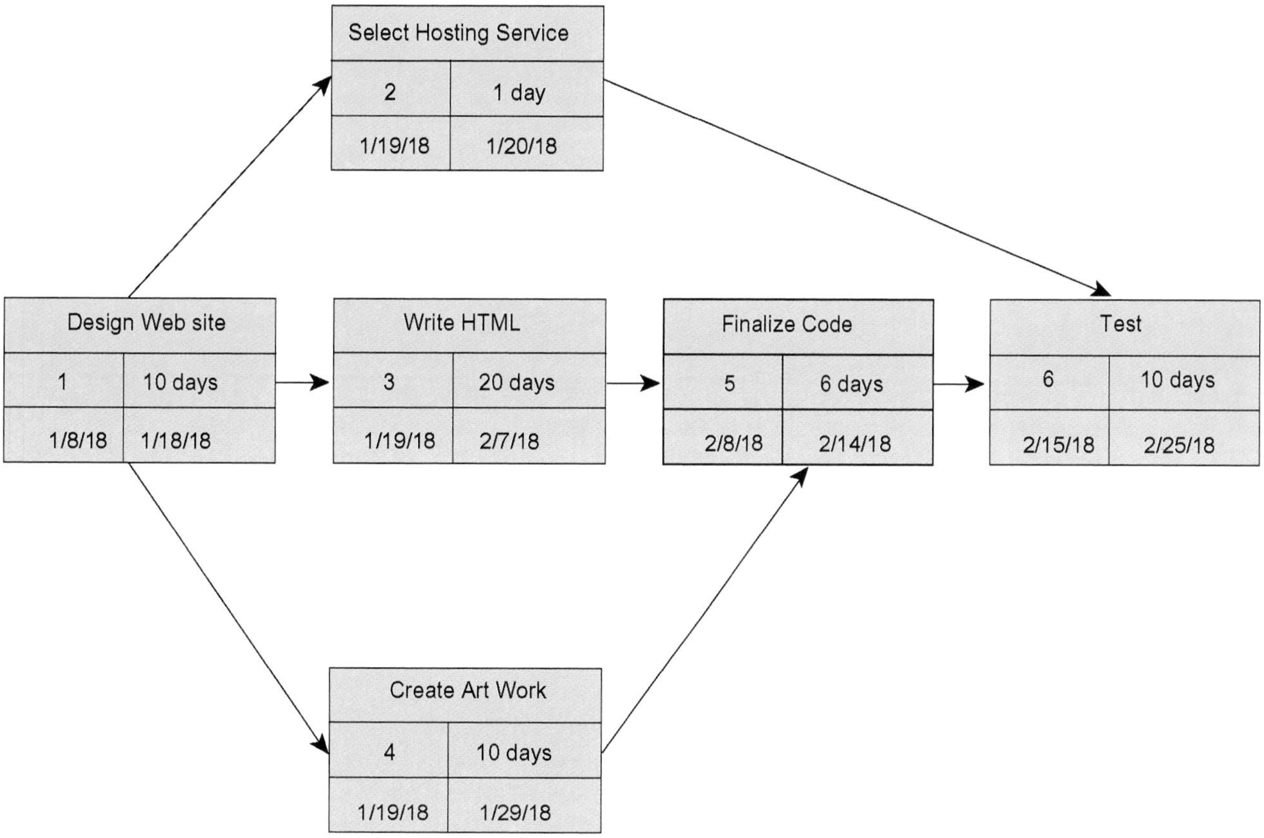

Figure 12.11
A PERT Chart
This is a simplified PERT chart for creating a small website. It shows the ordering of project tasks and the relationship of a task with preceding and succeeding tasks.

during the 1950s to manage the Polaris submarine missile program. A PERT chart graphically depicts project tasks and their interrelationships. The PERT chart lists the specific activities that make up a project and the activities that must be completed before a specific activity can start, as illustrated in Figure 12.11.

The PERT chart portrays a project as a network diagram consisting of numbered nodes (either circles or rectangles) representing project tasks. Each node is numbered and shows the task, its duration, the starting date, and the completion date. The direction of the arrows on the lines indicates the sequence of tasks and shows which activities must be completed before the commencement of another activity. In Figure 12.11, the tasks in nodes 2, 3, and 4 do not depend on each other and can be undertaken simultaneously, but each depends on completion of the first task.

Project Management Software

Commercial software tools are available to automate the creation of Gantt and PERT charts and facilitate the project management process. Project management software typically features capabilities for defining and ordering tasks, assigning resources to tasks, establishing starting and ending dates for tasks, tracking progress, and facilitating modifications to tasks and resources. The most widely used project management tool today is Microsoft Project. We should also point out that these traditional project management tools are being supplemented with some of the social business tools described in Chapter 2. For example, projects might use collaborative, shared workspaces, where project tasks are updated in real time or let activity streams inform team members of events taking place on a project as they occur.

INTERACTIVE SESSION: ORGANIZATIONS

Snohomish County Public Utility District Implements a New Human Resources System

Snohomish County Public Utility District (PUD) in Washington State provides electric power to 330,000 households and also provides water to 19,000 homes throughout a territory covering 2,200 square miles. In 2013, the Everett, Washington-based company realized that more than 35 percent of its 1,100-strong workforce was eligible to retire within the next five years. Many were highly experienced and capable employees. This impending staff turnover and need to recruit engineers, IT staff, and other technical positions spurred Snohomish PUD to revamp its Employee Resources department and recruitment systems.

An aging human resources (HR) system had been used for employee data and benefits, with access restricted to HR employees. Managers in other departments could not make changes to employee data or obtain information for their employees. Outdated processes included paper-based performance appraisals and manually entering employee data that originated in HR into the payroll system. Bogged down with routine day-to-day tasks, PUD's Employee Resources department could not concentrate on the career development and talent recruitment needed for future success.

CIO Benjamin Beberness and Employee Resources Director Kristi Treckeme began searching for a self-service system that would enable employees to access and update their own data. PUD decided to upgrade its SAP ERP system to consolidate and create a single system of record for the organization and to use SAP's cloud version to maintain its HR records. PUD also decided to implement in parallel SuccessFactors, SAP's cloud-based human capital management (HCM) suite, which features modules for workforce planning and workforce analytics.

To implement SuccessFactors, the project team used a wave approach in which pieces of software were released to employees in stages so they could gradually get comfortable with the new system. The Project Preparation stage began in March 2014. All fundamental business processes were examined and a business process design settled upon. Next, in the Business Blueprint stage, a detailed description of the business processes and system requirements was outlined to produce the project structure and documentation.

By May the team was ready to launch the first wave of the Realization stage. ADP Payroll and two SuccessFactors modules, Employee Central and Learning, were rolled out along with Benefitfocus, a benefits administration package. Employee Central is the core self-service human resources system in which employees can enter data about their skills, accomplishments, areas of concentration, and proficiencies and where managers can enter information such as promotions, salary changes, and terminations. Employee Central is linked to Learning, the talent management module in which curriculum can be developed, deployed, and managed.

From November 2014 to March 2015, the second wave rolled out SAP Jam, the social collaboration tool, and SuccessFactors modules for compensation management, performance and goals, succession management, career development and planning, and the competency framework. The third and final wave took place in August 2015, deploying SuccessFactors modules for recruiting management, recruiting marketing, onboarding, workforce planning and analytics, and advanced reporting. The Realization phase concluded when all business process requirements had been implemented.

In the Final Preparation stage, the SAP ERP system was integrated with SuccessFactors to complete the final configuration. All HR data were now linked to security access controls, all processes for employee time tracking, and ADP payroll. The Go Live & Support phase began in September 2015.

The wave rollout created a climate of persistently building on success. This and the meticulously assembled project team propelled the project forward. Headed by a functional lead from the Employee Resources department and assisted by several strategic subject matter experts (SMEs) who rotated in and out to perform system and end-user acceptance testing, the team also included SAP specialists from Deloitte Consulting.

As with any project, there were a few hiccups. Despite the full support of management, including the utility's board of commissioners, the project struggled with improper resource allocation. With all departments required to maintain normal operations, transferring team members in and out sometimes resulted in understaffing either departmentally or on the project team. Key Employee Resources staff members helped to navigate these rough waters with their thorough knowledge of HR processes and complete familiarity with SuccessFactors.

Change management was addressed up front and consistently emphasized. From the start, the project was presented as a company transformation as opposed to simply an IT initiative to foster an atmosphere of shared commitment. The Deloitte partners recommended "change champions." Groups of employees were inserted in various departments to make sure that their colleagues understood the system. They served as trainers, trouble shooters, helpers, and cheerleaders. Assisted by "super users," they used SuccessFactors' Learning module to make sure that all employees would be ready when Go Live day arrived. Each and every employee in the Employee Resources department participated in testing so that they were well versed in every aspect of the new system and capable of helping their fellow employees. A dedicated internal corporate communications team reinforced and encouraged these efforts.

Project objectives and targets were successfully met, in part because each core business process was assigned to a senior leader. These business process "owners" had developed backup procedures. This freed team members to make on-the-spot system implementation decisions without worrying about business process interruptions. It also meant that it was predominantly broader issues that were shuttled up the executive decision-making chain.

Centralized, transparent employee data have resulted not only in astonishing time savings but also in a noticeable companywide morale boost. Managers and employees can monitor goal setting and performance evaluations, enter feedback, and respond to comments in real time as opposed to the cumbersome paper system previously used. A number of antiquated HR systems and their attendant maintenance costs were eliminated. Employee Resources personnel are no longer dependent on the IT department to run reports and perform analytics.

Sources: Lauren Bonneau, "This Is Not Your Grandfather's Utility," *SAP Insider Profiles*, October–December 2015; "Snohomish County PUD SAP One Program," The Global Smart Energy Elites, 2016; "Metering and Smart Energy," 2016; www.successfactors.com, accessed April 13, 2017; and Craig Powers, "Snohomish PUD Went to the Cloud for HR: The Result? Success," asugnews.com, May 14, 2015.

CASE STUDY QUESTIONS

1. How important was the human resources project for Snohomish PUD? Why?
2. Classify and describe the people, organization, and technology issues the project had to address in order to implement the new system successfully. How did the project team deal with these issues?
3. Describe the composition of the project team. How important was this? Why?
4. Why do you think the implementation of Snohomish PUD's new human resource system was successful? Explain your answer.

Overcoming User Resistance

You can overcome user resistance by promoting user participation (to elicit commitment as well as improve design), by making user education and training easily available, and by providing better incentives for users who cooperate. End users can become active members of the project team, take on leadership roles, and take charge of system installation and training.

You should pay special attention to areas where users interface with the system, with sensitivity to ergonomics issues. **Ergonomics** refers to the interaction of people and machines in the work environment. It considers the design of jobs, health issues, and the end-user interface of information systems. For instance, if a system has a series of complicated online data entry screens that are extremely difficult or time-consuming to work with, users will reject the system if it increases their workload or level of job stress.

Users will be more cooperative if organizational problems are solved prior to introducing the new system. In addition to procedural changes, transformations in job functions, organizational structure, power relationships, and behavior should be identified during systems analysis, using an **organizational impact analysis**.

You can see some of these project management strategies at work in the Interactive Session on Organizations, which describes how the Snohomish County Public Utility District (PUD) implemented a new human resources system.

12-5 How will MIS help my career?

Here is how Chapter 12 and this book can help you find a job as an entry-level junior business systems analyst.

THE COMPANY

Systems 100 Technology Consultants, a Chicago-based professional technology services firm, provides staffing and information technology consulting services to other U.S. companies and has an open position for an entry-level junior business systems analyst. The company provides business and technology consultants to more than 150 firms in financial services, healthcare, communications, transportation, energy, consumer goods, and technology, helping them implement business and technology initiatives cost-effectively.

POSITION DESCRIPTION

A junior business systems analyst is expected to work in project teams throughout all phases of the software development life cycle, including defining business requirements, developing detailed design specifications, and working with application developers to build or enhance systems and business processes. Before undertaking assignments, new business systems analysts receive training in the background they will need to succeed in their assignments.

The first assignment is to work on a contract basis for a startup data analytics company in Michigan serving mid-sized organizations. The junior business systems analyst would work with a team of data scientists to help clients integrate data sources, cleanse and organize messy data, and improve understanding of patterns and trends.

JOB REQUIREMENTS

- Upcoming or recent college graduate, with BA in Management Information Systems, Finance, Psychology, or related field
- 3 to 6-plus months of corporate work or internship experience, including experience working with a project team
- Strong analytical, communication, and problem-solving skills
- Ability to work comfortably in a team environment
- Knowledge and understanding of the software development life cycle and business process improvement
- Knowledge of MS Office applications
- Exposure to SQL desirable but not required

INTERVIEW QUESTIONS

1. What information systems courses have you taken, including MIS, database, data analytics, and systems development? Can you write SQL queries?
2. Have you worked on any systems development projects? If so, what exactly did you do? What systems development practices did you use?

3. Have you worked on any other kinds of projects, and what role did you play? Do you have samples of the writing or output you produced for these projects?
4. Which Microsoft Office tools have you used? What kinds of problems have you used these tools to solve?
5. Do you have any experience with Agile software development?

AUTHOR TIPS

1. Review the discussion of business processes in Chapters 2 and 3 and Chapter 12 on developing systems and IT project management and implementation. Be prepared to talk about any systems development experience you have had, including analyzing or redesigning business processes. Also be prepared to discuss contemporary systems development practices.
2. Inquire about how you would be using SQL and Microsoft Office tools for the job and what skills you would be expected to demonstrate. Bring examples of the work you have done with this software.
3. Bring examples of your writing (including some from your Digital Portfolio described in MyLab MIS) demonstrating your analytical and business application skills and project experience.

Review Summary

12-1 **What are the core problem-solving steps for developing new information systems?** The core problem-solving steps for developing new information systems are: (1) define and understand the problem, (2) develop alternative solutions, (3) evaluate and choose the solution, and (4) implement the solution. The third step includes an assessment of the technical, financial, and organizational feasibility of each alternative. The fourth step entails finalizing design specifications, acquiring hardware and software, testing, providing training and documentation, conversion, and evaluating the system solution once it is in production.

12-2 **What are the alternative methods for building information systems?** The systems life cycle requires information systems to be developed in formal stages. The stages must proceed sequentially and have defined outputs; each requires formal approval before the next stage can commence. The system life cycle is rigid and costly but useful for large projects.

Prototyping consists of building an experimental system rapidly and inexpensively for end users to interact with and evaluate. The prototype is refined and enhanced until users are satisfied that it includes all their requirements and can be used as a template to create the final system. End-user-developed systems can be created rapidly and informally using user-friendly software tools. End-user development can improve requirements determination and reduce application backlog.

Application software packages and SaaS eliminate the need for writing software programs when developing an information system. Application software packages and SaaS are helpful if a firm does not have the internal information systems staff or financial resources to custom-develop a system.

Outsourcing consists of using an external vendor to build (or operate) a firm's information systems. If it is properly managed, outsourcing can save application development costs or enable firms to develop applications without an internal information systems staff.

Rapid application design, joint application design (JAD), cloud-based platforms, DevOps, and reusable software components (including web services) can be used to speed up the system's development process. Mobile application development must address multiple platforms, small screen sizes, and the need to conserve resources.

12-3 What are the principal methodologies for modeling and designing systems? The two principal methodologies for modeling and designing information systems are structured methodologies and object-oriented development. Structured methodologies focus on modeling processes and data separately. The data flow diagram is the principal tool for structured analysis, and the structure chart is the principal tool for representing structured software design. Object-oriented development models a system as a collection of objects that combine processes and data.

12-4 How should information systems projects be selected and managed? To determine whether an information system project is a good investment, one must calculate its costs and benefits. Tangible benefits are quantifiable, and intangible benefits cannot be immediately quantified but may provide quantifiable benefits in the future. Benefits that exceed costs should then be analyzed using capital budgeting methods to make sure they represent a good return on the firm's invested capital.

Organizations should develop information systems plans that describe how information technology supports the company's overall business plan and strategy. Portfolio analysis and scoring models can be used to evaluate alternative information systems projects. Information systems projects and the entire implementation process should be managed as planned organizational change using an organizational impact analysis. Management support and control of the implementation process are essential, as are mechanisms for dealing with the level of risk in each new systems project. Project risks are influenced by project size, project structure, and the level of technical expertise of the information systems staff and project team. Formal planning and control tools (including Gantt and PERT charts) track resource allocations and specific project activities. Users can be encouraged to take active roles in systems development and become involved in installation and training.

Key Terms

Acceptance testing, 441
Agile development, 449
Component-based development, 453
Computer-aided software engineering (CASE), 453
Customization, 445
Data flow diagram (DFD), 450
DevOps, 449
Direct cutover strategy, 442
Documentation, 442
End-user development, 444
Ergonomics, 463
Feasibility study, 439
Formal planning and control tools, 459
Gantt chart, 459
Implementation, 458
Information requirements, 438
Information systems plan, 455
Intangible benefits, 455
Joint application design (JAD), 449
Maintenance, 442
Mobile web app, 447
Mobile website, 447
Native app, 447
Object-oriented development, 451
Organizational impact analysis, 464
Parallel strategy, 442
PERT charts, 459
Phased approach, 442
Pilot study, 442
Portfolio analysis, 457
Process specifications, 451
Production, 442
Project, 454
Project management, 454
Prototyping, 443
Rapid application development (RAD), 449
Request for Proposal (RFP), 445
Responsive web design, 447
Scope, 454
Scoring model, 457
Structure chart, 451
Structured, 450
System testing, 441
Systems analysis, 437
Systems design, 440
Systems development life cycle (SDLC), 443
Tangible benefits, 455
Test plan, 441
Testing process, 441
Unit testing, 441
User–designer communications gap, 459

MyLab MIS™

To complete the problems with **MyLab MIS**, go to EOC Discussion Questions in MyLab MIS.

Review Questions

12-1 What are the core problem-solving steps for developing new information systems?

- List and describe the problem-solving steps for building a new system.
- Define information requirements and explain why they are important for developing a system solution.
- List the various types of design specifications required for a new information system.
- Explain why the testing stage of systems development is so important. Name and describe the three stages of testing for an information system.
- Describe the roles of documentation, conversion, production, and maintenance in systems development.

12-2 What are the alternative methods for building information systems?

- Define the traditional systems life cycle and describe its advantages and disadvantages for systems building.
- Define information system prototyping and describe its benefits and limitations. List and describe the steps in the prototyping process.
- Define end-user development and explain its advantages and disadvantages.
- Describe the advantages and disadvantages of developing information systems based on application software packages and cloud software services (SaaS).
- Define outsourcing. Describe the circumstances in which it should be used for building information systems. List and describe the hidden costs of offshore software outsourcing.
- Explain how businesses can rapidly develop e-business applications.
- Describe the issues that must be addressed when developing mobile applications.

12-3 What are the principal methodologies for modeling and designing systems?

- Compare object-oriented and traditional structured approaches for modeling and designing systems.

12-4 How should information systems projects be selected and managed?

- Explain the difference between tangible and intangible benefits.
- List six tangible benefits and six intangible benefits.
- List and describe the major components of an information systems plan.
- Describe how portfolio analysis and scoring models can be used to establish the worth of systems.
- Explain the importance of implementation for managing the organizational change surrounding a new information system.
- Define the user–designer communications gap and explain the kinds of implementation problems it creates.
- List and describe the factors that influence project risk and describe strategies for minimizing project risks.

Discussion Questions

12-5 MyLab MIS Discuss the role of business end users and information system professionals in developing a system solution. How do both roles differ when the solution is developed using prototyping or end-user development?

12-6 MyLab MIS It has been said that systems fail when systems builders ignore people problems. Why might this be so?

12-7 MyLab MIS Why is building a system a form of organizational problem-solving?

Hands-On MIS Projects

The projects in this section give you hands-on experience evaluating information systems projects, designing a customer system for auto sales, and analyzing website information requirements. Visit **MyLab MIS** to access this chapter's Hands-On MIS Projects.

MANAGEMENT DECISION PROBLEMS

12-8 The Warm and Toasty Heating Oil Company used to deliver heating oil by sending trucks that printed out a ticket with the number of gallons of oil delivered that was placed on customers' doorsteps. Customers received their oil delivery bills in the mail two weeks later. The company recently revised its oil delivery and billing system so that oil truck drivers can calculate and print out a complete bill for each delivery and leave customers with the bill and a return envelope at the time the delivery takes place. Evaluate the business impact of the new system and the people and organizational changes required to implement the new technology.

12-9 Caterpillar is the world's leading maker of earth-moving machinery and supplier of agricultural equipment. The software for its Dealer Business System (DBS), which it licenses to its dealers to help them run their businesses, is becoming outdated. Senior management wants its dealers to use a hosted version of the software supported by Accenture consultants so Caterpillar can concentrate on its core business. The system had become a de facto standard for doing business with the company. The majority of the 50 Cat dealers in North America use some version of DBS, as do about half of the 200 or so Cat dealers in the rest of the world. Before Caterpillar turns the project over to Accenture, what factors and issues should it consider? What questions should it ask? What questions should its dealers ask?

IMPROVING DECISION MAKING: USING DATABASE SOFTWARE TO DESIGN A CUSTOMER SYSTEM FOR AUTO SALES

Software skills: Database design, querying, reporting, and forms
Business skills: Sales lead and customer analysis

12-10 This project requires you to perform a systems analysis and then design a system solution using database software.

Ace Auto Dealers specializes in selling new vehicles from Subaru in Portland, Oregon. The company advertises in local newspapers and is listed as an authorized dealer on the Subaru website and other major websites for auto buyers. The company benefits from a good local word-of-mouth reputation and name recognition.

Ace does not believe it has enough information about its customers. It cannot easily determine which prospects have made auto purchases, nor can it identify which customer touch points have produced the greatest number of sales leads or actual sales so it can focus advertising and marketing more on the channels that generate the most revenue. Are purchasers discovering Ace from newspaper ads, from word of mouth, or from the web?

Prepare a systems analysis report detailing Ace's problem and a system solution that can be implemented using PC database management software. Then use database software to develop a simple system solution. In MyLab MIS, you will find more information about Ace and its information requirements to help you develop the solution.

ACHIEVING OPERATIONAL EXCELLENCE: ANALYZING WEBSITE DESIGN AND INFORMATION REQUIREMENTS

Software skills: Web browser software
Business skills: Information requirements analysis, website design

12-11 Visit the website of your choice and explore it thoroughly. Prepare a report analyzing the various functions provided by that website and its information requirements. Your report should answer these questions: What functions does the website perform? What data does it use? What are its inputs, outputs, and processes? What are some of its other design specifications? Does the website link to any internal systems or systems of other organizations? What value does this website provide the firm?

Collaboration and Teamwork Project

Preparing Website Design Specifications

12-12 With three or four of your classmates, select a system described in this text that uses the web. Review the website for the system you select. Use what you have learned from the website and the description in this book to prepare a report describing some of the design specifications for the system you select. If possible, use Google Docs and Google Drive or Google Sites to brainstorm, organize, and develop a presentation of your findings for the class.

BUSINESS PROBLEM-SOLVING CASE

The Philly311 Project: The City of Brotherly Love Turns Problems into Opportunities

Philly311 is the City of Philadelphia government's centralized non-emergency contact center that is accessible to all residents, businesses, and visitors. Using Philly311, you can find out how to start a business, contact your local police district, obtain a smoke alarm, and issue requests for services such as fixing broken traffic signals, repairing potholes, or removing graffiti. You can also use Philly311 to report abandoned vehicles, unsafe/improper housing conditions, and complaints. Philly311 can be contacted by phone, by visiting its website, or by using a mobile app. Philly311 receives more than a million calls each year.

Requests for service through 311 generally have expected time frames for action or resolution. After receiving a request for service, Philly311 will provide a citizen with a reference number to track the status of that request as it moves through different departments by calling the Philly311 Call Center, visiting the Philly311 website, or using the mobile app. Residents can relay photos to city officials for more effective response to service calls and receive real-time updates on their requests. The city is able to mine data from the Philly311 system to identify trends that will help city employees to discover and address the needs of citizens. Philly311 also features a Neighborhood Community portal that allows citizens to engage with fellow residents on shared concerns and interact with each other and city departments and officials directly. The system includes GPS integrative mapping so the public and city government can view service requests by location.

Philly311 has been extremely popular with citizens, earning a customer satisfaction rate of 98 percent. Moreover, Philly311 is much, much more than a traditional government call center. Residents can connect with Philly311 by telephone, email, mail, a walk-in center, or the Philly Mobile App. Philly311 has also extended its service through social media. The Philly311 Facebook and Twitter accounts are managed by an experienced agent who responds to questions and enters service requests based on user interaction. Since the beginning of 2012, Philly311 has seen a 360 percent increase in its social media followers.

Philly311 started out as a traditional 311 call center. (The telephone number *3-1-1* is a special telephone number used by many communities in Canada and the United States to provide access to non-emergency municipal services.) The first version of Philly311 was designed to provide the public with quick, easy phone access to all city services and information.

When Mayor Michael A. Nutter came into office in 2007, he called for a more transparent and efficient government, increasing integrity, more open data practices, and improving government accountability. The Nutter administration wanted to empower Philadelphians and work with them on government-related issues that citizens care most about. According to Rosetta Lue, Philadelphia's Chief Customer Service Officer, the customer may always be right, but that only goes so far if the customer can't be heard. Philadelphia's citizens are its customers, and city government should use the best tools possible to make sure every citizen is connected and can be heard loud and clear. In the past, when Philadelphians called 311 with a service request, such as a pothole they wanted fixed, they would have no idea when the city would get around to addressing it, which led to frustration for residents and repeated calls to the city.

The project timeline for upgrading Philly311 was ambitious, aiming for making the new center operational by the end of 2008. Managers Jeffrey Friedman and Patrick Morgan engaged an external consulting group to develop a plan and scope for the 311 system. In June 2008, Mayor Nutter and City Managing Director and Executive Sponsor Camille Barnett approved the implementation strategy. Lue joined the Philly311 project team in May 2008. The team worked collectively to develop civil service testing requirements for contact center agents. Thirty representatives from various city departments helped populate the Philly311 knowledge base with more than 2,000 articles about city services and municipal information.

In September 2008, the national financial crisis caused a drastic cut in Philly311's budget, affecting the Philly311 implementation. At the same time, however, the crisis created an opportunity to improvise creatively by developing a fairly low-cost solution using established city services and technologies. Instead of implementing new software for a customer relationship management (CRM) system, the Philly311 project team worked with the city's Department of Technology to implement a less expensive web-based solution with CRM functions. This web-based system was integrated with other systems so, for example, agents were able to look up municipal information and directly enter service requests into the integrated work systems of servicing departments. Philly311's new budget constraints also put a brake on hiring and head count. Instead of hiring experienced contact center agents, Philly311 hired internal transfers and employees who would have been laid off due to budget cutbacks. Delays in the implementation timetable gave Lue and her team more time to study the problem and develop a sound solution.

Lue wanted to make sure that the system would be easy for customers to use, so local citizens were involved in the new Philly311 design from the beginning. Bringing users in early in the process also saved time during system implementation and rollout. They were able to bring together about 100 people from different city departments to say what they liked and what they didn't like about the technology and new business processes. They had a chance to see how data were coming in, how they would be used, and how Philadelphia could be more efficient and effective.

The Philly311 project had full executive support from Mayor Nutter and the city's managing director. The upgraded call center opened on December 31, 2008, and the new Philly311 website went online in January 2009. The website had many of the same functions as the call center: customers could connect with 311, report an issue, or ask about public services through email. To make Philly311 even more accessible to citizens through multiple channels, the city launched a social media campaign and expanded its public reach through social media in October 2009. Philly311 established a Twitter account that provided citizens a new way to receive information.

With a city as large as Philadelphia, which has an above-average percentage of residents living below the poverty line, city leaders realized they needed to work on establishing trust within individual communities to educate and provide access to Philly311. The city hired a community engagement coordinator to address community concerns and to oversee the Neighborhood Liaison Program (NLP), which trains volunteers to record items discussed during community meetings and encourages standout community leaders to bring their neighbors' public service concerns straight to Philly311. In the program's first year, 600 neighborhood liaisons were trained, and two years after the program's launch, the number of neighborhood liaisons had doubled.

Philly311 launched its mobile application in 2012. The app provides another way for residents to connect to Philly311, and it also allows customers to add on-site and real-time images to their service requests. The app is free to the public and can be downloaded onto a smartphone. Add-on widgets, such as a widget for election days and after-school programs, can be incorporated when needed. The mobile Philly311 app was the first 311 app to be offered in 16 different languages. This app now accounts for 18 percent of the requests Philly311 receives.

Philly311's traffic volume steadily increased, and by the end of 2012, Philly311 had taken its 5 millionth call. The popularity of the service demonstrates the tremendous benefit and popularity of the system, but it also created operational strain. In 2011, an independent gap analysis found that the existing system did not have the capacity to continue supporting Philadelphia's growing service requirements. The system was not built to handle very large volumes of data, nor could it easily archive data about citizen calls, complaints, and follow-ups. These technology limitations prevented the city from crunching data or from changing business processes to improve workforce efficiency.

The time had come to invest in new technology to keep pace with current demands and to position the city for future technology and business developments. After months of planning, a solution was finalized: The project planning process took special care to define a detailed set of business and technical requirements for the new system. The solution selected contained several modules, allowing city management to pick and choose which features were most critical. One called the Neighborhood Community portal allows citizens to communicate with neighbors and like-minded residents about concerns and issues relevant to them. Mayor Nutter finally obtained $120 million in funding for capital investment projects to upgrade technology infrastructure and chose Philly311 as one of those investments.

After a rigorous RFP selection process, Unisys was chosen to lead the IT implementation for this project, and Salesforce's cloud computing platform was selected as the underlying technology for the system. Unisys had implemented similar 311 systems on the Salesforce platform for Hampton, Virginia, and Elgin, Illinois. The city chose Salesforce.com in part because of its capabilities as a platform. In addition to full-featured CRM functionality, Salesforce.com has its own app store and cloud platform for building and running apps. That way, the city can leverage its investment to take advantage of other apps that work on the Salesforce platform.

The new CRM system, released in December 2014, is much more robust, integrating the city's knowledge base, service departments' work order systems, and community engagement programs in a single customer portal. The system improves the city's ability to share knowledge and work interdepartmentally and creates a social platform that facilitates conversations between neighbors and stakeholders who want to collaborate, share best practices, and organize events to improve their community. The new Philly311 helps the city capitalize on a variety of communications, including social media data, to better understand the needs of its citizen customers.

Philly311 has been widely embraced by Philadelphia residents, and has received numerous accolades. It was selected as a winner of the 2015 Government Computer News Awards for IT excellence. In 2015, Philly311 became a finalist for the United Nations' Public Service Award for demonstrating attention to its international audience, and in 2013 Philly311 was named an ICMI Global Call Center award finalist. The system has expanded its reach and has even become a resource and example for those outside of Philadelphia. Philly311 has helped build a more reliable city government and make Philadelphia a welcoming and connected city.

Sources: Rosetta Carrington Lue and Cory Fleming with Amanda V. Wagner, "Creating a Welcoming and Connected City: The Philadelphia Experience," www.phila.gov, accessed January 11, 2017; Derek Major, "Philly 311: Innovation That Was Worth the Wait," *Government Computer News,* October 15, 2015; Jake Williams, "Philadelphia Rolls Out Innovation Blueprint, 311 Upgrade," statescoop.com, February 19, 2015; City of Philadelphia, "Mayor Nutter Announces Successful Launch of New Philly 311 System," February 18, 2015; and Lauren Hertzler, "Philadelphia Unveils Enhanced 311 System at Innovation Summit," bizjournals.com, February 19, 2015.

CASE STUDY QUESTIONS

12-12 Assess the importance of the Philly311 project for the city of Philadelphia and its citizens.

12-13 What problems was the Philly311 project designed to solve?

12-14 Why was the Philly311 project so successful? What people, organization, and technology factors contributed to its success?

12-15 What risk mitigation strategies did Philadelphia use for its Philly311 project? How did they help?

MyLab MIS

Go to the Assignments section of MyLab MIS to complete these writing exercises.

12-18 Describe four system conversion strategies.

12-19 Compare the two major types of planning and control tools.

Chapter 12 References

Appan, Radha, and Glenn J. Browne. "The Impact of Analyst-Induced Misinformation on the Requirements Elicitation Process." *MIS Quarterly* 36, No. 1 (March 2012).

ArcTouch. "Functional but Unfriendly: A Study of Enterprise Mobile App User Experience." (2017).

Bayerl, Petra Saskia, Kristina Lauche, and Carolyn Axtell. "Revisiting Group-Based Technology Adoption as a Dynamic Process: The Role of Changing Attitude-Rationale Configurations." *MIS Quarterly* 40, No. 3 (September 2016).

Benaroch, Michael, Yossi Lichtenstein, and Lior Fink. "Contract Design Choices and the Balance of Ex Ante and Ex Post Transaction Costs in Software Development Outsourcing." *MIS Quarterly* 40, No. 1 (March 2016).

Bloch, Michael, Sen Blumberg, and Jurgen Laartz. "Delivering Large-Scale IT Projects on Time, on Budget, and on Value." *McKinsey Quarterly* (October 2012).

Bossert, Oliver, Chris Ip, and Irina Starikova. "Beyond Agile: Reorganizing IT for Faster Software Delivery." McKinsey & Company (February 2015).

Brock, Jon, Tamim Saleh, and Sesh Iyer. "Large-Scale IT Projects: From Nightmare to Value Creation." Boston Consulting Group (May 20, 2015).

Brown, Karen A., Nancy Lea Hyer, and Richard Ettenson. "Protect Your Project from Escalating Doubts." *MIT Sloan Management Review* (Spring 2017).

Browning, Tyson, R., and Ranga V. Ramases. "Reducing Unwelcome Surprises in Project Management." *MIT Sloan Management Review* (Spring 2015).

Cecez-Kecmanovic, Dubravka, Karlheinz Kautz, and Rebecca Abrahall, "Reframing Success and Failure of Information Systems: A Performative Perspective." *MIS Quarterly* 38, No. 2 (June 2014).

Chandrasekaran, Sriram, Sauri Gudlavalleti, and Sanjay Kaniyar. "Achieving Success in Large Complex Software Projects." *McKinsey Quarterly* (July 2014).

Chen, Yuanyuan, Anandhi Bharadwaj, and Khim-Yong Goh. "An Empirical Analysis of Intellectual Property Rights Sharing in Software Development Outsourcing." *MIS Quarterly* 41 No. 1 (March 2017).

Comella-Dorda, Santiago, Swati Lohiya, and Gerard Speksnijder. "An Operating Model for Company-Wide Agile Development." McKinsey & Company (May 2016).

Debane, Francine, Katya Defossez, and Mark McMillan. "Developing Talent for Large IT Projects." *McKinsey Quarterly* (August 2014).

Florentine, Sharon. "More Than Half of IT Projects Are Still Failing." *CIO* (May 11, 2016).

Flyvbjerg, Bent, and Alexander Budzier. "Why Your IT Project May Be Riskier Than You Think," *Harvard Business Review* (September 2011).

Gnanasambandam, Chandra, Martin Harrysson, Rahul Mangla, and Shivam Srivastava. "An Executive's Guide to Software Development," McKinsey & Company (February 2017).

Henningsson, Stefan, and William J. Kettinger. "Understanding Information Systems Integration Deficiencies in Mergers and Acquisitions: A Configurational Perspective." *Journal of Management Information Systems* 33, No. 4 (2016).

Han, Kunsoo, and Sunil Mithas. "Information Technology Outsourcing and Non-IT Operating Costs: An Empirical Investigation." *MIS Quarterly* 37, No. 1 (March 2013).

Hoehle, Hartmut, and Viswanath Venkatesh. "Mobile Application Usability: Conceptualization and Instrument Development." *MIS Quarterly* 39, No. 2 (June 2015).

Information Builders. "Yellow Pages Uses WebFOCUS to Demonstrate ROI to Advertisers." www.informationbuilders.com, accessed March 30, 2015.

Keil, Mark, H. Jeff Smith, Charalambos L. Iacovou, and Ronald L. Thompson. "The Pitfalls of Project Status Reporting." *MIT Sloan Management Review* 55, No. 3 (Spring 2014).

Kendall, Kenneth E., and Julie E. Kendall. *Systems Analysis and Design,* 9th ed. (Upper Saddle River, NJ: Prentice-Hall, 2014).

Kim, Hee Woo, and Atreyi Kankanhalli. "Investigating User Resistance to Information Systems Implementation: A Status Quo Bias Perspective." *MIS Quarterly* 33, No. 3 (September 2009).

Kloppenborg, Timothy J., and Debbie Tesch. "How Executive Sponsors Influence Project Success." *MIT Sloan Management Review* (Spring 2015).

Kotlarsky, Julia, Harry Scarbrough, and Ilan Oshri. "Coordinating Expertise Across Knowledge Boundaries in Offshore-Outsourcing Projects: The Role of Codification." *MIS Quarterly* 38, No. 2 (June 2014).

Kovacs, Mandy. "Developing Mobile Both Important and Challenging: OutSystems Report." *Canadian CIO* (April 2017).

Kudaravalli, Srinivas, Samer Faraj, and Steven L. Johnson. "A Configural Approach to Coordinating Expertise in Software Development Teams." *MIS Quarterly* 41 No. 1 (March 2017).

Levina, Natalia, and Jeanne W. Ross. "From the Vendor's Perspective: Exploring the Value Proposition in Information Technology Outsourcing." *MIS Quarterly* 27, No. 3 (September 2003).

Li, Xitong, and Stuart E. Madnick. "Understanding the Dynamics of Service-Oriented Architecture Implementation." *Journal of Management Information Systems* 32, No. 2 (2015).

Mani, Deepa, and Anitesh Barua. "The Impact of Firm Learning on Value Creation in Strategic Outsourcing Relationships." *Journal of Management Information Systems* 32, No. 1 (2015).

McGrath, Rita. "Six Problems Facing Large Government IT Projects (and Their Solutions)." *Harvard Business Review Online* (October 10, 2008).

Nelson, H. James, Deborah J. Armstrong, and Kay M. Nelson. "Patterns of Transition: The Shift from Traditional to Object-Oriented Development." *Journal of Management Information Systems* 25, No. 4 (Spring 2009).

Overby, Stephanie. "The Hidden Costs of Offshore Outsourcing." *CIO Magazine* (September 1, 2003).

Polites, Greta L., and Elena Karahanna. "Shackled to the Status Quo: The Inhibiting Effects of Incumbent System Habit, Switching Costs, and Inertia on New System Acceptance." *MIS Quarterly* 36, No. 1 (March 2012).

Project Management Institute and Boston Consulting Group. "Executive Sponsor Engagement: Top Driver of Project and Program Success." (Newtown Square, Pennsylvania: PMI/BCG, October 2014).

Ryan, Sherry D., David A. Harrison, and Lawrence L. Schkade. "Information Technology Investment Decisions: When Do Cost and Benefits in the Social Subsystem Matter?" *Journal of Management Information Systems* 19, No. 2 (Fall 2002).

Schwalbe, Kathy. *Information Technology Project Management*, 8th ed. (Boston: Cengage, 2016).

Sharma, Rajeev, and Philip Yetton. "The Contingent Effects of Training, Technical Complexity, and Task Interdependence on Successful Information Systems Implementation." *MIS Quarterly* 31, No. 2 (June 2007).

Sircar, Sumit, Sridhar P. Nerur, and Radhakanta Mahapatra. "Revolution or Evolution? A Comparison of Object-Oriented and Structured Systems Development Methods." *MIS Quarterly* 25, No. 4 (December 2001).

Sykes, Tracy Ann. "Support Structures and Their Impacts on Employee Outcomes: A Longitudinal Field Study of an Enterprise System Implementation." *MIS Quarterly* 39, No. 2 (June 2015).

Valacich, Joseph, and Joey George. *Modern Systems Analysis and Design*, 8th ed. (Upper Saddle River, NJ: Prentice-Hall, 2017).

Wiener, Martin, Magnus Mähring, Ulrich Remus, and Carol Saunders. "Control Configuration and Control Enactment in Information Systems Projects: Review and Expanded Theoretical Framework." *MIS Quarterly* 40, No. 3 (September 2016).

Whitaker, Jonathan, Sunil Mithas, and M. S. Krishnan. "Organizational Learning and Capabilities for Onshore and Offshore Business Process Outsourcing." *Journal of Management Information Systems* 27, No. 3 (Winter 2011).

Glossary

3-D printing: Uses machines to make solid objects, layer by layer, from specifications in a digital file. Also known as additive manufacturing.

3G networks: High-speed cellular networks based on packet-switched technology, enabling users to transmit video, graphics, and other rich media in addition to voice.

4G networks: Ultra high–speed wireless networks that are entirely packet switched, with speeds between 1 Mbps and 1 Gbps.

5G: Next generation of wireless networking technology expected to transmit very large amounts of data in the gigabit range over short distances, with fewer transmission delays.

acceptable use policy (AUP): Defines acceptable uses of the firm's information resources and computing equipment, including desktop and laptop computers, wireless devices, telephones, and the Internet, and specifies consequences for noncompliance.

acceptance testing: Provides the final certification that the system is ready to be used in a production setting.

accountability: The mechanisms for assessing responsibility for decisions made and actions taken.

advertising revenue model: Website generating revenue by attracting a large audience.

affiliate revenue model: E-commerce revenue mode in which websites are paid as affiliates for sending their visitors to other sites in return for a referral fee.

agile development: Rapid delivery of working software by breaking a large project into a series of small subprojects that are completed in short periods of time using iteration and continuous feedback.

analytic platform: Preconfigured hardware-software system that is specifically designed for high-speed analysis of large data sets.

analytical CRM: Customer relationship management applications dealing with the analysis of customer data to provide information for improving business performance.

Android: Open source operating system for mobile devices Google and the Open Handset Alliance developed; currently the most popular smartphone operating system worldwide.

antivirus software: Software designed to detect, and often eliminate, computer viruses from an information system.

application controls: Specific controls unique to each computerized application that ensure that only authorized data are completely and accurately processed by that application.

application server: Software that handles all application operations between browser-based computers and a company's back-end business applications or databases.

application software: Programs written for a specific application to perform functions specified by end users.

apps: Small pieces of software that run on the Internet, on a computer, or on a mobile phone and are generally delivered over the Internet.

artificial intelligence (AI): The effort to develop computer-based systems that can behave like humans, with the ability to learn languages, accomplish physical tasks, use a perceptual apparatus, and emulate human expertise and decision making.

attributes: Pieces of information describing a particular entity.

augmented reality (AR): Technology for enhancing visualization that provides a live view of a physical world environment whose elements are augmented by virtual computer-generated imagery.

authentication: The ability of each party in a transaction to ascertain the identity of the other party.

backbone: Part of a network handling the major traffic and providing the primary path for traffic flowing to or from other networks.

balanced scorecard method: Framework for operationalizing a firm's strategic plan by focusing on measurable financial, business process, customer, and learning and growth outcomes of firm performance.

bandwidth: The capacity of a communications channel as measured by the difference between the highest and lowest frequencies that can be transmitted by that channel.

banner ad: A graphic display on a web page used for advertising. The banner is linked to the advertiser's website so that a person clicking it will be transported to the advertiser's website.

behavioral targeting: Tracking the click-streams (history of clicking behavior) of individuals across multiple websites for the purpose of understanding their interests and intentions and exposing them to advertisements that are uniquely suited to their interests.

benchmarking: Setting strict standards for products, services, or activities and measuring organizational performance against those standards.

best practices: The most successful solutions or problem-solving methods that have been developed by a specific organization or industry.

big data: Data sets with volumes so huge that they are beyond the ability of typical relational DBMS to capture, store, and analyze. The data are often unstructured or semi-structured.

biometric authentication: Technology for authenticating system users that compares a person's unique characteristics, such as fingerprints, face, or retinal image, against a stored set profile of these characteristics.

bit: A binary digit representing the smallest unit of data in a computer system. It can only have one of two states, representing 0 or 1.

blockchain: Distributed ledger that stores permanent and tamper-proof records of transactions and shares them among a distributed network of computers.

blog: Popular term for weblog, designating an informal yet structured website where individuals can publish stories, opinions, and links to other websites of interest.

blogosphere: The totality of blog-related websites.

Bluetooth: Standard for wireless personal area networks that can transmit up to 722 Kbps within a 10-meter area.

botnet: A group of computers that have been infected with bot malware without users' knowledge, enabling a hacker to use the amassed resources of the computers to launch distributed denial-of-service attacks, phishing campaigns, or spam.

broadband: High-speed transmission technology; also designates a single communications medium that can transmit multiple channels of data simultaneously.

bugs: Software program code defects.

bullwhip effect: Distortion of information about the demand for a product as it passes from one entity to the next across the supply chain.

business: A formal organization whose aim is to produce products or provide services for a profit.

business continuity planning: Planning that focuses on how the company can restore business operations after a disaster strikes.

business intelligence (BI): Applications and technologies to help users make better business decisions.

business model: An abstraction of what an enterprise is and how the enterprise delivers a product or service, showing how the enterprise creates wealth.

business performance management (BPM): Methodology for measuring firm performance by using key performance indicators based on the firm's strategies.

business process management (BPM): Tools and methodologies for continuously improving and managing business processes.

business process reengineering (BPR): The radical redesign of business processes to maximize the benefits of information technology.

business processes: The unique ways in which organizations coordinate and organize work activities, information, and knowledge to produce a product or service.

business-to-business (B2B) electronic commerce: Electronic sales of goods and services among businesses.

business-to-consumer (B2C) electronic commerce: Electronic retailing of products and services directly to individual consumers.

BYOD: Allowing employees to use their personal mobile devices in the workplace.

C: A powerful programming language with tight control and efficiency of execution, portable across different microprocessors and used primarily with PCs.

C++: Newer version of C programming language with capabilities for working with software objects.

capacity planning: The process of predicting when a computer hardware system becomes saturated to ensure that adequate computing resources are available for work of different priorities and that the firm has enough computing power for its current and future needs.

carpal tunnel syndrome (CTS): Type of RSI in which pressure on the median nerve through the wrist's bony carpal tunnel structure produces pain.

centralized processing: Processing that is accomplished by one large central computer.

change management: Giving proper consideration to the impact of organizational change associated with a new system or alteration of an existing system.

chat: Live, interactive conversations over a public network.

chatbot: Software agent designed to simulate a conversation with one or more human users via textual or auditory methods.

chief data officer (CDO): Individual responsible for enterprise-wide governance and usage of information to maximize the value the organization can realize from its data.

chief information officer (CIO): Senior manager in charge of the information systems function in the firm.

chief knowledge officer (CKO): Responsible for the firm's knowledge management program.

chief privacy officer (CPO): Responsible for ensuring that the company complies with existing data privacy laws.

chief security officer (CSO): Heads a formal security function for the organization and is responsible for enforcing the firm's security policy.

choice: Simon's third stage of decision making, when the individual selects among the various solution alternatives.

Chrome OS: Google's lightweight operating system for cloud computing using a web-connected computer or mobile device.

churn rate: Measurement of the number of customers who stop using or purchasing products or services from a company; used as an indicator of the growth or decline of a firm's customer base.

click fraud: Fraudulently clicking an online ad in pay-per-click advertising to generate an improper charge per click.

clickstream tracking: Tracking data about customer activities at websites and storing them in a log.

client: The user point of entry for the required function in client/server computing; normally a desktop computer, workstation, or laptop computer.

client/server computing: A model for computing that splits processing between clients and servers on a network, assigning functions to the machine most able to perform the function.

cloud computing: Model of computing that provides access to a shared pool of computing resources over a network, often the Internet.

collaboration: Working with others to achieve shared and explicit goals.

community provider: Website business model that creates a digital online environment in which people with similar interests can transact; share interests, photos, and videos; and receive interest-related information.

competitive forces model: Model used to describe the interaction of external influences, specifically threats and opportunities, that affect an organization's strategy and ability to compete.

component-based development: Building large software systems by combining preexisting software components.

computer abuse: The commission of acts involving a computer that may not be illegal but are considered unethical.

computer crime: The commission of illegal acts through the use of a computer or against a computer system.

computer forensics: The scientific collection, examination, authentication, preservation, and analysis of data held on or retrieved from computer storage media in such a way that the information can be used as evidence in a court of law.

computer hardware: Physical equipment used for input, processing, and output activities in an information system.

computer literacy: Knowledge about information technology, focusing on understanding of how computer-based technologies work.

computer software: Detailed, preprogrammed instructions that control and coordinate the work of computer hardware components in an information system.

computer virus: Rogue software program that attaches itself to other software programs or data files and activates, often causing hardware and software malfunctions.

computer vision syndrome (CVS): Eyestrain condition related to computer display screen use; symptoms include headaches, blurred vision, and dry and irritated eyes.

computer vision systems: Computer systems that try to emulate the human visual system to view and extract information from real-world images.

computer-aided design (CAD) system: Information system that automates the creation and revision of designs by using sophisticated graphics software.

computer-aided software engineering (CASE): Automation of step-by-step methodologies for software and systems development to reduce the amount of repetitive work the developer needs to perform.

consumerization of IT: New information technology originating in the consumer market that spreads to business organizations.

consumer-to-consumer (C2C) electronic commerce: Consumers selling goods and services electronically to other consumers.

controls: All of the methods, policies, and procedures that ensure protection of the organization's assets, accuracy and reliability of its records, and operational adherence to management standards.

conversion: The process of changing from the old system to the new system.

cookies: Tiny files deposited on a computer hard drive when an individual visits certain websites; used to identify the visitor and track visits to the website.

copyright: A statutory grant that protects creators of intellectual property against copying by others for any purpose during the life of the author plus an additional 70 years after the author's death.

core competency: Activity at which a firm excels as a world-class leader.

cost transparency: The ability of consumers to discover the actual costs merchants pay for products.

critical thinking: Sustained suspension of judgment with an awareness of multiple perspectives and alternatives.

cross-selling: Marketing complementary products to customers.

crowdsourcing: Using large Internet audiences for advice, market feedback, new ideas, and solutions to business problems; related to the wisdom-of-crowds theory.

culture: Fundamental set of assumptions, values, and ways of doing things that has been accepted by most members of an organization.

customer lifetime value (CLTV): Difference between revenues produced by a specific customer and the expenses for acquiring and servicing that customer minus the cost of promotional marketing over the lifetime of the customer relationship, expressed in today's dollars.

customer relationship management (CRM) systems: Information systems that track all the ways in which a company interacts with its customers and analyze these interactions to optimize revenue, profitability, customer satisfaction, and customer retention.

customization: In e-commerce, changing a delivered product or service based on a user's preferences or prior behavior.

customization: The modification of a software package to meet an organization's unique requirements without destroying the package software's integrity.

cybervandalism: Intentional disruption, defacement, or even destruction of a website or corporate information system.

cyberwarfare: State-sponsored activity designed to cripple and defeat another state or nation by damaging or disrupting its computers or networks.

cycle time: The total elapsed time from the beginning of a process to its end.

data: Streams of raw facts representing events occurring in organizations or the physical environment before they have been organized and arranged into a form that people can understand and use.

data administration: A special organizational function for managing the organization's data resources, concerned with information policy, data planning, maintenance of data dictionaries, and data quality standards.

data center: Facility housing computer systems and associated components, such as telecommunications, storage and security systems, and backup power supplies.

data cleansing: Activities for detecting and correcting data in a database or file that are incorrect, incomplete, improperly formatted, or redundant. Also known as data scrubbing.

data definition: Specifies the structure of the content of a database.

data dictionary: An automated or manual tool for storing and organizing information about the data maintained in a database.

data flow diagram (DFD): Primary tool for structured analysis that graphically illustrates a system's component process and the flow of data between them.

data lake: Repository for raw unstructured data or structured data that for the most part have not yet been analyzed.

data management software: Software used for creating and manipulating lists, creating files and databases to store data, and combining information for reports.

data management technology: Software governing the organization of data on physical storage media.

data manipulation language: A language associated with a database management system that end users and programmers use to manipulate data in the database.

data mart: A small data warehouse containing only a portion of the organization's data for a specified function or population of users.

data mining: Analysis of large pools of data to find patterns and rules that can be used to guide decision making and predict future behavior.

data quality audit: A survey and/or sample of files to determine accuracy and completeness of data in an information system.

data visualization: Technology for helping users see patterns and relationships in large amounts of data by presenting the data in graphical form.

data warehouse: A database, with reporting and query tools, that stores current and historical data extracted from various operational systems and consolidated for management reporting and analysis.

data workers: People such as secretaries or bookkeepers who process the organization's paperwork.

database: A group of related files.

database administration: Refers to the more technical and operational aspects of managing data, including physical database design and maintenance.

database management system (DBMS): Special software to create and maintain a database and enable individual business applications to extract the data they need without having to create separate files or data definitions in their computer programs.

database server: A computer in a client/server environment that is responsible for running a DBMS to process SQL statements and perform database management tasks.

decision-support systems (DSS): Information systems at the organization's management level that combine data and sophisticated analytical models or data analysis tools to support semi-structured and unstructured decision making.

deep packet inspection (DPI): Technology for managing network traffic by examining data packets, sorting out low-priority data from higher priority business-critical data, and sending packets in order of priority.

demand planning: Determining how much product a business needs to make to satisfy all its customers' demands.

denial-of-service (DoS) attack: Flooding a network server or web server with false communications or requests for services to crash the network.

design: Simon's second stage of decision making, when the individual conceives of possible alternative solutions to a problem.

DevOps: Organizational strategy to create a culture and environment to promote rapid and agile development practices by emphasizing close collaboration between software developers and the IT operational staff.

digital asset management systems: Systems that classify, store, and distribute digital objects such as photographs, graphic images, video, and audio content.

digital certificates: Attachments to an electronic message to verify the identity of the sender and provide the receiver with the means to encode a reply.

digital dashboard: Displays all of a firm's key performance indicators as graphs and charts on a single screen to provide one-page overview of all the critical measurements necessary to make key executive decisions.

digital divide: Large disparities in access to computers and the Internet among different social groups and different locations.

digital goods: Goods that can be delivered over a digital network.

digital market: A marketplace that is created by computer and communication technologies that link many buyers and sellers.

Digital Millennium Copyright Act (DMCA): Adjusts copyright laws to the Internet Age by making it illegal to make, distribute, or use devices that circumvent technology-based protections of copyrighted materials.

digital signature: A digital code that can be attached to an electronically transmitted message to identify its contents and the sender uniquely.

digital subscriber line (DSL): A group of technologies providing high-capacity transmission over existing copper telephone lines.

direct cutover strategy: A risky conversion approach by which the new system completely replaces the old one on an appointed day.

direct goods: Goods used in a production process.

disaster recovery planning: Planning for the restoration of computing and communications services after they have been disrupted.

disintermediation: The removal of organizations or business process layers responsible for certain intermediary steps in a value chain.

disruptive technologies: Technologies with disruptive impact on industries and businesses, rendering existing products, services, and business models obsolete.

distributed database: Database stored in multiple physical locations.

distributed denial-of-service (DDoS) attack: Attack that uses numerous computers to inundate and overwhelm a network from numerous launch points.

distributed processing: The distribution of computer processing work among multiple computers linked by a communications network.

documentation: Descriptions of how an information system works from either a technical or end-user standpoint.

domain name: English-like name that corresponds to the unique 32-bit numeric Internet Protocol (IP) address for each computer connected to the Internet.

Domain Name System (DNS): A hierarchical system of servers maintaining a database enabling the conversion of domain names to their numeric IP addresses.

domestic exporter: Form of business organization characterized by heavy centralization of corporate activities in the home country of origin.

downtime: Period of time in which an information system is not operational.

drill down: The ability to move from summary data to increasingly granular levels of detail.

drive-by download: Malware that comes with a downloaded file a user unintentionally opens.

due process: A process by which laws are well-known and understood and provide an ability to appeal to higher authorities to ensure that laws are applied correctly.

dynamic pricing: Pricing of items based on real-time interactions between buyers and sellers that determine what an item is worth at any particular moment.

efficient customer response system: System that directly links consumer behavior to distribution, production, and supply chains.

e-government: Use of the Internet and related technologies to enable government and public sector agencies' relationships with citizens, businesses, and other arms of government digitally.

electronic business (e-business): The use of the Internet and digital technology to execute all the business processes in the enterprise; includes e-commerce as well as processes for the internal management of the firm and coordination with suppliers and other business partners.

electronic commerce (e-commerce): The process of buying and selling goods and services electronically, involving transactions by using the Internet, networks, and other digital technologies.

Electronic Data Interchange (EDI): The direct computer-to-computer exchange between two organizations of standard business transactions, such as orders, shipment instructions, or payments.

email: The computer-to-computer exchange of messages.

employee relationship management (ERM): Software dealing with employee issues that are closely related to CRM, such as setting objectives, employee performance management, performance-based compensation, and employee training.

encryption: The coding and scrambling of messages to prevent them from being read or accessed without authorization.

end users: Representatives of departments outside the information systems group for whom applications are developed.

end-user development: The development of information systems by end users with little or no formal assistance from technical specialists.

enterprise applications: Systems that can coordinate activities, decisions, and knowledge across many functions, levels, and business units in a firm; include enterprise systems, supply chain management systems, customer relationship management systems, and knowledge management systems.

enterprise content management (ECM) systems: Systems that help organizations manage structured and semi-structured knowledge, providing corporate repositories of documents, reports, presentations, and best practices and capabilities for collecting and organizing email and graphic objects.

enterprise software Software built around thousands of predefined business processes that reflects best practices and integrates the major business functions of the organization..

enterprise systems: Integrated, enterprise-wide information systems that coordinate key internal processes of the firm. Also known as enterprise resource planning (ERP).

enterprise-wide knowledge management systems: General-purpose, firm-wide systems that collect, store, distribute, and apply digital content and knowledge.

entity: A person, place, thing, or event about which information must be kept.

entity-relationship diagram: A methodology for documenting databases illustrating the relationship between various entities in the database.

ergonomics: The interaction of people and machines in the work environment, including the design of jobs, health issues, and the end-user interface of information systems.

e-tailer: Online retail stores from the giant Amazon to tiny local stores that have websites where retail goods are sold.

ethical no-free-lunch rule: Assumption that all tangible and intangible objects are owned by someone else, unless there is a specific declaration otherwise, and that the creator wants compensation for this work.

ethics: Principles of right and wrong that can be used by individuals acting as free moral agents to make choices to guide their behavior.

evil twins: Wireless networks that pretend to be legitimate Wi-Fi networks to entice participants to log on and reveal passwords or credit card numbers.

exchanges: Third-party Net marketplaces that are primarily transaction oriented and that connect many buyers and suppliers for spot purchasing.

executive support systems (ESS): Information systems at the organization's strategic level designed to address unstructured decision making through advanced graphics and communications.

expert system: Knowledge-intensive computer program that captures the expertise of a human in limited domains of knowledge.

Extensible Markup Language (XML): A more powerful and flexible markup language than hypertext markup language (HTML) for web pages, allowing data to be manipulated by the computer.

extranets: Private intranets that are accessible to authorized outsiders.

Fair Information Practices (FIP): A set of principles originally set forth in 1973 that governs the collection and use of information about individuals and forms the basis of most U.S. and European privacy laws.

fault-tolerant computer systems: Systems that contain extra hardware, software, and power supply components that can back a system up and keep it running to prevent system failure.

feasibility study: As part of the systems analysis process, the way to determine whether the solution is achievable, given the organization's resources and constraints.

feedback: Output that is returned to the appropriate members of the organization to help them evaluate or correct input.

field: A grouping of characters into a word, a group of words, or a complete number, such as a person's name or age.

file A group of records of the same type.

File Transfer Protocol (FTP): Tool for retrieving and transferring files from a remote computer.

FinTech: Start-up innovative financial technology firms and services.

firewall: Hardware and software placed between an organization's internal network and an external network to prevent outsiders from invading private networks.

foreign key: Field in a database table that enables users to find related information in another database table.

formal planning and control tools: Tools to improve project management by listing the specific activities that make up a project, their duration, and the sequence and timing of tasks.

franchiser: Form of business organization in which a product is created, designed, financed, and initially produced in the home country, but for product-specific reasons relies heavily on foreign personnel for further production, marketing, and human resources.

free/freemium revenue model: E-commerce revenue mode in which a firm offers free basic services or content while charging a premium for advanced or high-value features.

Gantt chart: Chart that visually represents the timing, duration, and human resource requirements of project tasks, with each task represented as a horizontal bar whose length is proportional to the time required to complete it.

general controls: Overall control environment governing the design, security, and use of computer programs and the security of data files in general throughout the organization's information technology infrastructure.

genetic algorithms: Problem-solving methods that promote the evolution of solutions to specified problems using the model of living organisms adapting to their environment.

geoadvertising services: Delivering ads to users based on their GPS location.

geographic information systems (GIS): Systems with software that can analyze and display data using digitized maps to enhance planning and decision-making.

geoinformation services: Information on local places and things based on the GPS position of the user.

geosocial services: Social networking based on the GPS location of users.

Golden Rule: Putting oneself in the place of others as the object of a decision.

Gramm-Leach-Bliley Act: Requires financial institutions to ensure the security and confidentiality of customer data.

graphical user interface (GUI): The part of an operating system users interact with that uses graphic icons and the computer mouse to issue commands and make selections.

green computing: Practices and technologies for producing, using, and disposing of computers and associated devices to minimize impact on the environment.

grid computing: Applying the resources of many computers in a network to a single problem.

group decision-support system (GDSS): An interactive computer-based system to facilitate the solution to unstructured problems by a set of decision makers working together as a group.

hacker: A person who gains unauthorized access to a computer network for profit, criminal mischief, or personal pleasure.

Hadoop: Open-source software framework that enables distributed parallel processing of huge amounts of data across many inexpensive computers.

hertz: Measure of frequency of electrical impulses per second, with 1 hertz (Hz) equivalent to 1 cycle per second.

HIPAA: Law outlining medical security and privacy rules and procedures for simplifying the administration of health care billing and automating the transfer of health care data between health care providers, payers, and plans.

hotspots: Specific geographic locations in which an access point provides public Wi-Fi network service.

HTML5: Next evolution of HTML, which will make it possible to embed images, video, and audio directly into a document without using add-on software.

hubs: Very simple devices that connect network components, sending a packet of data to all other connected devices.

hybrid cloud: Computing model by which firms use both their own IT infrastructure and public cloud computing services.

Hypertext Markup Language (HTML): Page description language for creating web pages and other hypermedia documents.

Hypertext Transport Protocol (HTTP): The communications standard that transfers pages on the web. Defines how messages are formatted and transmitted.

identity management: Business processes and software tools for identifying the valid users of a system and controlling their access to system resources.

identity theft: Theft of key pieces of personal information, such as credit card or Social Security numbers, to obtain merchandise and services in the name of the victim or to obtain false credentials.

Immanuel Kant's categorical imperative: A principle that states that if an action is not right for everyone to take, it is not right for anyone.

implementation: All the organizational activities surrounding the adoption, management, and regular reuse of an innovation, such as a new information system.

implementation: Simon's final stage of decision-making, when the individual puts the decision into effect and reports on the progress of the solution.

indirect goods: Goods not directly used in the production process, such as office supplies.

inference engine: The strategy used to search through the rule base in an expert system; can be forward or backward chaining.

information: Data that have been shaped into a form that is meaningful and useful to human beings.

information asymmetry: Situation when the relative bargaining power of two parties in a transaction is determined by one party in the transaction possessing more information essential to the transaction than the other party.

information density: The total amount and quality of information available to all market participants, consumers, and merchants.

information policy: Formal rules governing the maintenance, distribution, and use of information in an organization.

information requirements: A detailed statement of the information needs that a new system must satisfy; identifies who needs what information and when, where, and how the information is needed.

information rights: The rights that individuals and organizations have with respect to information that pertains to them.

information system (IS): Interrelated components working together to collect, process, store, and disseminate information to support decision making, coordination, control, analysis, and visualization in an organization.

Information systems audit: Identifies all the controls that govern individual information systems and assesses their effectiveness.

information systems department: The formal organizational unit that is responsible for the information systems function in the organization.

information systems literacy: Broad-based understanding of information systems that includes behavioral knowledge about organizations and individuals by using information systems as well as technical knowledge about computers.

information systems managers: Leaders of the various specialists in the information systems department.

information systems plan: A road map indicating the direction of systems development: the rationale, the current situation, the management strategy, the implementation plan, and the budget.

information technology (IT): All the hardware and software technologies that a firm needs to use to achieve its business objectives.

information technology (IT) infrastructure: Computer hardware, software, data, storage technology, and networks providing a portfolio of shared IT resources for the organization.

informed consent: Consent given with knowledge of all the facts needed to make a rational decision.

in-memory computing: Technology for very rapid analysis and processing of large quantities of data by storing the data in the computer's main memory rather than in secondary storage.

input: The capture or collection of raw data from within the organization or from its external environment for processing in an information system.

input devices: Device that gathers data and converts them into electronic form for use by the computer.

instant messaging: Chat service that allows participants to create their own private chat channels so that a person can be alerted whenever someone on his or her private list is online to initiate a chat session with that particular individual.

intangible benefits: Benefits that are not easily quantified; they include more efficient customer service or enhanced decision making.

intellectual property: Intangible property created by individuals or corporations that is subject to protections under trade secret, copyright, and patent law.

intelligence: The first of Simon's four stages of decision making, when the individual collects information to identify problems occurring in the organization.

intelligent agents: Software programs that use a built-in or learned knowledge base to carry out specific, repetitive, and predictable tasks for an individual user, business process, or software application.

"intelligent" techniques: Technologies that aid decision makers by capturing individual and collective knowledge, discovering patterns and behaviors in very large quantities of data, and generating solutions to problems that are too large and complex for human beings to solve on their own.

Internet: Global network of networks using universal standards to connect millions of networks.

Internet Protocol (IP) address: Four-part numeric address indicating a unique computer location on the Internet.

Internet service provider (ISP): A commercial organization with a permanent connection to the Internet that sells temporary connections to subscribers.

Internet of Things (IoT): Pervasive web in which each object or machine has a unique identity and is able to use the Internet to link with other machines or send data; also known as the industrial Internet.

Internet2: Research network with new protocols and transmission speeds that provides an infrastructure for supporting high-bandwidth Internet applications.

interorganizational system: Information systems that automate the flow of information across organizational boundaries and link a company to its customers, distributors, or suppliers.

intranets: Internal networks based on Internet and World Wide Web technology and standards.

intrusion detection systems: Tools to monitor the most vulnerable points in a network to detect and deter unauthorized intruders.

iOS: Operating system for the Apple iPad, iPhone, and iPod Touch.

IPv6: New IP addressing system using 128-bit IP addresses. Stands for Internet Protocol version 6.

Java: An operating system–independent, processor-independent, object-oriented programming language that has become a leading interactive programming environment for the web.

Joint application design (JAD): Process to accelerate the generation of information requirements by having end users and information systems specialists work together in intensive interactive design sessions.

just-in-time strategy: Scheduling system for minimizing inventory by having components arrive exactly at the moment they are needed and finished goods shipped as soon as they leave the assembly line.

key field: A field in a record that uniquely identifies instances of that record so that it can be retrieved, updated, or sorted.

keyloggers: Spyware that records every keystroke made on a computer.

key performance indicators (KPIs): Measures proposed by senior management for understanding how well the firm is performing along specified dimensions.

knowledge base: Model of human knowledge that expert systems use.

knowledge management: The set of processes developed in an organization to create, gather, store, maintain, and disseminate the firm's knowledge.

knowledge management systems (KMS): Systems that support the creation, capture, storage, and dissemination of firm expertise and knowledge.

knowledge work systems (KWS): Information systems that aid knowledge workers in the creation and integration of new knowledge in the organization.

knowledge workers: People such as engineers or architects who design products or services and create knowledge for the organization.

learning management system (LMS): Tools for the management, delivery, tracking, and assessment of various types of employee learning.

legacy systems: Systems that have been in existence for a long time and that continue to be used to avoid the high cost of replacing or redesigning them.

liability: Laws that permit individuals to recover the damages done to them by other actors, systems, or organizations.

Linux: Reliable and compactly designed operating system that is an open-source offshoot of UNIX, can run on many hardware platforms, and is available free or at very low cost.

local area network (LAN): A telecommunications network that requires its own dedicated channels and that encompasses a limited distance, usually one building or several buildings in close proximity.

location analytics: Ability to gain insight from the location (geographic) component of data, including location data from mobile phones, output from sensors or scanning devices, and data from maps.

location-based services: GPS map services available on smartphones.

long tail marketing: Ability of firms to market goods profitably to very small online audiences, largely because of the lower costs of reaching very small market segments.

machine learning: Study of how computer programs can improve their performance without explicit programming.

mainframe: Largest category of computer, used for major business processing.

maintenance: Changes in hardware, software, documentation, or procedures to a production system to correct errors, meet new requirements, or improve processing efficiency.

malware: Malicious software programs such as computer viruses, worms, and Trojan horses.

managed security service providers (MSSPs): Companies that provide security management services for subscribing clients.

management information systems (MIS): Specific category of information system providing reports on organizational performance to help middle management monitor and control the business.

management information systems (MIS): The study of information systems, focusing on their use in business and management.

market creator: E-commerce business model in which firms provide a digital online environment where buyers and sellers can meet, search for products, and engage in transactions.

market entry costs: The cost merchants must pay simply to bring their goods to market.

marketspace: A marketplace extended beyond traditional boundaries and removed from a temporal and geographic location.

mashups: Composite software applications that depend on high-speed networks, universal communication standards, and open source code and are intended to be greater than the sum of their parts.

mass customization: The capacity to offer individually tailored products or services on a large scale.

massive open online course (MOOC): Online course made available on the web to very large numbers of participants.

menu costs Merchants' costs of changing prices.

metropolitan area network (MAN): Network that spans a metropolitan area, usually a city and its major suburbs. Its geographic scope falls between a WAN and a LAN.

microblogging: Blogging featuring very short posts such as those using Twitter.

micropayment systems: Systems that facilitate payment for a very small sum of money, often less than $10.

microprocessor: Very large-scale, integrated circuit technology that integrates the computer's memory, logic, and control on a single chip.

middle management: People in the middle of the organizational hierarchy who are responsible for carrying out the plans and goals of senior management.

mobile commerce (m-commerce): The use of wireless devices, such as cell phones or handheld digital information appliances, to conduct both business-to-consumer and business-to-business e-commerce transactions over the Internet.

mobile device management (MDM): Software that monitors, manages, and secures mobile devices the organization is using.

mobile web app: Application residing on a server and accessed through the mobile web browser built into a smartphone or tablet computer.

mobile website: Version of a regular website that is scaled down in content and navigation for easy access and search on a small mobile screen.

modem: A device for translating a computer's digital signals into analog form or for translating analog signals back into digital form for reception by a computer.

multicore processor: Integrated circuit to which two or more processors have been attached for enhanced performance, reduced power consumption and more efficient simultaneous processing of multiple tasks.

multinational: Form of business organization that concentrates financial management and control out of a central home base while decentralizing production, sales, and marketing.

multitouch: Interface that features the use of one or more finger gestures to manipulate lists or objects on a screen without using a mouse or keyboard.

nanotechnology: Technology that builds structures and processes based on the manipulation of individual atoms and molecules.

native advertising: Placing ads within social network newsfeeds or traditional editorial content, such as a newspaper article.

native app: Stand-alone application specifically designed to run on a mobile platform.

natural language processing: Technology that makes it possible for a machine to understand spoken or written words expressed in human (natural) language and to process that information.

near field communication (NFC): Short-range wireless connectivity standard that uses electromagnetic radio fields to enable two compatible devices to exchange data when brought within a few centimeters of each other.

net marketplaces: Digital marketplaces based on Internet technology linking many buyers to many

network: The linking of two or more computers to share data or resources such as a printer.

network economics: Model of strategic systems at the industry level based on the concept of a network when adding another participant entails zero marginal costs but can create much larger marginal gains.

network operating system (NOS): Special software that routes and manages communications on the network and coordinates network resources.

networking and telecommunications technology: Physical devices and software that link various pieces of hardware and transfer data from one physical location to another.

neural networks: Hardware or software that attempts to emulate the processing patterns of the biological brain.

nonobvious relationship awareness (NORA): Technology that can find obscure connections between people or other entities by analyzing information from many sources to correlate relationships.

non-relational database management system: Database management system for working with large quantities of structured and unstructured data that would be difficult to analyze with a relational model.

normalization: The process of creating small, stable data structures from complex groups of data when designing a relational database.

n-tier client/server architecture: Client/server arrangement that balances the work of the entire network over multiple levels of servers.

object: Software building block that combines data and the procedures acting on the data.

object-oriented development: Approach to systems development that uses the object as the basic unit of systems analysis and design. The system is modeled as a collection of objects and the relationship between them.

Office 365 : Hosted cloud version of Microsoft Office productivity and collaboration tools as a subscription service.

offshore software outsourcing: Outsourcing systems development work or maintenance of existing systems to external vendors in another country.

on-demand computing: Firms off-loading peak demand for computing power to remote, large-scale data processing centers, investing just enough to handle average processing loads and paying for only as much additional computing power as they need. Also called utility computing.

online analytical processing (OLAP): Capability for manipulating and analyzing large volumes of data from multiple perspectives.

online transaction processing: Transaction processing mode in which transactions entered online are immediately processed by the computer.

open source software: Software that provides free access to its program code, allowing users to modify the program code to make improvements or fix errors.

operating system: The system software that manages and controls the activities of the computer.

operational CRM: Customer-facing applications, such as sales force automation, call center and customer service support, and marketing automation.

operational intelligence: Business analytics that deliver insight into data, streaming events, and business operations.

operational management: People who monitor the day-to-day activities of the organization.

opt-in: Model of informed consent permitting prohibiting an organization from collecting any personal information unless the individual specifically takes action to approve information collection and use.

opt-out: Model of informed consent permitting the collection of personal information until the consumer specifically requests the data not to be collected.

organizational impact analysis: Study of the way a proposed system will affect organizational structure, attitudes, decision making, and operations.

output: The distribution of processed information to the people who will use it or to the activities for which it will be used.

output device: Device that displays data after they have been processed.

outsourcing: The practice of contracting computer center operations, telecommunications networks, or applications development to external vendors.

packet switching: Technology that breaks messages into small, fixed bundles of data and routes them in the most economical way through any available communications channel.

parallel processing: Type of processing in which more than one instruction can be processed at a time by breaking down a problem into smaller parts and processing them simultaneously with multiple processors.

parallel strategy: A safe and conservative conversion approach in which both the old system and its potential replacement are run together for a time until everyone is assured that the new one functions correctly.

partner relationship management (PRM): Automation of the firm's relationships with its selling partners using customer data and analytical tools to improve coordination and customer sales.

password: Secret word or string of characters for authenticating users so they can access a resource such as a computer system.

patches: Small pieces of software that repair flaws in programs without disturbing the proper operation of the software.

patent: A legal document that grants the owner an exclusive monopoly on the ideas behind an invention for 17 years; designed to ensure that inventors of new machines or methods are rewarded for their labor while making available widespread use of their inventions.

peer-to-peer: Network architecture that gives equal power to all computers on the network; used primarily in small networks.

personal area networks (PANs): Networks linking digital devices that are close to one person.

personal computer (PC): Small desktop or portable computer.

personalization: Ability of merchants to target their marketing messages to specific individuals by adjusting the message to a person's name, interests, and past purchases.

PERT chart: A chart that graphically depicts project tasks and their interrelationships, showing the specific activities that must be completed before others can start.

pharming: Phishing technique that redirects users to a bogus web page, even when the individual types the correct web page address into his or her browser.

phased approach: Introduces the new system in stages either by functions or by organizational units.

phishing: A form of spoofing involving setting up fake websites or sending email messages that look like those of legitimate businesses to ask users for confidential personal data.

pilot study: A strategy to introduce the new system to a limited area of the organization until it proves to be fully functional; only then can the conversion to the new system across the entire organization take place.

pivot table: Spreadsheet tool for reorganizing and summarizing two or more dimensions of data in a tabular format.

platform: Business providing information systems, technologies, and services that many other firms in different industries use to enhance their own capabilities.

podcasting: Method of publishing audio broadcasts through the Internet, allowing subscribing users to download audio files to their personal computers, smartphones, or portable music players.

portal: Web interface for presenting integrated personalized content from a variety of sources. Also refers to a website service that provides an initial point of entry to the web.

portfolio analysis: An analysis of the portfolio of potential applications within a firm to determine the risks and benefits and to select among alternatives for information systems.

predictive analytics: Use of data mining techniques, historical data, and assumptions about future conditions to predict outcomes of events.

predictive search: Part of a search algorithm that predicts what a user query is looking for as it is entered, based on popular searches.

price discrimination: Selling the same goods, or nearly the same goods, to different targeted groups at different prices.

price transparency: The ease with which consumers can find out the variety of prices in a market.

primary activities: Activities most directly related to the production and distribution of a firm's products or services.

primary key: Unique identifier for all the information in any row of a database table.

privacy: The claim of individuals to be left alone, free from surveillance or interference from other individuals, organizations, or the state.

Privacy Shield New framework for exchanges of personal data for commercial purposes between the European Union and the United States.

private cloud: Proprietary network or data center that ties together servers, storage, networks, data, and applications as a set of virtualized services that users inside a company share.

private exchange: Another term for a private industrial network.

private industrial networks: Web-enabled networks linking systems of multiple firms in an industry for the coordination of trans-organizational business processes.

process specifications: Specifications that describe the logic of the processes occurring within the lowest levels of a data flow diagram.

processing: The conversion, manipulation, and analysis of raw input into a form that is more meaningful to humans.

production or service workers: People who actually produce the products or services of the organization.

production: The stage after the new system is installed and the conversion is complete; during this time, the system is reviewed by users and technical specialists to determine how well it has met its original goals.

profiling: The use of computers to combine data from multiple sources and create electronic dossiers of detailed information on individuals.

program: Series of instructions for the computer.

programmers: Highly trained technical specialists who write computer software instructions.

programming: The process of translating the system specifications prepared during the design stage into program code.

project: A planned series of related activities for achieving a specific business objective.

project management: Application of knowledge, skills, tools, and techniques to achieve specific targets within specified budget and time constraints.

protocol: A set of rules and procedures that govern transmission between the components in a network.

prototyping: The process of building an experimental system quickly and inexpensively for demonstration and evaluation so that users can better determine information requirements.

public cloud: Cloud maintained by an external service provider, accessed through the Internet, and available to the general public.

public key encryption: Encryption using two keys: one shared (or public) and one private.

public key infrastructure (PKI): System for creating public and private keys by using a certificate authority (CA) and digital certificates for authentication.

pull-based model: Supply chain driven by actual customer orders or purchases so that members of the supply chain produce and deliver only what customers have ordered.

push-based model: Supply chain driven by master production schedules based on forecasts or best guesses of demand for products; products are pushed to customers.

quality: Product or service's conformance to specifications and standards.

quantum computing: Use of principles of quantum physics to represent data and perform operations on the data, with the ability to be in many states at once and to perform many computations simultaneously.

query Request for data from a database.

radio frequency identification (RFID): Technology using tiny tags with embedded microchips containing data about an item and its location to transmit short-distance radio signals to special RFID readers that then pass the data on to a computer for processing.

ransomware: malware that extorts money from users by taking control of their computers or displaying annoying pop-up messages

rapid application development (RAD): Process for developing systems in a very short time period by using prototyping, user-friendly tools, and close teamwork among users and systems specialists.

record: A group of related fields.

referential integrity: Rules to ensure that relationships between coupled database tables remain consistent.

relational database: A type of logical database model that treats data as if they were stored in two-dimensional tables. It can relate data stored in one table to data in another as long as the two tables share a common data element.

repetitive stress injury (RSI): Occupational disease that occurs when muscle groups are forced through repetitive actions with high-impact loads or thousands of repetitions with low-impact loads.

report generator Software designed to take data from a source such as a database and use the data to produce a report in a polished format.

Request for Proposal (RFP): A detailed list of questions submitted to vendors of software or other services to determine how well the vendor's product can meet the organization's specific requirements.

responsibility: Accepting the potential costs, duties, and obligations for the decisions one makes.

responsive web design: Ability of a website to change screen resolution and image size automatically as a user switches to devices of different sizes, such as a laptop, tablet computer, or smartphone.

Eliminates the need for separate design and development work for each new device.

revenue model: Description of how a firm will earn revenue, generate profits, and produce a return on investment.

richness: Measurement of the depth and detail of information that a business can supply to the customer as well as information the business collects about the customer.

risk assessment: Determining the potential frequency of the occurrence of a problem and the potential damage if the problem were to occur. Used to determine the cost/benefit of a control.

risk aversion principle: Principle that one should take the action that produces the least harm or incurs the least cost.

robotics: Use of machines that can substitute for human movements as well as computer systems for their control, sensory feedback, and information processing.

router: Specialized communications processor that forwards packets of data from one network to another network.

RSS: Technology using aggregator software to pull content from websites and feed it automatically to subscribers' computers.

safe harbor: Private, self-regulating policy and enforcement mechanism that meets the objectives of government regulations but does not involve government regulation or enforcement.

sales force automation (SFA) Software that helps sales staff increase productivity by streamlining and automating important sales processes.

sales revenue model: Selling goods, information, or services to customers as the main source of revenue for a company.

Sarbanes–Oxley Act: Law passed in 2002 that imposes responsibility on companies and their management to protect investors by safeguarding the accuracy and integrity of financial information that is used internally and released externally.

scalability: The ability of a computer, product, or system to expand to serve a larger number of users without breaking down.

scope: Defines what work is or is not included in a project.

scoring model: A quick method for deciding among alternative systems based on a system of ratings for selected objectives.

search costs: The time and money spent locating a suitable product and determining the best price for that product.

search engine marketing: Use of search engines to deliver sponsored links, for which advertisers have paid, in search engine results.

search engine optimization (SEO): Process of changing a website's content, layout, and format to increase the site's ranking on popular search engines and to generate more site visitors.

search engines: Tools for locating specific sites or information on the Internet.

Secure Hypertext Transfer Protocol (S-HTTP): Protocol used for encrypting data flowing over the Internet; limited to individual messages.

Secure Sockets Layer (SSL): Enables client and server computers to manage encryption and decryption activities as they communicate with each other during a secure web session.

security: Policies, procedures, and technical measures used to prevent unauthorized access, alteration, theft, or physical damage to information systems.

security policy: Statements ranking information risks, identifying acceptable security goals, and identifying the mechanisms for achieving these goals.

semantic search: Search technology capable of understanding human language and behavior.

semi-structured decisions: Decisions in which only part of the problem has a clear-cut answer provided by an accepted procedure.

senior management: People occupying the topmost hierarchy, who are responsible for making long-range decisions, in an organization.

sensitivity analysis: Models that ask what-if questions repeatedly to determine the impact of changes in one or more factors on the outcomes.

sentiment analysis: Mining text comments in an email message, blog, or other social media.

server: Computer specifically optimized to provide software and other resources to other computers over a network.

service level agreement (SLA): Formal contract between customers and their service providers that defines the specific responsibilities of the service provider and the level of service the customer expects.

service-oriented architecture (SOA): Software architecture of a firm built on a collection of software programs that communicate with each other to perform assigned tasks to create a working software application.

shopping bots: Software with varying levels of built-in intelligence to help electronic commerce shoppers locate and evaluate products or service they might wish to purchase.

Six Sigma: A specific measure of quality, representing 3.4 defects per million opportunities; used to designate a set of methodologies and techniques for improving quality and reducing costs.

slippery slope rule Ethical principle that an action that may bring about an acceptable small change now would bring unacceptable changes in the long run if it was repeated

smart card: A credit-card-size plastic card that stores digital information and can be used for electronic payments in place of cash.

smartphones: Wireless phones with voice, messaging, scheduling, email, and Internet capabilities.

sniffer: A type of eavesdropping program that monitors information traveling over a network.

social business: Use of social networking platforms, including Facebook, Twitter, and internal corporate social tools, to engage employees, customers, and suppliers.

social CRM: Tools enabling a business to link customer conversations, data, and relationships from social networking sites to CRM processes.

social engineering: Tricking people into revealing their passwords by pretending to be legitimate users or members of a company in need of information.

social graph: Map of all significant online social relationships, comparable to a social network describing offline relationships.

social networking: Online community for expanding users' business or social contacts through their mutual business or personal connections.

social search: Effort to provide more relevant and trustworthy search results based on a person's network of social contacts.

social shopping: Use of websites featuring user-created web pages to share knowledge about items of interest to other shoppers.

software as a service (SaaS): Services for delivering and providing access to software remotely as a web-based service.

software localization: Process of converting software to operate in a second language.

software package: A prewritten, precoded, commercially available set of programs that eliminates the need to write software programs for certain functions.

software-defined networking (SDN): Using a central control program separate from network devices to manage the flow of data on a network.

software-defined storage (SDS): Software to manage provisioning and management of data storage independent of the underlying hardware.

solid state drive (SSD): Storage device that stores data on an array of semiconductor memory organized as a disk drive.

spam: Unsolicited commercial email.

spoofing: Tricking or deceiving computer systems or other computer users by hiding one's identity or faking the identity of another user on the Internet.

spreadsheet software Software displaying data in a grid of columns and rows, with the capability of easily recalculating numerical data.

spyware: Technology that aids in gathering information about a person or organization without their knowledge.

SQL injection attack: Attack against a website that takes advantage of vulnerabilities in poorly coded SQL applications to introduce malicious program code into a company's systems and networks.

streaming Method of publishing music and video files that flows a continuous stream of content to a user's device without being stored locally on the device.

structure chart: System documentation showing each level of design, the relationship among the levels, and the overall place in the design structure; can document one program, one system, or part of one program.

structured: Refers to the fact that techniques are carefully drawn up, step by step, with each step building on a previous one.

structured decisions: Decisions that are repetitive, routine, and have a definite procedure for handling them.

structured knowledge: Knowledge in the form of structured documents and reports.

Structured Query Language (SQL): The standard data manipulation language for relational database management systems.

subscription revenue model: Website charging a subscription fee for access to some or all of its content or services on an ongoing basis.

supercomputer: Highly sophisticated and powerful computer that can perform very complex computations extremely rapidly.

supply chain: Network of organizations and business processes for procuring materials, transforming raw materials into intermediate and finished products, and distributing the finished products to customers.

supply chain execution systems: Systems to manage the flow of products through distribution centers and warehouses to ensure that products are delivered to the right locations in the most efficient manner.

supply chain management (SCM) systems: Information systems that automate the flow of information between a firm and its suppliers to optimize the planning, sourcing, manufacturing, and delivery of products and services.

supply chain planning systems: Systems that enable a firm to generate demand forecasts for a product and develop sourcing and manufacturing plans for that product.

support activities: Activities that make the delivery of a firm's primary activities possible; consist of the organization's infrastructure, human resources, technology, and procurement.

switch: Device to connect network components that has more intelligence than a hub and can filter and forward data to a specified destination.

switching costs: The expense a customer or company incurs in lost time and expenditure of resources when changing from one supplier or system to a competing supplier or system.

system software: Generalized programs that manage the computer's resources, such as the central processor, communications links, and peripheral devices.

system testing: Tests the functioning of the information system as a whole to determine whether discrete modules will function together as planned.

systems analysis: The analysis of a problem that the organization will try to solve with an information system.

systems analysts: Specialists who translate business problems and requirements into information requirements and systems, acting as liaison between the information systems department and the rest of the organization.

systems design: Details how a system will meet the information requirements as determined by the systems analysis.

systems development: The activities that go into producing an information systems solution to an organizational problem or opportunity.

systems development life cycle (SDLC): A traditional methodology for developing an information system that partitions the systems development process into formal stages that must be completed sequentially with a very formal division of labor between end users and information systems specialists.

T1 lines: High-speed data lines leased from communications providers, with a transmission capacity of 1.544 Mbps.

tablet computer: Mobile handheld computer that is larger than a mobile phone and operated primarily by touching a flat screen

tacit knowledge: Expertise and experience of organizational members that has not been formally documented.

tangible benefits: Benefits that can be quantified and assigned a monetary value; they include lower operational costs and increased cash flows.

teams: Formal groups whose members collaborate to achieve specific goals.

telepresence: Technology that allows a person to give the appearance of being present at a location other than his or her true physical location.

telnet Logging on to one computer system and doing work on another.

test plan: Plan prepared by the development team in conjunction with the users; it includes all the preparations for the series of tests to be performed on the system.

testing process The exhaustive and thorough process that determines whether a system produces the desired results under known conditions.

text mining: Discovery of patterns and relationships from large sets of unstructured data.

token: Physical device, similar to an identification card, that is designed to prove the identity of a single user.

total cost of ownership (TCO): Designates the total cost of owning technology resources, including initial purchase costs, the cost of hardware and software upgrades, maintenance, technical support, and training.

total quality management (TQM): A concept that makes quality control a responsibility to be shared by all people in an organization.

touch point: Method of firm interaction with a customer, such as telephone, email, customer service desk, conventional mail, or point of purchase.

trade secret: Any intellectual work or product used for a business purpose that can be classified as belonging to that business, provided it is not based on information in the public domain.

transaction costs Costs of participating in a market.

transaction fee revenue model: E-commerce revenue model in which the firm receives a fee for enabling or executing transactions.

transaction processing systems (TPS): Computerized systems that perform and record the daily routine transactions necessary to conduct the business; they serve the organization's operational level.

Transmission Control Protocol/Internet Protocol (TCP/IP): Dominant model for achieving connectivity among different networks. Provides a universally agreed-on method for breaking up digital messages into packets, routing them to the proper addresses, and then reassembling them into coherent messages.

transnational: Truly global form of business organization where value-added activities are managed from a global perspective without reference to national borders, optimizing sources of supply and demand and local competitive advantage.

Trojan horse: A software program that appears legitimate but contains a second hidden function that may cause damage.

tuples: Rows or records in a relational database.

two-factor authentication: Validating user identity with two means of identification, one of which is typically a physical token, and the other of which is typically data.

unified communications: Integrates disparate channels for voice communications, data communications, instant messaging, email, and electronic conferencing into a single experience by which users can seamlessly switch back and forth between different communication modes.

unified threat management (UTM): Comprehensive security management tool that combines multiple security tools, including firewalls, virtual private networks, intrusion detection systems, and web content filtering and anti-spam software.

uniform resource locator (URL): The address of a specific resource on the Internet.

unit testing: The process of testing each program separately in the system; sometimes called program testing.

UNIX: Operating system for all types of computers, which is machine independent and supports multiuser processing, multitasking, and networking; used in high-end workstations and servers.

unstructured decisions: Nonroutine decisions in which the decision maker must provide judgment, evaluation, and insights in the problem definition; there is no agreed-upon procedure for making such decisions.

user interface: The part of the information system through which the end user interacts with the system; type of hardware and the series of on-screen commands and responses required for a user to work with the system.

user–designer communications gap: The difference in backgrounds, interests, and priorities that impede communication and problem solving among end users and information systems specialists.

utilitarian principle: Principle that assumes one can put values in rank order and understand the consequences of various courses of action.

value chain model: Model that highlights the primary or support activities that add a margin of value to a firm's products or services where information systems can best be applied to achieve a competitive advantage.

value web: Customer-driven network of independent firms who use information technology to coordinate their value chains to produce a product or service collectively for a market.

virtual company: A company that uses networks to link people, assets, and ideas, enabling it to ally with other companies to create and distribute products and services without being limited by traditional organizational boundaries or physical locations.

virtual private network (VPN): A secure connection between two points across the Internet to transmit corporate data. Provides a low-cost alternative to a private network.

Virtual Reality Modeling Language (VRML): A set of specifications for interactive three-dimensional modeling on the World Wide Web.

virtual reality systems: Interactive graphics software and hardware that create computer-generated simulations that provide sensations that emulate real-world activities.

virtual world: Computer-based simulated environment intended for its users to inhabit and interact through graphical representations called avatars.

virtualization: Presenting a set of computing resources so that they can all be accessed in ways that are not restricted by physical configuration or geographic location.

Visual Basic Visual programming tool and environment for creating applications that run on Microsoft Windows operating systems.

visual programming language: Allows users to manipulate graphic or iconic elements to create programs.

visual web: Refers to web linking visual sites such as Pinterest where pictures replace text documents and where users search on pictures and visual characteristics.

Voice over IP (VoIP): Facilities for managing the delivery of voice information using the Internet Protocol (IP).

war driving: An eavesdropping technique in which eavesdroppers drive by buildings or park outside and try to intercept wireless network traffic.

wearable computer: Small wearable computing device such as a smartwatch, smartglasses, or activity tracker.

Web 2.0: Second-generation, interactive Internet-based services that enable people to collaborate, share information, and create new services online, including mashups, blogs, RSS, and wikis.

Web 3.0: Future vision of the web when all digital information is woven together with intelligent search capabilities.

web beacons: Tiny objects invisibly embedded in email messages and web pages that are designed to monitor the behavior of the user visiting a website or sending email.

web browsers: Easy-to-use software tool for accessing the World Wide Web and the Internet.

web hosting service: Company with large web server computers to maintain the websites of fee-paying subscribers.

web mining: Discovery and analysis of useful patterns and information from the World Wide Web.

web server: Software that manages requests for web pages on the computer where they are stored and delivers the page to the user's computer.

web services: Set of universal standards using Internet technology for integrating different applications from different sources without time-consuming custom coding. Used for linking systems of different organizations or for linking disparate systems within the same organization.

website: Any of the World Wide Web pages maintained by an organization or an individual.

wide area networks (WANs): Telecommunications networks that span a large geographical distance. May consist of a variety of cable, satellite, and microwave technologies.

Wi-Fi: Standards for wireless fidelity and refers to the 802.11 family of wireless networking standards.

wiki: Collaborative website where visitors can add, delete, or modify content on the site, including the work of previous authors.

WiMax: Popular term for IEEE Standard 802.16 for wireless networking over a range of up to 31 miles with a data transfer rate of up to 75 Mbps. Stands for Worldwide Interoperability for Microwave Access.

Windows 10: Most recent Microsoft client operating system.

wireless sensor networks (WSNs): Networks of interconnected wireless devices with built-in processing, storage, and radio frequency sensors and antennas that are embedded in the physical environment to provide measurements of many points over large spaces.

wisdom of crowds: Belief that large numbers of people can make better decisions about a wide range of topics and products than a single person or even a small committee of experts.

workflow management: The process of streamlining business procedures so that documents can be moved easily and efficiently from one location to another.

workstation: Desktop computer with powerful graphics and mathematical capabilities and the ability to perform several complicated tasks at once.

World Wide Web: A system with universally accepted standards for storing, retrieving, formatting, and displaying information in a networked environment.

worms: Independent software programs that propagate themselves to disrupt the operation of computer networks or destroy data and other programs.

zero-day vulnerabilities: Security vulnerabilities in software, unknown to the creator, that hackers can exploit before the vendor becomes aware of the problem.

Index

Name Index

Organizations Index